LAY CULTURE, LEARNED CULTURE

LAY CULTURE, LEARNED CULTURE

Books and Social Change in Strasbourg, 1480–1599

MIRIAM USHER CHRISMAN

YALE UNIVERSITY PRESS   NEW HAVEN AND LONDON

Designed by Nancy Ovedovitz
and set in VIP Bembo type by The Composing Room of Michigan.
Printed in the United States of America by The Alpine Press,
Stoughton, Mass.

Library of Congress Cataloging in Publication Data

Chrisman, Miriam Usher.
  Lay culture, learned culture.

  Bibliography: p.
  Includes index.
    1. Strasbourg (France)—Intellectual life. 2. Print-
ing—France—Strasbourg—History. 3. Strasbourg (France)
—Imprints. I. Title.
DC801.S577C47   001.1′0944′3835   82-2771
ISBN 0-300-02530-0   AACR2

10   9   8   7   6   5   4   3   2   1

*For Nicholas
and
For Abbott*

CONTENTS

ILLUSTRATIONS

FIGURES

TABLES

PREFACE

This book owes many things to many people, but above all it represents consistent support from my family, an acceptance of my work on the book as an on-going element of family life.

The book started with a very simple question. As I worked on my first study of Strasbourg during the Reformation, I was curious to know what ideas and information an ordinary citizen had to draw on when he made his decision to accept the Reform or to remain within the traditional church. It occurred to me that the books published in the period would provide insight into the larger intellectual milieu. I broached the idea to Docteur Jean Rott, suggesting that I might investigate everything published in the city from 1510 to 1530. M. Rott replied, with a smile that no one could resist, "You would have to do at least 1480 through 1545." So the book is, in essence, his. His interest and support never flagged. He helped me to develop the first tentative subject-matter classifications. He encouraged quantitative analysis of the data when no one else did. Finally, he rigorously proofread the manuscript of the bibliographic volume—a real task of Sisyphus. All these things were done with the assumption that they were mere courtesies, extended from one scholar to another.

The research was a family project from the start. When we began the job of recording each book, our sons, Nicholas and Abbott, needed some supervision at the Strasbourg swimming pool. The parent who was pool watching did the book entries. As the study progressed and the data began to accumulate, these same sons insisted that I would have to use a computer. They became IBM card punchers, data processors, computer programmers, and relentless, but friendly, critics.

David Aronson, Devon Schneider, Maryelise Lamet, and Sterling Lamet all helped with the recording process. Nicholas and Abbott Chrisman shouldered the work of transferring the data onto IBM cards. Nicholas developed and ran the first computer programs. These were refined by Abbott, and the final programs were the work of Wayne Johnson of the University of Massachusetts Computer Center. Bonita Warner made the final corrections on the computer tape. Glen McDougall worked from the cards to make the typed bibliography from which the companion volume, *Bibliography of Strasbourg Imprints, 1480–1599,* was developed.

For the past ten years the Archives Municipales at Strasbourg has served as my major base. Dr. François-Joseph Fuchs creates a center for scholarly work. The historians at the University, under the leadership of Professeur Georges Livet, have been unfailingly supportive. Docteurs Marc Lienhard, Jean Lebeau, Jean-Pierre Kintz, Bernard Vogler, and Françoise Lévy-

Coblentz all shared their current work with me. The particular quality of the Strasbourg community is reflected in the fact that one's fellow workers are not competitors but colleagues. I have relied heavily on the other American scholars, Jane Abray, Thomas A. Brady, Jr., James Kittelson, Steven Nelson, and Kenneth Thibodeau. Jane Abray took notes for me from the *Ratsprotocol* on anything having to do with censorship or the printers. Tom Brady taught me how to use the Chambre de contrats materials, read the manuscript, and showed me its weaknesses. This kind of help is rare in the scholarly world and I am grateful for it.

The late Harry Harrison of the Circulation Department of the Sterling Library at Yale University, Mr. Ferenc Gyorgy of the Yale Medical Historical Library, and the Beinecke Library at Yale made it possible for me to carry on my research in this country. In Strasbourg the staff of the Bibliothèque Nationale et Universitaire provided unfailing, courteous service summer after summer.

Nancy L. Roelker read an early draft at a critical stage. Her comments, and those of Phillip Bebb, helped me to clarify the central theme. Helen Swartz gave invaluable editorial criticism and did much to develop the unity of the book. Abbott Chrisman drafted the original versions of the graphics, which were then executed by Suzanne Simon with Virginia Simon of the Department of Medical Illustration of the Yale University School of Medicine.

The book required a team of typists. Marjory Erikson, Barbara Rowe, the Lamets, Betty Wallace Hunter, and Jan Peene worked on early drafts. Nancy and Ross Scott provided the final copy, including the camera-ready copy for the companion volume, *Bibliography of Strasbourg Imprints, 1480–1599*. The staff of the Yale University Press made the final move from chaos to order.

My husband, Dr. Donald Chrisman, has been the pillar of the whole enterprise. It has been a slow piece of research, taking nearly twelve years, which is a long time to live with an idea and to spend your vacations in libraries not related to your own field. I could never have attempted to consider the scientific materials without his help. He worked on the earlier medical texts with me until I felt competent on my own and helped particularly with the pharmaceutical materials. More important, he has always assumed that my work was equal in importance to his own.

The whole family owes much to Madame Mathilde Goehry and her daughter, Marianne Faivre, who, beginning in 1961, created a foyer for us abroad. This book is an attempt to express the affection of our family for our friends in Strasbourg and our admiration for the city and its people.

Northampton, Massachusetts

GENERAL EDITORIAL NOTE

SPELLING CONVENTIONS

The spelling of proper names in the sixteenth century is a problem all its own. Few men or women spelled their names the same way at all times. Learned men, moreover, were likely to spell their Christian names in Latin when appropriate, and some, of course, changed their patronyms to Latin forms. Wolfgang Capito, the reformer, was born Wolfgang Köpfel. The printer Wolfgang Köpfel was his nephew and namesake. Luckily for us, the one used only Capito, and the other used only Köpfel. The inconsistencies caused by sixteenth-century indifference to standardized spelling are compounded by the custom of modern German and French scholars. German scholars use German forms for all individuals and places; French scholars use French forms. As a result, all Alsatians have two names, the form depending upon the nationality of the modern scholar. The *Ammeister* Jacob Sturm becomes Jacques Sturm in French; François Lambert of Avignon is called Franz Lambert by the German historians.

My general rule has been to leave all names of persons in the native language of the individual concerned, on the theory that one does not change one's name when traveling. When referring to an author in the text, I have used the form most often found on the title pages of his works. In the bibliography, however, the name is left as it appears in the book, since this is the form used in library catalogues and other references.

My most difficult problem was with the name of the humanist Jean/Johann Sturm: he was born in Luxembourg, educated in France, and long resident in Strasbourg. As an author he used the Latin form Johannes; but what did his friends call him? I have finally decided to depart from the precedent established by Thomas A. Brady, Jr. and have used the German form, since this and the very similar Latin form appear on the title pages of his books. It is well to remember that Jacob Sturm, the patrician nobleman, early protagonist of the Reform and supporter of the new Gymnasium, was not related to Johann Sturm, who was called to the city to become a teacher, later the rector of the new Gymnasium.

In order to make it easy to check locations on modern maps, place names have been given in the standard spelling used in English gazetteers. Villages have been left in the modern French form rather than the German.

REFERENCES

To simplify references in the footnotes, every book is referred to by the number under which it is listed in the companion volume, *Bibliography of*

Strasbourg Imprints, 1480–1599. The number provides a codified description of the book. Each number is preceded by an alphabetic letter denoting the class of the book: C stands for Catholic, P for Protestant, H for humanism, A for antiquity or editions of the classics, S for science, T for school texts, L for law. The first number stands for the subject matter. For example, Protestant books are divided into the following subjects: 1. statements of doctrine; 2. sermons; 3. polemic; 4. anabaptism; 5. devotionals and prayer books for lay use; 6. hymnals and liturgies; 7. manuals for the clergy. Thus the number P1 means that the book is a Protestant statement of doctrine. The next number, separated by a decimal point, denotes the topic within the subject matter category. Protestant statements of doctrine are broken down into statements by Martin Luther, statements by other Protestant reformers, statements by Strasbourg reformers, and so forth. The final number in the sequence, again separated by a decimal point, denotes the chronological position of the book within the topic. A book with the number P1.1.30 tells you immediately that there were many books on this particular topic. A lower-case letter is used to denote multiple editions. The first edition of any book is automatically designated *a*, though this is not used unless there were subsequent editions. The second edition is *b*, and so forth. The number P1.1.30m would mean that the book was popular.

References to the Bürgerbuch are complicated by the fact that one portion of the records has been published; the remainder is in manuscript form. Acquisition of citizenship was recorded in the Bürgerbuch, with separate records for citizenship acquired by purchase and citizenship acquired by marriage. The earliest section of these records was published from 1948 to 1961 by Charles Wittmer with the title *Le Livre de Bourgeoisie, 1440–1530*. There is a lacuna in the records after 1530. The manuscript records of acquisition by purchase resume with 1543 and run to 1618; those by marriage run from 1559 to 1730. These manuscript volumes are referred to collectively as the *Bürgerbuch*.

INTRODUCTION

HAT DID THE MEN AND WOMEN OF THE
sixteenth century think, believe, and know? We
have assumed that two major intellectual movements, the Renaissance and the Reformation,
shaped their thoughts, influenced their decisions,
and guided their actions. But is this view entirely
accurate? Were all social groups affected in the same
way by these movements? Were there other important intellectual forces,
which we have failed to identify? My earlier study of the Reformation in the
city of Strasbourg led me to question whether examining the work of the
major figures, the humanists and the reformers, was enough. Their ideas
needed to be considered within the perspective of the larger setting of
thought and belief within which they worked. It was essential to examine a
larger corpus.

Printed books, I decided, could serve as the major source in my attempt
to reconstruct this whole context. Books printed in a given year, whether
the work of living or dead authors, record the ideas currently in circulation.
They are cultural artifacts which reflect the questions, doubts, assumptions,
and certainties of their time. As historians we have tended to use books in a
limited way to examine the work of an individual or a school of thought.
The totality of books published in a given time can be used to provide
insights into the cultural and social forces operating in a period.[1] Based on
all the surviving books published in the city of Strasbourg from 1480 to
1599, this study attempts to recreate the context of sixteenth-century
thought in one place, to discover the range of ideas available to individual
writers or to common citizens as they developed their own intellectual
interests and fashioned their own world views.[2]

As the study progressed new questions developed, particularly with regard to the process of communication in the sixteenth century. The new
technology of the printing press has long been regarded as the major instrument in the dissemination of the ideas of the humanists and the Protestant
reformers. We have assumed that their ideas filtered down to the lower
levels of society like wine grapes pressed through a sieve, creating a thinner
potion from which ordinary men and women could extract their beliefs.
Scholarly attention has focused on the work of the humanists and theologians, since it was believed that their formulations shaped the thought and
actions of the men and women of the time. The evidence from the study of
book publication forces us to take a second look at this assumption. When

one examines the total production of books it becomes clear that there was a sharp division according to language. Half of the books were written by scholars and theologians and published by the more prestigious presses. The other half were written in German and published by a different group of printers. Careful analysis of this phenomenon revealed that two cultures were present in a sixteenth-century city: a Latin culture dominated by the universities and the churches and a vernacular culture rooted in the interests of ordinary men and women. This division was hardly new. The development of printing, however, served to increase or formalize the distance between them.

The Latin culture and the vernacular culture conformed to the modern anthropological definition of culture.[3] Each had its own language of communication which, in turn, influenced the manner in which thought was formulated. The Latin writers' grasp of rhetoric and dialectic made it possible for them to develop logical, conceptual forms. The vernacular writers, ignorant of these skills, wrote descriptively rather than analytically. The two cultures used different sources and diverse criteria of evidence, although they shared one important source of knowledge, the Bible. But even the Bible was interpreted distinctively. From these disparate sources each culture developed its own system of values and beliefs: the Latin culture was based on the ethics and philosophy of ancient Rome, the Bible, and the Church Fathers; the lay culture was based on the laws and commandments of Scripture.

The Latin culture was formulated and controlled by the schools, the universities, and the churches. The lay culture developed outside of the scholarly institutions. Each group, lay and learned, developed its own scientific corpus. The university mathematicians and doctors of medicine based their work on the Greek and Roman physicians and on Euclid. Military surgeons, barber surgeons, apothecaries, applied mathematicians, and technicians worked from observation and wrote popular medical manuals and how-to books. The interrelationship between the two cultures during the century is illustrated in figure 1. In the earliest decades the Latin culture was ascendant; vernacular books constituted only a fifth of the output. With the Reformation, however, the German culture made a sudden burst and vernacular culture predominated until 1574.[4]

Vernacular culture experienced its own particular evolution within the time span 1519–74. For a brief decade, from 1519 to 1528, theologians and scholars articulated the hopes and aspirations of ordinary people and promulgated the message of the new faith in German. After 1530, however, the Protestant clergy returned to the use of Latin for their religious books and by 1538 the aristocracy and the upper middle class, educated at the newly established humanist schools, became deeply involved in the Latin culture.

The middle class, the artisans and craftsmen, found little inspiration in Cicero or Demosthenes. They developed their own cultural life centered on theatrical groups, popular music, novels, and history. Their lively interest in the everyday world was manifested in the growth of popular journalism. These publications sustained the primacy of vernacular publication until 1580. In the very last decades, both cultures were maintained at essentially the same level.

Language, then, created a primary division within the intellectual world. There were further fundamental divisions along the lines of the broad fields of human thought: among the books produced were theological books, scientific books, legal treatises, popular stories written in the vernacular, and editions of the classics. Each of these represented widely different tastes, interests, or states of knowledge.

I have established nine major divisions to serve as a basis for classification of the books of the period: Catholic, Protestant, humanist, classical, scientific, vernacular, biblical, school texts, and legal literature. Each book was assigned to its appropriate division and the production of each major type of book was charted on a computer (see Appendix A). The results for all areas but law are shown in figures IV–X. These graphs reveal a highly diversified cultural milieu. Production patterns varied widely, and no one field reproduced the configuration of total production shown in figure II. There was no single course of evolution. Each field expanded and contracted according to its own rhythm, represented in the graphs by a series of peaks and troughs; for example, figure V shows that the outpouring of Protestant polemic from 1522 to 1528 was followed by a trough from 1532 to 1544 and then by an almost total collapse. From 1560 to 1580 production of Protestant books revived and was relatively stable. The timing of the peaks and troughs changes significantly from graph to graph.

What caused the peaks and troughs? What do they represent? Obviously, some of them show the results of external events, the turbulence of the early years of the Reform, the disarray of war. Most of the peaks, however, represent the work of groups of people, men working together as an intellectual generation. The development of each field of knowledge was shaped by groups of men who shared the same intellectual aims and purposes. Each of these groups had its own particular definition of learning. It had its own accepted sources and its own standards of style and form. In most cases the groups held together for a period of from twelve to twenty years. Cohesion was then lost because of death or changing circumstances, or because the group's ideas were no longer well received.

The generational groups comprised important subgroups within the broader pattern of linguistic cultural division. The Latin culture was divided into two important groups, the theologians and the scholars. Generational division among the theologians stemmed from differences in doctrine. The Catholic theologians were replaced by the early reformers, Martin Bucer and Wolfgang Capito, with their distinctive theology of the Eucharist. The later theologians, led by Johann Marbach and Johann Pappus, were orthodox Lutherans. The scholarly generations were differentiated by the sources they used. The first generations of scholars, the early humanists, were primarily interested in poetry and literature. They were succeeded by the biblical humanists. After 1538 a new group of humanists, teaching in the Gymnasium, diffused a Ciceronian classicism. By the end of the century the professors at the Academy had returned to Aristotle as the ultimate source.

The groups involved with vernacular culture were less formalized, in part because they had no institutional bases like the church, the school, or the chapters. In a few instances printers' shops brought them together. The earliest vernacular writers were military surgeons, an apothecary, and other technicians. The religious interests of the laity were expressed in a burst of polemic literature written by local figures and by a small group of Anabaptists, active from 1522 to 1535. The thirties saw an increase of publication by medical and technical writers. From 1538 to 1560, a group of writers, most of them civil servants in surrounding towns, articulated ethical ideals based on burgher life. The last decades were dominated by the satirist Johann Fischart, who worked as proofreader, in-house author, and editor for his printer brother-in-law, Bernard Jobin.

The generational groups bear witness to the constant changes taking place within the intellectual milieu. Ideas are not constants, providing unalterable truths from generation to generation. Rather, they are continually restated and applied to the particular circumstances of a given moment. The great truths are those that can be adapted, restated, and revitalized over and over again.

The city of Strasbourg provided the physical setting within which the intellectual changes could be examined. Ranked third among the principal cities of German language publication, Strasbourg was large enough to be important in local, regional, and even international book trade,[5] but it did not produce the overwhelming number of books that would be found in great centers like Paris, Lyons, or Venice. Strasbourg was a medium-sized printing city. This does not mean that it reflects the intellectual currents of other medium-sized German and Swiss cities, that it can serve as a standard or a norm. Local studies that have proliferated in recent years force us to recognize the uniqueness of development in each place. Restricting research to one city permits the historian to study the data in depth and to observe the interaction of a multiplicity of factors.

I cannot state strongly enough that the study does not claim to provide a total view of sixteenth-century culture. Quite obviously it leaves out all the books that were not printed in Strasbourg but circulated freely within the city, having been purchased at the Frankfurt book fair or from booksellers in the city. The intellectual milieu was not a closed system, but the fact remains that we have no way of discovering what books came from outside. By limiting my study to the repertoires of the local printers, it was possible to establish a solid base of empirical evidence that provides some insight into the relationships between different groups in one intellectual community.

Situated on the southeastern border of the Holy Roman Empire, Strasbourg was the largest city in Alsace, a free imperial city with a population of some twenty thousand persons.[6] Privileges granted in the thirteenth century gave it a high degree of political autonomy. It was responsible for its own defense, it could raise its own army, and it could hire troops at will. It levied its own taxes and was subject to no regular levies of the Holy Roman Empire.[7] It formulated its own foreign policy, receiving and sending ambassadors. It sent delegates to the Diet who spoke in the name of the city. Thus it functioned as an independent political unit, its independence furthered by a special relationship with its bishop.

The city was a bishop's seat. The diocese straddled the Rhine from the Black Forest to the crest of the Vosges. In 1262, however, the city authorities had shaken off the political control of the bishop.[8] The peace treaty concluded at that time provided that the bishop would live outside the city walls in Saverne. Thus, Strasbourg was the center of the diocese but the bishop was nonresident.[9] In practice this meant that the administrative and judicial affairs of the church were carried on by the bishop's officials, who continued to live in the city. The arrangement diminished neither the power of the church nor the clerical presence.

The church was a dominant force. There were two large, powerful chapters, one in the cathedral, the other at the Church of Saint Thomas. The cathedral chapter drew its members from the highest ranks of the German nobility, leading Erasmus to remark that Christ himself would not have gained admittance.[10] The chapter of Saint Thomas represented the Strasbourg patriciate, creating a base from which they could control land, rents, and appointments. There were three smaller chapters, one at Old Saint Peter, another at New Saint Peter, and a third at All Saints. The chapters controlled the appointment of clergy to many of the seven parish churches, thus profoundly influencing the spiritual life of the city. Both monastic foundations and the preaching orders were well represented. The convents of the Franciscans and the Dominicans were situated in major squares in the center of the city. Several of the smaller houses, the Carthusians' and some of the women's convents, lay at the edge of the city, still within the walls, often controlling large tracts of land worked by citizens hired as day laborers. Two noble orders, the Knights of Saint John and the Teutonic Knights, maintained their foundations in considerable luxury.

The economy was mixed. The city functioned as a major agricultural market and transportation center, and it had its share of manufactures. One reason for its prosperity lay in the fact that no one activity prevailed. Strasbourg dominated the Alsatian plain, where wheat, rye, and other grains grew in abundance. Where the plains stopped, the hills, covered with vineyards, began. Both the wine and the grain moved out onto the European markets from the city docks and warehouses. These were the major source of Strasbourg wealth, for the city was a natural transportation center. It was at a crossroads north and south, east and west, as the Romans had recognized when they established a *castra* there. Medieval engineers had improved upon nature by constructing a series of causeways and pontoon bridges that traversed the Rhine. This bridge, situated northeast of the city, was Europe's northernmost bridge over the river. It made Strasbourg a major gateway for commerce coming up the Rhone Valley, passing over into Upper Germany, Swabia and Württemberg, Nuremberg, and points north. Similarly, it provided access for goods coming from eastern Europe, Poland, and Bohemia into France or down the Rhine. The river was another major line of communication, not only for the cities on its banks, but between Switzerland and the Low Countries, and for Italian goods moving through Switzerland to Flemish and Dutch cities. All of this was important to the book trade. Venice, Lyons, and Basel, major centers of book production, lay within Strasbourg's established network of trade.

Manufacturing activity in Strasbourg was balanced. There was no one specialty like the fine cloth-making of Florence or Ypres, the metal-working of Nuremberg. Strasbourg turned out cheap, sturdy loden cloth; a heavy-duty black linen; and wool, cloth, and leather goods.[11] By the fourteenth century, paper manufacturing had become important and there was a playing card industry, which may have encouraged the development of printing.[12]

The city was governed by a patriciate whose power had been confirmed in a constitutional revision in 1480. Administrative, legislative, and executive powers were rarely separated in the fifteenth and sixteenth centuries. The Strasbourg constitution, in recognition of this principle, created a series of interlocking committees and councils. There was a senate, made up of twenty burghers, elected by the guilds, and ten nobles. There were two major privy councils or standing committees, the Council of XV, which was responsible for internal affairs, and the Council of XIII, responsible for foreign affairs. The major decision-making group for the city was composed of the XV and the XIII together. Called the XXI, it actually included thirty-two men, about one-third of them nobles, the other two-thirds commoners.[13] The whole group of the senate and the members of the councils was referred to as the *Magistrat,* or the *Rat.*

The presiding officer for the city was the *Ammeister,* always a burgher and a commoner, chosen by the twenty guild members sitting in the senate. Four *Stettmeisters,* chosen from the nobility, assisted the ammeister in carrying out his duties. Each stettmeister presided for two three-month terms during his two years in office. All appointments to lesser city offices were made by one of these five men. Committees and officials proliferated. There were financial officials, tax collectors, treasurers, and recorders. One committee (the church wardens) supervised the Reformed church, another (the school board) ran the schools, while a third (the school visitors) kept watch to see that the policies of the school board were carried out. There was a welfare board, a hospital committee, and an orphan committee, and certain members of the Magistrat patrolled the market daily to see that the fishwives sold only fresh fish. It was a complex system. The patriciate that controlled it was a rentier-merchant aristocracy. Few ordinary citizens penetrated to the seats of power.[14]

Citizenship, or *Bürgerrecht,* was a privilege acquired through purchase or by inheritance.[15] As a citizen, a man had the right to vote within his guild for the senator from that guild. Citizenship gave him the protection of the city and the right to exercise a trade or enter into commerce. Once purchased, these rights passed automatically to all legitimate children. An artisan moving into the city could acquire citizenship by marrying the daughter of a citizen, a procedure common among the printers. For those who wished to purchase citizenship, however, the price was high.[16] The established artisan or craftsman could afford the fee; the laborer could not. He was only able to purchase half-citizenship, *Schultheissenbürgerrecht,* which provided neither economic nor political rights but gave access to alms from the city. A considerable number of the men and women within the walls were simply *Inwohner* or inhabitants with no rights or privileges.

Burgher, schultheissenbürgher, and inwohner: the city walls embraced them all. These diverse groups were separated according to birth, wealth, and occupation.[17] In the early seventeenth century the city's sumptuary code distinguished among six different classes, several of them subdivided into two levels.[18] In the sixteenth century these divisions were implicit rather than explicit, although city ordinances made special provisions for particular social groups, namely, artisans, handworkers, inwohner, and the poor.[19]

The noble canons of the cathedral chapter were at the apex of Strasbourg's social pyramid. Many of them younger sons of the greatest and most powerful families of the Empire, they held benefices as one form of family privilege. Although they played little part in the day-to-day political or social life of the city, which they considered beneath them, they were nevertheless an important presence. Their secretaries and administrators played leading roles in the humanist movement of the early decades. The dean of the chapter himself turned Protestant and wrote in defense of the new faith. In 1590 the city nearly bankrupted itself in a war to protect the rights of those cathedral canons who had become Protestant. The cathedral chapter involved the city in ecclesiastical and imperial politics, albeit often against the will of the Magistrat.

Below the canons came the aristocracy. This included, first, the local landed nobility, resident in the country, who might own houses in the city but were not obliged to maintain permanent households there. They were granted the privilege of *Ausbürgertum,* associate citizenship.[20] More important were the urban aristocracy for whom Brady uses the term *patriciate*.[21] These families bore arms and owned lands in the city, in the country, or both. They lived on rents, dues, and interest from investments and were distinguished from the rest of the burghers by the fact that they neither practiced a craft nor involved themselves in commerce.[22] They were gentlemen; the local term was *Constofler*. Exemption from guild membership confirmed their special status; the constofler voted in their noble clubs rather than in one of the twenty guilds. Their original wealth might have come from commerce or from land; the source was not important. They were the city's most honored citizens, the leaders in military and diplomatic affairs. They served in the Rat, in the privy councils, and as stettmeisters, their political importance vastly outweighing their numerical strength.[23] The group played an important role culturally. Jacob Sturm, one of the important early humanists, came from a patrician family and was actively involved in the introduction of the Reform. Patrician families encouraged the foundation of the new Latin schools and the Luxembourg humanist Johann Sturm's Gymnasium became a preparatory school for their sons. Eckhart zum Treubel, of an old and honorable family, vigorously championed the Reform in a series of religious treatises that were published. He was joined by another noble, Matthias Wurm von Geudertheim.

Closely associated with the patriciate were the big merchant families, the Ingolds, the Prechters, the Ebels, the Miegs, and the Johams. Unlike the aristocracy, the merchants were still engaged in trade—Europe-wide, large-scale trade and banking. Often this was a step on the way to ennoblement, for once enough revenues were acquired, trade was left behind and the family attempted to gain admittance to a constofel. Their success was by no means assured since the patricians reserved the right to vote on each applicant. One negative vote was enough to destroy the social mobility of even the most wealthy.[24] In economic interest and life-style, the merchants closely resembled the aristocracy. Their political role was played within the guilds, and they were perhaps less active politically than the urban aristocracy or the smaller merchants and artisans, partially because their economic interests took precedence. As individuals they took little part in cultural life. They were minimally involved. The Prechters might provide occasional banking services for Erasmus, but they did not serve as patrons.[25] Daniel Mieg's enthusiastic espousal of the Reformation was exceptional within the group.

Merchants, most of them cloth merchants engaged in regional and local trade, made up the next level of the social pyramid. While great merchants like the Prechters and the Ingolds invested in mining on a large scale and in trade with Italy and the Low Countries, the lesser merchants bought and sold cloth in the local area. Their ties and loyalties were regional. They had to have the same grasp of credit arrangements and business organization as their wealthier colleagues, but the scale of their operations was smaller.[26] As a group the cloth merchants were well respected in the community. Mattheus Geiger and Martin Herlin were both ammeisters. Mathis Pfarrer, Hans Stösser, and Luke Messinger all served on the privy councils and on other important committees.[27] Two merchants, Martin Herlin and Hans Lindenfels, together with Claus Kniebis, led the most militant Protestant party, which fostered a political-military alliance with the Zwinglian Swiss cities.[28]

The master artisans formed the backbone of the community. Their political power, however, was not equivalent to their numerical strength. There were many guildsmen, but their political influence was nominal. They were the middle class, the true burghers, whose economic existence and social status depended on their urban residence. Independent, running their own shops, within their own guilds they were still autonomous. "The masters of even very ordinary crafts," Brady points out, "were genuine *masters,* both in the sense of commanding the tools and lore of their crafts . . . and the labor and loyalty of the journeymen and apprentices."[29] There was an established hierarchy of prestige among the guilds. In Strasbourg the shippers' and the merchants' guilds were preeminent.[30] Among the craft guilds, the *Stelz,* which combined goldsmiths, engravers, and painters, commanded greater respect and honor than the guilds of furriers, gardeners, and fishermen. As masters of a new technology, the printers were immediately granted special respect and assigned to the Stelz. Because of the very nature of their craft, the printers had strong links with the intellectuals and with the clergy.

This brings us to the problem of assessing the social position of the intellectuals, both clerical and secular. Where did they fit in the urban social structure? In the old church, social differences were maintained among the clergy. Canons who were born into the nobility preserved their privileges and prestige. The upper hierarchy of the church was selected from this pool of aristocrats. Sons of ordinary burghers who became priests represented a lower class within the church and could move upward only by exhibiting truly exceptional gifts as a preacher or administrator. The new church achieved a major social change. Leadership in the Protestant church came from the group that formerly would have risen no further than the priesthood. Many of these men came from the artisan class.[31] The intellectuals who taught in the schools and universities came from the middle ranks or higher, from merchant families or from families in the upper levels of the civil service. By the end of the century a significant number were the sons of professors and teachers.[32] In the sumptuary law of 1628, scholars holding the doctorate were given the same rank as patricians. Those without the doctorate were placed at the level of large-scale merchants. Teachers in the Gymnasium were considered the equals of civil servants.[33]

The intellectuals were one of the most mobile groups in Strasbourg society. A university education raised a young man to a higher social status. Since this status rested on his grasp of Latin, the language of learning, he was unlikely to write in the vernacular. The clergy preached in German, but they wrote their important treatises in Latin, reserving written German for polemic and propaganda purposes. Although many scholars and clerics sprang from the very middle of burgher society, they did not necessarily remain spokesmen for their class of origin. This role was often filled by men without formal education: civil servants, surgeons, apothecaries, artisans.

The lower levels of the society included those referred to in the documents of the time as handworkers. This included workmen of all types, most of them working in shops supervised by a master. These could vary in size from a unit employing from twenty to thirty men, to a shop with one master and one assistant. By the sixteenth century the system of advancement through the guild was in decline. Mastership was granted only within an inner circle of the guild. The journeyman had become a subordinate, permanently relegated to inferior status, dependent on a money wage that was rarely sufficient to support a wife and family.[34] Some were citizens, often by birth. Others could afford only schultheissenbürgerrecht or were merely inhabitants. The guild provided them with a few privileges—perhaps a yearly banquet, perhaps a fund to cover funeral expenses. If they were citizens, they could vote in their guild for their representative to the Senate. Otherwise they were powerless, except for their ability to instill fear in the hearts of authorities. This was the urban group most likely to protest, most likely to riot in the streets.[35]

Below the journeymen came the day laborers, men and women with no permanent jobs who had to find work on a day-to-day basis. Below them came the poor, unable to work, or without jobs. Clearly, the boundaries here were blurred and many people moved from one status to another. Their lives were characterized by economic insecurity, political impotence, and social alienation. They poured into the parish churches to hear the sermons of the reformed clergy, they sang the new hymns, they sang political songs in the tavern. Again, their power lay in the fear they engendered.

The social structure was a combination of a hierarchy of estates and a class system. There was a well-established order of estates, particularly apparent in the distribution of political power and authority. The estates included, in descending order, the landed nobility, the urban nobility, men of magistral rank, and the upper clergy. These men had higher rank and authority than guildsmen who held no office, the parish clergy, or schoolteachers. Journeymen, apprentices, day laborers, and the poor, were, as a rule, outside the political process, though a few individuals from these groups were able to vote.

Side by side with this hierarchy was another based on occupation, wealth, and economic power. Here the wealthy merchant could stand as an equal with the nobleman. A well-trained lawyer could rise above his father's status as an artisan and attain a higher rank in the society. A large-scale, successful printer commanded more respect than the job printer running his own small shop.

The intellectual world was divided according to yet another factor. Here men were separated by language, a characteristic not exclusively tied to social status or wealth. Latin was originally reserved to the clergy, the scholars, and educated members of the upper class. Yet, in the early decades of the sixteenth century, a classical education was still exceptional, even for the sons of patrician and merchant families. Of the 105 men included in Brady's study of the Strasbourg ruling class from 1520 to 1555, only thirteen (13.5%) had received a university education.[36] Most of these were from rentier families; four of them were merchants. Five other men, all but one of them merchants, could speak and read French.[37] This meant that the majority of the upper class spoke and read only the vernacular language.

With the establishment of the Gymnasium in 1538 this changed. A humanist education came to be regarded as essential for the sons of the urban nobility and the merchants. The lack of a matriculation register for the Gymnasium makes it impossible to know how far this penetrated among the master craftsmen's families. We do know of individual sons of certain printers who were pupils of the school, but solid, statistical evidence is lacking. Parish schools that taught reading and writing in German were established under the supervision of the reformed clergy by 1531.[38] These probably met the needs of the majority of artisanal families. However, the acceptance of humanist education as part of the rite of passage from child-hood to manhood for the sons of the upper bourgeoisie made the language division more of a class matter as the century wore on.

These social differences were reflected in what was printed. Printers attempted to meet the needs of all—nobles, patricians, merchants, guildsmen, craftsmen, artisans, engineers, builders, and men and women of all religious persuasions. The intellectual milieu was far from unified. The discords and antagonisms that hovered below the surface are portrayed visually in Matthias Grünewald's Isenheim altarpiece. Grünewald's surrealistic demons, the idealized young Virgin and the child, the brutally realistic dead Christ, and the transcendent ascent into heaven reveal conflicting and contradictory perceptions of the world. These same dissonances were present in the written culture.

PART I
THE BOOK TRADE

CHAPTER ONE · THE PRINTERS

RINTERS WERE NEW MEN IN THE FIF-
teenth and sixteenth centuries. By traditional defini-
tions they were artisans and craftsmen. In practice,
they enjoyed a higher status. Contemporary documents refer to printing as an art, distinctive because
its product is uniquely valuable to mankind. Fascinated by the technology and mechanics of printing,
their contemporaries recognized the printer's special achievement—technical mastery over the machine combined with the ability to influence human
thought.

Printing was an art, a technique, a business, and an innovative force
within the intellectual community. Despite its status as one of the wonders
of the age, the printing industry was subject to all the hazards that beset the
late medieval craft guilds, and, at least in Strasbourg, the new industry
lacked the capital needed for long range economic security. The graph of
total book production (figure II) shows that the local printing industry
experienced well-defined economic cycles. In 1480 the printing industry
was in the final phase of a fairly long, slow, developmental period with
production below forty books a year. This phase was followed by a boom
from 1508 to 1528, when production doubled to about eighty books a year.
From 1529 to 1544 the output began an erratic decline, ending in a sharp
depression from 1546 to 1556. Gradually in the last decades of the century
there was a return to stable production of fifty books a year, substantially
below the level of the boom years.

These cycles are evidence of the impact of the Reformation on the printing industry. The most stable and secure market for the printers was the
Roman church with its host of cathedral schools and monastic and chapter
libraries. Reformation polemic monopolized the presses from 1521 to 1528.
The Protestant church, however, did not have the same needs as the old
church, and, with demand falling, the printers were faced with the task of
discovering new markets.[1] The establishment of the Gymnasium and the
development of the Academy created new institutions which provided a
steady demand, but the printers were forced to seek other outlets as well. In
Strasbourg, a sizable market was found for scientific and vernacular books.
This helped to create the recovery from 1531 to 1544, and the more stable
conditions from 1560 to 1599. The printers moved from boom conditions,
to instability and depression, and finally to a tenuous equilibrium.

From 1480 to 1599 some seventy-seven printers established themselves in

3

the city of Strasbourg long enough for each to print one book bearing his name. In addition, at least sixty-five men served as journeymen or assistants in the printing shops, but there is no evidence that they printed under their own names.[2] This study is confined to the seventy-seven men whose signatures, colophons, or emblems appeared in the books examined.

A preliminary classification of the seventy-seven was made according to the total number of books each man produced. Clearly, a man who had printed 250 books in his lifetime was working on a very different scale from a man who had printed only 30. This particular measure of productivity divided the printers into four different groups: major printers who produced over 100 books; intermediate printers who produced between 50 and 99 books; minor printers who produced between 20 and 49 books; and occasional printers who produced between 1 and 19 books (table 1). The last group is a special case and is not included in the discussion of overall conditions in the industry. The figures revealed important differences in terms of the size of shops and made desirable a more accurate measure of productivity.

In table 1, each book—whether a huge folio volume, a short treatise, or a four-leaf song sheet—is counted as one publication.[3] All books in the study, however, can be reduced to a common unit, the number of pieces of paper that went into the printing press. Every book was printed on folio-sized sheets of paper. After being removed from the press, these sheets were folded, once to produce a folio book, twice to produce a quarto book, or

Table 1. Printers by Number of Books Produced (arranged chronologically)

Major Printers	Total Editions	Intermediate Printers	Total Editions	Minor Printers	Total Editions
(100 or more books)		(50–99 books)		(20–49 books)	
Georg Husner	129	Martin Flach II	94	Heinrich Knoblochtzer	23
Johann Prüss	177	Johann Herwagen	67	Martin Schott	35
Johann Grüninger	389	Reinhardt Beck	55	Bartholomäus Kistler	36
Martin Flach I	108	Samuel Emmel	76	Ulrich Morhard	28
Matthias Hupfuff	175	Balthasar Beck	76	Johann Schwan	23
Johann Knobloch	429	Jacob Frölich	97	Christian Egenolff	41
Johann Schott	229	Nikolaus Wyriot	91	Heinrich Seybold	19
Matthias Schürer	297	Christian Mylius	85	Peter Schöffer	21
Johann Prüss II	135	Christian Mylius II	55	Johann Albrecht	21
Wolfgang Köpfel	185			Matthias Biener	22
Wendelin Rihel	197			Georg Messerschmidt	47
Crato Mylius	103			Paul Messerschmidt	30
Theobald Berger	160			Jost Martin	29
Theodosius Rihel	108			Lazarus Zetzner	45
Josias Rihel	281				
Bernard Jobin	285				
Anton Bertram	171				

three times to produce an octavo book.[4] One foliosheet, printed on both sides, was the product of each turn of the press.

The format and length in leaves are known for approximately two-thirds of the books in the study.[5] The number of leaves has been divided by two, four, or eight, depending on the format, thus creating a new variable, foliosheets, for each book.[6] The number of foliosheets could then be totaled for each printer by year and for his whole career. It is not possible, however, to determine accurately the number of copies made of any one book. Although a standard press run probably averaged about 1,250 copies, this figure could be incorrect by as much as 300 to 800.[7] To arrive at a standard measure of production it is best to think in terms of a masterforme, the large, two-sided frame used to print both sides of the foliosheet of paper. All the masterformes produced in a given year would constitute a set of type-filled formes, set by the typesetters and used by the pressmen to print the foliosheets that were folded to make books. The masterforme and the foliosheet are the same except that the foliosheet is finite, representing a unique copy. The masterforme is capable of producing multiple copies. Production of the Strasbourg shops will be described in terms of masterformes.

One can visualize all the masterformes produced in a given year as creating a set of books on display in the printer's shop. A yearly production of 300 masterformes could consist of three folio books of 200 leaves each, or six quartos of 200 leaves each, or twelve octavos of 200 leaves each. Or it could be broken down in other ways, for example one folio volume of 200 leaves, three quartos of 200 leaves, and two octavos of 200 leaves each. The average annual production of a large-scale shop in Strasbourg was 338 masterformes, often represented by one folio, three quartos, and two octavos.

Ranking by masterformes suggested four different classifications: large-scale shops, medium-scale shops, one-man shops (table 2), and non-established printers (table 3).[8] These are comparable to but more precise than the classifications in table 1.[9] There are fewer large-scale shops; the number of medium-scale shops is far greater; and the number of one-man shops exceeds the number of minor printers. The ranks established in table 2 provide a better picture of the industry because they are based on a more accurate estimate of the work load and reflect the number of presses in operation. By correlating the masterforme production figures with the evidence available from Leon Voet's study of the Plantin press in Antwerp, the labor force in each type of shop can be reconstructed.

A printing shop employed a team of four men: two compositors and two pressmen. The compositor's work was the least standardized. He had to cope with differences in type sizes and formats. A small octavo volume,

Table 2. Shops by Average Number of Masterformes Produced Annually[a]

Large Scale Shops	Average Annual Master-formes	Medium Scale Shops	Average Annual Master-formes	One-Man Shops	Average Annual Master-formes
Theodosius Rihel[b] (1555–99)→1620	597	Wolfgang Köpfel (1522–54)	191	Rémy Guédon (1548–49)	40
Wendelin Rihel (1535–54)	428	Georg Husner (1479–1505)	190	Christian Egenolff (1528–31)	40
Crato Mylius (1536–47)	424	Johann Schott (1500–44)	190	Johann Prüss II (1512–51)	37
Matthias Schürer[c] (1508–20)	413	Johann Prüss I (1480–1510)	181	Jacob Frölich (1533–57)	31
Lazarus Zetzner (1585–99)→1616	366	Christian Mylius (1555–68)	170	Heinrich Knoblochtzer (1480–84)	30
Johann Knobloch (1500–28)	333	Balthasar Beck (1527–51)	169	Nikolaus Wyriot (1568–83)	28
Martin Flach (1477–1500)	313	Martin Flach II (1501–25)	166	Konrad Kerner (1517)	26
Josias Rihel (1555–98)	309	Ulrich Morhard (1519–22)	154	Heinrich Vogtherr (1538–40)	26
Johann Grüninger (1483–1531)	289	Johann Albrecht (1532–38)	146	Jost Martin (1590–99)	25
Bernard Jobin (1570–94)	243	Georg Messerschmidt (1541–48)	140	Blase Fabricius (1549–58)	24
Johann Herwagen (1521–28)	232	Reinhardt Beck (1511–22)	135	Johann Wähinger (1502–04)	23
Georg Ulricher (1529–36)	229	Bartholomäus Grüninger (1532–38)	135	Sigismund Bundt (1539–45)	23
Samuel Emmel (1553–70)	226	Johann Knobloch II (1530–32)	124	Theobald Berger (1551–84)	23
		Jacob Cammerlander (1531–48)	124	Bartholomäus Kistler (1497–1510)	21

(continued)

requiring complex placement of the pages, was more difficult to set than a folio volume. The size and style of type also made a difference in how quickly the work could be done. Voet's figures, based on the Plantin account books, show that it took one day for two compositors to set the two sides of the forme required to print both sides of one foliosheet. One compositor was responsible for the recto side, the other for the verso side.[10] Each masterforme in this study represents a minimum of one day's work by two compositors. In several examples in the Plantin records the compositor completed only half the forme in a day, producing a total of from two and one-half to three formes in a week.[11] Since the standard work year was 260 days,[12] the maximum one compositor could prepare was 130 masterformes a year; the team could produce 260. If the material was difficult the rate for the team could fall to as little as 130 masters annually.

Table 2. *Continued*

Large Scale Shops	Average Annual Master- formes	Medium Scale Shops	Average Annual Master- formes	One- Man Shops	Average Annual Master- formes
		Matthias Biener (Apiarius) (1533–37)	124	Peter Schöffer (1529–39)	20
		Matthias Hupfuff (1492–1520)	111	Heinrich Seybold (1528–33)	10
		Paul Messerschmidt (1555–66)	106	Johann Schwan (1524–26)	10
		Printer of *Vitas Patrum* (1483–94)	104	Matthias Brant (1496–1500)	4
		Anton Bertram (1584–99)	98	Karl Kieffer (1586–98)	4
		Martin Schott (1481–99)	85	Peter Hugg (1563–71)	4
		Christian Mylius II (1570–81)	85	Nikolaus Faber (1573–83)	1
				Nikolaus Waldt (1583–95)	1

aSee also note 8.

bAverage figures given for men like Theodosius Rihel whose printing career extended beyond 1599, include only those books published up to 1599.

cJosef Benzing, on the basis of careful examination of the typographical evidence, has identified a printer using the German typefonts that had belonged to Matthias Schürer after the latter's death. He calls this press Schürer Erben. I have included the books listed by Benzing in the bibliography, but I have not listed the Schürer Erben as a separate press since the evidence is so scant. The Erben would extend the activity of the Schürer press to 1525 and add another 415 foliosheets to the total output. Production of the Erben was well below the norm for Matthias Schürer, averaging only 83 mastersheets per year.

The pressmen also worked as a team. They received the folio-sized forme from the compositors and locked it into the press. They could pull 1,250 sheets, printed on both sides, off the press in a single day. If the majority of Strasbourg press runs were for 1,250 copies from a masterforme, the number of working days of two pressmen (with a maximum 260 days) would equal the number of masterformes produced per year.

This maximum of 260 masterformes was not attained in most of the Strasbourg shops. The average annual output of both large-scale and medium-scale shops was 218 masterformes, based on the output of thirty-four shops using at least forty-six presses. An average yearly production of this size means that production ran at 85 percent of capacity—an estimate that is probably more realistic than 100 percent capacity. The figure of 220 masterformes (rounding off from 218) will be used as the yearly production norm for the city throughout this study.

Table 3. Nonestablished Printers by Number of Books and Masterformes Produced (arranged chronologically)

Printer	Number of Books Produced	Average Annual Masterformes
Thomas Anshelm (1488)	1	164
Peter Attendorn (1489)	2	9
Friedrich von Dumbach (1497–1499)	2	82
Wilhelm Schaffner (1498–1515)	6	6
Hieronymus Greff (1502)	1	16
Beatus and Sixtus Murner (1510)	1	2
P. Götz (1514)	1	20
Carthusian Monks (1533)	1	—
Amandus Farkal (1530)	1	28
Johann Schwintzer	2	6
Sigismund Bund (1539–45)	4	17
Hans Grimm	1	—
Jacques Poulain (1555–58)	2	5
Urban Wyss (1556)	3	—
P. Schmidt (1561)	1	16
Pierre Estiart/François Perrin (1558–64)	8	188 (in 1558)
Paul Acker (1568)	1	—
Gillotte le Pords (1587)	1	—
Simon Meyer (1592)	2	9
Elias Baldus	2	2

In Strasbourg each of the large-scale printers had at least two presses in operation. Production was usually very low in the first years of operation, but once the shop was underway the average yearly total was 440 master-formes. Sixty-three percent of Theodosius Rihel's work required more than two presses. For seven out of thirty-five years his annual production was over 1,100 masterformes, indicating that he had as many as five presses working at a time. By contrast his father, Wendelin Rihel, reached 760–800 masterformes, printed on four presses, only twice. Eighty percent of the time he had only two presses in operation.

There is a problem in interpreting the data in these cases. The sharp variations in output of masterformes, which are shown vividly in figures XIII–XV, are also typical of the production patterns of individual printers. For example, Wendelin Rihel produced 301 masterformes in 1538, 764 in 1539, 808 in 1540, and 323 in 1541. It is possible that some of the master-formes which appear in 1539 were made in 1538, as the first part of a large book that was completed in 1539. On the other hand, elevated production over two successive years means that he must have used extra presses at some point. Most of the large-scale printers maintained their higher levels of production over some consecutive years, thus substantiating my conclusion that these printers must have used several presses. The majority of large-scale printers used two presses 60 to 70 percent of the time and three or four presses 30 to 40 percent of the time, although Bernard Jobin, Johann Herwagen, Georg Ulricher, and Samuel Emmel used additional presses less frequently than the others. Variation in the number of presses used was common at the Plantin press, which indicates that this was a usual pattern in the industry.[13] The larger output could also reflect work put out on commission to other printers, either in Strasbourg or in other cities. The fact remains that the larger printers commanded more presses.

In the large-scale shops specialized workers were used in addition to the compositors and pressmen. The corrector was responsible for reading the proofs and informing the compositors of corrections that had to be made. In most cases during this period he worked directly from the formes as they had been prepared by the compositors. The corrector, particularly for Latin publications, was a man with scholarly training.[14] A collector took up the sheets printed by the pressmen and placed them in order, a job regarded as of minor importance and therefore poorly paid.[15] A large-scale shop, working at full capacity, could have employed as many as ten to twelve men, counting the master-owner. There were four large-scale shops in the period 1480–1530, only two in the period 1531–55, then five in the last four decades.

Medium-scale shops were, as is clear from table 2, the backbone of the industry. In terms of organization, they followed much the same pattern as the large-scale shops except the majority of their work was done on one press instead of two. Of the nineteen medium-scale printers, seven never produced more than could be printed on a single press; these were Johann Albrecht, Reinhardt Beck, Johann Knobloch II, Paul Messerschmidt, the Printer of *Vitas Patrum*, Anton Bertram, and Christian Mylius II. Five other men, Ulrich Morhard, Georg Messerschmidt, Jacob Cammerlander, Bartholomäus Grüninger, and Martin Schott, each worked at a two-press level only once during his entire career. Wolfgang Köpfel operated at a two-press level for six of thirty years, but each year of high output was preceded by a year of very low production, indicating that a large book was being accumulated. Johann Prüss seems to have used two presses from 1503 to 1509, Christian Mylius produced at a two-press level for four consecutive years, and Georg Husner probably made use of more than one press. The most interesting example is Johann Schott. He opened his shop in 1500, but for the first twenty-nine years never operated more than one press. In 1530 he must have purchased a second press—from then until the very end of his life, he ran a two-press shop. Schott's shop was an exception among medium-scale shops, most of which operated one press, with occasional use of a second. The working group in these shops would have included one team of compositors, a team of pressmen, and the master, with the latter performing some of the composition or presswork himself.

Both large- and medium-scale shops accepted work from other printers or publishers, in many cases from shops outside of Strasbourg. Johann Grüninger printed editions for Martin Flach of Basel, Peter Drach of Speyer, and Anton Koberger of Nuremberg. Johann Knobloch worked for Johann von Ravensburg at Cologne, Strasbourg publisher Paul Goetz, Urban Kaym of Buda, and Johann Haselberger. Johann Schott worked on commission both for Paul Goetz and for the Alantsee press in Vienna.[16] This practice seems to have been less usual among printers at the end of the century, except for Lazarus Zetzner, who probably functioned more as a publisher than a printer. In books printed under his auspices, his signature was accompanied by the identification "Bibliopola" or "Verleger."[17]

One-man shops were exactly that. The printer-owner worked alone doing both the composing and the printing, with perhaps some help from an apprentice. In an average year he could set up and print between 25 and 40 formes, roughly one-fifth the output of the medium-scale shops. In this case, one man literally performed the skills of five. For most of these men, printing was their livelihood, though for a few it was peripheral to their other work. Heinrich Knoblochtzer, Christian Egenolff, Jacob Frölich, Jost Martin, and Theobald Berger all made their living as printers. Egenolff specialized in scientific and technical publication, Knoblochtzer pioneered popular illustrated books,[18] Berger concentrated on popular music. Their products commanded particular markets. Peter Hugg, Nikolaus Faber, and Nikolaus Waldt were job printers, printing broadsheets, songs, and legal documents, keeping themselves busy with work around the Ratshaus. Heinrich Vogtherr was an engraver and Heinrich Seybold a doctor; their printing activities were ancillary to these other pursuits. Two of the small printers, Rémy Guédon and Peter Schöffer, were religious propagandists. These small shops prove that a man operating his own press could make a living even though his production was low in comparison with other shops.

In addition, there were several men who each printed in his own name but published fewer than six books during his career in Strasbourg. I have labeled this group of twenty-one the nonestablished shops, since none of the printers established permanent shops in the city (see table 3).

There is no evidence that any of these men operated his own shop for a continuous period. Peter Attendorn, a pupil of Wimpheling, followed his teacher to Strasbourg and worked with the Mentelin-Rusch press until 1482. In 1489 he attempted to establish a small press. Despite encouragement from Wimpheling, he was not able to maintain a steady production and eventually turned to bookselling.[19] Thomas Anshelm arrived in the city in 1488 apparently with the intention of establishing himself, but left before the year was up after having printed a German edition of the Gospels and Epistles. The press he founded in Tübingen became an important center for the humanist movement there.[20] Hieronymus Greff, an artist, produced a pirated edition of Dürer's series on the Apocalypse with the statement on the title page "printed at Strasbourg by Hieronymus Greff, the painter."[21] Wilhelm Schaffner was an itinerant printer, carrying his press with him from one town to the next, turning out works that were familiar and sure to sell, such as Morgenstern's sermons, Perotti's Latin grammar, and Wydenbusch's *Hortulus animae*.[22] Sigismund Bundt, a printer in Haguenau, had a workshop in Strasbourg for a few years.[23] Friedrich Ruch von Dambach, an obscure figure, seems to have had sufficient connections to print a missal for Warmia in Ermland and then be commissioned by the diocese of Breslau to do a liturgy for the Vratislavian church.[24] After his work for these eastern dioceses was completed, it appears that he either died or moved on to continue elsewhere. Beatus and Sixtus Murner were based in Frankfurt, but their desire to publish the works of their brother Thomas led them to bring out one of his treatises on poetics in Strasbourg.[25] All these men worked in the early period, and their careers reflect the mobility that was possible in the developing phase of the printing industry.

Most of the works of other nonestablished printers were expressions of their religious convictions. Johann Schwintzer, an enthusiastic follower of Schwenckfeld and a student of Valentin Krautwald, arrived in the city seeking employment. He learned the printing trade from Peter Schöffer and then used these skills to publish Schwenckfeldian treatises and Anabaptist works while serving as an assistant in Schöffer's shop.[26] As the religious crisis deepened, an increasing number of Protestant printers from other areas came to the city and attempted to support themselves by their trade. By 1548 the names of French printers began to appear on books published in Strasbourg: Rémy Guédon, Jacques Poulain, Pierre Estiart, and Gillotte le Pords. As refugees they wished to print propaganda leaflets and treatises for French markets. Whether they brought presses with them or purchased equipment in Strasbourg remains questionable. It is believed, for instance, that Rémy Guédon was protected by the eminent physician Johann Guinther von Andernach and that he printed his two editions of Guinther's treatise on the plague and an edition of Marot's psalms in Guinther's house.[27] Having arrived in 1547, Guédon left the city shortly after the publication of the Interim. He followed Bucer to Cambridge, where he became an important and well-regarded printer.[28]

The most productive of the French refugee printers were Pierre Estiart and François Perrin. Estiart, a bookseller with business connections in Geneva, Lyon, and Basel, purchased citizenship in Strasbourg in 1555, using the city as a base from which he traveled forth to other cities.[29] Rodolphe Peter's relentless search has uncovered at least seven books published by order of Estiart. Those printed in 1558 were probably done by François Perrin on his own press, which he had set up in the Kansgässlein. Perhaps because there was a well-trained printer like François Perrin available, Estiart commissioned the publication of Francisco de Enzinas's *Histoire de l'estat du Païs Bas,* Bullinger's sermons on the Apocalypse in a French translation, Sleidan's *Histoire de la religion,* and a summary of the latter work.[30] These were all large books (the Sleidan ran to 950 modern pages), and it was certainly the largest production of any refugee printer. The level attained in 1558, however, was not maintained. Peter points out that work continued to appear under Estiart's signature after his death in 1564 but believes it had simply become a convenient false name.[31] The work that was accomplished by these two men in a single year was probably made possible because Estiart had sufficient funds to finance it from his other activities.

By the end of the century the treatises from the small presses were increasingly political. Gillotte le Pords published an account of the efforts of Henry of Navarre and Duke Casimir to raise troops in 1587.[32] Elias Baldus wrote and printed stirring accounts of the Protestants' struggle during the Bishop's War.[33] It is difficult to determine whether any of these propagandists owned a press. They may have worked in the shops of established printers sympathetic to their causes, who permitted them to bring out one or two treatises on the shop presses.

The work of the nonestablished printers stands as proof of the availability of presses to those with the skill to use them. These men, however, do not figure in the rest of the chapter; the discussion is confined to the established printers listed in table 2.

The fortunes of the printers were intimately tied to external events. The economic periods already described are confirmed by the totals for masterformes (figure III). There was slow but steady growth from 1480 to 1507, then a period of high production from 1508 to 1525, averaging about 1,800 masterformes. In contrast to the startling increase in the number of books produced during the years 1523 through 1528 (figure II), the number of masterformes fell to 1,400. The early years of the Reform were marked by a pamphlet war, not a battle of books. For the first time the printers were faced by a decrease in their net output. Production of masterformes was high briefly from 1538 to 1544 and then depressed from 1545 to 1566, when the city was caught in the struggle of the Schmalkaldic War, the crisis over the introduction of the Interim religion, and internal religious factionalism. After 1570 production of masterformes returned to the 1490 level, except in

1594 and 1596, when the Bishop's War created another local crisis. The production figures, whether in terms of the number of books or the number of masterformes, bear witness to the economic vulnerability of the printers.

Economic conditions in the printing trade were never stable. In the face of these circumstances which they could not control, the printers knit themselves together with strong social ties. Although they were essentially newcomers, both as craftsmen and citizens, the printers rapidly developed protective social forms and traditions.

Few of the Strasbourg printers were native born. Of the seventy-seven printers only ten can be firmly identified as having been born in the city: six of these were sons of Strasbourg printers.[34] The majority of the printers (88 percent of the seventy-seven) had immigrated to the city. Records exist for forty-one of these immigrants, and the place of birth of eight of these men can be identified.[35] For the rest, the roster of new citizens serves as evidence of their arrival and relatively rapid assimilation into the community: sixteen purchased burgher status,[36] and nineteen acquired citizenship by marrying Strasbourg women.[37]

The high immigration rate reflects the demographic realities of sixteenth-century urban life. Because of the high death rate inside its walls, particularly during outbreaks of plague, the city had to renew itself from the outside.[38] All urban trades were dependent on a constant flow of immigrants. In the years 1544–65, for which adequate records exist, 105 textile workers, woodworkers, and metalworkers; 46 locksmiths, ironworkers, and leather workers; and 54 shoemakers entered the city. Eight printers arrived in these years, supplemented by 11 bookbinders and 8 typefounders.[39] Over the whole period 1480–1599 the printers were only a small part of a larger stream but were among those who had traveled the longest distances, coming from as far away as the Low Countries, Switzerland, and the lower Rhineland.[40] Nine of the large-scale printers were immigrants, able to establish a flourishing trade within their own lifetimes.

There were several avenues by which one might become a printer. Georges Husner was a goldsmith; Jacob Cammerlander, Hieronymus Greff, and Heinrich Vogtherr were engravers; Bartholomäus Kistler was a painter.[41] These particular arts provided easy entry into the printing trade, since many of the same skills were required. Some of the men who emigrated to the city had already served as apprentices or journeymen in print shops before their arrival. Johann Grüninger was trained at Basel, Wendelin Rihel at Haguenau, Peter Schöffer at Mainz, and Augustin Fries at Zurich.[42] Others acquired their skills in Strasbourg: Martin Flach under Johann Mentelin and Adolf Rusch, Matthias Schürer under his cousin Martin Flach II, Reinhardt Beck under Johann Prüss.[43] The scholarly world provided another entrée. A substantial proportion of the printers had attended univer-

Table 4. Education of Printers (arranged chronologically)

Printer	Education/Foreign language	Source
Heinrich Knoblochtzer	Heidelberg, matric. 1486	F. Ritter, *Hist.Impr.*, p. 55
Georg Husner	Heidelberg, 8 yrs.	*ADB*, 13, p. 457
Martin Flach	Magister	Ritter, *Hist.Impr.*, p. 76
Johann Prüss	Ingolstadt, matric. 1474	Benz, *Buchdrucker*, p. 410
Martin Schott	Latin	Ritter, *Hist.Impr.*, p. 70
Johann Grüninger	Magister	*ADB*, 10, p. 53
Matthias Hupfuff	Unknown	
Johann Schott	Freiburg, Heidelberg, Basel	Benz, *Buchdrucker*, p. 412
Johann Knobloch	Elementary Latin	Ritter, *Hist.Impr.*, p. 194
Martin Flach II	Basel, matric. 1503	*Matrikel der Univ. Basel*, I, p. 270.
Matthias Schürer	Magister, Cracow, Sélestat Grammar School	Benz, *Buchdrucker*, p. 413
Reinhardt Beck	Unknown	
Ulrich Morhard	Tübingen, matric. 1523	Ritter, *Hist.Impr.*, p. 306
Johann Herwagen	University educated	Ritter, *Hist.Impr.*, p. 309
Wolfgang Köpfel	Greek	A2.3.4 preface, A2.3.9
Balthasar Beck	Unknown	
Georg Ulricher	Unknown	
Johann Knobloch II	Unknown	
Johann Albrecht	Unknown	
Jacob Cammerlander	Magister, Mainz	Benz, *Buchdrucker*, p. 416
Bartholomäus Grüninger	Unknown	
Wendelin Rihel	Latin	Ritter, *Hist.Impr.*, p. 566
Crato Mylius	Wittenberg, Melanchthon student	Benz, *Buchdrucker*, p. 418
Georg Messerschmidt	Hebrew[a]	Ritter, *Hist.Impr.*, p. 215
Paul Messerschmidt	Unknown	
Samuel Emmel	Unknown	
Christian Mylius	Unknown	
Josias Rihel	Strasbourg Gymnasium	Ritter, *Hist.Impr.*, p. 268
Theodosius Rihel	Strasbourg Gymnasium	Ritter, *Hist.Impr.*, p. 268
Bernard Jobin	Unknown	
Christian Mylius II	Unknown	
Anton Bertram	Unknown	
Lazarus Zetzner	Unknown	

[a]Georg Messerschmidt was able to print Hebrew text.

sities, proceeding from the university classrooms to the printing shops where they served their apprenticeships (table 4).

When a printer purchased citizenship or acquired it through marriage, he was assigned to the Steltz, a large guild which included artists, engravers, and goldsmiths. This has been interpreted as an attempt on the part of the Strasbourg Magistrat to control the new industry.[44] Guild membership in Strasbourg had political as well as economic significance. The trade guilds made up the twenty corporations established by the city constitution. Every citizen voted and fulfilled his political obligations within the corporation to which he was assigned. The requirement that the printers serve in a guild simply meant that they were being assimilated into the political system.[45]

The printers tended to settle in the city in one of three favored locations. The earliest printing shops were located in the little stalls clustered around the base of the cathedral and in the adjoining streets. Three men, Johann Mentelin, Johann Prüss, and Matthias Hupfuff, had shops there before the turn of the century. The square near the Dominican convent, where faculty and students came and went to the Gymnasium and Academy (occupying the old convent building), became another important location. Two major printers, Wendelin Rihel and Bernard Jobin, established shops there, the Rihel shop within the very door of the school. The area around the city hall, close to the city offices and the law courts, provided yet another group of potential customers.[46] These three areas are all within a five minute walk of one another—one could make the circuit in ten minutes. The smaller shops were located in the side streets and alleys of this same central district.

Like most sixteenth-century crafts, printing was a family industry and success was closely linked to a printer's familial ties and his associations with intellectual families in the city. Of the thirteen large-scale printers, 62 percent were directly related to printing families; two of the others, Johann Herwagen and Bernard Jobin, had important ties by marriage or family to the intellectual community. Of the medium-scale printers, 65 percent were members of printing families, often by marriage. The masters of only 27 percent of the one-man shops enjoyed family connections within the trade. None of the nonestablished printers had this advantage. These percentages underscore the familial nature of sixteenth-century business organization.

Five major families dominated the printing trade in Strasbourg, maintaining their influence for several generations, although infrequently through direct male heirs.[47] Johann Mentelin established a press in 1460 and eventually created a printing dynasty through his daughters. Salome, the eldest, married a printer, Adolf Rusch, who carried the shop on from the time of Mentelin's death in 1478 until his own death in 1492. Martin Schott, the printer husband of the second daughter, then inherited the business. In 1499, he left it to his son, Johann, who became more successful than his father.[48] Martin ran a small medium-scale shop, exceeding the capacity of one press only once in his sixteen years of activity. For twenty-two years his son was content to follow this pattern. After the Reformation, in which he played an active role in the diffusion of Protestant polemic and doctrine, Johann added another press and doubled his original production. He remained active for forty-four years, keeping the Mentelin-Schott family in continuous presence in the Strasbourg printing community for ninety years and achieving a three-generation succession.

In 1480 Johann Prüss, originally from Württemberg, established himself in Strasbourg. The first five years were difficult. He managed to produce no more than sixty-six masterformes in the best year, but by 1486 his production had begun to expand. By 1498 he was often using two presses to keep up with his commissions, in particular the missals for which he established a reputation.[49] He had at least two children—a daughter, Margarethe, and a son, Johann II, who carried on the shop after his father's death in 1510. Margarethe, however, married her father's typographer, Reinhardt Beck, who took over the shop in 1512, forcing Johann II to find a new location.[50] Whether he lost his father's contacts, whether he was not interested in specializing in missals, or for some other reason, by 1521 Johann II's production decreased to about 30–40 masterformes per year. Many of these were devoted to Martin Luther, Joachim Vadian, Ulrich Hutten, and other Protestant polemicists. He ran a one-man shop and kept it going until 1550. Reinhardt Beck, in the meantime, carried on the family shop at one-press capacity, also deserting the Catholic repertoire of his father-in-law for humanist works and, as early as 1521, Lutheran tracts. In 1522, Beck died. Margarethe supervised the shop for three years until her marriage to Johann Schwann, a Lutheran, formerly a Franciscan, who had probably worked in the shop for Beck.[51] Schwann, however, lived only two years. In 1527, a year after Schwann's death, Margarethe married yet another printer, Balthasar Beck.[52] Balthasar operated at a relatively high level of production for a one-press shop and, for at least four years, he kept two presses running. He was well known among the Anabaptist community, publishing the work of Anabaptist and Spiritualist theologians and leaders. The original Prüss press lost its Catholic commitment and became, essentially, two presses, both marked by a strong, if heterodox, religious focus.

The evolution of the Flach-Knobloch press reflects the strains which could result from the remarriage of a widow and the effects of such a marriage on the inheritance of the son. Martin Flach was already middle-aged when he set up his own press in 1487, having apprenticed under Mentelin and Rusch as early as 1469.[53] Flach's press got off to the usual slow start—40 masterformes a year for three years—but by 1487 he was running one press at capacity. By 1489 he had two presses, which were in full use for six of the next twelve years. The shop produced 419 master-formes in 1500, the year of his death.

Martin Flach II carried on without any break after his father's death, turning out 690 masterformes under his own name in 1501, although these must have already been in press. Johann Knobloch, recently arrived from Zofingen, Switzerland, was already working in the Flach shop and had begun to publish under his own signature by 1500. In 1501 he married Catherine Dammerer, the elder Flach's widow, and took over the direction of the Flach shop. Martin Flach II moved out and started a new shop in the St. Barbaragasse near his father-in-law, the printer Johann Wähinger.[54] Martin II was no longer a young man at this time: he must have been at least thirty since his son was old enough to enter the University of Basel in 1503.[55] According to Benzing, Martin II remained on good terms with Knobloch, the latter providing him with type, initial letters, and even some commissions.[56] Nevertheless, the hardships of establishing his own enter-prise were refelected in his production. In 1503 Flach II produced only 16 masterformes; from 1504 to 1507 we have records of nothing printed under his name. From 1508 to 1512 business was a little better—he averaged 64 masterformes a year, with a big year in 1513 when he brought out Petrus de Natalibus's *Catalogus sanctorum et gestorum,* which required 209 master-formes.[57] This was followed by another gap from 1514 to 1516. By 1519 he was publishing Luther; by 1520 Luther, Karlstadt, and Hutten.[58] Even this new activity could not fend off a financial crisis. After 1523 his production dwindled to one short treatise a year. He sold his house in 1522; his shop was closed by 1525.[59] Three years later, in 1528, he attempted to recover half of his mother's 1,000 florin dowry from Knobloch's second wife and widow, Magdalene. The court found in Flach II's favor, but he had insuffi-cient funds to carry the case further when Magdalene appealed to a higher court. In 1536 the Magistrat issued him a certificate of indigence.[60]

Meanwhile, under Knobloch's direction, the original Flach press became one of the most important in the city. By 1501 he was using two presses and, after 1516, often used a third. Three years after Martin Flach had been forced to close, Knobloch died. Johann Knobloch II, Knobloch's son by his second wife, assumed direction of the shop. A year later, Magdalene, Knobloch II's mother, married Johann Albrecht, who had operated his own printing shop in Haguenau. According to Benzing, the stepfather and son shared the Knobloch shop.[61] Knobloch II drew on his father's repertoire, publishing further editions of the Tengler *Layenspiegel* and a third edition of Crescentius's agricultural treatise. Two treatises by Melchior Hoffmann are also attributed to him.[62] After 1532 no books appear under the younger Knobloch's name.[63] Albrecht maintained the Knobloch shop at a one-press level, printing items whose market was assured, such as Brant's *Richterlich*

Clagspiegel and more editions of Tengler. To these he added Cocles's physiognomy book, a work of popular science, Latin texts, and a few humanist writings.[64] Family continuity was maintained by using the signature "ex officina Knobloch." In 1541 the shop was acquired by Georg Messerschmidt, who was joined by his brother Paul in 1555. Georg modified the signature to "ex officina Knoblochiana." The name was used for its prestige, but the press was no longer a family press. By coincidence the three early printing families, the Flach-Knoblochs, the Mentelin-Schotts, and the Prüss-Becks, had died out by 1550. They were replaced by two new printing dynasties.

The Rihels were the only family who managed to keep a large-scale shop going for two generations, successfully passing it down from the father to two sons. Originally from Haguenau, Wendelin Rihel, the founder, purchased citizenship in Strasbourg in 1525 and established his press in 1535,[65] starting out immediately with two presses on which he produced 400 masterformes in the first year. He kept the two presses operating relatively close to capacity for sixteen of the next twenty years, printing classical editions and texts for the new Gymnasium. When Wendelin Rihel died in 1554, two of his sons, Josias and Theodosius, inherited the press. The brothers ran the shop together for a brief period, disagreed on business matters, and divided the inheritance within a year of their father's death.[66]

Both shops operated on a large scale. Josias continued the family shop near the school, publishing the classical editions and texts needed by the students, as well as various works by the faculty, with whom he enjoyed close associations.[67] For the first twelve years after the split Theodosius maintained much the same pattern as his brother, although he produced less. His work required no more than one press. In 1568 he added at least one additional press and began to reprint Sleidan's *De statu religionis . . . Carolo V,* originally brought out by his father.[68] By 1570 he was using at least four presses, producing 1,000 masterformes a year. Although he dropped back to three presses from time to time, throughout the decade of the eighties his average was well over 1,000 masterformes a year. He published Johannes Schneidewin's commentaries on Justinian's *Institutes,* one of the few important legal publications to come off a Strasbourg press. The shop had to be large to handle it. It ran to 400 foliosheets and Theodosius Rihel reprinted it nine times.[69] He also did numerous editions of Josephus and Hegissipus.[70] Printing these big volumes may have been expedited by Rihel's owning a papermill, since paper was the largest factor in determining the cost of printing.[71]

Other members of the Rihel family were also involved in the book trade. A third brother, Wendelin, appears in the baptismal records as a bookbinder.[72] In 1558 Sarah Rihel, a sister, married her second husband, the printer Samuel Emmel, who had previously been married to the widow of Balthasar Beck.[73] Emmel was already established in his own one-press shop. Indeed, in 1557 he had entered into an association with the printer Jacob Froschesser and the binder and bookseller, Christopher Riedlinger, to expand his printing activity. According to the terms of the contract, Emmel was to furnish all the equipment for the enterprise as well as pay the wages. Froschesser and Riedlinger were to furnish the paper and together would share half the profits.[74] This association had little effect; Emmel's shop remained a one-press operation for the next six years. Then there was a substantial jump to a two-press level in 1564, which peaked in 1569 with a production of 671 masterformes. In that same year Emmel declared bankruptcy. François-Joseph Fuchs suggests that Emmel may have been unwise in the books he chose to print.[75] The marked increase in his output began with the publication of several Biblical commentaries in German by Cyriacus Spangenberg—88 percent of his press space in the last disastrous year went to these commentaries.[76] Clearly this was far too large a segment. Spangenberg was a disciple of Flacius Illyricus, whose doctrine on Original Sin was considered unorthodox. Although Emmel may have been a disciple of Spangenberg, it was impossible for him to dispose of the commentaries, which were regarded as theologically dangerous.

The Rihel family was entangled in the failure. Emmel's creditors included his brother-in-law Josias Rihel and the merchant Nikolaus Goetz,[77] who complained that, among other things, Theodosius Rihel was reprinting works from Emmel's repertoire although more than 2,000 copies remained for sale in Emmel's stock room.[78] Furthermore, they claimed these were editions for which Emmel had purchased a privilege. Theodosius Rihel replied only that he would turn over the works in question for 300 florins. The creditors claimed damages of 6,000–7,000 florins, and by 1571 Emmel had closed his doors. His brothers-in-law made no attempt to rescue him financially. Three years later Emmel was able to establish himself in his own printing shop in Cologne although the record is silent about where he obtained the money.[79]

The Mylius press was the second family press to emerge into prominence after 1555, but it is almost impossible to determine the nature of the family relationships involved. The press was founded in 1536, within a year of the establishment of Wendelin Rihel's shop. Crato Mylius (the name was actually Müller but all members of the family preferred the latinized version) was a nephew of Mathias Schürer and, like him, a scholar. Educated at Wittenberg, he studied under Philipp Melanchthon[80] and devoted much of his press space to the publication of humanist literature and Protestant theology, in particular the works of Melanchthon, and of Jodocus Willich and Caspar Cruciger, both associates of Melanchton.[81] Mylius purchased his shop from Georg Ulricher and immediately established a high level of production, turning out 643 masterformes the year after he opened. For six of nine years he operated two or more presses. Having quickly made his mark within the intellectual community and among the Magistrat, he was asked to carry out several diplomatic assignments for the city. In the course of one of these missions in 1547 he was killed, at the age of forty-one, at the battle of Mühlberg,[82] leaving his wife, Ottilia, and a one-year-old son named Phillip.[83] It is possible that there were some older children as well. The bereaved Ottilia struggled to keep the shop going. In 1549 she married the humanist Blase Fabricius, one of Crato's assistants.[84] They managed to maintain a minimal level of production—one or two books comprising a total of 40 masterformes a year. It would seem from this that Fabricius was working alone.

In 1555 books began to appear under the signature of one Christian Mylius. Fabricius continued to print under his own name, carrying on with a book or two a year until 1559. In 1558 Christian Mylius was able to produce 476 masterformes in one year, although he quickly fell back to a one-press level of 100 masterformes a year. Then, in 1564, his production rose again to a one and one-half or two press level, probably because he had taken over the house and shop of his father-in-law, Jacob Frölich. He had, however, used Frölich's equipment and press marks since the latter's death in 1557,[85] thus his earlier spurt in production may have reflected his association with Frölich rather than a revival of activity for the Mylius press.

Who was Christian Mylius? Johannes Ficker and Otto Winckelmann identify him as the son of Crato. Ritter believes, based on the age difference between Christian and Phillip, that he was the brother of Crato. Benzing says he was a relative of Crato.[86] All the answers leave unsolved questions. If he was the son, there was a large age gap between him and his brother Phillip. If he was the brother, why was it necessary for Ottilia and Fabricius to keep the press during the interim period? Furthermore, why was Christian so willing to leave the original Mylius shop and establish himself in the Frölich house on the Kornmarkt and to use the signature, from then on, "auf dem Kornmarkt"?

To complicate matters further Christian Mylius's production began to diminish in 1568, and then in 1569 and 1570 books appeared with the signature "Christian Mylius Erben."[87] From 1570 to 1580 fifty-seven books appear with the signature "Christian Mylius." Both François Ritter and Josef Benzing believe that he is a different individual. To clarify matters somewhat I have designated him Christian Mylius II and refer to the earlier printer as Christian Mylius. Given the lack of evidence, it is impossible to establish the exact relationship between these two men, or between them and Crato Mylius.[88] The only element that seems clear is a desire to maintain the continuity of the Mylius name despite changes in management.

Family connections were important to those entering the printing trade and establishing a shop. The family provided vocational security and continuity. It could not, however, provide financial backing or support. The periods of transition that followed the death of a printer indicate that there was very little accumulated capital to hold things together for even one or two years. The drop in production after death was, in most cases, precipitous—only Martin Flach II was able to carry on without a break and his production was probably sustained by books already in press. Each generation had to begin again to accumulate its capital, to acquire the contacts that would bring trade into the shop. The disarray that followed Crato Mylius's death is particularly telling. Mylius had successfully operated a large-scale shop. He was respected by the community and had strong support from the theologians, the intellectuals, and the Magistrat. Yet, his widow and his journeyman could barely keep the press going after his sudden death in the service of the city. The decline in production on the death of a printer and the slow build-up by his successor indicate that few customers could be passed along from one generation to the next. The printers worked on a thin margin of profit from year to year. Family influence was more a matter of prestige, of status, and of tradition than of money.

The crisis for any one of these presses was the death of the founder. Even direct succession from father to son by no means guaranteed that the press would continue at the same level of productivity. Indeed, in all cases but two, inheriting sons did not do as well as their fathers. Seven of the large-scale and medium-scale presses passed directly from father to son. Only three sons, Johann Schott and the brothers Josias Rihel and Theodosius Rihel, were able to maintain or exceed their fathers' levels of production. Johann Prüss II, Martin Flach II, and Johann Knobloch II were less successful than their fathers—Flach II ending in bankruptcy, Knobloch II printing only five books in his own name. Johann Prüss II operated only a one-man shop. In several instances the sons sold the family press within a few years of their fathers' deaths. For example, Bartholomäus Grüninger directed the Grüninger press when the aged Johann was overwhelmed by the factionalism caused by the religious changes. Bartholomäus operated the shop at a substantially lower level after his father's death in 1531, but in 1539 he left for Cologne, perhaps because it was Catholic.[89] The sons of Wolfgang Köpfel carried on only briefly as his heirs before leaving the city.[90] In all these cases the sons were old enough to have carried the responsibility and had been trained by their fathers, yet the presses prospered in only half the transfers.

Marriage of a printer to the widow or daughter of another printer seems to have been as important as inheritance from father to son in insuring the continuity of a press. Transfer of the property through women was as frequent an occurrence as transfer through sons. There were seven instances where the press went from the husband to the widow and then to the second husband, who assumed direction of the press.[91] This does not include Johann Herwagen, the Strasbourg printer who married the widow of Johann Froben and thus became the head of the most important press in Basel.[92] In addition, six printers' daughters married printers, and four shops then passed to the sons-in-law.[93] Thus, Strasbourg presses were transferred in eleven instances through women, as against seven transfers to male heirs. Since three of the female transfers were through Margarethe Prüss, the ratio could be given as nine to seven. The press suffered the same problems of reorganization under the widow or daughter. In only two instances did the production levels increase after the transfer. Women did, however, play a pivotal role in the complex web of family relationships which characterized the printing trade.

Catherine Dammerer Flach demonstrates the strong position of a widow in the sixteenth century in determining the continuity of property. Her second marriage to Johann Knobloch put the Flach press in Knobloch's hands. Her large dowry also fell to him and, at his death, to his second wife who managed to keep the money from Catherine's own son, Martin Flach. Martin had been forced to leave his father's shop at Catherine's remarriage and had also lost his share of her money; his rights as an heir were clearly subordinate to hers.

Printers' daughters occupied a special position in the trade. Their marriages to printers reflected the pattern of endogamous marriage common in all the trades of the city.[94] A printer's daughter not only brought useful connections with her, she probably had specific skills which were useful to a printer husband. Christophe Plantin, the Antwerp printer, taught his five daughters to read by the age of four or five and the four eldest all worked as proofreaders until they were twelve. The fourth daughter, Magdalene, carried the proofs of the folio-size Polyglot Bible to the house of the scholar Montanus and read from the originals in Hebrew, Chaldean, Syriac, Greek, and Latin. When one scholar questioned a friend of the Plantin family about Magdalene's linguistic skills it was explained that she could read the texts but did not understand their content.[95]

Among the daughters of the Strasbourg printers, Margarethe Prüss emerges as the most energetic figure. During two intervals of widowhood she directed the family shop by herself. She seems to have had strong religious convictions and probably strengthened the Anabaptist commitment of the press by her selection of marriage partners. Her second husband, Johann Schwann, continued the publication of Carlstadt's work which Margarethe's brother had started, in addition to publishing the work of other radical reformers. When Schwann died, Margarethe married an even more pronounced radical, Balthasar Beck, who became a leading Anabaptist publisher. Anabaptist preachers came to Strasbourg to meet Beck and arrange for publication of their work.[96] Since the Spiritualist-Anabaptist direction was maintained from one husband to the next and since Margarethe provided the element of continuity, it is impossible to believe that she was not a strong factor in determining the ideological commitment of the press. The heterodox tradition in the family was further demonstrated by the marriage of Margarethe's daughter in 1542 to Sebastian Franck, after Balthasar had published his *Chronica*.[97]

Another Strasbourg woman, Walpurg Wähinger, the unmarried daughter of the printer Johann Wähinger, purchased citizenship in 1525 and belonged to the guild, zur Steltz, like other printers.[98] There is no evidence that she printed any books in her own name but she may have worked as a proofreader or corrector. The important element is that she wanted to be publicly recorded as a member of the guild although, as a woman, she could enjoy none of the political rights that were associated with membership.

Family connections within the printing trade could influence the scale of production, the number of commissions a press received, and ultimately its financial success. Equally important were connections with the intellectual community. Many printers at all levels enjoyed close relationships with writers. The printer Matthias Brant, for example, is believed to have been the brother of Sebastian Brant, the humanist.[99] Sixtus and Beatus Murner printed the works of their brother Thomas, the humanist-satirist.[100] Martin Schott, the printer, was the son of a highly respected Strasbourg family. His father was a well-known sculptor. The printing family used the same coat of arms as the Peter Schott family. The younger Peter Schott, a canon of New Saint Peter chapter, was one of the founders of the humanist movement in Alsace and through him Martin seems to have had ties to other members of the group. Wolfgang Köpfel, the nephew of Wolfgang Capito, enjoyed similarly close associations with the Strasbourg reformers. Bernard Jobin was the brother-in-law of Johann Fischart, the satirist and propagandist.

Patronage relationships between printers and intellectuals moved in both directions. The writers encouraged the printers; the printers provided work for the writers. Jacob Wimpheling, for instance, encouraged his pupil Peter Attendorn to learn the art of printing. Wimpheling aided him directly by turning over to him several of his own treatises.[101] When Peter Schöffer was in difficulty with the Magistrat at Worms because of his sectarian publications, he wrote to Capito for help. The latter, with Martin Bucer, presented the case to the Strasbourg authorities and Schöffer was given permission to settle in Strasbourg.[102] Shortly before, Bucer and Capito had welcomed another refugee, Johann Schwintzer, whose espousal of Schwenkfeld's ideas had forced his departure from Liebnitz; Schwintzer learned his printing skills in Strasbourg.[103] Later the two reformers were instrumental in obtaining an appointment for Matthias Biener as official printer to the city of Berne.[104] Paul Fagius, professor of Hebrew at the Academy, probably gave the Hebrew type he had used on his own press at Isny to Georg Messerschmidt, enabling Messerschmidt to print Fagius's edition of the *Targum,* the first Hebrew work to be printed in Strasbourg.[105] Elias Schad, who occupied the same chair of Hebrew at the end of the century, had his own press for Hebrew editions and permitted Simon Meyer to use it.[106] Thus, both theologians and scholars used their influence to further the careers of the printers and even provided equipment for them.

From the very beginning of the century the printers, for their part, supported the cause of learning by employing scholars as correctors and proofreaders and by encouraging writers to undertake translations, new editions of the classics, or original works. Several members of the Strasbourg *sodalitas literaria,* among them Matthias Ringmann and Nikolaus Gerbel, served as correctors and scholarly advisors—Ringmann for Johann Prüss, and Gerbel for Matthias Schürer.[107] Beatus Rhenanus, another member of the sodalitas, performed similar services for Joannes Froben in Basel. Johann Adelphus Müling supported himself by working as a proofreader for Grüninger and Prüss.[108] He also translated a variety of medical and literary works, which were printed by Flach, Prüss, and Grüninger.[109]

Examples of printers employing scholars are many. Matthias Ringmann traveled to Italy to pick up the manuscript of the complete works of Giovanni Pico della Mirandola, which the author had promised to Thomas Wolf during a visit to Strasbourg. Ringmann then worked closely with Johann Prüss, preparing the text and supervising the volumes through the press.[110] Thomas Vogler served as an editor for Martin Schott and Johann Grüninger and worked on Grüninger's edition of Ptolemy with Lorenz Fries. He was responsible for editions of Poggio Bracciolini and a complete Terence.[111] Matthias Schürer asked Nikolaus Gerbel to undertake the translation of the *Noctium Atticarum* of Aulus Gellius, a task which Gerbel complained was too difficult for him because he was unable to read the Greek passages.[112] According to Ficker and Winckelmann, Francisco de Enzinas, the Spanish humanist, supervised Spanish translations of Plutarch, Lucian, and the complete Livy for the Strasbourg presses.[113] The most prolonged relationship between a printer and a writer was that between Bernard Jobin and Johann Fischart. Fischart lived in the Jobin house. Jobin provided Fischart with commissions and Fischart worked perennially as a proofreader. Until Fischart finally managed to obtain a civil service appointment in Forbach, Jobin provided his major means of support.[114]

Scientific editions involved substantial underwriting by the printers. Johann Schott brought together a team of men—the scientist Michael Herr, an apothecary surgeon, and the artist Hans Weyditz—who worked together for several years to insure the accuracy of Otto Brunfels's botanical treatise.[115] Wendelin Rihel printed David Kyber's Latin translation of Hieronymus Bock's *Kreuterbuch*. Later Josias Rihel sent David Kandel, a young Strasbourg artist, to live with Bock and prepare the drawings for a new edition of the work.[116] Christian Mylius printed two editions of Paracelsan texts prepared by Michael Toxites, and Christian Mylius II later continued to support Toxites in this venture.[117] Walter Ryff worked as a house author and editor over a considerable period of time for both Balthasar Beck and Josias Rihel, compiling one edition after another of his popular medical texts.

A significant element in the support which the printers provided was that it went to scholars, linguists, and scientists who did not have ecclesiastical or academic appointments. The majority of men mentioned above had no regular positions within the intellectual establishment. The printers played a vital role in making it possible for these men to support themselves independently.

By the middle of the century familial ties between the intellectuals and the large-scale printers had become closer. In part this may reflect the fact that the later printers tended to have more education than the earlier group. The Rihels were particularly closely bound to the intellectual community. Josias, the eldest son of Wendelin Rihel, was baptized by Wolfgang Capito while the Rihel family was still living in Haguenau.[118] Thus the friendship between these two families was strong. By 1535 Wendelin had opened his shop in Strasbourg, where his friendship with Johann Sturm created a strong bond with the new Gymnasium. The young Rihel sons, Josias, Theodosius, and Wendelin II, attended the new school while Sturm was one of the most influential rectors in Germany. The faculty included the humanist-lexicographer Peter Dasypodius, the humanist Johann Schwebel, as well as Wolfgang Capito and Martin Bucer. Wendelin Rihel printed Peter Dasypodius's Latin-German dictionary.[119] The relationships between the families went beyond business. Wendelin Rihel and Peter Dasypodius served as godfathers to the daughter of Christian Herlin, the mathematician at the Gymnasium. Wendelin II later married the Dasypodius daughter, Judith.[120] Josias Rihel printed the mathematical treatises of Conrad Dasypodius, who was probably his classmate or near contemporary at the Gymnasium.[121] The Rihel sons remained loyal to their old rector, Johann Sturm, and supported him during his long controversy with Johann Pappus. Theodosius Rihel was criticized by the Kirchenkonvent on the grounds that his editions of classical authors undermined the morals of the young,[122] a criticism similar to allegations leveled against Sturm. Throughout the sixties and seventies while the controversy raged, Josias Rihel continued to publish Sturm's texts and editions of Cicero.[123] The Rihels clearly provided strong support for the Sturm faction within the Gymnasium. The continued publication of Sturm's work is an indication of the popularity of his methods in other humanist schools.

The Rihels were also closely associated with Jean Sleidan. Luxembourgeois by birth, Sleidan arrived as a refugee from Paris and became one of the leading intellectual figures of the German Reformation. His history of the reign of Charles V expressed the highest hopes of the new movement. Wendelin Rihel printed the first edition in the last year of his life. Two reprintings, necessary in the next year, were brought out by the brothers Josias and Theodosius. Theodosius continued to reprint the book through 1576.[124] Crato Mylius was also closely associated with Johann Sturm, whom he accompanied on diplomatic missions, and with Sleidan. Sleidan's wife stood as godmother to Mylius's baby, Phillip.[125]

Connections with authors were important to the printers. In all cases in which a printer undertook to publish a large body of work by a single author—such as Sleidan, Paracelsus, or Fischart—or an important book—such as Otto Brunfels's *Kräuterbuch* or Peter Dasypodius's dictionary—there were preexisting ties between the writer and the printer. Business life and intellectual life in the sixteenth century were based on personal relationships. The intricate network of relationships between the intellectuals and the large-scale printers indicates that the two were not separated by social differences. The intellectuals of the period tended to come from the upper artisanat.[126] As we have already seen, the majority of the large-scale and at least half of the medium-scale printers had some form of higher education (see table 4). Those who read Latin were the social equals of the theologians, the humanists, and the scientists and were accepted within the intellectual community. The printers with less education ran the smallest shops and occupied the status of artisans, except for professional men like Heinrich Seybold and some of the refugee printers.

Social differences within the trade were reflected in patronal relationships between the large-scale printers and those who owned smaller shops. Baptismal records show that a large-scale printer or a member of his family often stood as godparent to the child of a far less prestigious printer. It was the custom to ask persons of superior social standing to assume this responsibility. The Protestant clergy often appeared in this guise, as did members of the Magistrat and their wives. Among the printers it was usual for an employer or patron of a young printer to stand at the font for the latter's child.[127] The paternal relationships of the traditional guild system were thus maintained in the new trade. Their presence indicates that the guilds were still important in providing social cohesion, although economically they no longer provided an assured ladder of advancement.

Politically the printers played only a very small role in the city of Strasbourg. The printers, as craftsmen, could hardly expect to enter the inner circles of the patriciate. The immigrant status of most of them reduced this possibility even further. There were, as we have seen, a few native-born printers who had family ties within the Magistrat. Martin Schott's cousin's family had long been active in city politics,[128] but neither Martin nor his son, Johann, pursued political honors.

Not until 1530 was any printer called on to undertake civic responsibilities. Crato Mylius, born in Sélestat and closely related to the Schürer family, received exceptional recognition on his arrival in Strasbourg. He was quickly accepted by the intellectual community, perhaps because he came as the new Gymnasium was being organized and there was need for more scholar–printers. In any case, although he did not serve in the Rat and thus was ineligible for appointment to other councils, he carried out diplomatic missions for the city. It was during one such mission that Mylius was killed.

The Rihels were the only printing family to achieve any position of political influence. Josias was elected to the Rat and served nine years between 1563 and 1579.[129] The presence of only one printer in the Rat during the entire century is a gauge of the standing of the printers among the governing elite. Printers were artisans—clever artisans with special skills, but artisans. Their importance within the intellectual community made little difference to the patriciate.

The governing authorities and the printers encountered one another chiefly in matters of censorship. Although the Rat and the Council of XXI passed a fairly strict censorship edict and had a committee of censors, supervision was relatively lax. The first recorded incident involving censorship of the printers occurred in February 1504. A set of defamatory verses had been published in late 1503 or early 1504 by Johann Schott under the title *Margarita, opus rursus exaratum pervigili nova itemque*. Schott and several other printers were called before the Rat and admonished to refrain from printing anything that would undermine the morals or reputation of the city. Schott responded to the warning by publishing a second edition in March 1504.[130] In 1524 the first formal censorship edict was promulgated, with the provision that each printer was responsible for submitting a copy of every book, treatise, or other publication to the Magistrat for inspection. The criterion was that nothing should be published "that would provoke the ordinary Christian man to attack or ridicule his neighbours."[131] The aim was not to control theological ideas or establish a particular brand of orthodoxy. A committee of two or three Ratsherren made up the board of censors. This does not seem to have been a permanent group like the school committee or the church wardens, but functioned as an ad hoc committee.[132] Basically, enforcement was the responsibility of the city secretary, but individual Ratsherren were appointed to handle particular books. The committee had no well-defined policy.

Serious actions resulting in the destruction of an entire press run were rare. Notable examples are the steps taken against Johann Grüninger for printing Thomas Murner's *Von dem grossen Lutherischen Narren* in 1522. The Rat confiscated the copies. Grüninger, convinced that the poem was no worse than the polemic the Protestants had published, held aside part of his stock and issued it for sale again, having added an apology for Murner's work. The Rat took action again, and everything was confiscated. Grüninger felt disgraced and alienated.[133] A second major incident occurred when Balthasar Beck printed Sebastian Franck's *Chronicle* in 1531. When Beck appeared before the censors he stated that the book was a standard history book. It is fairly clear that the censors had not read the book, for only after publication was there an uproar. Franck's account of the Hapsburgs was critical rather than laudatory. In particular, he described the Hapsburg eagle as a bloody bird, which was tantamount to an insult to the crown. Franck's religious views were unorthodox and original. He included in the book short biographies of people who were believed to be heretics but who had, in his view, contributed much to the church and to their community. It was a list of those he admired, and it included Erasmus. Erasmus did not understand the compliment. He wrote to the Rat in fury, demanding they control this dangerous writer and the printer who unleashed such filth. The Rat responded by confiscating the entire press run. All Beck's copies of Melchior Hoffmann's *Prophesy order weyssagang* and *Prophetisch gesicht* were also destroyed.[134]

Suppression of the latter treatises constituted religious censorship, of which there were other incidents as well. The gardener Clement Ziegler, a self-appointed preacher, appeared before the Rat on several occasions, requesting permission to publish his religious treatises. Associated with the Anabaptists in the minds of the Ratsherren, after 1536 he was invariably refused: in one instance the Rat suggested he stick to his work or else face punishment.[135] The Magistrat also took action against the established clergy. They forced Johann Marbach to restrain his attacks on the Calvinists in a set of published sermons, and removed a section of the preface to another sermon.[136]

Censorship did not weigh heavily on the printers. The magistrates were more concerned with so-called *Schmahschriften,* slanderous or libelous works, than they were with theological unorthodoxy or political polemic. This is evident from the fact that Strasbourg was an important center of Lutheran publication from 1522 on, well before the magistrates had accepted the Reform.[137] It was also important for the diffusion of Anabaptist ideas.[138] Inflammatory attacks upon the papacy were permitted during the 1530s and at the time of the Council of Trent.[139] The city presses were used by Huguenot publicists all during the French wars of religion.[140] There were equally concerted drives against the Hapsburgs' invasion of the Low Countries and against the Jesuits.[141] It is hardly possible to conclude that the printers were seriously restricted by the political authorities.

The importance of the printers lay in neither birth, wealth, property, nor political power, the essential elements in determining a man's status in the sixteenth century. It lay in their control of the printed word. Ultimately their decision to print or not to print a particular book or tract could have an immediate effect on political and religious events and, in a time of rapid change, on institutions. The most striking example of their influence can be seen in the religious publication of the pivotal years of the Reformation. The decision to print Protestant works in the earliest years reflected an individual conviction on the part of the printer, a sign of his own commitment to the new faith.

Matthias Schürer, Johann Schott, Martin Flach II, Reinhardt Beck, and Johann Prüss II took considerable risk in printing Lutheran treatises as early as 1519 and 1520 and merit designation as reforming printers. No one could foretell Luther's eventual success at that time. The Magistrat had by no means adopted a favorable position toward the Reform. It is particularly significant that Schürer, whose interests were predominantly classical and humanist, was the first to print a Lutheran treatise in the city.[142] The press believed to have been operated by his heirs published nothing but Protestant polemic. Martin Flach II printed both the *Appeal to the German Nobility* in 1520 and Luther's answer to the Papal Bull that condemned him.[143] The strongest Protestant supporter in the early years, however, was Johann Schott. He issued Luther's *Treatise on the Babylonian Captivity* in both German and Latin in 1520[144] and, out of personal admiration, became Ulrich von Hutten's major printer. As Hutten became increasingly radical and isolated from his former humanist circle, Schott continued to encourage him and print his work.[145] Schott protected and encouraged Otto Brunfels when the latter left the Carthusian monastery; Schott also continued to publish his theological and scientific works. In so doing, Schott again chose a nonconformist, since Brunfels was regarded as too Lutheran by the Strasbourg theologians.

Johann Prüss II was another enthusiastic supporter of the Reform, printing Lutheran tracts, in several cases in pirated editions.[146] His zeal was further reflected in his publication of treatises by French converts, which were designed to spread Lutheran ideas into France.[147] Johann Herwagen advanced the Protestant cause by publishing Protestant biblical commentary, including exegetical works by Philipp Melanchthon, Martin Luther, Johann Bugenhagen, and François Lambert,[148] books essential to the Reformers in preparing their own sermons and lectures.

Wolfgang Köpfel, Capito's nephew and namesake, was a strong and convinced Protestant from the beginning of his career. The very first book off his press was a polemic letter from Luther to Hartmut von Cronberg.[149] When the controversy over the marriage of the clergy raged between the bishop and the reformers in 1523–24, Köpfel helped to gain support for the married pastors by printing their treatises on marriage.[150]

These printers helped to determine the course of events. The decision to publish the work of a particular writer, say Hutten, at a particular time had a substantial influence on the evolution of the Reform. Precisely because they began to publish Luther's treatises very early, Schott and Prüss affected the speed with which the new doctrines were spread throughout Germany, although, in the long run, production by the Augsburg, Nuremburg, and Wittenberg printers exceeded that of the Strasbourg presses.[151] Locally the Strasbourg printers had significant impact. Herwagen's publication of the biblical commentaries essential for evangelical preaching and Köpfel's publication of the arguments of the reformers against the bishop on local issues influenced the evolution of the Strasbourg Reformation.

The reforming printers risked the success of their businesses for their religious ideas. The printers who printed the work of the Spiritualists and the Anabaptists took even greater risks. Again Martin Flach II and Johann Prüss II appeared in the vanguard, printing Karlstadt's work as early as 1520: Prüss continued to publish Karlstadt after he had become unpopular with the Strasbourg reformers, issuing four of his treatises in 1524 alone.[152] Johann Schwann, Prüss's brother-in-law, followed his lead. Balthasar Beck printed the treatises of Johann Buenderlin, Caspar Schwenckfeld, and Melchior Hoffman as well as Sebastian Franck's scandal-provoking chronicle.[153] Peter Schöffer and Johann Schwintzer, often working together, carried on the publication of Schwenckfeld's work.[154] Since it was difficult for the sectarians to propagate their views either orally or in print, the efforts of these Strasbourg printers were vital to the diffusion of Anabaptist and Spiritualist theology.

After 1550 this type of religious commitment on the part of the printers is far less evident. It was not because of highly organized or effective censorship. Rather, the inner energy seems to have disappeared. Bernard Jobin and Theodosius Rihel were the exceptions who adopted and maintained an ideological position. By publishing Johann Fischart's polemic tracts, Jobin promulgated a veritable flood of religious and political propaganda supporting the Huguenots in France and the Protestants in the Netherlands, while bitterly attacking the Spanish Inquisition.[155] Fischart's work was clearly pro-Calvinist and it was printed during a period of intense Lutheran orthodoxy. Jobin may also have printed Musculus's dialogue against Nicodemites and others who temporized with their faith. Eugénie Droz assumes that he had some connections with the French refugee community and the preparation of materials to be sent to France.[156] Theodosius Rihel was also identified with the Calvinist cause, which led to the suppression of his edition of the Bible for several years.[157] After 1570 the majority of printers, however, preferred to avoid controversy, whether political or religious.

The repertoire of each large-scale and medium-scale printer is summarized in tables 5 and 6. What these tables show most strikingly is the printers' range of choices. No two printers produced the same kinds of books in the same proportions. As table 7 shows, until the Reformation both large-scale and medium-scale printers published most of their books in Latin, though Johann Grüninger, Martin Schott and Matthias Hupfuff were exceptions. After 1530, however, the large-scale printers began to dominate the Latin market, chiefly because they functioned as printers to the Gymnasium, the Protestant clergy, and the Academy. Matthias Biener, with his musical publications, and Anton Bertram, who printed student theses for the Academy, were the only medium-scale printers after 1530 with an important portion of their work in Latin. A division of the market seems to have taken place. The large-scale printers commanded Latin publication. The medium-scale printers, joined at the end of the period by Bernard Jobin, turned to vernacular books and helped to mold and create the vernacular culture.

Specialization was another characteristic that differentiated the output of the large shops from the outputs of the medium and one-man shops (table 8).[158] Among the large-scale printers only Martin Flach, in the very earliest decades, had more than 50 percent of his total oeuvre in one field, in this case publication for the church. With the possible exception of Johann Herwagen, the rest of the large-scale shops diversified, offering a broad choice to the buyer: religious treatises, school texts, classical editions, humanist works, history, and science. The medium-scale and smaller printers, conversely, found it was practical to develop one field, establishing a clientele among the writers and readers of certain types of books.

In the first decades three medium-scale printers concentrated on the clerical market, printing editions of sermons and doctrinal classics for chapter and monastic libraries. Johann Prüss had a subspecialty in breviaries. As we have seen, many printers shifted to Protestant publication as the Reformation developed. Wolfgang Köpfel became, in a sense, the semi-official printer of the Strasbourg reformers, printing most of the treatises written

Table 5. Publication Programs of Large-Scale Printers

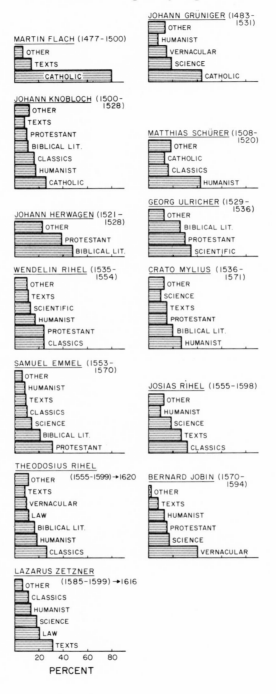

MARTIN FLACH (1477–1500)

JOHANN GRÜNIGER (1483–1531)

JOHANN KNOBLOCH (1500–1528)

MATTHIAS SCHÜRER (1508–1520)

JOHANN HERWAGEN (1521–1528)

GEORG ULRICHER (1529–1536)

WENDELIN RIHEL (1535–1554)

CRATO MYLIUS (1536–1571)

SAMUEL EMMEL (1553–1570)

JOSIAS RIHEL (1555–1598)

THEODOSIUS RIHEL (1555–1599)→1620

BERNARD JOBIN (1570–1594)

LAZARUS ZETZNER (1585–1599)→1616

PERCENT

Table 6. Publication Programs of Medium-Scale Printers

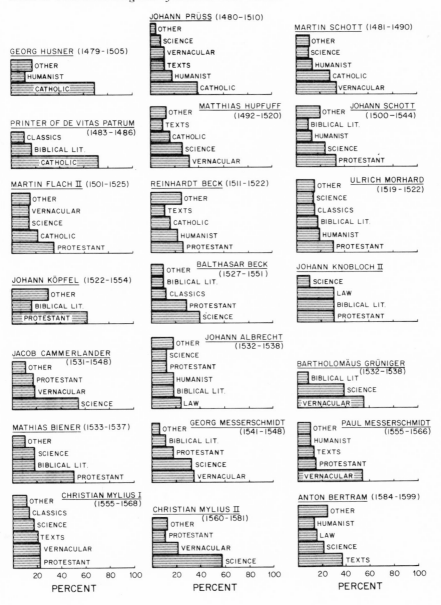

GEORG HUSNER (1479-1505)
OTHER
HUMANIST
CATHOLIC

PRINTER OF DE VITAS PATRUM (1483-1486)
CLASSICS
BIBLICAL LIT.
CATHOLIC

MARTIN FLACH II (1501-1525)
OTHER
VERNACULAR
SCIENCE
CATHOLIC
PROTESTANT

JOHANN KÖPFEL (1522-1554)
OTHER
BIBLICAL LIT.
PROTESTANT

JACOB CAMMERLANDER (1531-1548)
OTHER
PROTESTANT
VERNACULAR
SCIENCE

MATHIAS BIENER (1533-1537)
OTHER
SCIENCE
BIBLICAL LIT.
PROTESTANT

CHRISTIAN MYLIUS I (1555-1568)
OTHER
CLASSICS
SCIENCE
TEXTS
VERNACULAR
PROTESTANT

20 40 60 80 100
PERCENT

JOHANN PRÜSS (1480-1510)
OTHER
SCIENCE
VERNACULAR
TEXTS
HUMANIST
CATHOLIC

MATTHIAS HUPFUFF (1492-1520)
OTHER
TEXTS
CATHOLIC
SCIENCE
VERNACULAR

REINHARDT BECK (1511-1522)
OTHER
TEXTS
CATHOLIC
HUMANIST
PROTESTANT

BALTHASAR BECK (1527-1551)
OTHER
BIBLICAL LIT.
CLASSICS
PROTESTANT
SCIENCE

JOHANN ALBRECHT (1532-1538)
OTHER
SCIENCE
PROTESTANT
HUMANIST
BIBLICAL LIT.
LAW

GEORG MESSERSCHMIDT (1541-1548)
OTHER
BIBLICAL LIT.
PROTESTANT
SCIENCE
VERNACULAR

CHRISTIAN MYLIUS II (1560-1581)
OTHER
PROTESTANT
VERNACULAR
SCIENCE

20 40 60 80 100
PERCENT

MARTIN SCHOTT (1481-1490)
OTHER
SCIENCE
HUMANIST
CATHOLIC
VERNACULAR

JOHANN SCHOTT (1500-1544)
OTHER
BIBLICAL LIT.
HUMANIST
SCIENCE
PROTESTANT

ULRICH MORHARD (1519-1522)
OTHER
SCIENCE
CLASSICS
BIBLICAL LIT.
HUMANIST
PROTESTANT

JOHANN KNOBLOCH II
SCIENCE
LAW
BIBLICAL LIT.
PROTESTANT

BARTHOLOMÄUS GRÜNIGER (1532-1538)
BIBLICAL LIT
SCIENCE
VERNACULAR

PAUL MESSERSCHMIDT (1555-1566)
OTHER
HUMANIST
TEXTS
PROTESTANT
VERNACULAR

ANTON BERTRAM (1584-1599)
OTHER
HUMANIST
LAW
SCIENCE
TEXTS

20 40 60 80 100
PERCENT

Table 7. Language of Publication of Large-Scale, Medium-Scale, and One-Man Shop Printers (arranged chronologically)

Large Scale Printers	% Latin	% German	Medium Scale Printers	% Latin	% German	One Man Shops	% Latin	% German
Martin Flach (1477–1500)	100	—	Georg Husner (1479–1505)	100	—	H. Knoblotzer (1480–84)	50	50
Johann Grüninger (1483–1531)	39	61	Johann Prüss (1480–1510)	68	30	Matthias Brant (1496–1500)	66	33
Johann Knobloch (1506–28)	66	33	Martin Schott (1481–99)	27	73	B. Kistler (1497–1510)	12	88
Matthias Schürer (1508–20)	93	7	Printer of *Vitas Patrum* (1483–86)	100	—	J. Wähinger (1502–04)	80	20
Johann Herwagen (1521–28)	100	—	Matthias Hupfuff (1492–1520)	12	85	Johann Prüss II (1512–51)	31	69
Georg Ulricher (1529–36)	78	21	Johann Schott (1500–44)	57	42	Konrad Kerner (1517)	33	66
Wendelin Rihel (1535–54)	55	45	Martin Flach II (1501–25)	70	32	J. Schwan (1524–26)	—	100
Crato Mylius (1536–47)	77	23	Reinhardt Beck (1511–22)	87	11	C. Egenolff (1528–37)	57	42
Samuel Emmel (1553–70)	22	77	Ulrich Morhard (1519–22)	96	4	H. Seybold (1528–33)	100	—
Josias Rihel (1555–98)	54	42	Wolfgang Köpfel (1522–54)	10	85	P. Schöffer (1529–39)	72	28
Theodosius Rihel (1555–99)	55	45	Balthasar Beck (1527–51)	15	85	J. Frölich (1533–57)	17	83
Bernard Jobin (1570–94)	30	69	Johann Knobloch II (1530–32)	1	99	H. Vogtherr (1538–40)	—	100
L. Zetzner (1585–99)	64	36	Jacob Cammerlander (1531–48)	7	92	S. Bundt (1539–45)	—	100
			Bartholomäus Grüninger (1532–38)	1	98	R. Guédon (1548–49)	70	30
			Johann Albrecht (1532–38)	40	59	B. Fabricius (1549–58)	82	18
			Matthias Biener (1533–37)	78	22	T. Berger (1551–84)	2	98
			Georg Messerschmidt (1541–48)	36	62	P. Hugg (1563–71)	—	100
			Paul Messerschmidt (1555–66)	48	51	N. Wyriot (1568–83)	58	30
			Christian Mylius (1555–68)	31	55	N. Faber (1573–83)	—	100
			Christian Mylius II (1570–81)	1	82	N. Waldt (1583–95)	18	82
			Anton Bertram (1584–99)	63	35	K. Kieffer (1586–98)	90	10
						J. Martin (1590–99)	15	66

by his uncle, Wolfgang Capito and by Martin Bucer. Matthias Biener specialized in printing music for the new Protestant liturgies, encouraged by the reformers themselves. Johann Schwann and Peter Schöffer were Anabaptist printers.

Scientific publication was another important area of specialization. Six men devoted from 40 to 98 percent of their press space to scientific tracts, prognostications, medical books, and technical manuals. Among these,

Table 8. *Specialization among Large-Scale, Medium-Scale, and One-Man Shops (40% and over in one subject matter field)*

Large-Scale Shops	Subject	%	Medium-Scale Shops	Subject	%	One-Man Shops	Subject	%
Martin Flach (1477–1500)	Catholic	79	Georg Husner (1479–1505)	Catholic	69	Bartholomäus Kistler (1497–1510)	Vernacular	47
Johann Grüninger (1483–1531)	Catholic	44	Printer of *Vitas Patrum* (1483–86)	Catholic	72	Johann Schwann (1522–24)	Protestant	74
Matthias Schürer (1408–1528)	Humanism	48	Johann Köpfel (1522–54)	Protestant	62	Peter Schöffer (1529–39)	Protestant	43
Johann Herwagen (1521–28)	Biblical commentary	48	Balthasar Beck (1527–51)	Science	40	Christian Egenolff (1528–31)	Science	51
Bernard Jobin (1570–94)	Vernacular	40	Jacob Cammerlander (1531–48)	Science	54	Heinrich Seybold (1528–33)	Science	89
			Bartholomäus Grüninger (1532–38)	Vernacular	54	Jacob Frölich (1533–37)	Vernacular	50
			Matthias Biener (1533–37)	Protestant	50	Heinrich Vogtherr (1538–40)	Science	95
			Paul Messerschmidt (1555–66)	Vernacular	53	Peter Hugg (1563–71)	Vernacular	98
			Christian Mylius II (1570–81)	Science	57			

Heinrich Seybold, a well-trained doctor and professor of medicine, probably developed the publication of medical manuals on his own press as an adjunct to his practice. Heinrich Vogtherr, an engraver and oculist, based his publications on these specialized interests. The others, however, may have had very different reasons for their scientific interest. Jacob Cammerlander was violently anticatholic, publishing some of the sharpest attacks against the papacy to appear in the city. Balthasar Beck was known as an Anabaptist. Publication of popular medical works by these two men may have served as a cover for their religious activities or may have helped to underwrite the religious publications, since the medical manuals commanded an assured market.

Popular literature became increasingly important as a field of specialization after 1530. Bartholomäus Grüninger reprinted popular works from his father's repertoire, probably to avoid the religious issue. Jacob Frölich found that stories, novels, and plays provided a stable base for his small operation. The high percentage of vernacular publications by Paul Messerschmidt, Peter Hugg, and, most important, Bernard Jobin, bear witness to the steady growth of the popular audience. By the end of the century Jobin could risk devoting the major part of his press space to popular books and journalism.

In conclusion, the evidence shows clearly the difficulties faced by the sixteenth-century printers. They were confronted by religious and political changes, which altered very rapidly what they were able to sell, and they had few economic safeguards. Throughout the century they had to adapt to constantly changing market conditions. The Reformation cut back their international markets not only because the unity of the old church was lost but because Protestant doctrine itself became regional and local. Lutheran communities were hostile to Bucerian doctrine in the thirties and forties; the orthodox Lutheran Strasbourg of the 1570s strongly rejected Calvinism. While printing was essential to the propagation of the Reformation, in the long run the Reformation created chaotic conditions for the printers.

As early as 1480 the printing industry was characterized by differences in the scale of production, determined by the number of workers employed and the number of presses that could be kept busy. All through the century the larger shops were invariably linked to the ecclesiastical or academic establishment. Religious books, scholarly works, and text books had the most sales. Medium-scale printers were forced to look for different types of material, and many of them found popular medical texts, how-to books of various types, calendars, vernacular religious books, and popular literature. The printers were more than mere craftsmen, greatly as these skills were admired. By their decisions to print or not to print they helped to mold the culture and thus became important adjuncts to the intellectual community.

CHAPTER TWO · THE INTELLECTUAL COMMUNITY

 HO WERE THE INTELLECTUALS IN A SIX-
teenth-century community? Obviously, the clergy,
the teachers, the humanists—but who else? In this
study, an intellectual has been defined as anyone
who shared his ideas by writing and publishing,
whatever the subject matter. It is a definition that is
at once broad and narrow. It includes men who are
usually ignored: doctors, apothecaries, botanists, astronomers, mathematicians, accountants, veterinary surgeons, popular playwrights, and minor
civil servants. It excludes the friends of humanists or theologians who were
well known within their circle, but who never published.

A total of 1,133 authors are represented in the study. The classical writers, the church fathers were long dead. Even if we leave them aside, however, we face a bewildering number of German, French, and Italian humanists, theologians of all persuasions, and a miscellany of men who may have
been important in their own age but are now obscure or unknown. The
problem was to determine the significance of all these writers in their own
time, to establish their associations with one another.

The computer brought to light generational groupings which helped to
define the structure of the intellectual community.[1] Few intellectuals wrote
or worked in isolation. They were affected by the problems and issues of
the moment in which their own ideas matured. Each found other men,
writers and printers, who shared his interests and convictions. Each of these
groups dominated the work in a particular field for a period of ten to
fourteen years. Writers were not, of course, limited to the local community
for their friendships and acquaintances. They mirrored the interests of the
broader European community and became involved in publishing not only
their own work but also that of like-minded men: Italian and French humanists, Luther, Melanchthon, Bugenhagen, Italian medical writers, and
Viennese and English mathematicians. The generational groups created the
pattern of publication that appears so clearly in figures IV–X.

The elements that drew these men together, creating the bond of common thought, consisted of more than simply friendship, discipleship,
shared experience, or affinity of age. The intellectual groups in Strasbourg
were composed of men who perceived the world in the same way, who
agreed with regard to what needed to be changed and how that change

37

Table 9. Clergy, Scholars, Scientists, and Popular Authors Resident in Strasbourg or Was Published (dates in parentheses indicate the years in which the authors were

Theologians	Scholars and Teachers
Catholic Theologians (1500–1517)	*Linguists* (1502–1519)
Johann Geiler von Kaysersberg	Sebastian Brant (1494–1549)
(1482–1522)	Jacob Wimpheling (1495–1530)
Jacob Otther (1508–13)	Hieronymus Gebwiler (1519)
Johann Adelphus Müling (1511–14)	Nikolaus Gerbel (1515–17)
Johann Pauli (1520–22)	Ottmar Nachtgall (1515–42)
Johann Hug (1504)	Thomas Vogler (1511–22)
Thomas Wolf, Jr. (1508)	Matthias Ringmann (1505–12)
Peter Schott (1498–1506)	Johann Adelphus Müling (1509–13)
Reforming Clergy (1520–1548)	Thomas Murner (1506–19)
University Trained Clerics	*Christian Humanists* (1515–1529)
Martin Bucer (1521–79)	Martin Bucer (1527–55)
Wolfgang Capito (1523–39)	Wolfgang Capito (1526–39)
Matthias Zell (1523–35)	François Lambert (1524–26)
Caspar Hedio (1524–58)	Otto Brunfels (1527–35)
François Lambert (1523–31)	*Classical Humanists* (1538–1550)
Otto Brunfels (1524–45)	Johann Sturm (1538–97)
Symphorian Altbiesser (Pollio)	Peter Dasypodius (1535–99)
(1525–30)	Valentin Erythraeus (1541–61)
Conrad Pellican (1527)	Johann Sapidus (1539–42)
Sigismund von Hohenlohe (1525)	Theophilus Goll (1541–49)
Leonhart Brunner (1530)	Michael Toxites (1540–54)
Sebastian Meyer (1524)	Johann Bitner (1550)
Jean Calvin (1539–61)	Justus Velsius (1544)
Abraham Loescher (1548)	Jacob Bedrot (1539–40)
Anabaptists and Spiritualists (often without	Ludwig Bebio (1571)
University education or degrees)	Nikolaus Gerbel (1540)
Caspar Schwenkfeld (1530–34)	Christian Herlin (1566)
Melchior Hoffmann (1530–32)	Jonas Bitner (1550)
Martin Cellarius (1527)	*Academic Humanists* (1574–1599)
Andreas Carlstadt (1520–24)	Conrad Dasypodius (1565–96)
Johann Bünderlin (1529–30)	Michael Beuther (1566–93)
Sebastian Franck (1542–61)	Valentin Erythraeus (1566–76)
Lutheran Clergy (1560–1589)	Michael Bosch (1578–91)
Johann Marbach (1552–81)	David Wolckenstein (1585)
Johann Pappus (1564–99)	Melchior Junius (1585–99)
Ludwig Rabus (1552–71)	Hubert Giphanius (1572–75)
Melchior Specker (1555–68)	Johann Bentz (1589–94)
Cyriacus Spangenberg (1560–85)	Johann Ludwig Hawenreuter (1576–93)
Isaac Kessler (1566)	Theophilus Goll (1572–99)
Nikolaus Florus (1576–86)	Georg Obrecht (1586–99)
Kaspar Heldelin (1575)	Laurentz Tuppius (1565)
Samuel Neuheuser (1575–95)	Melchior Sebiz (1593–99)
Daniel Schadeus (1585)	Nikolaus Reusner (1578–99)
Georg Miller (1585)	Paul Crusius (1598)
Johann Avenarius (1582–91)	
Erasmus Marbach (1586)	
Philip Marbach (1596)	
Elias Schadeus (1592)	
Matthias Flacius Illyricus (1562)	

Surrounding Alsatian Towns, 1500–1599, Arranged by Decade in Which Their Work published, sometimes posthumously)

Men of Science	Vernacular Writers

First Scientists (1500–1520)
  University Trained
    Johann Adelphus Müling (1505–13)
    Hieronymus Gebwiler (1509–13)
    Matthias Ringmann (1505–11)
  Non-University Trained
    Hieronymus Brunschwig (1497–1537)
    Hans von Gersdorff (1517–42)
Second Scientists (1530–1542)
  University Trained
    Lorenz Fries (1518–48)
    Otto Brunfels (1526–39)
    Michael Herr (1533–46)
    Johann Guinther von Andernach
      (1542–65)
    Sebald Hawenreuter (1539–44)
    Heinrich Seybold (1528–38)
  Non-University Trained
    Nikolaus Prügner (1532–51)
    Heinrich Vogtherr (1537–59)
    Georg Vogtherr (1539–44)
    Heinrich Vogtherr II (1537–51)
    Georg Wälckl (1536)
    Walter Ryff (1530–99)
    Jacob Scholl (1537)
Third Scientists (1570–1596)
  University Trained
    Conrad Dasypodius (1565–96)
    Johann L. Hawenreuter (1571–93)
    Andreas Planer (1571–76)
    Michael Beuther (1580–84)
    Nikolaus Reusner (1585)
    Gallus Etschenreuter (1571–99)
    Melchior Sebiz (1570–92)
    Israel Spach (1590–99)
  Non-University Trained
    Michael Toxites (Paracelsus edit.)
      (1564–84)
    Lucas Bathodius (1586–95)
    Elias Röslin (1578–97)
    Georg Höflin (1586)
    Daniel Specklin (1589–99)
    Wendelin Dietterlin (1593)
    Caspar Reuschel (1593–99)

Satirists and Light Fiction
(1508–1520)
  Sebastian Brant (1494–1518)
  Johann Adelphus Müling
    (1513–20)
  Thomas Murner (1511–19)
  Johann Murner (1520)
Lay Polemicists (1523–1536)
  Stephan von Buellheim
    (1523–24)
  Eckart zum Treubel (1522–39)
  Katherine Zell (1523–24)
  Clements Ziegler (1524–36)
Burgher Moralists (1536–40,
1556–77)
  Georg Wickram (1539–55)
  Theobald Gart (1540–59)
  Jacob Frey (1556–76)
  Martin Montanus (1560)
  Matthias Holtzwart (1568–81)
  Christian T. Walliser (1568)
  Johann Rasser (1574)
  Christian Zyrl (1572–92)
Propagandists, Playwrights, Musicians
(1572–1590)
  Johann Fischart (1570–1590)
  Hieronymus Schütz (1576)
  Tobias Stimmer
  Nicodemus Frischlin
  Sixtus Kargel

should occur. Each of the Strasbourg groups was faced by different pragmatic circumstances and events and thus defined its goals distinctively. The essential factor in terms of membership or belonging was not a man's age, but how he comprehended his society and his role within it. Members of the same generational group could be widely separated in terms of age. Matthias Zell and Wolfgang Capito, for instance, were fourteen years older than their colleagues, Martin Bucer and Caspar Hedio. Jacob Wimpheling and Sebastian Brant were twenty years older than most of the members of the *sodalitas literaria*. Yet in both cases the older men shared a common world view with the younger members of their respective groups. Intellectual groupings involved more than mere coexistence; they reflected the inmost concerns of their members.

The life span of most generations was fourteen to twenty years. Only the exceptional man was influential for a longer period. This was because men were both products and agents of time, and their ideas were rooted in specific conditions or problems. Once these conditions had changed or the problems had been solved, the next generation could never totally understand the forces that had molded their predecessors. Neither could the older generations fully appreciate the concerns of the younger. Only very rarely could a man develop a world view, conceive of a program of change, carry some of it through or see it fail, and then, twenty years later, begin the process again. Both men and their ideas were bound by time.

Thirteen different groups made up the intellectual community in Strasbourg between 1480 and 1599. In this chapter the developments during these years within each major field of intellectual activity—religious, humanist, scientific, and vernacular—and the role of the intellectual generations in these changes are considered.

The general evolution of religious publication, the work of Catholic and Protestant churchmen, can be followed in figures IV and V. Catholic production was well established by 1480; one peak was reached in 1488, the other in 1500 (see figure IV). This latter, however, is a false peak stemming from modern attribution of undated books to the year 1500; thus classified as incunabula, the books are considered to be more valuable. In actuality the peak was probably rounded, integrated into a pattern of steady production for the period 1508–24. The earliest years of the Reform brought an enormous outpouring of Protestant publication. The peak of religious production for the century was reached between 1522 and 1528 (see figure V). This was followed by a dramatic decline from 1529 to 1531, with a period of recovery from 1532 to 1548. After the religious war, Protestant publication never achieved the levels it had in the past. The group of Lutheran ministers who led the Strasbourg church from 1560 to 1589 did not have to fight the same polemic battles that had occupied their predecessors, and they wrote and published less.

The Catholic churchmen of the period 1480–1520 were divided into two groups, each one a generation in itself. The first group, gathered around Geiler von Kaysersberg, was active from 1490 to 1510, when Geiler died. The second was comprised of devoted followers who edited, translated, and published Geiler's sermons and other works from 1508 to 1522.[2] None of these Catholic theologians were ordinary parish priests. They were drawn from the upper clergy and the learned: chapter members, cathedral clergy, monks, and humanists. Peter Schott, Johann Hug, and Thomas Wolf, Jr., all members of the first group, were young, beneficed clerics from patrician families who had little contact with any of the congregations in the city.[3] Johann Adelphus Müling, Johann Pauli, and Jacob Otther were scholars from widely different backgrounds: Müling was a university-trained physician, Pauli a converted Jew who had become a Franciscan friar, Otther an amanuensis to Geiler.[4] Geiler was their common inspiration. His preaching would bring about a Christian renewal and lead to the moral reform of society.[5]

Geiler and his disciples believed that the key to overcoming the corruption of their time lay in repentance. The essential problem was the sinfulness of each individual. If men were made aware of the consequences of their evil ways and were led to repent, then true order would be restored to the Christian commonwealth. Geiler and his disciples deplored the weaknesses of the church and wrote persuasively of the damage wrought by an uneducated clergy who were given no decisive leadership. Solving these problems, they believed, was the responsibility not only of the clergy but of individual Christians and the secular authorities as well. The Ratsherren should restore the church to its ancient position of autonomy, recognizing again the primacy of its authority. Then the church could cleanse itself. More important, each Christian should recognize his accountability for the immorality and decadence of society. The task of the clergy was to arouse men from their torpor, to awaken their consciences, and to lead them to repentance.

Geiler's attempts at reform revealed that even the most dedicated individual clergymen could not bring about the moral and financial reform of the church. Although he begged the bishop to undertake a full visitation of the diocese, his own energies were consumed in the pursuit of smaller and more limited goals. He fought against the restrictions laid on the church by the secular authorities. He banished the town prostitutes from the chancel steps in the cathedral. He defied the Magistrat by insisting on his right to administer the Sacrament to criminals on the way to execution. His sermons were enthusiastically attended and widely circulated in print. His popularity helped to create a new demand for devotional literature for the use of laymen. But the church remained unchanged.

In the decade of the twenties the reforming clergy played a very different role in the community. More than twenty men were involved in preaching and writing for the Protestant cause; a few were Lutheran, others followed the theological leadership of Bucer, and there was a substantial group of Anabaptists. Unlike the earlier theologians, these men were primarily ministers or pastors. Although some were eventually given chapter appointments, they had earned them through their contributions to the new church. Even as canons, these reformers remained involved in the parish ministry as their primary activity. The influence of the chapters was broken; the parishes emerged as the important centers of the new church, each led by an Evangelical preacher.

There was wide disparity within the reforming group in terms of age and background. Matthias Zell, who began to preach from the Epistle to the Romans in 1521, was forty-four years old at the time. Wolfgang Capito was forty-two. Martin Bucer and Caspar Hedio, Capito's protegé, did not arrive in the city until 1523; Bucer was then thirty-two, Hedio twenty-seven. Their experiences had been very different. Zell had been a preacher in the cathedral, Bucer an unwilling Dominican.[6] Capito was a distinguished humanist who already had a brilliant career in the court of the Archbishop of Mainz.[7] These men formed the core of the reforming group. Rather quickly, priests from many of the parish churches joined them, including Symphorian Altbiesser (Pollio) and Anton Firn.[8] Sigismund von Hohenlohe, dean of the cathedral chapter, also accepted the Reform.[9] Otto Brunfels, Michael Herr, and Sebastian Meyer came from the monastic orders. The arrival of refugees from France, Italy, and other German cities and states, including Anabaptist and Spiritualist leaders, caused the group to grow in size throughout the decades of the twenties and thirties.[10] The printers Johann Schott, Johann Knobloch, Johann Herwagen, and Wolfgang Köpfel played their own important role in the dissemination of the reformed theology.

The reformers went beyond the penitential focus of their predecessors and strengthened their call for institutional reform. They turned to the Gospels for solutions to social and religious problems. The disorder in the church and the secular world came, they believed, from the internal weakness of the church, in particular from the corruption and ignorance of the clergy. Deprived of strong spiritual guidance, many people had followed their own desires instead of the laws of God and had moved away from God's commandments. The reformers believed in turning back to God. Hearing the Gospel, men would be opened to God's saving grace and would then lead virtuous lives.

These ideas of the reformers were first developed in the polemic writing that created the flood of publication after 1521.[11] By 1524 the Strasbourg reformers had begun to develop their own doctrinal statements as the split from Rome became irreparable, culminating in the publication of the church ordinance and catechism of 1531–34.[12] After 1534 doctrinal publication diminished; the compelling drive to define the new belief was over. Attempts to establish a unified doctrine for the German Protestant churches, beginning at the conference of Regensburg, pulled the city clergy back into the center of ecclesiastical controversy. Bucer wrote and published thirteen treatises and reports between 1540 and 1548, but these were attempts at accommodation rather than new doctrinal statements.[13]

By 1548 the work of the reforming theologians was over in Strasbourg. Capito and Zell had died. Bucer was forced into exile in England. The Schmalkaldic War and the unsuccessful attempt to introduce the Interim religion after the Protestant defeat created an entirely new set of circumstances for the men who had to lead the reformed churches after 1555.[14]

The orthodox Lutheran clergy, who emerged as the theological leadership at the end of the sixteenth century, were slightly more numerous but less active in terms of publication than the reforming generation had been. Serving as parish clergy or professors of theology at the Academy, several of them were the sons of ministers, thus a hereditary pattern within the clerical vocation was already evident.[15] The parish clergy continued to play one of the most important roles in the intellectual life of the community. They were responsbile for overseeing the elementary schools within each parish and for catechizing all the young men and women in the parish. They were in intimate contact with the lives of their parishioners. The theological faculty of the Academy were more remote, commanding the prestige formerly granted to the chapter canons.

The world view of the Lutheran theologians Johann Marbach and Johann Pappus was shaped by the war and the establishment of Calvinism in the Rhineland. As members of a post-war generation which had experienced the military defeat of the city, they were frightened both by the possibility of Calvinist subversion and of Catholic insurgence. The policies of the previous generations, they believed, had undermined and weakened the city. The reformers, particularly Bucer, had been mistaken in attempting to create their own particularist confession of faith, which had undermined Protestant unity. The goal of Lutheran theologians was to establish the Confession of Augsburg as the official faith of the city. Yet even when this was achieved, the Lutheran theologians were never convinced that the Magistrat would defend the Augustana. For this reason Marbach and Pappus continued to elucidate and summarize the tenets of Lutheran doctrine.[16] They were helped in their task by younger members of the parish clergy. A catechism was prepared which taught the major doctrinal points and provided a historical summary of the development of the Strasbourg church. The catechisms, along with the text of the Augustana, were frequently reprinted.[17] The establishment and maintenance of purity of doctrine was the central concern of this later generation of clergy. The current of theological ideas had moved from a highly traditional Catholicism, through a period of renewal, to a new orthodoxy; a normative pattern for the evolution of religious reform, according to Anthony F. C. Wallace.[18]

Scholars, teachers, humanists, and literary men were the other important contributors to the Latin culture. Whereas the theologians were divided between Catholic and Protestant, and doctrinal differences later separated the Protestants, the scholars and teachers, despite religious differences, enjoyed greater unity and continuity. Each generation built on the experience and knowledge of its predecessors. The activity of the different groups is depicted in figures VI and IX. The major production of humanist works from 1502 to 1529 was accomplished by the linguists who introduced humanism to the city. They were followed by the Christian humanists who developed biblical studies from 1518 to 1529 (figure IX). The classical humanists flourished from 1538 to 1550, as shown in figure VI. They founded the Gymnasium, which institutionalized the new learning. The academic humanists, active from 1575 to 1590, focused their attention on dialectics and Aristotle, in contrast to the Ciceronian emphasis of the preceding generation.

The first group, whom I refer to as the Linguists, were characterized by an intense enthusiasm for classical antiquity. They believed that social and religious order could be restored through the revival of learning. Through their efforts classical learning began to be disseminated on a broader scale, reaching beyond clerical circles to the upper levels of burgher society. The group was composed of clergy, teachers, and lawyers scattered around the city in the chapters, in city offices, or in the chapter schools. A *sodalitas literaria* established around 1510 fostered an informal association among them. Correspondence between Jacob Wimpheling and Erasmus provides a list of the members: Sebastian Brant, Jacob Wimpheling, Hieronymus Gebwiler, Nikolaus Gerbel, Ottmar Nachtigall, Johann Rudolphinger, Peter Heldung, Thomas Vogler, Jacob Sturm, Johann Ruser, Johann Guida, Thomas Rupp, Stephan Tieler, and Matthias Schürer.[19] Some of these men were dilettantes who contributed at most a few dedicatory verses for a colleague's work, an oration, or a short biographical note. The others were professional men: lawyers, teachers, and educators who, in addition to carrying on their regular responsibilities, dedicated themselves to preparing and editing classical texts and the works of contemporary French and Italian humanists.

Their work covered a wide range—histories, grammatical treatises, editions of classical authors, pedagogical essays.[20] Their emphases, however, were on the study of the Latin language and on poetry. They understood the complementary relation between language and thought, perceiving that words control the ideas expressed. Learning Latin was not a mere end in itself; it was a basic step in the development of logical thought and clarity of expression. The Linguists were not prepared, however, to move toward philosophic speculation or to confront epistemological questions. They edited grammatical works by Greek and Latin authors or by Italian and French humanists, but they poured most of their energy into poetry. They delighted in every poetic form. Pastorals, elegies, lyrics, epics, and odes, editions of ancient and contemporary poets flowed from the presses.[21] They themselves wrote elegies to German princes, epigrams to their friends, and odes and carmina to the Virgin Mary.[22]

In addition to their literary activity, they began the process of educational reform in the city. Wimpheling was convinced that clerical control of the schools had subverted the educational system and undermined the moral integrity of the community. In a treatise dedicated to the Strasbourg Magistrat, he proposed that the schools should be placed under lay control.[23] Although no action was taken by the authorities, the humanists were successful in bringing a lay scholar, Hieronymus Gebwiler, to assume the rectorship of the cathedral chapter school and in encouraging others to open private schools. Ottmar Nachtigall inaugurated the study of Greek in the city, editing and publishing the texts needed by his adult students.

Because of the efforts of the Linguists, particularly the work of the printer, Matthias Schürer, the literature of classical Rome became easily available in the city. In the preceding decades only sixteen editions of the Greek and Latin classics had been printed in Strasbourg. Schürer printed 101 editions of these authors in twelve years and an equal number of contemporary humanist works. These inexpensive editions helped to kindle the interest of the educated laymen in the ancient world.

The Linguists hoped to strengthen the ethical standards of their own society by reestablishing the value system that had guided the late Roman Republic. They failed to achieve this goal, in part because their energies were diffused in the pursuit of literary enthusiasms and rancorous personal quarrels. They did, however, communicate a genuine intellectual excitement and opened the upper levels of burgher society to the broader movement of German humanism. Natural factors of death, age, and illness terminated their activities by 1518.

Christian humanism was introduced to Strasbourg by Matthias Schürer who, in 1515, published Erasmus's *Enarratio in primum psalmum* in an edition of the *Lucubrationes*.[24] This initiated serious biblical scholarship in the city, to be further developed by the reformers, supplemented by French and Italian refugees and by colleagues and associates in other cities. The roster of Christian humanists included Erasmus, Martin Luther, Philipp Melanchthon, Martin Bucer, Wolfgang Capito, Caspar Hedio, François Lambert, Conrad Pellican, Otto Brunfels, and Oecolampadius. Publication of their work was concentrated in the period 1515–29.

The goal of this group was to open the Christian sources to the community. Their major means of communication was through preaching. Preparation of their sermons required a thorough knowledge of the Scriptures. It was essential to have careful, scholarly interpretations of biblical texts available to ministers; therefore, the reformers, most of whom had some humanist training, turned their linguistic and textual skills to biblical commentary. Between 1515 and 1529, Latin commentaries were prepared for nearly every book of the Bible and were published by the Strasbourg presses.[25] The language division was distinct in this case. German commentaries, with the exception of a few short explications by Luther or short expositions of a single psalm,[26] were written by men whose theological ideas were not accepted by the inner circle of scholars and reformers[27] or by Anabaptist and Spiritualist leaders.[28] The established Christian humanist wrote for his learned colleagues, not for the ordinary layman.

The texts needed by the ministers were completed by 1529. In the next decade, work on the biblical sources was continued by a few individuals with genuine exegetical interests. Wolfgang Capito, for example, continued to work on the Hebrew prophets. In these later commentaries, however, he used the Scriptures to support his doctrinal concepts instead of limiting himself to textual analysis.[29] The work of the humanist exegetes was crucial to the success of the Reform and it was accomplished quickly, allowing the reformers to move on to other tasks. Eventually, Christian humanism was absorbed into the very movement it had fostered.

The third group of humanists—the classical humanists—gathered around the Strasbourg Gymnasium and its charismatic first rector, Johann Sturm. Founded in 1538, the Gymnasium created a new focus of intellectual life in the city. For the first time there was an established center for scholarly work outside the church. Printers like Wendelin Rihel and Christian Mylius devoted most of their press runs to work for the school. The Classical humanists, who were the faculty of the school, achieved the goals that had eluded their predecessors. They were able to carry out the pedagogical reforms envisioned by the linguists and to incorporate Erasmus's ideal of the Christian commonwealth into the organization of the school The restoration of classical learning became a reality for the upper levels of the community. The curriculum of the Gymnasium, as devised by Sturm, provided a thorough grounding in the Latin culture. The student did not learn by rote but was given the tools to understand the ancient language. He was trained to think and to speak in Latin. This accomplished, he moved on to Greek. The purpose was to open the treasure house of classical knowledge. Cicero was the model for ethics, morality, philosophy, and style. Dialectics and oratory provided training in logic and analysis. With the founding of the Gymnasium, the Latin culture was strengthened and institutionalized.

Between 1538 and 1548 thirty-six teachers and scholars taught in the school.[30] There were six Latin classes, or forms, and a further two-year program referred to as the Upper Classes. These provided advanced work in theology, Greek, Latin, mathematics, and law for students who did not go on to university. The first teachers of the Latin classes were recruited from the old private and chapter schools. By 1545 they had been replaced by younger men who were themselves graduates of the Gymnasium. The Upper Classes were taught by scholars from all over Europe, a good number of them religious refugees from France and Italy. Others, attracted by the new school and the leadership of Johann Sturm, came from Swabia, Württemberg, the Tyrol, and Holland.[31] Thus, the intellectual community expanded and became more international.

The scholarly activity of this group was remarkable. Sturm provided a sense of common purpose, and the *esprit de corps* was high. Half of the faculty published. Although the teachers of the more elementary Latin classes contributed very little, the overwhelming majority of the professors in the Upper Classes were publishing scholars. Teachers of the more advanced classes wrote their own textbooks and prepared editions of classical authors for their classes.[32] These texts, developed by Sturm and his faculty for use in their own carefully planned curriculum, were used in schools all over Germany. The Gymnasium was a center not only for the city but for the whole upper Rhineland.

From 1550 to 1574 the academic community faced a series of crises. The work of the Classical humanists, like that of the reformers, was brought to an abrupt halt by the Schmalkaldic War. The faculty of the Gymnasium shrank from sixteen men to seven.[33] After the war Sturm never resumed his unquestioned leadership of the school. His strongest supporters, Bucer, Capito, and Jacob Sturm, were dead, and the aging rector was faced by young, orthodox Lutherans who knew they must control the school if they were to control the doctrines and teachings of the Strasbourg church. There was a prolonged struggle for power from 1561 to 1581.

Concurrently, the school was reorganized. By an imperial privilege granted in 1566, the school gained the right to confer the bachelors degree.[34] The Upper Classes were abolished and replaced by the new Academy, which covered the entire university curriculum from rhetoric, dialectic, ethics, Hebrew, Greek, and history, to law, medicine, and theology. The new institution was obviously the more prestigious and became the focus of the intellectual community, while the Gymnasium dropped back to the level of a preparatory school. There was a similar change for the faculty.

The Gymnasium instructors ranked as teachers; the Academy faculty were professors.

The academic humanists who published between 1574 and 1599 were all on the Academy faculty. Their task was to build up the reputation and prestige of the new institution as rapidly as possible. Their focus was professional and institutional. The aim of the Gymnasium had been to provide a general literary education based on Ciceronian humanism. The academic humanists left the literary preparation to the school and began to develop the rigorous training in dialectic and rhetoric that would prove essential to the legal profession, the emerging bureaucracy, and the church.[35] Sturm had included dialectic as the basic training in logic for his students; at the Academy, its study was now significantly furthered.

The Academy faculty was large. There were eight major divisions: rhetoric, philosophy, mathematics, philology, history, law, medicine, and theology; but two of these, theology and law, had more than one professor. In all, forty-one individuals held professorships between 1566 and 1599. Of these forty-one, twenty-one were publishing scholars, a smaller percentage than among the classical humanists, of whom sixteen men of the Academy faculty of twenty-two wrote and published. In part this lower rate of performance was due to a high rate of turnover. Many men served only two or three years before moving on to another post, usually to a more prestigious university. The backbone of the faculty consisted of a small group who held their professorships for several decades and created vital continuity and stability. These men included Johann Marbach (1546–81); Johann Pappus (1576–1610); Theophilus Goll (1572–1600); Johann Ludwig Hawenreuter (1572–1618); Conrad Dasypodius (1562–1601); Georg Obrecht (1575–1612); Laurentius Tuppius (1572–1600); and Melchior Sebiz (1586–1612).[36] Approximately half of the faculty were Strasbourg born, had attended the Gymnasium, and then pursued further studies at the universities. The Academy also attracted scholars who were known throughout Europe, like the historian Michael Beuther, the mathematician David Wolckenstein, and the lawyers Hubert Giphanius, Nikolaus Reusner, and Denys Godefroy who made the Academy a center of humanistic jurisprudence.[37] It was an able faculty, devoted to the new rhetorical interest and to the reintroduction of Aristotelianism. It was international, bringing in men from Swabia, Franconia, the Netherlands, and France. Even those men who later moved on to other universities, such as Jena or Tübingen, linked the Academy to a larger network.

Publications by this group were frequently grammar books, legal treatises, or handbooks of rhetoric and dialectic.[38] Most important numerically, however, were the student theses, which reflect the emphasis on rhetorical training. After 1578 every student receiving a degree was required to publish a formal disputation.[39] These usually ran from four to sixteen pages and summarized the propositions defended or the conclusions of the argument. The subjects of the theses show that, while Sturm's students had emulated Cicero, the Academy students took Aristotle as their model. Aristotle was used as the basic text for philosophy, physics, ethics, and dialectic, and the preferred topics for theses were drawn from his works: Aristotle on youth and age; Aristotle on life and death; Aristotle on meteorology; the books of the Nichomachean Ethic.[40] The subjects were rigidly drawn, and the argument followed the most formal rules of dialectic reasoning, but the standards of eloquence were high. This strict dedication to professionalism was, ironically, the final result of the educational reforms that the earlier generations of humanists had believed would revitalize society.[41] The enthusiasm engendered by the linguists and by Johann Sturm's impassioned revival of classical antiquity was gradually lost as educational needs became more specifically defined. The diffuse ardor of the earlier humanists was replaced by greater philosophic and logical rigor.

The classicists and the theologians were the guardians of the established culture, sharing a common concept of knowledge. All the valid truths had been discovered in the past, either by the ancients, the patriarchs, the prophets, by Jesus and his disciples, or by the church fathers. The duty of the intellectual was to search for those truths which had been lost, to uncover the forgotten sources, but above all to preserve and maintain the whole corpus of learning through the universities and the church.

Yet there were other intellectuals who functioned outside these institutions or on their peripheries. Among these were the men with scientific interests. They were not scientists in the modern sense, having no concept of experimental method or of the need to test hypotheses by standard and accepted criteria. They were practical men: doctors, military surgeons, apothecaries, mathematicians, astrologers, and men with technical interests. As a group, like other groups of intellectuals in Strasbourg, they were divided between the Latin culture and the vernacular culture. In this group, however, vernacular publication thrived, because even august doctors of medicine with university degrees wrote in German to provide advice on health care to the common man.

Three generational groups devoted themselves to scientific inquiry in Strasbourg during the sixteenth century. The first group of scientists was active from 1500 to 1520; the second group from 1527 to 1543; the third group from 1570 to 1584, with a brief concluding flourish from 1589 to 1593 (figure VII).

Little original medical or scientific work was published in Latin during the first period. Few university-trained physicians resident in Strasbourg from 1500 to 1520 undertook to edit or publish medical works. The majority of the university-educated scientists in the first group were scholars and teachers. Johann Müling, Hieronymus Gebwiler, and Matthias Ringmann were all members of the humanist circle[42] and followed the usual pursuits of men of letters—writing poetry, historical works, and grammatical studies. To these they added the translation and editing of scientific treatises.

These scholar-scientists flourished in the city between 1500 and 1513. They supported themselves in part by performing editorial work for the printers. Matthias Ringmann earned part of his living as a proofreader for Johann Prüss and for Matthias Grüninger, but he was free to direct much of his energy to geographic studies. He edited some of the first accounts of voyages to the New World, making them available both in Latin and German. After 1507 he joined Martin Waldseemüller at St. Dié. There, under the patronage of the Duke of Lorraine, the two worked on a new map of the world and a revision of Ptolemy's geography.[43] Ringmann edited the text, working from a newly discovered Latin manuscript. Johann Müling, like Ringmann, served as a corrector, but he also prepared a world geography and edited medical texts.[44] Hieronymus Gebwiler was able to combine his responsibilities as rector of the cathedral school with editing scientific texts, including Lefevre d'Etaples's *Paraphrases on Aristotle's Physics,* for his students.[45] In following their scientific pursuits these men were performing their usual scholarly roles as editors and translators. They did not produce new work, nor did they seek out new sources among the ancients. The Arab, Latin, or Greek authorities were not questioned by the first group of scientists. When the discovery of the New World made Ptolemy's map obsolete, the scholar-scientists set out to correct it by adding the New World to the old map.[46] The existing body of knowledge was revised, not reexamined.

Original scientific work came from two vernacular writers, Hieronymus Brunschwig, a surgeon and apothecary, and Hans von Gersdorff, an army surgeon.[47] Brunschwig's *Distillierbuch* was a traditional botanical compendium. Its originality lay in the author's explanation of new techniques he had developed for distillation.[48] His method for extracting the essence from plant materials was an important contribution to the evolution of chemistry and to the development of alcoholic beverages, which would have such a profound effect on the European diet.

Gersdorff, an army surgeon, wrote his surgical treatise to share the fruits of his "experiments" with his colleagues. It went well beyond the standard manuals, providing instructions for the treatment of wounds, for prosthetic devices, and for making braces for fractured limbs.[49] As ordinary practitioners of their crafts, Gersdorff and Brunschwig could add their own observations to the established sources, a risk the academic doctors were less willing to take.

The second group of scientists, active from 1527 to 1543, responded to the currents of change that had already profoundly transformed the humanists and the theologians. In 1530, doctors, botanists, and mathematicians began to search for new sources of scientific knowledge and to reassess traditional procedures. Concurrently a lively interest in technology and applied mathematics emerged. There were more scientists than in the earlier period and they played a more active role in the community. The university-trained men were, in this generation, mostly doctors of medicine. Lorenz Fries, having achieved a reputation as an important physician in Colmar, moved to Strasbourg around 1520.[50] He was joined in 1527 by Heinrich Seybold from Heilbronn.[51] As the Reformation developed, two learned Carthusians, Otto Brunfels and Michael Herr, joined this group. Herr was a doctor of medicine; Brunfels was a scholar-humanist who was encouraged in his scientific studies by the Lutheran pastor Johann ab Indagine.[52] Paracelsus practiced in the city for a brief period from December 1526 to February 1527.[53] Johann Guinther von Andernach, trained at the University of Paris, and Sebald Hawenreuter, with a degree from Tübingen, both established themselves in the city at the very end of the period, around 1540.[54] The number of university-trained physicians was thus substantially increased.

By 1530 the Strasbourg group was drawn into controversy regarding the sources of medical knowledge. The merit of the Arab physicians had been questioned by several university faculties and a return to the Greek sources had been proposed. In 1530 Lorenz Fries entered the dispute with a vigorous defense of the Arabs,[55] which was rebutted by Leonhard Fuchs, professor of medicine at Tübingen.[56] The debate led Otto Brunfels to read the newly published Greek sources. Impressed by their clarity, he began a major compilation of the botanical knowledge of the Greek medical writers.[57] Most important, he added to these descriptions his own notes based on precise observation of plants in the field. Johann Schott, the printer, supported his work by commissioning a gifted artist to illustrate each plant. The collaboration of the three created a new type of scientific book based on accurate description from nature. Brunfels's friend and associate Michael Herr attempted to make a similar study of animals.[58] At the same time, the university-trained physicians moved away from the generalized texts of the past to treatises that focused more precisely on one disease or condition. This trend was reflected in the work of Heinrich Seybold, who edited and published the treatises of the Italian, Georgio Valla,[59] the gynecological work of Ludovico Bonaccialo,[60] and Berengario's anatomy.[61]

Much of the initiative for vernacular scientific publication in this period came from the printers. A small number of men earned their living in scientific pursuits, in part through working for the printers, turning out health manuals and other popular scientific works. Nikolaus Prügner arrived in Strasbourg in 1538, having lost his pulpit because of his violent criticism of the Pope.[62] Instead of continuing his career as a cleric, he used his skills as a mathematician and astronomer to prepare calendars, prognostications, and astronomical texts for the printer Jacob Cammerlander, who was also an extreme anti-papist.[63] Heinrich Vogtherr, engraver, oculist, printer, and artist, published treatises in all his fields of interest.[64] Walter Ryff, one of the city physicians, compiled popular medical books for Balthasar Beck.[65] Treatises on agriculture[66] and veterinary medicine and hunting,[67] design books for goldsmiths, engravers, and cabinet makers,[68] practical accounting texts, and books on metallurgy[69] came off the presses of Vogtherr, Cammerlander, Beck, and Christian Egenolff. These publications reflect an intense curiosity about technology and a new attitude toward technical skills. Printing made it possible to disseminate the practical knowledge gained by artisans through centuries of experience.[70]

The second generation of scientists, like the first, had few institutional ties and were not closely associated with one another, with the exception of Brunfels and Herr. There was no scientific community nor did the Gymnasium emerge as a center of scientific learning. Geometry, taught by Christian Herlin, was included in the curriculum from the very beginning, and Johann Guinther von Andernach and Sebald Hawenreuter gave poorly attended lectures on medicine in the Upper Classes. Nevertheless, the school did not stimulate scientific inquiry. The impetus came from the burgher's own concerns: their interest in health, in the world of nature, in applied mathematics, and in practical skills.

Scientific publication suffered a profound decline during and after the Schmalkaldic War. The activity of the third group of scientists did not begin until 1570. They flourished until 1584, declined briefly from 1584 to 1589, and then experienced a revival from 1589 to 1593. The composition of the group changed significantly from those of their predecessors, as did their interests. Scientific disciplines were now incorporated in the curriculum of the Academy, providing an institutional base for the scientific community for the first time. University-trained scientists were now part of the Academy faculty.[71] Among them were Conrad Dasypodius, a mathematician, and his friend and colleague David Wolckenstein, a musician as well as a mathematician. Andreas Planer and Johann Ludwig Hawenreuter both taught physics and medicine. After 1586 the medical lectures were taken over by Melchior Sebiz and Israel Spach. Several faculty members, following the pattern of the first generation of scientists, combined literary and scientific pursuits. Michael Beuther, a linguist and polyhistorian, was also an accomplished astronomer.[72] Nikolaus Reusner was a poet, geometer, and mathematician.[73]

The work of the academic scientists of the third generation was centered on Aristotle and Euclid. Johann Ludwig Hawenreuter worked on Aristotle's physics.[74] Conrad Dasypodius edited the complete corpus of Euclid and prepared a monumental mathematical compendium and a mathematical dictionary.[75] All the surviving student theses in the sciences were written on Aristotelian topics.[76] Thus Aristotle was restored to his primary position in the Latin scientific culture.

The most important vernacular scientists at the end of the century were Paracelsans. The leader of the group was Michael Toxites who, having been dismissed from the Gymnasium faculty for drunkenness, began a new career as a doctor.[77] An enthusiastic disciple of Paracelsus, he undertook the Herculean task of editing and publishing the master's works. The skills developed while working with Johann Sturm on Cicero were put to new use. His editions of Paracelsus, most of them in German, came out in the 1570s.[78] Lucas Bathodius and Elias Röslin, both doctors, were also Paracelsans, drawn to the study of the effect of the elements of the cosmos on human life.[79] Bathodius supported himself by publishing prognostications;[80] Röslin wrote geographic, astronomical, and astrological treatises.[81]

The applied and technical interests of the previous generation were carried over in work that was increasingly professional in quality. Daniel Specklin, an engineer for the city, published a detailed study of military architecture.[82] Wendelin Dietterlin brought out an extraordinary architectural treatise which anticipated the elaboration of rococo.[83] The agricultural and hunting texts were continued with a new emphasis on contemporary French authors.[84]

The term "vernacular writers" refers to those men who wrote songs, plays, novels, religious polemic, moral tales, and news accounts for the vernacular audience. Literary works in German, designed to amuse or enlighten the common man, were part of the printer's repertoire by 1481. Production of vernacular literature was not as great as production in some other fields, but it was one of the most stable. There were three generations of vernacular writers. The satirists wrote between 1508 and 1520. The burgher writers began to be active between 1536 and 1540, but they were interrupted by the Schmalkaldic War. They resumed activity from 1556 to 1577. The final group, the propagandists, playwrights, and musicians, overlapped with the burgher writers, experiencing their major activity from 1572 to 1590.

The first period, the period of the satirists, was characterized by a split similar to that found in the scientific community. Several university-trained men, learned humanists, wrote in the vernacular, although their work hardly expressed the ideas and values of ordinary laymen. Concurrently, three printers, Johann Knobloch, Johann Grüninger, and Matthias Hupfuff, printed amusing tales and stories that had long been part of the oral tradition. The aim of the vernacular works, in both cases, was to entertain.

The humanist satirists included Sebastian Brant, the city secretary, Johann Müling, the scholarly doctor, Thomas Murner, the Franciscan friar, and his brother Johann.[85] Müling wrote several popular historical works,[86] and the other men wrote satires for the amusement of their learned friends and colleagues, which were also enthusiastically received by the broad public. Brant's *Narrenschiff* and Thomas Murner's *Narrenbeschwörung* and *Mühle von Schwindelsheim* ridiculed everyday life.[87] The burghers and peasants in these tales were dishonest, grasping, ambitious, driven by vain desires to achieve a higher position in society. This desire to rise above one's ordained station in life created chaos and disorder, which the poets described in detail. Wise men would reject these worldly goals and devote themselves to an ascetic way of life. Few men, however, were wise.

The satires were one type of vernacular publication in a period when the growing national consciousness encouraged even learned men to write in the vernacular tongue. It was a short-lived phenomenon. More numerous than satires were medieval tales, lives of the saints, and popular histories, which had long been part of the oral tradition and were now printed by the enterprising Knobloch, Grüninger, and Hupfuff. These three men, recognizing the potential of the popular market, commissioned artists to do woodcuts and presented the tales in illustrated editions which were attractive and easy to read. The books had a dual function. They were entertaining and they encouraged literacy. This didactic purpose was further developed by a variety of self-help manuals. Thus the role that books could play in self-education was recognized and exploited.

During the years of the Reformation, publication of vernacular literature declined, displaced by religious polemic in German. It did not revive until the end of the 1530s, when an entirely new group of vernacular writers appeared. They began to write and publish between 1536 and 1540, after which their development was hindered by the Schmalkaldic War. Once the war was over the group emerged in strength and from 1556 to 1577 the burgher writers functioned as an independent cultural group, tied neither to the church nor to the schools. Drawn from the middle ranks of burgher society, they wrote unaffectedly of the dignity of burgher life, the superiority of the married estate, and the virtues of family life. The burgher writers rejected the elitist criticism of the satirists and stated their own moral values, values whose importance the intellectuals had failed to understand.

Few of these burgher writers were resident in Strasbourg itself. They came from the smaller Alsatian towns, but their work was published in Strasbourg and their plays were produced by the Strasbourg burghers. The leader of this group was Georg Wickram, the illegitimate son of a Colmar patrician family. Wickram, through his father's influence, held a middle civil service post in Colmar.[88] Jacob Frey was the burgormeister of Marmoutier,[89] Matthias Holtzwart held the same office in Zellenberg,[90] and Theobald Gart served as burgormeister of Seléstat.[91] Christian Zyrl[92] and Christian Thomas Walliser[93] were school masters in similar towns, while Johann Rasser was a clergyman who ran a school.[94] Thus, these men were part of the everyday life which they described. Burgher society no longer had to depend on the scholars or the literati to articulate its beliefs. It could produce its own writers from within the culture.

Vernacular writing explored a variety of literary modes. Wickram wrote novels,[95] a form which Montanus also used, though less skillfully.[96] All of them wrote plays, which were produced in their own cities or in Strasbourg, as drama played an increasingly important role in urban community life.[97] There was an outpouring of popular music, published by Theobald Berger, and books on instrumental music.[98] The heros and heroines of these plays, songs, and novels were drawn from the Bible, from Roman legends, or from contemporary society, but there were common elements that all shared. Depictions of courtships and happy marriages stressed the development of reciprocal respect between the two partners. The goal was a stable relationship, with loyalty and friendship as secondary themes. The contempt and ridicule which had permeated the satirists' writing on marriage was replaced by a strong affirmation of the value of family life. These writers, in contrast to their predecessors, idealized marriage and created an ethic based on the social needs of the urban community.

The last generation of vernacular writers was somewhat comparable to the first, in that it was comprised of a group of printers and, in this case, one particularly prolific writer.

Johann Fischart was the outstanding vernacular writer from 1572 to 1590, although some playwrights were also active. Born in Strasbourg, Fischart attended various foreign universities, returning to the city around 1570. His brother-in-law Bernard Jobin was already established and was beginning to build up an important press. Fischart worked as his proofreader and as an in-house author.[99] Fischart was a brilliant satirist and his poems were enlivened by the illustrations of Tobias Stimmer. These works, particularly a long poem loosely modeled on Rabelais's *Gargantua et Pantagruel,* had little relationship to the work of the burgher moralists.[100] His more important contribution to burgher culture was through polemic journalism. From 1572 to 1590 Bernard Jobin and Theobald Berger published a steady stream of broadsides and newspapers, most of them written by Fischart. These described the dangers of the Catholic revival, in particular the threat offered by the Jesuits and the war policies of the French and Spanish monarchs.[101]

He emphasized the danger to the political order and to the Protestant churches. His message was dramatized by the stunning woodcuts and engravings of Stimmer. The realities of the last decades were reflected in these polemic works. The division of Christendom had become a basic fact of life. A Protestant city like Strasbourg had to be able to defend itself physically and spiritually from the Catholic opposition. The reformers' attempts to restore the moral order of society had become a struggle for survival.

The intellectual generations were an important manifestation of the social dimension that influenced the flow of ideas. With the important exception of the original reformers and perhaps some of the popular writers, each generational group, whether theologians, humanists, scientists, or vernacular writers, addressed a particular audience. The Catholic theologians, except Geiler von Kaysersberg, wrote and published for a clerical audience. They thought in terms of communicating to the broader audience through the spoken word, and therefore attempted to improve the level of training and discourse for preachers. The reformers actually carried this intent into practice, their sermons reached the whole community. The enthusiastic response of the laity to the sermons and to their written polemic, the laymen's interpretation of the call for reform in their own social and political terms, caused the reformers to draw back, particularly after the Peasant's War. They continued to write doctrinal and polemic works but the latter were increasingly directed to those in positions of political responsibility. The later Protestant theologians tended to write for a narrow circle of fellow theologians and the upper ranks of the political hierarchy. Through their polemic they attempted to change opinions at these upper levels. Only a few treatises and their catechetical works were aimed at the broad population. Their task, as they saw it, was to defend the new church against any erosion from the Calvinists, the Catholics, or the dissonant Lutherans.

Each humanist group wrote for a different audience. The linguists had perhaps the broadest appeal. They attempted to convey their enthusiasm for Latin literature to the learned members of burgher society by writing Greek grammars for self-instruction and editing classical texts. Sebastian Brant wrote German poetry and popular histories of Rome or accounts of the Holy Land in the vernacular. In the next generation Luther carried the Bible directly to the laity, but the rest of the biblical humanists intended a more circumscribed diffusion of their commentaries. These were scholarly works written for other scholars and theologians. Exegesis of the Scriptures was still regarded as belonging exclusively to the clergy. The classical humanists, for their part, created a curriculum that would form the basis of western European education for the next three centuries, but their students were drawn from the patrician group and the middle level of urban society. A humanistic education became a mark of breeding, of upper-middle-class life.

Scientists of the first generation seem to have directed their work toward a relatively broad audience. The division between the learned and the lay communities was less sharply drawn in this area of knowledge. The translations of the reports of the new voyages were clearly aimed at a popular audience, though Ptolemy appeared only in Latin. Brunschwig and Gersdorf, writing medical manuals in German, were essentially addressing fellow apothecaries and surgeons, not the broader literate public. By the 1530s, when the second group of scientific writers began to be active, Otto Brunfels and Michael Herr could make a conscious attempt to make the best scientific knowledge available to the general public. Though Brunfels wrote his botany in Latin, Herr must have worked almost simultaneously on the German translation since, it appeared only two years after the first Latin edition. Herr followed this with his book on the animal world, in German, and his translations of Latin agronomy texts. Several printers, including Vogtherr and Balthasar Beck, published popular health manuals, how-to books, and technical manuals. The latter were obviously compiled for artisans and craftsmen. By the end of the century there was less interest in the popular dimension among the scientific writers and publishers. Scientific information was fragmented once more. Latin works were directed to the academic mathematicians and doctors of medicine. Popular publication consisted of Paracelsus's work, edited and published by Michael Toxites. The result was still a broader dissemination of information.[102]

It is impossible to establish the audiences reached by the vernacular writers. Since their work was written in German, it could have been read by any literate person. The work of men like Sebastian Brant and Thomas Murner was read at all social levels. We know, for instance, that the *Narrenschiff* could be found in the libraries of a humanist and of a wealthy patrician widow. A copy of the joke book *Schimpff und Ernst* appeared in the living room of an ordinary middle-class family.[103] The work of Georg Wickram and the other moralists of the mid-century indicates that they were attempting to reach a broad spectrum of their fellow citizens. The title page of Wickram's early joke book states that these are tales to be told when traveling—on ships, in wagons, at the barber's, and at the bath house—certainly places frequented by the most ordinary persons.[104] *Knaben Speigel* was dedicated to the mayor of the town of Ruffach for his children.[105] Again and again the plays of the period note that they were presented by the honorable *burgherschaft*, probably meaning the artisans and craftsmen who had traditionally acted in the plays since the thirteenth and fourteenth centuries, of the city or town. Thus, much of the vernacular literature would seem to have penetrated to the middle and artisanal level of the society, though it may have been read by the patriciate, the scholars, and the humanists as well.

The sixteenth-century city held strongly to the myth of the unity of the urban society. Both political and religious leaders appealed again and again to the vision of an integrated society that served the needs of all. An analysis of book publication reveals, instead, wide diversity within the community, mirrored in differences within the intellectual community. Each discrete intellectual group tended to write for a specific audience, creating further distinctions. The final element was the factor of individual taste and interest. The Latin reader could and did buy vernacular as well as Latin books. The vernacular reader was free to choose for himself within the area of German publication. Some indication of the range of choices can be found by looking at individual libraries.

CHAPTER THREE · THE READING AND BOOK-BUYING PUBLIC

T IS ONE THING TO DISCOVER WHO wrote the books and who published them. It is far more difficult to determine who bought them and, presumably, read them.[1] This chapter uses the scattered data that is available to arrive at a rough view of the reading public.

There are two main sources. Testamentary inventories in the Strasbourg Archives provide references to books owned by Strasbourg citizens. These are analyzed in the first section of this chapter. Inventories of private libraries owned by clergy, scholars, doctors, and lawyers provide another source. These can be found for libraries all over western Europe, including Paris, upper Alsace, the Rhenish states, and other parts of Germany. I have used them to reconstruct a general impression of the market for books among these particular occupational groups. It is important to emphasize that in most cases neither the will nor the library inventories specifies where a book was printed. The library inventories have been used solely as guides to determine the types of books that were attractive to different groups of readers.

The most important source on book ownership in sixteenth-century Strasbourg was destroyed during the bombardment of the city in 1870. The libraries of the Gymnasium and the city were burned, including the catalogues. Libraries given to the school by sixteenth-century donors were thus lost from the record. The sixteenth-century books now in the collection of the Bibliothèque nationale et universitaire were donated by other libraries and by private donors from all over German-speaking Europe. Provenance of these books, as recorded on the fly-leaves, was irrelevant to this study since few of the books had been owned locally.

We know that more private libraries existed than those for which we have inventories or catalogues. In 1553 Jacob Sturm, for example, left his books to the Gymnasium. They became the foundation of the academic library in the city, but the books and the original catalogue were among those burned in 1870.[2] There is a list of the books owned by Martin Bucer when he was in the Dominican convent.[3] When he was forced into exile from Strasbourg in 1548, he arranged for his books to follow him. His wife, Wibrandis, packed them into crates and barrels and carried them with her when she traveled to join him in England. After his death in England the books were divided, but no inventory exists of the whole collection.[4] It is also known from references in letters that Matthias Zell had a library, which was probably left, along with his other property, to Katherine, his wife. Her will, however, makes no mention of personal property. It was a testament in the true meaning of the word—a statement of her religious beliefs, together with arrangements for the care of her nephew.[5] We can assume that Johann Sturm, Jean Sleidan, Peter Dasypodius, and Wolfgang Capito all had scholarly books in their possession. There is contemporary evidence that Conrad Dasypodius[6] had a considerable collection of books, and a modern scholar has located books belonging to the writer Johann Fischart.[7] Johann Pappus left his library to the Academy upon his death in 1614, but, again, the catalogue did not survive the fire.[8] Since at least ten libraries existed of which no trace remains, the libraries for which we have clear evidence represent a minimum of the private collections.

The earliest collections in Strasbourg were made by the clergy. For example, Paul Munthart, canon of Saint Thomas, on his death in 1480, left a library of 64 books, which included 43 volumes in manuscript and 20 printed books. There were no books in German. It was essentially a lawyer's library—52 of the 64 books were legal treatises. But Munthart also had his particular religious interests. He owned the commentaries of Nicholas of Lyra on the Gospels and the Epistles and a printed Bible in two volumes. There were Albertus Magnus's volume in praise of the Virgin Mary, the *Moralia* of Saint Gregory, and *Speculum historiale,* a collection of historical works.[9]

When Ludwig von Odratzheim, dean of Old Saint Peter, died some nineteen years later, his library bore witness to the shift from script to print. He owned 127 books, nearly twice as many as Munthart, but only 7 of them are recorded as manuscript volumes. One would like to be able to conclude that the expansion of printing meant that he could afford more books. The collection was still legal in focus, but law books dropped to 49 percent. The rest of the books revealed wide-ranging interests. There was a small collection of Greek and Latin classics (Virgil, Aesop, and Plutarch, but no Cicero), balanced by a representative group of Italian humanists, including Valla, Francesco Filelfo, Aeneas Silvius Piccolomini, and Petrarch. Odratzheim had a serious interest in philosophy and had purchased several collections, including two different editions of *Lives of the Philosophers* and *Writings on the Philosophers* in Latin, as well as volumes of Aristotle and Boethius. He owned a Bible but had nothing that would come under the heading of a breviary, a prayer book, or a devotional, except a little book in praise of Saint Ann. His other interest was natural philosophy. He owned a volume of Euclid, Aristotle's *On the Nature of Things* and *On Heaven and Earth,* Albertus Magnus's *On the Properties of Plants and Minerals,* another herbarium, and Versoris's *Physics*.[10] Clearly, Odratzheim was interested in the physical world around him.

An even larger library, owned by another canon, has only recently come to light.[11] The senior Thomas Wolf, a canon both of Saint Thomas and of New Saint Peter, died in 1511, leaving a library of nearly 300 volumes, almost twice as large as that of Odratzheim. Did it become easier in each succeeding decade to put together a library? Lawbooks constituted 46 percent of the library, a figure close to that of the Odratzheim library. Curiously, there was a good deal of duplication. Wolf apparently never had enough copies of the *Decretals,* and he was always eager to purchase yet another edition. There was a similar duplication of copies of the *Codex* and the *Panadectae—Digestum,* together with all the principal learned commentaries on each. Religious literature, chiefly editions of the church fathers, breviaries, and prayer books, made up fourteen percent of his collection. His major personal interest, however, was in the classical world. One quarter of his library was devoted to the Greek and Latin classics, history, and humanist works. He owned both Vitruvius's *De architectura* and Leon Baptista Alberti's *De re aedificatoria*.[12] Wolf's library can best be compared with those of the secular lawyers.[13] He devoted the largest portion of his library to legal treatises and clearly spent a great deal of time and energy on his function within the church as a canon lawyer.

The library of Ludwig Gremp von Freudenstein, a lawyer who was active in the middle of the century, provides some interesting contrasts to these early canonical libraries. Gremp von Freudenstein studied at Tübingen and Ingolstadt and served on the faculty of the latter institution, but eventually had to leave because of his Lutheranism. In 1540 he became lawyer for the city of Strasbourg, serving as one of the city's representatives at most of the major diets of the Empire: Ulm, Augsburg, and Regensburg.[14] He was an important political counselor and advisor but apparently had his enemies as well. In 1566 he complained before the Rat that Theobald Berger and two typesetters had maliciously accused him of not paying his debts. He reported that they had also said that he was so unpopular in Strasbourg that if he were condemned to death no one would raise a penny in his defense.[15]

Whatever his personal popularity, he built up a large library, which he left to the University of Tübingen. The quality of the collection can be ascertained from the list kept by his bookbinder of 431 books bound between 1557 and 1563.[16] The binding of 400 books in a six-year period indicates steady acquisition. Unfortunately, the binder listed only 200 of the books by title; for the rest he simply stated, "Item, nineteen pieces bound in octavo. Item, fourteen pieces bound in octavo."[17] The books with titles indicate that Gremp's primary interest in these years was theology, particularly the controversy with regard to the Eucharist; 78 of the 200 were religious works. Gremp purchased at least 25 volumes of Protestant doctrine and 23 volumes of biblical commentary. Furthermore, he did not limit himself to orthodox Lutherans. He had several doctrinal works by Peter Vermigli, the *Decades,* a volume of sermons of Heinrich Bullinger, and numerous commentaries by Cyriacus Spangenberg. His favorite author, however, would seem to have been Melanchthon. He owned two complete Bibles, one in three parts, edited by Robert Estienne, and a Frankfurt Bible in two parts. In addition he had the Epistle of Matthew in a separate volume, four different editions of the Psalms, a biblical concordance, and a book on Jerusalem that included a map of the Holy City.

Only 30 of the 200 books were legal treatises, which may simply show that he had previously purchased the basic core of his legal library. It is noteworthy that, as part of the process of building a professional library, he acquired the edicts of the *Kammergericht* and of various territorial states and added them to his collection. He routinely had laws, ordinances, and other legal documents concerning the city of Strasbourg bound together to facilitate their use over a long period of time. In a sense he treated them as a modern scholar might treat professional journals.

His literary interests were rather evenly divided between humanism and history. Since the study shows that the publication of Italian humanism fell off by the middle of the century, it is important to note that he owned a complete Pica della Mirandola, a folio copy of Valla, and a volume of Joannes Baptista Mantuanus. Even more interesting was his possession of the complete works of Sir Thomas More. His historical books included five volumes of church history, including a history of the Jewish people, the lives of the fathers of the church, and various chronicles of German history. Interests in geography and exploration were manifested in two cosmographies, including that of Sebastian Munster, and a world map. The books Gremp purchased in these six years were contemporary in their focus. He bought books that offered sober discussion of the controversies of his time and books that gave conflicting points of view.

The library of Beatus Rhenanus can serve as an example of the collection of a scholar-writer. Rhenanus was a member of the Alsatian humanist circle and, like Jacob Wimpheling, was able to support himself without a church benefice. He made his living first as a proofreader, later by his pen. He created a remarkable library of 1,020 volumes, which attested to his interest in Greek and Latin linguistics, in the literature of these two cultures, and in contemporary humanist writing, Italian, French, and German.[18] The size of the collection and the presence of duplicate copies may indicate that he received some of his pay as a proofreader in books.

He owned 3 editions of the Bible, 2 copies of the Greek Bible published by Köpfel in 1526, and Froben's Latin Bible of 1530. Like Erasmus,

Rhenanus remained faithful to the Roman church, but he was well abreast of biblical scholarship with 12 editions of biblical commentaries. His favorite devotional was the seven Penitential Psalms, of which he owned 3 copies. His collection of the Greek and Latin classics was broad and well chosen. He had 12 editions of Cicero, perhaps an index of the shift to Ciceronian Latin. It was, however, the contemporary humanists—Italian, French, and German—that were his passion. He had 124 volumes by Italian humanists, one of his favorites being Faustus Andrelinus, and 94 works by German humanists. His close friendship with Erasmus, as well as his service to the latter as an editor, is demonstrated in Rhenanus's ownership of 96 copies of Erasmian works, many in duplicate.

Rhenanus's books on natural philosophy indicate the close relationship between the humanists and the natural philosophers, particularly in the early decades before the Reform. He had a complete collection of Aristotle, the scientific works as well as the general philosophical works. To these he added the 3 volumes of commentary by Egidio Colonna. He bought widely in mathematics, including the arithmetical books of Severinus Boethius, edited by Lefèvre d'Etaples, and those of Thomas Bradwine and Petrus Cirvellus. He owned a Euclid and more than 10 astronomical treatises, beginning with the traditional Sacrobusto and carrying through to Regiomantus.[19]

His major scientific interest was geography. The earliest geographical treatise in his collection was a 1499 edition of *Dionysus Cosmographia*. He also owned Pomponius Mela and a handsome, printed edition of Ptolemy's world atlas with maps painted by hand.[20] In 1505 he purchased Vespucci's Latin account of his voyage to the New World and, in 1507, the account of the voyage sponsored by the king of Portugal to India. He was particularly interested in Ethiopia and bought anything he could find, geographic or historical, on this region.[21]

His medical collection was uneven. He had an undated Leipzig edition of Mundinus's *Anatomy,* although he could have purchased far more up-to-date anatomical charts. He had four different botanicals, including the Latin edition of Brunfels's *Herbarium,* which suggest that he kept abreast of new botanical work but was not interested in the work of men like Hans von Gersdorff or Walter Ryff. He did have a veterinary text. It is worth noting that, among technological books, he bought a Vitruvius and two copies of Vogtherr's *Kunstbüchlein.*

A notable element in Rhenanus's collection was its balance between the old and the new. He had all the basic works of classical philosophy and literature, but he also had books by contemporary authors. He owned editions of all the classical historians, but he also had 30 journalistic accounts of recent events as well as 20 other works, often speeches or letters, dealing with contemporary political issues. Similarly, he kept himself informed about Protestant developments. He had about 20 works of Catholic polemic against the Protestants, including Leo X's bull against Luther and a litany to be used in German churches to protect the faithful against the heresy of Luther. But he also had 6 works of Protestant polemic, including Andreas Bodenstein von Carlstadt's disputation against Johann Eck. He owned 31 Lutheran books; among them, the original letter on indulgences addressed to the pope, the *Theologia Teutsch,* the treatise on the powers of the pope and on the Eckish Bull. He had, however, neither the *Appeal to the German Nobility,* the *Babylonian Captivity,* nor the *Freedom of a Christian.* Most of his Lutheran books were exegetical; he owned the *Auslegung der 109 psalm, Die 7 Busspsalmen,* the *Pater Noster,* the exception was Luther's treatise on usury. He had all the important individual works by Melanchthon and the complete works as well. In addition he bought Huldrych Zwingli's *Apologeticus.*[22] His library included John à Lasco's dispute with the Anabaptist theologians, published in 1545, the biography of Thomas Muntzer, published in Hagenau, and a 1535 account of the Anabaptists at Münster,[23] a further indication that Rhenanus followed developments in the Protestant world.

Rhenanus's library represents an extraordinary breadth of interests. While the canon lawyers at the turn of the century spent their money on books they needed for their work, Rhenanus was able to buy books that gratified particular interests—a thirst for knowledge about Ethiopia (or the Baltic area or Russia), a profound concern for the church, which fed his interest in Reformation theology. His library shows that men did not limit their collections to books that supported their own particular views. Rhenanus's library, like that of Gremp, was contemporary in emphasis. Although this trend would not be defined until the seventeenth century, modern authors were already beginning to pull ahead of the ancients.

The library of one member of the Protestant community in Strasbourg has survived, though it suffered some deletions. Peter Vermigli (Peter Martyr) took refuge in the city and taught in the Gymnasium, later accompanying Bucer to England. On his death he left his books to his servant Giulio Santerenziano who offered them for sale in 1565. Purchased by the city of Geneva, which was eager to build up the library of the newly-established Academy, the books were sent from Zurich to Geneva in three barrels. Since the freight charges were large, the town council sent back some of the books.[24] The collection as it now exists is not complete, but John Donnelly has recently compiled a list of what did survive from the catalogue of the Bibliothèque publique et universitaire at Geneva; 135 books can be identified as having belonged to Vermigli.

The collection was heavily theological in focus and indicates the importance of the church fathers to the Reformers. Martyr had editions of the Greek fathers, including Justin, Clement of Alexandria, Athenaeus, Chrysostom, Gregory of Nazianzus, Basil, and John of Damascus, all in the original Greek. Donnelly notes that these were the most beautiful volumes in the collection.[25] In addition Martyr had the complete works of Augustine and Jerome, but only one volume of Aquinas.[26] Like Beatus Rhenanus he did not restrict his book buying to one side of the religious controversy, but continued to buy works of contemporary Catholic theologians, in particular the English prelates—Stephen Gardiner, Alban Longdail, and Reginald Pole.

Twenty-eight percent of his books were devoted to Protestant theology and sermons, and here his own theological tastes are quite clear. He owned ten works by Heinrich Bullinger, five by Johannes Brenz, four by Calvin, and only two very minor works by Luther—his defense against Henry VIII and his German tract against processions. However, like Rhenanus, he had the complete works of Melanchthon, in this case in five volumes. Of works by the Strasbourg reformers, he owned only Capito's *Responsio de Missa, Matrimonio et iure magistratus in Religionem.*[27]

His Bibles and works of biblical commentary were the most exceptional part of his collection. He did not have a complete Bible with both Old and New Testaments; instead, he had two rabbinical Bibles with commentaries, Sebastian Munster's Hebrew grammar and dictionary, and Capito's two volume *Institutionum Hebraicarum.*[28]

Martyr's choices from among the humanist and classical writers show a marked taste for Cicero, the ancient philosophers, and the basic classic historical works. The library, as a whole, provides further evidence of the extent to which traditional sources and the work of contemporary scholars and theologians were successfully blended by the sixteenth-century churchmen.

Another library of a Protestant pastor for which we have an inventory is that of Georg Federer, a Zwinglian who served as chaplain to the lord of Rappoltstein (Ribeaupierre) and as pastor in the adjacent town of Ribeauvillé from 1562 to 1583.[29] As in the other libraries, there was the usual concentration of books needed for his function as preacher and teacher. Forty-six percent of his library consisted of religious works: the Bible and biblical commentary, treatises on Protestant doctrine, source volumes of the fathers of the church. The majority of his doctrinal works were those of the Swiss reformers: Bullinger, Oecolampadius, Zwingli, and Calvin. Federer also had *Loci Communes* and the commentaries on Colossians and on Genesis by Melanchthon, Luther's Bible and the *Quaestioni Sacrarum,* and Bugenhagen's *Annotatio.* The doors between the different Protestant groups were not yet finally closed.

The Augustinian revival is reflected in Federer's comprehensive selection of the "Divinus Aurelius," including two volumes of doctrine, the *City of God,* and the complete commentary on the Old and New Testaments and the Psalms. There was also a life of Augustine.[30] Other Catholic writers represented included Cyprian, Anselm, Gregory of Nazianzus, and Jean Gerson.[31]

Federer's function at Ribeauvillé was not limited to the curing of souls. He and his wife were also responsible for the school,[32] which probably accounts for the substantial number of grammatical treatises in his library. Melanchthon was the primary authority, represented by the *Grammatica absolutissima,* the *Annotationes in grammaticam,* and the *Exempla in grammaticam.* In addition, Federer had two Greek and three Hebrew grammars, a Latin-German dictionary, a Latin-Greek dictionary, a Hebrew dictionary, and two dictionaries specifically designed for school boys.[33] There were several plays, the comedies of Terence and Rudolph Walther's *Nabal,* which may have been performed by the students. The library itself demonstrates that throughout the sixteenth century the communication of religious truth was inextricably tied to the study of language and grammar.

A common characteristic of these professional libraries is that a substantial portion of the books in each was directly related to the owner's work. In the libraries we have surveyed, the number of professional books was never below 30 percent. For the canon lawyers Munthart and Odratzheim, 80 percent and 59 percent of their collections, respectively, were law books. The library of Thomas Wolf, another canonist, was 49 percent law books. Johann Protzer, who had practiced both types of law in Nuremberg, devoted 33 percent of his library to legal texts. He then bequeathed the books to his native city of Nördlingen. Beatus Rhenanus, a writer, had a major portion in grammatical works, linguistic studies, and the work of his fellow writers. Eighty percent of Georg Federer's library was devoted to books he needed as a pastor or a schoolteacher. Clearly, a professional man, whether a lawyer, minister, or writer, had to rely on his own library. In buying books his first aim was to meet the requirements of his work. Only later would he be able to indulge his own particular interests. A private library built around a particular profession would have a long-term influence on the creation of professional elites and probably remained important through the seventeenth century. A library was an investment in the profession. Sons who grew up in a household surrounded by law books, if they were readers at all, would have familiarized themselves with the major sources before they matriculated at a university. The same would be true of sons of the clergy. The books in the family library would influence their interests and their choices of career.

One Strasbourg library, that of Johann Schenckbecher, stands as an example of the tastes and interests of an educated and cultivated patrician. Born in Obernai (Oberehnheim), Schenckbecher was descended from an old and distinguished Strasbourg family, the Drachenfels, through his mother.[34] Johann himself received his early education in Strasbourg, perhaps at the Gymnasium under Johann Sturm. His university years were spent in France and Italy, and thereafter he served as a diplomat in the court of Duke Albert von Mecklenberg. Finally, he returned to Strasbourg to marry and to uphold his family tradition of service to the city. He served on the Council of XV. He inherited a large fortune but was childless.

Schenckbecher died in 1590, leaving a remarkable will in which he gave all his worldly goods—his house, his money, his books—to the city of Strasbourg. The will, drawn up in 1577, established two scholarships to enable poor young men to prepare themselves for careers in law and medicine. Each recipient was to have sufficient funds to attend universities in France, Germany, or Italy for five years. On the completion of his doctorate, each was to return to Strasbourg to live in the Schenckbecher house for three months while he found a position.[35] The house and its furnishings, along with Schenckbecher's library, his manuscripts and paintings, and his collections of antiquities and minerals, were all part of the foundation. The library would continue to be used by his protegés.

It was a remarkable collection of books in German, French, Latin, and Italian, unlike Rhenanus's library, which was predominantly Latin. In the Schenckbecher library the numbers of books in the vernacular and in Latin were nearly equal: 147 books (52 percent) were in Latin; 136 books (48 percent) were in a vernacular tongue—22 percent in French; 20 percent in German; 6 percent in Italian; and one book in Spanish.[36]

The subject matter of these books differed markedly from that of the books in the professional libraries. Schenckbecher was wider ranging in his interests and more inquisitive about other parts of Europe and the world, perhaps as a result of his diplomatic career. His major interest was history—history of the past, but especially history of his own times. He acquired 92 historical works (33 percent of his library) in his quest for information about the Turks, the Danes, the Spaniards, the Poles, the French, and the Swedish, and rounded off his collection with biographies of Mary Queen of Scots and Suleiman the Magnificent. He had the historical treatises of Guiccardini, Machiavelli, and Johann Sleidan.

Schenckbecher's next interests were music and the theater; books in these areas constituted 14 percent of the total library. In this musical household, the collection ranged from music for the lute and quindern (a small violin) to vocal music: five-part motets in Italian, three- and four-part French songs, motets for four and five voices in Latin, the Psalms set to music, and Luther's hymnal. The plays covered the usual range from the comedies of

Terence and the tragedies of Sophocles and Euripides to the popular biblical plays of the time—Judith, Adam and Eve, Lazarus, and Tobias.

The popular literature that Schenckbecher collected was sometimes in German, but more frequently in French. He took pleasure in Rabelais's *Pantagruel* and in various dialogues, poems, and plays about the joys of love and the virtues of women. His collection of the classics was small, comprised of only 12 books. He was not deeply interested in humanism, and owned only 17 humanist books.

It was the collection of an individual, but it can also be seen as an indication of a movement away from the tastes and interests that had dominated the early decades of the century. Schenckbecher's interests in history, drama, and popular literature are all borne out by the general production graphs for Strasbourg printing. By the end of the sixteenth century, men did not buy only the histories of Greece or Rome or of the church. They were eager to inform themselves about the causes of the tumultuous events of their own century and the relationships between these events. There was also a shift in literary form. The humanists of the early decades saw poetry as the ultimate form of human discourse. By the end of the century there was an increasing emphasis on music and drama, and burghers and school children were participating in performances of plays and chorales.

Libraries, it must be assumed, were usually owned by men who had received some higher education. All the collections examined belonged to men who had had some university training. But what about the ownership of books among ordinary people—men and women who were literate but without formal education?

The art of the period provides some evidence of the increasing availability of books at all levels. Books appear in paintings, although usually they are placed in the hands of a clergyman or a religious figure. The Virgin Mary in the Annunciation, for instance, is often depicted reading a book when the angel appears before her. In a portrait painted in 1479 of a donor, probably a canon, the cleric holds not only a book but also a pair of glasses. Another canon, portrayed in 1538 by Baldung Grien, firmly clasps a black leather-bound book.[37] A signboard painted by Hans Holbein in 1516 gives evidence of reading and literacy in the lower levels of burgher society. The sign, painted for a schoolmaster, shows two grown men working at a table with their teacher. Private classes of this sort carried the major responsibility for teaching ordinary citizens to read until public schools were established during the Reform.[38] Holbein's client described his abilities clearly to his fellow burghers:

> If someone wishes to learn to write German and to read in the shortest way that can be conceived, [let him come]. Someone who cannot even

recognize the alphabet can quickly grasp this system and can learn to write and read by himself. If anyone has not the aptitude for this and cannot learn, I will not charge him anything.

So, whether one be a burgher, an artisan's apprentice, a matron, or young woman, if you wish to learn, enter. You will be conscientiously taught for a fair price. But young boys and little ones should come after the ember day fasts as is customary.[39]

Evidence of the reading activities of ordinary burghers can be found through a study of will inventories. While full notarial records are not available in Strasbourg for the period 1500–80, scattered inventories do exist. Ungerer published 25 lay wills drawn from the hospital archives and the folders of the Kontraktstube.[40] An additional 120 inventories were examined from these two sources and from the notarial register of Daniel Strinz, who was active as a notary at the end of the century.[41] Of these 120 inventories, 20 had to be rejected as being too fragmentary. This was especially true of the material from the Hospital archives, where the will was often made at the point of death and only a very summary indication of possessions (usually money and jewelry) was given. It was possible, however, to achieve a statistical sample of 100 inventories. Random selection was assured by taking them in the order in which they appeared. The notarial inventories were taken as recorded over a three-year period. The Kontraktstube creates its own random series, and so the inventories were taken as found, scattered through the mass of other documents.

A wide social spectrum was represented. Those whose property was inventoried at death were not only the rich and the powerful. People from the lower levels of burgher society might also draw up such lists for one reason or another. The lower the social stratum, however, the higher the proportion of people who died intestate. The really poor, being without property, leave no record at all. Yet the sample includes members of the Magistrat, civil servants, a printer's wife, a shoemaker, a fisherman, several gardeners, a miller, a mason, a day-laborer, a boatman, and a man who made wooden lasts for shoes. Of the total sample of 100 individuals, 44 owned a book, several books, or other printed materials. This means that books were in the possession of over 40 percent of the citizens, including artisans and workmen.

These Strasbourg figures reflect a higher incidence of books in the lower strata of society than Doucet found in Paris. He lists 194 will inventories that included books for the period 1493–1560.[42] Nevertheless, Natalie Davis found that, of his 94 inventories drawn from the years 1540–60, only 10 percent represented "persons below the commerical or legal elite."[43] Of the forty-four Strasbourgeois who were bookowners, eleven, or 25 percent, were artisans or working people: Hecklin, the shoe last maker; Metziger, the miller; Anna Madner, the mine foreman's widow; Sara Trens, the tanner's wife; Sigrist, the linen weaver; Barbara Wüchterin and Künigund Kraut, both shoemaker's widows; Salome Schwinger, the furrier's wife; Salome Schmid, the cloth dyer's wife; Ehrle, the baker; and Wurms, the mason.

In the Strasbourg inventories, most of the people who owned books had more than one book. Ten people in the study possessed only a single volume. Twenty-one people, the largest number, had from two to five books; ten people not counting those with larger libraries who have already been discussed, had more than ten books. Unfortunately, unless there was a fairly large number of books, the notary or his clerk did not bother to record them by individual title. Moving from room to room, surrounded by kitchen utensils, eating utensils, articles of clothing, and furniture, the clerk would simply record "three old books." Thus the subject matter of the books in lay hands cannot be precisely ascertained, even when the existence of books was recorded. In two instances no books were listed in the inventories, though other evidence shows that books were among the property of the deceased. In one case, a specific note was made on the last page of the dossier stating that, since the widow had no desire to keep the books, they would be given to a son and a granddaughter.[44] In the other, two books appear in the list of goods sold at auction to settle the estate.[45] For this study, all printed materials listed in the inventories were counted, including maps and calendars.

Among those individuals who owned only one book, Heinrich Martin, a burgher of Strasbourg who died in 1496, left a considerable estate, with silver and gilt goblets and twelve rings, including four set with diamonds. His house had a private chapel with an altar, pictures hanging over the altar, and, as part of the equipment for the chapel, a mass-book.[46] Paulus Lauffenberger the elder (d. 1542), for whom we have no biographical information, was also a wealthy man with a large inventory of household goods, money, and clothing. No books were listed, but he did possess a map of the world.[47] At the other end of the economic scale, Hannsen Hecklin (d. 1556), who made wooden lasts for shoes, owned a Bible,[48] as did Hans Metziger, the miller at the hospital mill,[49] and Appolonia Stöckler, wife of Conrad Müller, a stone mason.[50] The Stöckler inventory explicitly states that it was a German Bible. Thomas Lendysen, who lived with his wife, Margaret Swendin, on the wine market, also had a German Bible.[51]

Dr. Andreas Waldner, the administrator of the orphanage,[52] and Anna Madner, the widow of a mine foreman, had *calendar-tafeln*.[53] These were long calendars, often nearly eighteen inches in length, which provided not only the days of the month, the saint's days and festivals, but also astronomical information and information regarding the stages of the moon, planting, and the proper times for undergoing various types of medical treatment.[54] Both Waldner and Madner's husband would have made use of this kind of information in the ordinary routine of their work.

Only two inventories listed single books of other sorts. Oswald Kastner, a furrier and former customs officer at the Rhine bridge, owned one small book.[55] Hans Göpp, a flour merchant, had in his possession "ein buch deckel."[56] Whether this was just the cover of a book (namely, a wooden chest) or an actual book is uncertain.

The individuals who owned from two to five books came from a similarly broad economic and social spectrum. Veronica Körberin, widowed by the death of Hans Hasen, a burgher of Strasbourg, became a pensioner at Saint Barbara's cloister. On her death in 1530 she left her money to the hospital, which was a part of the convent. Her personal property was not particularly distinguished, and the entire inventory covered only two pages. The major property may have been sold when she entered the hospital. In any case she had a silver ring, a gold ring, and seven rosaries, but she also owned a German Gospel, both the winter and the summer volumes of the *Lives of the saints,* as well as other "assorted old books, bound in parchment."[57] Agnes Götz, the wife of Jörg Kunmann, owned two houses, although each was small, one (described as a "cleynin kammerlin") having four rooms and the other having only two rooms. Yet in the *Stube* or main room of the first house were three "tutsche büchen." In the stube of the other were the Old and New Testaments and *Schimpft und Ernst,* a popular joke book.[58] This is rather striking for this woman had no money, no jewelry (at least none that was listed), and two tiny houses; yet, she owned five books. Unfortunately, no biographical material survives for either the husband or the wife in this family.

Clara Eckart, the widow of the notary Eckart Wyhersheim, occupied a high level of wealth and social position.[59] Her husband was a notary for the great cathedral chapter, and the money in her possession exceeded 1500 gulden. She owned four books, two of which had certainly been used by her husband professionally. There was one copy of the *Vitae Patrum,* the lives of the saints, in Latin, and another copy in German. There were two dictionaries, *Vocabularius rerum* and *Vocabularius breviloquus.*[60] Obviously, as a notary, Wyhersheim was fluent in Latin, but the German copy of the lives of the saints may have been purchased for his wife. There is an equally intriguing question raised by the inventory of Eva Müller, widow of the stone mason Mathis Heussel. This otherwise undistinguished list (one gold piece, three rings) includes "etliche latinische büchlin."[61] One of them must have read Latin.

Margaretha Röttel, the wife of the printer Theodosius Rihel, died in 1599. Rihel was a wealthy man, one of the most important printers at the end of the century. Yet in her own personal possession Margaretha had only a Bible, a church postil, and other small books.[62] George Flügel, a furrier, husband of Catherine Bing, left a more extensive list: a Bible, printed in Nuremberg; a house postil; a copy of Virgil; and five assorted books in octavo.[63] It is worthy of note that since Catherine Bing did not wish to exert her rights over this property, the house postil, the Virgil, and the other books were left to a granddaughter, Catherine Holander. The Virgil was a Latin copy. Do we assume the granddaughter could read it?

Lucretia Weber, the daughter of Isaac Weber, an organist in Baden-Baden, left three books, described as two old books and one small book.[64] Similarly Sara Trens, wife of Hans Schott, a tanner, had three German books in her possession,[65] as did Bartholomeus Dietrich, who was simply listed as a burgher of Strasbourg.[66] Ludwig Sigrist, a linen weaver, had "assorted old small books."[67]

The books most commonly found in the hands of laymen were the Bible or parts thereof, postils or prayer books, and calendars, in different combinations. Johann Etlin, another administrator, owned all three items: a full Bible, a house postil, and a calendar-tafel.[68] Barbara Wüchterin, a shoemaker's widow, had a calendar-tafel and "one old book."[69] Künigund Kraut, another shoemaker's widow, possessed a calendar-tafel and "one old book."[70] Salome Schwinger, a furrier's wife, had acquired a Bible and a calendar-tafel.[71] Salome Schmid, whose husband was a cloth worker and a dyer, could boast of a Bible, a prayer book, and two psalters.[72] In an auction to settle the estate of Ludwig Bozen, a Bible and a bound book were sold,[73] while the matrimonial inventory of the property of Samuel Ehrle, the appointed representative of the baker's guild, recorded a Bible and a postil in his possession.[74] The death inventory of Philip Wurms, a mason who died in 1541, listed, along with hammers and saws and other tools of his trade, "zwey bücher syendt ingebunden das newtestament das ander distch."[75] It is possible that the second item was a manual for the carpenter's trade.

One other Bible deserves special mention. In May 1569 Nikoläus von Türckheim, a merchant who had been ennobled in 1552, and his wife, Agnes Rietschin, left a legacy to support a student, who was to pursue a degree in Evangelical theology. It was stipulated that if the student so requested he could use, on loan, the eight-volume Hebrew Bible that was part of the estate.[76]

Catherine von Offenburg, widow of Wolfgang Bissinger, died in 1546 an extremely wealthy woman. Philip Ingold, a member of one of the leading commercial families in the city, was the guardian of her younger children. One of her older daughters was married to Jacob Cammerlander, the printer. The inventory of the property included a four-page list of the citizens of Strasbourg who owed them money, a six-page list of village and country debtors, and a six-page list of bad, and presumably uncollectable, debts. In the smaller sitting room of the house, the notary recorded, were two German Bibles, one in one volume, the other in four volumes. In addition there were three treatises by Sebastian Franck and a copy of Brant's *Narrenschiff,* together with a framed picture of Christ at the Last Supper.[77] This important family of wealth and standing owned three books by the arch-nonconformist Franck. Although Franck had been banished from the city and was pursued from one place to the next, the Bissingers had purchased and preserved his writings.

In general, wealth does not seem to have been a necessary factor in the acquisition of books. Long inventories that looked promising were often disappointing. In the case of Dorothy Ebel, the wealthy widow of Reynard Wyd, the inventory was organized by types of property: jewelry, linen, wooden work, tableware, embroidered goods, chair covers, but no books.[78] A relative, however, Catherine Arg, daughter of the ammeister Peter Arg and wife of Frederick Wyd, left at least six books, since the third of her estate that went to Gabriel Wyd included two books as part of his share.[79]

It is true, however, that individuals who owned more than ten books were at a higher economic and social level than those who have already been reviewed. The first of these, Catharine Brunck (d. 1530), a pensioner at the beguinage *zum Spiegel,* was the sister of a cleric, Mathis Brunck, who had predeceased her. She left a considerable amount of money, more than 126 gulden in different denominations and currencies, tied up tightly in little individual sacks. In the list of possessions were three bound books and a separate chest containing thirty-six more books, including Lyra's *Commentaries on the Old and New Testaments,* a *Catholicon* or dictionary, numerous collections of sermons, a curate's manual, breviaries, a register of all the clergy in the Strasbourg diocese, several volumes of Marian verse, and a copy of Thomas à Kempis's *De Imitatione Christi.*[80] Since the late Mathis Brunck's seal was tied up in one of the little sacks of money, we must assume that he had left his worldly goods to his sister. According to the *Livre de bourgeoisie* he purchased citizenship in Strasbourg in 1514, having originally served as a member of the clergy in Blienswiler.[81] The books, while in the hands of a lay woman, are clearly more representative of clerical tastes and use. It is important, however, to remember that Catharine owned three books of her own.

The next set of books were, unfortunately, not inventoried. Bernhard Schlitzer, who had served as the secretary to the very important secret Council of XV, died in March 1543, having made a will on his death bed that assigned all his property to the common chest for poor relief in the city.

There were only two exceptions made to this bequest: a yearly income of two gold gulden and all his books were left to the new Gymnasium.[82] Since only the will is left, we have no further knowledge of the books themselves, but Schlitzer may have owned a fair number of books.

In February 1600, Heinrich Seüpell, who had served the city as a member of the Magistrat, left seven folio-sized books, twelve quarto books, "others in octavo," and a new calendar-tafel.[83] Lux Schwarz, an administrator for the orphanage, left a Bible, a postil, and from six to eight German books.[84]

Evidence of two other collections of books appears in the protocols of the *Ratsherren*. In June 1570, ratsherr Adolf Braun rose in defense of a citizen whose religious ideas were being questioned on the basis of the books that he owned. Braun, who represented the Lucern guild, rejected this as simplistic. Merely having a book in one's house did not mean one agreed with it. He, himself, had papist books, Lutheran books, and books by Zwingli, Carlstadt, Calvin, Pantaleon, Erasmus, and Zanchi.[85] In another entry the Ratsherren recorded that among the effects of Wilhelm Plumen [Plum], the Anabaptist miller, "quite a lot" of books and other Anabaptist writings were found.[86]

The second part of the analysis of the reading public is based on the larger Strasbourg private libraries and on holdings in private libraries in other German cities and in Paris, as well. In these larger libraries the titles of the books are recorded,[87] and considerable recent scholarly interest in these collections has made them more accessible. Thus, the books in each library could be classified according to the system used in this study, and the percentages of holdings in theology, humanism, biblical texts, science, and law determined.[88] These percentages provide a rough overview of the kinds of books likely to appear in the library of a clergyman, a doctor, a lawyer, or a scholar. Once the markets for particular kinds of books were determined in this way, the figures were compared with the yearly Strasbourg production figures for those categories of books. The reader-market graph (figure XXI) illustrates to what extent the printers attempted to serve these markets during the period from 1480 to 1599. The classes of books which constitute the different reader-markets appear in appendix C.

The most striking feature of the reader-market graph is the change in the number of books printed for the clerical market. At the beginning of the period the clergy was the largest group of readers, a fact that will be borne out in detailed analysis in chapter IV. This reflected, in part, the size of the traditional church, which included not only the parish clergy but also the cathedral chapter, the monastic clergy, the administrators and officials in the bishop's service, and the canon lawyers attached to the ecclesiastical courts. The abrupt drop in publication for clerical readers after 1527 gives further evidence of the rapid laicization of much of the priesthood. The declining interest in the clerical market after 1550 probably corresponds with the smaller number of clergy in a reformed community. Originally the most important group of readers, it became the smallest.

The curve for scholarly readers is probably skewed from 1508 to 1530 by the exceptionally large output of the scholar-humanist printer Matthias Schürer. Nevertheless the extraordinarily large library of Beatus Rhenanus shows the soaring humanist interest in that period and the eagerness to put together a collection of both the Greek and Latin classics and the works of modern Italian and German poets and essayists. Production for the scholarly market was cut back during the Reform, but the foundation of the Gymnasium and the establishment of the Academy created a new scholarly cadre. This became the most important or the second most important group of readers and buyers from 1540 to 1560 and, at the end of the century, they were again emerging to a primary position.

Production of books for the professional market (doctors, lawyers, notaries, civil servants) was at first smaller than that for the clerical market, but it grew slowly and steadily. After 1550 professional readers formed a solid and important audience. Production for popular readers was established by 1500 at a moderate but steady rate, which was maintained until 1540. Output for this reader-market doubled after 1550, and, from 1558 to 1582, it was larger than for any other group of readers.

If one puts all the evidence together—the production of books for the different reader-markets, the professional libraries, the teaching of reading and writing to adults, the testamentary inventories—it is clear that reading was not limited to the scholars and the educated. There was probably a fairly high literacy rate among the urban population, and these readers seem to have read a surprising variety of books. A furrier could own a Latin Virgil, and a wealthy man three treatises by Sebastian Franck. Reading contributed to the creation of a more diversified society; indeed it may have helped to break down the cohesion of urban life.

PART II
CLERICAL DOMINANCE
1480–1520

THE POLITICAL AND RELIGIOUS SETTING

From 1480 to 1520 Strasbourg experienced an unaccustomed interval of peace. For forty years there was relative peace and stability; the threat of invasion was minimal. The respite was the product, in part, of a redistribution of external political forces. From the time of the Hundred Years War, the Dukes of Burgundy had dreamt of restoring the ancient Carolingian Middle Kingdom, linking their Burgundian and Netherlandish territories by a Rhenish state. Charles the Bold attempted to establish himself in the Breisgau, the county of Ferrette, and the Sundgau during the 1470s, but his ambitions terminated on the battlefield at Nancy in 1477. Once the drive for an independent Burgundy was lost, political pressures were more sharply polarized. Good relations with the Swiss cities needed to be maintained, but this had to be balanced against the Hapsburg-Valois rivalry, which overshadowed all foreign policy decisions in this period.

Strasbourg was loyal to the Holy Roman Empire and to the Hapsburgs, and Maximilian was warmly welcomed in the city as he moved back and forth between his Rhenish and Austrian territories. The city's imperial allegiance was based partially on a deep distrust of the Valois, partially on a strong feeling of German nationalism, and partially on a genuine admiration for Maximilian. Although the cost was financially heavy because of Maximilian's increased imperial demands for revenue, the city was willing to break its relation with the Swiss cities, which were drawing closer to France and pursuing their campaign against the Hapsburgs.[1] The peace did not depend upon Strasbourg's own policies. It stemmed from the fact that both the Hapsburgs and the Valois were engaged elsewhere.

Within the city, equilibrium had been achieved with the confirmation of the new constitution in 1483. The bitter quarrels between the guilds and the patricians were forgotten, and the foundations of long-term political stability established. With internal and external affairs relatively quiescent, attention shifted to the church. The rivalry between chapters and the bishop, the lack of discipline among the monastic and chapter clergy were hardly new. Geiler von Kaysersberg, however, made these central issues for twenty years. Installed as preacher in the cathedral in 1479, he raised the call for reform, and two successive bishops, Robert von Bayern and Albert von Bayern, were forced to respond, however reluctantly.

Geiler conceived of the type of reform which Jean Gerson had envisioned. Each local area of the church would proceed to put its own house in order. To achieve this, Geiler recommended the holding of a diocesan synod to bring the clergy together, to make them aware of their common goals, and to communicate the sincerity of the bishop's commitment to reform. The synod would be followed by a series of diocesan visitations in which the state of each parish could be observed, the parish clergy examined, and the financial conditions of each church assessed. Although Albert von Bayern called a synod in 1482 and, in 1491, established a visitation committee that included Geiler, both moves were aborted. The clergy met at the synod and listened to a persuasive sermon by Geiler outlining the need for discipline, education, and dedication. They disbanded without taking action. The program of visitation was stopped when the cathedral chapter violently objected to any interference within the parishes they controlled. Since they possessed revenues the bishop needed, the project was abandoned. By 1492 Geiler realized that there was little hope that Bishop Albert would undertake the leadership of any fundamental reforms. The same proved true of his successor, Wilhelm von Honstein.[2] Over the course of the four decades, however, a few monastic houses were restored to order.

The attempt to reform the church and the failure to do so demonstrated the need for radical changes within the institution. Yet the self-interest of each competing group was so strong that even the most popular cleric in the city could do nothing to disturb the established patterns of power. The bishop was far more interested in maintaining his fiscal solvency than in creating a disciplined and pious clergy.

CHAPTER FOUR · CATHOLIC PUBLICATION AND THE FIRST HUMANISTS

UBLICATION OF RELIGIOUS BOOKS DOM-
inated the Strasbourg presses in the period
1480–1520. The extraordinary number of Catholic
books and mastersheets produced was never
reached again in any category in the eighty years
that followed (figure XVI). Catholic publication
constituted 35 percent of what was actually available
in the Strasbourg printing shops from 1480 to 1520 (figure XXII). Another
26 percent of the total was devoted to literary works, grammar books, and
classical texts prepared by the humanists, many of whom were clerics.
Vernacular and scientific publication together comprised only 23 percent of
the total in this period.

The production of this Catholic literature, much of which involved the
printing of standard works from the Christian corpus, did not reflect a
conscious use of the presses by the Roman hierarchy to educate the secular
clergy or to reawaken the religious interests of the laity. It was this element
that would make a marked difference between Catholic publication and the
Protestant publication to come. The Protestant reformers, from the very
beginning, recognized the usefulness of the printing press to their cause, and
they used it to propagandize both clergy and laity, to educate the clergy,
and to instruct their congregations. The Roman church, in the forty years
before the Reform, used the printing presses without fully realizing their
potential for diffusion of the faith. They had no comprehensive program of
publication, and the selection of what was to be printed was made in the
scattered centers of power within the Roman church by bishops, monastic
clergy, or chapter clergy. Each, as was so often the case in this period, was
taking care of its own particular needs without much attention to the needs
of the whole church.

Much of the initiative seems to have come from the printers. From their
standpoint, the church provided the safest, firmest market. In the decades
before 1500, three printers had over 70 percent of their oeuvre in publication
for the church. In these years the church market provided a secure foundation for the development of the printing industry. There was, however, a
significant evolution over the forty years from 1480 to 1520. The percentage
of Catholic publication within the total output of books shows a consistent

decline. From 1480 to 1489 Catholic works comprised 60 percent of the total production. In the next decade the proportion declined by five points to 55 percent, and by the period from 1500 to 1509 it was reduced to 34 percent. In the decade immediately preceding the Reform, Catholic works made up only 23 percent of the whole. These figures are obviously reflected in the proportion of work that individual printers committed to Catholic publication. In the first two decades the majority of printers devoted 40 percent or more of their press space to Catholic publication. In the decades from 1500 to 1520, 28 percent was the highest figure for any one printer; the average for the eight most active printers was 21 percent. Thus, well before the Reformation, the market for standard Catholic works was no longer as sure in this one printing center. All the printers were reaching out to develop other markets as well.

What group or groups were responsible for the publication of Catholic literature? The contribution of the local clergy to the total production has to be described as minimal. Only a tiny group of Strasbourg clerics were involved in writing and publishing theological treatises and sermons, or in editing texts. These men—Peter Schott, Jacob Han, Thomas Wolf, Jr., Johann Hug, and Jacob Otther—gathered around Johann Geiler von Kaysersberg, who was appointed preacher to the Strasbourg cathedral in 1478.[1] Geiler was a scholastic theologian who poured his energies into preaching and the reform of the church rather than into scholarly writing on theological themes.[2] He worked on an edition of the works of Jean Gerson, but his own sermons, which were central to the religious life of the city, were not published until two years before his death in 1510.

The interests of his followers were more literary than ecclesiastical. Thomas Wolf, Jr., enjoyed the revenue of four benefices. His writing was confined to a brief life of Cato; a preface to a collection of essays by Plutarch, Epictetus, and others; and short expositions of several psalms.[3] He spent more time collating the Latin inscriptions he had brought back from student days in Italy than in pursuing questions of doctrine or theology. Peter Schott, the son of a magistral family, lived the life of a wealthy dilettante. His contributions to the literary and religious interests of his circle were limited to letters to his friends and Latin verses written to enliven the Saint Nicholas day festivities.[4] His early death cut short what others believed would have been a promising literary career. Johann Hug was the only member of the group to address questions of church polity, to analyze the relation of the church to the secular authority. In his treatise *Quadruvium Ecclessie,* he called for greater autonomy for the church, a theme Geiler had developed in his sermons. The expansion of lay control over the church, Hug wrote, had destroyed the traditional, established religious order. To restore the proper balance the church should have complete financial independence and the ecclesiastical courts should once again take precedence over secular courts.[5] These works had little impact on the community at large. They were written for and circulated within the ecclesiastical world of canon lawyers, the chapter canons, and the bishop's administrators.

The Strasbourg printers were more important than the local clergy in the dissemination of Catholic ideas and Catholic forms of worship. They had their own network of connections within the church hierarchy and among the monastic and preaching orders. Significantly, in the early decades, the international market was more important for several of the local printers than the local market. Johann Prüss and Johann Grüninger, for example, had a monopoly of printing breviaries and missals for fourteen dioceses of the Holy Roman Empire.[6] The bishops of Breslau, Mainz, Worms, Hamburg, and Halberstad each commissioned two service books, a breviary, and a missal, arranged according to the rite of their diocese.[7] The bishops of Constance, Speyer, and Olmütz commissioned new breviaries,[8] and the bishops of Warmia, Cracow, Bremen, and Basel had new missals printed.[9] Thus, the work of the Strasbourg printers was clearly well known and well regarded in northern centers like Hamburg and Halberstad; in the easternmost areas of the Empire, Silesia and Pomerania; and beyond in the kingdom of Poland. The bishop of Ermland (modern Latvia) commissioned Friedrich von Dumbach to print a missal for his diocese.

The monastic orders also commissioned service books. Johann Grüninger printed missals for the Cistercians and the Praemonstratensians. The Knights of the Order of Saint John worked with Johann Prüss.[10] The Carthusians requested that Heinrich Eggestein publish the life of Ludolph of Saxony, their prior. Eggestein moved his press to the monastery and, while there, instructed several of the monks in the techniques of printing.[11] Similarly, Johann Schott moved to the Carthusian house in Freiburg to print his edition of Gregorius Reisch's *Margarita philosophica,* Reisch being the prior there.[12]

These commissions give evidence of the network of contacts which existed between printers and churchmen. It is much more difficult to determine precisely where the initiative lay for the major Catholic publications: the volumes of doctrine, the editions of the writings of the church fathers, and the great sermon collections. Information on title pages in these decades tends to be meager, and the editors are rarely named. A volume of the sermons of the Franciscan Antonio Bitonto states that they "were diligently examined by the venerable father of the order, Brother Philipp of Rhotingo."[13] An edition of a confessional manual states that it was edited by "our brother, Antonius, archbishop of Florence of the Franciscan order,"[14]

and an edition of the sermons of the Dominican Vincentius Ferrerius included a short life of Peter Ransanus, professor of sacred theology and also a
Dominican.[15]

No correspondence between the printers and particular churchmen survives that sheds light on the publication of such works. There are a few
scattered references on title pages, in colophons, or in prefatory materials.
Grüninger's 1489 edition of the *Liber antidotarius anime* states that Nikolaus,
abbot of Pomerania, gave the volume to the "industrious printer Johann
Grüninger" in the city of Strasbourg.[16] Nikolaus Wydenbusch, the abbot of
Baumgarten, commissioned Grüninger to print the Cistercian missal in
1487. He followed this with an order for a prayer book which he himself
had compiled.[17]

This evidence, limited though it is, provides some indication that the
preaching orders were interested in publishing the work of their own theologians, living or dead. On the other hand, the printers may have selected
these works because they knew they would sell well. A study of the appearance of popular volumes of sermons in other printing centers shows a
distinct clustering of editions within a twelve- or fifteen-year period. The
sermons of Vincentius Ferrerius were published in Cologne, Strasbourg,
Basel, Nüremberg, and Lyons from 1487 to 1497. Roberto Caracciolo's
Sermones . . . de poenitentia were printed over and over again in Venice,
Cologne, and Basel between 1472 and 1485. There were Strasbourg editions
in 1473, 1485, and 1497. Johannes de Verdena's *Sermones dormi secure* followed a similar pattern.[18] This clustering of publication suggests that
printers were apt to follow the lead of a successful printer, even a printer
from another city. If sermons were selling well, printers in every publishing
center would put out their own editions, using any text available to them.
The scant information on most title pages suggests that the majority may
have been pirated editions. Volume after volume lists no editor, no worthy
patron, nothing but the name of the author and the title of the work.

The heart of Catholic publication in Strasbourg from 1480 to 1499 was the
printing of sermons, sermons of the great preachers of the past. Of the total
of 770 Catholic books published, 192 (25 percent) were sermons, the majority printed before 1500. These sermons constituted 3 percent of all books
published in the entire period of the study.

The sermons were penitential sermons on the unchanging themes of sin
and repentance. Roberto Caracciolo, an Italian Franciscan, was one of the
great popular preachers of the fifteenth century. His *Opus quadragesimale*
alone went through eighty editions.[19] His sermons described to his listeners
the life of Christ and his incarnation, the divine love shown by God in
sending Christ to mankind, and the immense benefits in this gift. God, he
preached, knows all; those who realize this will be moved to genuine repen-

tance; and, for those who are penitent, God remits all sin.[20] Antonio Biton-to, another fifteenth-century Franciscan, had traveled the major cities and towns of Italy, often invited to preach a special Lenten or Advent sequence.[21] His collection of sermons followed the course of the church year, but Bitonto laid particular emphasis on the development of moral character. He preached on the virtue of humility, on the sin of pride, and on the anger that created impatience and frustration and thus led men to lead vicious lives.[22] These sermons, according to contemporary accounts in Italy, stirred men to greater devotion and dedication.[23] The German Dominican, Johannes Herolt, preached in a similar vein. His sermons described men's sinful actions and the evils of daily life, such as sloth, adultery, and blasphemy. Men must abandon the old way, confess their sins, and thus experience a reawakening of conscience and genuine contrition. Having reformed himself, the Christian could then turn to help his brother, teaching him, in turn, the way of humility, obedience, prayer, and patience.[24] The volumes of Vincentius Ferrerius reiterated the same themes. Vincentius, a Spanish Dominican, was one of the most charismatic penitential preachers of the fifteenth century. Riding on the back of a donkey, he had journeyed from Catalonia through southern France, Lombardy, Geneva, Lausanne, and as far north as Freiburg, followed by thousands of enthusiastic men and women who had been called by his preaching to live new lives.[25] Another popular volume of sermons, indeed the most frequently reprinted, was published under the name of Petrus de Paludanus, general of the Dominican order in 1317. They were probably, in fact, the work of a fifteenth-century theologian.[26] The pseudo-Paludanus preached the renunciation of the secular world. Having free will to choose his way of life, man should follow the teachings of the Gospel and flee the world to seek tranquility and a peaceful heart. The Paludanus sermons made clear that he who had money could enter the kingdom of God only with great difficulty, for no one could serve both God and mammon.[27]

These sermon collections kept the words of the reforming preachers of the fifteenth century in circulation. In the early decades the printers were drawing their materials not from local writers, not even from German preachers, but from the sermon writers of Italy and France. A major purpose of these collections was to provide parish priests with ready-to-preach sermons, as was explicitly stated by Johannes de Verdena, a German Franciscan. In the introduction to his *Sermones dormi secure,* he explained that his book contained a sermon based on a Gospel reading for every Sunday in the year. His title, *Sleep without care,* was chosen, he wrote, because it allowed every priest to have a good sermon for his people without having to study or to make the effort of writing.[28]

The sermon collections were supplemented by handbooks and manuals of all sorts. As in the case of the sermons, these volumes were selected from the writings of the past and the editions were printed in clusters. Many of these books appeared simultaneously in several cities. Giovanni Balbi's *Catholicon* had been prepared in the thirteenth century and was, indeed, one of the very first books to be printed.[29] It was a classic. Guido di Monte Rocheri, a fourteenth-century preacher, wrote a curate's manual that was frequently reprinted in the 1490s.[30] Johannes Melber's *Vocabularius praedicantum,* the most recent of these, was compiled from the sermons of Judocus Eichmann in the mid-fifteenth century.[31]

Both Melber and Balbi started with the basics of Latin grammatical construction—information that was essential for the preacher whose Latin was weak. Balbi then went on to exegetical explanations of biblical texts, arranged in encyclopedic form for easy reference.[32] Both these books were preaching manuals. Guido di Monte Rocheri's book, however, was a guide to the administration of the sacraments. The institution of the sacraments was described, then the meaning of each explained, along with its effect for the recipient. The proper forms to be followed in its ministration were outlined step by step. Throughout the manual Guido spoke to the cleric directly, telling him what to do in many specific situations. A final section outlined the principal articles of the faith, prayers of penitence, and the Ten Commandments.[33] These books by well-respected preachers (note that most of them were Italian) provided the instruction needed by the secular clergy, yet there is no indication that they were envisioned as part of a program of education for the parish priests.

Postils were yet another form of reference book for the clergy, providing expositions of the Epistles and Gospels for every Sunday in the year and suitable homilies for each reading.[34] Jacobus de Varagine's *Legenda Aurea* was another type of informational manual; it supplied biographical material for every saint in the church year and a homily for the day. Although some of the postils were published in German, probably for the less-educated clergy and perhaps for the literate parishioner, the *Legenda aurea* appeared only in Latin. It was, furthermore, full of difficult Latin abbreviations, which would have made it difficult to use for anyone without a university education.[35]

Eight Bibles, seven in Latin and one in German, were printed in the two decades from 1480 to 1499.[36] There was then a hiatus until 1520. Eleven Bibles were published between 1520 and 1599. During the Catholic years, no separate Old Testaments, New Testaments, or individual books of the Bible were published. Biblical commentaries were printed, but these were in the style of curates' manuals and were not scholarly expositions of the Bible text. The most popular of these were Johannes Marchesinus's biblical dictionary, the *Mammotrectus,* and Juan de Torquemada's exposition of the psalter, both of which were designed to explain scriptural passages to the officiating priest.[37] Torquemada's expositions were, in fact, meditations on the psalms rather than analyses of the text. There was little exegetical work to which the parish priest could refer.

It is possible to make some connections between the books that were printed and the books that were purchased during these first decades. The inventories of clerical libraries provide some insight into what was owned. The legal focus of the chapter clergy stands clearly revealed by information, already discussed, about the content of their libraries. Paul Munthart, canon of Saint Thomas, died in 1480 leaving a library of 43 manuscript volumes and 20 printed volumes. The overwhelming majority were works of canon law, primarily the *Decretals* and a variety of commentaries thereon. He did, however, own a two-volume Latin Bible, a *Catholicon,* and the commentaries of both Augustine and the Carthusian, Ludolph, on the Gospels.[38] Ludwig von Odratzheim, dean of the chapter of Old Saint Peter, left an even larger library of 127 books. Again, the majority were law books he needed for his profession, but he also had a Bible, the sermons of Saint Bonaventura, and the confessional manual of Antonius Florentinus.[39]

It was Matthias Brunck, a churchman from Blienswiler, who had the library that almost perfectly reflected the stock of the Strasbourg printing shops. He died between 1514 and 1532. No Bible is listed, but he had a psalter, Balbi's *Catholicon,* and the commentaries of Nikolaus of Lyra for the Old and New Testaments. He also had separate commentaries for the book of Matthew and the book of wisdom. He had three collections of sermons in addition to Johannes de Verdena's essential *Sermones dormi secure.* He had a preaching dictionary and two editions of Jacobus de Varagine's *Legenda aurea.* In addition he owned a breviary for the Strasbourg rite and a register of the clergy of the Strasbourg diocese. His personal spiritual needs were met by Thomas à Kempis's *De imitatione Christi.*[40] All these he could have purchased from Strasbourg printers.

Chapter and monastic houses formed a particularly important element of the market for these ecclesiastical materials, and their inventories of books closely reflect what the printers were printing. The Carthusian house listed 240 printed books in one inventory and 78 books, most of which were printed, in the other.[41] There were 2 copies of a Latin Bible with a preface by Jerome, the commentaries of Nikolaus of Lyra on the Old Testament, the Epistles of Paul, and Acts. There were special editions of the psalter according to the Carthusian order and breviaries for their rite. Indeed, there were more than 12 editions of the psalter, 3 of them in German.[42] There were dictionaries and a concordance of Biblical terms,[43] the works of the theologians Augustine and Thomas Aquinas, and 34 collections of sermons. There was also a basic collection of canon law. This inventory and those of the libraries of individuals bear witness to the fact that printed materials were diffused among both the secular and the regular clergy.

Before 1500, the printers had drawn from the corpus of Catholic literature: the church fathers, the important theologians of the Middle Ages, the great penitential preachers of the fourteenth and fifteenth centuries. After the turn of the century there was a pronounced shift. Editions of the church fathers and theologians remained the same, but publication of the large volumes of collected sermons in Latin plummeted. Only 35 of these Latin collections were published between 1500 and 1520, as against 106 in the twenty years before. The sermons of Geiler von Kaysersberg, the local popular preacher, however, went through 47 editions, mostly richly illustrated German versions that were clearly aimed at the popular market. The same number of curate's manuals were printed, but, as in the case of the sermons, these were now written by contemporary clerics.

The decade 1500–09 saw a new vitality among the local clergy, and the printers selected works of neighboring German and Swiss preachers. Most important was a change to publishing religious material that could be used by the laity. There was a marked increase in the publication of devotionals for private use and of lay manuals of the Christian life. Popular religious music appeared on the Strasbourg presses for the first time. Thus, twenty years before the Reformation, religious publication turned away from the institutional, ecclesiastical market to attract the lay reader as well as the secular clergy.

The devotionals seem to have come first. The *Hortulus animae* was a classic work of devotional literature. It began, as was traditional, with the ecclesiastical calendar and listed the major saints' days and the calendar for movable feasts. The festivals for the four seasons were accompanied by a description of the four humors of man. These introductory materials were followed by meditations on the Virgin and the Passion and by prayers: prayers to be said on entering church and after entering church; prayers to be said at baptism, before communion, and after communion; prayers to individual saints.[44] The Latin *Hortulus* were part of the basic repertoire of at least four Strasbourg printers, who produced twelve different editions.[45] By 1501 they began to print the book in German as well, with a total of nine German editions.[46] There were also German books of consolation, a German meditation on the Passion, a manual on penance and another on prayer, and books on preparing for death.[47] The most important of these was Geiler's sermon on the death of a child, which was published as a book of consolation and a guide to families facing the problems of illness, death, and final separation. Geiler reached out to provide spiritual support during that profound period of sorrow that was both a normal and frightening part of family life. Men, he wrote, should not bewail death. " 'Now,' you say, 'how shall I not cry at the death of my child or my friend. That is natural.' "[48] Geiler agreed that it was natural and that Christ himself had wept at the death of his special friend, Lazarus. The preacher said, however, that Christ was not weeping over death but because he wished to awaken others to the wretched life Lazarus had suffered. Geiler believed that it was not unnatural to mourn but he hoped that his book would show men and women how to face death with understanding.

"Death is a friend," he wrote. These were words of great comfort in a period of high and sudden mortality. No one should indulge himself in immoderate or convulsive grief. Rather, one should rejoice with the friend who had died; even the man who had sinned and would suffer the pains of hell was better off in the long run, for God sees to everything according to men's needs. If the bereaved indulged in disorderly sorrow, however, death lost its purpose. A good woman, Geiler explained, lost her talented son. She wept without ceasing until one night in a dream she saw a group of handsome young men enjoying themselves in a beautiful place. Asked why her son was not with them, they told her that the weight of her tears dragged him down, so that he was excluded from their companionship.[49]

These devotional books signal a renewal or reawakening of spiritual life among the laity. A further indication is the publication of the sermons of Geiler, certainly one of the most important elements of the repertoires of the Strasbourg printers from 1508 to 1519. There were 49 editions of Geiler and only 26 editions of Erasmus during these years. Although Geiler preached in the city from 1483 until his death in 1510, no attempt was made to publish the sermons until just before his death. The publication history of the sermons indicates that individuals, not the church, took the initiative to bring out the volumes. Jacob Otther, his amanuensis, began the task of editing the sermons while living in Geiler's household. When Geiler died, however, his nephew, Peter Wickram, succeeded to his pulpit, immediately assumed full responsibility for publishing his uncle's works, and took the notes from Otther. At the same time, Johann Müling, a member of the humanist circle who worked for several of the Strasbourg printers, published German versions of some of the sermons. Johann Pauli, guardian of the Strasbourg Franciscan house, then put out his edition of the German sermons, stating that he had been in attendance at the cathedral every day for the last four years of Geiler's life and had written down each sermon from memory at the time.[50] Quite obviously, each of these men was working on his own, or on his own with a printer. A major motive in publishing the sermons was profit, and publication of Geiler's sermons showed that the printers recognized the potential of the lay market. No scholarly references were included in the German versions, and the volumes were illustrated. The books were a publishing success, judging from the number of reprintings and successive publications year after year.

Geiler had preached these sermons in direct, idiomatic, everyday German. They read as they had sounded. He was direct and personal in his address. "I am telling you this," he would say. "This is something you need to know." "I know this is true and you should listen to me." Other sermon writers, Vincentius or Bitonto, discussed sin impersonally and addressed a generalized person—a Christian—rather than an individual. Intensely subjective, Geiler described the everyday lives of his listeners, the kinds of problems they were apt to meet, and offered solutions.

How should a person in these days, he asked, direct his life so that he might honor God and receive salvation? He should follow the examples of Lazarus, Mary, and Martha. Lazarus provided men with the most worthy example: the death of a poor soul who receives, in return for his death, a new and pious heart. Men and women should, in the same way, devote themselves to godly and brotherly love and to good works, which they should attempt to accomplish with the help of God. Above all, they should offer up their hearts to God daily.[51]

He described the religious struggles of three different kinds of men: one was cold, unable to feel the grace of God; the second had a bad conscience; the third was tempted by doubt. He would talk about these problems according to the teachings of Jean Gerson. It was not sinful to suffer doubt or temptation. The error occurred only when these feelings impeded the working of the grace of God. Through prayer and confession, men could break out of the cycle of sin and begin anew.[52]

In an epiphany sermon, Geiler used the symbols of the gifts. The myrrh, he said, symbolized good works and a healthy penitential life; the gold wisdom; the frankincense love. Each person must offer these to God. Each person's soul, he continued, was made up of three elements: an intellectual potential, an affective potential, and an effective potential. Through the first a man could understand and know what he should do. The second gave him the inclination and the will to do it. The third provided the actual power. Geiler's sermons gave men a strong sense of their own ability to overcome their sins.[53] The story of the vineyard workers provided another example. It did not matter how sinful men had been, nor how old they were. They could always turn to God and find complete acceptance.[54] Geiler drove home the point that men must do all in their power to help themselves. They could not merely throw themselves on God's mercy and expect God to do everything. They must work and cultivate the fields of their own spiritual lives. "Do therefore what you can and notice what you do," he said.[55]

Geiler was a conservative theologian. He made no attempt to break with the traditional emphasis on sin and penance, nor did he attempt to integrate humanist elements into his preaching.[56] He did not turn to the Roman citizen as a useful model for the burghers of Strasbourg. He was interested in reestablishing firm, Christian discipline. Human merit, he believed, would always be essentially insufficient, and no man could ever be certain that he had achieved a state of grace. But, he should always hope that he would be saved.[57] His sermons brought strength and promise to his listeners, for he taught that God would never abandon those who repented of their sin and that a new life could be attained through contrition and penance. The numerous editions of the sermons meant that Geiler's words remained a vital part of the religious life of the community up to the eve of the Reformation. Although he was himself convinced that he had failed to achieve the changes he had hoped for,[58] he had begun the process of awakening men and women to a deeper spiritual life.

This reawakening was reflected in the increase in private devotional literature already described. In these same years popular religious music also began to appear on the Strasbourg presses. There were essentially only a handful of songs, eight in all, on the same familiar themes: the Eucharist, the Annunciation of the Virgin, the seven last words of Christ, and death.[59] Yet even this small number indicates a greater religious activity among the laity and the exploration of new forms of individual communion with God.

Among the clergy, there seems to have been an increased professionalism after 1500. The generalized, traditional curates' manuals were no longer printed. The preferred manual of this period was the work of Johann Ulrich Surgant, priest and canon at Basel, a friend of Sebastian Brant's. Surgant took preaching very seriously. The task of the preacher was to open the word of God to the congregation. In his manual he attempted to cover every possible impediment to effective preaching. In twenty-five chapters, he laid out the proper course for each priest to follow from his salutation to the people, to his gestures (don't point with your finger), to the need for a clear outline.[60] The message was perfectly clear—it was the responsibility of the preacher to open the word of God to the people.[61] A collection of hymns for the church year was designed to make it possible for the priest to integrate the music of the service with the other elements. The meaning of each hymn was explained so that he could communicate this to the congregation before the hymn was sung.[62] A concordance was prepared by the Franciscan Wigand Trebellius, friend of Jacob Wimpheling, as an attempt to instill the sermons of the secular priests with some of the knowledge of the humanists. The volume provided summaries of the thought of great philosophers: Aristotle, Cicero, Julius Caesar, and Augustus, as well as Bonaventura, Christ and, Pope Pius II.[63] The quality of what was available to the clergy improved substantially in the decades immediately preceding the Reform. Publication, however, was still the work of individual clerics, rather than the result of a concerted effort on the part of the institutional church. The humanists, many of whom were clergy, were far more effective than the church in their use of the presses to diffuse the vital materials of intellectual renewal.

The early humanists introduced the new classical and linguistic learning that they had acquired abroad, leading to a renewal of Latin culture in the city. Since these humanists were primarily interested in language, I have referred to them as the Linguists. The movement began with the arrival of Sebastian Brant in 1501. His literary career was already behind him. He had been a professor of poetry at the University of Basel. His seminal work, the *Narrenschiff,* had been published in 1494. Called back to his native city to serve as syndic, an important civil post, he concentrated his energies on the law, publishing little literary work after his return.[64] His importance to the humanist group lay in his established reputation, which attracted other writers and young intellectuals to the city. Jacob Wimpheling, another well-known humanist, played a more important role and emerged as the mentor of the humanist circle. As a professor at Heidelberg he had taught the sons of several Strasbourg patrician families. Geiler asked Wimpheling to assist him in editing Gerson's works, and Wimpheling came, without a teaching post and with neither an ecclesiastical nor a civil appointment to support him.[65]

By 1503 the presence of these two began to create a new intellectual atmosphere in the city. Young humanists came to Strasbourg in hopes of an appointment; others were invited by Wimpheling and Brant. Matthias Ringmann arrived, hoping to found a new school. Johann Gallinarius was appointed to teach grammar and rhetoric in the chapter school of New Saint Peter. Beatus Rhenanus arrived in 1507. In 1509 Wimpheling and Brant prevailed upon Hieronymus Gebwiler to leave his post as rector of the Sélestat grammar school to undertake the reform of Strasbourg's cathedral chapter school.[66] They encouraged Nikolaus Gerbel, a well-trained lawyer and humanist, to open a private Latin school in the city. The school failed, but Gerbel remained and applied himself to literary tasks. He drew Otto Brunfels, a member of the Carthusian house in Strasbourg, into the circle. Ottmar Nachtigall—a musician, an accomplished Greek scholar, widely traveled in Greece and eastern Europe—returned to his native city because of his admiration for Brant and Wimpheling. He settled in the city by 1514; the following year he was appointed organist at Saint Thomas.[67]

A *sodalitas literaria* was established, probably in 1510, to bring the humanists together. By 1514, when Wimpheling invited Erasmus to visit the city, the group included, in addition to the above, Johann Rudolphinger, musician and vicar of the cathedral; Peter Heldung, comptroller of the cathedral chapter; Thomas Vogler (Aucuparius), lawyer and almoner of the cathedral; Jacob Sturm; Johann Ruser von Ebersheim, a friend of Beatus Rhenanus; Johann Guida, amanuensis of Wimpheling; Thomas Rapp; Stephen Tieler; and Matthias Schürer.[68] The majority of the group were clerics, supported by benefices in the cathedral, Old and New Saint Peter, and Saint Thomas. The exceptions were Brant and Gerbel, both lawyers; Sturm, who in 1517 would become secretary to the dean of the Strasbourg chapter; Wimpheling; and Schürer, the printer. We have no information with regard to the meetings of the *sodalitas* other than the banquet which they gave in honor of Erasmus. The close friendships between the members of the group, however, are reflected in references in correspondence.[69] There were also profound differences among them. Those who arrived after 1507 were critical of basic institutions within the church—monasticism and the papal power— and were no longer content merely to remonstrate against ceremonies and other usages. They understood the full implications of Erasmus's thought and were ready to move toward new interpretations of biblical and patristic texts. For them, Brant and Wimpheling represented an older generation.[70] By 1510 the group was also substantially larger than the small handful that had gathered around Geiler. This in itself was an indication of the quickening tempo of German intellectual life. The influence of the group on the community was considerable. As members of the city administration and as rectors and teachers of the schools, they were in close touch with patrician society and with members of the Magistrat.[71]

The humanists encouraged new approaches to the classical texts and introduced particular skills, including stylistic analysis, critical reading, and historic and aesthetic sensibility.[72] The Linguists were most interested in style and in aesthetics, but they also made an important contribution to historical studies. Their work included not only their own literary compositions, but the editing of Greek and Latin texts, the preparation of editions of contemporary humanists, and the writing of school texts. All these are considered in the analysis of humanist work in this and in later chapters. The evolution of the whole humanist movement is shown in figure XX.[73] The contribution of the Linguists was unlike that of any later period, because they disseminated the work of other writers. They were particularly dependent on the work of their contemporaries, both German and Italian humanist scholars. They encouraged the printers to publish the poetry, letters, and historical works of classical authors and contemporary Italians, but they undertook little original work of their own. They were disseminators rather than originators, but they had a clear purpose, from which they developed their program of reform.

Latin was their primary interest. They approached language with moral and religious fervor; to be a good linguist was as important to them as to be a pious Christian. This was not mere scholarly zeal. They were aware of the connection between language and culture. They realized that the ideas which a society formulates are shaped by the language in which they are expressed. To restore Christian thought to its fundamental meaning, it was essential to return to the classical Latin in which it was originally communicated by the apostles and the early church fathers.

Their first aim was to purify Latin grammar by ridding it of its medieval accretions. They looked with horror on the traditional texts by Donatus and Alexander de Villa Dei, which had been used for centuries. Eighteen editions of Alexander's *Doctrinale* had been printed in Strasbourg by 1500, supplemented by five editions of Donatus.[74] After the arrival of Brant and Wimpheling, only two editions of each were printed. The disappearance of these texts signaled the establishment of humanism as an important force in the city. Hieronymus Gebwiler selected Johann Cochlaeus's new Latin grammar for the cathedral school.[75] Strasbourg publishers quickly printed the grammatical texts written by other northern scholars. The works of Herman Torrentius, brother of the Common Life and teacher at Groningen, Johann Brassicanus of Tübingen, Jacob Heinrichmann, and Erasmus poured from the Strasbourg presses.[76]

The new grammars still demanded much from the student. Few authors or printers thought of presenting declensions or verbs in tabular form, which might have made it easier for the student to comprehend. In Wimpheling's *Elegantiae majores,* the Latin text was set in Gothic type. There was no attempt to explain the structure of the ancient language, the word order, or the problems of declension. Each element of the language was presented separately with no indication of how it was related to the others. There were no selections of prose or poetry for the student to read.[77]

Matthias Schürer's edition of Erasmus's *De duplica copia* (1513) was one of the few grammatical texts that departed from the traditional presentation. The text was broken into sections so that the student was not confronted with a solid page that had to be memorized. Chapter headings in large type provided an outline. The text was liberally scattered with examples, which served as models of style.[78]

An innovative approach to grammar was made by Matthias Ringmann, an intimate of the Strasbourg circle of teachers and writers. His *Grammatica figurata* was published in 1501 in Saint-Dié. It presented the basic principles of Latin grammar in the form of a card game. Nouns and pronouns were characterized as priests; adjectives were his vicars. The verbs were kings; adverbs queens; the participle served as a monk. The conjunction was a cupbearer; the preposition a church warden; and the interjection a fool.[79] The relationships between the various parts of speech were thus personified for the student. These texts, written by Wimpheling, Gebwiler, Gerbel, and Ringmann and printed by Johann Prüss II, Matthias Hupfuff, and Matthias Schürer, improved the quality of Latin instruction.

Ottmar Nachtigall introduced the study of Greek in Strasbourg, editing Greek texts for those individuals who wished to pursue the more ancient language. In these decades the study of Greek was limited to adults who already knew Latin. It was one of the new acquisitions of the Renaissance. Nachtigall's handbooks were not schoolboy texts, but provided the elements of Greek grammar so that a trained scholar could work out his own translation with the aid of a bilingual Greek and Latin text.[80] Nachtigall also provided selections of Greek epigrams, poetry, and prose suitable for the adult amateur of the language.[81] In 1513 Matthias Schürer had published a Greek grammar which merely listed nouns, pronouns, verbs and adjectives, providing an example of each declension or conjugation. Nachtigall's text, published by Johann Knobloch in 1517, provided a clear and logical introduction to the language, starting with the alphabet and a chart on the use of the diphthong, as well as an explanation of pronunciation and accent. The parts of speech were introduced separately, but Nachtigall was careful to show how each was used in the construction of a sentence.[82] His work, together with Ringmann's, reflects a growing awareness of the importance of structure in language.

The Strasbourg humanists made use of the grammatical work of the Italian humanists. Lorenzo Valla's *Elegantiae lingua Latinae* was published by Matthias Schürer in 1517. It was a careful, scientific analysis of grammar— the most advanced of the time, particularly in terms of the inner structure of the language.[83] Schürer's publication of five editions of the *Dialectica* of George of Trebizond was another indication of the persistent search for clarity, precision, and the logical ordering of words and ideas.[84] Collections of letters of the Italian humanists were used as models of style, and there were numerous editions of these: nine editions of Francesco Filelfo's letters; eight editions of the moral letters of Faustus Andrelinus, the professor of Latin literature who had taught Matthias Ringmann, Ottmar Nachtigall, and Sebastian Murr.[85]

The restoration of classical Latin was, however, a means to a more important end. The ultimate goal was to arouse men to higher levels of moral consciousness and, finally, to open them to a deeper spiritual life. Here the Linguistic humanists turned to their Italian contemporaries rather than to classical authors. Their consuming passion was poetry, but they were not fully prepared to present to students the Latin poets with all the complications involved in terms of moral and religious ideas. The Christian poets, particularly their own teachers, like Faustus Andrelinus, were more congenial. The result was a wave of publication of Italian authors (figure XX). Most of these books were printed by Matthias Schürer, who brought out 117 editions of the Italian humanists. Thirty-seven editions were printed by Johann Schott, Johann Prüss II, Matthias Grüninger, and Renatus Beck. If reprintings are an indication of popularity, the favorite Italian authors of the Strasbourg humanist circle were Joannes Baptista Mantuanus, Francesco Filelfo, P. Faustus Andrelinus, Giovanni Pico della Mirandola, George of Trebizond, Lorenzo Valla, Aeneas Silvius Piccolomini, and Poggio Bracciolini, in that order.

Mantuanus's popularity can be explained in part because he was regarded by the northern humanist school masters as a Christian counterpart of Virgil. His Latin was considered equal in purity to that of the Latin poet, and the content of his writings was untainted by paganism. The frequent reprints of his work indicate that it was widely read.[86] The most important was his epic poem, the *Bucolica,* which mirrored the profound conservatism of the Linguistic humanists. They could undertake the reform of grammar, they could adopt new forms of expression, particularly poetry, but they did not change their ideas about the nature of man and his world. Faustus, the hero of Mantuanus's poem, was a simple shepherd seduced from the honesty of his calling by a pretty village girl. The story retold the Fall, and the *via contemplativa* emerged as the ideal way of life. The love of a man for a woman was shown to be dangerous, exposing the lover to the perversity and duplicity of women and to the craft of the devil. There were long descriptions of the corruptions and evils of the world. One section was devoted to Faustus's journey to Rome, which was climaxed by his arrival in front of Saint Peter's, accompanied by his sheep. The citizens of Rome were inconsiderate, lacking in love and Christian concern, heedless of their country brother. The problems of the Roman church, however, were alluded to only very generally. Faustus was shocked by the power, the influence, and the accumulation of wealth that he saw around him. For Faustus, the alternative to accepting these evils was to flee the valleys, to return to the mountains and live close to God, while caring for his flock.[87]

Obviously the poem was more Christian than classical. The humanists accepted the dichotomy between the spiritual and material worlds. On the very eve of the Reform they did not question the superiority of the celibate life. The books they used with their students affirmed the old values; indeed, Wimpheling and Geiler, attempting to carry the ideal into practice, planned to withdraw to a hermitage to flee the pressures of everyday life.[88] The conservatism of the Linguistic humanists was manifested in other ways as well. The books they neglected, and which the printers passed over, were as important in defining the intellectual environment as those that were printed.

Certain major works of the Italian humanists were never published in Strasbourg. Lorenzo Valla's grammatical work was acceptable, but his *Annotations on the New Testament,* his *Dialogue on Free Will,* and his essay *On the True Good* were not printed. Similarly, the translations from Greek by Francesco Filelfo and George of Trebizond, which included Chrysostom's *Commentaries on Matthew* and the major works of Aristotle, were disregarded by both the printers and the humanists. Poggio Bracciolini's joke book went through several editions, but his philosophical writing was neglected. Giovanni Pico della Mirandola was the only Italian humanist whose philosophical and theological work was published in its entirety in the northern city.[89] As Baillet points out, his religious sensitivity made him attractive to the Alsatians.[90]

The absence of these works by Poggio, Valla, and Pomponazzi, coupled with minimal publication of Plato and Aristotle, is an indication that the Linguists failed to move on to the metaphysical phase which was so important to the later Italian Renaissance.[91] The Strasbourg circle, as long as it was led by Wimpheling and Brant, did not undertake publication of the philosophical or critical works of men like Valla or Pomponazzi because they regarded them as too radical and unorthodox. They admired the grammatical works of Erasmus and his pedagogy, which were published in multiple editions. His critical essays, however, warranted only single editions.[92] Linguistic studies and poetry could be pursued without disturbing the central core of their faith. They did not wish to move away from the religious and philosophical principles they had learned at the university. In the decade from 1510 to 1520, men like Gerbel and Brunfels were not yet prepared to develop their own views.

When they turned to the classical corpus, the Linguists were drawn to poetry and *belles lettres*. Virgil was their favorite Latin author: there were fifteen editions of the *Aeneid* and the *Georgics* in this period.[93] Cicero was next with fourteen editions of the essays and letters, but only two editions of the orations.[94] In comparison with classical publication in the later decades, this period was characterized by a far wider-ranging selection. Juvenal, Martial, Symmachus, Lucian, and Aules Persius Flaccus were represented along with Ovid, Horace, Cato, Pliny, and Sabellicus.[95] Most important, in comparison with the later oeuvre, were the numerous editions of Ovid, a favorite of Matthias Schürer. Schürer began with *De remedio amoris* in 1514 and brought out seven more works of Ovid before 1519.[96] Knobloch added an edition of the *Heroides* in 1522. These were the only editions of Ovid published in sixteenth-century Strasbourg.

In reviewing the publications of this period it becomes clear that the Linguists were interested in content as well as style. Their focus was moral. They searched for examples from the classical past which provided apt models for the Christian life.[97] Aesthetics and virtues were intertwined; clarity of style led to purity of life.

The early humanists had a compelling vision of educational reform. Here their intellectual interests were translated into action, an action which was profoundly religious in nature. The reform of the Christian community could come only through spiritual rebirth which was dependent on the restoration of learning. The role of the clergy in the process was vividly set forth by Wimpheling. The clergy were meant to serve as models for the rest of society. Because they ignored their role of moral leadership and led debauched lives, society reflected their corruption, and the educational system, which they controlled, was subverted.[98] The solution was to reform the schools to provide a genuinely Christian education. For both the theologians and the humanists, the ultimate aim was the same—the restoration of the Christian community.[99]

Wimpheling's *Adolescentia,* first published in 1500, made far-reaching proposals with regard to the financing of schools, the organization of instruction, and the curriculum itself. It was an eloquent and early statement of the need for publicly supported secondary schools, going far beyond the recommendations of any of the Italian humanists. One of Wimpheling's primary concerns was that insufficient provision was made for poor students, who had to beg or accept jobs in wealthy families in order to support themselves. Either solution was degrading, exposed the student to vicious habits, and made him overly concerned with money.[100] Wimpheling, therefore, advocated public support of the schools, which would relieve the student of the necessity of paying high fees. The money needed could be obtained by turning over existing church benefices to students and scholars.[101] In a later treatise, Wimpheling proposed that every German city should establish a Gymnasium, an intermediate school to serve as a link between the grammar schools and the universities.[102]

Wimpheling's plan for curriculum reform stressed careful organization and planning. The pupil should progress from one well-defined task to another, so that from elementary school onwards he would find himself adequately prepared for the next step. He applied this principle not only to academic learning but to moral education as well. After the student had been initiated in the fundamentals of Latin grammar and elementary Latin texts, the basic moral rules of life should be thoroughly inculcated. With these rules of life firmly in hand, sure of his moral values, the student would be able to go on to the Latin poets and not be undermined by their different standards.[103] The *Adolescentia* provided selections for ethical instruction drawn from more than fifty sources: Tobias, Horatius, Bonaventura, Ecclesiasticus, Seneca, Poggio, Augustine, Jerome, and Sebastian Brant.[104]

Wimpheling's program was practical. He was not interested in outlining an ideal education based on purely theoretical assumptions. His proposal for an intermediate school would eventually bear fruit in the establishment of the Strasbourg Gymnasium in 1538. Hieronymus Gebwiler suggested a similar plan in his preface to Lefevre d'Etaples's *Introductio in physicam paraphrasim* (1514). The students in his school would be divided into three groups: the beginners to concentrate on grammar, vocabulary, and prose reading from classicial or neo-Latin texts; the second group would continue their language study, but begin dialectic, including oral exercises, in this art; the most advanced group would move on to moral and natural philosophy, using Aristotle for their text.[105]

Erasmus's pedagogical ideas were widely diffused by the Strasbourg printers. His treatise *De ratione studii ac legende interprete* went through eight editions in nine years.[106] It was, in fact, only a minor work of Erasmus, written in Paris when he was struggling to support himself by tutoring.[107] It outlined an orderly curriculum, providing for the academic progress of the student from grammatical studies through the complexities of dialectic and philosophy. Erasmus applied the concept of sequential learning even to infants in his *De pueris statim ac liberaliter instituendis*.[108] Here he proposed that the education of a young child should proceed in stages: first the primary education undertaken by the mother or nurse; then, from age three to age six, an elementary education based on games; then the beginning of systematic instruction in the fundamentals of grammar, reading, and writing.[109]

Toward the end of the period, Otto Brunfels, then a member of the Carthusian community in Strasbourg, presented his plan for a curriculum that would integrate mathematics and medicine into the work of the school. To defend this departure he quoted Pythagoras, who believed it was not possible to understand the truth without geometry, and Philo, who wrote that mathematics was essential to understanding the eternal qualities of nature. The study of medicine was justified by Hippocrates and Avicenna.[110] In view of the interest in mathematics later in the century, Brunfels's proposal was almost prophetic.

The pedagogical treatises, with their emphasis on a careful progression from one subject to the next and the preparation of the student for each task, led to a more highly structured school organization. Philippe Ariès sees this development as playing a significant role in the changing attitude toward childhood. The separation of students into well-defined classes, each with its specified objectives, would help to create a differentiation between childhood and adolescence and would lead to a variation in expectations for the different groups.[111] This concept was already well established among the

Italian humanist schoolmasters of the early fifteenth century. The German humanist treatises introduced it to the north by the first decades of the sixteenth century.

Although language and education were the first priority of the Linguistic humanists, they were active in other ways as well. Wimpheling was embroiled in a series of bitter scholarly quarrels with the Franciscan Thomas Murner, with Jacob Locher, and with the Swiss.[112] His savage personal attacks destroyed the effectiveness of his criticism, particularly in the case of his diatribes against the monastic orders. These literary disputes, however, were an accepted element of intellectual life that would surface later in the polemic warfare of the Reform period. The humanists wrote in glowing terms of the life of Christian piety and devotion. They failed to practice these virtues in their relationships with one another.[113]

The early humanists were strong German nationalists. Their work helped to stimulate the development of a conscious, German identity in the face of the cultural cohesion of France or Italy. Resenting the assumed superiority of the latter, the German writers turned to discover their own independent heritage. They produced eulogies and panegyrics celebrating the virtues and leadership of particular German men and rulers;[114] there were carmina in praise of German cities such as Freiburg and Strasbourg;[115] most important were the histories. In 1505 Wimpheling published a collection of historical writings, one of the first important histories of Germany written by a German citizen. Wimpheling broke away from the medieval chronicle style, which started with Adam, and began his account with the first reference to the Germanic peoples by a Roman writer. He described the Roman conquest and the reign of each Roman emperor, but the heart of the account was the invasion of the Roman Empire by the German-speaking tribes and the history of the new imperial dynasty, beginning with Charlemagne. A chapter on the national character extolled German constancy, German courage, and German liberality. The book ended with a summary of the contributions of the German peoples to the civilization of Europe, again a departure, since he wrote not of politics and military exploits but of culture and the arts—specifically, the invention of printing and the perfection of Gothic architecture.[116]

Heinrich Bebel, a Tübingen humanist, was widely published in Strasbourg. Influenced by Aeneas Silvius Piccolomini's history of Germany, Bebel turned the attention of his fellow humanists to medieval historians like Einhard and Otto of Friesing.[117] His treatise on the merits of the German language, and another on the superiority of German proverbs to classical adages, went through five editions on the Strasbourg presses.[118] Ironically, the treatises were written in Latin and the German proverbs, which were cited to illustrate their superior wisdom, were carefully translated into Latin. Several of the Strasbourg humanists wrote biographies. Johann Müling wrote an account of Frederick Barbarossa in German, and Hieronymus Gebwiler a history of the Archduke Ferdinand, which was expanded to include the whole Hapsburg family.[119] Previously unexploited sources were opened up, and German historical development began to be freed of its dependence on Rome.

The success of the Linguists depended heavily on the printers, in particular, Matthias Schürer, Johann Knobloch, and Johann Schott. The Strasbourg circle was able to write only a fraction of the books and treatises needed to institute a more analytical study of Latin. The printers supplemented these by publishing the work of Italian and German humanists, Erasmus, and classical texts. It was Matthias Schürer, in particular, who made the full spectrum of humanist literature available in the city. He printed cheap, clear editions of a full panoply of classical and humanist authors. In the seventeen years from 1490 to 1507, only 16 editions of the Greek and Latin classics were printed in Strasbourg. In the twelve years that Schürer was active, before his untimely death in December 1519 or January 1520, there were 116 editions. Schürer's contribution to the total of humanist publication is dramatically summarized in table 10.

Schürer's interest in the classics, particularly the Latin poets, the historians, and Cicero, was balanced by his acumen in selecting the most significant contemporary humanists. He published the more important Italian grammarians and stylists and began the publication of the works of Erasmus in Strasbourg (at first in a pirated edition). Erasmus respected the young printer, encouraged him, and, until Schürer's death, gave him a virtual monopoly on publishing his works in the city. Schürer was a scholar himself, trained at the University of Cracow. He had genuine interest in language and an enthusiasm for Latin literature. As a scholar-printer he was able to mold the public taste. More than any other member of the *sodalitas literaria* he was responsible for opening the doors to Roman antiquity for the educated burghers and patricians of Strasbourg.[120]

Table 10. *Publication of the Greek and Latin Classics and Humanist Works, 1502–1519*

	Humanism	Classics	Total
Totals for the Period	*196*	*141*	*337*
Matthias Schürer	105	74	179
Johann Knobloch	30	34	64
Johann Schott	8	8	16
Totals of these 3 printers	143	116	259

Both the traditional theologians and the Linguists sought to reform their society. Of the two, the latter would have a more lasting effect. Their focus on style and language was an important step in the process of change. New conceptual formulations cannot be stated in the vocabulary of the past, which in itself inhibits the scope of the thought. There is a need for a language heard and perceived freshly, without the overlay of past usage and assumptions. The early humanists provided a new language, together with the linguistic and grammatical equipment essential to the work of the Christian humanists and the reformers. Furthermore, their sensitivity to language and to the relationship between thought and expression gave words a pre-eminence that came to characterize the intellectual life of the century. The Protestant reformers spent decades attempting to unravel what was meant by the words "This is my body." The words "baptism," "trinity," and "communion" created deep and permanent divisions among people. The agony of definition started with the linguistic humanists and their respect for words. Faced by conflicting ideas and contradictory values, the men of the sixteenth century attempted to control them with words.[121] Words became weapons.

CHAPTER FIVE · ILLUSTRATED BOOKS FOR THE LAYMAN, 1490–1520

THE LATIN CULTURE SET THE INTELLEC-tual tone of the city in the late fifteenth century, reaching out beyond the clergy and the chapters to the city bureaucracy and the patrician circle. In these earliest decades the printers, with the exception of Heinrich Knoblochtzer, looked to the clergy as their major market, and few vernacular books were published. Not until the turn of the century did this change. In the first decade of the sixteenth century, Johann Grüninger added vernacular books to his already extensive stock, and Matthias Hupfuff began to develop the new market in preference to ecclesiastical publication, where the competition may have been too great for him. From 1508 to 1520, popular vernacular books constituted approximately twelve percent of the total volume of books produced in the city.

The vernacular culture in these days was, nevertheless, molded by the learned. Johann Geiler von Kaysersberg, Sebastian Brant, Jacob Wimpheling, and Thomas Murner not only wrote in the vernacular, they were responsible for the best-sellers of the period. Animated by the ardent German nationalism of the time, Sebastian Brant wrote his *Narrenschiff* in German (it was also duly translated into Latin for the humanists). The poem, describing the vagaries of every familiar social type, was enormously popular. Thomas Murner modeled his *Narrenbeschwörung* on Brant's poem and wrote a series of satirical poem-stories, which quickly went through several editions. These publications by Brant and Murner comprised 6 percent of the vernacular books published between 1490 and 1520. The sermons of Geiler von Kaysersberg, together with his devotionals and the book of consolation, represented 17 percent of the total. Thus, approximately a quarter of the vernacular books were the work of learned men. The remainder, over 75 percent, were chivalric tales, folk stories, lives of the saints, and Bible stories drawn from the oral tradition. The majority of the vernacular publications of this period were illustrated. The printers, drawn by the possibility of selling to a larger market, established workshops of trained artists and spent much of their time and energy perfecting the techniques for printing with woodcuts.[1] These illustrated books encouraged literacy. They made it easy for an adult to learn how to read and laid the foundation of an independent popular culture.

The popular books by the learned were written with a moral purpose. Brant's tone in the *Narrenschiff* was melancholic, rueful. He depicted men's faults with little hope that they would change their ways. Although he singled out a few individual fools—ignorant scholars, beneficed clergy, gamblers, adulterers, prostitutes, cooks, and waiters—his major concern was the foolish behavior of all sorts and conditions of men. They were too easily influenced by popular opinion, seeking material wealth and comfort instead of tending to the salvation of their souls. They were thoughtless, inflicting troubles on others, and disloyal to their friends.[2] The all-pervasive theme was their lack of wisdom. God had provided the Scriptures as a guide to life, but few listened to wise advice.[3] Instead they ignored their eternal life, their own salvation. They relied on their own power, although they were powerless. One of the longest stanzas attacked the desire to learn about cities and countries all over the world, the foolish attempts of the geographers to measure the earth. Why explore foreign lands when you did not understand yourself? Self-knowledge was the gateway to eternal life; knowledge of the world itself was fruitless.[4] A separate woodcut depicting the foolish action embellished each stanza of the poem.

Thomas Murner was more sarcastic and biting, almost savage in his attack.[5] His *Narrenbeschwörung* [The fools' exorcism] was a harsher version of Brant's *Narrenschiff*. The first object of attack was the clergy. Murner depicted them as arrogant and insensitive, boasting that they were indispensable because no one else could interpret the holy texts. In reality, he stated, they contributed very little to the community, at great expense to everyone else. They claimed to know the way to heaven but never showed it to the people; in short, the clergy took care of the faithful as well as a wolf takes care of a flock of sheep.[6] If, however, men were venal, crafty, selfish, and untrustworthy, women were worse. They were the major cause of trouble in the *Narrenbeschwörung*. The man who married was trapped forever and would find no peace. Murner stated he would give a thousand gulden to see all the women who led men around by the nose laid flat out.[7]

Murner's misogyny was fully developed in the satirical tale *Die Mühle von Schwindelsheim,* the story of a miller and his unfaithful wife.[8] The miller's wife had granted her favors far and wide. When the bell rang for her funeral, priests, monks, burghers, counts, and princes streamed to do her honor, bearing expensive gifts. The poor miller, overwhelmed, turned to the merchant to find who had bought the gifts and discovered the depth of his wife's deception. The merchant's books showed all the presents that priests, noblemen, and burghers had given over the years in return for his wife's favors. Murner's point was that all human activity was characterized by dishonesty and cheating. The priests accumulated benefices illegally and broke their vows. The miller had given short weight to his customers. All were caught in the same web of dishonesty; but, the root cause was the excessive demands made by the miller's wife. Women caused the fall of men.[9]

Like Wimpheling and Geiler, Murner felt that one solution to the falseness of the world was withdrawal to the contemplative life, the strengthening of one's own inner religious life. His book *Ein Andechtig Badenfart* offered a meditative retreat which even an ordinary man could achieve.[10] Murner's own experience at the healing baths at a nearby spa was used as an allegory of the spiritual pilgrimage that an individual could undertake to purify himself. The woodcuts in the Strasbourg edition strengthened the allegory. God was shown preparing the water for the bath with his own hands. Jesus stoked the furnace to heat the water and, in another picture, made a nourishing soup for the invalid.

In the text the metaphor of the cure was carefully developed. Each step in the routine followed by the bather was given a spiritual interpretation. At the beginning the individual should recognize his uncleanness and commend himself to the healing powers of the bath, as the prodigal son submitted himself to his father. The bather must then purge himself of sin and ugliness, and strip himself to stand naked before God. At the end of the bath, the bather, wrapped in a warm, clean bathrobe, would rest quietly before journeying home, so the soul should be clean and ready at all times for the final journey.[11] This was the most empathic of Murner's works, written with a basic assumption that men would heed the advice and renew themselves spiritually. The reeditions of the book, two in seven years, reflect its popularity. The mixture of a gentle piety with scenes of everyday life, the comparison of bodily health with the welfare of the soul, had broad appeal.

Neither Brant nor Murner were social critics. They did not attempt to describe social conditions. Such descriptions emerge, if at all, only secondarily. Nor were they attempting to articulate the aspirations of artisans, businessmen, peasants, or journeymen. They were moralists. Their purpose was to awaken men, to bring about the same spiritual reforms envisioned by Geiler and Wimpheling. The popularity of their books would indicate that readers enjoyed the criticism, even when it was directed against them.

The diffusion of a wider variety of vernacular literature was the direct result of the efforts of the printers themselves. They created a market among ordinary readers by developing illustrated books. Recent scholarship suggests that reading these books was a transitional phase between listening to a story and reading; looking at the picture took the place of hearing the words.[12] An illustrated book was a book designed for lay use, whether the laymen could read or not. Thus Brant, in a foreword to an illustrated version of the *Narrenschiff,* stated explicitly that those who could not read could see their foolishness reflected in the woodcuts.[13] Illustrated books played a vital role in making the world of print accessible. After the 1520s, the use of illustrations diminished,[14] though the Strasbourg figures for illustrated books show a slight rise in the percentage of total production during the decade 1530–39 (table 11). This rise in the 1530s was due to the publication of scientific manuals. The high proportion of illustrated books was not maintained throughout the century in part because the illustrations were no longer necessary. Pictures were needed when literacy was low. As more people learned to read, the number of illustrated books was substantially reduced. Furthermore, the illustrations were used differently in the later decades. In the period before 1515, they were designed very clearly to elucidate the text. Later they were often merely intended to embellish or ornament the book.

Heinrich Knoblochtzer was the first Strasbourg printer to exploit the possibilities of illustrated editions. Borrowing the pictures from editions of an Augsburg printer, he issued an illustrated version of the story of *Belial* in 1477, which went through four editions. He followed this with the story of *Herzog Ernst* and a version of the Lucretia story.[15] This repertoire was representative of the materials that would remain popular.[16]

Knoblochtzer left Strasbourg in 1485 to set himself up in Heidelberg. His innovative use of illustrations, however, had already been picked up by other Strasbourg printers. In 1483, Johann Prüss brought out an illustrated version of *Melusine,* followed by an edition of the story of the three kings. Fifty of the fifty-eight pictures he took from Knoblochtzer.[17] Martin Schott used woodcuts in almost all his editions.[18] Johann Grüninger, with the largest volume of any printer in this period, adapted illustrations to a broad range of work and encouraged the development of new techniques. In his

Table 11. Editions of Illustrated Books by Decade, 1480–1599

Decade	Number	% of Total Production	Decade	Number	% of Total Production
1480–89	14	5	1540–49	42	10
1490–99	26	8	1550–59	29	9
1500–09	91	21	1560–69	30	8
1510–19	121	17	1570–79	40	9
1520–29	79	8	1580–89	35	10
1530–39	73	14	1590–99	36	9

earliest illustrated editions he, like the other Strasbourg printers, borrowed from the Knoblochtzer woodcuts or from illustrations done by printers in other cities.[19] After 1500, however, he began to commission new wood-cuts, calling on major artists like Hans Baldung Grien, Johann Schaufelin, and Johann Wechtelin.[20] Matthias Hupfuff specialized in vernacular pub-lication. A veritable flood of stories, songs, calendars, and prognostications flowed from his press, almost all of them illustrated. The pictures borrowed heavily from the work of other printers.[21]

These illustrated books helped to create a new mass of readers. The text and illustrations were combined so that the story could be followed easily, and a direct effort was made to reach the common reader. This is evident from the title pages, which anticipated the jacket blurb of a modern novel. The title itself was often enticing: "a pretty little story," "a good read," "a useful story." The subtitle led the reader further, listing the episodes to be found in the book: an attack on a lovely queen by a frightful dragon; her rescue by a great army of kings, counts, knights, and squires;[22] the adven-tures of a true and brave knight;[23] the knightly deeds and prowess of Hugh de Capet, climaxing in his coronation as king of France.[24] In these title pages, an early form of advertising, the printer depended on the glamour and romance of court life to sell the book. Knightly life was accepted as a suitable model for burgher society: "the Knight of Turn or the Mirror of valor and honor, with very pretty and valuable stories in examples for instructing your children," read one of the subtitles.[25]

Other fruitful sources for popular books were the medieval versions of Roman and Greek legends, in particular the *Gesta Romanorum,* Leo the Archpresbyter's version of the life of Alexander the Great, the destruction of Troy, and Livy's history of the city of Rome.[26] The *Gesta Romanorum,* a traditional medieval collection, included the stories of Lucretia, Cincin-natus, Julius Caesar, Domitian, and all sorts of other "noble and valiant Roman knights" whose lives reflected loyalty, responsibility, and devotion to duty. The original Roman legend was retold with emphasis on individual heroism, patriotism, and selflessness. The Latin editions show that these were used by the clergy as sources for their homilies in the same way that they used the lives of the saints.[27] By 1512 they were translated into Ger-man and incorporated into popular literature. Each tale was given a highly allegorical interpretation and was followed by a "moral," which provided a pious Christian version of the event. The rape of Lucretia, the reader was told, symbolized the struggle between the soul (Lucretia) and the devil (Sextus). Calatinus's villa (referred to as his castle) represented the heart which Sextus forced open. The sword with which Lucretia killed herself stood for penitence.[28] The fact that Lucretia was hardly a willing participant to any of this was completely neglected by the Christian adaptor. The life of

Iß jar wurden in dem acker Euclij Pacilij deß schreibers zů Rom vnder dem berge Janiculo genennt/zwen steynen Kasten bei acht schůch langk vnnd vier schůch breyt funden (do die bawleüt die erden tieffer graben wolten) die waren mit decken belegt vnd mit bley vergoßen/ vnd war eyn jetlich mit Latinischen vnd Griechischen büchstaben gezeichnet vnd üschriben/das inn dem eynen Kasten Numa Pompilius Pomponis sůn/der eyn Römisch König gewest/ vnd inn dem andern die bücher Nume Pompilij begraben weren. Da aber der herr deß ackers mit radt seiner freünd die zwen Kasten hett öffnen vnd auffbrechen laßen/ ward der eyn (darauff der Tittel deß Königs Pompilij aldo begraben geschriben ward) gantz leer vnd ledig funden on eynig anzeyge eyns menschlichen leibs oder anders die weil alle ding durch so vil jar verwesen vnd verfeület waren/inn dem andern Kasten waren funden zwey gebundt inn wächßen kertzen gewickelt/ die hetten inn sich jetlich siben bücher/nicht alleyn gantz vnd vnuerseeret/sunder auch an der gestalt seer newe. Die siben Lateinischen waren von dem geystlichen rechten/die siben Griechischen waren von der zucht vnd kunst der weißheyt/die zů der zeyt sein mocht. Valerius Antias der historien beschriben hat/ sagt es weren gewest die bücher Pythagore deß hochgelerten meysters/ vnd leget zů dem gemeynen wahn vnd gerücht eynen glauben mit eyner glaublichen lügen/inn dem das es geglaubt vnd darfür gehalten wirt Numa Pompilius der Rö-

Plate 1. Everyday life in the Roman forum. The burning of the books of Numa Pompilius from Livy's *Römanische History*, Johann Grüninger, 1507.

Alexander the Great, the *Historia Alexandri,* was also first published in Latin.[29] In 1488 Martin Schott came out with a German edition, based on a 1444 translation by Dr. Hartlieb. This German edition had already been published in Augsburg in 1472;[30] Schott's edition brought it to the attention of the other Strasbourg printers, who promptly copied it.[31]

The contrast between the Latin and German editions of the *Gesta* and the *Historia Alexandri* reflect the different audiences they were intended to attract. The Latin editions were done in clear Roman type, without illustrations. The initial letter for each section was still painted in by hand. A small letter was printed in the space to guide the artist, and the finished letters vary in size, shape, and style in such a way that they could not have been produced by type. To add to the beauty and variety of the page, the artist used red ink to fill in or draw a line through the first letter of every sentence and all capital letters.[32] These hand details indicate that the copies for the Latin reader were still designed to imitate manuscripts.

Martin Schott's 1493 German edition, by contrast, was set in Gothic type. There were one full-page illustration and twenty-five smaller woodcuts. No captions were given, and there were large chunks of text without pictures. In some cases, the initial letters for the paragraphs were never finished; the space was left, but the final decoration was not completed. The illustrations provided a medieval setting for the life of Alexander, the majority depicting men in armor performing knightly deeds.[33] The story gave the artist some special opportunities: a confrontation between the Indian army, mounted on elephants, and Alexander's troops, equipped with cannons; and Alexander's descent into the sea in a diver's bell, which was shaped like a smallish lobster pot.[34] The fall of Troy provided equally rich opportunities. The writer and the illustrator started with Jason and the golden fleece, went on to Jason's seduction of Medusa, to the abduction of Helen, and finally to the siege of Troy. There was a conscious effort to present the marvelous, the sensational.

The story of Dietrich von Bern is an excellent example of a knightly tale prepared for the popular audience.[35] The presentation was not unlike a modern comic strip with the text running under the woodcuts. Like a comic strip hero, everything happened to Dietrich von Bern. He left his home and devoted wife to do battle against a giant who menaced the countryside. Right away he met a wild man who attacked him, smiting him to the ground. Dietrich recovered with sufficient speed to cut off the head of his assailant. He next encountered a dwarf who guided him to the giant. A prolonged battle ensued. Dietrich won the first round, striking so hard with his sword that sparks flew from it. The giant retaliated by tearing up a tree by the roots to use as a weapon. With this he overcame Dietrich, tied him up, and carried him off to a cave inhabited by a dragon. An elderly knight

wie Jason mitt eynem tracken ficht.

Arnach gieng er man lich zū dem tracken/vnnd do er jnn sach zū jm kommen/ do ließ er dē scheyn des steyns dē jm Medea geben hett scheynē in des tracken augē/võ wegen des steyns krafft mocht er keynē flammen fürbas auß seynē mund lassen· Den selben steyn fyndet man in jndia:als vnnß schreybet der meyster Jsidorus/vnnd heyst bey vnnß schmarag dus· Des krafft ist also· Welicħe verr giffte thier oder würm mann den steyn hebt für die augen/ vnd als bald er des steyns entpfyndt/ so mūß der würm oð das thier zū stund sterben· Vnd do der tracke des scheynes entpfand/ do mocht er dem Jason nitt mer schaden· Zū hād nam Jasonn das schwert/vnnd schlüg jnn als lanng auff die schüpeln des ruckens/wann die waren als hart vnnd als vest als ob er auff ein anboß schlüge/doch so schlüg er als lang biß er tod gelage·

Do ficht Jason mitt vier gewapneten ritter die gewachsen seynd auß des tracken zen geseet jn das erdtreych dz do wz vmb geackert mit den ochsen

Plate 2. Woodcut from Knobloch's 1510 edition of *Ein hübsche histori do der küniglichen stat Troi wie si zerstorett wart*. The caption reads: "How Jason fought with the dragon." Below is the caption for the next illustration, the fight with the warriors who spring from the dragon's teeth. Note that equal space is given to the woodcut and to the text.

attempted the rescue, but he, too, was overpowered, tied, and imprisoned in the giant's bedchamber. Nevertheless, the captured rescuer escaped his bonds and slew the dragon. The stark black and white of the woodcuts intensified the contrasts: the dwarf and the giant; the helplessness of Dietrich, trussed like a chicken bound for the market under the arm of the giant; the exaggerated length of the ladder used to rescue Dietrich from the dragon's cave.[36]

In marked contrast to the women who would appear in the vernacular stories in the middle of the century, female heroines were infrequent in the early decades. Indeed the theme was often the moral weakness of the woman, her infidelity, and the collapse of her marriage. Hupfuff's edition of Salomon and Morolf began with King Fore, surrounded by his knights and squires, asking where he might find a beautiful wife worthy of him.[37] The answer was Queen Salme, unfortunately already married to Salomon, the king of Jerusalem. Messengers were sent. A fierce hand-to-hand combat between the kings ensued and Fore was taken prisoner.[38] Placed in the

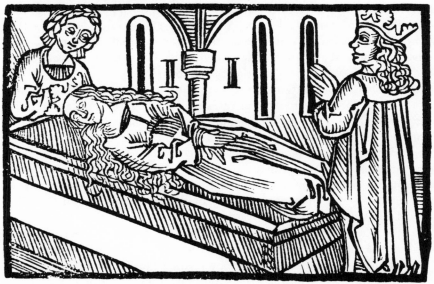

Plate 3. The death of Salme, from Hupfuff's 1499 edition of *Salomon und Morolff*. The caption reads: "Here King Solomon orders an expensive coffin to be made and lays the dead queen in it."

stocks, Fore gave Salme a magic ring. Bewitched, she fell in love with Salomon's brother Morolf, died, and was placed in a casket by her heart-broken husband. The major part of the book was devoted to Morolf's adventures after his departure from his brother's court.[39] In the end they were reunited and reconciled. Brotherly love conquered all. The illustra-tions carefully followed the narrative.

Melusine was a story of female guile. That the lady was bewitched was no excuse. Melusine had closed her father up in a high mountain because of his unkindness to her mother. As punishment she was condemned to become a serpent from the waist down every Saturday as long as she should live. Knowing this, she nevertheless married Raymond, Count of Lusignan. Much was made of the wedding in the illustrations. One woodcut showed Melusine and Raymond in a well-appointed chapel with a bishop receiving their vows. Another showed the magnificent banquet where Raymond himself served his bride. Next they were shown in their marriage bed, surrounded by the bishop and acolytes as the match was blessed. Yet all this time Melusine knew that she could never fulfill her marital duties. Thus, in a later scene, again when the two were in bed, she had to explain that she must leave Raymond every Saturday and that he must never attempt to see her. The secrecy, however, was too much. Raymond visited the little bower and saw her transformation.[40] Melusine, her secret discovered, was then forced to quit Raymond—she fled through the window to wander as a specter for the rest of earthly time. She had been deceitful and false and this was her just reward. In this instance there were copious illustrations, cap-tions for each, and a full text. The reader could choose between reading the text or looking at the pictures and the captions.

In some cases illustrations were used simply to make the book more attractive. In these instances the pictures might have little application to the text. Grüninger's 1500 edition of the *History von eines küniges tochter von Frankreich* used a stock set of woodcuts—a king and queen, knights being received in court, a banquet scene—which sometimes fit the story and sometimes did not.[41] Repeated throughout the text, the illustrations were handsome: a full page of a court ball, complete with musicians in the gal-lery; the siege of a city with a battery of cannons; and a queen traveling toward Paris in a cart drawn by two horses.[42] They were obviously de-signed for a quarto volume, but Grüninger put them side by side in a folio volume, and the ill matching of the plates was obtrusive. The reader could, however, follow some sort of story by reading the captions, although the actual text might not be related to the illustrations. Bartholomäus Grü-ninger used the same cuts later for an edition of Hug Schapler.[43] The emphasis of the chivalric tales was on the extraordinary, rather than the ordinary. They were stories of high adventure and the characters were of

O nun Melusina dise wort alle volbzacht vñ do te=
sy vor inen einen sprung vng sprang gegen einem
venster vnd schos also zů dem fenster aus vnd waß
zů stunde eins augenblicks vnder dem gurtel nid
wider ein vientglicher vngehüer grosser lannger
wurm worden·des sy sich sere alle verwunderten·
den niemant vnder in allen sy vormals also in dem
stat gesehenn noch vernomen het dann allein Rey
mond O der ellenden stund do er mit ir zů stoß kam von Goffrops wegen
als ir gehört hant Melusina schos hindannê durch den lüfft gar schnell
als sy flüg vnd vmbfür das schlos zů dem dritten mol vnd lies zů iegli=
chê mol ein grossen schrey gar zů mol erbermbklich vñ schos also durch
den lufft hin schnell das sy in kurtzem alles volcks niemät sy me gesehê
möcht·Reymond stund aldo bey den seinen vnd was in grossem vnsegli=
chem leid vnd in grosser qual·er schrey vnd weinet bitterlichen· vñ rüfft
im selbs sein löck auß vnd flüchet dick vnd vil der stnnd dar an er ye ge
bozen wart·vnd do er voz leid so vil sprechen möcht do rüffte er vñ spra
che Nun gesegne dich got mein schöner gemahel mein liebste freundin
aller selden ein kron·Gesegne dich got mein gluck vnd gesuntheit·Gese
gne dich go du mein susse meisterin·Gesegne dich got mein freude vnnd

Plate 4. Melusine's flight from the window of the palace, having become again "a
great long serpent." From the Heinrich Knoblochtzer edition, undated.

heroic order. The reader was offered the glamour of journeys to far-off places and the luxury of elaborate palaces.

One of the few popular works based on everyday life were the *Hausrat* poems, which dated from the fifteenth century, and were often included in the repertoire of the meistersingers.[44] Hampe points out that they stemmed from the medieval love of lists and from a practical desire to inform a betrothed couple of all the equipment they would need to set up housekeeping.[45] The first printed version appeared in Bamberg in 1493.[46] The genre became a part of the popular stock. They were lavishly, if crudely, illustrated. The stanzas might be set in the middle of the page and completely surrounded by woodcuts of everything from beds, to sausages, to garden equipment, to casks of wine.[47] The *Hausrat* poem published by Matthias Hupfuff in 1511 was a New Year's greeting in which the household articles were listed as gifts the poet would bring to his young wife from the Netherlands. He started with two key baskets (not too small), the symbols of her position of authority in the house,[48] and went on through all kinds of kitchen equipment: a mustard mill; fire tools; stone and steel; a mirror; a hammer and nails; a bed cover; a book stand so that her chronicles, the Bible, Brant's *Narrenschiff,* and the lives of the saints would be close at hand;[49] a harp; a lute; an organ; articles of clothing; herbs and pharmaceuticals; and a great basket of fish were each carefully named.[50] "So," concluded the poet, "with all these things I have taken care of you and provided you with your household needs."[51] The poem provides an insight into burgher attitudes toward material goods. Whatever the preachers or Sebastian Brant might say about the virtues of asceticism, the poets of the artisanal class saw nothing corrupting in the goods of this world. They loved every article, and they enjoyed the comforts these goods would provide. Their poems, in different forms, remained popular until at least the middle of the century.[52]

Gradually the printers extended themselves beyond the traditional repertoire to create new types of vernacular books, which were directed at the religious interests of the laity. Popular versions of the Bible and bible stories had long been available. The *Biblia pauperum,* for example, was one of the earliest block books, printed from wooden blocks rather than with movable type.[53] It was a picture book with very little text, depicting the fulfillment of Old Testament prophecies in the events of the New Testament. For example, the Old Testament episodes of Moses and the burning bush and Abner before King David were paired with the birth of Christ, since both incidents were prophecies of the coming of the savior.[54] The Strasbourg *Biblia pauperum,* published by Matthias Grüninger (1490) and Johann Prüss, was a type of curate's manual. The earliest popular biblical publications were stories of particular individuals: Belial, Job, Daniel, Noah.[55]

The *Somnia Daniel* provides an example of adaptation for popular biblical publication. The book was actually a secular text in the guise of a bible story. The title page had two woodcuts, the upper one showing Daniel in bed, surrounded by seven learned men; in the lower illustration, Daniel appears before two queens proclaiming "I am the prophet Daniel."[56] On the back of the title page was a highly abridged, inaccurate version of Daniel's appearance before Nebuchadnezzar. The king, according to the text, had asked Daniel to interpret his dream. Daniel replied that there were three types of dreams: dreams occurring in the first hours of sleep, when one had eaten and drunk too much, and which therefore had no meaning; dreams in the second phase of sleep, when the stomach had settled and the blood had run out to the various members of the body, which meant that these dreams could not be regarded either; and dreams in the third phase of sleep, when the blood had returned from its journeys and the body was at peace. These last dreams warranted attention.[57]

The rest of the book was a traditional dream book, listing what might be seen in a dream and its meaning. To see farmland meant work. To see someone reading a letter meant there would be good news. Someone learning from a book meant gain or profit. The number of things that might be seen were relatively large, but the interpretations were repetitive. One might have good luck or bad luck, illness or good health, happiness or trouble; the interpretations rarely exceeded these limits. Significantly, few dreams had religious meaning, and very few religious symbols were listed among those that might appear in a dream. To see a church full of people meant sorrow. To dream of going to church meant special sorrow. To pray to Christ meant joy. To see oneself bearing a cross meant slander.[58] In *Somnia Daniel,* the biblical setting was simply a vehicle for secular precepts.

Until 1500, the most common religious books for the lay reader were lives of the saints. The collection made by Otto of Passau, a Franciscan friar in Basel, with the title *Die vier und zwanzig Alten,* went through five editions between 1483 and 1500.[59] There were other accounts of individual saints, the most favored being Brendan, Ursula, and Katherine.[60] It is noteworthy that two of these latter accounts involved tales of travel to distant lands, which allowed the reader to enjoy the adventures and wonders of distant lands, along with stories of the pious life.

In 1502, Sebastian Brant edited a collection of saint's lives based on a late fifteenth-century German text.[61] Printed first by Grüninger, this was frequently reprinted, and copies of it turned up in several local will inventories.[62] Brant's collection was divided into two parts, a summer section and a winter section. It was richly illustrated with a picture on nearly every page. It included, in addition to the traditional saints, such local saints as Ita, Diebolt, Imma, Adolf, Weinrat, and Fridlin, none of whom appeared in the

Latin collection of Jacobus de Varagine. After the appearance of the Brant
edition, the Varagine collection, which had been published for the clergy,
was not reprinted. Since Hupfuff and Knobloch quickly followed Grüninger's lead with their own lives of the saints in German, the lay market
was clearly emerging as important to the printers.

In 1506, Johann Knobloch published a folio edition of the Passion of
Christ as described in the four Gospels, based on a harmonic text that he
asked Geiler von Keysersberg to provide. There was an illustration for each
page of text. Two editions, one Latin, one German, were published in the
same year.[63] The illustrations were the work of Urs Graf. Charles Schmidt
believed that, since the coat of arms of Johann Schott was included in the
illustrations, Schott may have made the original contract with Graf but was
then unable to complete the volume.[64] The immediate popularity of these
illustrated volumes is reflected in the fact that Knobloch brought out new
German editions in 1507 and 1509, and new Latin editions in 1507 and
1508;[65] Grüninger and Hupfuff then published their own versions, heavily
dependent on the Knobloch text, although Grüninger used different
illustrations.[66]

These editions were a significant departure. The biblical text was presented to the ordinary reader in a version close to the Vulgate. The accounts
from all four Gospels were included so that the reader could discover the
different details provided in each version. The biblical sources were carefully noted in the margin, with a reference in some cases to the time of year
when the verses were to be read. At the very end of the 1506 edition,
Knobloch included an admonition to the reader: The book had been printed
so that every thoughtful reader could seek out the story more frequently,
and thus experience the bitterness, the compassion, the godly sorrows,
which the Savior had suffered. It would perhaps not affect moralistic sinners
so deeply, but God's companions [Gott gesellen] would be truly moved.[67]

The account began with Jesus in the temple at Jerusalem, the resurrection
of Lazarus, and the visit to Bethany to the house of Mary and Martha, with
Martha's statement of her faith as a foreshadowing of what was to come.[68]
The next scene depicted the Jewish priests discussing means to destroy the
growing power of Jesus.[69] The scene then changed to the supper on the
road to Jerusalem, the entry into Jerusalem, Judas meeting with the priests,
and his agreement to betray Jesus.[70] Following this were the familiar scenes
of the last supper, the Mount of Olives, and the events of the Passion.[71]
When necessary the text ran to six or eight pages between illustrations to
include a full Gospel text. The synoptic character of the text carried the
narrative at a compelling rate.

The illustrations sharpened the impact of the text. Urs Graf was a powerful draftsman, and these woodcuts were conceived as a sequence. Certain

figures, besides Christ himself, were carried over from one picture to the next. Contrasts were provided in different ways. The foreground figures were much larger than those in the background; therefore, two or three events could be shown occurring at the same moment, with one event given more importance than the others. In the woodcut of Jesus ready to enter Jerusalem on the donkey, small figures in the background tore palm branches off the trees. There were differences in clothing: Jesus and the apostles, the Marys, and Salome were dressed in biblical robes; the Jews, the Roman military, and Joseph of Arimathea were in sixteenth-century clothing.

There was a dramatic opposition between the calm, unmoved, accepting, and somewhat withdrawn Jesus and the crowd, the Jews, and the Roman soldiers, shown as hostile, aggressive, menacing. In each woodcut action swirled around the central figure of a passive Jesus. In the first scene Jesus, leaving the temple at Jerusalem, was confronted by an angry group of scornful men—one ready to stone him, his lips drawn back in hatred; two others dressed as merchants, one particularly fat and gross.[72] In the later scene of Christ preaching in the temple, these same men were there, gesticulating, obviously arguing and disputing the words of Jesus.[73] In the scenes before Caiaphus and Pilate, the soldiers were shown in aggressive postures, their arms upraised and ready to strike, swords and whips brandished, and, always in the background, men with lances and banners signifying military power.[74] Graf's presentation of the event centered on the hostility of the populace, the rejection of Jesus by his people, the cruelty of the military, but Jesus himself was serene. The very last woodcut was of the resurrected Christ surrounded by all the instruments of the crucifixion: the money, the cock, the cross, the nails, the whip, the dice. Above these Christ rose, radiant in his triumph over death and pain.[75]

These versions of the Passion reveal an important element in the religious life of the laity in the opening decades of the sixteenth century. There was a special devotion to the mysteries of the death of Jesus,[76] which led to the frequent and sometimes gruesome depiction of the sorrowing Christ, his endurance of suffering in a hostile world, the physical pain of the crucifixion, and the instruments of torture and death. At the same time, a new image of Christ can be discerned. In these illustrated lives of Christ printed in Strasbourg, Christ never appears as a judge. In the Urs Graf illustrations, in particular, he is a man, his humanity made deeper by his humiliation and suffering. Furthermore, he is living in a city with other men and these latter are driven by hatred and suspicion. A strong suggestion of conspiracy emerges. Rich and prosperous citizens, the wealthy and the powerful, gather together to plot his overthrow. Thus, the divisions within an urban community are hinted at.

Plate 5. The Jewish priests (notice the label "concilium pontificum") conspiring to kill Jesus, who is shown preaching in the background. From *Der Text des Passions oder lidens christi*, Johann Knobloch, 1506.

Plate 6. Jesus after he has preached in the temple, showing the hostility of the crowd. From *Der Text des Passions oder lidens christi,* Johann Knobloch, 1506.

The success of the illustrated editions of the Passion shows the thirst for biblical knowledge. With the appearance of the accounts of the life of Christ, publication of vernacular lives of the saints decreased. Well before the Reformation, the laity themselves had begun to turn away from the more legendary accounts of saints and martyrs to find the source of their faith in the life of Jesus himself. Significantly, the editions appeared at least ten years before the first local publication of Erasmian Christian humanists. Though local humanists and theologians translated the texts, initiative for the publication of these biblical texts in German came from the printers.[77] The learned community was not eager to have the Scriptures available to the laity. As late as 1525, the humanist Noel Beda admonished Erasmus: "You are totally misled to believe, under the pretext of piety, that it is useful for the church to translate the Scriptures . . . without realizing the danger to souls and the trouble the church will suffer."[78]

Knobloch's success with the story of the Passion may have stimulated Grüninger to publish Geiler von Kaysersberg's sermons in German. Printers watched each other carefully and they were on the lookout for usable manuscripts.[79] Geiler's sermons suited the popular taste for moral and didactic tales. Grüninger presented the sermons in different forms, presumably with different groups of readers in mind. *Das Irrig Schaf* and *Hasenpfeffer* were printed with only one illustration, based on the sermon theme; in these, the emphasis was on the text. The *Evangelibuch* was based on Geiler's weekly homilies on the Gospel readings, rendered in a short, digested version by the Strasbourg Franciscan Johann Pauli. After the biblical text was summarized, the homily dealt with details of the story; such as, that Jesus had no pillow when he slept in the boat. In the story of Christ's healing of the woman with the flux, Geiler was careful to point out that the woman was not just suffering from womanly sickness. He then went on to list seven reasons why Christ healed her; including, that she was a woman and, therefore, needed more protection than a man; that she had been sick a long time; and that she had had many doctors and was not getting better.[80] The full-page illustrations in the *Evangelibuch,* however, went even further than those of the Passions in developing the theme of Christ participating in everyday life. As Jesus told the parable of the sower, a peasant was depicted on one side of the picture planting his field.[81] The miracle of the loaves and the fishes showed a town in the background. A group of men, a woman, and one child had come out into the field where Jesus was preaching. The disciples clustered around Jesus, visibly concerned about the meagerness of the two fishes and the two round loaves.[82] A full-page illustration accompanied the story of the man with the mote in his eye. A traveler who had sustained some sort of injury was being cared for by a well-dressed man. The mote in the latter's eye was the size of half the shaft of an arrow. The scene was filled with homely details: a peasant's hut surrounded by a wattle fence, a garden, the road wending its dusty way through the village. Christ stood at one side, commenting on the scene to his disciples.[83] In all of these Christ was firmly placed within the familiar milieu of daily life. There was no separation between him and his disciples, between him and the people around him.

The theme of another set of Geiler's sermons was the ant, from whom humans could learn to store up in summer what they would need for the winter. In the text, the industry of the ants, each with his own task, was compared favorably with the idleness of human beings. Both action and inaction, however, led inevitably to death. The illustration emphasized co-operative labor. The division of labor practiced by the ants could be duplicated at planting time. In the woodcut, one man ploughed, another harrowed, a third repaired drainage ditches, a fourth chased storks from the newly planted grain with great clappers. A fifth man shot the birds.[84] In a later illustration captioned "Laboris communitas," men were shown working in a vineyard, each performing a separate task, but with a common purpose. Thus, one man on a ladder trimmed the vines, another pruned the stems, a third burned the excess twigs and shoots.[85] The sermons belabored the frailty of human life, the imminence of death. The illustrations idealized work and cooperative endeavor. The work ethic was clear.

These publications reflect the religious search of ordinary citizens. They were eager to know more about the life of Christ. They were anxious to develop their own religious insights, to strengthen their inner, spiritual lives. Yet there was a schism between the laity and the clergy. There were churchmen, like Geiler, who genuinely hoped to change the moral climate. The theologians at the University of Tübingen wrestled with specific issues like the heavy burden of the tithes, usury, and witchcraft.[86] But, as Rapp shows, lay distrust of the clergy was changing to hatred.[87] In the early decades of the sixteenth century many theologians and clerics lived hermetically sealed off from their contemporaries, their eyes closed to the broader needs of the church.[88] While the lay culture still drew on traditional works conserved or created by the clergy, it was beginning to develop its own original spirit based on a practical view of the world.[89] This was articulated, as had not been possible in the past, in printed books.

One other genre of publication shows the response of the printers to this spirit: the book for self-instruction.[90] A spate of books printed between 1480 and 1520 offered basic instruction in speaking and writing, the most popular written by Heinrich Geissler of Freiburg.[91] It provided models to follow in the daily round of business. The first section was given over to rhetoric, meaning proper forms of speech: what to say before the *Landrichter* or how to make a formal presentation before the magistrates of a city. These were followed by a long section that provided the proper title and form of address for myriad individuals. The rest of the book furnished set letters to use for various purposes: a letter of quittance for debt, a letter to accompany a promissory note, a letter with regard to the title for a mill, a letter leaving one's worldly goods, another petitioning for release from imprisonment, and a letter of apology addressed to a father by a son.[92] This book appeared in various forms; sometimes the letter section was left out, or only the list of titles was given.[93] Another version, written by Stephanus Fliscus, the rector of a school in Ragusa, gave similar formularies in both German and Latin, clearly for the use of notaries or other court officials.[94] One particularly interesting text was a teach-yourself Latin grammar and vocabulary. The title page promised that the book would make it possible for any layman who so desired to learn Latin.[95] It is perhaps significant that nineteen of these self-teaching manuals were published between 1480 and 1520; after that there were only eight, most of them ABCs for children, along with a popular phrase book for businessmen.

Vernacular books did not begin to appear in print until the first decade of the sixteenth century. In the first two decades the vernacular culture was only nascent. The major vernacular writers were clerics or scholars who wrote poetry, satire, and popular religious works. The development of the vernacular audience was furthered by the printers themselves and was probably a result of the commercial pressures under which they labored. The majority of the printers came from the artisanal stratum and knew the tastes of their friends and fellow artisans—didactic books and instructional manuals, along with the traditional tales and histories to amuse. To cater to this readership, they originated new genres of popular literature, like the stories of the Passion, Geiler's sermons, illustrated books, and self-help manuals, creating thereby a new group of readers. These readers would become increasingly important during the course of the century.

CHAPTER SIX · SCIENTIFIC PUBLICATION, 1480–1520

CIENTIFIC PUBLICATION FROM 1480 TO 1520 covered the entire spectrum of contemporary interests in the world of nature. At one end were popular works, like calendars, prognostications, *Bauernpraktik,* physiognomy books, astrology manuals, and popular health manuals. At the other end were scholarly medical treatises in Latin and the standard medieval encyclopedias on such subjects as mathematics, astronomy, geography, and medicine. In between were innovative works that described new techniques and skills. At the beginning of the period science was still defined in very general terms, and scientific writers relied heavily on the traditional Arab and Roman sources. By 1520 new forces were apparent. Several scientific writers based their treatises on their own "experiments" and drew their conclusions from their personal observations, although never questioning their own methods.

The men of science in the early decades were a mixed group.[1] Two of the major scientific writers were not resident in the city. They lived up the valley, using the Strasbourg presses to publish. These were Gregorius Reisch, the prior of the Carthusian monastery in Colmar who served as supervisor for the neighboring houses, including the one in Strasbourg; and Lorenz Fries, a doctor of medicine who practiced in Colmar, and who later moved to Strasbourg. The active members of the Strasbourg medical community who wrote and published were Hans Gersdorff, an army surgeon, and Hieronymus Brunschwig, a surgeon-apothecary. Neither had attended university. In addition to this handful, there was an important group of humanists who pursued scientific work. By the middle of the fifteenth century, the Latin literary sources had been fully exploited. The aspiring humanist was forced to turn to scientific texts to demonstrate his ability as a translator.[2] Several Strasbourg humanists followed this pattern. Johann Adelphus Müling, a doctor of medicine from Tübingen, attached himself to the Strasbourg humanist group, writing and working as a proofreader and editor. He edited the first anatomical work published in the city and translated geographic treatises into German. He was informally connected with the group of geographers based in Saint-Dié at the court of Réné II, duke of Lorraine.[3] Matthias Ringmann, a poet and linguist, was an important member of the Strasbourg *sodalitas literaria.* After struggling to establish a Latin school in Strasbourg, he moved to Saint-Dié to work on a new edition of Ptolemy.[4] Hieronymus Gebwiler, rector of the cathedral school, wrote grammatical texts, edited the plays of Plautus, and annotated Lefevre d'Etaples's *Commentaries on Aristotle's Physics* for his pupils. The humanists thus played a vital role in making scientific texts available.[5] Furthermore, their love of nature led to more careful observation of natural phenomena.[6]

The men involved in scientific pursuits were, as we have already observed, divided in terms of training and interests. The medical community, in particular, had long had its own social hierarchy. The most prestigious were doctors of medicine holding university degrees. By established custom they never used their hands when treating a patient. They were learned men who knew Galen, Hippocrates, and the Arab physicians. Their function was to observe, diagnose, and prescribe. Any manual work was performed by an assistant.

The surgeons, represented in Strasbourg by the military surgeon Hans Gersdorff and the surgeon-apothecary Hieronymus Brunschwig, ranked substantially below the doctors of medicine. Originally the surgeon was not highly trained. He was a barber who took care of open wounds in addition to his other functions. Gradually, responding to the needs of the military, surgeons began to handle fractures, gunshot wounds, head wounds, and other traumas. Working directly with their patients, they developed a corpus of practical knowledge, which they supplemented with close reading of the Arab and Greek physicians. By 1500 they were well educated and well trained, and many of them practiced general medicine as well as surgery. The separation between them and the university doctors remained, however, because the surgeons used their hands and thus continued to be regarded as menials. Several of the highly skilled surgeons practicing in Strasbourg called themselves *wundartze* to distinguish themselves from the traditional *scherer* or barber surgeons. Rivalry between these two groups was keen, and there was intense competition among them for positions in the city as welfare and health officers.[7] The wundartze and the university doctors remained separated, although during the course of the sixteenth century the surgeon's work would come to be more highly regarded.[8]

Dentists, occultists, and *blatterartze,* who took care of syphilis, were another group of specialists within the general fields of medicine or surgery. Bathhouse attendants (who took care of skin problems), midwives, nurses, and *kreutler* or *würzler,* who collected herbs and roots for the apothecaries, occupied the lowest ranks of the health care hierarchy.[9]

The monastic orders were perhaps second in importance in training men of science and encouraging scientific interests. Gregorius Reisch, the prior of the Carthusian monastery in Freiburg, wrote an important encyclopedia; Otto Brunfels, the major scientist in the later period 1530–1540, was originally a member of the Strasbourg Carthusians, raising the question whether the order had particular interests in scientific inquiry. Thomas Murner, a member of the Franciscan community, wrote treatises on astronomy and polemic against astrology.[10]

Unlike the theologians or the literary humanists, however, these men who were interested in scientific inquiry were not brought together by an institution, nor did they form close bonds of friendship. There was no scientific community; rather, there were independent individuals engaged in scientific work. This alone made printing far more important in the scientific field than in literary studies. The scientists themselves were conscious of the value of publication. Several of the general surgical and apothecary manuals state that they were written for the use of ordinary practitioners or blatterartze.[11] Printed works bridged the social divisions. Texts edited by the scholar-humanists became available to the practicing physician or apothecary. Furthermore, new work, like that of Gersdorff, could then provide a point of departure for others. Scientific knowledge began to become cumulative.[12] The printing press made this possible.

The accepted scientific concepts of the turn of the century are conveniently summarized in Gregorius Reisch's *Margarita philosophica,* a conventional late medieval encyclopedia of scientific information. It was widely used as a university text and probably served as the introduction to natural philosophy for most of the scientists in our study, until 1530. The treatise began with a two-page diagram outlining the branches of knowledge.[13] Philosophy was divided into two parts: theory and practice. Theory included, in order, theology, humane letters, mathematics, and physics. Thus the sciences were regarded as third in order of importance. They provided knowledge of the physical world as God made it, the astral movements, the material components of the universe, and the essence of animal and human life. Practice involved activities like ethics, politics, mechanical works, agriculture, and medicine.

From this broad definition, encompassing all knowledge, Reisch turned to arithmetic and a review of the basic skills of addition, subtraction, multiplication, and division. The most complex techniques covered were the rules of geometric proportion and harmonic numbers. His demonstrations of addition and subtraction incorporated the technique of reckoning "on the line." The problem was given in arabic numbers, and the active elements of the problem were separated from the solution by a line; for example:

4679	number which should be added to
3232	number to be added
——	interjected line
7911	product.

For multiplication and division, however, Reisch reverted to the traditional style, writing the problem out:

> Say that you have to divide a number into its essential parts, and say that you take 8 and also 3, or 11 and 4; then you must see whether the minor part can be contained in the major part.[14]

A full discussion of solid as well as plane geometry was accompanied by careful diagrams of every procedure. Euclid's assumptions and definitions were replaced by a dialogue between student and teacher, a style Reisch adopted for the whole book. The student could be depended upon to ask the convenient question—"What is a right angle?"—to which the teacher could then reply, "It is an angle resulting from a straight line crossing a perpendicular line."[15]

The section on astronomy included astronomical charts of the location of major stars and constellations at different times of the year and the position of the planets in relation to the earth and the sun, followed by a short treatment of lunar eclipses. The student raised the question of the shape of the earth—was it round? This was very possible, according to the teacher, since by the laws of physics, all round things were apt to be round. Furthermore, mathematical law established that all unified bodies were round, and, finally, the action of the polar motion would lead one to conclude the earth was round. Since the book was probably finished by 1493, it provides further evidence of the general acceptance of the spherical shape of the earth, an essential element of Ptolemaic astronomy and Aristotelian cosmology.[16]

In the same chapter Reisch strongly criticized the astrologers. Citing Augustine, Reisch asserted that the heavenly bodies had less effect on men and events than philosophy or theology. No matter what the astrologers might claim, God controlled the world, and his actions could be understood by reason and the Bible. Thus, if one wanted to probe the possibility of war, revolution, famine, or sedition, it was wiser to consult philosophers and other learned men than astrologers.[17]

Human physiology was Reisch's weakest field. His description of human conception showed that he was still dependent on a rather garbled version of Aristotle's *De generatione animalium*. The fetus, Reisch said, was formed in a fixed order: first the heart, then the liver and the brain, followed by the umbilical cord, the stomach and the testicles, and finally the hands and feet. The whole process required a minimum of thirty-five days for a male child, although seventy days were required to perfect all the vital elements. Reisch claimed that the cause of death in premature infants was the incomplete development of their living processes at the time of birth.[18]

At the end of the treatise Reisch reviewed various theories with regard to the nature of the primary material of the universe.[19] A woodcut at the beginning of this chapter showed Adam lying comfortably under a tree while God drew Eve from his rib. The newly-formed human couple were surrounded by a variety of horned beasts, fish, birds, and snakes. Whatever the learned theories, the widely accepted version of the creation remained biblical.

Reisch's encyclopedia reflects the assumptions of late medieval natural philosophy. God had created the universe. It was entirely his, and he was still active within it. At the same time the natural world was made for man to use. All matter had a reason for existence as part of God's great plan. Plants were there to provide food for men or animals or to be used as healing herbs. This Galenic view made it difficult for a sixteenth-century botanist to look at a plant as an independent element, living within its own system in relation to other plants. To move away from this teleologic view was an essential step in the transition to modern scientific thought. The acceptance of God as both the primary and the final cause, so evident in Reisch, made it difficult to recognize that man, himself, could control certain forces of nature.[20] Reisch represented the state of scientific learning and its limitations at the turn of the sixteenth century.

The herbal was another type of traditional work, which began to be printed not only for use by the scientific community but to provide information on the curative powers of plants for the laity.[21] Ten editions of these compilations appeared between 1500 and 1520.[22] Like Reisch's encyclopedia, these books reveal the knowledge of the natural world at the beginning of the sixteenth century, in particular the extent to which men remained dependent on the ancients. Their information about plants, minerals, and animals came from the Greek texts of Dioscorides and Aristotle, as translated by the Arabs, or from Pliny. As a result, they considered only the plants or animals included in these sources to be genuine or real. A northern European species of a plant was simply regarded as an aberrant phenomenon. Galen remained the strongest influence.

In the *Ortus sanitatis,* the description of each animal, bird, flower, insect, or mineral terminated in a description of its *wirckung,* its use or effect.[23] These could range from the obvious—the wool, lanolin, meat, and cheese supplied by sheep—to the semi-magical properties ascribed to stones. A diamond made a man strong against his enemies and gave him good dreams. Lapis lazuli could make a man's eyebrows fall out; hung around the neck of a child, it would protect him from fear.[24] The uses ascribed to minerals and metals, on the other hand, were straightforward, reflecting the empirical knowledge gained from mining activity. Properties of the major metals were described, and directions given for refining. The differences between substances like coal and anthracite were made clear.[25]

The illustrations in the *Ortus* were stylized; realistic portrayal of nature was still nascent. In some cases this was because the artist had never seen the animal in question. Pliny, for instance, described an animal brought by the Roman army returning victorious from the East. He called it a *cephes* and said it had feet and legs like a human, paws closely resembling the human hand, and a body like a donkey. Exerting a bit of imagination, the modern

Plate 7. Pliny's *Cephes,* which he described as having "legs and feet like a human, paws like human hands, and a body like a donkey." The artist followed Pliny's description exactly. From the *Gart der Gesuntheit,* Balthasar Beck, 1528.

reader can recognize in this a generalized description of a chimpanzee. The sixteenth-century artist who prepared the woodcuts, however, could only follow the text literally and delineated an upright body of a donkey with the head, hands, and feet of a human.[26] Fish presented another challenge, since the artist was familiar only with river or lake fish. The dog fish was therefore provided with four legs, paws, and a dog's head, while the body was neatly fitted out with fins.[27] The illustrations for birds and insects that the artist himself could have observed were recognizable. The plants, in these early editions, were never more than generalized designs, and the same woodcut was often used for different genera or species. The *Ortus sanitatis* provided a view of the world that mixed the real and the fabulous, ancient truths and timid contemporary descriptions.

Certain standard medical texts continued to be popular throughout the first two decades of the century. There were eight editions, compiled by different editors and published under various titles, of the *Regimen of Salerno,* a set of thirteenth-century common sense rules of personal hygiene that was regarded as authoritative because it had originated in Salerno, an early medieval medical center.[28] The *Margarita medicinae* was another example of the unchanging nature of the medical corpus in these early decades. Compiled by Johann Tollat at the University of Vienna, it was based on the work of his professor, Doctor Michael Schrick, who had died in 1472. The short treatise was crammed with references to the ancient physicians; in particular, Pythagoras, Dioscorides, and Galen. Despite its title, it was a pharmaceutical handbook rather than a medical text, providing remedies for everything from colds to snakebite; in fact, it recommended the same herb, the gold lily, for both conditions, as well as for kidney problems.[29] Preparations were supplied for all types of stomach complaints, for bringing on menstrual periods, for infertility, and to encourage lactation.[30] Another handbook, much in the style of Tollat's, furnished answers from Aristotle, Avicenna, Galen, and Albertus Magnus to common medical questions, all squeezed into twenty-four pages.[31]

Whatever their divisions among themselves, the doctors and surgeons of the period saw their role in society clearly. Their responsibility was to make the knowledge they had accumulated available to their fellow men, and the printing presses were a means of achieving this goal. Almost every medical book, text, or treatise was dedicated to the needs of the common man. Tollat, for example, stated that poverty or distance from the city might make it impossible to seek a doctor. His book would provide remedies for ordinary health problems.[32] The doctors wanted every man to be able to maintain himself and his family in good health, to achieve the seventy years of life which God had fixed as his normal life span. The overwhelming majority of medical and botanical treatises in this period were, therefore, written and published in German.

Plate 8. The dogfish and the owl from Beck's *Gart der Gesuntheit,* 1528. The artist had to depend on a written description of the fish, "a sea animal which has little feet and a big body and his feet are like those of a cow. . . . He is the dog of the sea, the most frightening of all animals." The artist had seen an owl.

These traditional medical texts were only a small proportion of the total medical publication of the period. Medical knowledge was advancing rapidly. There were concerted efforts to develop and perfect new techniques for preparing medicines and new treatments for diseases and injuries.[33] Important anatomical investigations were undertaken by university-trained physicians, dissections were carried out on human corpses, and a series of anatomical charts were published by Strasbourg printers. Doctors began to address themselves to limited and specific medical problems; their work resulted, in these decades, in surgical manuals, a gynecological text, several treatises on plague, and some of the first studies of syphilis.

The development of new medical knowledge in the city of Strasbourg was initiated by the surgeons. The university-trained, Latin-speaking doctors were more remote from the needs of the community. The practical *wundartz* carried the larger responsibility in terms of daily health care[34] and developed new methods and techniques. It was through their work that knowledge gleaned from active practice was given the same weight as the ancient sources. Hieronymus Brunschwig was a botanist and apothecary as well as a surgeon. Born in Strasbourg, he worked there all his life and was regarded as a sound man who followed the Arab physicians.[35] He published a traditional surgical manual, *Buch der Chirurgia, Hantwirkung und Wundartzney,* in 1497, followed by a treatise on the plague in 1500.[36] The *Chirurgia* drew heavily on Arab and classical texts, but practical instructions for the treatment of wounds, based on Brunschwig's own experience and that of other surgeons, were included.

Brunschwig's most important contribution was to lay the groundwork from which chemical medicine could develop. The process of distillation was already well known. Alcohol had long been used for medicinal purposes, and, since it heated the body, it was widely adopted as a remedy for the plague, and its use had spread during the fifteenth century.[37] Brunschwig brought together existing knowledge of distillation and applied it to the distillation of herbs and plants for medicinal purposes. The text was enhanced by woodcuts which clearly depicted the necessary equipment and the various processes. The illustrations made it possible for any apothecary or winemaker to make alcohol or other distilled waters. Thus it was an important contribution to technical knowledge, recognized in the publication of fifteen editions in Strasbourg alone.[38] It may have contributed to the increased use of alcoholic beverages which characterized the sixteenth century.[39]

Until Brunschwig, the accepted pharmaceutical practice was to use the leaf or root of a plant in its original form. Three or four herbs were crushed, lacerated, or macerated and mixed with liquid to produce remedies that could be taken internally. Plasters or compresses were made by the same procedure, the mixtures bound by oil or unguent. Roots were ground up in similar fashion and then mixed with the necessary liquid. Brunschwig realized that these methods were inefficient as a means of employing the curative elements of a plant; furthermore, it was difficult to prescribe exact dosages. His chemical techniques made it possible to distill the essence of a plant from either leaf, flower, or root. The strength of these liquids could be measured, and accurate doses prepared and repeated. The first section of his book described techniques for extracting five elements contained in every plant.[40] The rest was devoted to various distilling procedures. One illustration showed a warm water bath with six crucibles floating in it, each draining off into a separate flask. Others showed how to construct a proper oven, or a flat stove capable of heating thirteen crucibles at the same time.[41] His careful description of the technique he had developed allowed chemical preparation of herbal remedies to spread rapidly throughout Europe.[42]

Hans von Gersdorff's *Feldtbuch der Wundartzney* (1517) was another innovative work.[43] Gersdorff, a citizen of Strasbourg, served as an army surgeon in the field in Alsace, Lorraine, and Switzerland. Gersdorff compiled the *Feldtbuch* on the basis of what he had seen in his own time, in his own practice. He had evaluated these procedures, which had won the approval of many doctors of medicine, and friends had requested that he describe his surgical "experiments." Instead of leaving these secrets of his art to his sons, he had decided instead to share his discoveries with other barbers and surgeons for the common good.[44]

The book began with two full-page human anatomies, one of the skeletal frame, the other of the organs.[45] These were from the Schott anatomical charts of 1517, which were based on the dissections of doctor Wendelin Hock and drawn by Hans Wächtlin.[46] Although the organs were properly placed in terms of their position in the body cavity, and while each organ is identifiable, the details of skeletal and arterial anatomy, which would distinguish the work of Vesalius, were missing. The most detailed presentation in the organ chart was that of the head. Six different views were given, all from the superior position, proceeding by successive steps from a view of the entire brain to a view of the empty cranium. The skeletal chart itself was accompanied by German verses, which introduced a religious note. If you found this skeleton terrible and frightening, said the verse, so it was: it should stand as a warning to all that they must honor God, so their souls might achieve everlasting life and leave their bodies to their particular destiny.[47] The contrast between these verses and those under the organ plan was striking. The latter chart was described as a useful mirror of the skillful arts of the doctor. The organs were exposed so that men could understand the function of each and their interrelationships, since none could work independently of the others. The skeleton, even in a medical text, was the symbol of death to the men of the sixteenth century; the organs could be viewed objectively.

The first book of the treatise was devoted to the anatomy of the human body. Each part was described separately, beginning with the skin, the muscles, and the ligaments—in other words, following the procedures involved in a dissection. In the second book Gersdorff proceeded to forms of treatment. The section was preceded by a stock wound chart, the figure of a man suffering from every abuse available to the hands of his enemies. While the reaction of the modern viewer is at first repugnance or amusement, closer examination reveals that it provided a relatively precise indication of the kinds of wounds a surgeon of the period would face. The head would suffer club wounds and dagger or sword cuts; arrows would tend to hit the upper or lower torso; swords would be directed at the heart and chest cavity; cannon balls would tend to shatter the extremities, particularly the wrist or the lower leg.[48]

Careful illustrations in this section of the text demonstrated a series of surgical procedures. A screw device was shown for trepanning the skull.[49] Cauterization of wounds was shown with the necessary instruments and an open charcoal fire for heating them.[50] The illustrations of correcting a twisted or crooked arm indicate that Gersdorff had obviously availed himself of the services of an armorer during his military career. A device fashioned like a piece of armor was fitted with a screw between the upper and lower arm, which would be thus extended or flexed. Another for the lower leg bore the caption "with this leg-vestment a crooked leg is immediately straightened." There was a traction apparatus—a large wooden screw on which a patient's leg could be stretched if muscles or ligaments had tightened.[51] Gersdorff used the armorer's skills to develop appliances that functioned as orthopedic braces. His use of traction reflected an understanding of the function and flexibility of the musculo-skeletal system.

The tone of Gersdorff's text was very different from that of earlier medical works, like Tollat's. Gersdorff did not continually refer to Greek, Roman, or Arab sources. He listed his own sources—Hippocrates, whom he believed had never erred in anything with regard to medicine, Galen, Avicenna, Nichomachus, Rhazes, Johannes, Averoes, Rabbi, and the saints Cosman and Damian[52]—but there was a self-assurance evident on the very first page of the book. He was working from his own knowledge and his own experience and did not feel he had to support his observations with references to the ancients. It was a move toward intellectual independence.

As an army surgeon, Gersdorff had had long experience with gunshot wounds. Until his book appeared there was a general belief that gunshot wounds were poisonous and must be closed off to prevent spreading of the poison. Gersdorff recognized that the powder was not poisonous but acted

Plate 9. Device for straightening a stiff elbow, from Hans
Gersdorff's *Feldtbuch der Wundartzney,* Johannes Schott, 1517. The
caption reads: "I make a stiff arm straight and give it its natural
alignment. If the arm remains rigid, with art I teach it to go
forward."

as an irritant and therefore should be removed.[53] The patient, he directed, should be placed on his back. The surgeon should then dilate the wound very carefully with a surgical chisel, great care being taken to prevent any further damage to the tissue. *Sanguinoletis,* putting a finger into the wound and compressing the gaping blood vessels, as recommended by Galen, should be used to stop the bleeding.[54] After the wound had been washed with warm water (note the absence of boiling oil), a bandage of cotton soaked in oil should be applied. Ambroise Paré's substitution of an unguent of egg yolk, oil of roses, and turpentine for the boiling oil he could not procure for treating wounds is usually looked on as a landmark in medical treatment.[55] Yet, Paré's use of unguent occurred in 1536, almost twenty years after the publication of Gersdorff's book, and clearly Gersdorff had used the techniques he described for many years. Establishing priority of invention is not a particularly useful historical activity; what is important is Gersdorff's independence, his professional confidence, his belief that treatment should be based on observation and experiment.

Gersdorff's work demonstrated growing familiarity with the functioning of the human body, based on increased knowledge of human anatomy. In this instance the evolutionary development can be clearly traced. Johann Schott's 1503 edition of Reisch's *Margarita philosophica* included a chart of the human organs done by an artist who had observed a dissection but was still hesitant to make precise and fully accurate drawings.[56] In the Grüninger edition of Reisch the following year, the organ chart was more exact; it had to have been done after an autopsy. The wings of the lungs were properly divided, the right lung showed the three lobes, and both the kidney and the urethra were accurately drawn. Wieger believed that since the drawing of the liver was not very detailed, the autopsy was probably performed by a barber-surgeon without a doctor of medicine in the chair to supervise. Organ charts were thus incorporated into medical texts by 1503 and 1504. In 1513 Martin Flach II published an organ chart and part of the anatomical text of Mondino dei Luzzi. The chart was crudely done. The lungs were represented as three-pronged. Directly below them was the stomach, which led into an extremely attenuated set of intestines, which ended in a balloon-shaped bladder.[57]

In 1517 Wendelin Hock performed a public dissection of a human corpse in Strasbourg.[58] It was during this event that Hans Wächtlin prepared the innovative skeletal and organ charts that appeared in Gersdorff's *Feldtbuch*.[59] Johann Schott, who printed the book in that same year, also published both the skeletal figure and a chart of the organs as separate broadsheets. The two charts were incorporated into many medical books at the time.[60] The role of the printer should not be minimized. Johann Schott not only made Gersdorff's work available to a professional audience, he transmitted the revelations of Hock's dissection directly to ordinary laymen. Publication of the charts is one more indication that a cadaver was no longer regarded as abominable; the human body was given new value.[61]

Lorenz Fries's *Spiegel der Artzney,* published first by Matthias Grüninger in 1518, the year after Schott published the *Feldtbuch,* exemplifies the difference in approach of the university-trained doctors of medicine. Where Gersdorff began with anatomy, Fries began with a broad philosophic description of man, based on the four humors and the members: the head, the heart, the spleen, the soul.[62] Most of the book consisted of remedies for common diseases and recipes for pharmaceuticals and simples. The chapter on gynecology, however, when compared to the Reisch explanation, reveals the variation in knowledge of the period. Fries drew from Avicenna. He described the human seed at the beginning as no more than a foam, which nevertheless bore within it the materials essential to the human form. In the middle of the foam a vesicle, a tiny bubble, would develop, which was the beginning of the heart. Another blister would become the liver, a third formed the navel. Natural forces then created a little cave in which the fetus could grow and develop without harm, like the crust around a piece of bread. Within this cover were small holes or arteries through which the blood of the mother was drawn to nourish the fetus. Within two days of conception the rest of the body began to take shape; within five days blood flowed through the whole fetus; and within nine days the blood became flesh. In the next nine days the head accomplished its separation from the shoulders, and within thirty days the whole human form was completed in all its members and characteristics.[63] Fries's description reflects some observation of animal fetuses and a more assured knowledge of the role of the sperm and the ovum. At no point in his book, however, did he refer to his own observations or to knowledge gained from practice. His learning came from books.

The two great epidemic diseases of the fifteenth and sixteenth centuries, plague and syphilis, encouraged the physicians to break away from their dependence on the Greek and Roman sources and to develop their own diagnoses from observation.[64] Faced by recurring outbreaks of plague, the medical community attempted to isolate the circumstances in which it developed, determine its cause, and provide information for citizens threatened by the devastating disease. Six manuals on the plague appeared in these decades, an earlier one having been published in 1491.[65] The doctors could not determine the origin of the disease nor identify the way it spread. They were convinced there was contagion in the air. Philip Beroaldus, the poet and humanist, linked the incidence of plague to earthquakes, which destroyed the proper balance of nature. Once the equilibrium between hot and cold, dryness and wetness was disturbed, forces which stimulated the immoderate, intemperate qualities in men were released.[66] Johann Widmann, a Strasbourg physician,[67] provided more practical advice. It was essential to avoid contaminated air or any place where people had died of plague.[68] When plague broke out, individuals should move to a place where there had been no plague deaths in the last three months. Once contaminated by the disease, an area would remain unsafe for half a year. An essential precaution was to keep one's house light, airy, and well-ventilated. Fresh herbs, like rosemary, sage, and onions, should be burned throughout the house and others, like roses, violets, and marjoram, should be kept in the rooms.[69] Widmann advised individuals to observe moderation in all things, especially in diet and sleep. A little piece of coriander carried in the mouth or precious stones, such as sapphire, garnet, or ruby, also provided protection to the wearer. Energetic exercise or activity, indeed any tension, excitement, anger, or fear, should be avoided.[70]

Widmann recommended the same regime both for those hoping to avoid the disease and those who contracted it. If all precautions failed and one was stricken, the body was to be cleansed and purified by the usual, drastic courses of laxatives and purges for at least a week. All moist elements in the body—gall, mucous, or melancholy—should be eliminated by using special plague pills. The patient should never be bled.[71] There was strong division among doctors over the practice of bleeding for the plague—Guinther von Andernach would later advise against it. Remedies for the plague varied little from those recommended for a broad spectrum of other diseases. Sixteenth-century medicine was helpless before the menace.

Syphilis, however, lay more within their control. Its first appearance in the Rhine Valley, shortly before 1495, had an even more profound impact on the mentality of the period than plague. Reports of cases of syphilis by town authorities and physicians reflect terror and helplessness.[72] The disease was introduced by *Landsknechts* returning from the Italian wars, where they had had contact with Spanish troops.[73] By 1495 the ammeister of Strasbourg had mentioned "the bad pox" in a mandate, and treatises describing the new disease began to be published in the city.[74] Geiler saw the disease as a punishment for the lusts of the flesh and preached against the "sins of the mouth" which led to catching the pox. In medical circles, the venereal element in transmission was early recognized. Johann Widmann, in one of the best early treatises on the disease,[75] wrote that it was essential to avoid any contact with a woman who had pustules; indeed, one must not touch a woman who had had contact with a man infected with pustules.[76] Hieronymus Brunschwig correctly described the symptoms and characteristics of the disease in a German tract published in 1500.[77] There were two favored cures. Wendelin Hock, who performed the first public dissection in Strasbourg, prescribed mercury.[78] Ulrich von Hutten, suffering from the disease himself, recommended the curative powers of the American wood guaiacum, which was taken as an infusion.[79] The authorities moved quickly to isolate those suffering from the disease. In 1500 the Rat forbade surgeons, barbers, and bath attendants to take care of persons with syphilis. By 1520 the city had established a separate hospital for these patients. The nature of the infection and the need for quarantine were recognized, and measures to protect the public were inaugurated.[80] Castiglione sees this rapid control of syphilis as an indication of the success of the new medicine based on observation rather than theory.[81]

A gynecological handbook written by Eucharius Roesslin serves as an example of the popular diffusion of medical knowledge. Roesslin was the city physician at Frankfurt am Main and attended the Countess Katherine von Braunschweig, who encouraged him to publish his obstetrical treatise. *Der Schwangeren Frauen Rosengarten* became the first manual for the instruction of midwives. Roesslin followed a careful outline. The appearance and condition of normal pregnancy were described, the process of delivery explained step by step, with considerable attention given to complications. Diagrams provided clear examples of possible difficulties—breech birth, twins, even Siamese twins.[82] In fact, these varied little from the standard problem births depicted by Soranus, and the text itself was a compilation of standard Greek and Roman sources. Its importance lay in the diagrams and the use of vernacular language, which made the material available to lay persons.[83] Printed first in Strasbourg, it went through one hundred editions in the sixteenth century.[84]

Medical, botanical, and distilling treatises comprised the bulk of scientific publication in the first decades of the sixteenth century. Astronomy and mathematics, which would later become important, were minimally represented.[85] Geography, however, enjoyed a burst of popularity. The voyages to the New World had an immediate and obvious impact, and the publishers were quick to exploit this. Seventeen geographic works were published in the twenty years between 1500 and 1520, whereas, in the seventy years that followed (1520–1599), only eleven geographical works appeared.[86] Amerigo Vespucci's description of his third voyage, in 1501 and 1502, was published in Strasbourg by 1505; it was printed with a German translation the next year. In 1509 there was a longer, illustrated account of the four Vespucci voyages, Vespucci having returned to Spain in 1505. King Manuel's report to the Pope on India and the conquest of Malacca of 1511 was published in both Latin and German versions.[87] These were topical items and thus apt to attract the attention of the book buyer; the speed of the printers meant that the voyages were known in northern Europe in some cases within two years of the explorer's return.

The Strasbourg and Alsatian humanists made a major contribution to cosmography and geography. Matthias Ringmann, Johann Adelphus Müling, and Martin Waldseemüller were involved in the translations of the voyages of discovery and, more important, in amending Ptolemy in terms of the new information. Ptolemy was the definitive source of geographical knowledge. His maps, lost during the Middle Ages, had been painfully reconstructed from his directions in the fifteenth century.[88] The discoveries controverted Ptolemy's cosmology, but the humanist geographers did not face the conflict. They simply extended Ptolemy's map, adding on the new continents from Vespucci's drawings. Under the patronage of Duke René II of Lorraine, these men worked at Saint-Dié on a new edition of Ptolemy and on maps. In 1507 Waldseemüller published in Strasbourg a revised map of the world in which the "islands" of the New World were joined for the first time into a single land mass.[89]

The Waldseemüller-Ringmann edition of Ptolemy, published by Johann Schott in 1513, became one of the standard sixteenth-century versions. The two men prepared twenty new maps, based on the modern discoveries, to accompany their carefully edited text.[90] The map of the upper Rhineland in this edition is regarded as the first published map based on systematic field observation. Close examination by modern cartographers has revealed that the latitudes of the chief cities were correct to within 18' and their angles of position were also accurate within a few minutes of the arc. This degree of precision could only have been achieved by field survey.[91] Waldseemüller and Ringmann were capable of carrying out accurate measurement in the field, probably using a *polimetron,* a type of surveying instrument, together with the pocket compass, or dial.[92] They had acquired new technical skills and new empirical evidence, but they never questioned the authority of Ptolemy.

The new Ptolemy immediately led to others. Schott reprinted the 1513 edition in a shortened version in 1520; Georg Ubelin, a Strasbourg lawyer, served as the major editor.[93] In 1522 Grüninger, using badly executed copies of Schott's woodblocks, brought out another edition with the help of Lorenz Fries, the doctor, and Thomas Vogler.[94] Grüninger's version was a retrogression in that the old medieval figures—monsters, castles, and cannibals with heads of dogs—were added to the maps.[95]

The geographers and the printers quickly incorporated the new techniques of map making. In 1511 Waldseemüller prepared and published an itinerary map of Europe to be used with a traveler's pocket dial.[96] Those dials, developed in the fifteenth century by Nuremberg craftsmen, made it possible for a traveler to determine north. In 1492 Erhard Etzlaub, a Nuremberg cartographer, issued a map that included a printed facsimile of a compass dial, enabling the traveler to place his own instrument on the map and determine his own route with assurance and accuracy. Waldseemüller's

European itinerary was the second published map to incorporate the dial; thus it combined scientific cartographical information with the most advanced technology of the day.[97] Later, in 1527, Johann Grüninger published a large, world map, prepared by Waldseemüller, which incorporated the discoveries made by the Portuguese and the major shipping routes to Africa, India, and the Far East. Woodcuts depicted some of the major cities and the inhabitants of the different continents. New features of the map were crosshatching and the indication of degrees of latitude and longitude in the margins. Place names were indexed and the coordinates given for each city.[98] In this rare instance, we have some information about the arrangement for publication. Grüninger was ready to print the map as early as 1519, but hoped to receive financial assistance from Anton Koberger of Nuremberg.[99] When this failed to materialize, Grüninger went ahead on his own after eight years of delay. The edition was reprinted within three years. There was also sufficient demand for Grüninger to publish a map and itinerary of Europe in 1527.[100]

Natural philosophy in this period remained descriptive. The doctors, botanists, and geographers were observers, anxious to convey their knowledge about the natural world to their fellow citizens. There was a new delight in nature, stemming in part from the humanists and their interpretation of the Latin poets. At the same time there was greater curiosity about man, reflected in the anatomical works, and about the globe on which he lived. Particular conditions—the battlefield, gunpowder, urban communities threatened by plague and syphilis—stimulated a search for new solutions, but the traditional Greek, Roman, and Arab sources remained unquestioned.

In the decades from 1480 to 1520, the church was the dominant intellectual institution. Most members of the intellectual community were clergymen, and the bulk of publication was for the use of the church. These books did little to close the gap between the clergy and the ordinary men and women who made up their congregations. Volumes of fourteenth- and fifteenth-century sermons were put into the hands of priests and curates. Sermon after sermon called for penitence, the individual's recognition of his need to acknowledge his faults and approach the altar only after complete contrition. Confessional manuals laid down rigorous standards for examination of the conscience. These elements helped to create the heavy psychological and social burdens of late medieval religion, which the laity found onerous.[101] Only the sermons of Geiler von Kaysersberg dealt with the problems of everyday life.

The burghers had their own social and moral standards, based on order, the virtue of hard work, the value of knowledge and education, and a respectable, settled family life.[102] They found meaning in the Gospel accounts of the Passion of Christ,[103] in Geiler's sermons, and in popular tracts which dealt with virtuous moral behavior and the problems of coping with death.[104] Legislation passed by the Strasbourg Magistrat provides further evidence of a consistent desire to create an ordered environment. They wanted to establish moral order in the city, to abolish concubinage and harlotry, and to protect the sanctity of married life.[105] They wanted religious order, seemly conduct at church services, and an end to blasphemy and the swearing of oaths.[106] They wanted public order, and an end to personal feuds and brawling.[107]

The importance of work to the burgher ethic and the burgher desire for learning were reflected in the scientific manuals and autodidactic books. Gersdorff and Brunschwig, in their treatises on surgery and distilling, described the techniques they had discovered, so that others might avail themselves of this knowledge. Notarial manuals, books on how to read and write could help any citizen to acquire basic skills of literacy. These books, in turn, were supplemented by the illustrated books, which stimulated the beginning reader. Sebastian Brant in his *Narrenschiff* might rail against those fools who attempted to measure the earth instead of attending to the salvation of their souls, but this did not prevent Matthias Ringmann and Martin Waldseemüller from developing better techniques of surveying and incorporating them into maps, which were then made available to businessmen and other travelers.[108] Accounts of the voyages of Columbus, Vespucci, and the Portuguese were quickly translated into German; men knew about the expansion of European trade to the East and the discovery of the New World.[109]

The two cultures were already discernible, Latin and vernacular. The theologians, scholars, and humanists who shaped the Latin culture continued to fulfill their function as curators of that vast body of knowledge which had accumulated since ancient times. The humanists approached the writings of antiquity with new understanding and with better philological tools. With their popular satires, on one hand, and their translations of Roman scientific works, on the other, they also made an important contribution to the vernacular culture. Many of the vernacular writers of the period were technicians. Their approach to knowledge was empirical, and their work was based on their own pragmatic experience. They were therefore less dominated by the ancient authorities. The Latin culture was based on the very deepest elements of traditional Graeco-Roman-Christian values. The vernacular culture drew far less from antiquity. It was Christian in its religious and moral ideas, empirical in its approach to the material world. These differences would become more distinct in later decades.

PART III
FORCES FOR CHANGE
1515–1549

THE POLITICAL AND RELIGIOUS SETTING

Between 1520 and 1549 Strasbourg experienced a series of religious, social, and political changes which brought it to the brink of revolution and ended in war and bitter defeat. Three groups were involved in these changes: the Protestant clergy, the Magistrat, and the populace. The goals of the three differed, but each was subject to or influenced by the others. The changes occurred in uneven, lurching steps, usually when two groups were able to ally themselves briefly.

The movement for religious reform began in 1522 when Tilman von Lyn, reader at the Carmelite house, began to preach the Word of God according to Luther. Quickly dismissed, von Lyn was followed by others. In 1521 Matthias Zell, the people's priest in the chapel of Saint Lorenz in the cathedral, defended Luther from his pulpit and announced that he would preach the pure Gospel, starting with the Epistle to the Romans. This announcement set off a protracted struggle between the bishop and the cathedral canons. The former insisted that Zell be dismissed. The latter regarded this as an interference with their privileges to appoint and supervise their parish clergy. In the course of the struggle the humanist Wolfgang Capito, recently appointed provost of the chapter of Saint Thomas, joined Zell, and several parish priests began to preach in an evangelical way. In 1523 Martin Bucer returned to his native city after being dismissed from several pastorates for his reforming sermons. Bucer, Capito, and Zell, joined by Capito's protégé Caspar Hedio, became the leaders of the new movement, creating a theology that was neither Lutheran nor Zwinglian, but unique to Strasbourg.[1]

Luther's doctrine of justification by faith was softened. God, they taught, did not conceal his gift of faith. If a man believed, he knew he was elect. The power of the Word of God was given greater efficacy. Through the Word all men could be opened to God and to his grace.[2] The Strasbourg reformers, led by Capito, rejected Luther's doctrine of consubstantiation, accepting a more spiritual interpretation. Denying the real presence, they taught that the Supper was a memorial, in which the individual shared with Christ and was renewed in faith and love.[3]

The reformers believed, at first, that the changes they envisioned could be made within the Roman church, that the preaching of God's word could be reestablished in the Catholic service. Instead, their preaching set off a series of changes which forced a break with the old church. Criticism of the lack of discipline and the mores of the Roman clergy led to an attack on clerical celibacy which ended, in 1524, with the marriage of the reformed clergy and their excommunication by the Catholic church. In 1525 many monastic clergy deserted their convents, and these institutions, except for four women's convents, were closed down. These changes were followed by a concentrated attack on the Catholic Mass from 1526 to 1529. The reformers were convinced that the Mass would have to be abolished in all the churches of the city so that pure forms of worship could be inaugurated. The Protestant clergy appealed to their parishioners on the issue and, in face of the threat of civil unrest, the Mass was abolished in February 1529.

At the Diet of Augsburg in 1530 the preachers and the civil authorities feared they would be called to account for abolishing the Mass. Instead, they were asked to present a formal confession of faith. Unwilling to accept the Lutheran confession, later known as the Confession of Augsburg, the Strasbourg delegates sent for Capito and Bucer to prepare a statement that would enable the city to maintain its ties with the Swiss cities.[4] The *Confessio Tetrapolitana* was drawn up and accepted by only three other cities, Memmingen, Constance, and Lindau. This separate statement of faith created a deep distrust of Strasbourg among the German Lutheran cities, adding to the tensions within the Protestant camp.

At home the preachers faced increased attack from the sectarians who challenged the truth of their preaching, taunting them with their failure to bring about a moral renewal. The clergy turned to the Magistrat in hopes of creating a new ecclesiastical order that would give them the power and authority to deal with the dissidents. A synod was held in 1533. The problem of discipline was ignored, but Articles of Faith for the Strasbourg church were agreed upon. These were meant to conform to the Augustana, which Strasbourg had signed in 1532. Article IX, on communion, was vague, but it did omit the statement that communion was received spiritually.

> In communion it is Christ himself . . . which is offered to us and thus we are offered his real body and his real blood but in such a way that the bread is not inevitably the body of Christ Himself and the wine his blood, that the bread and wine are not transformed into the body and blood and that these are in no way enclosed locally . . . for thus the immortal body and blood of Christ would become a perishable food and drink. But with the bread and wine and with the words, we are offered the true body and the true blood, that is to say, the true community of Christ.[5]

Despite this attempt to assuage the Lutherans, relations with other Protestant churches and cities remained difficult. The nature of the Eucharist provoked endless debate within the city over the next decades.

No religious changes would have been achieved by the reformers without the support of the populace. The sermons of Zell, Capito, and Bucer fused the populace into a political force, willing to resort to violence to achieve its aims. When Zell began to preach in 1521 and the St. Lorenz chapel grew too small for his audience, the cathedral canons refused to unlock Geiler's great stone pulpit in the nave of the cathedral. A group of carpenters made a portable wooden pulpit that was borne into the cathedral for each sermon and then carefully removed and stored away.[6] When the bishop threatened to end the preaching by placing Zell on furlough there was a rumor of an uprising. The next year an itinerate anti-papist preacher provoked a riot. By 1523 popular feeling had united behind the married priests. When the chapter clergy deposed one married preacher, his parishioners arrived in church the next Sunday armed to defend him. Within a month five more of the clergy married. In 1524 popular discontent shifted to the monastic orders. Two hundred burghers invaded the Dominican cloister and were quelled only by the arrival of the ammeister himself. A few weeks later a mob of six hundred attacked Augustinians, then attacked Carthusians. In these same months the congregations of five parishes petitioned the Rat to confirm the appointments of preachers who had been appointed by the parishioners without due authorization.

In the fall of 1524 there was an outbreak of iconoclasm. Pictures were taken down in some churches, and small street shrines were subject to vandalism and mutilation. The Magistrat intervened by ordering that all pictures and statues should be removed from the churches and cloisters and put away carefully. By January 1525 the authority of the church over ecclesiastical property was more directly challenged. The gardeners and the wagoners joined in requesting that the Rat take over all the possessions of the clergy and distribute them among the burghers. When the Rat failed to respond, except to decide that it would be necessary to hire a battalion of soldiers, the gardeners of the parish of St. Aurelia announced that they would no longer remit their rents to the chapter of St. Thomas, nor would they pay any fixed dues or tithes. As proof of their intention a delegation of gardeners attacked the *Pfennigthurm,* which housed the city treasury. These incidents within the city were overshadowed by open revolt in the countryside. The violence of the Peasants' War spread over all of Alsace and was felt especially in convents and monasteries, which were particularly vulnerable. Inside the city the Magistrat went from guild to guild, polling them on the loyalty of their membership. All pledged their support to the Rat.

The outbreaks of popular feeling were spontaneous and undirected. The campaign which the preachers organized to abolish the Mass was more carefully orchestrated. "We are," wrote Capito to Zwingli, "directing every trick against the Mass."[7] A stream of petitions poured forth from the preachers, from groups of burghers, from the guilds, asking that the Mass be abolished and replaced by the preaching of the pure word of God. It was a propaganda campaign in which the burghers were used to bring pressure on the Magistrat. By the time the synod of 1533 was organized, there was genuine confusion with regard to the role the laity should play in it. The original plan made the sessions open to all who felt they had grievances or anyone who wished to listen to the divine doctrine being explained. When the meeting actually took place the only nonofficial laymen in the audience were elected representatives from each guild. An ordinance, issued three days before the meeting, had abjured everyone else to stay at home and be quiet.[8] The laity had been used to bring down the old church, but they were not permitted to help in the construction of the new. Indeed, neither were the clergy.

The Magistrat, pushed by the clergy and the populace to accept the religion unwillingly, in the end were able to gain from the changes, extending their own power and authority. The Rat itself was deeply split by the religious issue as Thomas A. Brady, Jr., has shown. There were the "Zealots," militant Evangelicals who tended toward a Zwinglian theology and were pro-Swiss in foreign policy; the "Politiques," who were more moderate in their theology and convinced of the need to ally the city with the Lutheran princes and cities; and the "Old Guard," who maintained their Roman Catholicism.[9] In the first decade of the Reform, the Zealots were in the ascendant. They supported the appointment of Protestant preachers to parish churches, and they envisioned a strong alliance between Strasbourg, Basel, and Zurich, to defend the new faith against the Emperor. After the abolition of the Mass and the presentation of the *Tetrapolitana* at the Diet of Augsburg, the Politiques took power and began the gradual process of disengaging the city from the Swiss, seeking an alliance with the Lutheran princes, and, eventually, the Schmalkaldic League.[10]

Within the city the secular authorities began, in the early years of the Reform, to assume the powers wrested from the Roman church. While the bishops and the canons wrangled over their right to control the parish clergy, the parish churches had taken matters into their own hands; they selected reforming preachers and then turned to the Magistrat to confirm their actions. In August 1524 a decree of the Rat established the right of the civil authorities to appoint parish priests. Clerical immunity was abolished, and, in December, all clergy were required to take the burgher oath.

Voluntary dissolution of the monasteries led to further extension of secular authority. Monks appeared before the Rat complaining of maladministration of the convents by their orders. The Ratsherren were loathe to become involved in these internal disputes but stated that, if the monks decided to leave the convents, the Rat would take over the revenues. A committee called the curators of the convents was already responsible for supervising the administration of convent property. In the spring of 1525 the Rat provided that the curators should inventory the possessions of all convents, chapters, and churches. In response several convents closed voluntarily, and a new committee, the convent supervisors, was established to administer both the real estate and the revenues of the former monastic units.

As the Reformation evolved, the civil authorities took action to eliminate the overlapping jurisdictions that had impeded them in the past and attempted to keep authority over the new church firmly in their own hands. A marriage court composed of three senators and two ratsherren was established in 1529. The court had jurisdiction over all aspects of marriage—the question of the consent of both parties, the procedure for publication of the bans, the question of consanguinity and forbidden degrees of relationship, and the problems of divorce and remarriage.[11] Authority over these matters had long been disputed between the civil and the ecclesiastical courts. The Magistrat needed no petitions from the citizens in this instance. They moved quickly to establish their power.

The Magistrat were equally quick to place themselves in a position of authority over the new church. In March 1531 the reformers proposed the establishment of three-member lay committees within each parish. These men, called church wardens, would have the authority to supervise the moral behavior of the parish clergy and to assess the truth of their teachings. Once established, these committees became the basic administrative unit of the Strasbourg church. Meeting as a body, these parish committees, or church wardens, made decisions for the church as a whole. At the synod of 1533 the reformers proposed that the parish church wardens, together with the pastors, be given responsibility for maintaining purity of doctrine. This suggestion was ignored by the Magistrat, who again took full authority into their own hands. A special examining committee was created, consisting of two ratsherren, three church wardens, and two preachers, to hear clerics whose doctrines were in question. Those whose teachings were doubtful were then referred to the Rat itself. The Magistrat had no intention of permitting the Protestant clergy to develop the privileges and immunities that the Catholic clergy had enjoyed.

Provision was made for the ministers to meet in an assembly of the clergy called the *Kirchenkonvent*. Three church wardens, however, always met with the assembly and had the right to remove any matter from its hands to the church wardens or to the Rat. Responsibility for the administration of the new church was in lay hands. The function of the clergy was to teach and to preach under the supervision of the lay authorities.

After 1533 the thin and temporary alliances among clergy, magistrates, and people fell apart. The populace, which had been strongly attracted to the reformers' ideal of the city as a sacral corporation, was no longer needed.[12] The reformers, realizing they had failed to acquire control of the church, assured the Magistrat of their allegiance but turned from local political activity to theology and broader political activity with other German states.

Within the city the Magistrat had emerged in a strong position, but outside the city their acceptance of the teaching of Bucer and Capito made them vulnerable. Jacob Sturm, aware of the city's increasing isolation by 1528, had begun to evolve a policy by which the city could draw close to the Lutheran princes, abandoning its traditional urban alliances. By 1530 Sturm was preparing a reconciliation with the Elector Frederick of Saxony.[13] In late 1531 and early 1532, the negotiations were fruitful. Strasbourg was admitted to the Schmalkaldic League and signed the Confession of Augsburg. Encouraged by Sturm, Bucer corresponded with Melanchthon and Luther. In 1536, agreement with regard to the Eucharist was achieved and the Wittenberg Concord was signed; thus, Strasbourg publicly affirmed its adherence to Lutheran theology. Bucer was an active participant in the conferences and colloquies that attempted to bring religious peace to the Empire in the 1530s and early 1540s.

The hopes for peace collapsed in 1545. The Schmalkaldic War began in 1546. A year later Strasbourg, like other southern German cities, was left defeated and vulnerable by the collapse of the League. The Protestant princes showed little concern for their allies but scurried to protect themselves. Strasbourg was faced by an ultimatum from the emperor to accept the Interim of Augsburg, which was designed to provide religious peace in the Empire until a council could make the final decisions. Acceptance of the Interim would have required abandonment of the XVI Articles, the Confession of Augsburg, and the Wittenberg Concord. Essentially, it demanded a return to a modified Catholicism. The debate on accepting the Interim was the final crisis of the early Reformation in Strasbourg. The populace strongly opposed signing a treaty with the emperor and were equally unwilling to forsake their religious beliefs. Bucer, supported by a young preacher named Paul Fagius, once again stirred his audience from the pulpit, urging military resistance. Jacob Sturm, the diplomat, knew this was impossible in view of the collapse of the League and the empty city treasury. Many members of the Magistrat deserted the city to save their own skins, knowing that the Emperor could seize their possessions or place them under ban if the city resisted.[14] The divisions which had been hidden from the very beginning finally surfaced. In the end, Sturm, using his extraordinary negotiating skills, made a special arrangement between Strasbourg and the emperor. Three churches were returned to the Catholics, but the Interim was never formally accepted. The patricians came back into the city. Life resumed.

CHAPTER SEVEN · CHRISTIAN HUMANISM AND PROTESTANT PUBLICATION, 1518–1548

HE LAITY AND THE CLERGY WERE brought together by the Reformation only intermittently. For a brief moment, at the height of its revolutionary phase, the clergy seemed to articulate the thoughts and aspirations of a large sector of the society. As time went on, however, each group interpreted the message of the Reformation in its own way and according to its own particular needs. The Protestant clergy, who were not politicized by becoming burghers, did not remain the chief spokesmen for their parishioners. They continued in their traditional roles as learned men and religious leaders. In these roles they were respected, even revered, but the differences in interest and focus between the learned and the nonlearned were maintained.

The movement for change had begun within the Latin culture. The Biblical humanists applied the methods of textual and linguistic analysis developed by earlier generations of humanists to the study of the Bible. Their aim was to restore the Christian sources to their original purity, but they also began to develop new interpretations of the texts. In Strasbourg the scholarly study of the Bible rapidly became part of the work of the Reformation. That the reformers were the Biblical humanists indicates the closeness of the two movements.

Biblical humanism was introduced to Strasbourg with the publication of Erasmus's biblical commentary, although somewhat later than in other centers. Matthias Schürer included Erasmus's short commentary on the first psalm at the end of his 1515 edition of the *Lucubrationes*.[1] Although Erasmus's New Testament, the *Paraphrasis* on Romans, and the treatise on biblical exegesis had all appeared in other cities by 1516,[2] Schürer, who had a virtual monopoly on Erasmian publication in Strasbourg, neglected these in favor of the literary works, which he preferred personally. Thus, there were no Strasbourg editions of the Erasmian New Testament or the commentaries until after Schürer's death in 1519 or 1520.[3] One edition of the *Paraphrasis* appeared without a printer's signature in 1519, which indicates that the printer did not wish to compete openly with Schürer by publishing an edition of Erasmus. In 1520, however, Ulrich Morhard brought out a

German edition of the Erasmian New Testament, and six Latin editions, by Morhard, Johann Knobloch, and Johann Herwagen, were published in the two-year period from 1522 to 1523. At the same time Knobloch began publishing Erasmus's commentaries on individual books of the New Testament and on the letters of Paul. Six editions, all in Latin, were completed between 1522 and 1525.[4] The educated—a few patricians, university graduates from the upper and middle strata—could read these Erasmian works, but they were closed to ordinary citizens, particularly artisans, craftsmen, and laborers.

In these earliest years of the Reform, from 1522 to 1523, Erasmus served as a leader of the leaders, but by 1523 he had lost this position. His bitter attacks on Ulrich von Hutten in the *Expostulatio* and the even more mordant *Spongia adversus asperigines Hutteni*[5] created a break with the Strasbourg intellectual community. Publication of his work decreased dramatically until by 1526 nothing of his came off the Strasbourg presses. This drop was mostly due to the theological differences that had developed between Erasmus and the Strasbourg reformers. Capito broke with him in 1524 on the question of free will.[6] Angry letters were exchanged, but the final blow came when Erasmus accused the Strasbourg reformers of being false preachers in an attack in 1529.[7] The Strasbourg preachers attempted to maintain some vestige of their personal relationship with Erasmus,[8] but in the meantime the task of editing biblical texts and writing biblical commentaries passed into the hands of the reformed theologians. Their work as Christian humanists was confined to a remarkably brief period. In the five years from 1523 to 1528, 65 percent of all biblical commentaries printed during the century came off the presses. The peak came in 1525, when twenty-one editions of biblical commentaries and two biblical texts were published in one year.[9]

The Strasbourg reformers relied on the Erasmian New Testament, on Luther, and on other members of the Wittenberg group for their basic biblical texts in this period. Luther's Latin Bible was published once; his German New Testament went through five editions from 1522 to 1528; three editions of his German psalter and one of the German Old Testament were printed.[10] In addition Johann Lonicer's Greek testament and Leo Jud's German translation of the Apocrypha were published. By the end of the decade Bucer had translated Tzephaniah into Latin and prepared a Latin translation of the Psalms direct from the Hebrew.[11] Most of the biblical texts were prepared by the Wittenberg circle.

The local reforming clergy devoted themselves to the writing of biblical commentaries. Again, in the early phases of the movement they had to depend on commentaries written by Luther, Melanchthon, and the Pomeranian reformer Johannes Bugenhagen,[12] but by 1524 the Strasbourg reformers, with the help of François Lambert, began to prepare and publish their own commentaries. Lambert was a recently arrived French Franciscan who had left his order in 1522 to study in Wittenberg under Luther. Having unsuccessfully attempted to preach the Gospel in francophone Metz, he was welcomed to Strasbourg by Bucer and Capito and given a stipend to lecture on the Old Testament and the epistles of Paul.[13] He combined these Latin lectures with concentrated work on biblical commentary, publishing first an exposition of the Song of Songs and Luke. By 1525 he was working steadily through the Old Testament prophets—Joel, Moses, Amos, Jonah— eventually completing commentaries on nine biblical books as well as a treatise on his method which addressed the problem of choosing between the letter and the word of the text.[14] Lambert's work reflects a high degree of cooperation among the reformers in this early period. It was difficult to place Lambert, a French-speaking refugee, in the pulpit. His work on the commentaries permitted his colleagues to concentrate on preaching and administration. Theological differences, however, terminated Lambert's stay in Strasbourg. He was too close to Luther and moved on to Hesse in 1526.[15]

After his departure most of the Latin biblical commentary published in the city was written by the Strasbourg reformers. By 1527 Bucer had completed one treatise on Paul's epistle to the Ephesians and another on the synoptic gospels.[16] The following year he completed the Gospels with a book on John and filled some of the gaps left by Lambert with commentaries on Job and, in 1532, on Ecclesiastes.[17] Wolfgang Capito's major work, his commentary on Habbakuk, was published in 1526, followed by another on Hosea in 1528.[18] These latter were particularly important because Capito was one of the distinguished Hebrew scholars of the time. The commentary on Hosea created disarray in the ranks of the Strasbourg reformers for several months because Bucer felt it leaned in the direction of Anabaptism.[19]

The commentaries were, then, as much vehicles of doctrine as they were explications of the biblical texts. Lambert's departure from the city and the brief furor over Capito's *Hosea* are indicative of the role commentaries played in shaping theological truth. They were written by the clergy for other clergy. If they had been intended for educated laymen, they would have continued to be published in the latter part of the century. The aim of the reformers was to have a revised interpretation for every book of the Bible, based on reformed theology and on the new scholarship. Once this was done the task of opening the Scriptures was completed, and the reformers could turn to other tasks.

Despite the rhetoric of the priesthood of all believers and the promulgation of the pure Word of God, the reformers did not encourage the laity to interpret Scripture. That was the responsibility of the clergy, as is indicated by the paucity of biblical commentary published in German. With the exception of Luther's expositions of Deuteronomy, Habbakuk, and Jonah, German commentaries treated only portions of biblical texts;[20] entire books were rarely outlined for the lay reader. The commentary most readily available to the Strasbourg laity was Otto Brunfels's *Pandectarum Veteris et Novi Testamentum*.[21] Brunfels was a scholarly Carthusian who had turned early to the Reform. His compendium, published by Johann Schott in both Latin and German, provided biblical passages to support the major tenets of Lutheran doctrine. The first book described the nature and properties of God, His miraculous works, His revelation of Himself.[22] Brunfels took a strong stand against free will, admonishing men never to confide in their own reason, for the number of the elect was small indeed.[23] Divine election was elucidated in his popular biographies of men and women of the Bible—those chosen by God were followed by those rejected.[24] Brunfels's books were, in part, expositions of doctrine and, in part, biblical texts. Their significance lies in the fact that they were available in the vernacular and that eight editions were printed in three years.[25]

Cyriacus Spangenberg, a strong supporter of the gnesio-Lutheran Flacius Illyricus, was the only reformer, except the Anabaptists, who consistently published his biblical commentary in German.[26] Both he and Brunfels were excluded from the inner circle of the established Strasbourg reformers: Brunfels, because he was regarded as too Lutheran by Bucer and the others; Spangenberg, because of his ties with Flacius Illyricus. What motivated them to write their biblical commentaries is not clear: they may have wanted, primarily, to disseminate their own ideas or they may have written them as statements of defiance. Melchior Hoffman, another writer of biblical commentaries, shows both intentions in his claim that his spiritual insights were superior to those of formally trained theologians. He declared that he could discover the original sense of the Scriptures where the others failed.[27] Whatever the motive of their writers, the vernacular commentaries were usually the work of disaffected individuals. Thirty-seven percent of the German commentaries were written by opponents of the Strasbourg reformers or by men whom the reformers distrusted, such as Anabaptists or self-appointed lay theologians like Clements Ziegler.[28]

The totals for biblical publication in Strasbourg force us to look closely at some common assumptions. It is generally accepted that publication of the Scriptures in the vernacular was one of the decisive changes effected by the Reformation. Yet the actual number of complete Bibles published in Strasbourg was quite low—ten during the entire century.[29] This figure is similar to the number of German Bibles printed in other German cities in the same period. The catalogue of the British Museum lists, for the period from 1520 to 1599, twelve Luther Bibles printed in Frankfurt, and twelve in Wittenberg, as well as twelve editions of the Swiss version printed in Zurich. There were eight editions of the Catholic vernacular Bible printed in Cologne during the same time. The British Museum collection lists fifty-two editions of German Bibles printed during the period 1500–99.[30] Assuming a press run of 1,250 copies in each edition, one arrives at a total of 65,000 German Bibles; press runs of 2,000 copies would bring the total to 104,000, still not a very large number for a population which, by a low estimate, was about sixteen million.[31] In the study of Strasbourg will inventories, only sixteen (35 percent) of the forty-four persons owning books were in possession of a Bible.[32]

The old image of the Protestant family seated around the table with the father reading the Bible is based on seventeenth- and eighteenth-century examples of Puritan and Pietist families. It is probably an optimistic view of the sixteenth century. The ordinary sixteenth-century family was more apt to own a psalm book, especially psalms set to music,[33] or the New Testament than a complete Bible.[34] In his bibliography of Luther's German Bible, Paul Pietsch lists 117 German New Testaments printed from 1522 to 1546, 11 percent of which were printed in Strasbourg. He lists only twenty entire Bibles, nine published in Wittenberg, three in Strasbourg and one each in Augsburg, Frankfurt, Zurich, and Worms. The Old Testament appeared in three sections, the first with the title "The XXIIII Books of the Old Testament, The first Book of Moses to the fourth Book of Moses," in 1523. By 1527 the other two volumes were completed. The second began with Joshua, the third with prophets. Pietsch's list indicates that most printers printed one volume at a time. Only five printers did all three volumes together; the other sixty-four editions were of volume I, II, or III. Pietsch lists thirty-four editions of the German psalter and fifty-five editions of individual biblical books. The Strasbourg figure reflects the general pattern found in Pietsch's work. There were few entire Bibles. The New Testament was the most available of all biblical texts. For the Strasbourg printers the psalter was the next in importance, but Pietsch does not include the psalms set to music, which were so important to the Strasbourg oeuvre.[35] The Strasbourg evidence further indicates that the average sixteenth-century layman remained dependent on the clergy for his understanding of the Scriptures. He might own a New Testament or the psalms but he was far less likely to own a book of commentaries. The reformed clergy did not give up their clerical prerogative, their control over correct interpretation.

Scholarship for the learned; polemic for the common people. The new faith was not communicated in well-reasoned, dispassionate sermons or carefully argued doctrinal works. It was presented in polemical pamphlets that violently attacked Catholicism, the Pope, the bishops, and the teachings of the church.[36] The printing presses made these pamphlets possible; a propaganda campaign of this size was an entirely new phenomenon. In the critical years of the new movement, from 1520 to 1523, the learned abandoned their roles as guardians of the culture to assault it from within, becoming publicists and propagandists for the new belief. Enthusiastic laymen joined the attack and printers diffused the tracts on a scale previously inconceivable. The printing presses served as the cutting edge of the new movement.

Figures on Protestant publication reflect this early propaganda campaign. The majority of Protestant books was published before 1548, indeed, by 1528. Doctrinal works, sermons, and liturgies never equalled the totals achieved by the polemic tracts (table 12). Thirty-seven percent of Protestant publication consisted of polemic works; 75 percent of these were published before 1528. These tracts were clearly the most important element in shaping men's understanding of the Reformation and determining their actions. They cannot be dismissed as "mere polemic." In this phase of its evolution, the Reformation was a vernacular movement. The overwhelming majority of the polemic, as well as the doctrinal works and the sermons, were published in German until 1525. Thereafter, both polemic and doctrinal works dropped off (table 13).

Clergy, laymen, and printers worked together in the early years. Luther and Melanchthon were the central figures, but early propaganda also came from Ulrich von Hutten, a layman. By 1523 the initiative in Strasbourg had shifted to the local men: Martin Bucer, Wolfgang Capito, Matthias Zell, Caspar Hedio formed the core of the Strasbourg reformers. Rather quickly,

Table 12. Protestant Publication by Subject Matter by Period

Subject Matter	1515–1548	1549–1569	1570–1599
Anti-Catholic polemic	294	26	37
Doctrine and theology	129	32	26
Biblical commentary: Latin	90	5	3
Biblical commentary: German	51	14	3
Sermons	84	10	14
Anabaptist doctrine	44	1	1
Polemic against Anabaptists	23	0	0
Devotionals and prayerbooks for lay use	20	8	15
Hymnals and devotional songs	18	58	8
Manuals and aids for the clergy	63	3	6

Table 13. *Breakdown of Protestant Publication, 1520–1540*

Subject Matter	1520–1525	1526–1530	1531–1535	1536–1540
Polemic by Luther	54	0	8	1
Polemic by Strasbourg reformers	25	4	0	0
Polemic by laymen (including von Hutten)	58	2	4	2
Sermons by Luther in German (many polemic in nature)	49	2	1	2
Sermons by Luther in Latin	1	3	0	0
Doctrinal works on the Eucharist in German	10	6	1	0
Doctrinal works on the Eucharist in Latin	1	0	0	0
Other doctrinal works in German	40	6	0	1
Other doctrinal works in Latin	12	9	1	4

they were joined by priests from the parish churches, including Symphorian Altbiesser and Anton Firn, and by canons from the chapters. Capito was provost of Saint Thomas; Sigismund von Hohenlohe was dean of the cathedral chapter. Other men—Otto Brunfels, Michael Herr, Sebastian Meyer—came from the monastic orders. Refugees from France, Italy, and other regions in Germany swelled the size of the group throughout the decade of the thirties.

Spiritualist leaders began to arrive after 1525, as persecution began in other cities. Andreas Karlstadt, Martin Cellarius, and Caspar Schwenckfeld were each resident in the city for some period. The latter, in particular, had a devoted group of followers in the upper ranks of burgher society. Anabaptist leaders came and went, ministering to small congregations in the city.

In addition to the clergy and sectarian leaders, lay men and women actively supported the religious change by writing tracts. The writers were a varied group, ranging from the nobleman Eckhart zum Treubel and Matthias Wurm von Geudertheim to the gardener Clements Ziegler and Katherine Zell, wife of the reformer Matthias Zell. The printers Johann Prüss II, Johann Schott, Johann Knobloch, Wolfgang Köpfel, and Johann Herwagen committed themselves and their presses to the task of disseminating the new ideology in the early years, when this still involved a considerable personal risk. Similarly, Balthasar Beck, Peter Schöffer, and Johann Schwintzer undertook the publication of Anabaptist books. Luther and Hutten led the offensive in 1520 and 1521, but by 1520 other laymen were moved to write and publish. By 1524 the majority of the tracts being published were written by the Strasbourg reformers and laymen (table 14).

The polemic struck at the institutions of the church rather than the doctrines. Few tracts censured the Mass or indulgences.[37] Instead, the long pent-up frustrations against the church hierarchy, the clergy, and the ecclesiastical courts, so evident by 1510, were now poured forth in vituperative pamphlets. The first focus of attack was the pope himself.

Luther's charges against the papacy were published as early as 1520.[38] Ulrich von Hutten's followed with three anti-papal treatises published in one year, one of which went immediately through four editions.[39] Layman and humanist that he was, Hutten linked his criticism of the pope to his German nationalism. The pope, he charged, had consistently undermined the power and authority of the German emperors. When Leo X excommunicated Luther, Hutten saw this not only as a move to extinguish Christian truth, but as an attack on German freedom as well.[40] Thus the old issues raised by the pope's relationships with the secular powers were once again revived. One pamphleteer went back to King Edward III's protest against papal taxation, written in 1366, and published it as part of the new campaign.[41] An anonymous writer, probably a cleric, summarized the major papal bulls, from those of Innocent III to the *Unam Sanctam* of Boniface VIII, to show the relentless assumption of illegal and unauthorized power.[42] Heinrich von Kettenbach, a former Franciscan, published a series of papal bulls to expose their lack of consistency.[43] These pamphlets, whose purpose was to discredit the canon law and thus affirm the superiority of German law, were the most moderate of the anti-papal tracts. The more extreme forms were personal attacks on the pope himself or dialogues in which the

Table 14. Authorship of Polemic Works, 1519–1528

Author	1519	1520	1521	1522	1523	1524	1525	1526	1527	1528
Luther	3	13	11	9	12	5	2	0		
Hutten		13	6	3	3	1	0	0		
Strasbourg reforming group, including Brunfels			3	1	5	15	7	1		
Other reformers (Swiss or German)		3	3	6	4	5	6	2		
Laymen (published in Strasbourg)		2	4	5	10	8	1	0		
Foreigners (English or French)		1						0	2	2
Anonymous		1	5	1	1		1	3		

pope was unmercifully lampooned.[44] After 1523 this campaign was dropped and anti-papal propaganda did not appear again until the Council of Trent.

Instead the pamphleteers turned against the ordinary parish clergy. The immorality of the clergy was a well-worn theme in the late Middle Ages.[45] Geiler and the Alsatian humanists had consistently criticized the licentious behavior of priests and monks. The laxity of the priests had long been linked to the decline of religious and spiritual life among the people; this message was now repeated by the Protestant polemicists.[46] What was new was that the Protestants offered a solution. The clergy should marry.

Over the centuries the Roman church had legalized priestly incontinence. The priest who could not maintain sexual abstinence was permitted to live with a concubine, on payment of a fee. Children were tolerated, on payment of a cradle tax, and the canon law made it possible to legitimize these children. The Protestants attacked these measures as hypocritical. How, they asked, could a priest preach penance to his congregation when he, himself, was living a more sinful life than most of his flock? What was superior about celibacy if it led to such behavior? Marriage was equally worthy, indeed had been established by God. The priests should marry and maintain the same standards of morality they preached to the people. The repudiation of celibacy by the Protestant polemicists created a new attitude toward sex. If celibacy was the more estimable state, ordinary sexual relations were a mark of weakness, of lust, and were, by implication, sinful. Once marriage was declared to be as worthy of merit, sexual relations could be regarded as a normal part of human emotional life, and the family could assume a more central role in the social ethic.

A spate of tracts was written by priests to justify their own marriages. One of the first to be published in Strasbourg was by Johann Eberlin von Günzburg, a Franciscan who broke with his order in 1521. Going back to the Old Testament he demonstrated that marriage was part of the natural order, created by God for the benefit of mankind. The rule of celibacy subverted this normal arrangement and was thus against God's law.[47] In the fall of 1523 several of the Strasbourg priests married. Called before both the civil and ecclesiastical authorities, their defenses at these hearings were published almost immediately.[48] Other defenses followed. Matthias Zell, preaching at the wedding of Anton Firn, one of the first priests to marry, asserted that clerical marriage was not an innovation but a return to the true ordinances established by God but set aside for a long time. Woman was not a separate creature from man; she was made from man. Man could achieve full perfection only in marriage—this was what God had intended at the Creation.[49] When Zell himself married, his wife Katherine rose to defend the marriage against the bishop, who had placed the married priests under ban. The bishop's opposition, she wrote, was entirely a matter of money.

He could raise more from cradle taxes and levies on men living with concubines than from honest married folk. She had married Zell to save souls.
Many men had been damned to hell-fire for living out of wedlock. Only if
pious women were willing to enter into marriage vows with the clergy
could they be saved.[50] These justifications of clerical marriage played an
important role in breaking down the ethic of celibacy and placed family life
in a more positive light. The idea that there was one moral order for the
clergy and another for the laity was rejected.

The attack on monasticism was another facet of the general censure of the
clergy. Polemic against the orders began with Luther's tract on monastic
vows and the false spirituality of the cloistered life.[51] In Strasbourg itself the
debate over monasticism and the authority of the church was drawn between Conrad Treger, provincial of the Augustinian hermits, and the reformers.[52] The discussion was significant in that it went beyond the mere
repetition of salacious incidents to address the reasons for the corruption
and disintegration of conventual life. The problem was placed on a theological level, the general question of ecclesiastical authority was raised, and
the practice of taking lifetime vows was seriously questioned. Such vows,
the reformers argued, could not be perpetually binding because they sub-
stituted man-made rules for God's law.[53] Laymen quickly responded, particularly those who had sisters and daughters in convents. Matthias Wurm
von Geudertheim, who had placed one of this sisters in the convent of Saint
Nikolaus-in-Undis, questioned the wisdom of his action. The basis of his
argument was the same as Luther's: individuals could not take vows of
chastity, poverty, or obedience to other men or women since this robbed
God of his power and authority over human life.[54] He further questioned
the conventual life, with its emphasis on prayer, since the prayers were
addressed to saints. A long section of the treatise, thoroughly supported by
passages from Scripture, proved that these prayers were in fact blas-
phemous, since they invoked men, not God.[55] For these reasons he had
decided to remove his sister from the cloister to live a life of work and
virtue.[56] Jacob Schenck, another layman, wrote a letter to his sister, a nun,
to point out that the true Christian life could be found in marriage, caring
for a husband, and raising children to be good Christians.[57]

Criticism of the clergy and the papacy led in yet another direction: the
rejection of the power asserted by the clergy over individual Christians and
over their congregations. This was implicit in doctrinal statements such as
the *Freedom of a Christian Man,* but it was specifically developed by Luther in
a short treatise addressed to the town of Leisnig, where the efforts of the
parish to recognize and establish the Reformation had met with resistance
from the Abbot of Buch. Luther insisted that the congregation had final
authority over the affairs of their own church, because they had received the

authority of the Word through their baptism.[58] "The bishops, religious foundations, monasticism, and all associated with them have long since ceased to be Christians." Indeed, Luther claimed that Christ had taken the power from the bishops and scholars, and vested it directly in the people. Every Christian who had received the Word of God could thus assume the function and responsibilities of the priesthood.[59] While this concept of congregational authority would later be substantially restricted, in 1523 Luther's treatise stood as a major statement of the doctrine of the priesthood of all believers and the power of the individual Christian. In that same year a Bavarian noblewoman took Luther at his word and asserted her authority as a Christian to question an ecclesiastical procedure. The University of Ingolstadt had forced a young member of the faculty to repudiate his Lutheran views in a public and humiliating ceremony. Argula von Grumbach, rising in defense of the young scholar, wrote a vigorous protest to the University faculty, stating that they had no authority over the Word of God, nor could they judge the case by papal decretals drawn from Aristotle, since he was not a Christian.[60]

Laymen echoed the same themes as the reformers, describing the inability of the clergy to exert leadership, their corruption, their immorality, their greed for money. Most important, the clergy consciously manipulated the laity for their own purposes. This was described by Eckhart zum Treubel, an Alsatian nobleman and citizen of Strasbourg. Between 1521 and 1528 he wrote and published a series of pamphlets addressed to his fellow citizens. Since one of them went through three editions he clearly struck a receptive audience.[61] In vigorous, idiomatic German, he set forth his own reaction to the Catholic clergy:

> It must indeed be a grossly foolish Christian who does not see or notice how adroitly our so-called clergy have managed us up until now. They have . . . shown us the way to their money bags but never, or seldom, to heaven. . . . They are not ashamed to mount drunk to the pulpit, to forget the gospel and lie under the chair . . . and unashamedly cry Porter, Porter. . . . As soon as a preacher beats around with his bagpipes, I am bored and annoyed . . . then another [priest] does exactly the same thing. And thus they destroy Christ's flock instead of gathering it around them and protecting it. . . . It is the time, God will have it, when the flocks in the field can speak. . . . It is the time, as the heart says, when the stones must talk. Oh pious Christendom, all noble and non-noble are . . . cautioned against tolerating such a pitiable and lamentable situation. . . . It is especially in the churches that the greatest poison and evil lies. . . . How I praise God that it should be changed. . . .[62]

One of the most devastating lay attacks was written by the Bernese playwright, Niklaus Manuel. In his *Fastnachtspiel,* first published in 1522 and widely reprinted, he protrayed the deception of the clergy, their mockery of the intelligence and human concerns of the people. The pope extolled death because it was the key to controlling the laity. Men could always be frightened into doing penance, he said, by threats of hell-fire. Thus they could be forced to give money to the church, the priests and the bishops could become wealthy, and the church could emerge as the most powerful institution on earth.[63] The clergy were not only callous, they were consciously dishonest.

Both the Protestant clergy and the laity revealed a conscious desire to end the separation between the spiritual and the secular worlds in the early years of the Reform. The movement attracted ordinary men and women precisely because it promised to end the control the church had exerted over all phases of everyday life.[64] The dualism between church and state, which had developed in the Middle Ages, was seen as unnatural and divisive. A new society, a united Christendom based on shared responsibilities, was envisioned.[65]

While the polemicists attacked the old, they also held out a vision of the new. In particular, they established Luther as a charismatic hero, understanding of the problems of his time, able to defend his ideas against the Emperor, the cardinals, and the rest of established authority. The first of these defenses of Luther to appear in Strasbourg (1519) was written by Luther himself, summarizing the false accusations brought against him.[66] The burning of Luther's books on Louvain in 1520 provided Hutten with an opportunity to portray Luther as the victim of injustice.[67] A student named Lux Gemigger was moved by the incident to defend Luther and his doctrines. "If someone wants to know the author of the poem," he said on the title page, "it was done by a free student because they burned Luther's books."[68] Much of the poem was a recital of the inequity of the pope and the Romanists, but at the end Gemigger extolled Luther:

> This is what Luther has shown us and has explained to us the Word
>   of God and has increased faith in Christ.
> He has truly accomplished that which God commanded, as is stated
>   in the Gospel.
> Luther has driven the evil spirit out of us, which was the greatest
>   cause of all our problems.[69]

Luther's appearance before the Diet of Worms in 1521 made him a hero for many German people. Descriptions of his confrontation with the Emperor were rapidly disseminated. There were five editions in Strasbourg alone: two in Latin, three in German.[70] Many of these pamphlets and the songs celebrating the event included woodcuts of Luther, who became the standard bearer of German freedom. The songs were written by Michael Stifel, a former Augustinian monk from Esslingen.[71] Otto Brunfels published a eulogistic biography of Jan Huss, which connected the Czech to the new movement.[72] In all these accounts the apostle of truth was hindered and opposed by the forces of established authority. Thus the aims of German freedom were implicitly related to the success of the Reformation.

Locally, a citizen named Stefan von Bullheym rose to defend Matthias Zell after the bishop had attempted to dismiss him for Lutheran preaching. Bullheym, about whose life we have no details, wrote a dialogue in which a son warned Zell that he was in danger and explained Zell's new teaching to his father. The father was won over because he feared what might happen to Zell. Recently the magistrates at Bern had charged several Dominican monks with heresy, and the spiritual authorities had then condemned the monks. The father was afraid that if Zell fell into the hands of the ecclesiastical authorities he would suffer the same fate, for certainly one could not expect to receive justice in an ecclesisatical court.[73] The pamphlet reflected the layman's deep distrust of clerical authority. Bullheym genuinely feared that Zell might be taken by force, just as Gemigger feared that Luther would be subjected to bodily harm. The laity perceived ecclesiastical authority as capricious and vindictive.

The polemic broke the primacy of the Roman church, but it did little to provide something in its stead. This was achieved by doctrinal treatises which, from 1523 to 1524, were written and published in German. In the earliest years of the Reform, Luther and his Wittenberg followers were the major source of doctrinal writing. These works were published, as the Strasbourg figures bear partial witness, all over Germany. They formed the core for Reformation writing just as the work of Italian writers had formed the core for the early period of the humanist movement. Invariably the main flow of ideas was introduced from outside. Major Lutheran treatises introduced new doctrines with regard to penance and the Eucharist.[74] Abolition of private masses was recommended.[75] Other doctrinal treatises covered the role of the Christian in society: his obedience to secular authorities;[76] his behavior in a period of turmoil and unrest;[77] his responsibilities in the marketplace.[78] Issues of family life, the responsibility of parents for their childrens' education, and marriage were discussed in separate tracts.[79]

With the exception of Bucer's *Das ym selbs niemant,* there were few summaries of the meaning of the new faith. There was, however, a general reordering of beliefs and practices.[80] Indulgences, and the penitential theology based upon them, disappeared without regret. Man's sinfulness was placed within a larger social context. Preachers, magistrates, and laymen condemned men for their sinfulness because it hindered the achievement of a truly Christian commonwealth.[81] There was a new emphasis on law, especially the laws of God, both those of the Old Testament and the New. To disobey was blasphemy. The commandment of the New Testament was embodied in Justification by Faith. Men must love God with their hearts and souls and place their faith in him, rather than relying on their own efforts.[82] God gave men faith and he had redeemed mankind through Christ. His death on the cross secured forgiveness for all men for eternity.[83] The basic elements of Reformed theology were knit into religious writing, not as doctrinal truths which had to be explicated and defended, but as fundamental assumptions.

The exception to this was the doctrine of the Eucharist. Because the Strasbourg reformers had their unique interpretation, it was essential for them to publicize and defend it. Treatises on the Eucharist were written and published in German precisely because the reformers hoped to win others to their belief. These doctrinal works had a polemic quality. Of the eighty doctrinal works published after 1525, 48 percent grappled with the problem of the meaning of the Eucharist.[84] Other treatises included sections on the Eucharist within the context of a broader theological summary.[85]

The first publications gave the Lutheran position. Luther's very short treatise on the meaning of the Sacrament, on the scriptural basis for communion in both kinds, and on the veneration of the sacramental body of Christ was first published in 1522.[86] His other early writings condemned Roman practices, but did not develop his own views. These first appeared in 1525 in the treatise *Against the Heavenly Prophets,* written to repudiate and correct the doctrines of Karlstadt, a refugee in Strasbourg since 1524.[87]

In 1525 the Strasbourg reformers also began to publish their particular views, although Capito had put forth a Spiritualist interpretation before it was ever a matter of controversy.[88] Oecolampadius's Latin treatise on the meaning of the phrase *Hoc est Corpus Meum* supported Capito's point of view.[89] Bucer's first statement of his interpretation of communion went through two editions in rapid succession.[90] While he attempted to take a neutral stand, he asserted that the bread and wine, as material and external elements, had no intrinsic value.[91]

In 1526 the first confrontation over the significance of communion occurred between Luther and Bucer. The latter had agreed to translate Luther's German postill into Latin for use in Italy and France. The first three volumes of these homilies, published by Johann Herwagen, had pleased Luther; but in the fourth, which appeared in July, he found that his meaning had been twisted by Bucer's translation of the commentary on 1 Corinthians, chapters 9 and 14. Bucer had given a Zwinglian or "Swiss" interpretation to his teaching of the Sacrament and to the meaning of the words "the rock was Christ.''[92] Luther immediately wrote to Herwagen, stating that Bucer's erroneous translation amounted to a monstrous blasphemy against the Sacrament, and reaffirmed his literal interpretation of the words *Hoc est Corpus Meum*.[93] Bucer reacted to this by publishing his preface to the fourth volume the following year, with a letter defending his position.[94]

By 1528 Bucer had moved to a more conciliatory position. In that year Luther published his *Von Abendmal Christi, Bekendnis* [Treatise concerning the Lord's Supper, a confession]. This treatise, ready for sale at the Frankfurt book fair,[95] was not published in Strasbourg. Bucer was convinced by reading it that Luther's definition of the real presence of Christ in the Sacrament did not extend to an outward physical presence, but involved a sacramental union. In his *Vergleichung D. Luthers, unnd seins gegentheyls* [A comparison of the positions of Luther and his opponents], Bucer pointed out the similarities between Luther and the other reformers, asserting that the two points of view were not irreconcilable.[96] Bucer's optimism influenced Philip of Hesse to call the Marburg Colloquy in 1529, although in fact the break was far too deep between the two sides. The schism was symbolized by Luther's refusal to let the Zwinglians receive communion at the end of the Colloquy.[97]

After the collapse of his efforts to achieve unity at Marburg, Bucer drew back from his efforts at reconciliation. The doctrine of the Lord's Supper, as practiced in Strasbourg, was formally drawn up in a series of statements; these defined the Eucharistic beliefs of the city and culminated in the Tetrapolitana and the Articles of Faith of 1533.[98] Concentration on the Eucharist meant that other issues were neglected. The question of penance was entirely laid aside. The dispute over priestly marriage was considered to be settled, and nothing was written on the matter from 1530 to 1540.[99] Although the Strasbourg church was struggling with the difficulties of organization, there were no treatises on church polity. These matters were worked out on a day-to-day basis, but no attempt was made to systematize the experience. Thus the process of creating a new church to replace the old proceeded in a lopsided fashion.

After 1525 the Reformation lost its original fervor. The intense enthusiasm of the laity was channeled in different ways. The reformers developed their role as preachers, leaving aside their function as propagandists except in the campaign against the Mass. The new faith was now integrated into the everyday life of the people through the liturgy, through music, and through private devotional literature. These new liturgical forms strengthened religious and communal life. The ordinary burgher was no longer a passive observer of the religious service. Through music, hymns, the singing of the psalms and prayers, he was swept into active participation. The liturgy and the sacred music bound the congregations to the new faith.

The new order of service took shape early in the movement. In 1520, 1522, and 1524, prayer books compiled by Luther and his followers were printed.[100] By 1524 Luther's liturgy for the German Mass and the first edition of what would become the Strasbourg liturgy—*Teutsche Mess und Tauff wie sie yetzund zu Straszburg Gehalten Werden*—were published.[101] This latter was revised, enlarged, and reedited from decade to decade until 1550.[102] Its language was at once dignified and expressive; the prayers and collects mirrored the spiritual concerns not only of the Strasbourg congregations but of other Reformed churches, as well. Widely copied, it had an important influence on the development of liturgies in other German states and cities, in Geneva, and in French Reformed congregations.

The most enduring change in the church service was in religious music. In the Catholic church, hymnals and graduals had been used by the clergy, the choir master, and the trained choir. Luther's hymns were written for the entire congregation. Through hymns and music essential elements of the new doctrines were disseminated among the common citizens. As early as 1524 Bucer recommended the singing of the Ten Commandments and the Creed, as well as songs of praise and the psalms. Set to music, the psalms could be learned by every man, woman, and child, forming an important part of their religious life.[103] Congregational music created a new form of religious communication. It was a means of increasing devotion as well as strengthening popular understanding of the Scriptures.[104]

The enthusiasm for music manifested itself early in the Reformation, reaching its major development in mid-century.[105] Fifteen editions of Protestant hymns were published, together with forty-eight editions of the Psalms set to music, sixty religious songs, and several editions of prayers set to music. Luther's hymns were available by 1525. The Strasbourg liturgies included the *Gesangbuch,* which gave the psalms and hymns used in the Strasbourg churches and suggested appropriate music for weddings, baptisms, and the communion service. Another volume gave musical settings for all the psalms. In these editions the music was given at the beginning of each psalm or hymn, and the books were often illustrated with woodcuts for the pleasure and instruction of those who used them.[106] An average of two psalters, hymn books, or individual songs were published every year after 1539, reflecting their importance to the new church. Through congregational singing the laymen learned the psalms in German, and the words of the Scriptures became an intimate part of their own thoughts and prayers. Music thus played an important role in opening up the Scriptures to the laity. Through singing they became familiar with the Word.

Prayer books were another important form of Protestant publication for the laity, together with short catechisms for families to use in the religious education of their children. The prayer books were a conscious attempt to break the use of old books like the *Hortulus animae,* which the Protestants felt were too heavily directed toward Catholic feast days and prayers to the saints. The reformers returned to simpler forms of prayer, with an emphasis on prayers for the common man, to be used in daily life. The Ten Commandments were often included in these books, as well as readings or meditations to help in preparation for communion. Thus, we can see that there was a conscious effort to deepen the spiritual life of the individual.[107]

Children's books were a new departure in lay devotionals. These were compiled for children or for parents to use with their children. The earliest of these books was Luther's exposition of the Lord's Prayer, published in 1520. In 1527 Capito prepared a book of instruction for children, an early catechism with questions on the basic points of the Christian faith.[108] Melanchthon's *Little Book for Laymen and Children* introduced children to the devotional life, providing prayers for parents and children to recite together.[109] Another book provided graces, accompanied by salutary quotations from Scripture to be learned by heart.[110] By the middle of the century, first communion had begun to assume its central role in the life of the individual Lutheran. A special manual, written to prepare boys and girls for Holy Communion, went well beyond a catechism to include a self-examination which young people should use to determine their readiness for presentation at the Lord's table.[111] They were urged to probe their own inner desires, to face their faults and shortcomings directly and honestly.[112] The Protestant church recognized the special needs of young people, and the family was regarded as having an integral role in religious instruction.

The new liturgy was centered on prayers, songs, and hymns, on the praise of God rather than on the sacrament of the Mass.[113] Communion was no longer an individual rite, preceded by the personal dialogue between priest and penitent in the confessional. It was a public act of worship in the tradition of the Hebrew literature and the congregational assemblies described by Peter and Paul. The liturgical publications from 1525 to 1550 made the new rituals familiar to the parishioners of every church in the city. The hymnals, together with the psalms set to music, created a spirit of triumph and exaltation, a celebration of the power of God and His protection of His people.

The sequence in which the different types of Protestant works appeared is, in itself, significant. Furthermore, this sequence was related to Catholic publication in the preceding period. Religious publication from 1480 to 1550 followed the pattern of evolution which has been defined as a revitalization movement.

"A revitalization movement," according to the anthropologist Anthony Wallace, "is a deliberate, conscious effort by members of a society to construct a more satisfying culture."[114] As a form of cultural change it is distinctive in that the persons involved in the process perceive their culture, or major parts of it, as a system, are dissatisfied with it, and undertake to create a new system.[115] The process involves five evolutionary phases, which may blend into one another.

At the beginning, the society is operating under relatively stable conditions. A "steady state" obtains in which the existing sociocultural system is able to absorb the stresses felt by most members of the population. According to Wallace, the process of change starts when an increasing number of individuals experience tensions and stresses which they are not able to resolve by socially accepted techniques. This initiates a period of cultural distortion when the elements of the system are no longer harmonious, but conflicting. Among individuals the discord may be expressed in intragroup violence, in irresponsible actions on the part of public officials, in states of depression and self-reproach. This period of tension leads into the revitalization movement.[116]

The essential purpose of revitalization is to reformulate the "maze way," or the mental image of the society and its culture which is the essential frame of reference of every individual member.[117] This reformulation occurs through the activity of one person, a prophet or leader, who is able to restructure the culture, often drawing on elements already present in nascent form. The insight of the leader enables this person to envision an internally consistent system. Usually this occurs suddenly; the leader may receive a vision of the new system in dreams or through other forms of revelation. Sharing this experience with others is the next phase—the stage of communication, in which the leader conveys the revelation to the people. The message usually involves two fundamental elements: the individual convert will receive special protection from the deity, and the individual will benefit materially from a change in the cultural system. The preaching of the message attracts disciples and followers, who help to continue the process of communication.[118]

A new organizational structure begins to take shape. At this point the movement inevitably meets with some opposition or resistance either from another faction within the society or from outsiders. A process of adaptation must occur in which the original doctrine of the leader is modified to meet criticisms and demands of the broader culture. Once this has occurred, a cultural transformation has taken place, which must then be rationalized. The new system becomes the norm; a new steady state has been reached.[119]

The socio-evolutionary process described by Wallace is remarkably appropriate for viewing the diverse stages of the Reformation movement as a comprehensive whole. The dissatisfactions with their society, which are so evident in the work of Brant, Murner, and Geiler, were expressions of the cultural distortion that was beginning to be felt. The publication of the great sermons of the past reflect the desire among the clergy to maintain the steady state of that past. Yet, for the individual member of the society, the penitential system was no longer an acceptable means of resolving individual tensions. The profound anticlericalism of the burghers was a syndrome of intragroup violence and distrust.

The revitalization process began with the preaching of Luther, which was communicated by the tracts and treatises that flowed from the presses. The local leaders—Zell, Bucer, and Capito—then joined Luther. The polemic literature communicated the new ideology. The earliest tracts helped to establish Luther's position as a heroic and invincible leader. Tracts against indulgences and the Mass helped to destroy the old maze way, at the same time offering the Protestant convert a new relationship with the deity and the promise of a better way of life. The controversy over the Eucharist and the struggle over the marriage of the clergy were part of the process of adaptation. In these instances the new ideas were carefully examined, subjected to criticism, and revised. The Anabaptist formulations received similar scrutiny and, in Strasbourg, were rejected as too radical. Routinization began with the Synod of 1533. It was articulated in the confessions of faith, the catechisms, and the liturgy, which together created a new form of religious experience. A new steady state was established after 1570. The Wallace model enables us to see the relationship of Catholic publication to the later movement and the contribution of each type of Protestant publication to the larger course of events. All were part of the process of change.

CHAPTER EIGHT · SCIENTIFIC PUBLICATION, 1530–1548

I N 1530 PUBLICATION OF SCIENTIFIC books outstripped religious publication. This was not a passing phenomenon, for protestant publication soon leveled off to an average of six editions a year, a norm maintained by the printers until the end of the century. By contrast, scientific editions— including scientific treatises by university professors, medical works, technical manuals, and pseudo-science such as calendars and prognostications—averaged nine a year over the same period (this difference in volume can be seen by comparing figures V and VII). The number of scientific masterformes produced ran consistently higher than the number of Protestant masterformes (figures XII and XIV). Somehow, interest in the material world became increasingly important to the culture.

One historian of science has argued that the scientific changes were conscious attempts to carry the religious reform further, that the questioning of traditional doctrines in one area led to transformations in other fields as well.[1] I would suggest that it was the result of a combination of factors, which happened to converge at roughly the same time. There were men ready to carry out innovative work. Otto Brunfels and Michael Herr were drawn to the Reform and had attempted to participate in the creation of the new church. Their Lutheran beliefs separated them from the Strasbourg reformers, and they were excluded from the scholarly community. Both had strong scientific interests, which they began to develop after 1525. It is hard to determine, however, whether their work represented a counter movement to the religious reform or an application of the principles of the religious reform to the scientific field.

There were practical, economic factors at work. Several printers whose major interest was in scientific and technical publication arrived in the city and set up shop at just this time. These included Christian Egenolff (1528–1531), Heinrich Vogtherr (1538–1540), and Jacob Cammerlander (1531–1548). Johann Schott, like his friend Brunfels an enthusiastic supporter of Luther, published Lutheran polemic and the pamphlets of Ulrich von Hutten. He was less eager to publish the works of the Strasbourg reformers.[2] There were, then, several printers available and interested in printing scientific works at exactly the right time. The sale of Reformation polemic had uncovered the potential of the lay market. During the twenties the printers had responded to the demand for religious tracts, prayer books, and psalters. As the intense interest began to flag, however, they were left in a vulnerable position. The Catholic market was permanently lost as far as the Strasbourg printers were concerned. The Protestant market was now proving to be shaky. The printers needed noncontroversial books which would appeal to a broad market. Popular medical books and technical manuals, which catered to the everyday needs and material well-being of ordinary people, filled both requirements. Science, however, could also serve as a cover for religious heterodoxy. The men who published the treatises of Anabaptist and Spiritualist leaders also printed scientific works.[3]

These economic circumstances were complemented by intellectual factors. There was a genuine interest in the physical universe. Sixteenth-century men were fascinated by the world of nature. They were curious about the structure and functioning of the human body. They wanted medical information. Plants and animals, agronomy, and veterinary medicine all interested them. They were eager to extend their computing skills and their knowledge of techniques of measurement and simple mechanics. The scientific publication of the period indicates that concern for the life in the world to come was balanced by strong interest in the here and now. The scientific books, the majority published in German, are another index of the strength of the lay culture.

The scientific community continued to be split between Latin writers and vernacular writers. In a sense the divisions became more distinct. Although the university-trained doctors continued to publish a few works in German, for the most part they, together with the teachers of science in the Gymnasium, wrote in Latin. Two groups wrote almost exclusively in German: a small but extremely prolific group of medical popularizers; and those applied mathematicians and skilled craftsmen and workers who wrote and edited technical manuals.

The circle of university-trained doctors who edited and published expanded considerably in this period to include four men: Lorenz Fries, Johann Guinther von Andernach, Sebald Hawenreuter, and Heinrich Seybold. Two of them undertook to print their own editions. Heinrich Seybold had his own press, while Andernach established a press for the French refugee, Rémy Guédon, in his house.[4]

Lorenz Fries was by now the dean of the medical community. He had published a major medical text in 1518, as well as other scientific works, including an edition of Ptolemy. In 1525, grieved by Strasbourg's acceptance of the Reform, he renounced his citizenship and moved to Metz. He continued to use the Strasbourg presses, however, so his work must still be considered as part of the local scene. His physical absence accentuates the divisions within the community. From 1526 to 1527, Fries's young friend,

Theophrastus von Hohenheim Paracelsus, practiced in the city before moving on to become city physician at Basel.[5]

In 1527, Heinrich Seybold, a learned doctor from Heilbronn, purchased burgher rights and began to practice in the city.[6] He used his own printing press to publish the work of the Italian humanist-physician, Giorgio Valla, who had translated the Greek sources of medicine and botany into Latin. Seybold left the city in 1538, and there is no record of further printing activity.[7]

In the 1540s two new doctors arrived. Johann Guinther von Andernach had trained in Paris and was there from 1526 to 1539, serving as personal physician to Francis I. His acceptance of the Reform forced his departure from Paris; he arrived in Strasbourg in 1544. Known to be a follower of Schwenckfeld, he was protected by the Magistrat because of his skills as a physician.[8] His strong religious loyalities show up in his protection of the refugee printer Rémy Guédon, whom he provided with work and shelter. While two of his treatises were published in this period, his impact on the community was greater after 1555.

Sebald Hawenreuter, educated at the universities at Wittenberg and Tübingen, arrived in the city at much the same time as Andernach. The two lectured on medicine in the early years of the Upper Classes at the Gymnasium, although neither was apparently gifted as a teacher. Hawenreuter held the position of city physician for forty-nine years, from 1540 to 1589.[9] The number of trained physicians had increased, and all of them had some commitment to teaching or disseminating medical knowledge.

The formal study of science was introduced by Christian Herlin in 1538. Nephew of the Strasbourg ammeister, Martin Herlin, Christian taught for several years in one of the struggling lay schools. When the Gymnasium was organized in 1538, he was given responsibility for teaching mathematics.[10] In 1547, with mathematicians Nicholas Prügner and Michael Herr, Herlin was commissioned to rebuild the Strasbourg clock.[11] A nucleus of men interested in mathematics had been created. It would be extended by Herlin's pupil, Conrad Dasypodius.

Closely tied to the academic medical community, the Strasbourg physicians were drawn into the debate over the authoritative sources of medical knowledge. Doctors had begun to search for the original medical texts, just as the humanists earlier in the century had pursued the original texts of classical authors and the Bible. In 1525 the medical faculty at the university of Paris condemned the Arab physicians, the traditional medieval authorities, as mere compilers and encyclopedists and recommended a return to the original texts of the Greek physicians, in particular Galen and Hippocrates.[12]

The debate was carried to Strasbourg by Lorenz Fries. In 1530, although he had already moved to Metz, he published a treatise in Strasbourg that came out firmly on the side of the Arabs.[13] The Paris medical faculty, he charged, had been carried away by the general enthusiasm for classical literature. Swayed by the example of the humanists, they were subjecting medical knowledge to literary standards. While Fries praised the humanists for their contribution to learning, he insisted that there were significant differences between science and literature. The humanists were concerned with words, with style, and with modes of expression. A doctor, who was responsible for the health of his patients, should have a different set of priorities. Fries was concerned that overzealous adoption of the Greek physicians would lead to bad medical practices and a mountain of errors. In particular he feared that the procedures of diagnosis so painstakingly developed by the Arab physicians were being ignored. The Grecophiles identified their patient's illnesses from the diagnoses of the Greek physicians and proceeded to prescribe for the patient without making any physical examination.[14]

Fries's treatise opened the discussion within the Strasbourg medical community. From 1529 to 1546, the opposing factions prepared and published materials to support their positions. Thirteen texts were published in all, six by Greek physicians, seven by Arab.[15] In addition there was Giorgio Valla's work drawn from Greek sources. The editions of the Arab sources were essentially reprints of the traditional texts. Michael Herr prepared a German translation of Abu Ali Jahiah ben Ife ben Dschesda, but he worked from Gerald of Cremona's Latin text. The Arab sources were made available in Latin or German.[16]

Leonhard Fuchs, the professor of medicine at Tübingen,[17] wrote the major rebuttal to Lorenz Fries. First published in 1531, Fuchs's treatise appeared in Strasbourg in 1535. The Arab physicians, Fuchs pointed out, had themselves depended on the Greek sources. Copying from the Greeks, they had often changed the text in the process; thus it was essential to return to the originals to purify medical learning of its irrelevant accretions.[18]

The doctors were, however, ill equipped to carry their search back to the original texts of Hippocrates or even Galen since few of them read Greek. Instead they turned to the Greek physicians of the Roman and Byzantine period whose work was available in Latin. The first text to be published in Strasbourg was that of Theodosius Priscianus, a fourth-century Byzantine doctor who had translated his own treatises from Greek into Latin.[19] Paul of Aegina, a sixth-century Greek, had compiled a summary of the major Greek medical writers of the past. This was adapted by the Arab Henain Ibn-Isaak, better known by his Latin name of Johannitus. The three editions of Paul of Aegina provided secondhand versions of the original texts of Dioscorides, Galen, and Theophrastus.[20]

The Greek party in Strasbourg, Heinrich Seybold in particular, drew heavily on the work of Giorgio Valla for translations or compendia of the older Greek medical texts. Valla, a late fifteenth-century Italian physician, was also a humanist and an accomplished linguist. He went back to Dioscorides, Hippocrates, and Herodotus and summarized their texts in Latin.[21] Seybold devoted his press to Valla's works, thus reintroducing the Greeks. Valla's *De inventa medicina* traced the development of medicine as a Greek art. He began with Aescalapius, followed through to Galen, and then on to Serapion of Alexandria, and Appolonius Mys. There was brief mention of the theories of the four humors from Johannitus and from Avicenna.[22] His *De simplicium natura* was drawn straight from Dioscorides. The *De universi corporis purgatione* used Paul of Aegina, Celsus, Galen, Hippocrates, and Herodotus as sources.[23] Thus Seybold was instrumental in incorporating the knowledge of the Greek physicians into the standard medical corpus.

The only Strasbourg physician who worked directly from Greek texts was Johann Guinther von Andernach. His Latin translation of Paul of Aegina, which appeared in Paris in 1532, was recognized as the best translation of the period, far superior to that of Albanus Torinus, published in the same year.[24] The most important Greek text, Dioscorides's *De materia medica,* was made available through the translation of French physician Jean Ruel, whom Andernach may have known in Paris.[25]

The doctors of medicine had opened the debate on the merits of the Greek and Arab sources, but they could not carry their search back to the classical Greek physicians. Lacking the necessary language skills, the Grecophiles were content to discover Galen through Paul of Aegina or Dioscorides through Giorgio Valla. The fundamental exploration of original Greek texts, in this case botanical texts, was accomplished by the humanist-scholar-teacher-reformer Otto Brunfels. Brunfels was accepted neither in the scholarly, the scientific, nor the religious community, though he was well educated and an accomplished linguist. He was also a scientist, though the source of his training is uncertain. He had been a member of the Carthusian community in the city, and the Carthusians may have had particular interest in natural history.[26] During his years in the monastery, however, Brunfels was more involved with humanist studies and his conversion to Lutheranism than with natural philosophy.[27] In 1521, Brunfels and his close friend, Michael Herr, were kidnapped from the convent by some of Hutten's soldiers.[28] Johann Schott, the printer, housed them, provided them with secular clothing, and protected them. Herr was forced to return to the convent, but Brunfels escaped and spent several years near Frankfurt under Hutten's protection. Here he was close to Johannes ab Indagine, a Lutheran pastor with deep interests in natural philosophy.[29] Brunfels at this point, however, was working on his biblical commentaries, rather than on scientific pursuits. In 1524 he returned to Strasbourg to teach in the school that the reformers were attempting to organize.[30]

Brunfels's relationship to Schott grew closer after the latter published his defense of Hutten. Both men were cited before the Rat,[31] an incident that could have had severe consequences for the printer. Schott, however, referred to Brunfels as his dearest friend.[32] Sometime after 1525, with constant encouragement from Schott, Brunfels began to work on the Greek sources with the aim of writing a new botany. Brunfels recognized the task could not be carried out by one man. Aldus Manutius of Venice, he pointed out, had started work on a botany, but the project had ended with his death. A botanical book required a variety of skills and knowledge. It needed the experience of apothecaries and herb gatherers, who knew the effects of different plants. Accurate drawings must be made by a skilled artist. The learning of a trained physician was essential.[33]

Schott drew together the working team: Brunfels, Michael Herr, Nikolaus Prügner, several apothecaries and herb gatherers, and the artist, Johann Weyditz. Herr had by then completed his formal training as a doctor at Basel.[34] He performed the functions of translator, medical consultant, and editor. Prügner, another monastic refugee, gathered botanical samples for Brunfels.[35] Heinrich von Eppendorf was a peripheral member of the group.[36] All these men were deeply committed to the Reform but were never accepted by the inner circle of reformers in the city. The group maintained some kind of continuity for at least eleven years, since their final volume did not come out until 1536, completed by Herr after Brunfels's death. Held together by the leadership of Schott and their personal loyalty, they were the first scientists in the city to work collectively.

Brunfels's knowledge of the ancient languages was crucial to the project. During the debate over the Greek and Arab sources, he had studied the newly published Greek texts available from Paris and Venice and was struck by the superiority of the work of Galen and Dioscorides. Convinced that medical practice should henceforth be based on their work, his botany was based on descriptions drawn from the original texts of all the ancient Greek and Roman authors. He applied techniques he used in working on ancient and biblical texts to these medical sources. For each plant he went back to the definitions of Hippocrates and Dioscorides, Galen and Pliny. These definitions were then examined in the light of the findings of contemporary scientists, such as Giovanni Mainardo of Ferrara, Leonhard Fuchs, Joachim Schyller, and Hieronymus Trager.[37]

The modern reader opening the Latin edition of Brunfels's *Herbarium vivae icones* recognizes that an invisible line has been crossed. The natural world is perceived in a new way.[38] Each plant is presented systematically, with comparable data provided for each specimen. The presentation is logical, clear, and ordered. In Brunfels's Latin edition each plant was first shown graphically, usually in a full-page illustration of the genus, followed by illustrations of the species and subspecies. Thus *Plantago major* was accompanied by *Plantago minor* and *Plantago rubea,* and the student could see the relationships between the different specimens.[39] While much credit must go to the illustrator, Johann Weyditz, for the clarity and precision of the woodcuts, the conceptualization of these presentations was certainly in part the responsibility of Brunfels himself, since he mentions the need to observe the plant over the entire season. His was a dynamic concept of nature. He saw the natural world as being in a state of change or flux. Each plant was presented developmentally.[40] In the illustration of plantain, on one stalk a small seed cap was shown, just emerging out of the leaves at the base. Another seed cap, more fully developed, but still hard and compressed, was represented on a longer stalk. On two shoots the seeds had matured and half of them had fallen off or blown away. The formation of the leaf was clear, showing the matting effect and the crispness of the central rib. The roots of all specimens were included as an integral part of the plant. The text gave the name of each plant in Greek, Latin, and German, and then gave a description of all components: leaf, flower, seeds, roots, and habits of growth. Major references to the species by Greek authors were summarized before Brunfels went on to describe the medical uses. In most cases Dioscorides' prescription was given first, followed by those of Aurelius, Pliny, and other Greek or Latin authors. The Arab writers and fifteenth-century Italian writers like Barbaro and Vergilio were also cited, as were, finally, the most recent physicians.[41]

One of the impressive elements in this Latin edition was the economy of presentation. There was no superfluous material. The clarity of the text was aided by Johann Schott's use of a clear, large, Roman type. An alphabetical index made the information easily available. Schott's technical skills of book design, Weyditz's ability as a draftsman, Brunfels's competence in research created a new model for the dissemination of systematic, classified, standardized scientific data.

Two years after the Latin edition was published, Schott printed Brunfels's German translation of the first volume. This project was later completed by Michael Herr, who, after the death of Brunfels, finished the German translation of the second volume as well as the third Latin volume.[42] The German version provides an important insight into the difference between a book prepared for the scholarly reader and books for the popular market. The 1532 German edition was still printed in folio size, with the illustrations of the same dimensions. By 1534 the volume was reduced to quarto format, which meant that the illustrations were reduced

Plantago Maior.

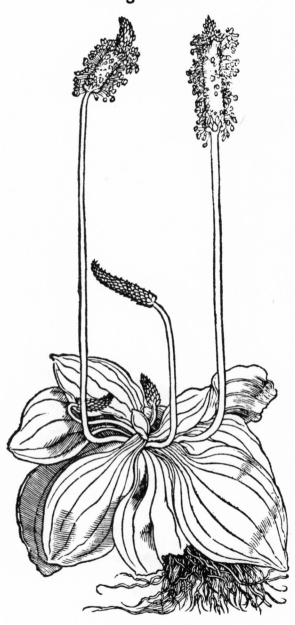

Breyter Wegrich.

Plate 10. Weyditz's illustration of the plantain with its
evolution from seed cap to maturity. From Otto
Brunfels, *Herbarum vivae icones,* vol. 1, fol. 23, Johann
Schott, 1530.

De N A R C I S S O, & Hermodactylo,
Rhapfodia Vicefima.

❡ N O M E N C L A T V R AE.

Græcæ, νάρκισσος. αὐτογινίς. βόλβος ὁ ἐμετικός. λίριον. ἄννδρος.
Latinæ, Narciſſus, Hermodactylus.
Germanicę, in Marcio, **Hornungs blům**. In Septembri, **Zeytlöſlin.**

P L A C I T A A V T O R V M de Narciſſo.

Hiftoria Narciſſi, fecundum D I O ⸗
S C O R I D E M, lib.ℛ.

N A R C I S S V S folia Porro fimillima habet, tenuia, multo mi⸗
nora, & anguſtiora:caulis uacuus, & fine folijs, fupra dodrantem attolli⸗

Plate 11. A full page from the Brunfels botany showing the illustration, the Greek
names, the Latin names, and the German names, as well as the beginning of the
Latin text. From Otto Brunfels, *Herbarum vivae icones*, vol. 1, fol. 129, Johann
Schott, 1530.

by at least half. Many were reduced even more and appeared as small cuts at
the top of paragraphs, instead of as full-page pictures. The book had
changed from a scientific treatise to a popular field guide. Brunfels greatly
simplified the text. The name of the plant was given with brief references to
the names used by Pliny and Dioscorides, but that was all that was given
from the classical sources. A description of the plant followed which included its season of growth, when it should be gathered, and its medical
uses. Aaron's beard, for example, was good for healing fractures or for a
reducing diet, since it caused loss of appetite.[43] Most strikingly, the logical,
clear style of the Latin text disappeared completely. The same quality of
information, the rational presentation, was not offered to the layman.

Michael Herr was dedicated to diffusing scientific information at a popular level. He was an indefatigable worker, translating Seneca and Plutarch as
well as scientific writers. His scientific treatises included a translation of
Simon Grynaeus's description of the New World and the agricultural treatise of Cassianus Bassus.[44] Having completed Brunfels's *Herbarium* after his
death, Herr attempted a companion volume on animals, in German. He
limited his study to animals native to Europe, which he himself had seen, or
to descriptions by Roman writers who had observed the animals brought
back to Rome from faraway lands. He was careful to explain that he had left
out many animals portrayed in previous books because of contradictory
accounts or ridiculous claims of miraculous powers.[45] The illustrations
were again drawn from life and the details were finely done. The cloven
hooves of the deer and boar were meticulously drawn; the boar's teeth, his
small tusks, the variations in his coat were clearly shown. The text, however, had none of the systematic quality of Brunfels's Latin botany. It was
informative, not scientific. It was assumed that the popular reader was not a
scholar and did not need the same quality of information. Books for the lay
market were simplified and made easy to read.

With the exception of Herr and a few writers of vernacular medical
treatises, such as Fries and Günther von Andernach, the university-trained
doctors of medicine confined themselves to serious, scholarly studies, written in Latin. A different group undertook the project of communicating the
medical knowledge of the time to a mass audience. Walther Ryff, a resident
of the city by 1532, was the most successful of these. Probably trained as an
apothecary, he received no formal medical education, but he made an enormous reputation publishing popular medical books for home use. He practiced as a physician in the city from 1532 to 1540 and was appointed city
physician.[46] In 1544 he was forced to leave because of a law suit for plagiarism. Three Strasbourg printers, Jacob Cammerlander, Balthasar Beck, and
Josias Rihel, used him as an in-house writer for medical handbooks.[47]
Heinrich Vogtherr, engraver, printer, and oculist, contributed anatomical

charts and treatises on the eye to the popular market. Jacob Scholl, an astrologer, was another popular medical writer. The work of this group was quite clearly differentiated from that of the university-trained doctors and scientists, and there were no established relationships between the two sets of men.

The popular medical manuals continued the tradition of bringing medical information "to the common man who cannot request a doctor's help or who, in time of need, cannot get to him" and of giving advice on the care of "headaches and croup among the poor folk."[48] Walter Ryff's books were widely distributed by Frankfurt as well as by Strasbourg presses. They went through edition after edition, indeed reeditions were still being printed by the Strasbourg presses in 1599. In all he compiled and published more than fifteen different medical books: some of these were pharmacopia and herbals; others were general medical texts or treatises on specific illnesses.[49] His largest selling books were his manuals for making laxatives and purgatives at home. There were seven editions in Strasbourg of his treatises on making these home remedies—a reflection, in part, of the diet of the period. In these manuals there was little emphasis on diagnosis; a two-line description of the disease was followed by a fairly lengthy recipe for the remedy.[50] His advice, at best, summarized the work of men like Gersdorff or Leonhard Fuchs; at worst, it passed along standard remedies from the medieval pharmacopia. He transmitted some of the medical knowledge of the academic community to popular levels.

Anatomical information was also broadly disseminated by popular treatises and anatomical charts. In 1530, Heinrich Seybold published Jacopo Berengario's important Latin anatomical treatise, first printed in Italy in 1522.[51] Berengario taught at Bologna and all his drawings, both of the skeleton and of the organs, were based on dissections. Seybold may actually have intended that his edition be used by the professional medical community. Whatever his intention, however, several popular anatomies were compiled and published within that same decade.

Heinrich Vogtherr, whose skills ranged from engraving to printing to optometry, published a series of tracts with elaborate titles, claiming to present "anatomies or reproductions of the entire body of a man." In fact they did not, but offered only very crude and highly generalized diagrams of particular organs. A rather elementary paragraph describing the action and function of the heart was probably plagiarized from Fuchs.[52] It was preceded by a small (1½ inches) drawing of the heart, which looked more like the heart on a modern valentine than the actual working organ. The stomach, liver, and kidney were hardly better,[53] though the treatise on the eye was more complete. The major drawing was a horizontal cross-section of the eye. This at least showed the cornea, the lens, the vitreal chamber, and the retina as separate chambers, but there was no attempt to render them in proper scale.[54]

A more complete anatomical treatise was compiled by Walter Ryff in 1541. Ryff was notorious for his plagiarism, but in this instance he showed acumen by copying from Vesalius. He presented his borrowed materials in an original form. The human body was presented in terms of its development over the lifespan of an individual. The book opened with diagrams of the fetus in the womb, which Ryff took from the Roesslin gynecological text. The next figures were a side view of the adult skeleton, a back view, and a drawing of the vascular system, all from Vesalius's *Tabulae sex*.[55] The organ charts were specially prepared for this edition, probably by Hans Baldung Grien. Two classical Renaissance figures (one male, the other female) were shown seated, the man holding his intestinal tract on his right arm to give the reader a clearer view of his lungs, diaphragm, liver, stomach, and kidneys. The female figure had no intestinal tract; only her female organs were shown. The organ plans were the work of someone who had observed a dissection. Each organ was well drawn and their placement in the body cavity was essentially correct. They were frequently reproduced in other anatomies during the course of the century or included in general medical texts.[56] The significance of these anatomical publications hardly needs to be underscored.

The publication of Vesalius's *Fabrica* in 1543 was a landmark in the development of medicine and science. The earlier charts and treatises indicate, however, that a fairly accurate knowledge of the human body was not restricted to the medical profession and allied practitioners. By 1541 it was quite possible for an ordinary family to own a medical book that included relatively accurate illustrations of the skeleton and the organs. Although knowledge of anatomy did not mean that a layman could cure himself of the plague or the French disease, it contributed to breaking down the barrier of ignorance about the human body and its functions. The secrets of nature were becoming a little less secret. The numerous editions of Ryff's work indicate that the laity wanted to know more, and that they were particularly curious about themselves. The popular medical books also reflect a concern with health and physical well-being which confirm the break with the other-worldliness of the past. The medical manuals assumed that good health and longevity were major human goals.

The third group of scientific writers were neither university-trained nor popular scientists, but technicians. Since many of the technological treatises were published anonymously, the printers were the most important element in disseminating technical knowledge. Christian Egenolff, educated at the university of Mainz, worked as a journeyman for Wolfgang Köpfel from 1524 to 1528. In the latter year he set up his own shop, devoting his press space almost exclusively to technical books. In 1530 he moved on to Frankfurt, where he continued with much the same repertoire.[57] His Strasbourg shop was purchased by Jacob Cammerlander, who maintained the production of technical books which Egenolff had begun. In 1525, Heinrich Vogtherr arrived in the city and worked as an engraver for various printers. In 1537, with the help of his son, he opened a printing shop and published his own *Kunstbüchlein* (a manual for engravers, goldsmiths, and other artisans), how-to books, and popular medical books. The books these men printed came from the guilds, the shops of artisans and workmen, the classrooms of the city *Rechenmeister*. They grew out of the pragmatic needs of daily life and reflected a popular interest in self-education and a desire to acquire new skills.

These technical manuals were the most important form of vernacular scientific publication. Strictly defined they are not scientific treatises, yet their publication reflected a new attitude toward the material world, a desire to use material things to make everyday life more comfortable and enjoyable. Quantitatively, they were significant. During the course of the century some eighty-five of these technical manuals were published, which may be compared with the total of ninety-five Catholic and Protestant devotionals over the same time span (1500–99) or with the total of forty-eight editions of the psalms set to music, another important vernacular genre. Of the eighty-five technical manuals, thirty percent were printed between 1528 and 1549, in part because of the particular efforts of Christian Egenolff, Jacob Cammerlander, and Heinrich Vogtherr.

The materials in these manuals were not necessarily new; several of them were medieval treatises that had circulated in manuscript form in the fifteenth century.[58] Thus, the ideas were not innovative. What was unusual was the dissemination of technological information at the artisanal level. Publication of formulae for metallurgy, techniques of tempering iron and steel, different methods of dyeing cloth, meant that the mysteries of the guilds were no longer sacrosanct. Men could acquire trade information without being members of a guild. The information in the manuals was based on the pragmatic observations of individual workmen. It rested on principles derived from experience rather than on a theoretical understanding of mechanical laws or forces. The technical manuals of the sixteenth century were how-to-do-it books; they were not a sign of the beginning of a technological revolution. For that, it would be necessary to go beyond empirical observation to conceptual formulations based on experiments with statics and mechanics.[59]

The manuals provide a fresh look at the daily life and activities of all levels of sixteenth-century society. They offered instruction in an astonishing variety of skills. There were hunting manuals for the nobleman, including specific treatises on hunting birds and on fishing.[60] The young nobleman could improve his skills with a fencing manual or he could learn to box,[61] while noble and burgher women could find new embroidery patterns for the numerous cushions that filled the living quarters of their houses.[62] There were accounting books for businessmen,[63] books on techniques for artisans,[64] surveying manuals for the estate manager,[65] books on making wine for the householder and the vintner, and books on how to store the wine once it was made.[66] One of the bestsellers of the period was a manual on how to make a sundial in your own backyard.[67] Among other things, the manuals help the modern reader to understand the extent to which men and women at every level of society used their own hands. They also show that craftsmen and artisans had sufficient education and technical mastery to write a book. They were able to write descriptively, analyzing their work procedures systematically and clearly. Men without formal education were just as quick to use books for their own purposes as the educated elite.

One of the most active fields was applied mathematics. The needs of business and commerce created a demand for mathematical instruction and the development of techniques applicable to the practical problems of commerce. Instruction of merchants was taken seriously in Strasbourg. Schools which taught the basic skills were fairly common, and there were special schools for instruction in French. Sons of businessmen were then sent as apprentices to Metz to perfect their French. Special apprenticeships in accounting gave the young men training in the art of bookkeeping.[68] In addition rechenmeister taught arithmetic, geometry, and accounting. In 1534 Georg Wälckl petitioned for and was granted the privilege of opening a school of accounting. In 1560 Georg Hohenlohe from Ingolstadt asked permission to establish himself in the city for the same purpose. In October of 1559, Matthias Seydenschuher asked the city to provide him with a house that could contain both his dwelling and his schoolroom; otherwise, his expenses would be too great. He emphasized that, despite financial pressures, he had continued to teach both older men and young boys.[69] Urban Wyss, who printed Johann Heckel's *Lauten-buch* in 1566, described himself on the title page as "Rechenmeister und burgher zu Strasbourg."[70] In 1580 Johann Schlenck appeared in the city records as a "master of accounting."[71] In 1586 one Georg Höflin, "Von Bregentz, Burger und Rechenmeister zu Strasbourg," published an account book for household and business use.[72] Thus at least six of these applied mathematicians were resident and teaching in the city in the period from 1530 to 1586.[73]

The rechenmeister taught techniques of bookkeeping and systems of business accounting. While they used geometry for problems of measurement, they also recognized the utility of algebra and were among the first to teach algebraic methods. They profited from the work of the cossists, academic mathematicians whose study of the Arab sources had led to the rediscovery of algebraic equations.[74] In 1525 the first edition of one of the most important cossist treatises was published in Strasbourg by Wolfgang Köpfel.[75] Written by Christoph Rudolph von Jauer, professor of mathematics at the university of Vienna, the treatise demonstrated the flexibility to be gained by using algebraic techniques, as well as making an important contribution to the development of standard mathematical symbols.[76] The signs now used for plus and minus had been utilized by another Viennese mathematician, Johann Widmann, as abbreviations. Rudolph, however, adopted them to denote the basic arithmetic functions of addition and subtraction and also developed the symbols for square root, cube root, and fourth root, which are still in universal use.[77] He also concerned himself with the pragmatic problems of the business community. Seeking to simplify the computation of compound interest, he developed decimal fractions. He did not, however, devise the decimal point but used a vertical bar to mark the separation of the fraction from the integer.[78]

Rudolph's work led to greater facility in calculation and to simpler and more efficient procedures. The modern reader must realize that, until this development of symbols and the technique known as "reckoning on the line," mathematical problems were presented verbally rather than numerically. This made it difficult to comprehend the problem as a whole or to visualize the logical steps of the solution. A modern scientist has stated that the development of symbols was necessary to proceed "from the inertness of traditional syllogistic schemata of Greek mathematics to the mobility of symbols and functions and mathematical relationships."[79] Significantly, it was the rechenmeister and the business community, not Rudolph's academic colleagues, who picked up his work. Academic mathematics remained Euclidean, while the needs of business and technology pushed practical mathematics forward.

While it is not possible to establish a direct relationship between Rudolph and the Strasbourg rechenmeister, Georg Wälckl, in 1536 the latter published a treatise which applied the principles of algebra to business problems and practices.[80] Wälckl did not use the plus and minus symbols as Rudolph had, but he taught reckoning on the line and trained his readers to use algebraic equations to solve everyday problems of exchange and profit and loss. He used the word "proportion" to describe an equation, stating that it involved two quantities or things that were equal and the same.[81] The definition provides a good example of the mathematical reasoning of the time. If the number of things on two sides of an equation was not equal, Wälckl continued, the result was an unequal proportion; but if the smaller number could be contained in the larger, a rational inequality was achieved.[82] The balance was arrived at by algebraic procedures.

The ordinary calculations performed by businessmen were demonstrated in the actual examples presented to the readers. Four pages involved simple matters of exchange: changing pounds into florins or Rhenish gulden, changing ducats into heller, and other exercises. These were followed by more complex questions, such as whether it would cost more to buy 34 pieces of cloth in Venice at 21 ducats, 14 groschen or to buy 36 pieces of cloth at 32 Bernese pounds.[83] After several pages of multiplication examples, Wälckl settled down to seven more pages of problems involving exchange, usually in reference to paying up accounts at the Frankfurt fair. An Altdorf businessman owing 400 hörnisch gülden and 6 stüber had to pay back the amount in Frankfurt in Rhenish gold. How much gold must he take?[84] The problems of exchanging silver for gold and of accounting in both metals were covered, but the heart of the text, twenty-two pages, was about the computation of profit and loss, usually profit. This section started out with the simple example of buying a cloth for 12 florins and selling it for 14 florins; it went on to an example, requiring far more complex operations, in which a merchant bought nails in Nuremberg and cloth in France, both to be sold in Strasbourg, while another bought wax in Nuremberg to take to Cologne.[85] Several pages were devoted to investment in a company, the buying and selling of shares, and the calculation of profits from such an investment. The problems bear witness to the skills required of the sixteenth-century businessman. He had to have a firm grasp of the intricacies of a variety of currencies, all denominations of these currencies, and the value of each unit. He also had to know the different standards of measurement used by every city for its cloth and the different weights used for other goods. Most computations involved both variables.

Ulrich Kern, a Freisen rechenmeister, addressed himself to the problems of variation in weights and measurements in an exceptionally clear text, published in Strasbourg in 1531.[86] In his preface Kern noted that he was a pupil of Christoph Rudolph von Jauer and promised to teach his art to the reader, who would then be able to perform the procedures by himself in all lands and places in the whole world.[87] The book explained the measurements used by different cities; the basic rules of measurement; the computation of the size of circles; the measurement of solids. In his solutions, Kern demonstrated the extraction of roots and the use of geometric progression. While he used Rudolph's symbols for roots, he did not use the plus and minus signs. His tables, diagrams, and mathematical demonstrations were not only clear, but elegant. A significant addition to the book was a section on surveying land accurately with a rod and a sight.[88]

The *Vocabularius latinis, gallicis et theutonicis* was yet another aid to the businessman, which proved to be useful enough to warrant four editions during the century, in 1521, 1535, 1575, and 1590.[89] It provided the basic vocabulary that a man might need in the course of his travels in Latin, French, and German: the days of the week, holidays, parts of the body and illnesses, food, ordinary utensils, as well as prayers and the Ten Commandments. These were followed by phrases for everyday use. "Have you been to Mass today?" was still printed in the 1535 edition. In 1575 it had been changed to "Have you been to the sermon?" In both cases the respondent answered affirmatively, but claimed that the service had been badly celebrated.[90]

Other than the *Vocabularius,* all but two of the technical books were published in German. The other exceptions, both in Latin,[91] were a handsome edition of Alberti's *De re aedificatoria* published in 1541 and, two years later, the first edition of Vitruvius's *De Architectura,* printed in Germany. In 1547 Walter Ryff made a German translation of the Vitruvius, which was published in 1547.[92] These books demonstrate the influence of Italian artistic styles and models after Italian literary influence had effectively disappeared among the city's intellectuals. Although Italian poets were no longer fashionable, classical models were adopted for the handsome wooden chairs, desks, and *casten* that reflected the wealth and comfort of upper and middle rank burgher families. Significantly, Renaissance motifs were used in furniture before they were adopted for the outside decoration of houses.[93] The classical models to be followed in making furniture were described in the guild ordinances of the *schreiner,* or cabinet makers. In the guild ordinances of 1571, the master cabinet makers required that every guild member presenting a masterpiece must make a large chest incorporating the principles and proportions of the five classical orders. The ordinance established with great detail the decoration of the various parts of the chest, which had to include a Renaissance window (*Welch Fenster*) on one of the doors.[94] The Vitruvian influence is confirmed by the requirements for order, symmetry, and proportion established by the ordinance. The guild ordinance provides direct evidence of the dependence of artisans on printed books.[95]

Until these Latin treatises were published in the 1540s, artisans could refer to the model book compiled by the local printer-publisher Heinrich Vogtherr. His *Kunstbüchlein* included fifty-one engravings of the human body, studies of the head in full face and in profile, studies of hands, and pages of intricate armories and ornamental motifs.[96] These were to serve as models of the new Italian styles for goldsmiths, engravers, sculptors, cabinet makers and carpenters, but, as Lévy-Coblentz points out, they reflected the artistic barrenness of the first years after the Reform.[97] The human models lacked correct classical proportions or grace; the armories (hardly a classical form at best) were contorted and extravagant; and it was hard to recognize any Doric, Ionic, or Corinthian elements in the capitals of

Vogtherr's columns. Whatever its artistic merits, Vogtherr's book must have filled some of the needs of the artists and craftsmen to which it was addressed, since it was a bestseller of the period, going through six editions in twelve years. It continued to be reissued in different forms and under different titles, often with no attribution to Vogtherr, throughout the century.

Artisans and craftsmen recognized the usefulness of printed books for mastering the skills of their trades and keeping themselves informed of new techniques or styles. They provided a market large enough to permit the fairly high degree of specialization of printers like Egenolff and Vogtherr. They also sought out books that would appeal on a broad scale. Christian Egenolff initiated his technical publications in Strasbourg in 1529 with a treatise on gunpowder.[98] Written in 1420, the treatise had long circulated in manuscript form but was not printed until 1529, when a large, handsome edition was done in Augsburg by Heinrich Stainer. As the modern editor commented, the noblemen and city officials who had access to the manuscript in the fifteenth century did not wish to have it circulate among their enemies.[99] Egenolff's Strasbourg edition was somewhat shorter than Stainer's. It was reissued by his own heirs in Frankfurt in 1569 and 1589 and, indeed, was still reprinted as late as 1619. It was known as the definitive book on artillery and gunmaking and was liberally pirated by French, Italian, and English writers of the period.[100] While an attempt at theoretical discussion of the properties of gunpowder, fire, saltpeter, and various types of ammunition was made at the beginning, the treatise was essentially a series of instructions for making munitions. Special fireworks for pageants and spectacles were also included.

In 1530 Egenolff published an important edition of a metallurgical treatise called the *Probierbüchlein*.[101] This, again, was a compilation of instructions for mixing different metals, assaying, and other techniques, probably originally culled from manuscripts kept by individual artisans and first printed in Magdeburg in 1524. A good deal earlier a book on mining practices, entitled *Bergbuch,* had made its appearance. Egenolff combined the two: the basic techniques of mining were described first; instructions for melting and assaying followed.[102] Both treatises were important because they constituted the first printed works to deal with the technology of mining and metallurgy. They were used by Georg Agricola in writing his *De re metallica,* which appeared in Basel in 1556.[103]

Egenolff's text was crammed with information and included a thorough index at the back for easy reference. It provided a good introduction to metallurgical techniques, but no theoretical framework. Detailed instructions were given for the making of different types of touch needles, and their uses were outlined. A table of standard assay weights (in pounds) was also included.[104] Directions were given for building an assaying oven. There was a careful discussion of the proper materials to be used for each part, and diagrams were provided for each step: the foundation, the crucible, the muffle, with a cross-section of the finished whole.[105] This was followed by directions for placing the crucible in the oven and for regulating the intensity of the fire throughout the process.[106] Further information was provided on the properties of various ores, chemical compounds to use in the assay process, and means of recognizing the different elements as they appeared.[107] One section of the book was directed to mint-masters, with descriptions of a wide variety of techniques, including the separation of gold from silver or copper from gold, essential to the making of coins.[108] The section on mining was limited to the definition of terms used within the mine and a very brief description of the division of the different tasks among the workers.[109]

In contrast to the complicated and demanding instructions contained in the *Probierbüchlein,* a treatise on steel and iron, addressed to armourers, goldsmiths, brass founders, and stamp and seal cutters, was a mere thirteen pages long and contained only rather summary directions for achieving different tempers of metal.[110] The layout of the book was clear. A large type font was used and each set of instructions was set off from the next by a wide margin, making the page easy to read. In a short preface the author explained that his object was to share the alchemists' knowledge of the properties of metals with the metalsmiths.[111] Different techniques were described for working with cold or hot metals, and various recipes for tempering steel were given; for example, the steel could be placed in a water bath made from the leaves and root of ox-tongue plant.[112] A chemical compound of sal ammoniac (ammonium chloride) and salts was recommended to prepare steel for etching or engraving, and the technique of soldering was outlined.[113] There were no illustrations of equipment or tools, and the tone was less professional than it had been in other manuals. This was also true of two treatises on fabrication of dyes and techniques for preparing cloth for the dyeing process.[114] These differences in the style and presentation of the pamphlets indicate an awareness of the level of training and the demands placed on the worker in different trades. Another manual, published in 1518, included a set of tables for the use of money changers, and, at the end of the century, a unique twelve-page publication described all the coins minted in the Holy Roman Empire. In this latter broadsheet, both faces of each pattern thaler were illustrated and the inscription was given. A separate section depicted the coins that were illegal in the Empire; namely, Swedish, Danish, Polish, Swiss, Netherlandish, or the coins of any Italian city. Finally the valuations of all coins—Spanish, Italian, Portuguese, Roman, Papal, Hungarian, French, and English—were given in terms of

Strasbourg currency. Clearly, this was designed to be a useful manual for businessmen, merchants, and money changers.[115] In 1580, a detailed and highly professional text on land surveying, written for rechenmeisters as well as surveyors, appeared.[116]

Instructional manuals were not printed only for urban craftsmen and workers. In the very earliest decades there were several farmer's almanacs, as well as three editions of Peter de Crescentiis's medieval compilation on agriculture.[117] In the period 1529–46, the indefatigable Michael Herr translated the treatises of Columella and Cassianus Bassus into German, in the hope of making the techniques of these ancient agronomists available to the German peasant.[118] In his preface Herr set forth his purpose in making the translation.

> Poverty, is admired by the learned and they teach their particular arts only to the rich. No one, however, does anything to teach the artisans and craftsmen and they have to shoulder all the hard burdens of the earth. Yet what is the most honorable and useful art, the one from which all others are created? The blessed, honorable art of agriculture. Without it no man can live on earth. If a man has no food what are all the other arts? Nothing. If I say I do not need the work of the farmer, then the farmer can even more easily say 'I do not need the work of the clever orator, the rechenmeister, the singer, the geometer.' Every merchant, every noble, every handcraftsman who lives in the city is dependent on the farmer.[119]

The text of the book contained solid, practical advice, including long sections on orchards and the various techniques for fertilizing, enriching, and testing their soil; crops to plant in different types of soil; the use of reservoirs for rainwater; and, at the end, principles of veterinary medicine for common farm animals.[120] The Greek source from which Cassianus had drawn his information was included in each selection. By combining Apuleius, Diophanes, Tarantinus, Zoroaster, and such Roman sources as Quintilius and Florentinus, Cassianus made the work of the ancient agronomists available in a way that was useful to the German husbandman. Herr did not write the book for the noble landowner with a great estate, but for the working farmer, although it was probably bought by estate managers. It was popular enough to warrant five editions in twenty years.

In addition to these manuals and treatises aimed at the needs of particular tradesmen and workers, there were how-to books of a domestic nature, essentially cookbooks, books on making and preserving wine, and a very popular treatise on making sundials. In all there were seventeen of these handy household books printed between 1507 and 1599. The first of the cookbooks was published by Hupfuff in 1507 and went through two later editions.[121] It was well organized, with separate sections for meat dishes, fowl and game, and vegetables. There were numerous recipes for river crab, which indicate that the book was probably locally compiled since these were common in the marshy sections of the Rhine.[122] A considerable portion of the book was devoted to the needs of invalids, since a housewife had to be able to rise to the responsibilities of nursing.[123] Instructions for making various types of sundials—square, cylindrical, and mounted on a gold ring—were compiled by Georg Vogtherr and published by his brother Heinrich. By the end of the century they were reprinted without reference to the author.[124] At the very end of the century two books of embroidery patterns were printed with an introductory poem addressed to the skilled lady embroiderer.[125]

Investigation of the world of nature played a more important role in the intellectual life of the city after 1530, both in the Latin culture and in the lay culture. The number of men engaged in serious scientific pursuits increased, and the quality of their training was higher. In the early decades there had been only one university-trained doctor of medicine practicing and writing in the city; now there were three—or, counting Paracelsus, four. Instead of a handful of humanist-scholars undertaking translations of ancient scientific texts as a secondary interest, Otto Brunfels, Michael Herr, and the men around them spent at least seven years of concentrated effort on the new botany. For the first time a group of scientific men worked as a team, a model which would be followed later by Josiah Rihel during the production of Hieronymus Bock's botanical treatise.[126] The repertoires of the printers reflected the change as well. Johann Schott, Heinrich Seybold, Christian Egenolff, Jacob Cammerlander, and Balthasar Beck all devoted an important part of their press space to medical books and technical treatises. The study of mathematics and of medicine were established as part of the curriculum of the new Gymnasium.

The examination of the Greek sources, the controversy between the followers of Arab and Greek authorities, contributed to a change in attitude toward the sources. The ancient writers were still assumed to be correct. But which one was superior? This new element in the analysis would lead, in the long run, to a more critical consideration of the Greek and Roman writers. Furthermore, Brunfels, Fuchs, Paracelsus, and Herr added their own observations to the ancient descriptions. Gersdorff and Brunschwig had done this in the earlier decades, but they were surgeons. The later men were university graduates, and this change meant that eventually the universities would add to the knowledge of the past instead of simply conserving it.

Science remained, however, primarily descriptive, not theoretical or investigative. The quality of the descriptions, however, improved greatly in these decades. The rediscovery of the Greek sources of medicine resulted in better diagnostic models. Brunfels's botany heralded a new emphasis on accurate and painstaking observation. The achievement of Vesalius was based on the same technique. The discoveries of these trained scientists were made available to the broad spectrum of burgher society through the medium of illustrated books. These books took the place of a technical vocabulary, which had not yet developed.[127]

Study of the world of nature was accessible to all levels of society. In the early decades men were fascinated by the new voyages, but few could join in the explorations. Everyone could investigate the physical universe. Flowers, plants, animals, and fish could be discovered and identified by simple herb women as well as by trained botanists. Peasants could observe the stars. Technology and mathematical rules and techniques provided a sense of mastery of a given skill. People had begun to discover their physical and material environment with their own eyes. As Juan de Vives wrote in 1531, "truly to man was opened up his plane."[128]

CHAPTER NINE · CLASSICAL EDUCATION, 1538–1550

HE GROWTH OF LAY CULTURE IN THE 1520s and 1530s did not mean that the learned culture declined. Both flourished. The Magistrat, supported by the reformers, carried out the proposals of the earlier humanists by establishing a school system supported by public funds. In 1538 the Strasbourg Gymnasium was founded. It institutionalized the Latin culture, providing a center in the city for scholars and teachers, opening the world of ancient Rome to the sons of the patricians, upper class burghers, and master guildsmen. Mastery of Greek and Latin was no longer restricted to clerics, scholars, lawyers, and other professionals. For six to eight years during adolescence students drawn from the elite were immersed in the ancient languages. A separate academic culture began to take root, with its own set of values, a mixture of Christianity and Ciceronian Stoicism. The values of the late Roman republic were combined with the teachings of the Gospel to create a socially oriented, urbanized Christian ethic.

Late Italian Renaissance thought had juxtaposed two intrinsically contradictory sources, Stoicism and Augustinianism.[1] These same dissimilar traditions were now incorporated into the educational institutions established by the Northern humanists. The Stoic view was essentially rationalist. Man, because he had within him the divine spark, could comprehend the order of the universe and understand the will of God. Man could achieve perfection through his reason, since the mind would control the irrational elements of human nature.[2] Augustinianism reversed this order. Man was a creature of God, subject to Him. His reason was by no means powerful, nor was it able to fathom the will of God. The essence of Man's being was not his reason but his heart; his other attributes—his body, his intellect, and his emotions—had to be comprehended as part of a larger whole.[3]

The curriculum of the Strasbourg Gymnasium, developed by the classical humanist Johann Sturm, was Stoic in morality and method. Cicero was presented to the students as a model to emulate. His orations and the *De Officiis* furnished ethical norms. The power of reason was stressed. Reason could control mankind's disorderly instincts, bringing men closer to the Ideal.[4] By constant exercises in dialectic, the school trained the students to think clearly, to analyze, and to build a logical structure of thought.

The Augustinian influence in Strasbourg was more subtle; indeed, it tended to be overshadowed by the competing Christian doctrines of the reformers. In fact, however, these doctrines were based in Augustinian thought. The reformers believed that ultimate truth was essentially a mystery, not discernible to the human mind, which came from God as part of his gift of Grace. Man's self-knowledge came from the same source.[5] The religious objective of the school was to open this knowledge to each student, to initiate his search for grace. To Johann Sturm and his teachers there was no conflict between reason and grace; both, were ultimately, gifts of God. The two strands of thought, Hellenistic and Christian, were harmoniously intertwined.

The development of a strong school system was one of the early concerns of the reformers. In August, 1524, they petitioned the Magistrat to appoint and support pious, learned schoolmasters who would provide the youth of the city with a Christian knowledge of God and of the useful things of this world, thus benefiting the whole community.[6] The Magistrat was unable to move as swiftly as the reformers desired, and the reformers, following the example of Wimpheling and Brant, encouraged two scholarly men, Lucas Hackfurt and Otto Brunfels, to open private schools. In 1526 the Rat established a permanent school board, drawn from the very highest ranks of the Ratsherren. Three men were made responsible for school policy and administration, with the aid of a two-man visiting committee, drawn from the preachers and teachers.[7] Within that same year the various schools and classes and lectures in the city began to be supervised by these two committees, but relationships between the thirteen separate schools and classes were not clearly defined and, inevitably, there was duplication and rivalry. In late 1537 the school board and the visitors concluded that consolidation was essential, and by 1538 a plan to combine the Latin schools and the theological classes into one unit, called the Gymnasium, was accepted.[8] Johann Sturm, who had been called to Strasbourg the year before to teach rhetoric, was appointed rector.

The organization of the new school was complex. There were six classes, from VI to I, which provided a secondary education based on mastery of classical languages. Two preparatory classes were gradually incorporated, so that, in effect, the Gymnasium had eight classes. In addition, two Upper Classes provided the opportunity for advanced study in theology, Greek, Hebrew, mathematics, geography, law, and, eventually, medicine. The reformers gave the theology lectures in the Upper Classes, and lectures in the other subjects were given by men with university degrees. The purpose of the Upper Classes was to provide work at the university level for students who could not afford to go elsewhere or whose parents wished to keep them at home. In 1563, under a new charter granted by the emperor, the Upper Classes were transformed into a degree-granting institution, the Academy, which had the right to bestow the master's degree.[9]

When Sturm assumed the rectorship in 1538, he was faced by a faculty riven with the usual tensions and jealousies of academic life. Two of his teachers were disappointed at having been passed over for the rectorship. Peter Dasypodius, a distinguished teacher and lexicographer, had directed his own school most successfully and was hardly eager to work under a much younger man.[10] Johann Sapidus, who had also run his own school, was subject to numerous complaints from the families of students, who found him erratic and bristly. His ire was further provoked because in the reorganization a younger man, Simon Lithonius, whose Greek was better, had been promoted to a post above his own.[11] Jacob Bedrottus, an established Greek scholar, had devoted ten years of his life to the Strasbourg schools.[12] Thus there was a firmly established old guard who did not benefit from the change. Sturm's success in creating a united faculty from this base is both an indication of the quality of his leadership and of the degree of intellectual unity which characterized the Strasbourg reform movement in this decade. The teachers were united in dedicating themselves to the creation of a new Christian commonwealth. By 1545, Sturm had elevated Dasypodius and Bedrotus to the Upper Classes. The faculty of the Latin Classes, mostly younger men who themselves had graduated from the Gymnasium, had been trained and selected by Sturm, himself.[13]

The faculty of the Upper Classes included the reformers Capito, Hedio, and Bucer, who lectured on theology and the Bible. In addition, there were scholars from all over Europe, a good number of them religious refugees from France and Italy. The school gave them employment and a salary. Peter Vermigli, Jean Calvin, and a young Venetian named Fontanus taught theology; Michael Délius from France and Immanuel Trémellio from Ferrara taught Hebrew. The school also drew men like Paul Fagius from Swabia, Ludwig Bebio from Württemberg, Michael Toxites, a poet and humanist from the Tryol, and Justus Velsius, a professor of philosophy from Holland. The Upper Classes offered advanced work in mathematics, taught by Christian Herlin, a nephew of one of the ammeisters. Lectures on Justinian's *Institutes* were the responsibility of the city jurist, Wendelin Bittelbronn. The intellectual community was broadened by these new faculty members. The early humanists, the Linguists, had been predominantly from Alsace or the Rhineland region. By the middle of the century, the scholarly group had become international, drawing its members from as far away as Italy and Holland. As the school developed this became an established pattern. Local men taught the Latin Classes; internationally known scholars taught the Upper Classes. Altogether, some thirty-seven individuals held teaching posts at the Gymnasium between 1538 and 1550. Twenty of them, half of the total staff, published work in Strasbourg. Among the staff of the Upper Classes alone, the proportion of publishing scholars was even more impressive: sixteen of a total of twenty-two professors.[14] Far from being dependent on the work of other scholars, as the Linguistic humanists had been, the Classical humanists supplied texts and scholarly editions for other schools in France, Germany, and Switzerland.

The Gymnasium played an important role in the institutionalization of the Reform. It helped to insure the continuity of the movement by creating a close association between the clergy, the teachers, and the upper levels of burgher society. The burghers had always claimed that chapter and monastic schools pulled their sons away from home into clerical life. The aim of the Gymnasium was to educate and train the good citizen, to prepare the student for the secular world. Attendance at the school became a rite of passage for patrician sons and the sons of business and upper guild families. As adults, the former students supported both the school and the church.

This sixteenth-century educational institution was designed to educate the sons of the upper classes, particularly for the civil service and the law. Money from the chapter of Saint Wilhelm was set aside to support intellectually gifted but poor students called to the Protestant ministry but, with that exception, a classical education was the prerogative of wealth and standing. As time went on the Gymnasium became more rather than less exclusive. It was patronized increasingly by sons of the urban patriciate from Strasbourg and other cities, by the sons of intellectual families, and by young noblemen from all over Germany and as far away as England, Styria, and Poland.[15] The Classical humanists were not interested in mass education; the purpose of education was to train those who would lead. This elitism was generic to humanism. Erasmus had put it very bluntly that "the mind of him who pants after Christ should disagree first with the deeds of the crowd, then with their opinions."[16] With its emphasis on learning and speaking Latin, the Gymnasium made only more pointed the difference between those who were educated and those who were not.

In the earliest classes the emphasis of teaching was on grammar and still more grammar. In his instructions to the teacher of one of the elementary classes Sturm wrote that each student should be given a specific number of words to learn every day, but, so that the students would learn from each other, they should each have different words. Young Romans, he pointed out, were totally surrounded by the language from their cradles—everyone spoke Latin to them and they learned quickly. Since the students had neither parents, servants, friends, nor even magistrates who spoke Latin, this deficiency had to be compensated with the ingenuity of the teacher.[17]

Mastery of grammar was the first instructional goal of the school. Sturm believed this was closely connected to the acquisition of virtue, as he wrote to one of the teachers in the lower Latin classes:

> What you do, you do for the good of the state. I know that you would like to teach a more advanced class but now we need you as a fighter in the arena against the barbarous gladiators who destroy the party of Latin. But eventually the Latin language will spread and bear great fruit in public and judicial life, in the Magistracies and the Councils, in the churches, everywhere in the Christian Republic.[18]

The second goal was to train the student in rhetoric, which encompassed far more than the ability to speak well. Rhetoric, in the minds of the Classical humanists, was the noblest of the human arts, the attribute which distinguished men from animals. Through the gift of speech, men had learned to guide and control society. The original state of nature had been chaotic, without agriculture, family life, or laws. The useful arts had been established by an orator who had first introduced them, then persuaded men to use them.[19] The humanists of the sixteenth century believed that as rhetoric had been a civilizing instrument in the past, so it could solve the problems of conflicting interests, disorder, and endemic violence that now plagued the urban community.[20] The inchoate groups within the city walls—businessmen, artisans, craftsmen, nobles, lawyers—could be led to discover their common interests by rhetoric. It was vital to the tranquility of the city that the leadership be trained in the art.

In the Strasbourg Latin Classes training in oratory began in class III. In each succeeding class, additional time was spent on style, the rules of rhetoric, public disputations, and theatre (table 15).[21] The texts which Sturm prepared for classes III–I not only provided techniques and styles of oratory but gave the students insight into the political confrontations and bitter personal strife of an earlier period of urban crisis.

Their guide was Cicero. His *De Inventione* showed the students how to develop valid arguments and organize their ideas logically. The orator, Cicero taught, was the catalyst of the society. The all-encompassing knowledge of the philosopher by itself was useless. Through rhetorical skill, however, knowledge could be shared and thus become beneficial to others.[22] The orations provided lessons in civic responsibility but they did not always idealize Roman society. Cicero's critical *Phillipics against Antony* was a favorite text. In the second speech of this series Cicero attacked Antony for being drunk much of the time, for arriving at public ceremonies too drunk to stand up, for hauling his mistress around with him when on military duty, and for indulging in orgies with low companions. There were intimations of homosexuality and an account of Antony's shady finan-

Table 15. *Johann Sturm's Graded Curriculum for the Strasbourg Latin Classes, 1538*

Class	Class
VI. Reading 　Declensions and Conjugations 　Explication of selected texts 　Catechism V. Learning of Grammar 　Parts of Speech 　　Irregular Declensions and 　　　Conjugations 　Syntax 　Latin reading and explication 　Cicero's *Letters* 　*Bucolics* 　Catechism IV. Review of Grammar 　Comparison of verbs 　Consideration of verbs and 　　nouns 　Rare forms and variants to 　　grammatical rules 　Conjugation of words and 　　sentences 　Preparation of brief proof 　Scanning the rhythm of poetry 　General and perpetual rules of 　　versification 　Reading and explication 　Cicero 　Virgil's *Aeneid* 　The Gospel of Matthew	III. General Review of Latin Grammar 　Introduction to 　　Cicero's *Orations* 　　*Georgics* 　　Caesar 　Classification of formulae of 　　recapitulation 　Styles of free and concise 　　discourse 　Metaphors and figures of speech 　　in Rhetoric and Dialectic 　Greek Grammar 　Reading of selections from 　　Aesop's fables in Greek 　The Book of Acts II. Review of Greek Grammar and 　　rules of order and arrangement 　Analysis and explication 　　Demosthenes 　　Cicero or Sallust 　Principles of Dialectic commonly 　　ascribed to Aristotle 　Principles of Rhetoric primarily 　　drawn from Herennius and 　　Hermogenes 　Style 　Practice in disputation (debating) 　　and extemporaneous speech 　Gospel of John I. Review of Dialectic and Rhetoric 　Cicero 　　On Oratory, Demosthenes, 　　　Homer 　　On Categories 　Style 　Practice in Disputation 　The Epistles of Paul

Source: AST, 324, Mémoire de Johann Sturm sur l'organisation de Gymnase, February, 1538.

cial deals.[23] The anti-hero, of course, made Cicero's virtue more compelling.

Moral lessons may have been taught by confronting the student with choices. The advanced classes were given Plato's defense of Socrates and the speeches of Aeschines and Demosthenes after the ill-fated second embassy to Philip of Macedon.[24] The student could be faced with the task of defining justice and virtue. How would he have cast his vote at Socrates' trial? Which of the two men sent to treat with Philip was right? In the court the patriotism of the two men, their loyalty to Athens, was never questioned. Each student could decide which of the two men had pursued the right course of action.

The stage was another vital part of life of the school. Cicero's orations were not permitted to become merely classroom texts—read but not heard. Students from classes III–I declaimed them before the assembled school on Fridays. Plays gave the students another chance to use their Latin. Not only did acting provide an opportunity to speak Latin unselfconsciously, but, Sturm believed, the productions created a healthy spirit of competition among the classes.[25] The student began with Terence in the sixth and fifth classes; in the four advanced classes all the comedies of Plautus and Terence were presented in the spring semester. In the second class the students were assigned a comedy of Aristophanes and a tragedy by Euripides or Sophocles.[26] In the first class a play was presented every week during the school year, and each student appeared on the stage at least once a month.[27] In these years the performances were intramural. Their purpose was to give the students the opportunity to use their Latin as a spoken language; there was no idea of presenting the plays to the public. Not until 1557 did the students begin to petition the magistrates for permission to act before a larger audience,[28] a custom which would become increasingly important in later decades.

The years from 1538 to 1550 were a golden age for the school. There was close cooperation between Sturm and the reformers, and an exceptionally close relationship developed between Sturm and the faculty; even those who had been displeased at the time of his appointment became his supporters. The esprit de corps is reflected in the dedicated work of the faculty in preparing the classical texts, grammar books, and other materials needed by the school.

Sturm's own contribution was staggering. In these twelve years alone, he brought out three volumes of Cicero's letters, a commentary on the form and structure of Cicero's orations for the use of class III, a commentary on dialectical method, an edition of Aristotle's *Nicomachean Ethics,* three volumes of Cicero's orations, and a collection of Cicero that included the speeches to Herennius.[29] In addition, for the use of class I, he edited Plato's defense of Socrates, the *Crito* and the *Georgics;* for classes I and II, he prepared Cicero's philosophical books, the *De Officiis,* and the speeches of Aeschines and Demosthenes.[30] His editions of Cicero were reprinted sixty times in Strasbourg alone.[31] They were printed in Paris, Basel, Bern, Frankfurt, and London, as well.[32] His text on dialectics was widely adopted in other humanist schools in Germany and was printed in thirteen editions.[33] Valentin Erythraeus, a teacher at the school, later organized Sturm's material in simplified, tabular form, which went through five editions. These diagrams represented a new teaching method and became increasingly important at the end of the century.[34] Sturm's texts were not critical editions, but emphasized dialectic goals and purposes.[35] The poetry selected for the different classes in the school was arranged by Sturm in a popular six-volume anthology; individual volumes were reprinted a dozen times before the end of the century.[36]

The faculty assumed the responsibility for the materials needed in their own classes. Jakob Bedrotus published materials for instruction in Greek: first a Greek version of the *Odyssey* and the next year a Greek text of Aristotle's *Politics.*[37] Theophilus Gol wrote an elementary Greek grammar containing selections from Aesop that the student could begin to read immediately. This was used by the beginning Greek scholars and went through nine editions by 1597.[38] Valentin Erythraeus devised tables and diagrams of Cicero's orations for the students in the three most advanced Latin Classes.[39] Michael Toxites, working with Sturm, wrote commentaries on the Ciceronian orations assigned to the students.[40] Christian Herlin, the mathematics teacher, edited Euclid for his classes,[41] and the philosopher Velsius wrote a treatise extolling the virtues of mathematical knowledge.[42]

Peter Dasypodius had begun work well before 1538 on a Latin-German dictionary, an important tool if Latin were to be read in depth by students or by educated burghers. The first version (1535) supplied German meanings for Latin words.[43] By the next year the edition had grown to one thousand pages but was still limited to giving German translations of Latin words, although a short section at the end gave the Latin for the most familiar German words.[44] In 1537 a new edition included a full German-Latin section and a short Greek and Latin vocabulary.[45]

The theologians were less active in writing and preparing materials directly for the schools. The major biblical commentaries that they needed for their lectures had already been written in the twenties. Furthermore, much of their time was given to the delicate political negotiations that were then going on among the Protestant groups and between the Protestants, the emperor, and the princes. Bucer did prepare and publish a catechism specifically for the use of the school, providing a basic text for the religious instruction of the first two classes.[46] While serving as a teacher in the Upper Classes Calvin published his commentaries on Paul's letters to the Romans.[47] After Paul Fagius joined the faculty he brought out an annotated translation of an Aramaic version of the Pentateuch.[48] These latter books were not primarily for the use of the school, but they reflect the scholarly commitment of the faculty.

The establishment of the Gymnasium allowed Strasbourg to become a center for the publication of school texts, and the needs of the school changed the focus of humanist publication in the city. After 1538 at least two major printers were continuously involved in printing textbooks and editions of the classics for the schools. The early humanists had favored a broad spectrum of classical authors and stylistic forms, including satire: Plutarch, Ovid, Horace, Martial, Persius, Juvenal, Lucian, and Pliny were all published. With the establishment of the school the range was narrowed. Sturm's collection of poetry took the place of editions of the poets. Not until 1556 would there be new editions of Latin poets, first Virgil's *Bucolics,* then a new Horace in 1568, and a Martial in 1595. Ovid disappeared and the other satirists were no longer edited.[49] On the other hand, Greek texts in Latin translation were more readily available. One could now buy the poetry of Pythagoras and Phoclides, the speeches of Demosthenes, and the critical works of Prophyry. Fewer Latin authors and more Greek authors were published.[50]

How effectively was Sturm's educational ideal realized? Within the school he created a unique harmony and a dedication to learning. The students spoke, wrote, and declaimed in Latin and were immersed in the culture of the ancient world. But how this affected their later lives we cannot know. The Ratsprotokolle rarely recorded individual speeches of members of the Council. Thus we have no way of knowing whether Sturm's careful training made his students into persuasive statesmen. Schindling believes, however, that there was little direct effect on the political institutions of the city. Rhetoric remained a school subject, something one had learned in the past but did not apply directly to everyday life.[51]

Schindling points to the fact that Sturm's Ciceronian curriculum was not widely accepted by other cities and was quickly forgotten even in Strasbourg itself. The training in eloquence could not compete with the Aristotelian program advocated by Melanchthon; it lacked the rigor and the method essential to the professional faculties: law, medicine, and theology.[52] The continued publication of the Ciceronian texts, however, somewhat discounts Schindling's argument. Clearly Cicero still served as a model, athough more among school students than at the university level.

The school's most important effect was social. Humanist education led to a new relationship of equality among the patricians, the clergy, and the scholars.[53] The upper levels of the urban community, by learning Latin, broke down one of the barriers which had always separated them from the hierarchy of the Roman church. The Gymnasium and the Academy became training grounds for those who would hold office. At the same time the clergy and the faculty were integrated into the civil service and the urban social community. They became a loyal intellectual elite serving the political elite. The ancient polarization between the secular and ecclesiastical authorities was thus destroyed. The learned, whether clergy or faculty, were firmly tied to the upper social strata of the city, and conflicts among these groups were neutralized.[54] Neither the patricians nor the learned were brought any closer to the lower strata, particularly the artisans and craftsman, by the school.

The upper classes, for their part, were now better educated than ever before. The humanist schools created a common experience for young aristocrats and the sons of patricians and wealthy merchants. In France, Germany, and Italy, the young men from these groups shared the same core of knowledge and training in rhetoric and dialectic. They might go on to Italian or French universities. They could enter the civil service in other cities or regions. They had joined a European cultural system that crossed national borders but not class lines.

The establishment of humanist education helped to increase the distance between the culture of the educated and the vernacular culture at a time when this could have been bridged by the printing press. Since proficiency in Latin and Greek would remain the essential characteristic of the educated person, the ordinary citizen, however literate, could never aspire to true learning. He was left to make his own observations and to communicate them in the vernacular language. Whatever the ideal of the rhetor, the humanist reforms of the educational system strengthened rather than weakened class divisions.

PART IV
LAY ASCENDANCE
1549–1570

THE POLITICAL AND RELIGIOUS SETTING

Despite the defeat suffered in the Schmalkaldic War, the Interim, and the exodus of the aristocracy, the Magistrat retained its dominant position over the church, the schools, and the moral and religious life of the citizens and inhabitants of Strasbourg after 1549. Beginning with the synod of 1533, conflict between the Protestant clergy and the magistrates had been a constant of political life, with the clergy struggling to acquire a greater degree of independence and control within the church.[1] They fought to establish their right to maintain purity of doctrine by excommunicating dissenting clerics. The Magistrat regarded this proposal as a return to papism and a usurpation of their own newly established authority over the clergy.[2]

The church was shaken by the war, the Protestant collapse, and the settlement which permitted Catholic services in three city parishes. Bucer's vigorous denunciation of the settlement and his attempt to arouse the citizens to armed resistance forced him into exile. With Capito and Zell both dead, leadership of the church passed into the hands of younger men, educated at Wittenberg and single-minded in their Lutheran orthodoxy. They regarded the three Catholic services as a major threat. From just such a foothold the Catholics could once again reach out, proselytize, and overthrow the reformed church. Responding to this danger, they concentrated their efforts on ridding the city of the Catholic menace.[3]

The Magistrat was more pragmatic. However the citizens might dislike the settlement, they pointed out, it was better to permit Catholic services in the three churches, as the treaty with the bishop required, than to create further friction. There were enough churches in the city for all.[4] The clergy merely bemoaned the Catholic presence. The Rat took positive diplomatic steps to preserve the autonomy of the city and forestall further Catholic influence. From 1549 to 1570, there was little doubt that leadership, both in ecclesiastical and political affairs, was firmly in the hands of the secular authorities.

The church was further weakened by internal strife. Johann Marbach, strongly Lutheran, was appointed superintendent of the assembly of the clergy in 1552, the highest position in the local church. The original XVI Articles of Strasbourg were, to him, an anomaly from the past which separated the city from the rest of Protestant community. He believed it was essential for the Strasbourg church to formally abandon the XVI Articles and accept the Confession of Augsburg as its only Confession of Faith, fulfilling the pledge made at the Wittenberg Concord. Marbach was opposed by the faculty of the Upper Classes. The professors of theology not only trained the future clergy, both for the city and the region, but also held benefices in the chapters and were members of the Kirchenkonvent. Many of them were Italian, French, and Spanish refugees, often rather heterodox in theology, who had experienced their conversions in isolation. The issue was drawn as early as 1553, when the Italian Peter Vermigli returned from exile in England. The Strasbourg school board immediately reappointed him to his old position on the theological faculty. To Marbach he was a dangerous radical, holding unacceptable views on the Eucharist. Marbach was not yet strong enough to oppose the school board and Johann Sturm as well, but the other Lutheran clergy joined him in a campaign of harassment which forced Vermigli to leave the city permanently. In 1562 the struggle was renewed when Marbach accused Hieronymus Zanchi, another Italian, of teaching doctrines antithetical to Luther. Johann Sturm rose to defend Zanchi. The faculty split. In 1563 Zanchi, too, was forced to leave. Led by Marbach, the assembly of the clergy voted that from henceforth all faculty at the Gymnasium and the Academy would be required to affirm publicly the Confession of Augsburg.

Riven by factionalism, the clergy and the school faculty were not in a position to assert leadership in the community. The dispute between Sturm and Marbach lasted for nearly twenty years, each side indulging in the bitter back-biting characteristic of the learned men of the sixteenth century. There was a temporary vacuum of scholarly activity, a vacuum quickly filled by lay writing and publication.

CHAPTER TEN · VERNACULAR LITERATURE AND POPULAR SCIENCE

OR TWENTY-ONE YEARS, FROM 1549 TO 1570, vernacular publication exceeded Latin publication (figure I, table 16). The Latin culture was quiescent, drawing on work published in the past, producing little that was new. The vernacular culture, in contrast, was lively. New literary forms were developed. New lay writers appeared. More presses printed the work of vernacular writers.

The clergy were particularly inactive in this period. During the twenty-one years only nineteen doctrinal works were published, ten the work of Strasbourg theologians (table 16). In this period of crisis the Magistrat was particularly careful to prevent publication of polemic against the Interim, the emperor, or the Roman Catholic church. Major statements by the Protestant preachers were contained in remonstrances which never went further than the council chambers of the Senate and the XXI.[1] Unlike the attacks of the twenties, these protests were never printed. Church publication was limited to safe items: catechisms, prayer books, and reprintings of the Strasbourg hymnal. Vernacular religious works were popular. Fifty editions of popular spiritual songs and eleven editions of the psalms set to music were published.

The faculty of the Gymnasium and the new Academy, always on the defensive, were unable to pursue their scholarly interests with their previous intensity. A small group continued to edit classical texts for their classes,[2] Sturm prepared new manuals for the rhetoric classes,[3] and Jonas Bitner compiled two new grammars,[4] but the majority of school texts and editions of the classics which came off the Rihel and Mylius presses were reprintings of earlier Sturm editions, many of them destined for schools in other cities. It was a period of stability rather than growth for the Latin culture (figures X and XX).

Vernacular literature increased noticeably, particularly after 1554 (figure VIII). An average of eight vernacular editions appeared every year, as compared with four school texts and five Protestant books in Latin and German. While the large-scale printers continued to publish Latin books, medium-scale printers, in particular Jacob Frölich, Theobald Berger, and Georg and

Table 16. Number of Book Editions, by Language, in Selected Subclasses, 1549–1570

Book Editions	German	Latin	English or French
Protestant			
Doctrine of the Eucharist	4	5	1
Catechisms	8	1	0
Doctrine by Strasbourg theologians	5	5	0
Devotionals and prayerbooks	7	1	0
Hymn books	4	0	0
Popular spiritual songs	50	0	0
Biblical			
New Testament	1	0	0
Psalms set to music	11	2	0
Humanism			
German and Swiss humanists	0	15	0
Alsatian humanists	0	7	0
Histories in Latin	0	24	0
Classics			
Cicero	0	48	0
Greek classics	4	16	0
Drama	0	8	0
School Texts			
Oratorical texts	0	43	
Grammars	0	6	
Latin plays	0	5	
Vernacular Literature			
Medieval tales	20		
Moral treatises	5		
Burgher novels or stories	22		
Popular songs	25		
Instrumental music	5		
Biblical plays in German	22		
Histories	28		
Popular journalism	38		
Accounts of recent events	19		

(*continued*)

Table 16. *Continued*

Book Editions	German	Latin	English or French
Science			
Medicine	12	21	
Botany	10	5	
Geometry	0	9	
Natural history (Aristotle)	0	4	
Agronomy	4	1	
Alchemy	0	5	
Total	300	236	1

Paul Messerschmidt, specialized in vernacular novels, plays, sheet music, and journalism.

The lay writers who filled the vacuum left by the clergy and the scholars were unique to the period. They had no ties to the established intellectual institutions. They were not university educated. Most of them could not write in Latin. They were townsmen, not from the city itself but from the small market towns around Strasbourg, where they held lower civil service posts. These townsmen had a vision of the good life that was little influenced by humanism, drawn from their own reading of the Bible and their fundamental belief in a corporate unity which might find expression either in the town, the city, or the family. Aware of the mutability of political relationships, they reaffirmed the stability of the family—the foundation of society—and of family life. Each man and woman should live as a Christ to his neighbor and should create within his or her own family a haven of peace, love, and concord. Strong families would bring peace, order, and discipline to the rest of society.

Georg Wickram was the central figure in the development of a popular literature that addressed itself to the interests of the ordinary citizen. Wickram came from the middle level of urban life, markedly below the patrician or intellectual elite in which such men as Sebastian Brant had moved. He was of illegitimate birth, the son of a wealthy burgher of Colmar whose family tended to go into the learned professions—law, the church, teaching.[5] Georg's illegitimacy was a barrier between himself and his father and, while the father eventually made the boy his heir, Georg was not given an education. Instead, he was apprenticed early to a goldsmith and then, rather unexpectedly, was appointed bailiff to the Magistrat at Colmar.[6] This civil service post gave him the income that made it possible for him to write. It also put him in contact with publishers. The Colmar Magistrat maintained its own press as a municipal enterprise, and Wickram was sent to other cities, such as Speyer and Frankfurt, to deal with publishers there.[7]

Georg Wickram's development as a writer illustrates the changing literary tastes and concerns of the period. His first novel, *Der Ritter Galmy,* was published in Strasbourg in 1539. Like much of the traditional popular literature then being printed—the *Gesta Romanorum,* a tale of the emperor Octavius, or *Griselda*[8]—Wickram's novel is one more account of an ideal knight who rides to the defense of innocent women. The heroine, a countess, is suspected of adultery and condemned to death. Galmy, after a long journey, arrives at court, engages the slanderer in combat, and saves the innocent countess.[9] Wickram published another story of court life, *Gabriotto,* around 1551.[10] At the same time he was writing plays for the Colmar theatre, often on such biblical themes as the prodigal son or Tobias. In 1555, disappointed by his failure to achieve recognition, he broke away from Colmar and became municipal secretary to the town of Burkheim. In that same year he published *Der Jungen Knaben Spiegel,* which is regarded as one of the first German novels. The book reflects a new concern with the family and explores the relationships between parents and children. It also provides insights into prevailing attitudes toward education, the value of nobility, work, and leisure.

The main characters of the novel are traditionally aristocratic. The story involves a good and faithful knight, Gottlieb, who had given loyal service to his lord for fifty years but had never married. His lord rewarded him by providing a beautiful, pious, young bride named Concordia, the widow of another vassal. The marriage was happy, but after three years there was no child. A sturdy farmer lived on their lands who, with his wife, already had a large family, and yet another child was about to be born. The wife was asked to live in the knight's house with the baby. She and the baby, Fridbert, were given excellent care and Gottlieb provided land for the couple so that they would be able to bring up their other children in comfort. There was no attempt to adopt Fridbert or to break the family tie between him and his parents, but he remained in the knight's home to be brought up by Gottlieb and Concordia. Shortly thereafter Concordia bore a son. The novel plays on the contrast between the virtuous Fridbert, the product of common stock, and the dissolute brother, Willibald, the nobleman. The traditional knightly setting is retained, but the point of the story is the superiority of the foster son, a commoner.

When Fridbert was seven and Willibald six, Gottlieb and Concordia planned their education. It was decided to send them to school with the extra assistance of a tutor, "so that the children would be drawn towards learning happily and pleasantly rather than by force."[11] Fridbert threw himself into his lessons with such enthusiasm that both his schoolmaster and his tutor marveled. The tutor, to provide some diversion, took his two charges out into the fields and woods. Fridbert, reflecting the contemporary interest in science, was delighted by the beauties of nature. He examined and studied the flowers and plants and asked their Latin names. As soon as his tutor gave him the information, he wrote it on his slate or drew a picture of the plant.[12] Willibald was the opposite of his precocious foster brother. He sought out undisciplined companions instead of studying and ignored his tutor's attempts to correct him.

The story continues with the downward descent of Willibald. He drank and gambled. Finally, he struck his tutor with a knife in a tavern brawl, stole money from the father of a friend, and went off to Breslau. Fridbert, of course, went on with his education, became a well-respected lawyer and, eventually, while traveling on business, found his foster brother playing the lute for money in a tavern. He assumed responsibility for him and found him a position with a local noble and a rich young bride. Eventually he brought Willibald back to his old mother and father, and all was well. Both brothers married happily and were blessed with adequate wealth.

The contrast between these characters and the fools and cheaters depicted by Murner or Brant is dramatic. In place of the deceitful miller's wife Wickram presented Gottlieb and Concordia, who live together with joy and deep affection.[13] They share all parts of their lives and make their decisions together. For example, when the boys are old enough to go to school, Gottlieb "discussed it all in a friendly way with his wife so they decided together to carry it out."[14] Later, Fridbert holds the family together, comforting Gottlieb and Concordia when Willibald is lost. When the latter is found, Fridbert recognizes his responsiblity to help his brother. At the end of the book, Willibald's reformation is rewarded by happy, family life: "He became one of the most respected men in all of Prussia and his wife bore him many wonderful children, sons and daughters. . . . Fridbert lived honorably with [his wife] and children and acted in a brotherly manner toward Willibald, and their children were very friendly, as if they were blood relations."[15]

The value of a happy familial relationship was consciously put forward, perhaps idealized, by Wickram, to whom it had been denied, just as the illegitimate Alberti had praised a family cohesion he had lacked.[16] Education is a matter of great importance to both parents and children, essential to achieving a proper station in life. Work is a virtue. When Willibald turns from his dissolute life, the change is manifested in work. "He is a young, indefatigable boy," the chancellor of Prussia reports. "I have watched him perform his duties for three years now and have full confidence in him."[17] Eventually Willibald is able to take his father's place, as is proper. Willibald is shown to be careful with his own children, never permitting them to be idle, teaching them to work according to their God-given talents. The daughters learn from their mother to spin, sew, embroider, knit, and weave. To lift their spirits and fatigue with song, they learn to play the harp, the clavichord, and other musical instruments. The boys are sent to school to receive a thorough education.[18] Work would protect against the idleness which had led to the dissolute life and the sad wasting of Willibald's early years. The focus of Wickram's novel is the strength of the family. Willibald's disobedience to his parents, his running away, are redeemed by his return and their forgiveness. The future is assured in the happy families established by both Fridbert and Willibald.

Wickram's novel, *Von Güten und Bösen Nachbaurn,* published by Knobloch in 1556, develops the theme of friendship along with the theme of family life. The concept of loyalty, so important to the noble ethic, was now applied to relationships within the merchant class. There are no noblemen in the book. The heroes are businessmen, a merchant from Antwerp and his son-in-law. As in *Der Jungen Knaben Spiegel,* it takes more than one generation to develop the moral. Robert, a wealthy Antwerp merchant, had bad neighbors on one side of his house. The neighbor, a clothdresser, was rash and violent. His son was a troublemaker who stirred up divisions among his father's apprentices and pitted Robert's sons against each other.[19] All Robert's children, except his youngest daughter, died in a plague epidemic and Robert was weighed down by sorrow. He was consoled by the good neighbor on the other side of his house, who reminded him that God gives and God takes away.[20] Accepting his loss, Robert dedicated himself to the duties and obligations of friendship.

On a sea journey a young Spanish merchant, Richard, fell ill. Taken off the ship, he was cared for in the home of an older merchant, a friend of Robert. Robert, without knowing Richard's family, but out of respect and love for his friend, Richard's host, gave the young Spaniard his only remaining child, his daughter, in marriage.[21] Richard made friends with a young Antwerp merchant, Lazarus, and the two shared many adventures as they traveled together on business. While they were acting as good samaritans to a merchant set upon by robbers, they were ambushed. Lazarus was captured and sold to pirates, then rescued by Richard. At home Cassandra, Lazarus's wife, took care of Richard's wife in childbirth.[22] Later Cassandra also bears a child, and the end of the novel describes the love of the children for one another and their eventual marriage.

Wickram was concerned not only with the family but with the spiritual development of his characters through friendship. Luther in his *Freedom of a Christian* had defined a Christian as a man who was as a Christ to his fellowmen. Wickram, in *Von Güten und Bösen Nachbaurn,* spelled this out in everyday terms. The virtues he encouraged were human and social—concern for the sick and the stranger, gratitude, obedience, trust, obligation, acceptance of total responsibility for the burdens and needs of a friend.

Not only did Wickram express values directly applicable to the realities of lay life, but the travels and adventures which had always been associated with knightly prowess were now made a part of urban, middle-class life. Robert, the merchant, traveled to Lisbon. Richard and Lazarus, the young heroes, traveled to Spain. Lazarus was sold to Turkish pirates; one of Lazarus's servants could speak Turkish, which came in handy for the rescue. In the knightly tale the hero won through his individual boldness and gallantry. In *Von Güten und Bösen Nachbaurn* the goals are achieved by cooperation. Robert trusts his friend and gives his daughter to Richard. Richard and Lazarus work together. Richard's wife takes care of Lazarus's wife. The communal elements of the burgher ethic were thus explicitly affirmed.

Wickram wrote other novels, *Die Siben Hauptlaster, Der Irr Reitend Pilger,* and *Der Goldfaden,*[23] all published in Strasbourg in the decade of the 1550s. Their quick succession indicates that a ready market existed. The virtues commended in the earlier novels were confirmed. *Der Irr Reitend Pilger* is set in a simple peasant household where harmony, love, and obedience govern all familial relationships. In this novel Wickram develops the themes of the close relationship of father and son, the obedience of the son to the father, and the responsibility of father for the son.[24] Wickram's stories and novels, even his collections of fables and tales,[25] marked a new attitude toward burgher life. He saw merchants and tradesmen as having their own way of life, which no longer had to be considered inferior to aristocratic life.[26] The urban classes did not have to look to the court or the nobility for their heroes; they could create their own. Family relationships, a deep understanding between husband and wife, and responsibility toward children took the place of the romantic love of the chivalric tales.

Another aspect of urban culture was the development of a strong and flourishing popular theater in Strasbourg, Colmar, Marmoutier, and other Alsatian towns. These grew out of the long tradition of the medieval moralities, the Mardi Gras plays of the Middle Ages, but the sixteenth-century plays were very different in tone, subject matter, and structure.[27] The farcical elements of the Mardi Gras plays disappeared. Citizens now took to the stage to present three- to five-act plays, which were based on biblical themes or the moral questions of everyday life.

Before publishing his first novel in 1539, Georg Wickram had already published several plays. In 1540, Thiebold Gart put out a popular play based on the Joseph story.[28] Other popular plays by Matthias Holtzwart, Martin Montanus, and Jacob Frey were later published. It is impossible to determine whether these men were in touch with one another, but they had a remarkable number of things in common. They all came from the middle ranks of urban society. Wickram's illegitimacy deprived him of an education and placed him on a social level lower than that of his father.[29] Gart was the son of a Sélestat baker.[30] Three of the writers held minor civil service posts in their respective cities, Wickram as bailiff in Colmar, Holtzwart as town registrar in Zellenberg,[31] and Frey as town registrar in Marmoutier.[32] Gart eventually became the burgomaster of Sélestat.[33] Whether these posts provided them with time to write and a certain economic independence, or whether it was part of their official responsibility to provide pageants for city functions, all these men wrote plays which extolled the virtues of urban life, usually based on biblical themes.

Their work took a genuinely original direction. Independent of the church and the schools, they were concerned with the moral and ethical needs of ordinary men and women. The Protestant clergy, after 1530, no longer published sermons or treatises addressed to moral issues.[34] Lay writers were, however, eager to discuss problems of morality and good conduct. Instead of the Roman republic, the model of the Classical humanists, they turned to the Bible, particularly the Old Testament. In this they were undoubtedly influenced by the Reformation. The Bible, with its realistic stories of family life, fraternal rivalry, and divided loyalties, was far closer to the lives of the populace than were the philosophical speculations of Cicero or Plato. In this period of political and institutional crisis the family offered a viable focus for life.

It seems that the plays were an integral part of urban life, bringing men together in a common endeavor. The casts could include from ten to thirty-six or fifty people. The plays were presented publicly, often taking more than one day to perform. Theater had always been an important element in urban popular culture. Traditionally, there had been miracle plays, plays for special church festivals such as Shrove Tuesday and Epiphany, and the so-called *Bettelkömodie,* or beggars' plays, given by poor students to fill their empty purses or stomachs. By 1500 the Strasbourg Magistrat was firmly suppressing the latter because they disapproved of the students asking for money. The Reformation brought an end to the traditional farces, and new plays had to be written for Shrove Tuesday and Christmas.

In the 1530s plays began to be published in Strasbourg which had been presented by local citizen actors. It is important to recognize that these performances antedated the establishment of the school theater and were independent of it. There has tended to be confusion on this point. Jundt wrote, for example, that the school theater became a town theater, that school performances in mid-century were aimed at the burgher audience and became increasingly popular.[35] Edith Weber, in her list of plays published in Strasbourg, does not discriminate between plays prepared for the school and plays written for the burgher theater, though both she and Crüger emphasize that the school plays were intramural in the early decades after the founding of the Gymnasium.[36] Evidence of magistral disapproval of anything approaching the *Bettelkömodie,* coupled with the stated purpose of the school plays—to provide an opportunity for the students to practice their Latin diction—shows that the plays were essentially an academic game.[37] They were presented outdoors, but to a limited audience; alumni were admitted only as a special privilege, perhaps because it was customary for them to loan their costumes.[38] It would seem, then, that only the students, faculty, parents, and perhaps a few friends witnessed the performances. Not until 1557 did the students ask for permission to present a play to the general public, thus inaugurating a more popular phase of the school theater.[39]

The burgher theater, on the other hand, was already established before the founding of the Gymnasium in 1538. The first biblical play, *Die Zehen Alter,* was published in Strasbourg in 1533, fully five years before the establishment of the Gymnasium. The statement "von newen gespilt" in Colmar in the subtitle indicates that it had already been presented.[40] From 1538 to 1574, our incomplete record shows at least one performance every four years in Strasbourg.[41] All the plays published in German before 1556 were, with one exception, written by lay authors. Georg Wickram, Jacob Frey, Thiebold Gart, Martin Montanus have already been identified as civil servants from nearby towns. Guilelmus Gnapheus, whose German version of the prodigal son was published in 1535, was the secretary of the city of Antwerp and the official Ratspoet.[42] Alexander Seitz, the author of a biblical play printed in 1540, was a doctor of medicine practicing in Marbach, later in Switzerland.[43] The only playwright in this period who seems not to have been a layman was Thomas Sunnentag, for whom biographical information is incomplete, but who may have been a Protestant pastor.[44]

From 1556 to 1570, the burgher theatre continued to function relatively autonomously. Most plays were written by lay authors, such as Jacob Frey and Jacob Ruof, a surgeon and prolific playwright from Zurich.[45] Two Lutheran pastors, Thomas Naogeorgus and Andreas Hoppenrod, and two school teachers, Sixtus Birck and Christian Walliser, also contributed plays during this period.[46] After 1570, however, schoolmasters took over the function of writing German plays for the popular audience. Christian Zyrl, for example, was the schoolmaster at Weissenburg;[47] Andreas Meyenbrunn was a Latin schoolmaster, probably at Colmar;[48] Cornelius Crocus was the rector of a school in Amsterdam;[49] Hieronymus Schütz taught in the Strasbourg Latin Classes.[50] Plays were now seen as an important element in the moral instruction of both actor and audience and were thus integrated into the school curriculum, although they continued to be presented by the adult community as well.[51] Significantly, the period when the burgher theater was at its height, from 1550 to 1570, was also characterized by the dominance of lay publication.

The burgher theater was based on a repertoire of biblical and moral plays, though a few had classical themes. Biblical plays emerged as an important literary genre. There were thirty-one editions of twenty-four biblical dramas published between 1533 and 1570.[52] This should be compared to the fourteen editions of the psalms set to music printed in the same period, the psalms being the other most popular biblical work. Plays were clearly of primary importance in familiarizing people with biblical stories and personages. The Old Testament was the favorite source. Twenty-one of the plays were based on Old Testament stories or characters. Seven of them had women heroines: Susanna, Judith, Jephtha's daughters, Esther, and Rebecca. The most popular figure, however, was Joseph. There were three editions of Gart's version of the Joseph story, two by Christian Zyrl, and one by Cornelius Crocus.[53] The favorite New Testament story was that of the prodigal son; three different versions were printed in Strasbourg. Wickram's adaptation of the story was printed in Colmar by Balthasar Grüninger.[54]

Theobald Gart's *Joseph* demonstrates the engagement of lay people with the central religious issues of the time. Probably a graduate of the Sélestat grammar school, Gart nevertheless broke away consciously from the classical dramatic form to create a realistic version of the Bible story.[55] In Gart's play, the Old Testament is presented as a prophecy of events to come in the New Testament, the symbolism made paramountly clear by the presence on the stage of Jesus, Peter, and Daniel, who point out connections for the audience. The drama is an affirmation of justification by faith and the salvation of mankind through the Eucharist. The play is based on passages from Genesis, and Gart found no need to embroider the biblical account. He added deeper characterizations and more obvious associations between the Joseph story with the life and experience of Jesus. Thus, when the brothers sell Joseph, Peter steps forward to remind the viewers that so, too, will Christ be sold. Reuben's discovery of the empty well prefigures the empty tomb. The incident with Potiphar's wife is done in a straightforward manner, her attempt to seduce Joseph and his rejection of her occurring on the stage.[56] In Cornelius Crocus's version, this is handled offstage to protect the morals of the young.[57]

The midsection of Gart's play, the imprisonment and the interpretation of the dreams, follow the details of the biblical text. With the famine in Canaan and the journey of the brothers to Egypt, the symbolism again becomes richer, the will of God and the necessity of sacrifice are emphasized. Joseph, through his servant Tachpenes, demands that Benjamin be brought to Egypt and Simon left behind as a hostage. These sacrifices must be made if the brothers are to receive food for their people; Benjamin is the embodiment of the sacrifice, and Jacob consents to Benjamin's departure through faith that it is God's will.[58] The action builds to a climax in a banquet scene where Joseph's cup is discovered in Benjamin's sack. Again, Joseph demands that Benjamin's freedom be sacrificed for the cup.[59] In the final act, Jacob arrives from Canaan, the sacks of Israel are filled with bread, and Christ steps forward to state that, as Israel is saved from starvation by bread, so all men are saved through his body, the bread of the Eucharist.[60]

Gart, a layman, felt no hestitation either in interpreting the biblical story or in tackling the problem of the meaning of the Eucharist. Far from feeling that this was a complex matter that had to be left to the clergy, he developed the concepts of the Covenant, the sacrifice of Christ, and the redemption of mankind through the Eucharist. The symbolism of the grain, the bread, and the cup was constantly kept before the audience. Laymen were not deterred by the lack of German biblical commentary to which they might refer. Luther's *Lectures on Genesis* were available in German after 1525, but these stressed the trials of Joseph and the forgiveness of sin.[61] Gart developed his own interpretation and, in particular, his own characterizations of Joseph, Jacob, and Reuben. The year after the publication of Gart's play, Köpfel brought out Antonius Corvinus's *Commentary on the Story of Joseph* in German. Two years later Balthasar Beck published Wenesclaus Link's *Commentary on the Pentateuch*.[62] Were these in response to popular demand?

The plays on the prodigal son were more contemporary in their emphasis. They were plays about current social ills, in which the moral was spelled out at frequent intervals during the play. Luke's synopsis of the parable of the prodigal son was so general that it permitted the writer to develop his own details of the sequence of events and the setting. The earliest sixteenth-century German version was translated by Georg Binder from Guilelmus Gnapheus's Latin text and presented in Zurich in 1535.[63] It was published in Strasbourg around 1560. Gnapheus's play is heavily laced with humanist allusions. In his hands the prodigal son, Acolastus, is a self-centered young man who goes off with his inheritance to live a fantasy of classical life. The major scene takes place during his love affair with a prostitute, in which Acolastus has a bed made up and strewn with herbs and flowers, as in antiquity. The girl is compared to Venus herself.[64] In a later scene the gamblers appeal to Bacchus and Ceres in their joy over their success at relieving their young friend of his wealth.[65] At the end, when the prodigal repents, his one friend appeals to Pollux rather than to Jesus or to God.

Acolastus does mention forgiveness, but accepts his father as governor and sovereign over him: "[Thou art] my defender, . . . my savior."[66] That is as close as Gnapheus gets to a Christian concept.

Georg Wickram developed very different themes in his version of the prodigal son, which was presented in Colmar in 1540 and printed there by Balthasar Grüninger in the same year.[67] Wickram has no interest in a classical setting; instead, he makes a strong attempt to connect the New Testament story with the Old Testament. The father is given the name Tobias. The son is called Absalom. All the father's friends bear Old Testament names. The story follows the biblical outline, except that Absalom's fall is caused not only by his own actions, but by his father's failure to bring him up strictly and to teach him God's commandments. Thus, both father and son bore the guilt.[68] Wickram avoids the seduction scene; instead, Absalom falls into gambling, drinking, and decadence with a group of clever rogues who devote themselves to fleecing this lamb who has appeared in their midst. The gambling scene is the longest part of the play. Absalom plunges from one card game to the next, then attempts to recoup his losses through dice.[69] Having lost his money, his clothes, his new friends, and his self-respect, he is forced to beg, finally, as in the biblical accounts, casting himself onto the charity of a cruel and heartless peasant. The return home is closely modeled on the New Testament; the son confesses his sin and the father forgives. In the epilogue the herald knits together a series of biblical passages that refer to the forgiveness of sins, including some from Isaiah, the psalmist David, and Paul's letters.[70] No man can avoid sin, but Christ's purpose is to free all men from the consequences of his sin. God is the father; mankind the prodigal son. Wickram related the story directly to his own society. The relationship between fathers and sons, the tensions within the family, the aspirations of the parents, the desire for freedom on the part of the young: all these were familiar to his audience. There was no need for complicated symbolism; God's redemption of the sins of mankind through Christ was well understood.

Another play by Georg Wickram, *Tobias,* gives some idea of the scale of the burgher dramatic productions. The enormous cast of eighty-eight, all with speaking parts, was obviously designed to include as many burghers as possible. Wickram accomplished this by writing several court scenes with all sorts of counselors, advisors, and marshals surrounding the king. Sennacherib is given ten retainers, although three would be sufficient. When he dies and his son Sisarah succeeds, a whole new group of retainers is introduced. The scenes involving Tobias, the father, are similarly enriched by countless neighbors, maids, and young manservants. The sheer number of actors must have provided a sense of movement and bustle. The play is not divided into acts or scenes; rather, the narrative unfolds as various people come and go on the stage. Originally the play was meant to take two days to perform, with a break between the first and second days.

The play follows the biblical account to the last detail and then Wickram adds some of his own. When Raphael and Tobias arrive at the Tigris at the end of their first day's journey, Tobias goes down to the river because his feet hurt from walking in the sand all day, while Raphael combs the river-bank for firewood.[71] These homely needs lead to catching the fish. At the end of the play, when Tobias returns with his young wife, Sarah, there is much discussion of packing up the camels.[72] One wonders if the camel remained off-stage.

Unlike Gart's version of Joseph, Wickram made no attempt to connect Tobias with the New Testament. His play was a historical drama in which the plight of the Jewish community living under the tyranny of Sennacherib is clearly depicted. Sennacherib's retainers are shown to indulge in mindless violence, cold-bloodedly killing Jews while on their way home from the tavern. Tobias the father emerges as a leader of the Jewish community, respected because of his piety and his willingness to disobey the king in order to provide a religious burial for the murdered Jews. Resistance to temporal authority in the cause of religion is thus established as not only pious but right. After three such incidents Tobias the father is blinded by God to test his patience. Wickram does not connect this punishment to his civil disobedience. Tobias accepts his blindness as God's judgment on him for his sinfulness, but these sins are not defined.[73] What God gave, God could take away; thus Tobias settles to wait patiently until God lifts the veil from his eyes.[74]

While the first part of the play is devoted to Tobias the father, the second part, essentially a wedding play, is devoted to Tobias the son. The story of the son's journey, his arrival at the house of Raquel, and his betrothal to Sarah, whose seven former bridegrooms had died on their wedding night, establish for the audience the prerequisites for happy marriage. Sarah's previous marriages failed because her father had consented to suitors who were not of the proper lineage. Sarah was meant to marry Tobias; thus, all the previous grooms had died.[75] Tobias, himself, is somewhat frightened by the previous record, but Raphael reassures him that the seven died because they had approached the bride with lust. Tobias, counsels the angel, must not sleep with Sarah for three nights. Instead the two must spend these nights in prayerful vigil, consummating the marriage on the fourth night.[76] With the help of the stench of fish heart and liver, Tobias fends off the devil, who attempts to kill him as he has killed the others. Then Tobias and Sarah pray together, affirming that they marry not for lust but to have children, who will grow up to praise and serve the Lord.[77] Wickram ignores the much discussed question of parental consent for marriage. Raquel is by this time anxious to marry his daughter without losing one more bridegroom, and no attempt is made to send a messenger to Tobias's father and Hannah in Nineveh. The young Tobias is on his own, guided by the angel; indeed the marriage is God's decision.[78] The *Argumentor* provides the biblical citations that institute marriage as a holy estate.[79] Raquel, for his part, provides parental advice as to the duties of the bride: to be obedient, to run the household well, and to be a loving helpmeet to her spouse.[80] Marriage is depicted as the crowning moment in the lives of the two young people.

All the biblical plays illustrated familial and domestic virtue. In addition to those already discussed, *Nabal* portrayed the strength of Abigail, her loyalty to her husband, no matter how difficult he might be, and her role as keeper of peace and harmony.[81] Jephtha's daughter served as a model of filial obedience and total devotion to her father; her chastity was an added virtue.[82] Rebecca provided another example of obedience and the obligation of the young toward their parents.[83] The stories of Esther and Judith, published in both German and Latin, honored their patriotism, thus furthering the cause of national pride and dedication to one's city and to Germany.[84] Lazarus evoked the duty and responsibility of Christian charity. The heartlessness of the rich man was accentuated to make clear the perils of wealth: selfishness, greed, and eventual damnation.[85] Marriage was the dominant theme, reflecting the centrality of marriage in burgher life.

Christian Zyrl, the German schoolteacher at Weissenburg, wrote another wedding play, *Rebecca,* for his pupils, which they presented before their parents and the honored Magistrat of the city in 1572.[86] Zyrl supported the Protestant view that marriage was a family matter, not to be entered into without parental consent. Nevertheless, he did attempt to give Rebecca the responsibility for making her own decision. In the opening scene Melchia, Rebecca's mother, asks her daughter if she wants to marry Isaac and go off to the land of Canaan. Rebecca replies that her mother knows best and, whatever her mother decides, she will do. Her father repeats the question, stating she must go of her own free will and because her heart desires it.[87] Rebecca counters that her first responsibility is obedience to her father, but that she wishes to be the bride of Isaac because she has been bestowed on him by God. The play ends with Rebecca's arrival at Abraham's house and her acceptance into the new family circle after pledging that she will never do anything to shame her new parents. Isaac affirms his fidelity to her because God has sent her to him.[88] God, thus, not only commended marriage, but also arranged it all.[89]

Martin Montanus used Roman legends to develop similar themes. Though the plays are set in Rome, they reveal little knowledge of the historical sources. Christian and classical influences intermingle, as they had in the *Gesta Romanorum*. In one complicated play, Titus Quintus Fulvius and Gisippus, Roman youths who have been close friends since childhood, go to Athens to study. Titus's father sends him off with the usual parental admonition:

> You should visit the churches
> If you do that, you will be joyous.
> You must listen to the sermons willingly
> For they will teach you Christ's word—
> That you must love your neighbor
> And never deviate from His word.
> If you do this for the good of the Fatherland
> You will never fall into disgrace.[90]

On their arrival in Athens, the difficulties begin. Gisippus becomes engaged to Sophronia. Titus falls in love with her, too, and Gisippus offers to give her up, since Titus's happiness is more important than his own or that of Sophronia. The parents of Sophronia agree to the change in fiancés, but then Titus, recognizing the depth of Gisippus's friendship, feels he cannot usurp his friend's position. The two depart on several journeys, but the tension tears their friendship apart. Gisippus, waylaid by robbers, is rescued by Titus, and they once again recognize their bond. Sophronia is reunited with her rightful fiancé, and Gisippus swears his loyalty to Titus as a brother.[91] Titus emerges as the ultimate hero because his loyalty to his friend takes precedence even over his devotion to Sophronia, but respect for the sacredness of the engagement is also implicit in his decision. Neither marriage nor betrothal should be broken by other ties.[92] Sophronia, it should be pointed out, had no voice in the decisions at all. Her destiny was left to the men; her duty was to accept whatever decision they made.

The plays, biblical and not, were a vindication of secular life, a positive affirmation of the value of the layman's everyday activities. These same activities had occupied a subordinate position in Catholic theology or in the satires of Thomas Murner. Certainly, the family was idealized in both the novels and the plays, yet this in itself is a reflection of the search for new social norms. The plays also record a change in sexual attitudes, albeit implicit rather than explicit. The sexual relationship between men and women was openly recognized as sanctified and inviolable. The family created from it was regarded as the foundation stone of society.

The growth of historical publication in German in the years 1549–70 was a manifestation of the burghers' increasing interest in the world around them, their desire to know about and understand political events, and their curiosity about the lives of other people, both past and present. Significantly, historical works in the vernacular outstripped Latin editions after

1540, except during the decade 1550–59, when Sleidan's history was published (table 17).

Analysis of the most important of these German publications and their authors (table 18) indicates that even scholarly histories appealed to the broad literate public rather than only to the learned. The interest of the reading public lay in ecclesiastical and contemporary history, although there was a steady market for the works of Livy, which combined an idealized description of the Roman Republic and the moral examples that the sixteenth century enjoyed.

The most popular historical work of the period was Flavius Josephus's *History of the Jews* published both under his name and that of the Latin translator and adaptor, Hegesippus. Caspar Hedio's translation of this work went through ten editions between 1530 and 1562.[93] In 1574 Theodosius Rihel published a new, more complete version translated by Conrad Lautenbach, the pastor at Hunaweiler.[94] It is ironic that Josephus should have been so popular in the sixteenth century. He did not portray the Jews as a struggling minority, courageously defending their faith against the Romans, which would have been relevant to the Protestant minority. Josephus, a Roman Jew, was firmly on the side of the state. Sixteenth-century Protestant readers turned to these accounts to read Josephus's account of the beginnings of the Christian church, before it had become the Roman, papal church. Josephus was important in helping to create a new image of the Christian church, a process furthered by historical accounts of the decline and corruption of the Roman papacy. Caspar Hedio's translation of Baptista Platina's *Historia von der Bapst und Kaiser Leben,* which appeared in 1545 and 1565, and Jean de Hainaut's history of the church, published in

Table 17. German and Latin Editions of Historical Works, 1500–1599

	German	Latin
1500–09	6	10
1510–19	6	20
1520–29	5	6
1530–39	10	9
1540–49	15	8
1550–59	14	18
1560–69	12	9
1570–79	17	9
1580–89	17	12
1590–99	14	13

Table 18. Selected Authors of German Editions of Historical Works, 1500–1599

	Livy	Josephus	Comines	Sleidan	Krantz
1500–09					
1510–19					
1520–29					
1530–39		5			
1540–49		1	3		
1550–59		3	2	9	3
1560–69	2	1	1	5	
1570–79	2	6		2	
1580–89	2	4		1	
1590–99	3	5			

French,[95] both described the weakness of the old church, which had compelled the reformers to find new solutions.

Jean Sleidan's meticulous history of the Reformation was the most important contemporary historical work. Sleidan, as official historian to the Schmalkaldic League, had access to the documents in the possession of the League and used them to support his account. A humanist by training, a Protestant by faith, and a loyal imperialist politically, Sleidan attempted to maintain an objective attitude toward his sources; indeed his accounts of the Diet of Worms or of Luther's interview with Cajetan are more objective than those of many modern Protestants or Catholics.[96] He began his history with the issuing of indulgences by Pope Leo X and Luther's preaching and writing against them, and he included the complete text of Luther's theses and all of Luther's treatises on the indulgence question. The book also contained an equally careful review of the positions taken by Johann Eck and Silvester Prierio on the Catholic side.[97] The correspondences between the Emperor Maximilian and the pope, the Duke of Saxony and the pope, and Cardinal Cajetan and the Duke of Saxony were summarized and evaluated.[98] Sleidan did not attempt to make the Catholic side black, the Protestant side white. Instead he showed that the new church was the inevitable result of past developments. Protestantism was thus not a heretical error but the result of long-term historical evolution.

In the hands of men like Sleidan and Hedio, history was not only a means of memorializing the past; it was a means of understanding the present. This was reflected in the publication of Philippe de Comines's book, an important source for the recent history of France as well as for the Burgundian war, which had deeply affected Strasbourg and Alsace. Heinrich von Eppendorf translated a book on Turkish history, as well as Albrecht Krantz's histories of Sweden, Norway, and Denmark.[99]

Interest in areas outside Germany and in contemporary events was further manifested in journalistic reports. There were broadsheets on religious affairs in Poland, on the wars between Denmark and Schleswig-Holstein, and on the diplomatic and military struggles against the Turks.[100] Clearly, by the decades 1550–70, the burgher's world was no longer limited to his city and his region. His historical consciousness reached from the time of the Roman Republic through the German Empire, from the period of the founding of the Christian church through the events of the Reformation. Politically, he took a lively interest in events in northern Europe and in the struggle between the empire and the Turks. He was informed about the war between Phillip of Spain and the Netherlands and the struggle between the French Protestants and the king of France.[101] Much more would be published on these wars in the next decade, but history and journalism had already become major instruments in shaping the world view of the Strasbourg citizen.

Scientific publication continued to develop in two separate streams. The division within the scientific community between university-trained men and practitioners was evident. Latin medical publication dwindled, perhaps because of the lack of medical teaching at the Academy. Conrad Dasypodius, the professor of mathematics, however, began to publish the mathematical texts that would become increasingly important in the later decades. Between 1557 and 1570 he brought out six separate collections of Euclid, which were essential for his classes, as well as two treatises on planetary theory.[102] The scientific treatises of Aristotle also began to appear, including Dasypodius's edition of the book on meteorology, the principles of physics, edited by Girolamo Zanchi, and two treatises on natural history, *De Mundo* and *De Anima*.[103] These foreshadowed later scientific development at the Academy. Late sixteenth-century academic science would be firmly rooted in the Greek tradition, particularly in Aristotle.

Vernacular science, in contrast, developed in new directions. Strasbourg became a center for publication of the work of Theophrastus Hohenheim (Paracelsus), thanks to the extraordinary efforts of Michael Toxites to edit the corpus of the master. Paracelsan publication remained important through 1580, though a third of the total was printed between 1564 and 1570. The concurrent interest in alchemy reflects the similarities between Paracelsan medicine and alchemy, both being based on a chemical concept of nature. Half of the treatises published on alchemy during the century were printed between 1560 and 1572.[104]

Both Paracelsus and Toxites were nonconformists who, although university educated, had been forced out of established intellectual institutions and lived precariously on the perimeter. Lucien Braun points out that Paracelsus consciously ignored Latin, believing that it confined and bound men's thoughts, that it could not adequately express the spontaneity and energy of the natural world.[105] Overtly breaking with tradition, burning the works of Celsus as outdated, Paracelsus hoped to disseminate his vision of the natural world among the less educated and less prejudiced. In his *Tinctura physicorum* Paracelsus wrote that all the doctors would ignore him but that his theories, based on the light of nature, would begin to become green in the year 1558. There would be all sorts of incredible signs which would be understood by the artisans and the common people, and his truths would stand against the work of the sophist scoundrels.[106]

Paracelsus and Toxites reflected in their lives the tensions and discord within the scientific community in the period. Born in the small Swiss village of Einsiedeln in 1493 or 1494, Paracelsus grew up in Villach, Carinthia, where his father was a doctor for the Fugger mines.[107] There was an important mining school in the town and Paracelsus not only received medical instruction from his father but also had the opportunity to attend the school and work in the laboratory of the metallurgist Sigmund Fuger in Schwatz.[108] Thus, Paracelsus's roots were in the technical world of his time. Growing up in the mining communities, going early into the mine pits, working and training with metallurgists and chemists, writing the *Bergkrankenbeiten,* the first treatise on industrial disease, he was, in part, an innovator who contributed to a science based on observation. The knowledge of the properties of metals he gained in these years was basic to the development of his own medical and cosmological ideas. He left Carinthia and began his formal education. No matriculation records have been found that would prove his entrance into a German university. One of his most recent biographers believes that he probably started his liberal arts training at Vienna, returned briefly to Villach to work, and then went to Ferrara for his medical studies.[109] Whether he actually received a degree as a doctor of medicine is also in doubt, although a legal suit against him in Basel in 1527 stated "den er an sein Doctorat der loblichen Hohen Schul zu Ferraria getan."[110] After 1518 he served as an army surgeon in Denmark, the Netherlands, and Naples and in 1526 arrived in Strasbourg, apparently ready to settle down, since he purchased citizenship.[111]

By March 1527, however, he had already left Strasbourg to become the city physician at Basel, with teaching responsibilities at the University,[112] an appointment which proved to be disastrous. Paracelsus quickly became embroiled with his colleagues at the university, and in midsummer he burned some old medical texts publicly. In the fall he was made the butt of a student lampoon. In January 1528, having cured one of the important canons of the church, the latter paid him six gulden instead of the promised hundred gulden. Insulted, Paracelsus complained to the Magistrat, who were concurrently besieged by complaints from his enemies. In February Paracelsus was forced to flee the city.[113] The Basel episode set the pattern for the rest of his life. He wandered from one German or Austrian city to the next, eternally involved in quarrels with his rivals and various authorities. He died in 1541.

Michael Toxites's career had parallels with that of Paracelsus. He suffered similar frustrations at the hands of the academic establishment and the civil authorities. Arriving in Strasbourg in 1542 his brilliance was recognized by Johann Sturm, who engaged him to teach at the Gymnasium and turned over to him work on some of his own editions of Cicero. In 1544 Toxites appeared before the school committee to ask for an increase in salary because his wife had a serious illness. The following year he was fired for arrogant behavior, neglect of his classes, and drunkenness.[114] This became a recurrent pattern for him. Most of the time he remained in Strasbourg, with brief periods of employment as a poet, an editor, or a teacher. Johann Sturm remained his loyal supporter, often providing editorial work or a diplomatic assignment to tide him over.[115] From 1551 to 1553 he stayed for fairly long intervals with Dr. Sebald Hawenreuter and Dr. Guinther von Andernach, both of whom gave lectures on Galen and Hippocrates. Toxites, in the tradition of medical apprenticeship, accompanied Guinther on his visits to patients. This was the beginning of a new career. Gradually, like Brunfels before him, he deserted his humanist studies and poetry in favor of medicine. By 1564 he had adopted the title of doctor, although there is no evidence that he received a university degree, nor any interval of more than six months when he could have attended university lectures.[116] He was, however, an enthusiastic Paracelsan, and in 1564 began to publish Paracelsus's work on the Strasbourg presses, a full twenty-five years before a complete edition was undertaken by Johann Huser, the Basel printer.[117]

Some of the Strasbourg editions were printed by Christian Mylius, perhaps because Toxites was married to Mylius's mother-in-law.[118] However, Samuel Emmel, Theodosius Rihel, Nikolaus Wyriot, and Bernard Jobin were all involved in the printing and dissemination of Paracelsan ideas. Since Rihel and Jobin were two of the most important printers of the period and since they were both able businessmen, the assumption has to be drawn that these editions represented assured profits. On the other hand, eleven of these twenty-seven Strasbourg editions of Paracelsus appeared without a colophon or signature during a period when, by and large, anonymous publication was no longer usual. Whether the printers wished to protect themselves from censorship or from the controversy which Paracelsus's work might engender is a matter for speculation.

Like the lay novelists and playwrights, Paracelsus and Toxites were outside the established intellectual community and independent of institutional ties. One prestigious figure in the local medical world, Guinther von Andernach, adopted some Paracelsan methods, but greater support came from the popular level, from Lucas Bathodius, a doctor-astronomer-astrologer who supported himself by compiling prognostications, and from a disciple of Toxites named Valentinus Kosslitius.[119] Paracelsus also had a following among the lower classes who hoped to understand the secrets of nature through a combination of empirical observation, technical skill, and numerical codes based on occultism and alchemy.[120]

Paracelsus broke away from the ancients as the source of knowledge about the natural world.

> As long as we write medicine as the Ancients wrote it, we will simply be followers, although there are many doctors who by following the Ancients became very rich. But we wish to establish a true practice of medicine. . . . And first we must think what is most necessary to man, and what is noblest, in order to know the mysteries of nature. Thus it will be explained, what God is, what man is, what his aims are, both heavenly and earthly. From this develops what is theology and what is medicine.[121]

He struggled to set himself free from the past accumulation of knowledge, which he saw as obsolescent. He replaced the traditional theory of the four humors with the proposition that man's nature is composed of three elements: spirit, soul, and matter. The latter, the least important, consisted of the body, blood, and flesh, which simply housed the other parts. The spirit included the senses, those faculties of sight, hearing, taste, smell, and touch that are halfway between the material and immaterial. The ultimate element of man was his soul, defined by Paracelsus as the indwelling God within. The primary responsibility of the physicians was to maintain the material house of nature so the soul could fulfill its destiny.[122]

Matter was also conceived of as composed of three elements—sulphur, mercury, and salt—representing, in the material world, the body, the spirit, and the soul of man's nature. The association of these two concepts was difficult in itself, but Paracelsus's meaning was further obscured by his use of terms that already had definite meanings different from his own. Scientific thought in the sixteenth century was hindered by the lack of a specialized vocabulary. Paracelsus used the term *mercury* to mean those elements common to metals. *Sulphur* was used for matter that was changeable, subject to combustion, dissolution, or combination. *Salt* was used for permanent substances, indissoluble and incombustible.[123] Nature was composed of these essential metals and minerals. The description was innovative in that Paracelsus recognized that matter was interchangeable. Nature could not be reduced to a simple hierarchy of forms.[124]

The application of chemical knowledge to pharmacopia and treatment was the basis of Paracelsan medicine. Paracelsus hoped that the physician would become a chemist, carrying out his own experiments to find methods to extract essential natural substances from air, water, earth, and fire.[125] The "revolution in medicine" which he proclaimed meant using chemical substances in pharmacopia instead of the traditional composites made from herbs.[126] These would lead to purer substances and more effective cures. Much of his medical writings was devoted to outlining chemical procedures for separating mineral elements from metals, stones, resins, and vegetable and animal matter.[127] He drew heavily on the chemical and alchemical treatises of the time; indeed his methods closely resemble the instructions given in the *Probierbüchlein*.[128] His division of matter into three categories— metals, nonmetals, and salt—did, however, anticipate the classifications of nineteenth-century chemistry.

Paracelsus was an iconoclast who rejected the intellectual establishment of his day. He was also profoundly Christian. He condemned dependence on heathen authors and sought to create a Christian philosophy of nature based on the Scriptures and on observation of nature.[129] Chemistry attracted him as a method because it was not associated with the logic and mathematics of the university scientists; rather, it was based on the experiments of generations of alchemists.

His world view grew out of the analogy between the microcosm and macrocosm.[130] Man and the firmament, he believed, were inextricably interrelated. The firmament existed within man, and thus the study of astronomy and astronomical theory was essential to understanding the human body. The earth existed to create food and other resources for the use of man. Concomitantly, the human body had the same purpose: from within the body all the food was created to sustain the members of the body. The unity of the two worlds, man and the firmament, was made possible by astral emanations, "signatures," which God had given to earthly things so that men would discover the secrets of his creation. For Paracelsus, as Debus put it, "the universe was a living unit with occult or magical forces everywhere at work."[131] As a result, the pursuit of knowledge based on observation alone was incomplete. These observations had to be related to the whole of creation, the secrets that God had hidden in the universe. Paracelsus thus synthesized those technical and religious elements of the culture that were particularly important to the laity.

Hieronymus Bock's botany was yet another example of the efforts of scientists to share their learning with the populace.[132] Bock described the whole undertaking in the 1587 edition of his botany. Years before, he wrote, Otto Brunfels had sent plants to him by various visitors and had even come to Hornbach, on foot, to see Bock's garden and botanical collection. Afterwards, Brunfels had sent him many of his notes, and Bock had felt responsible for putting them in order and bringing together all that was known about German plants, as a service to the fatherland.[133] He also wished to correct the old botanical books, which contained much erroneous information and often caused further pain and distress rather than healing.[134] His aim was to provide the knowledge which poor people needed to keep themselves well. In the old days, he said, princes like Alexander the Great gave scientists like Aristotle a great deal of money to make botanical collections. Now, wealth was provided only to hospitals or schools, and men like himself and Conrad Gesner had to give their own time and efforts without recompense.[135]

Bock's *Kreütterbuch* was important because it focused on German plants and medicinal herbs. Brunfels had attempted to break away from Pliny and Dioscorides by describing plants that did not appear in the Greek or Latin corpus. Bock went further. He recognized the uniqueness of German plants and saw that they had medicinal characteristics unlike those of the plants described by the ancients. Nationalist to the core, he argued that German plants were far more effective for German diseases than plants imported from Italy, Greece, or India.[136]

Like the Brunfels botany, Bock's book required close cooperation between scientist, artist, and printer. Josias Rihel underwrote the expensive publication and shouldered the risk. In his preface to the 1546 edition Rihel explained that he had undertaken the work with its many illustrations because the pictures made it truly useful to the common man. He was determined not to spare any cost and had worked with Bock to perfect the edition in every way possible.[137] In a later edition Bock, in turn, praised Rihel. The printer had sent a young artist to work side by side with Bock and had also assumed the fatigue, the planning, and the expense.[138] The *Kreütterbuch,* however, was not as well executed as Brunfels's text. The artist, David Kandel, the son of a Strasbourg burgher,[139] was less gifted than Johann Weyditz. The plants were drawn from life, as Bock laid them out for him,[140] but they remained botanical specimens. The root was included, but the full development of the plant, from bud to maturity to seed, was not.[141] Information was standardized for each plant: the plant was described, its various names were listed, and its medicinal power, effect, and uses were given.[142]

The Brunfels botany was not reprinted after 1537, and, therefore, much of Brunfels's botanical knowledge was communicated through Bock's popular *Kreütterbuch.* Bock also passed on Brunschwig's techniques for distilling and extracting substances. Thus, the scientific knowledge accumulated during the course of the century was continually collated and made available to the lay reading public.

In the period from 1549 to 1570, there was a brief cultural revolution. A vernacular culture developed, independent of the intellectuals and such established institutions as the church and the schools. These institutions experienced a period of weakness, and lay writers were able to create new literary forms: the novel, popular biblical drama, and journalism. Scientific practise was transformed by Hieronymus Bock, who freed botany from its dependence on Greek and Roman sources, and by Paracelsus, who also rejected the traditional sources and attempted to create a new scientific world view based on a synthesis of observations from nature, the Scriptures, and a mystic understanding of numbers. Paracelsus and Bock challenged the authority of the university-trained physicians and began the slow process of breaking away from the ancient authorities.[143] Both in ethics and in science the lay culture had established new foundations outside the traditional boundaries prescribed by the Latin culture.

PART V
THE STRUGGLE FOR
RELIGIOUS AND
ACADEMIC ORTHODOXY
1561–1599

THE POLITICAL AND RELIGIOUS SETTING

In the 1560s, the long process of adaptation and synthesis began. The various religious formulations had to be assessed, rejected, or accepted, and the new religious and ecclesiastical institutions placed within the formal order of urban life. This had to be accomplished under very difficult political circumstances. Catholicism and the strengthened Calvinism, now entrenched to the north in the Palatinate and to the south in the Swiss cities, continued to threaten, though there was disagreement as to which constituted the greater menace. The magistrates, supported by the citizenry, were agreed that the reestablishment of Catholicism was not to be tolerated. How far the city should go in alliances with Calvinist forces, the French Huguenots, the Palatinate, or the Swiss, however, was open to question. This issue was hidden below the surface of every debate that occupied the Magistrat in these decades.[1] The wars of religion brought French troops into the city, creating the possibility of a countermove from the emperor. Every decision had political implications, and the intellectual life of these decades can only be understood against the background of these events.

The opening phase of the Marbach-Sturm controversy, the struggle to control appointments to the Academy faculty, has been described in the introduction to Part IV. In 1578 Johann Pappus, Marbach's protégé and eventual successor, renewed the attack on Johann Sturm in sixty-eight theses on Christian charity. The doctrine of love for one's neighbor, he wrote, meant that a true Christian must search out and condemn the errors of others. Specifically, he meant Sturm's errors. The reaction was immediate. Other theologians were involved in the pamphlet warfare and the preachers stirred up the burghers with sermons on one side or the other. The students at the Gymnasium stood firmly for Sturm, providing an escort for his protection. Sturm, then seventy-four years old, wrote three violent pamphlets against Pappus, which he published without submitting them first to the authorities. The Rat, influenced by Sturm's long service to the city, was willing to overlook this breach, but in 1581 the Elector Palatine wrote the Magistrat that Sturm's last pamphlet had wounded him personally and that he could accept neither Sturm's apology nor his justification. Faced with this complaint after twenty years of controversy, the Rat fired Sturm. The Lutheran clergy assumed leadership of the Academy and emerged firmly in control after 1581. Johann Pappus succeeded Marbach, who died in the year of his triumph over Sturm.[2]

In these very years when Marbach and Pappus were gradually establishing their authority over the schools, despite a firm alliance with Lutheran Württemberg, they were not able to establish equally close relations with other Lutheran cities and territories. In 1570 Jacob Andreae, urged by the Elector of Saxony and the Duke of Württemberg, drafted a proposal to pacify the two major groups that had developed within Lutheranism. He sent the draft to the Strasbourg Magistrat. Marbach asked for permission to attend the colloquy where the articles would be discussed, but his request was denied. The Strasbourg clergy, however, signed the articles, which would eventually become the Formula of Concord. The Magistrat refused to be involved in the matter, stating that attempts to settle religious disputes invariably led to division and bitterness.[3]

Ecclesiastical unity within the city was furthered by the abolition of the French parish in 1577. Despite the efforts of both the magistrates and the clergy, divisions within the French church, quarrels between its elders and ministers, forced the city to take action to neutralize what had become a disruptive force. The move was favorably regarded by the Lutheran clergy.[4]

The policies that led to stronger support for the Lutherans and the acceptance of the Formula of Concord by the ministers and the faculty were offset by what could be called a procalvinist foreign policy. Throughout the wars of religion the Rat loaned money to the Calvinist leaders, permitted recruiting in the city and its territories, and even paid for mercenary troops.[5] Again and again, these policies brought the war to the gates of the city. In 1568 and 1569 the duc d'Aumale, leading troops of the duc de Guise, swept across the Alsatian plain and warned the Strasbourg rulers that the city's acceptance of Huguenot refugees and its aid to the prince of Orange were hardly the acts of a neutral power. Since Orange was actually within the walls, the Rat asked him to leave; but five years later, in 1574, they permitted Henri de Bourbon, prince of Condé, to enter the city, and they again provided loans.[6] In 1579 the Guise troops were again in force on the plain. Throughout the 1570s, the threat of war was omnipresent.

During the 1580s the threat became a reality over the issue of control of the cathedral chapter. In 1584 four canons of the Cologne chapter were expelled from their benefices after their conversion to Calvinism. Enjoying plural benefices in the Strasbourg cathedral as well, they came to take up residence in the city. The Catholic canons acted quickly to deny them their benefices, but the dispute served to focus all the city's fears and divisions. The Calvinist canons urged the city to support them, pointing out that it only strengthened the Catholics to permit the canons to act unilaterally. Protestant noble families were not eager to see the traditional ecclesiastical benefices slip out of their reach. The emperor sent an imperial commission to the city to intervene. A strong party within the Rat believed that the solution lay in an alliance with the Swiss, since the latter could be counted on against the Catholic forces. Despite opposition from the citizens, the ministers, and many of the magistrates themselves, the Swiss alliance was concluded in 1588 and preparation for war went forward.[7]

The death of Bishop Johann von Manderscheid in 1592 precipitated the final crisis. The Protestant canons met and elected one candidate, a minor. The Catholic canons elected Charles, cardinal of Metz, a member of the Guise family. The inevitable consequence was war, with the city backing the Protestant faction. Little help came from outside; the Swiss departed when the Rat could not pay them. The city troops were badly led. There was little enthusiasm for the war, and the city was defeated. By February 1593 a truce was arranged.[8] The Calvinist alliance had not only been proved unwise, but had brought the city to the edge of bankruptcy.

The Lutheran clergy remained silent during the war. The Magistrat's policy, not theirs, had led to the conflict. After the war, however, the assembly of the clergy renewed its efforts to have the Magistrat accept the Formula of Concord as the official confession of faith for the city. In January 1598 the Formula was read by the Rat, accepted, and incorporated into a new church ordinance published in that same year. Seventy years after the abolition of the Mass, Lutheran doctrine was formally adopted in the city of Strasbourg.[9]

CHAPTER ELEVEN · THE PROBLEM OF RELIGIOUS ORTHODOXY

HE RELIGIOUS WARS CREATED A PRO-found psychological and intellectual shock for the men and women of the late sixteenth century. The initial response was to fall back on the certainty of absolute truth, to state firmly one's own orthodoxy in the face of conflicting views. This was the purpose of the Tridentine decrees, and the establishment of Lutheran orthodoxy in Strasbourg sprang from similar motivations. It was not only a normative phase in the movement for religious revival; it was a response to the loss of inner cohesion. Whereas the humanists of the early decades had thrown themselves with enthusiasm into the search for new sources of Christian truth, scholars and theologians now felt the need to define religious beliefs precisely. Catechisms and confessions of faith were bulwarks against rival religious formulations. After 1560 the final process of adaptation and routinization was taking place, as can be seen from the publications of the period.

The shock suffered from the wars is evident in the malaise that appeared at many levels of thought and expression. The buoyant optimism of the early part of the century began to disappear. People were no longer sure that a renewal of faith would lead to a restoration of the kingdom of God. The will of God, according to the sermons and songs of the end of the century, was inscrutable. While all things moved in conformity with his plan, he might have to frighten men into obedience by acts of power. Popular songs described the punishments sent by God to prove his people.[1] The religious wars were interpreted as tests of the faithful.[2] The title of a hymn revealed the somber mood: "Oh God, to whom should I lament?"[3]

The wars, not only the Schmalkaldic War but the revolt of the Netherlands and the French wars of religion, compelled men to take action to defend their religion. In Strasbourg, more and more religious decisions were made under the pressure of external political factors. In the earliest phase the ideas for the Reform had come from Wittenberg, but the movement was quickly internalized and the Strasbourg reformers evolved theological doctrines unique to the city. This phase was short lived. Diffusion of these doctrines never reached beyond the three other cities that accepted the Tetrapolitana at the Diet of Augsburg.[4] By 1532 the Strasbourg clergy

236

had signed the Augustana, and in 1536 they accepted the Wittenberg concord with Luther and the other German cities.[5] Bucer continued, without success, to try to bring the Lutheran and the reformed Swiss cities together,[6] but these efforts died with the Schmalkaldic War and the Peace of Augsburg.

After 1555, as a Lutheran city, Strasbourg had to establish firm connections with other Lutheran institutions to survive. Similarly, intellectual life was no longer merely a local or regional affair. Strasbourg was linked more than ever before to a Europe-wide culture. By the last decades of the century the city had become an international center of learning. The professors at the Academy were drawn from all over Europe, as were the students. The printers' shift to publication in Latin is yet another reflection of the growing intellectual internationalism.

When Johann Marbach assumed the presidency of the assembly of the clergy in 1552 he was faced with the urgent problem of rebuilding the Protestant church after the debacle of the war. He had worked closely with Bucer, but he believed that Bucer's doctrines had led toward a dangerous religious particularism. In Marbach's view the spiritual and political safety of the city required the establishment of the Lutheranism of the Augustana. His first priority was to appoint ministers dedicated to the principle of theological purity as defined in the Confession of Augsburg. The few ministers who continued to assert their loyalty to Bucer or to Swiss reformers were forced to leave: first Peter Martyr, later Girolamo Zanchi. Conrad Hubert, who devoted himself to the editing of Bucer's work, was dismissed from his position as canon of Saint Thomas.[7] The theologians who grouped around Marbach included his protégé, Johann Pappus, his own sons, Erasmus and Phillip, Johann Flinner, Nikolaus Florus, Elias Schadeus, and Melchior Speccer—men of sound, orthodox views, the majority having been educated at Wittenberg.

The stability which Marbach hoped to achieve was partially reflected in the span of office of the ministers. The Interim had created a period of disorder. When the cathedral, New Saint Peter and Old Saint Peter, were returned to the Catholics, the ministers of these churches had to be transferred. Paul Fagius of New Saint Peter went into exile, and Diebold Schwarz of Old Saint Peter went to Saint Aurelia; the cathedral clergy were moved into various posts.[8] After 1560, however, the preachers settled into a pattern of lifetime appointments, averaging fifteen or twenty years. In each church, there were only two ministers for the entire period from 1560 to 1599.[9]

The ministers were able to establish administrative stability within the assembly of the clergy, but they continued to feel threatened by the Catholics, the Calvinists, and the Magistrat's political policies. Their fear of the

Calvinists was well founded. Pierre Estiart, a French refugee printer, was using the city as a base for clandestine publications to be sent to France. He printed an attack on the Council of Trent in 1561. In 1559 Christian Mylius had published Calvin's confession of faith, which was in direct conflict with the provisions of the Peace of Augsburg.[10] Yet no action was taken by the magistrates against what was a clear threat to the security of the city. In a series of conflicts with the ratsherren, the ministers struggled to maintain their independence and their authority to determine doctrinal matters. They attacked the Catholics and the Calvinists from their pulpits, but these sermons were not committed to print.

The clergy's need to accommodate diversity led to a very different publishing program. Their intense and agonizing disagreements were not aired in public.[11] Pamphleteering was held in check. Sturm wrote three treatises to which Pappus responded, but both the attacks and the response were written in Latin.[12] While the tone of Sturm's Latin was particularly vehement, the debate remained scholarly, filled with references to the Scriptures and the church fathers and in no way directed to the popular audience. There is no record of publication in Strasbourg of other polemic tracts written by the ministers of this period except for a treatise by Pappus against the Catholic theologians, published in 1597. Thus, there seems to have been an effort to dampen the flames of religious discord. Marbach and Pappus were not eager to be involved in polemic warfare. Their responsibility was to construct firm doctrinal positions from which to base teaching and preaching, and they directed their writing to this goal.

Marbach's career as head of the Strasbourg assembly of the clergy and his confrontation with Girolamo Zanchi and Johann Sturm have been subject to various historical interpretations. The liberal historians and theologians of the nineteenth century saw the controversy as an example of intellectual independence against ecclesiastical rigidity. Recently, such scholars as James Kittelson and Bernard Vogler have placed the conflict within the larger context of the institutional and theological questions involved.[13] Anthony Wallace's analysis of the stages of revitalization makes a particularly useful contribution to this debate. The process of adaptation was an extended one in Strasbourg. In the early years, Bucer attempted to modify the new doctrines to achieve unity between the Lutherans and the Swiss. After the Peace of Augsburg, which made Zwinglianism and Calvinism illegal, Strasbourg established the doctrine accepted by other Lutheran cities and adapted any remaining particularist elements of their theology to the Augustana. Marbach carried out this stage of the adaptation. His successor, Johann Pappus, was responsible for the final routinization of the revitalization movement. Placing the struggles between Marbach and Zanchi or Pappus and Sturm in the broader perspective of the larger process of change, however, should not obscure the bitterness of their differences. The struggles between these men were disruptive precisely because major issues were at stake. Nevertheless, routinization was inevitable.

The basis of the doctrine of the Strasbourg church after 1552 was Lutheran, but no attempt was made in the city to publish Luther's major doctrinal works, his biblical commentary, or his sermons. The dearth of Lutheran publication after 1560 is striking. There was one summary of his teachings in 1578 and one reedition of his doctrine of the Eucharist in 1584; only the catechisms went through several editions.[14] Marbach and Pappus took the responsibility upon themselves to define and propagate correct doctrine. They had three aims: to make the Confession of Augsburg available and known, to explain clearly the Lutheran doctrines concerning the Eucharist and predestination, and to instruct adults and children in these doctrines. While they addressed themselves to other theological issues, particularly in their roles as professors at the Academy,[15] they were not deflected from their primary tasks.

All the major doctrinal writing in these decades was focused on exegesis of the Confession of Augsburg and the promulgation of the Lutheran doctrine of the Eucharist and predestination. These were written primarily in Latin for the use of the clergy rather than for the average member of the congregation. Thus the dialogue of the early decades was lost. The function of the clergy was to define right doctrine. The function of the congregation was to listen and to believe.

Valentin Erythraeus was the first to provide an exhaustive analysis of the Confession of Augsburg in a treatise published in 1565.[16] Each article was presented separately, first in Latin, then in Greek. Erythraeus used his dialectic skills to outline the theological implications of each element of doctrine in an elaborate scheme that filled a double page.[17] Under each point of doctrine references to the writings of the church fathers and the Scriptures were given, citing the source of that particular precept. Erythraeus intended to explain the meaning of each article and to provide the supporting evidence. The book was clearly designed for the use of theologians, ministers already established in their parish, or theological students who would thus be introduced to the basic doctrines of their faith.

In 1567 during the controversy with Johann Sturm, Johann Marbach addressed himself to the question of the Eucharist in a 1,200-page book, which he dedicated to the Magistrat of Strasbourg. Marbach's purpose was to provide a history of the whole controversy, to explain Zwingli's ideas and show where he erred, to give the ideas of the church fathers on the matter, and to clear the waters which had been muddied by Sturm's attacks.[18] The basis of error, Marbach explained, was the Zwinglian belief that Christ's body, like all other bodies, could be in only one place at one time; thus, after the ascension, Christ could never return to earth. According to Zwingli, Christ had been removed from the world and from the church,[19] and had spoken the words of institution only figuratively. Lutherans, in contrast, believed that Christ had spoken literally and had made it clear in the words of institution that his body and blood, the salvation of mankind, were present in communion.

In this treatise Marbach was anxious to establish the continuity of his own teaching with that of the early Strasbourg reformers. He did not wish to convey disagreement with them: "The Zwinglians have accused me and my brethren, the pastors and the curates, of establishing a different and strange teaching in the Strasbourg churches."[20] In fact he had served the city for twenty-three years with no other aim than to carry out his responsibilities in the Strasbourg churches and schools by teaching, preaching, and administering of the Holy Sacraments according to Scripture and the Augsburg Confession.[21] He considered himself a disciple of Bucer.[22]

In 1598, Johann Pappus made the final doctrinal synthesis. After the acceptance of the Formula of Concord, a revised edition of the *Kirchenordnung* was published where, in an eighty-four page introduction, Pappus showed the continuity of doctrine from Bucer to Marbach. Bucer's teaching, he claimed, was Lutheran in essence. The special articles on the Eucharist contained in the Tetrapolitana had been written to keep the Swiss within the Protestant camp and thereby maintain the unity of the new church. These conclusions were carefully supported by statements from Bucer's correspondence and from documents from the various religious colloquies.

Pappus began his historical summary by saying that the article on the Eucharist in the confession of the four cities was difficult to understand and that all parties, papal, Lutheran, Zwinglian, and Calvinist, had mistakenly assumed the four cities to be Zwinglian.[23] In fact, Pappus stated, the article was not purely Zwinglian. Bucer had written a letter to Johann Comandrum, a Protestant minister in Chur, admitting that he was wrong on several matters in the articles and that he wished to acknowledge his errors.[24] He had not realized that the doctrine of the Eucharist contained in the articles would lead to a split with Luther. Bucer recognized that he had expounded a "coarse" doctrine with regard to the presence of Christ, which he no longer accepted. He had changed his mind when he read Luther's *Grosse Confession von Abendmal* and realized from this that Luther in no way held that Christ was narrowly confined within the elements.[25] Bucer continued that he had not informed Luther that he had revised his doctrine because he wanted to avoid new bitterness and division among the Protestants.[26] He still hoped that the other Swiss cities would join the four cities. Pappus interpolated that, once the Swiss cities had joined the four, Bucer planned to unite them all with Luther and the Saxon cities. Pappus supported this theory by showing that Strasbourg and the Swiss cities had explained their doctrines to the Saxons at Schmalkald and that their interpretations had been accepted by the Lutheran cities and states.[27]

The Wittenberg Concord, according to Pappus, was another indication of Bucer's acceptance of Lutheran doctrine. Bucer and Capito had addressed an apology to Luther at that time, in which they greeted him as the chief teacher of the Gospel and stated their acceptance of his teachings on the Eucharist, baptism, and confession.[28] Furthermore, Pappus pointed out, Bucer never again mentioned the four cities confession after 1537 but always referred to the Confession of the Electors and Princes.[29]

Pappus's historical reconstruction created the synthesis essential to the final phase of adaptation. All the differences of opinion, the conflicts, and the discord, were buried, and a single thread of development was shown to have been present from the beginning. There had ever been but one truth. Bucer had, perhaps, stated that truth incorrectly, certainly intemperately, but his mistakes had been made in the larger cause of maintaining Protestant unity. The Strasbourg church could see itself as embodying one faith; there was no discord between the early phase and the later doctrines.

In the same decade Pappus wrote his own exposition of the Confession of Augsburg. Like the analysis of Valentin Erythraeus, it was written in Latin and it explained the doctrines article by article and word by word. The significant difference was the sources he used. Pappus appealed neither to the Scriptures nor to Luther. His exegesis was based on Augustine. In article after article he cited the *Civitate Dei*, the *Libro de natura et gratia*, the *Contra Pelagianus*, the *Confessions*, and the *Epistolae*, noting each reference carefully in the margin.[30] Pappus expounded Augustine's view that knowledge does not come from man's reason but through the relevation of God in the Scriptures. His belief that man is unable to triumph over evil through his own will tied Augustinianism firmly to the Lutheran tradition.[31]

The campaign to establish Lutheran orthodoxy did not manifest itself in a concerted attempt to write religious treatises for the laity. Marbach's statement in 1567 and Pappus's summary in 1596 were designed to be read by the citizens, but they did not raise doctrinal questions. They provided a historical explanation for and established the continuity of the new religious formulations. Doctrine itself was a matter for churchmen, not the laity.

New editions of the Bible were not published after 1545 until Theobald Berger and Theodosius Rihel published Luther's German New Testament in 1576 and 1588, respectively. In 1595 Rihel, after much difficulty, brought out a complete Bible.[32] The Rihel editions were believed to have a Calvinist bias by the Assembly of the church, and the clergy made every effort to stop their publication.[33] The only other editions of Scripture, an edition of the New Testament and a version of Proverbs,[34] were published in Hebrew, which limited their circulation to the learned community. Biblical commentary was similarly restricted to a few Latin commentaries by Lutheran pastors in other German or Scandinavian cities and a Latin commentary on the Pentateuch by Erasmus Marbach.[35] Melchior Speccer published two short commentaries in the vernacular on individual chapters of the New Testament and Pappus a history of the kings and prophets of the Old Testament.[36] Cyriacus Spangenberg's lengthy German commentaries on the New Testament,[37] the most important biblical commentaries of the period, were written in support of the particular doctrines of Matthias Flacius Illyricus and to win other Lutheran clergy over to these views.

What was available for the laity? Psalm books, hymnals, and prayer books—in other words, books of religious devotion. While the contents varied from book to book and from publisher to publisher, there were stock features. All included the Ten Commandments, the Lord's Prayer and the Creed. These were usually followed by a selection of psalms, but rarely by the complete book. Sometimes the psalms were set to music. Admonitions to the readers in the prefaces provide some insight into daily religious practices. Singing the psalms was recommended to Christian men and women because they would turn them away from vicious habits and self-indulgence and toward a decent, sober life.[38] Biblical verses, arranged for the days of the week, to be recited after every meal, could improve the religious life of a family, particularly if the mother or father would take it upon themselves to explain the meaning of the verse to others at the table: grandparents, relatives, apprentices, and children.[39] The verses were not given in order of their placement within the Scriptures and they did not develop a particular theological point. Two or three verses were simply presented for memorization. Some of the prayerbooks were closely based on the psalms, references were given to the psalms from which the passages were selected, but the purpose of the books was to provide a framework for individual devotion rather than to familiarize the reader with the sources.[40]

The most popular prayerbook, of which five editions were printed between 1560 and 1591, was Luther's own *Betbüchlein,* also published with the title *Beteglöcklin.*[41] In the early period of the reform Luther had admonished his followers to use the Our Father and to refrain from using prayers not found in the Scriptures. The prayers in the *Betbüchlein* were drawn from Luther's postils, from the *Freedom of a Christian Man,* from his commentaries on the Scriptures, and from his hymnal.[42] The forms of worship which Luther had helped to create were described in new editions for the ordinary parishoner. His great statements of the new faith were no longer printed.

The major means of introducing religious ideas to the laity at the end of the century were catechisms and the instructional books used to prepare young girls and boys for their first communion. Both were prepared in Strasbourg as early as 1525, the first catechism written by Matthias Zell.[43] Bucer's first catechism was published in 1534, followed by another in 1537.[44] In the latter part of the century the catechism most in use was one prepared specifically for the pastors and teachers of Strasbourg. The pastors were responsible for instructing all the young people in their parishes. This catechism was reprinted five times between 1559 and 1585. Bucer's catechism was given a new edition in 1567. Luther's *Kleine Catechism* was published in 1560 and 1570, and the longer version was printed in 1568.[45] The continued use of the special Strasbourg version is yet another example of the hegemony of religious ideas in this period. The local pastors felt no hesitation in using their own set of questions in preparing young people for communion.[46] This was a common practice in other German cities as well.

Like all the Protestant catechisms of the period, the Strasbourg edition emphasized the Ten Commandments, the Creed, and the Lord's Prayer. Its purpose was not only to teach the words by rote but also to train the young person in the basic elements of Christian discipline. He should know right from wrong, he should recognize his own inability to live righteously, and he should be trained to turn to God for help. The manuals of preparation for communion, for example, taught the young person to examine himself, to recognize his sinfulness and weakness, to throw himself on the saving Grace of Christ, and thus to redeem himself from the consequences of his wickedness.[47]

Catechetical instruction was a powerful instrument for creating social order and religious orthodoxy. Children, beginning at the lowest level in the parish schools, were drilled in the questions and answers. Parents were urged to aid the process of learning at home. Tests were given by pastors and by schoolmasters. Learning the catechism was part of the ritual of Protestant life. As the basic statement of the faith, it was a proven means of passing belief, untarnished, from one generation to the next.[48]

The attempt to establish one Confession of Faith for all the citizens and residents of Strasbourg was, nevertheless, not entirely successful. Conformity was required within the church itself and within the schools, but religious unity was by no means achieved. Differences with regard to policy and doctrine continued to plague the Magistrat, ministers, teachers, and professors throughout the last decades of the century. There were men who persisted in their belief in the original Strasbourg Articles of Faith, whatever they might repeat in church, and there were known Roman Catholics among the Magistrat. The Schwenckfelders continued to cling tenaciously to their beliefs.[49]

This lack of unity was further demonstrated by the continued presence in the city of theologians, poets, and polemicists who did not accept the Confession of Augsburg, or who had their own interpretations of its meaning. They used the Strasbourg presses to disseminate their own doctrines or the views of their particular parties. While the city had a long-established censorship law, it was rarely and ambivalently applied to these writers. The Magistrat wanted to keep peace within the city and were willing, after 1563, to accept the theologians' insistence that all ministers profess one creed. They were not willing, however, to turn away everyone with whom the theologians disagreed. All through the wars of religion in France, they accepted Huguenot refugees, provided them with food as a relief measure, and required them to register with the authorities. This posed a risk, and the Rat was somewhat fearful, but the policy was maintained.[50] For the Rat, censorship was a necessary political weapon, but they did not want to establish a Protestant inquisition. They were far more worried by political pasquils and broadsides, particularly those that might arouse the attention of their neighbors, than they were by learned theological treatises.

The dismissal of Johann Sturm from the rectorship of the school exemplified the Magistrat's policy toward internal discord and censorship. The Marbach-Sturm controversy, as we have seen, split the city. But the Rat equivocated. They listened to both sides and refused to act. Even when Sturm published his attacks on Marbach without first submitting them to the Rat, as the censorship ordinance required, they temporized, excusing him on the basis of his past service to the city. When the Count of Zweibrucken lodged a complaint, however, the Rat took immediate action. After twenty years of strife, Sturm was promptly expelled. The power of censorship was exerted when it brought the city into conflict with outsiders.

Despite the desire of the theologians to maintain tight control, diverse intellectuals were allowed to reside in the city. They were not given posts in the civil service, in the church, or in the schools, but they were allowed to publish their work on the Strasbourg presses without interference. Only if their opinions brought down criticism from outside was action taken to censure them or to banish them from the city. The political authorities had a fairly realistic view of the possibility of establishing complete ideological conformity. One poignant entry in the *Ratsprotokolle* illustrates their attitude. When the controversy between Sturm and Marbach was at its height in 1579, Osiander had attacked Sturm while Tessanius attacked Marbach. The treatises, published in Frankfurt, were brought to the attention of the Strasbourg Magistrat. "It was decided to let the matter drop," recorded the city secretary, "and to let them write against each other until they get tired of it."[51] A variety of opinions could circulate within the city; only if they created political difficulties would the Rat move.

Matthias Flacius Illyricus and Cyriacus Spangenberg were Lutherans whose theology did not conform to the formulations accepted by the Strasbourg *Kirchenkonvent,* yet they resided in the city, and Spangenberg published at least eight books supporting Flacius's views. Flacius Illyricus arrived in Strasbourg in 1567 as a hero, recommended to the Magistrat by the *Kirchenkonvent* because he had led the resistance against the Interim in 1548. The son of a Slavic father and an Italian mother, Flacius had been educated in Venice and had gone from there to Wittenberg, where he became a passionate Lutheran. When Melanchthon accepted the Interim, Flacius left Wittenberg to begin a career of religious writing.[52] More than any other writer of the later period, he continued to probe for the historical sources of Protestant doctrine. He was contentious by nature and poured his full intellectual and physical energy into the search for the truth as he saw it. He was constantly embroiled with men whose minds were less quick than his own, and he pursued his adversaries relentlessly.[53] Expelled from Saxony by the duke himself, he arrived in Strasbourg hoping to receive an appointment at the Academy. He and Marbach had been friends when they were students, but it quickly became apparent that Marbach could not accept Flacius's mature theological views, in particular his formulation with regard to original sin. Flacius affirmed that original sin was attributable to substance, not accident. To Marbach this meant that he came perilously close to claiming that people could effectively act to resist sin. Flacius refused to abandon the doctrine, and the continued publication of his work led to a split between the two men. Despite this Flacius remained in the city, working on his exegesis of the New Testament and maintaining himself and his family through his writing from 1567 to 1573. In September 1570 he asked permission of the Magistrat to print a short explication of his doctrine on original sin in answer to his adversaries. The Rat was willing to permit this, though Flacius was ordered to report to them where it was being printed.[54] In the following year, however, books were circulated in Frankfurt which accused Flacius of being a Manichean and damned him as a heretic. The denouement was the result of further intervention from outside. The Elector August was an avowed enemy of Flacius. His continued complaints led the emperor to warn the Strasbourg Rat against providing protection for Flacius.[55] Inevitably, Flacius was then banished from the city.

Flacius's *Glossa* on the New Testament, on which he worked during his residence in Strasbourg, was a major contribution to Lutheran theology. It brought together all the important exegetical analyses of the New Testament, starting with those by the early church fathers. Flacius developed a historical method, believing that Christian doctrine could be understood only when it was examined chronologically.[56] The *Glossa* was not, however, published in Strasbourg. Only one of his treatises, an obviously anti-

Catholic, Latin analysis of papal errors, was printed by a Strasbourg press.[57] Flacius's doctrines were actually disseminated in Strasbourg through the work of one of his disciples, Cyriacus Spangenberg.

Spangenberg, a Wittenberg-trained theologian, was the preacher to the Count of Mansfeld.[58] During the 1560s his biblical commentaries, which strongly supported Flacius's theological views, were printed by Samuel Emmel.[59] In contrast to almost all the other biblical commentary of the period these were written in German. In his prefaces Spangenberg explained his reason for writing. Unity with God the father was essential for all things, but within the last year (1561) the devil had tried to tear men apart and introduce unrighteousness.[60] People had lashed out against those whose teachings were different from their own and had damned their opponents as false and wrong.[61] Spangenberg hoped to remind everyone of the gift of unity, which God alone could bestow.[62] In a later preface addressed to the queen of Denmark, Spangenberg affirmed that Luther's writings, and Luther's alone, should serve as the basis of all Christian truth, though his words had been misinterpreted by such men as Osiander and his followers. It was Flacius and his disciples who had corrected these errors and made the truth available.[63]

The heart of Spangenberg's commentaries lay in their treatment of sin, righteousness, and faith. Flacius taught that to the clean, all things are clean. He did not mean, however, that the pure cannot sin. Christ spoke to the woman of Canaan saying, "Oh woman, great is your faith, it will come to pass what you wish." Christ did not mean by this that she could defy the Ten Commandments or the will of God. The woman was a believer who had already given herself to the will of God, and thus she would desire nothing against God's law.[64] Here lay the crucial problem. By implication, Spangenberg claimed that the hearts of the faithful were purified by their act of faith. By giving themselves into the hands of God, they delivered themselves from the dangers of sin. This doctrine the Strasbourg ministers were unable to accept; yet, it was stated vigorously, year after year from 1560 to 1569, in Spangenberg's commentaries.

Spangenberg's loyalty to Flacius had led him into interminable conflicts, which eventually forced his departure from Mansfeld. His attacks against Jacob Andreae and the Formula of Concord brought him to Strasbourg as a refugee at the very time that Strasbourg finally accepted the Formula. Spangenberg resided in the city from 1577 to 1581 and from 1595 to 1596.[65] In these years no action was taken against him by either the Magistrat or the assembly of the clergy. The leader, Flacius, was banished from the city, but his disciple was given refuge.

Calvinist views were promulgated in the city by Johann Fischart, whose work was printed by his brother-in-law Bernard Jobin. Fischart was born in

Strasbourg, his father, a grocer, having settled in the city from Trier. Fischart received a master's degree from the Strasbourg Academy in 1568 and attended university in Paris and Italy. Despite his education he did not elect to pursue a career in the civil service or in teaching. Instead, he worked for his printer brother-in-law, living as a member of his household.[66] Throughout the 1570s Fischart devoted himself to writing propaganda for the Huguenot cause in France and for the beleaguered Calvinists in the Netherlands. Because of his pamphlets, poems, and broadsheets, the city was identified as a center of pro-Calvinist propaganda. Again the ambivalence of the Magistrat is noteworthy. They permitted David Chytraeus to publish a treatise against the Calvinists in 1567 because it provided a clear analysis of the differences between Calvinist teaching and the Confession of Augsburg, thus making the errors of Calvinism clear.[67] Throughout the 1570s, however, Fischart's reports on events in France pleaded the cause of the Calvinists. Both factions in the city, Calvinists and anti-Calvinists, were permitted to express themselves.

Nicodemus Frischlin was another intellectual whose contentiousness made it impossible for him to find a university or civil service appointment.[68] He taught briefly in a series of grammar schools, but by the end of two years he had usually worn out his welcome and was forced to move on. He was in and out of Strasbourg during the 1580s, and he involved himself in the Sturm-Marbach controversy on the side of Marbach. He was not entirely unacceptable to the Strasbourg establishment; his plays were even performed on the Academy stage. His comedy *Phasma* was unquestionably orthodox in its description of the confusion and tension generated by competing doctrines of faith.

The play championed unity of belief and the struggle against heresy. In the opening speech Corydon, a peasant, asks his friend how anyone can know what to believe. Some, he says, follow the pope, others Luther, others Zwingli, and not a few follow Schwenckfeld. There are also the Flacians, many Anabaptists, and even more Calvinists.[69] At this point, the pope seats himself upon a throne and asserts that he is the head of the church. Christ then appears before him, but the pope and his courtiers, unfamiliar with the Scriptures, are unable to examine Christ's teachings. Zwingli and Karlstadt are called before Christ to defend their teaching but are ashamed because they have perverted God's word. So it goes with all the rest, until Christ turns to Corydon, the peasant, saying, "Now the day of the Lord has come in the valley of confusion and all heretics will disappear."[70]

Frischlin's imaginary scene was not far from reality. Divisions remained in the city despite the efforts of the Lutheran theologians. Only Christ himself could have established unity among the different Protestant groups.

CHAPTER TWELVE · THE ACHIEVEMENT OF ACADEMIC ORTHODOXY

HILE IT PROVED IMPOSSIBLE FOR EITHER the Magistrat or the ministers to enforce religious orthodoxy, it was easier to establish effective control of the educational institutions. To achieve religious unity the authorities would have had to prevail upon all inhabitants of the city: patricians, burghers, artisans, apprentices, and the lower orders. Controlling the school involved only a small group, probably never more than six hundred students and from twenty to twenty-four members of the faculty.[1] Furthermore, this group was easily distinguishable by custom and way of life. In 1501 Wimpheling had petitioned the Rat to create a publicly supported school. This had been achieved in 1538 with the founding of the Gymnasium. But public support also meant public control, and the administration of the schools provides an excellent example of the managerial skills of the sixteenth-century magistracy. Everyday responsibility was delegated to the school board, whose members carried out their offices with the help of the school visitors. The separation of policy formulation and administration was carefully maintained. The teachers and professors were directly responsible to the visitors.[2] The school board was made up exclusively of Ratsherren.[3] The visitors included one theologian, one faculty member, and one Ratsherr.[4]

In 1566 the Upper Classes became the Academy as the result of an imperial privilege that gave the new institution the right to grant the master's degree. The change reflects both a desire to reform Johann Sturm's original curriculum and the city's ambition to acquire a more prestigious educational institution. Johann Sturm, himself, wanted the Upper Classes elevated to university status. The city, however, was reluctant to establish a university that would be an independent corporate unit with an autonomous faculty.

By 1555 Johann Sturm's influence on the educational systems of other cities had reached its highest point. The Upper Classes in Strasbourg began to suffer locally from comparison with the German universities or with the privileged Hochschule, which gave degrees. Students wanted degrees that led to better opportunities in the civil service and higher social status. Thus many young men left Strasbourg to go to the universities. Students also had other complaints. In a university they could become members of a corporation with recognized privileges and freedoms. In Strasbourg, students in the Upper Classes were still disciplined by the teachers and professors. Young Strasbourgers who went off to university after two years in the Upper Classes were teased by their peers at Tübingen, Heidelberg, and Wittenberg for their lack of independence.[5] There were also criticisms of Sturm's curriculum.

Johann Marbach, while he agreed on the basic content of the curriculum, felt that Sturm overburdened the students. He believed the course of studies could be made more attractive and that some of the classical studies could be cut back to permit more theology.[6] Marbach, himself a gifted administrator, was distressed by Sturm's informal administration of the school. Marbach also hoped to clarify the complex relationships between the church and the school, which had become confused by the presence of semi-autonomous and overlapping bodies like the assembly of the clergy, the old chapters, and the school itself.[7]

Balancing the pressures to change the Upper Classes was the Magistrat's conservatism. They were quite willing to have the prestige which a full-fledged university would bring, but the price was too high, not only monetarily but also administratively. A university would function as an autonomous corporate unit within the city after the Magistrat had just succeeded in bringing the former ecclesiastical corporations under their control. They were not willing to lose these gains so quickly to a university faculty which, among other things, would probably not discipline the students effectively.[8] Finally there was the problem of acquiring the privilege to grant degrees. This could only come from the emperor himself and, until 1557, the emperor had been slow to grant these to Protestant cities or territories.

The solution to these problems was offered at the Diet of Augsburg in 1566. Strasbourg agreed help against the Turks and, in return, the imperial authorities were willing to grant the city the right to confer the master's degree.[9] In 1567 the imperial privilege arrived and the new Academy was founded. In a public ceremony all faculty members who did not hold degrees, including Conrad Dasypodius, Theophilus Gol, Michael Bosch, and Jonas Bitner, were granted master's degrees.[10]

With the reorganization the Academy emerged as the center of intellectual life in the city. The Gymnasium settled into a subordinate position as a secondary school. There was competition for teachers at the time, and the school committee could rarely afford to bring instructors for the Gymnasium from the outside. They drew on scholarship students who had themselves attended the Gymnasium and the Upper Classes.[11] While the majority of the Academy staff, at first, were also graduates of the Gymnasium, professors were gradually brought in from other universities. Supervision of the Gymnasium and the Academy remained firmly in the hands of the Magistrat, administered by the established committees.

The faculties of arts and medicine were marked by stability of personnel in this period. In part this can be attributed to the sheer longevity of the key members of the faculty. Jonas Bitner, professor of Latin; Theophilus Gol, professor of Greek, later of ethics; Johann Hawenreuter, professor of logic, physics, and ethics; Melchior Junius, professor of eloquence; Johann Pappus, professor of Hebrew and history; Conrad Dasypodius, professor of mathematics; and Melchior Sebiz, professor of medicine, all taught for periods of from thirty to forty years.[12] Five of these men, Bitner, Gol, Dasypodius, Hawenreuter, and Junius, had received their own educations at the Strasbourg Gymnasium, and so carried another thread of continuity. Most of them had been in the school in the early years when the *esprit de corps* had been very high. Their decisions to devote themselves to teaching reflected the impact Johann Sturm had had on their own lives. Thus the core of the faculty was comprised of native Strassburgers. Other professors, men of eminent reputation, were drawn from as far away as Hamburg, Pomerania, Silesia, and Holland. Some of these, like Andreas Planer in medicine, Nikolaus Reusner in law, and Ernst Regius in ethics, stayed for relatively short periods, moving on to more prestigious appointments. Others, like Hubert Giphanius, settled into the life of the Academy and the city. Giphanius married Johann Marbach's daughter, thereby strengthening his ties to the community.[13]

In the first decades after the reorganization of the Academy, the intellectual and daily life of the school were disturbed by the struggle for power between Marbach and Sturm. From 1567 until his demission in 1581, Sturm continued as rector of the Gymnasium and factions formed around him. The teachers in the Gymnasium remained loyal to Sturm to a man, as did Conrad Dasypodius, Theophilus Gol, Valentin Erythreaus, and Leonhard Hertel from the Academy. The theologians supported Marbach.[14] But, there were other divisive issues as well. When the privileges of the Academy first arrived there was a dispute over whether to have a formal, public ceremony at which to confer degrees upon those members of the faculty without university credentials. Johann Sturm, Theophilus Gol, and the candidates were very much opposed to making it a civic occasion. They considered it a private, academic matter. The school board, however, wanted to confirm their new authority openly.[15] The latter won. That same year Ernst Regius proposed to the school board a reform to permit periodic election of all officials in the school, including the rector, and several changes in the curriculum that would create a sharper differentiation between the Gymnasium and the Academy. This, again, led to a dispute within the faculty because it struck at the position of the Gymnasium teachers, who were already threatened. Because Regius had supported the Magistrat on the issue of a public degree-granting ceremony, the split which had developed then was deepened.[16] When Sturm was demoted, Melchior Junius was appointed rector by the school board, and not until 1594 was any attempt made to involve the faculty in the selection of the rector. In that year all the professors were sent out of the room and called in one by one. Each was asked to name four candidates, one from each faculty. The school board then named Johann Pappus rector.[17] These incidents demonstrate the rivalries and factionalism that splintered the Gymnasium and the Academy in the last decades. Although one faculty member was meant to sit on the assembly of the clergy, the clerical group became more independent, and the faculty moved toward the establishment of its own semiautonomous governing unit.[18]

The requirement that all members of the faculty publicly affirm their loyalty to the Confession of Augsburg was scrupulously enforced. Close academic supervision was also maintained. For example, after finishing the first book of Euclid's and Mela's *Rudimenta sphero,* the professor of mathematics was allowed to move on to the second book only after discussion with the rector and the school board.[19] The professor of physics was to use only the assigned texts; changes could be made only through the action of the entire school board.[20] By the end of the century the regulations were even more stringent. No professor could give any sort of lessons at home. No private reading courses or disputations could be held. As a means of control, the lecture notes of all students could be called in by the school committee for inspection at the time of the examination for the master's degree.[21]

The Gymnasium and the Academy remained humanist schools after the reorganization. Eloquence was given precedence over other fields—no other classes could conflict with the 8 A.M. lectures of the professor of rhetoric.[22] Philosophy was regarded as one of the liberal arts, like philology or history.[23] The Strasbourg schools were newly founded, and therefore avoided the struggles between the humanist disciplines and scholastic philosophy that were common in this period at the older universities.[24]

Schindling believes that Sturm's oratorical and dialectical texts did not have a continuing influence in the Strasbourg schools, nor, he asserts, were they used in schools outside the city.[25] Rott, however, points to the diffusion of Sturm's texts in Poland and, as late as 1726, in Jena.[26] The publication data confirms Rott's findings. Sturm's *Partitiones oratoriae* went through five editions between 1557 and 1565, and there were eight editions, in various forms, of the *Partitionum dialecticarum* from 1557 to 1591.[27] The basis of Sturm's method in both these texts was a meticulous form of diagramming by which each step of an orator's argument was broken down so that the student could understand the inner structure of the thought.[28] True, this was adopted in the Strasbourg schools as a means of improving oratorical skills, and neither Sturm nor any other member of the faculty went on to apply it to the whole structure of learning,[29] but eventually the methods evolved for young orators would be applied to scientific thought by Melanchthon and Ramus.[30] In the later decades it was Valentin Erythraeus, Sturm's pupil, who preserved the Sturmian techniques by incorporating them into the teaching at the Academy. He prepared and published diagrammatic tables of Sturm's texts on dialectics and of Cicero's speeches. He applied the method to theology as well in a diagrammatic exposition of the Confession of Augsburg.[31] Diagrams were also used by Johann Hawenreuter and the lawyers Nikolaus Reusner and Dionysus Gothofridus.[32] Whether derived from Sturm or from others, logical analysis was a fundamental element of the training and intellectual experience of the Academy student.

The ascendance of rhetoric in the Academy was reflected in the requirement, enacted in 1578, that each student participate in a formal, public disputation before receiving his degree.[33] Students were also required to publish their theses, and they provided a steady business for the printers, particularly Anton Bertram, who seems to have functioned as a semiofficial printer to the Academy. These theses were limited to between four and eight pages, in which the student gave his argument and his conclusions. The topics, assigned by the professors, were remarkable for their repetition of certain standard subjects. The Nicomachean Ethics was a favorite source, and propositions were drawn from every book. There were declamations on religious topics, on other books of Aristotle, and in praise of the liberal arts. Moral themes and the rules of grammar and dialectic were common topics.[34]

The Gymnasium faculty did not, as a rule, publish much during the last decades of the century. The Academy faculty also published less frequently than their predecessors. Forty-eight men served on the faculty of the Upper Classes and the Academy from 1555 to 1599, and, of these, only twenty-four published. (From 1538 to 1550 sixteen of twenty-two faculty members had published.) Publication of classical editions and textbooks was reduced, in part because the work had already been done. Sturm's texts and those of Erythraeus continued to be used through the end of the century. The rather dramatic decline in this type of publication is portrayed in table 19, which also bears witness to the continuing importance of Sturm's texts. These were used not only in Strasbourg but in other cities as well.

Editions of classical authors were, by the 1560s, relatively easy to obtain from either the local presses, Basel, or other cities. The Academy faculty

Table 19. Texts and Classical Editions by Academy Faculty, 1560–1599

	1560–70	1571–80	1581–90	1591–99	Total
Editions by Faculty Members Other					
Than Johann Sturm					
Latin classics	7	3	0	5	15
Greek classics	8	5	1	4	16
Classical drama	5	6	1	2	14
Rhetoric and oratorical texts	16	7	0	2	25
Dialectics and logic	4	2	0	1	7
Editions by Johann Sturm					
Latin classics	21	18	3	1	43
Rhetoric and oratorical texts	16	7	0	2	25
Poetry anthology	1	8	5	1	15

filled a few gaps here and there, mostly with editions of Greek authors. There was a revised version of Aesop's fables, an edition of Thucydides, and an edition of Xenephon.[35] Michael Bosch, professor of Greek, prepared Greek editions of the dialogues of Plato needed by the students—the defense of Socrates and the *Crito*.[36] The emphasis on the Nicomachean Ethics led Josias Rihel to print three editions.[37] Several members of the faculty, among them Melchior Junius, wrote or edited oratorical texts. Appointed rector after Sturm's demission, Junius did much to maintain balance and order in these difficult years.[38] His primary interest was, like Sturm's, Latin eloquence. He edited Cicero's speech to Marcus Brutus, several collections of examples of different oratorical styles, and an anthology of speeches drawn from Greek and Latin historians.[39] Johann Benz, professor of dialectics and mathematics, published commentaries on Cicero's orations and a Greek and Latin thesaurus that provided the popular *loci communes* needed by the students.[40]

The declining rate of production of classical editions indicates that the major work of preparing texts and scholarly editions had already been accomplished. The men of the later generation were, therefore, free to work in areas of their own particular interests. They tended to cross over from one field to another, and mathematics and history, which had formerly been peripheral, became more important.

That scholars could move from one academic discipline to another proves the strength of the university training of the period. The extent to which this was practiced underscores the breadth of interest of these men. David Kyber, for example, was the professor of Hebrew from 1550 to 1569, but his scholarly work was in the field of botany. He translated Hieronymus Bock's botany from German into Latin, making it scholarly for the learned world. He also compiled a trilingual botanical dictionary.[41] Johann Pappus, the theologian, wrote history.[42] Johann Ludwig Hawenreuter began his teaching career as a professor of dialectics, went on to become a professor of medicine, and finally devoted all of his attention to Aristotelian science.[43] Michael Beuther, professor of history, was trained in law and medicine as well as in letters. He published astronomical treatises.[44] Melchior Sebiz and Andreas Planer from the faculty of medicine translated a contemporary French text on natural philosophy and agronomy.[45]

Thus there was cross-fertilization between disciplines, and new academic fields were opened to students. The establishment of the professorship of history serves as an example of this. Despite the interest of the early humanists in historical studies, history was not included in the curriculum of the Gymnasium or the Upper Classes in 1538. Nikolaus Gerbel was named professor of history in 1541, but this appointment was more an attempt to placate him and his patron Jacob Sturm than it was an introduction of the formal study of history.[46] The most important work in history during the 1550s was done by a writer who was not connected with the schools, Jean Sleidan. History was officially added to the curriculum of the Academy in 1565, and Michael Beuther was appointed as the first professor. Trained as a lawyer, Beuther shared the broad-ranging interests of his generation. His publications included a treatise on Greek and Roman festivals, in which he showed an awareness of the importance of the organization of social life to culture; he also perceived the usefulness of events like the Olympic and Delphic games to create the chronological sequence of Greek history.[47] As professor of history at the Strasbourg Academy, Beuther turned his attention to the study of the origins of the Germanic peoples. He went back to the Roman sources to trace the development of tribal groups, such as the Vandals, the Slavs, and the Franks, and then followed their gradual intrusion into western Europe. It was a staggering task, and the book was published posthumously.[48] Beuther was a central figure on the Academy faculty, and his historical interests encouraged others around him.

Johann Pappus needed no encouragement. For him church history was secondary only to theology. He carried on the historical lectures between the time of Beuther's death and the appointment, in 1591, of Philipp Glaser.[49] He also wrote a short history of Germany, based on Roman sources, for the students. His history of the early church began with the period of persecution and carried through to the emergence of the great heresies, the schisms that split the eastern and western churches, and the work of the early church councils.[50] His account reflects a thorough knowledge of the sources and painstaking analysis and judgment. The interest of the Protestant theologians in the early church now bore fruit in these historical studies.

Nikolaus Reusner, professor of law at the Academy from 1585 to 1589, published a series of illustrated biographies of famous historical and contemporary figures.[51] These books were significant because he chose learned men and humanists, rather than popes, kings, and military figures. Intellectuals and scientists, he believed as important as, if not more important than, statesmen and military leaders. He included contemporaries like Martin Luther, Martin Bucer, Savanarola, Jean Calvin, Nikolaus Copernicus, Andreas Vesalius, and Paracelsus.[52]

The historical lectures established the study of the past as one of the liberal arts. Music and dramatics continued to be integrated into the curriculum of the Gymnasium. Performances by the students were now given publicly, and contemporary poets, like Nicodemus Frischlin, Georg Frischlin, Georg Calaminus, and Michael Hospeinius, wrote Latin plays for the student actors.[53] Biblical plays were regarded as useful for moral instruction, and two faculty members, Christopher Thomas Walliser and Hieronymus Schütz, adapted biblical stories for the school theater.[54] Classical drama, however, was the most important. Written notes in an edition of *Medea* in the Bibliothèque Nationale in Strasbourg permit us to reconstruct a production of the Greek tragedy at the end of the century. Christopher Thomas Walliser, the music master, presented the play in Greek on July 7, 1598.[55] On the fly leaf of his own copy Walliser listed the members of the chorus by name: twenty-five sopranos, eighteen tenors, fourteen altos, and seventeen basses. For their appearance in act 2 the chorus was lined up in six rows: the first, clad in red tunics, held a small net in one hand, a trident in the other; the second, in blue, carried maces and shields; the third, dressed like Moors in white shorts and boots, carried bows and quivers on their backs; the fourth wore similar white boots and carried brightly-colored balls in their hands; the fifth wore green and held sabres in one hand, scabbards in the other; the last row, dressed in yellow tunics, carried great stones on their shoulders and wore crowns or garlands on their heads.[56] At the end of act 3 the chorus represented Mars, his warriors, satellites, and knights. Led in by a knight with a banner, the warriors carried muskets and halberds. Footmen on one side wore motley; those on the other wore painted tunics.[57] It was a colorful production that involved as many of the students as possible, from the youngest, who could still sing soprano, to the older basses. The costumes leave the modern reader wondering who did the sewing—the mothers?

Music, particularly singing, was taught in both the Gymnasium and the Academy. Christopher Thomas Walliser served first as master of music at the Gymnasium, and then became professor of music at the Academy. His hymns and settings for the psalms were included in many Lutheran hymnals.[58] David Wolckenstein had a dual appointment as professor of music and of mathematics; he also directed the choirs and the orchestra at the Academy from 1586 to 1592. He, too, published settings for the psalms and music that he had composed for the school choruses.[59] The musical choruses followed the same metrical principles as the odes and epics of classical Latin, thus choral singing was yet another means of achieving the humanist goal of eloquence of diction.[60]

More scientific instruction was offered in the last decades, as Aristotle was firmly reestablished as the source of scientific knowledge. Johann Sturm had included the teaching of mathematics in his original curriculum, but this was extended significantly by Conrad Dasypodius. The study of Aristotelian physics was started by Zanchi in 1554/55, but after Zanchi's forced departure these lectures were assigned to the professor of medicine, who added them to his expositions of Galen and Hippocrates.[61] When the Academy was founded, Aristotle was established even more firmly in its curriculum. In 1567 Michael Beuther, the historian, appearing before the school committee, strongly recommended a greater emphasis on physics, by which he meant Aristotelian science. The students, he said, should spend eighteen months on mathematics and then proceed to physics using the Aristotelian texts, *De naturali auscultatione (Physica), De Caelo, De Mundo, Meteorologica, De Anima,* and the second book of Pliny.[62] The texts had already been prepared. Zanchi had edited *De Naturali* in 1553, Conrad Dasypodius had completed the *Meteorologica* in 1566, and *De Mundo* had been printed in 1565.[63] Beuther suggested that the lectures be split between Conrad Dasypodius and Johann Bruno,[64] a former Gymnasium student who had studied with Cardano in Italy. Bruno took over the physics lectures,[65] but his early death in 1541 halted the evolution of physics as an independent field. The lectures on Aristotle again became the responsibility of the professor of medicine, and not until 1589, when Johann Ludwig Hawenreuter decided to concentrate his energies on Aristotelian science, did physics emerge as an independent discipline.[66] Hawenreuter was one of the most popular teachers in the Academy, but his teaching did not go beyond providing a commentary on the text. Since Aristotle's *Physica* was too long to be covered in the two-year master's course, Hawenreuter made a summary of five of Aristotle's major works,[67] which meant that the students were using a secondary source rather than the original texts. Scientific teaching was not extended in new directions and there was no attempt to introduce methods based on observations from nature, but Aristotelian science was made more available.[68]

The same was true of mathematics. Conrad Dasypodius published many books, but his work remained traditional both conceptually and pedagogically. Preparing mathematical texts for the school was his first priority. In 1564 he published a section of Euclid for the Gymnasium under the name of his former teacher, Christian Herlin, by then deceased. In the same year he published his own complete Euclid, with commentaries based on Theon of Alexandria, for the Upper Classes. He revised these editions for the next twenty years, adding to them a Greek text of Heron that included a vocabulary of geometrical terms.[69]

Dasypodius's lifework was a *Summa mathematica,* which he hoped would bring together the whole corpus of mathematical knowledge. He gained the support of the emperor himself, who instructed the major universities to cooperate with Dasypodius and to provide him with any materials he might need.[70] Although this work was never completed, his two volume *Mathematicum* and his *Institutionum mathematicarum* summarized the academic mathematics of the time.[71] Algebra, traditionally, was excluded. For Dasypodius, mathematics consisted of geometry, arithmetic, logic, geography, and astronomy. He began his books with a description of arithmetical functions and continued through the application of mathematical principles to astronomy.[72]

Dasypodius embodied the conflicts which faced the academic scientists of his time. His humanist interest in languages and the classical sources were manifested in his mathematical dictionary.[73] He had an important collection of manuscripts by Greek mathematicians, including Appolonius of Perga, Aristides, and Diophanatos; yet, when he wrote his translation of Heron of Alexandria, he worked from a Latin translation.[74] He was tied to the ancient sources and continued to base his geographical descriptions on Ptolemy. Though he did feel obliged to mention the New World, named by Amerigo Vespucci in 1497, he was unable to accept the Copernican view of the world; in a sense he ignored it.[75] In his section on the theory of the spheres he described the earth as round, placed in the middle of the world, where it functioned as a fixed star.[76] He describes different forms of stellar motion. The first, described by Aristotle, was the movement of the sky from the orient to the occident in twenty-four hours. The planets and fixed stars move essentially in place, as well as over the poles and along the axis of the zodiac. He also discussed the problem of spherical motion, concluding that some of the stars move obliquely, but that the zodiac and the milky way maintain a circular motion.[77] In 1568 Dasypodius published a short lecture by the Wittenberg mathematician Caspar Peucer which described the Copernican concept of planetary tracks. This Dasypodius could accept because it did not depend upon the heliocentric system.[78] In his treatise on comets, Dasypodius gave a meticulous description of how an astronomer should determine the location, place, distance, magnitude, and motion of a comet, but then fell back on Ptolemy's description of the doleful effects of comets on mankind—sedition, fire, disease, insanity.[79] Dasypodius never pulled free from Aristotle or Ptolemy. He was unable to make fresh observations based on experience because he could not conceive of new truths. The truth had already been revealed.

The reorganized Academy established a faculty of medicine to replace the lectures which from time to time had been offered in the Upper Classes. Andreas Planer, a recent graduate of Tübingen, received the first appointment to the medical faculty in 1571. He remained until 1584, when he returned to Tübingen to fill a more prestigious chair.[80] Johann Ludwig Hawenreuter, whose father, Sebald, was a Strasbourg physician, took over the lectures until 1585, but after a short period resumed his post as professor of physics.[81] The medical chair then went to Melchior Sebiz, a student of Ambrose Paré, who had been serving as city physician at Haguenau.[82] At the end of the century Israel Spach, a Strassburger by birth, educated at the Gymnasium and in Paris, took over as professor of medicine. The presence of Academy increased the number of university-trained physicians practicing and working in the city, for these men attracted others.

The medicine that these men taught was the traditional Galenic-Hippocratic corpus.[83] Like their colleagues in the liberal arts, the professors of medicine published little. They appear in the publications of the period chiefly as the authors of theses presented by their students.[84] Israel Spach, however, published a gynecological text which represented the best of university medicine in his day. It was a huge volume, 1,080 folio pages, composed of recent treatises on gynecology. Many of the twenty-one articles in the collection had appeared in different languages and had been translated into Latin to make them available to medical students and professors. The contributors included Felix Platter; Moschionos, a modern Greek physician; Nicolas Roche, Jacques Roche, Maurice Cordeaus, and Ambrose Paré, all French; Ludovici Bonaciolo of Ferrara; and Ludovici Mercato, a Spanish physician. There were many more moderns than ancients, the latter including only Priscian and Albucasus, the Arab-Spaniard. This book indicates that physicians, unlike the mathematicians or physicists, were achieving a new independence. The doctors were convinced of the validity of their own observations and presented them to their colleagues. In certain ways Spach's gynecology resembled a modern medical journal, for it incorporated the findings of well-established and recognized experts in the field. Each treatise was directed to a different problem: female anatomy, menstruation and its problems, conception, pregnancy, and cesarean sections.[85] The book was meant to be used as a text, and thus indicates the efforts that were made by the end of the century to disseminate recent information among university-trained physicians.

The Academy also inaugurated more rigorous instruction in law, and the city became an important center of humanist jurisprudence. The teaching of law in the city predated the founding of the Gymnasium. In the 1520s the city jurist was assigned to lecture on the *Institutes* of Justinian on a weekly basis.[86] These lectures were then continued in the Upper Classes by Ludwig Bebio, whose commentaries on book 4 of the *Institutes* were published posthumously. Immediately after the war, the law lectures were given by two young Frenchmen, François Baudoin and François Hotman, refugees closely identified with the French school of humanist jurisprudence that had begun to look at the ancient law codes historically and philologically.[87] When the Academy was reorganized there were two chairs of law; by 1575 there were three. Hubert Giphanius lectured on the *Institutes* while Georg Obrecht developed a new method of teaching based on actual presentation of cases; Obrecht also initiated the study of feudal law. Nikolaus Reusner continued the tradition of humanist jurisprudence. Together these men created a center of legal studies in Strasbourg, which was responsible for a sharp increase in legal publications and disputations.[88]

The Gymnasium and the Academy were representative of humanist schools throughout the German states and cities, France, and Italy. The classical curriculum they offered became standard training for the nobility, the patricians, the Protestant and Catholic clergy, and the professions for the next three centuries. Based on a mastery of ancient languages and techniques of oratory and dialectic, the course of study produced ordered, disciplined minds. There was little room for original inquiry or speculation, but it was an extraordinarily effective system for transferring accumulated knowledge from one generation to the next.

Socially, the schools created a common cultural experience for the governing classes of western Europe. In the urban environment of Strasbourg they created new bonds of loyalty between the secular and spiritual leaders of the community. The students were drawn from patrician families, from the constofler, and from leading guild families. In addition, faculty sons, the sons of the clergy, and the sons of a few artisan families were admitted on scholarship.[89] More boys than ever before received an education which prepared them for holding public or church offices or for academic life. The very nature of their education set them apart from the rest of urban society. They were the privileged few, trained to govern and to lead. The schools helped to maintain an aristocratic system by creating a learned estate with a shared background and similar goals. The bonds formed in the school room were carried into adult life.[90]

CHAPTER THIRTEEN · PROPAGANDA AND JOURNALISM

Y THE END OF THE CENTURY VERNACU-lar publication had also become less varied. Bernard Jobin, the first major printer to devote a large proportion of his production to vernacular works, dominated the market and thus had narrowed the scope of vernacular literature. Johann Grüninger, in the earliest decades, had committed 20 percent of his total to popular books. Of Jobin's total production, 40 percent were popular books (table 6). In addition, Theobald Berger turned out a steady stream of popular songs after 1565 which amounted to 18 percent of the total. The situation was very different from what it had been in the middle of the century, when Christian Mylius I and II, Paul and Georg Messerschmidt, Jacob Cammerlander, and Josias Rihel were all printing vernacular works. Between 1570 and 1599, 251 vernacular works were printed, 93 of them by Jobin. Fifty-four percent of all journalism came from his press, and it represented his point of view or that of his brother-in-law Johann Fischart. Strongly anti–Catholic and pro-Calvinist, they impressed upon the German reading public the intolerable injustices suffered by the French and Dutch Protestants because of their faith. As in the 1520s, the presses were used to influence men's opinions and beliefs.

While the ministers struggled to establish the Confession of Augsburg as the Articles of Faith for the city of Strasbourg, the lay culture continued to develop its own forms of religious expression. The laity do not seem to have been deeply concerned by the arguments over the nature of the presence of Christ in the Eucharist. They accepted the fact that Christ was there and went on to other matters. Nor were they moved to express themselves about the Confession of Augsburg. The majority of the inhabitants of the city were certainly Protestant, but they were not especially anxious to define their own religious beliefs in precise terms.[1] Gerald Strauss suggests that formal religion, whether Catholic or Protestant, made little impact on the general adult population.[2] The publication data would indicate that the religious beliefs of the laity were often expressed without reference to formal creeds and doctrines in the plays, popular songs, religious songs, and journalism of the time.

The basis of popular religious belief was the all-encompassing power of God and his immanent presence in the everyday world. He was the God of the Pentateuch: omnipotent, patriarchal, judgmental, capable of great mercy, but also capable of punishing people who broke his commandments. This concept of God was reflected in the titles of popular religious songs: "Help me God, my creator, that I may succeed"; "God, the tender father, is wise"; "I call to Thee, my Father in Heaven"; "Oh Lord God of Sabeoth, we the poor cry out to thee"; "Oh God, I do not ask for pitilessness from you"; "God is generous and merciful"; and "The world moves by the help of God."[3] In these songs the writers and the singers appealed to the mercy of God, his wisdom, his tenderness, but his omnipotence was assumed. His was the ultimate force in the universe.

God's activity in the daily world was an integral part of almost every journalistic account of the time.[4] Whatever the event, whether the birth of quintuplets, a murder, or a war, it had happened because God had willed it. Every act, every occurrence, was the result of divine intention. Thus, when the sun appeared with two smaller suns or the moon was surrounded by a ring covered with crosses and stars, it was taken to mean that God wished to manifest his power. His wonderful works were not always revealed clearly to men, nor were they revealed in a way that men could understand, but he wished to show men what was around them. He might also use stars, the sun, and the moon as weapons against mankind.[5] Another broadsheet depicts two women washing and hanging out clothes while two workmen gazed at the sky, which rained drops of blood. This was a sign of God's anger; men must repent to turn his anger away.[6] A comet in 1556 led a journalist to pray that God would turn men away from the pursuit of earthly things to seek the new life offered in Jesus Christ.[7] Another writer, reporting the same comet, quoted from Luke 21: "When there will be signs in the heavens and upon the earth . . . look up and raise your heads because your redemption is drawing near."[8]

The ever-present fear of God was manifested in men's reactions to unusually productive plants. This phenomenon could easily have been interpreted as a sign that God recognized the needs of mankind and promised to provide ample food and drink. Yet, reports of remarkable wheat plants or vines stressed the power of God and the warning he intended. A wonderful sheaf of wheat bearing seventy-two ears of grain was depicted in a woodcut. The accompanying poem stated that everyone knew that such a sheaf could not have come from a single grain of wheat. What God purposed by this act each person would have to decide for himself, but the obvious lesson was that men should turn to God and seek his Kingdom before all else.[9] Another set of exceptional stalks of grain (one with five ears, the other with thirteen) recalled Pharaoh's dream. Knowing that God meant something by the seven ears, Pharaoh had sent for Joseph. Strasbourg had no Joseph, but at least three things were clear: first, that those who were now

Neuwe Zeyttung vnd Warhaffte geschicht/ so dises ge=
genwertigen M. D. LIIII. Jars/ von vilen Menschen zů Ingelstatt/ zů Regenspurg/
vnd zů Nürnberg am himel gesehen worden/ Wie dann inn diser hienach gesatzten Figur
vnd volgendem Text weytleüffiger Bemelt vnd angezeygt wirt.

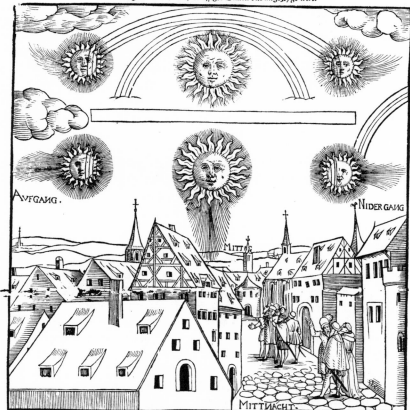

Erstlich seind zů Ingelstatt drey Sonnen am himel auff den vj. tag Marci zwischen acht vnd neün vhrn vor Mittag gesehen worden/ Jnn solcher gestalt wie durch die oberst Figur mit einem Regenbogen von beden neben Sonnen angezeigt ist/ On allein das der jnnerst Regenbogen mit sampt dem nebensichtigen Regenbogen gegen dem Nidergang nit darbey/ Auch seind die zwo neben Sonnen mit der farb eines Regenbogens nit bekleidet gewesen/ wie es inn der obern figur angezeigt vnd zů Nürnburg gesehen ist worden.

¶ Dann gleicher weiß wie sie zů Ingelstatt seind gesehen/ also e auch haben sie sich zů Nürnberg/ den xxiij. Marci am heiligen Karfreitag inn der ersten stund nach Mittag auch eraigt/ On allein das es innerhalb gegen der rechten Sonnen noch einen Regenbogen gehabt/ Auch zwo neben Sonnen mit einer farb des regenbogens halb bekleidet gewest/ vñ weit von der Sonnen gegen dem nidergang hat es noch ein schönen Regenbogen gehabt/ Zů solchem ist auch ein Weisser ring/ auß den zween neben Sonen/ sehr weit gegen mitternacht gegangen vnd beschlossen gewest/ Vnnd wie dann solicher weisser Reiff/ von wegen des regenbogens nit hat können gemacht werden/ sondern nur von den beden Sonnen ein wenig angezeigt ist/ auch hat es ein weissen strich mitten durch die recht Sonnen gehabt/ Zwů weilen haben sich solche Sonnen verloren/ vnd bald darauff wider hell sehen lassen/ das hat gewerdt/ biß inn die dritte stund vngeferlich/ ec.

Aber vor solchem/ ehe sie zů Nürnberg gesehen/ hat man sie den xx. Obberürte Monate zů Regenspurg auch gesehen/ Jnn solcher gestalt wie sie in der vndern Figur angezeigt sein/ Vnd die etwas weyt von einander/ vnd doch inn einer Parabel gestanden/ Jr anfang ist gewest vmb ein vhr nach mittag/ vnd jr wirckung ist zwüschen zwey vnd drey vhr am grössten/ vnd hat bey nahende/ biß in die vierdte stund gewert/ Auch haben solche drey Sonnen streym von sich gegeben/ gleich wie Cometen schwentz/ die recht mittel Sonn hat jre streym stracks gegen Mitternacht/ vñ die andern gegen auff vnd nidergang gehabt/ auch seind die neben Sonnen halb mit der farb eines Regenbogens bekleydet gewesen/ Vnd vber solche Sonnen einen langen weyssen strich/ oder balcken gehabt/ wie dann auß der vndern Figur zůsehen/ etc.

¶ Was nun solche zeychen bedeüten/ ist auß des Herren Christi worten von den letsten zeytten/ vñ seiner herrlichen zůkunfft/ was für grosse verfürung/ trübseligkeyt/ angst vnd not/ vor her gehn sollen/ dannocht die Welt darneben so frech/ böß vnnd sicher seind/ ec. leichtlich zůuerstehn/ Gott wöll das wir es erkennen/ vnser leben darnach besseren/ vnd soul gnaden erwerben/ das wir inn einer seligen stund betretten/ abscheyden/ vnd das ewig leben/ durch Jesum Christum vnsern lieben Herren erlangen mögen/ Amen.

¶ Zů Straßburg truckts Theobaldus Berger.

Plate 12. A wondrous sighting of three suns in the sky at Ingolstadt, Regensburg, and Nuremburg in 1554. "These are signs, in accordance with Christ's words, of the coming of the last days, for the world has become so evil that God wishes that we should know it so that we may live better." Printed by Theobald Berger, 1554.

in need would soon receive from five to thirteen times as much as before; second, that God would encourage the poor in this dreadful time by making every acre bear from five to thirteen times more; and third, that the rich should take warning. In this instance God's action was protective to the poor and threatening to the rich, but the writer concluded that God had made the grain stalk to create faith and fear.[10]

Monstrous births, particularly of animals with two heads or with the wrong number of legs, were also seen as warnings; this was the interpretation given to abnormal or unusual human births as well. A report of the birth of quintuplets was both sorrowful and accepting of God's will. The woodcut showed the mother in bed, propped up against pillows, looking exhausted and sad, attended by another woman. In the foreground, four infants were laid on a wide table in swaddling clothes while another woman swaddled the fifth. The account attested that Anna Risin had borne five living children on the Sunday before Christmas, all perfectly formed and normal. Since the children were weak they had been baptized at home, according to old Christian custom. They had lived two hours and then died. It should be noted, the report continued, that the same woman had borne triplets at another birth. What Almighty God wanted men to understand through such a wonderful occurrence could not be written in the newssheet, but it was clear that he wished men to know and recognize his majesty through a true understanding of the Christian faith and that men should praise and honor him for all his works.[11]

The laity perceived Christ's role in the world quite differently from God the Father's. More songs were addressed to God than to Christ—twenty-two songs invoked God and praised his actions or his qualities; only thirteen mentioned Christ. Many of these recounted an incident from the Gospels: the marriage feast of Cana; the resurrection of Lazarus; or Christ's own Passion.[12] In only three instances was Christ described as the mediator between God and man. In one case he was called the son who stands in the highest; in the other two cases the songwriter thanked God for his goodness in sending Christ.[13] Christ was depicted as a man living among men, taking action in the daily world. Even his role as intercessor was not strongly affirmed. That four of the thirteen songs were about the Passion or the Seven Words shows that the suffering Christ remained a powerful image. The only song of praise to Christ involved the theme of suffering, "Oh, Jesus, tender manifestation of God, a rose among the thorns."[14] With less emphasis on penance, there was less emphasis on Christ as the mediator between God and men. His gift of himself was more important.

The most popular religious book for the laity in this period, as we have already observed, was Luther's *Betbüchlein,* which went through five editions from 1560 to 1591. The prayer book was written early in the career of the reformer to provide an alternative to the *Hortulus animae* and the traditional books of hours. In a short preface Luther stated that every Christian person, no matter how humble, should be obliged to know the Ten Commandments, the Apostles' Creed, and the Lord's Prayer.[15] The *Betbüchlein* gave an exposition of each of these in turn. The exposition of each commandment came first, followed by the commandment itself.[16] The Creed was broken down into three parts—God, the son, and the holy spirit—and then explained under these headings,[17] though the full text did not appear. The Lord's Prayer, Luther explained, comprised seven divine petitions; the meaning of each was developed.[18]

The Creed, the Commandments, and the Lord's Prayer were the basis of Christian life. Questions about theological doctrine or the meaning of the Eucharist were rarely raised in the vernacular literature. There is, for instance, no song or poem on communion or on the elements. Even broadsheets that might have addressed themselves to questions of faith or doctrine avoided them. Thus, an early broadsheet on the martyrdom of Johann Hus gave an account of his trial and execution without mentioning his doctrines.[19] An encomium to Bullinger, published after his death, noted that he had gotten his grey hair in the service of God. His courage and understanding were known all over Switzerland. His books had explained God's word and testified to the power and glory of Christ. But there was no account of his teachings.[20] Doctrine was discussed in a broadsheet that recounted the heroic martyrdom of two young Dutch Anabaptist noblewomen. When asked what they believed, they had replied that they believed in Christ's teaching and in his holy word. They were then asked if they were Anabaptists. No, they replied. They had been baptized once according to Christ's teaching in Mark 16, and that was sufficient. Did they believe in the pope's mass and sacrament? No, they replied. They accepted no teaching from men, but only from God. They believed in Christ and in his word, in his testament before his death, his tender body in the morsel of bread, and his holy blood in the clear wine. These he had commanded us to drink for our sins.[21]

The reform had created a simple and direct faith. God's role as a powerful force in everyday life was accentuated more than his role as a judge. The earlier emphasis on sin and confession was replaced by a fear of God, a recognition that he demanded that commandments be kept. The Christ they imagined was the Christ of the Gospels, who went among the people, cared for the sick, cured the dying, and celebrated with the living; he was not omnipresent in daily life.

The religious ideas and religious identity of the laity were deeply influenced by political events. In the last decades, the political polemic engendered by the wars of religion in France and the Netherlands exerted an influence similar to that of the religious polemic written by the reformers. It crystallized men's ideas, it governed their actions, and it created sharp divisions between truth and error. This later polemic was written, not by the clergy, but by laymen, unassociated with the church or the Academy. The chief polemicist in Strasbourg was Johann Fischart, an educated man who showed no interest in a clerical or scholarly appointment, but who devoted himself to a campaign against the papacy, the Guise, and the Spanish Hapsburgs. He was supported by his brother-in-law, Bernard Jobin. Swiss by birth, Jobin had purchased citizenship in 1560 and established his own shop.[22] He then assembled a team of translators who worked tirelessly translating Huguenot tracts, treatises, and accounts of major events in the wars of religion. Fischart was the major force behind this enterprise.[23] A few accounts were published by Theobald Berger, but over fifty percent of these newssheets, poems, and pasquils were printed by Jobin. The accounts written by Fischart himself were strongly anti-papal and anti-Guise. These were no unbiased, objective narratives, but overt propaganda.

Fischart intensified the anti-papalism of the early period of the reform, and it became more bitter and more venomous. The pope became the scapegoat for all the evils suffered by mankind. He had fostered division among the Christian laity, repressed and suppressed the people. Belief in the pope's malevolence was a strong element in this propaganda. The broadsheet *Malchopapo* depicts the pope as having usurped the position of Saint Peter. A woodcut in the style of Tobias Stimmer shows Saint Peter with his right arm uplifted to strike the pope, grasping the key of ecclesiastical authority with his left hand. In the background, a small but lively devil relieves the pope of his staff. The text developed the theme of the woodcut. The pope had disregarded his duty to God and thought only of his own honor and authority. He had not preached God's word to the people and the people were pushed to murder and crime. Every responsibility of the pope had been abrogated; he had taught Christians false doctrines and had led them around by the nose.[24] In another broadsheet, *Der Gorgonisch Meduse Kopf,* the pope was depicted as Medusa, turning everyone who looked on him to stone. Medusa was an evil animal who sold various commodities: holy water, the elements of the sacrament, oil, salt, everything down to the peals of the church bells and the torments of purgatory.[25]

Fischart used every possible weapon in his campaign against the Catholic clergy. One of the interior pillars of the Strasbourg cathedral, dating from perhaps the twelfth century, depicted a collection of animals in ecclesiastical procession—a bear serving as the incense bearer, a deer carrying the cross, a hare carrying the candle, and a fox and a goat bearing the sacrament, which was a pig. Fischart took advantage of this grotesque, alleging that this was the kind of bad example the church and the priesthood had set for centuries.

Plate 13. "Malchopapo," 1577. The invective poem against the pope is attributed to Johann Fischart, the woodcut to Tobias Stimmer, and the printing to Bernard Jobin. "O blessed Christ, here you see the unequal battle / Waged between Peter and his steward the pope / Who calls himself his governor."

They had not respected those very elements whose sacredness they now protested. Indeed, the clergy were responsible for the blasphemy and laxness of the people. Fischart then turned the charge of blasphemy upon the Catholics. The animals represented the foulness and corruption of the Roman church. The sacramental sow stood for the Epicurean, benefice-seeking, acorn-fattened cattle who formed the pope's herd of clerics. The bitch following the procession represented the concubines and mistresses of the adulterous and lustful clergy. The laity were shown the evil and corruption of the false church. Fischart's point was that this must be replaced by the Lamb of God in his purity and simplicity.[26]

The Jesuits were another target for attack, and Fischart pursued the order and its founder with fire and brimstone. From their very founding, the Jesuits, according to Fischart, had been secretive, dangerous, and treacherous. In an early pamphlet Fischart threw doubt on the validity of Saint Ignatius's conversion, stating that his wound had provided him with a convenient excuse to leave his military career. His retirement to monastic life, therefore, was the result of cowardice.[27] A later pamphlet, entitled *The Four-Cornered Little Hats,* was Fischart's revision of a French tract that gained from his artful and malevolent imagination. The Jesuits were part of a longplanned campaign of the devil to regain control on earth from Jesus Christ. The devil had attempted through various means to reintroduce his own horrid followers on earth after the advent of Jesus. He had established the monastic orders for this purpose and had attempted to hide the horns of his followers within the hoods. He had created the mitres of bishops and the triple tiara of the pope for the same purpose, but still needed more soldiers for his army. The foundation of the Jesuits was his last attempt, and their four-cornered hats concealed the true identity of these cohorts of the devil more cleverly than had any other device.[28] Attacks of this nature created a solid foundation of distrust among the Protestant laity. Their loyalty to Protestantism was based, in part, on their fear of the papacy and their conviction that the Jesuits served as a secret arm of the pope's power.

The introduction of the Inquisition, the oppression of the Netherlands under the Duke of Alva, the Saint Bartholomew's Day massacre, and the assassination of Henry III gave further proof of what could be expected if the Catholics were in power. These events were reported in newssheets written by eye witnesses or by participants. The original accounts in French or Dutch were translated in Jobin's shop.

The oppressions of the Spanish Inquisition were well known in Strasbourg by 1563. An account was printed in a five-page pamphlet which quickly went through five editions. The actual form and procedure followed by the inquisitors was described. A report of this sort, with its careful attention to detail, must have been from the mouth of a person who had been questioned. Particular attention was given to the efforts of the inquisitors to ingratiate themselves with the accused:

> When someone is called before the inquisitors they say to him, as he enters, "My good friend, I came to the inquisitors yesterday and heard that they were talking about you. They gave me the task of speaking to you and telling you to mend your ways."[29]

or later:

> The inquisitors tell the accused he will not be troubled or fall into any difficulty if he will just tell everything a pious Christian should . . . . [They] appoint someone to watch these good people, to act as though they were their best friends, visit them everyday at home, and keep informed on what each individual really thinks in his heart.[30]

The injustice, the subtlety, the deceptiveness of the procedure was clearly established, creating a fear in Protestant hearts that would last for generations. Thus, the anti-Catholicism of the Protestant clergy was reinforced by popular journalism.

Accounts of battles and other events in the wars were more factual in nature, but the religious point was always driven home at the end. A five-page account of the battle of Friesland started with a straightforward description of the military encounter.[31] Only at the end did the reporter state that the German *landsknechts* would have preferred to take the captive Spaniards prisoner, but were deterred because the Spaniards hanged any enemy troops they captured.[32] As a result, the Spaniards who had taken refuge in a cloister were shot, and those who attempted to hide in the trees were shot down. Count Ludwig of Nassau was left wounded on the battlefield, but through God's help he had survived. All Christians should continue to invoke God's help and support for the victory of the Christians against the anti-Christ.[33]

A report of the Saint Bartholomew's massacre did not embroider the horror. Its brevity only made it more compelling. The death of the Admiral was recounted, as was the attempt of his followers to defend him. The report also described the four days thereafter, when people ran through houses all over the city and all males who were not papists were killed; more than one hundred women were chased through the streets and into the water. Everything that had to do with religion and evangelism was destroyed. The *"Ratsherren"* [sic] responsible for this tragedy were the "von Guise."[34]

Popular songs were yet another means of disseminating propaganda; the large number of attempts to censure *lieder* that were circulating in the city proves the effectiveness of the method.[35] In the earliest decades popular songs were about beautiful girls and heroic figures and deeds.[36] After Theobald Berger began to print popular music there was a marked increase in the number of songs produced, and the subject matter of the songs became increasingly topical and political. Berger's songs were often journalism put to music. There were songs which recounted the attack of the king of France on Germany; the battle between the kings of France and England; the battle between Condé and Guise; the tyranny of the Russians against the city of Reffel in Lapland; and the battle between the kings of France and Poland. The Bishops' War was reported in no less than five songs.[37]

The songs were not printed as broadsheets. Like newssheets, they were printed as small pamphlets, often with a woodcut on the title page. The music was not provided. Instructions were given that the new song was to be sung to the tune of "Es geht ein frischer summer daher" or "Ich hab mein Sach Gott heimgestelt."[38] Both secular and hymn tunes were used for popular music. The songs about the Bishops' War depicted the bravery of the Strasbourg troops and their German allies. One song described the battle of Dachstein, where many German soldiers were killed by Charles, cardinal of Lorraine. A French captain of German mercenary troops, who was in fact a spy, persuaded his men to take refuge in the city hall, which he had previously mined with explosives. At least three hundred German soldiers were killed in the terrible fire that followed, the result of Lotharingian deception. Lorraine betrayed the German soldiers just as it had betrayed the German peasants in 1525.[39] In another song the poet recounted the dangers of the restoration of the Catholics to power. They would put an end to Protestant services; they would restore the tyranny of the pope; they would infiltrate the schools; they would mislead the common man with sweet words and songs.[40] These songs and others like them idealized the Protestant cause and generated a deep distrust of the Roman church. The papacy represented a hierarchy of power beyond the reach of the layman and was thus particularly threatening. Implicitly the songs connected the papal power with the Catholic nobility.

Religious ideas were drawn not only from the Bible, sermons, and the Creed. They evolved out of the pragmatic experience of political events, the experiences of war and persecution. By the last decades Protestantism was characterized by a strong rejection of everything Catholic. Negative elements played as important a role in determining belief as positive factors. The Protestant was opposed to the ceremonies of the Roman church. He preferred congregational hymn singing to the Catholic liturgy and made a virtue of the simplicity of his religious service. He was Protestant because he abhorred the pope and the Roman curia—he mistrusted them and believed they would destroy peace and order. He hated the Jesuits and saw them as the masterminds of an immense conspiracy to destroy Protestantism and subvert secular government.

Interest in other peoples, other societies, near and distant lands created a thirst for history, geography, and compendia of general information. This was one of the areas where lay interests and humanist interests converged. The historical treatises of several of the Academy professors, the clergy, and other humanists were written or translated into German and thus made available to the literate laity. Some of these books or journalistic accounts were written by men outside the scholarly world.

Livy's work, translated into German by Conrad Lautenbach, a pastor, was a best-seller of the period; seven editions were published between 1574 and 1598.[41] The vernacular reader received a vivid impression of Republican Rome from Livy. Lautenbach also translated the five books of Hegisippus on the Jewish war and Flavius Josephus's history of the Jews.[42] There were fifteen editions of these last works after 1574, which indicates that the sources of Roman and church history became increasingly important. The lay person could now read the texts of these authors for himself; he did not have to rely on a summary made by a scholar. The chronicles and general introductions to ancient history disappear after 1569.[43] Serious histories of the German past were more numerous. Sleidan's history of the reign of Charles V continued to occupy an important place. There were seven editions after 1570.[44] Men turned to Sleidan's work to understand their own time. The great war continued to dominate their lives and they wanted to know what had occurred. There was a concomitant interest in detailed histories of other areas of Germany, such as Andreas Happenrod's account of the counts and nobility of Saxony and Cyriacus Spangenberg's Saxon chronicle, his chronicle of Henneberg, and several general accounts of the German emperors.[45] These were more professional than the history books of the earlier decades. A chronicle was no longer a mere compendium of events. The historian commanded a knowledge of the sources and usually attempted to describe major political, military, and religious events. This new professionalism did not, however, greatly affect the regional history written by Bernhard Hertzog.

Hertzog was an Alsatian, born in Weissenburg, where his father was the burgormeister. Bernhard was educated at the Strasbourg Gymnasium; he then studied law at Heidelberg and entered the civil service of Hanau-Lichtenberg.[46] His *Chronicon alsatiae,* which, despite its title, was written in German, was enormous—more than a thousand pages. Hertzog attempted to bring together histories of the great German noble families, accounts of military and political events and of the peasant revolts of 1493–1525, ecclesiastical history, the genealogy and history of the Alsatian nobility, and geographic information. It was a compendium rather than a well-constructed history, but it covered the activities of the emperor, the nobility, and the ecclesiastical hierarchy.[47] The book reflected men's desire to know about their immediate environment.

Helisaeus Röslin's book, *Der Elsasz und gegen Lotringen . . . Wasgawischer Gebirge Gelegenheit und Commodititen,* made another contribution to regional literature. Röslin was a doctor, a Paracelsan, and his book was a grand mixture of geography, geology, botany, medicine, chemistry, archaeology, and history. On the title page he states that he will discuss "old monuments, money and coins, inscriptions and characteristics of old buildings and houses, along with a lot of other worthy things, natural and political, spiritual and worldly, rulers and governors, religion, religious services, and also wars."[48] This list is a rather good description of the book. Röslin starts with a geographic description of Alsace, its topography and resources, with particular stress on its mineral wealth.[49] This leads to a long section on the mineral waters of the area and their medicinal uses according to Paracelsan principles.[50] One of the major mineral springs was at Niederbronn, and Röslin describes the Roman coins found there, devoting forty pages to illustrations and descriptions of the coins.[51] There is a final chapter on the history of Alsace from the time of the Romans to 1400. The book is an example of the eclecticism of the period and the fascination with ancient Roman remains. It betrays no scholarly training in the dialectic, which would have helped the author to achieve a firmer organization. Jobin printed Röslin's book only three years after he had published the Hertzog *Chronicon.* Large books, both required a considerable investment in labor and paper. Jobin must have been sure that these regional materials would sell.

Histories of European countries were not as popular in the last decades as they had been midcentury. There was one history of Italy.[52] Professors at the Academy published two vernacular histories: a general chronology of important events and a set of popular biographies.[53] Information about other peoples, religions, and cultures came from short, but very good, journalistic accounts. Accounts of military engagements were often written by eyewitnesses.

The war against the Turks continued to be a major focus of interest. A series of accounts reported the siege of Vienna in 1566.[54] The events at Malta were described in a letter written by a son of the Guevara family which circulated as a news story. Guevara reported the attack in Saint Elmo and the naval battle between the Christian and Turkish forces. The Christians overcame the enemy, some 1,000 or 1,500 prisoners were taken, and fifteen Turkish flags were captured. This was followed by a general attack by night. In the heavy bombardment of Saint Elmo's fortress, at least 9,000 were killed, including women, children and Christian soldiers.[55]

An uprising of the Janissaries and the Spahi against the Turkish sultan was reported. The revolt occurred because the men had been paid in worthless money. They did not ask for an increase in pay; they wanted viable currency. They also petitioned that Jewish officeholders be deprived of their appointments so their places might be filled by Turks. Thus, said the reporter, we can see with our own eyes that the authority of the sultan is threatened. Since the soldiers supported the young prince, either the father must turn against the son or the son against the father. So, he ended, may God stir up the disobedience of his people against the sultan.[56]

A broadsheet of 1575 described the misfortunes of Sultan Selim II: his military losses at the Tanais River and the destruction of his fleet at Lepanto. God in his mercy, the writer stated, had ended his difficulties by bringing about his death. His oldest son, Murat, had then hurried to Constantinople to assume the throne. Immediately on arrival he had summoned his brothers before him, whereupon he had them strangled or slain.[57] The woodcut depicted the casket of Selim II with the caskets of his five sons lying at his feet. God, it was hoped, would relieve the Turks from such tyrannical rulers.

The newssheets portrayed the Turks as tyrannical and cruel, but they also reported their strength and competence. The Europeans admired the discipline of the Janissaries and never underestimated the military power of this enemy. The only weak spot, they believed, was the sultan himself. Surrounded by rival factions, the problems of succession made him vulnerable.

There were more reports on the Turks than on any other foreign nation because of the war, but news filtered through from more distant parts. A terrible fire on an island off Peru was reported,[58] as were the depradations made by a crocodile in a town in Libya,[59] and Martin Frobisher's voyage of 1577 and discovery of Eskimos.[60] The crocodile broadsheet bears no indication of where it was published, but it represents the current interest in strange and wonderful things. The woodcut provided a precise and detailed picture of the crocodile. The length and girth of two animals, a male and a female, were given precisely. The text stated that these animals had perpetrated a great deal of damage on men and domestic animals in a city in Libya. An Italian businessman, imprisoned in Libya, heard of the destruction wrought by the pair and offered to destroy them. After digging a pit trap, he caught them and was freed by his captors. "I, Salvatore Flaminio," the writer declared, "was also imprisoned in Libya and saw all this with my own eyes."

The newssheet depicting the Eskimos bore the headline "A remarkable description and unique picture of a strange, unknown people [from] a new found land or island recently found by Sir Martin Frobisher." The account, published in 1578, described the Frobisher voyage of 1577 and dwelt on Frobisher's skill as a navigator and cosmologist and his interest in opening new trade routes. As the Frobisher vessels coasted along an island, they saw an Eskimo hunting in his kayak. They captured him and took him back to

Plate 14. "A Remarkable Description and unique Picture of a strange, unknown people from a New found land or island recently found by Sir Martin Frobisher." Strasbourg, no printer given, 1578.

England as proof of what they had found and to stir up interest in the new land. The account provided a remarkably accurate description of the Eskimos, starting with their height and stature, their physical features, their clothing, their diet, and other details of their way of life. It was noted that they ate only meat or fish, no bread. There was a particularly careful description of the kayak, the way it was made, and its navigability, and of the Eskimo weapons, such as the harpoon, and their uses. The woodcut showed a male and a female Eskimo, every detail of their fur clothing correct, with a kayak in the background from which another Eskimo had just harpooned a bird in flight.

By the end of the sixteenth century ordinary men knew a good deal about the New World, the Indies, and the Near East. They were aware that the people in these areas lived lives different from their own and had their own religious beliefs. Newssheets printed in other cities reported on life in Russia[61] and the ceremonies of the Eastern Orthodox Church.[62] There was even a report on Japan. The boundaries of the known world had been pushed back; all men lived in a larger cosmos. By and large these reports were free of any trace of superstition. When Flaminio wrote about the crocodile, he was afraid of it, but he recognized it as a natural creature and reported its size, dietary habits, and other characteristics objectively.

The scientific and medical knowledge of ordinary citizens in the last decades of the century were drawn in part from popular medical treatises, Paracelsan medicine, astronomy and astrology, and applied medicine. There was a renewed interest in agronomy and veterinary medicine. In fact, more scientific works were published in German than in Latin. The lay interest in scientific and technological information remained strong and provided a dependable market. The vernacular sciences, however, remained distinct from the science taught in the Academy. Aristotelian science was not diffused downward.

The schism between lay science and academic science was manifested by separate groups of physicians, resident in the city, who practiced Paracelsan medicine instead of the Galenic medicine of the academic physicians. Michael Toxites was perhaps the original leader of the group, although by 1572 he had left to become the city physician in Haguenau, where he died in 1581.[63] In 1564 he had been joined by Gallus Etschenreutter, a doctor with an established reputation as a chemist. Etschenreuter purchased citizenship in that year and became a respected physician in the community.[64] Helisaeus Rösslin settled in the city in 1586.[65] Lucas Bathodius, the son of Lucas Hackfurt, the welfare administrator, was already practicing in Strasbourg.[66] Guinther von Andernach, an elder statesman in the medical community by now, had accepted some elements of Paracelsan medicine.[67] Thus the Paracelsans were a sizable group, even when compared with the entire medical community of the early decades.

Faithful to the ideals of Paracelsus, who wished to disseminate medical knowledge among the poor and the peasants, these physicians were committed to publishing both his work and their own in German. Although publication of the work of Paracelsus had begun in the sixties, the peak was reached in the seventies when eighteen editions, all but four of them in the vernacular, were published. They were printed by Christian Mylius II, Bernard Jobin, and Nikolaus Wyriot.[68] Several of the treatises were addressed directly to the patient: a book on baths, on achieving longevity, on treating common diseases by yourself, and on the plague and syphilis were available. To these, Gallus Etschenreutter added an exhaustive treatise on German spas. Baths played an important role in Paracelsan medicine since natural waters made the healing qualities of minerals available. It was obviously a popular book for it was printed three times.[69] Etschenreuter also wrote an alchemical text; indeed, the Paracelsan regard for chemistry is reflected in the continued interest alchemical or chemical treatises received after 1572.[70] Lucas Bathodius provided astrological prognostications; these were important to Paracelsan medicine, and indeed to all medical practice, because the effectiveness of medicines and treatments was believed to be related to particular astrological signs.[71] In addition to these medical treatises, the layman could still purchase Walter Ryff's handy manual for home medical care, which Josias Rihel continued to publish.[72] Specialized medical treatises in this period were limited to works on gout.[73] The appearance of the Basel edition of Vesalius's *De humani corporis fabrica* in 1543 had an immediate impact. The completeness of the text, and the accuracy of the plates discouraged further work. In Strasbourg only two anatomical works, one a commentary, appeared after 1543.[74]

Lay mathematical publication continued, sharply differentiated from the Euclidian geometry of the academic mathematicians, usually published in Greek. Arithmetical and accounting manuals by the well-known English mathematician, Julius Caesar, were translated into German, and Georg Höflin, a Strasbourg rechenmeister, contributed a treatise on accounting systems.[75] The spurt of books on agriculture would seem to indicate greater concern with land management. Until 1570 the standard text had been that written by the Roman agronomists Columella and Cassianus Bassus. In 1579 Bernard Jobin published Melchior Sebitz's German translation of Jean Liebault's treatise in estate management and reprinted it three times.[76] Liebault had greatly enlarged the original text written by his brother-in-law, Charles Estienne. Instead of relying on Roman agricultural techniques, Estienne and Liebault described a typical French farm and then provided practical advice drawn from experience. It is interesting that at no time did they mention the three-field system. It was assumed that the landowner would plant according to the soil resources of the farm. There was an extensive description of soil types and the crops suitable to each type.[77] In addition to Liebault's book, a new manual on surveying summarized recent techniques useful to the estate manager.[78]

In these same decades there were three veterinary manuals on the care of horses. Caspar Reuschel, a Strasbourg riding master, wrote a riding manual that included various patterns for dressage. The direction of the rider was neatly indicated by horseshoes pointing in the appropriate direction.[79] Interest in the land was manifested in books on hunting, including Jacques Fouilloux's classic treatise and another book devoted entirely to wolf hunting.[80]

Laymen continued to purchase practical books that gave them information needed in their everyday life. Books on Paracelsan medicine, applied mathematics, and agricultural skills indicate that members of the lay culture continued to explore the physical world and to develop scientific and technical literature based on the pragmatic needs of business, agriculture, and health.

The scientific interests of the academic community and the lay world were brought together during the reconstruction of the cathedral clock. The Strasbourg cathedral had, from a very early period, boasted a clock, the first having been a sundial on the west porch of the building. In the fourteenth century a clock mechanism had been constructed, which was in disrepair by the middle of the sixteenth century. In 1547, the Rat appointed Michael Herr, Nikolaus Bruckner, and Christian Herlin to undertake the renovation. The war brought these efforts to a halt. Conrad Dasypodius was appointed in 1571 by the Magistrat to begin the task again. Dasypodius brought in his friend from Breslau, David Wolckenstein, who was a musician as well as a mathematician, and paid his salary from his own stipend. Tobias Stimmer was commissioned to paint the decorative panels and other ornamental work. The mechanical construction was in the hands of two Swiss clockmakers, Isaac and Josias Habrecht, whom Dasypodius had examined in 1571 and recommended to the Magistrat as qualified. The practical problems of building the clock forced a union of technology and scientific knowledge, but they also divulged the depth of the split between the university scientists and the technicians. In 1574 Dasypodius complained that the Magistrat had paid the Habrechts too much. Furthermore, he claimed, the clockmakers had assumed major credit for the clock when, in truth, he had himself conceived and created it. Each side put their arguments on paper; the Habrechts in a manuscript petition addressed to the Rat, Dasypodius in a small treatise published in 1578.

Dasypodius began by asking whether the moderns could ever equal the ancients. Were the Jews, the Greeks, and the Romans more learned than the modern men who practiced the free, liberal arts?[81] Starting with the building of the temple of Solomon, Dasypodius decided in favor of the moderns.

ℭ Ein gerechten Qua-
dranten zů machen.

ⅅV ſolt zům erſten ein ge-
den winckelhacken reiſſen/
wie zůforderſt glert iſt/ darnach
ſetz den circkel in den puncten a
mit dem andern fůß reiß ein circkel lini vom b biß in das c/als
groß du dan den quadranten haben wilt/ſo haſtu ein gerechten
quadranten/das iſt/ein viertheyl eines circkels/ Wiltu nun
den ſelbigen quadranten in ſeine 90 grad außtheylen ſo theyl
den circkelbogen erſtlich in 3. theyl/ darnach yetlich 3. theyl
aber in 3 theyl/ darnach yetlichs in 2 theyl/ zům letſten yetlichs in 5 theil/ ſo haſt du 90 theyl oder grad/ wie du hye obt
ſyheſt.

Volgt hernach wie man die Sonnen
vhr machen ſoll.

ⅇErſtlichen iſt zů diſem werck not/ zů machen das Recti-
ficatorium/das iſt/ein driangel gemacht von vier lini-
en/ als polus hőhe Equinoctialis/ Verticalis/ vnd hori-
zontalis/ den ſelben ſoltu machen alſo.   Setz fůr dich
den quadranten in 90 theyl getheylt/ wie du oben haſt le-
ren machen/ alſo das die linien a c überſich ſteh/ die lini
a b überzwerch in plano der erden gleich lig/ vnd der lim-
bus/ das iſt/ der bog mit den außgetheylten graden gegen
der lincken hand ſteh/ vnd die zal der grad ſoll eyngeſchri-
ben ſein/ Angefangen bey dem b/ vnd ſich enden geyen
dem

Plate 15. A sixteenth-century bestseller, published in six editions
from 1539 to 1582. "How to make a sundial." This is the first
page, which explains how to make the quadrant and then how to
place it in regard to the sun. From *Ein wolgegründs . . . Summari
Büchlin, aller Sonnen Uhr,* Christian Mylius I, 1559.

So many new arts had been established that there were now many more
skills, especially for war, printing, the construction of dikes and water-
works, and other free arts.[82] The art of the clockmaker, however, had not
progressed. The great clockmakers of ancient times were men like Archi-
medes and Heron, but contemporary clockmakers and artisans no longer
had the knowledge of geometry, arithmetic, and astronomy to create their
own plans.[83] The Habrechts were put in their place and the supremacy of
academic learning over mere technical skill firmly asserted.

In the rest of the treatise Dasypodius described the intricate mathematical computations, which required the use of astronomical instruments and years of experience. It was necessary to know the exact position of the stars and the seven planets for every hour of the year, as well as the different rates of motion of the planets. Because he felt that it was necessary to demonstrate the eternal quality of time, he had reckoned the movement of the planets over a whole century.[84] This required far greater skill than could be expected of a clockmaker. It involved the knowledge and proficiency of a trained astronomer. He regretted that the Habrechts were unable to see that the clock was a joint effort, requiring the cooperation of everyone who worked on it. The artisans and handworkers should rejoice in all they learned during the undertaking.[85] Dasypodius could not recognize the technician as his equal. The Strasbourg clock was one of the wonders of the age, and its repair required the work of both scholars and craftsmen; yet, in the end, it divided the lay world and the academic world rather than drawing them closer together.

The literary interests of the laity did not change radically. Theater continued to be important. There were regular performances of biblical plays and other dramatic works in the last decades although, as already noted, many of the plays were now written by school teachers and acted by their pupils.[86] The records indicate that a group of burghers and their sons presented *Judith* on the Cornmarket in 1564. Two years later the meistersingers requested permission to perform *Treuen Eckhart* but were rebuffed by the Magistrat, who said it would be better for them to stick to their work so that they could pay off their creditors and buy bread for their wives and children.[87] In September 1568 *Esther* was acted publicly, and in 1573 150 burghers of Colmar took part in a production of John the Baptist.[88] The burgher theater clearly was not replaced by the school theater.

There seems to have been an increase in musical activity at the end of the century, which can be attributed, at least in part, to Theobald Berger's printings of popular and religious songs. There are other indications, as well, of a greater demand for music. All but three of the known collections of instrumental music were printed after 1570. Three of these included arrangements for the lute and the zither. There were also arrangements of motets for four, five, and six voices.[89] The meistersinger of Strasbourg petitioned the Rat for permission to reorganize their group and, in 1598, a new set of ordinances were promulgated. Administered by twelve of the meister, the group greatly increased their strength to become more important in the following century.[90]

Fewer popular authors were published in Strasbourg after 1570. The civil servants who had been active in the previous generation were reprinted, but little new work appeared. Most of the novels or long poems published in Strasbourg in these years came from the pen of one man, Johann Fischart. Fischart was not cast in the same mold as Georg Wickram. He was the eldest son of a Strasbourg burgher, and his father's early death left him enough money to acquire an excellent education. He graduated from the Strasbourg Gymnasium, studied under Kaspar Scheit at Worms, then went to the Netherlands and the University of Paris, where he received his baccalaureate. In 1574 he acquired a doctorate in law from Basel.[91] Despite, or perhaps because of, his university years, he renounced the role in life for which he had prepared himself, rejected the academic establishment and a society based on a hierarchy of orders. His satires did for literature what Breughel had done for painting. His novels and poems were grotesque, bordering on the surreal. Drunk with words, he was unable to use two words to describe a person or a thing: he always used twenty. He drowned himself and his readers in words and sounds of his own invention. While the professors of the Academy taught their students to present their ideas according to the careful logic of dialectic, Fischart overflowed in a splendid disorder of phrase, thought, and meaning.

Fischart was not a burgher writer, extolling burgher virtues, searching for an ethic applicable to burgher life. His Gurgellentua was a drunken gourmand whose sexual appetites made Rabelais's Gargantua look like a celibate monk. Fischart also attacked the learned and the nobility as hollow frauds. Gurgellentua, with his love of material things, food, drink, clothes, comfort, and all the delights of the flesh, represented man's true nature.

Fischart's polemic works were different. In a political poem, *Das Gluckhafft Schiff von Zurich,* he extolled the virtues of burgher loyalty. The poem was written in a dangerous period, after the Saint Bartholomew's Day massacre when Henri de Bourbon was pressing the city for aid. The possibility of a Swiss alliance was in the air and Fischart wrote the poem to celebrate the feat of the Zurich boatsmen who, to demonstrate their city's loyalty to their ancient allies in Strasbourg, loaded a huge pot of hot porridge in their boat, rowed down the river, and delivered it while it was still steaming.[92] The poem praised burgher loyalty, the strength of the traditional friendship of the cities and the constancy and strong arms of the boatsmen. No task in the world was so difficult that it could not be overcome by work and effort.[93] In this case, as in Wickram's novels, the virtues of faithfulness, stability, and trust were primary, creating a community of mutual responsibility and responsiveness.

In a satire entitled *Der Flüh Hatz, Weiber Tratz,* Fischart ridiculed nobility, chivalry, and the knightly code. The epic was about a young flea. He was determined to desert the body of the sluttish woman, where he made his residence, and move to the body of a noble lady, where he would find honor and glory. His father warned him that such a step might lead to disaster, for he, himself, had led a band of highly noble fleas on just such a mission. His brave fleas had met terrible opposition from the noblewoman, and eventually the band was decimated. Those remaining had been reduced to common robbery and plundering.[94] The tale of the battle of the fleas was a masterpiece of satire; the chivalric ethic was made absurd and the heroic virtues irrelevant.

Fischart's *Geschichtklitterung,* which he described as a translation of Rabelais's *Gargantua,*[95] was, in fact, a new work. Three quarters of it consist of Fischart's own additions and insertions.[96] For example, when Rabelais's Gargantua is taught music by the humanist Ponocrates, he learns to play the lute, the spinet, the harp, the German flute, the viol, and the trombone.[97] In Fischart's embroidered version, the character learns the lute, the spinet, the harp, the German fife, the Polish bagpipes, the zither, the cornet, and, tucked under the arm, the Brunswick Hermeli. Irrepressible, Fischart goes on to mention the Alpine horn, the military horn, the flute with nine holes, the violin, the cymbals, and the sackbut, but these are left to be learned later.[98] This doubling or tripling occurs again and again. In the botanizing expedition in the same chapter Rabelais lists five useful implements for the amateur botanist; Fischart lists twenty.[99] He exaggerates obsessively: every act, every thing is multiplied ten times or more.

More important, the tone of the Fischart *Geschichtklitterung* was entirely different. Rabelais's Gargantua was secondarily a giant, but primarily a humanist and a prince. Fischart's Gurgellentua was all the human appetites collected in one being. Learning, manners, and morals were ridiculed. Furthermore, it is hard to see Gurgellentua as noble, let alone princely. His education, with its emphasis on mathematics, botany, and the nature of food, wine, and water, was closer to science than to humanistic studies; it was an education befitting a gourmand.[100] Fischart's Abbey of Thélème is founded not by gentlewomen and their noble lords but by "Männer und Frauen," and only once was the noble atmosphere of Thélème mentioned.[101] In fact, the Thélème episode does not fit into the rest of the work, which extolls the material joys of life. Fischart's poem had neither an element of asceticism and philosophic contemplation, nor a description of the joys of learning. His world delighted man in purely physical, sensual terms. Men simply had to reach out for these delights.

At the root of the lay culture was a deep-seated belief in the power of God and in divine providence. Religion bulwarked this belief and provided ethical and moral standards for everyday life in the Ten Commandments and the ideal of serving as a Christ to one's neighbor. God was imminent in the world: earthquakes, comets, and other natural events proved this. To be aware of the wonders of his creation was to honor God, and so men were encouraged to study and observe nature. Fischart's works affirmed the value of the activities of ordinary men. If one can find a moral in his Gurgellentua, it must be a confirmation of the pleasures of daily life, exaggerated to the extreme.

CHAPTER FOURTEEN ·
CONCLUSION

HO COMMUNICATED WHAT TO WHOM? Examination of book publication in the city of Strasbourg reveals that few ideas circulated among the entire community. Diffusion took place among specific groups; different forms of knowledge appealed to different interests. An individual's intellectual experience was determined by his education, by the social group to which he belonged, by the language or languages he spoke and read. Language was one of the most important cultural factors in the period. The use of Latin in the schools and universities created a sharp division between the learned, the professionals, and the rest of the society. Certain philosophic, theological, and scientific ideas were communicated only within the learned community. The German-speaking community received its religious ideology in part from the learned, but it also developed religious, moral, ethical, and scientific ideas for itself.

The debates over theological doctrine involved technical matters that could be discussed and argued only among theologians and scholars. Three doctrinal issues, however, were topics of popular concern during the period of the Reform: salvation by faith, the meaning of the Eucharist, and predestination. Since the first was central to conversion to Protestantism, and the others determined the type of Protestantism to which one belonged, these doctrines were expounded and disseminated in the vernacular language. The precise definition of the doctrines of the new church, however, remained the responsibility of the theologians. Some questions created profound differences among the reformers: the meaning of the law, the relationship between works and grace, the nature of original sin, the doctrine of predestination; and the nature of Christ himself. The attempt to establish doctrinal agreement on these matters led to prolonged controversies and culminated in confessional statements, the Augustana, the Tetrapolitana, the XVI Articles of Strasbourg, the Formula of Concord. The arguments for each point were written for and by the theologians, although the final confession was often circulated in German as well as in Latin. The laity's knowledge of doctrine came not from these learned disputations, however, but from catechisms that led neither to religious questioning nor to doctrinal speculation.

In the revolutionary years of the Reformation new doctrines were communicated to the laity. The doctrine of justification by faith replaced the penitential theology of the late medieval church. The concept of the priesthood of all believers gave the laity new importance. These changes were followed, however, by the need to formulate the new doctrines with an exactitude that would protect them from contamination by the conflicting beliefs of other sects.

Knowledge of the Bible seems to have been evenly disseminated among the whole Protestant population, though most Protestant laymen probably only heard the Bible read in their pastor's sermons. A significant minority, however, either owned Bibles or managed to get hold of biblical texts in one way or another. In 1530, the Alsatian nobleman Zorn von Plobsheim wanted to read the Bible. Luther's translation was not yet complete, so he gathered together what was available. He bought all the books that Luther had published in German, including the Pentateuch, the historical and poetical books, and the Gospels. He turned to the German translations of the prophets by the Anabaptists Hans Denck and Ludwig Hetzer. The Apocrypha he found in a translation by a Zwinglian, Leo Jud.[1] Undismayed by the theological differences of the translators, he bound the books together for his own use. For the most part, however, the Scriptures were available to the laity in short sections—the Gospels or single books from the Old Testament. The one part of the Bible every citizen could have owned was the book of Psalms, which was usually set to music. Plays based on Bible stories were another important means of making biblical texts familiar to the laity. The new exegesis of the Bible was confined almost exclusively to the learned. Most of the biblical commentaries published in German were written by theologians whose purpose was as much polemical as scholarly. In Strasbourg, these included Otto Brunfels and Cyriacus Spangenberg.

We cannot assume that the average Protestant of the sixteenth century knew the Bible in depth. He knew the psalms, because they were part of the liturgy. He was familiar with the stories in Genesis and the life of Christ. The laity understood the Bible in their own way. They did not approach it critically or analytically. They received it as the word of God. They turned to the Bible in their search for viable moral and ethical standards because the lives and problems of biblical people were relevant to their own. They were not unaware of the Christian symbolism to be found in the Joseph story, but they were also moved by its universal qualities: the jealousy between Joseph and his brothers; the favoritism of Isaac toward Joseph; the success story of the clever outsider at the pharaoh's court; the final victory of Joseph over his brothers. Most people met these same problems in their daily lives. The Bible provided examples to be followed or avoided. It demonstrated the strength and power which God had given to those who believed, and thereby suffused ordinary men and women with a spirit of hope and confidence.

The ideas and ideals of the humanists were communicated only among the learned. New institutions of learning were established as a result of the Reform. More burghers of Strasbourg were educated than before, but they were the sons of the elite or bright young men from the artisanal groups who would achieve higher social status through their education. The moral and ethical values imparted by a humanist education were drawn from antiquity and from the Christian Gospels. It idealized the *via activa,* a life of service to the community through politics, preaching, or teaching. This Ciceronian ideal was reinforced by Christian concepts of obligation and service. No effort was made, however, to communicate these classical values to ordinary citizens, except at the very end of the century when classical plays were presented in public in German. Latin and Greek authors were rarely translated into the vernacular. One hundred thirty-one editions of Cicero were printed between 1511 and 1597; none were in German. Pliny, Aulus Gellius, the Latin poets, Plato, Aristotle, and Homer were also available only to the Latin reader. Only Aesop, the historians—in particular, Livy and Josephus—and the playwrights were translated. Humanism shaped the cultural values of the learned, the academicians, and the clergy. It also provided them with the logical structure essential to critical analysis and with the tools of dialectic and rhetoric. Neither the values nor the methodology of humanism were shared with those outside the learned circle.

New scientific knowledge did not inspire serious questioning of accepted religious beliefs. God was at the center of the universe and at the center of men's lives. Even the controversy over the heliocentric universe, which historians have emphasized, was muted at the time by the assumption that, however the planets moved, the system was the work of God. Science, or natural philosophy, maintained its traditional subordination to theology and grammar. The scientists were divided by training and interests. The university-trained scientists were doctors of medicine or mathematicians. University-educated humanists joined them in their search for ancient scientific texts. They believed their function was to pass on the scientific knowledge of the ancients in its purest form. In the early decades of the century they concentrated on the works of the Arab physicians and the astronomical and mathematical compilations made by the medieval encyclopedists, which then served as the texts for the next generation of scientists. During the course of the century the sources were revised and improved. The Latin texts of Pliny and Ptolemy were corrected and re-edited. The works of the Greek physicians were searched out and published, usually in Latin translations. The books of Euclid were published in Greek. By the last decades Aristotle was once again established as the primary and indisputable authority of science. The function of the academicians was to make the ancient sources available, but they did not presume to add to them.

In medicine, however, new work was undertaken. Human dissections were carried out. Anatomical charts were prepared and broadly disseminated. There were careful studies of specific diseases, an important step in the development of precise investigation. The university-trained physicians communicated their information and knowledge to a larger public than did their other learned colleagues. They felt responsible for making general medical information available to the layman so that he might care for himself and his family. Many of the university-trained doctors wrote popular manuals, which described common ailments and recommended herbal remedies. They wrote special treatises, in German, about the plague and syphilis. Botany, whose methodology had become far more precise, was also published in German. This may have been done to serve the apothecaries, who needed the information but rarely read Latin. Otto Brunfel's important botanical treatise was written in Latin, but Michael Herr, a dedicated popularizer, translated it into German. Wendelin Hock wrote his botany in German and emphasized the importance of German plants unknown to Pliny or Dioscorides. The new botanies, the anatomies, and the manuals on the plague and syphilis, as well as traditional medical texts, were available to people at every level of society. Like the work of the cartographers, the anatomies and botanies charted the structure of the physical world.

Another type of science, based on observation from nature, began to develop. Descriptive in form, it was not tied to a larger cosmic view. Much of it was practical or applied, related to the needs of agriculture, the crafts, or commerce. These interests were reflected in translations of Roman agricultural treatises, books on mining, metallurgy, and architecture, treatises on surveying, and maps. The applied sciences and technology drew on several mathematical fields: businessmen used both algebra, which they learned from the Arab mathematicians, and arithmetic; artisans, wine-merchants, and surveyors used plane geometry and solid geometry.

Lay culture developed relatively independently of the culture of the learned. In the earliest decades, Brant and Murner wrote in the vernacular, and other humanists translated Roman scientific treatises into German. At the same time the printers discovered and exploited a market among the laity for handbooks and manuals and for entertaining tales and stories. The laity were searching for a deeper religious life and for moral and ethical standards appropriate to the needs of urban life. The printers responded to these needs first with versions of the Passion of Christ and with the popular sermons of

Geiler von Kaysersberg. Then, in the first decade of the Reform, evangelical preaching and the opening of the scriptures through sermons and lectures gave ordinary citizens a new faith and a more profound religious experience. They welcomed the campaign against the corruption within the old church. But when these reforms were accomplished the Protestant clergy failed to go further. Absorbed in their theological debates and the pressures of reorganization, they did not fully meet the moral search of the laity. Once they themselves were allowed to marry, for instance, they no longer wrote about marriage, a subject of focal importance to the townspeople. It was lay writers who emphasized family life. Georg Wickram and the lay playwrights developed the themes of the centrality of the family and the obligations of loyalty, friendship, and service. These writers picked up the reformers' theme of serving as a Christ to your neighbor and applied it to daily life.

The humanist ideal of the *via activa* did not penetrate to the lower levels of urban society. The Greco-Roman emphasis on service to the state was irrelevant to the townsmen who, at most, had the right of franchise and took the yearly oath of allegiance to the magistrates. The center of their lives was not the city but their families. The family was more than just the social unit in which each individual lived. It determined his occupation, his training, his choice of a marriage partner. Ordinary men and women needed an ethic that would help to solve the complex problems growing out of this intensive familial society. In addition they wanted amusement, entertainment, and information. These they found in plays, songs, and popular journalism. Lay culture had an independent vitality and its own forms of expression. It was founded on pragmatic knowledge that was not necessarily tied to learned sources.

Analysis of the pattern of dissemination of ideas contributes to a deeper understanding of the process of intellectual and social change. Fundamental change occurred when the intellectual interests of two or three groups converged. For a brief period the reformers became the spokesmen for ordinary men and women. Their program to reform the church, to abolish the priestly caste, to do away with the penitential rites of the Roman church, coincided with the desires of the townspeople. The Evangelical message of the Gospel found a direct response in the hearts of the laity. Because the interests of the laity and the learned were joined, major transformations in social and religious institutions were accomplished within a very short period of time. When it became necessary to formally define the nature of the new institutions, however, the divergence of interests again became evident, the groups resumed their separate paths of development.

Printing did not create a social revolution. Knowledge was dispersed on a far broader scale than before, but in the sixteenth century social differences were too firmly entrenched to be eradicated by technological change. The Latin culture remained dominant among the political, ecclesiastical, and intellectual elites and new institutions were founded that insured its continuity among them. Without this institutional structure, the lay culture was more dependent on the printing presses for its development and diffusion. From the sixteenth century until the twentieth, printers would play a major role in shaping the intellectual world of ordinary people.

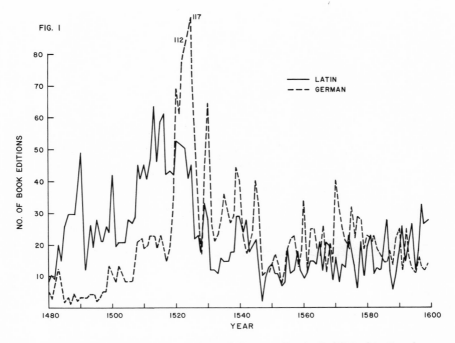

Fig. I. The Linguistic Division: Latin and German Books Published in Strasbourg, 1480–1599.

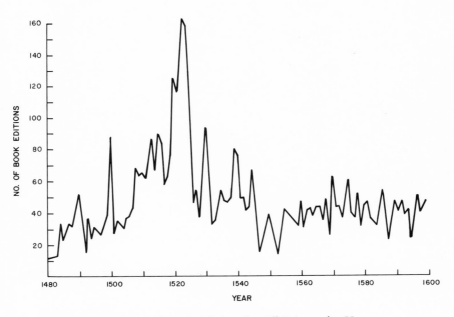

Fig. II. Total Production of Book Editions by All Printers by Year.

287

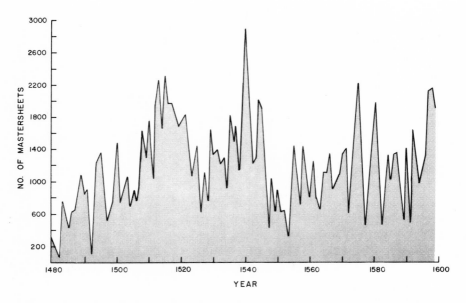

Fig. III. Total Masterformes Produced by Year by All Printers.

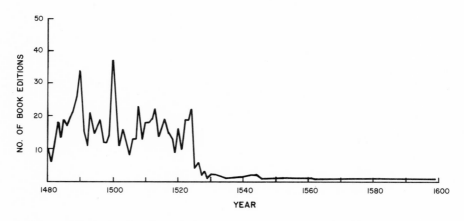

Fig. IV. Production of Catholic Literature in Strasbourg, 1480–1599.

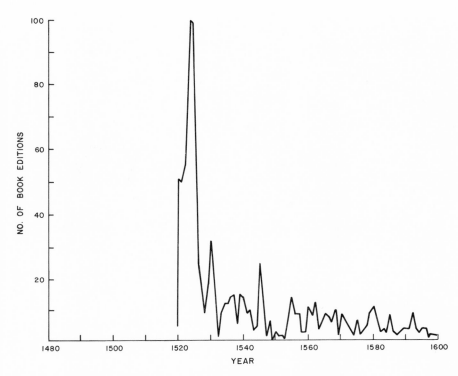

Fig. V. Production of Protestant Books in Strasbourg, 1480–1599.

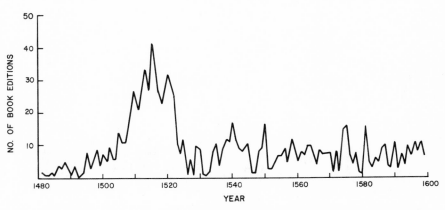

Note: For this figure, humanist editions and editions of the Greek and Latin classics have been combined, since the latter were often the work of the humanists.

Fig. VI. Production of Humanist Book Editions in Strasbourg, 1480–1599.

289

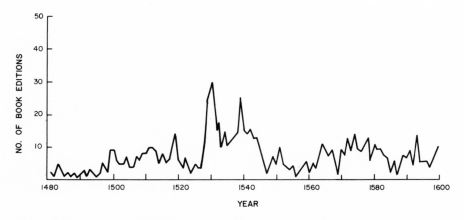

Fig. VII. Production of Scientific Book Editions in Strasbourg, 1480–1599.

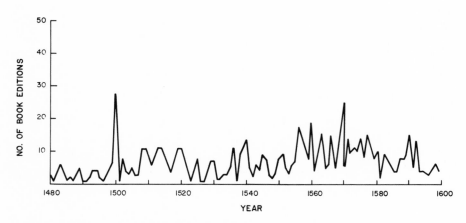

Fig. VIII. Production of Vernacular Literature Book Editions in Strasbourg, 1480–1599.

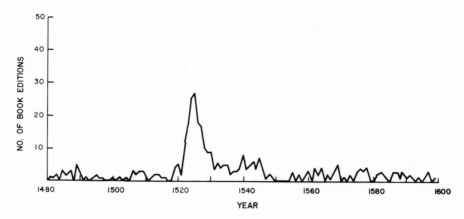

Fig. IX. Production of Bibles and Biblical Commentary in Strasbourg, 1480–1599.

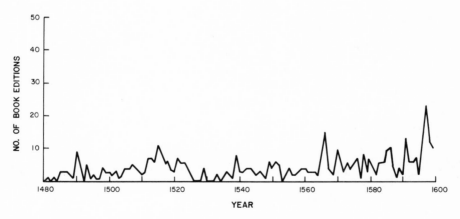

Fig. X. Production of School Texts in Strasbourg, 1480–1599.

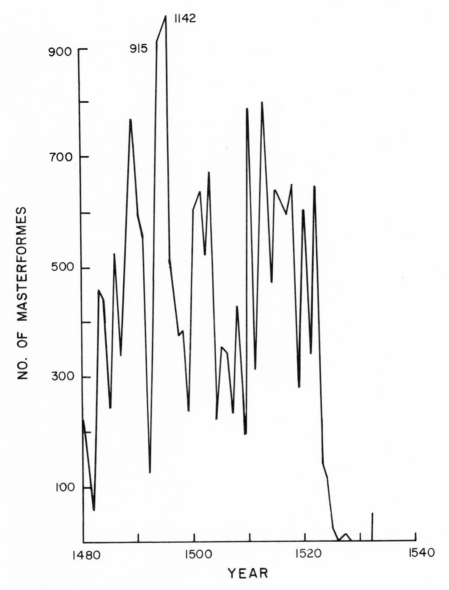

Fig. XI. Total Masterformes per Year for Catholic Books.

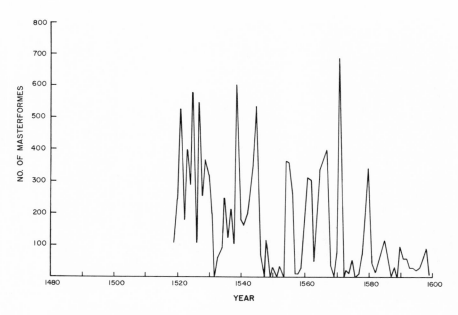

Fig. XII. Total Masterformes per Year for Protestant Books.

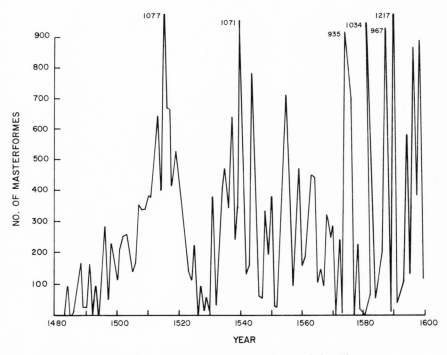

Fig. XIII. Total Masterformes per Year—Humanism and the Classics.

293

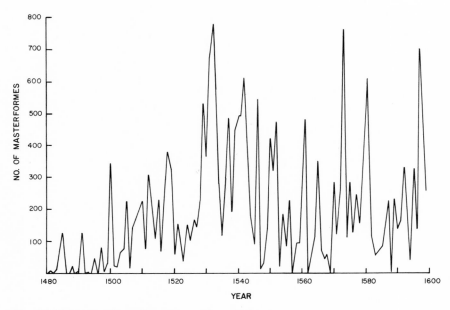

Fig. XIV. Total Masterformes per Year—Science.

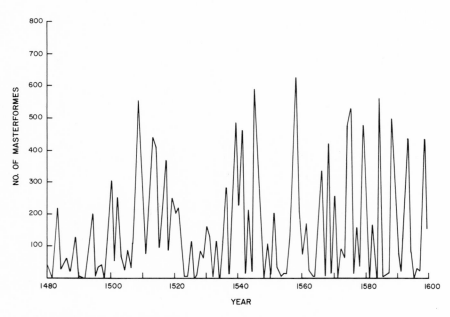

Fig. XV. Total Masterformes per Year—Vernacular Literature.

294

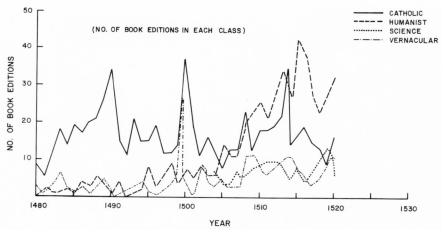

Note: Humanist combines humanist and classical (antiquity) books.

Fig. XVI. Composite Graph: Catholic, Humanist, Scientific, and Vernacular Publication, 1480–1520.

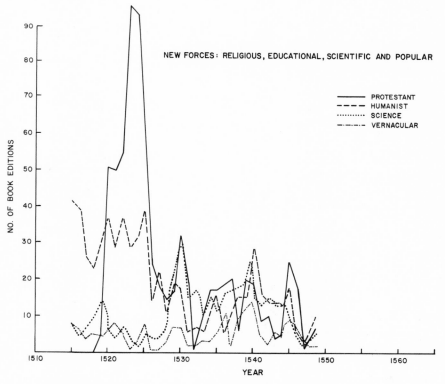

Note: Humanist includes humanist works, classical editions, and biblical scholarship.

Fig. XVII. Composite Graph: Protestant, Humanist, Scientific, and Vernacular Publication, 1515–1548.

295

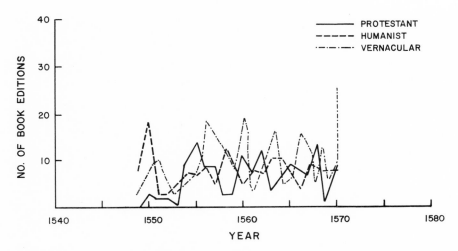

Note: Humanist includes humanist works and classical editions.

Fig. XVIII. Composite Graph: Protestant, Humanist, and Vernacular Publication, 1549–1577.

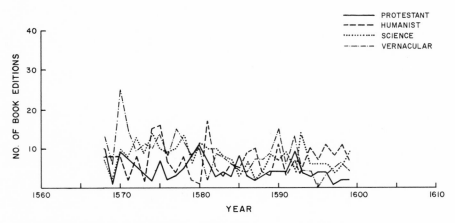

Note: Humanist includes humanist literary works and classical editions.

Fig. XIX. Composite Graph: Protestant, Humanist, Scientific, and Vernacular Publication, 1568–1599.

296

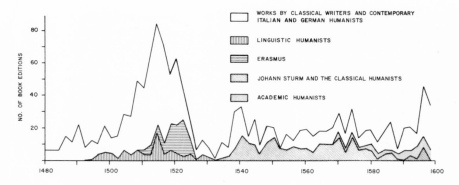

Fig. XX. Humanist Activity in Strasbourg, 1480–1599.

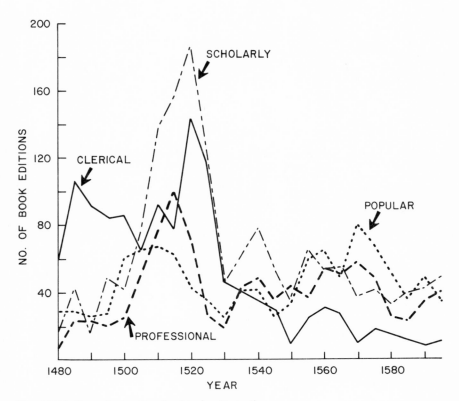

Fig. XXI. Cumulative Readership by Quintile.

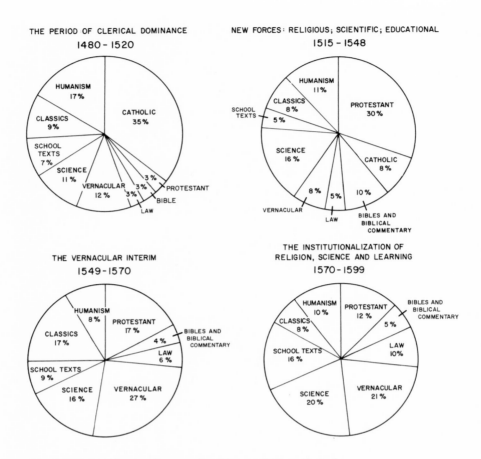

Fig. XXII. Publication Patterns by Class and Time Period.

298

APPENDIX A · DATA COLLECTION AND COMPUTER METHOD

Since computers have not been widely used in intellectual history, it may be helpful to summarize briefly the procedures followed in collecting the data and preparing it for computer analysis.

The first task was to establish the limits of the study and to collect all the data available. The opening date, 1480, was selected because it preceded the beginnings of Alsatian humanism and allowed for a sufficient sample of Catholic publication. A convenient closing date, 1599, was fixed arbitrarily. Every book, treatise, tract, broadsheet, or song sheet printed in Strasbourg and listed in an available catalogue or bibliography was included:

The catalogue of Charles Schmidt based on the repertories of the major printers from 1480–1520;

the catalogue prepared by François Ritter of books printed in Alsace from 1450–1600 which are now in the collection of the Bibliothèque Nationale et Universitaire de Strasbourg, and his catalogue of books in the collection of the Bibliothèque Municipale at Strasbourg;

the *Répertoire* prepared by François Ritter of books printed in Alsace not in the possession of the Strasbourg collections;

the revision of the Ritter catalogue by Mademoiselle Lilly Greiner of the Bibliothèque Nationale et Universitaire de Strasbourg;

the Strasbourg publications indexed in the collection of the British Museum, London, and in Pegg's bibliography of other libraries in the British Isles;

lists of publications in specialized catalogues of scientific books such as Zinner, Hirsch, and Bosse;

Charles Fischer's catalogue of astronomical tracts and treatises published in Strasbourg;

Jean Rott's bibliography of the work of Jean Sturm;

Josef Benzing's specialized bibliographies of Luther, Ulrich von Hutten, and Walter Ryff; and

Joseph Benzing's articles on the printers Christian Egenolff, Jacob Cammerlander, and Matthias Schürer Erben.

From these catalogues and bibliographies, a file was created in which the available data for each book was recorded: author, title, publisher, date of publication, language of publication, format, number of pages, and illustrations. The 5,677 cards, one to represent each published edition of a book, comprised the base of the study.

The books were then classified by subject matter. Nine major classes of books within which materials could be more closely analyzed were rather obvious from the start. Throughout the study these classes are designated by letters, as follows:

C   Catholic Literature
L   Legal Treatises and Documents
A   Literature of Antiquity (Classics)
B   Biblical Literature
T   School Texts
H   Humanist Works
V   Vernacular Literature
S   Scientific Writings
P   Protestant Literature

Identification of individual works was a slow process, complicated by the need to develop subject-matter designations that accurately described the contents of the books. Some seventy subject-matter categories emerged; many of them reflect particular ways in which books were used. For example, Catholic literature has been divided into sermons, service books to be used by the clergy, devotionals for laymen, curates' manuals, and so forth. The categories of all classes are listed at the end of this appendix, together with the topical breakdowns within each subject-matter category.[1]

The volume of data made the McBee retrieval system unwieldy and impracticable, and the information was transferred to IBM computer cards. Unfortunately, no acceptable system for recording the full titles of the books was found, and all authors' names had to be standardized. Once the coded data was on the computer cards, the cross-tabulations and graphic displays available in SPSS (Statistical Package for the Social Sciences) were used.[2] Standard programs exist which can be adapted to the needs of historical analysis—it is not necessary for the historian to become a computer programmer.

Simple frequency counts of each of the main classes of books were run first. The computer not only provided the raw numerical information but also drew six simplified bar graphs, or histograms, so that the material could be perceived visually.[3] One (figure II) delineates total production of all book editions by year for the study period. Figures III–VII showed total production by year for the most important classes: Catholic literature, Protestant literature, science, vernacular literature, and, on one graph, humanism, the Greek and Latin classics, and school texts. These graphs became a basic analytical tool. They provided new insight into the intellectual evolution of the period. None of the graphs by class repeated the pattern of the graph for total production, nor did the graph of any one class duplicate that of another. They showed that each field of intellectual activity had developed independently of the others, and that significant variations in chronological periodization existed from one field to another.

To permit further correlation each graph was put on a transparency. When they were superimposed one upon the other, a pattern of peaks and troughs emerged, leading to the identification of successive intellectual generations whose work created the peaks. These groups provided the organizational framework of the study.

The computer also made it possible to arrive at a viable estimate of the productivity of each printing shop. Page lengths were available for well over two-thirds of the books in the study. The format size of the book was also known, and so it was possible to recreate the actual number of folio-sized sheets on which a book was printed. It was thus possible to estimate each printer's yearly production.[4] Using the cross-tabulation program of SPSS, the yearly repertoire of every printer was analyzed by subject matter, and a precise picture of the activity of individual printers emerged.[5] Language patterns were traced by year and by decade, by subject matter class and by printer.

The computer made possible firm and explicit conclusions based on empirical evidence. It also brought things to my attention. Without the computer, the significance of vernacular publication would have gone unobserved, partially because my own training led me to assume Protestant publication and humanism would be preeminent. The computer also forced me to recognize that the pattern of intellectual generations, often discussed theoretically, was a phenomenon in all fields of learning.

While the historian tends to fear the computer as an alien element, which reduces human life to quantitative measurement, in fact the computer can serve as a liberating force, freeing the historian to examine all of the data. One of the frustrations of historical research is that, after amassing voluminous amounts of material over a period of years, one gradually forgets details that were once fresh in one's mind. If the material is in the computer, this cannot happen. The machine functions as a responsive memory which enables the historian to use every scrap of information effectively.

CLASSES, SUBJECT MATTER CATEGORIES, AND TOPICS

C. Catholic Literature
    C1. Catholic Doctrine and Theology Written before 1400.
        1. Works Printed before the Reform
        2. Church Fathers and Catholic Theologians Reprinted after the Reform.

C2. Catholic Doctrine and Theology Written after 1400.

C3. Catholic Sermons
    1. General Sermons.
    2. Sermons Preached by Johannis Geiler von Keysersberg.

C4. Catholic Curates' Manuals and Lives of the Saints for Priests.
    1. Catholic Curates' Manuals.
    2. Lives of the Saints in Latin.

C5. Catholic Sacred Music, Devotionals for Private Worship, Lay Manuals of Christian Life.
    1. Devotionals.
    2. Sacred Music for Church Worship.
    3. Popular Religious Music.

C6. Catholic Missals, Breviaries, and Sacramental Books.
    1. Breviaries.
    2. Missals.
    3. Books on the Administration of the Sacraments.

C7. Catholic Marian Verse, Marian Controversy, and Other Catholic Verse.
    1. Marian Verse and Marian Controversy.
    2. Other Catholic Verse.

C8. Intra-Catholic Controversy.

C9. Canon Law and Ecclesiastical Politics.

C10. Anti-Protestant Polemic.

L. Law and Politics.
  L1. Laws and Political Treatises.
    1. Imperial Politics, Letters and Ordinances.
    2. Law in Latin.
    3. Law in German.
    4. Statutes and Ordinances of Cities Other than Strasbourg.
    5. Political and Military Theory.
    6. External Political Matters involving Strasbourg.
    7. Edicts and Treaties.
    8. Legal Disputations.
  L2. Municipal Ordinances.
  L3. Notarial Manuals.

A. Literature of Antiquity.
  A1. Latin Classics.
    1. Cato.
    2. Horace.
    3. Virgil.
    4. Latin Poets.
    5. Other Latin Authors.
    6. Cicero.
    7. Ovid.
  A2. Greek Classics.
    1. Aesop.
    2. Greek Authors.

       3. Homer.
       4. Plato.
       5. Aristotle.
   A3. Greek and Latin Classics in German.
   A4. Classical Drama.
       1. Terence.
       2. Plautus.
       3. Other Dramatists.
       4. Classical Plays in German.
   A5. Classical Historians.
       1. Historical Works in Latin or Greek.
       2. Translations of Classical Historians.

B. Biblical Literature
   B1. Entire Bibles.
   B2. Psalters.
   B3. Bible Stories in Latin.
   B4. Psalms Set to Music.
   B5. The New Testament and Parts Thereof.
   B6. The Old Testament and Parts Thereof.
   B7. Biblical Commentary in Latin.
       1. Catholic Biblical Commentary.
       2. Erasmus.
       3. Melanchthon.
       4. Martin Luther.
       5. François Lambert.
       6. Other Reformers and Theologians.
       7. Strasbourg Reformers.
       8. Otto Brunfels.
   B8. Biblical Commentary in the Vernacular.
       1. Commentary by Martin Luther.
       2. Vernacular Commentary by Other Reformers and Erasmus.
       3. Commentaries by Laymen.
       4. Commentaries by Strasbourg Reformers.
       5. Commentaries by Anabaptists.
       6. Commentaries by Cyriacus Spangenberg.

T. School Texts
   T1. School Texts in Latin.
       1. Grammars.
       2. Rhetoric Texts.
       3. Oratorical Texts.
       4. School Vocabularies.
       5. Poetics.
       6. Dialectics and Logic.
       7. Musical Theory and Texts.
       8. Letters, Dialogues, Exercises.

      9. Song Books for the Gymnasium and Academy.

      10. Miscellaneous Texts.

   T2. Texts in Greek (often with Latin or German text).

      1. Greek Grammars.

      2. Greek Oratorical Texts and Examples.

   T3. Plays for the School.

      1. Latin Plays for the School Theater.

      2. Biblical Plays in Latin for the Gymnasium.

   T4. Academic Disputations and Theses.

      1. Theses, Disputations and Poems of Congratulation.

      2. Orations Given at the Academy.

H. Humanism.

   H1. Humanist Works in Latin.

      1. German and Swiss Humanists.

      2. Alsatian Humanists.

      3. Italian Humanists.

      4. Dutch Humanists.

      5. French Humanists.

      6. Other Humanists.

   H2. Humanist Collections.

   H3. Pedagogical Treatises.

   H4. Dictionaries and Vocabularies.

   H5. Historical Works in Latin.

      1. Ancient History.

      2. Ecclesiastical History.

      3. German and Imperial History.

      4. Other Historical Works.

V. Vernacular Literature.

   V1. Bible Stories in German.

   V2. Medieval Tales and Romances.

      1. Chivalric Tales.

      2. Monastic and Clerical Tales.

      3. Tales Based on Greek and Roman Sources.

      4. Ghost Stories.

   V3. Lives of the Saints in German.

   V4. Popular Textbooks and German ABC's.

   V5. Moral Treatises.

      1. On Marriage and Women's Position in Society.

      2. On Good Morals and Moral Advice.

      3. On Drunkenness and Gluttony.

      4. On Gambling.

      5. On Raising Children.

      6. On Charity.

      7. On Court Life.

V6. Popular Stories, Poems and Joke Books.
    1. Joke Books.
    2. Satire.
    3. Novels, Stories and Poems.

V7. Music Including Popular Songs.
    1. Popular Songs.
    2. Collections of Songs for Group Singing.
    3. Instrumental Music.

V8. Plays.
    1. Biblical Plays in German.
    2. Plays on other Themes.

V9. History in the Vernacular.
    1. General History and Chronicles.
    2. Ancient History.
    3. German and Imperial History.
    4. Ecclesiastical History.

V10. Popular Journalism.
    1. Accounts of Prophecies, Heresies, Religious Executions, and other Religious Occurrences.
    2. Accounts of Natural Disasters.
    3. Accounts of Marvelous and Monstrous Births.
    4. Accounts of Murders.
    5. Accounts of Wonderful or Exceptional Plants.
    6. Accounts of Marvelous and Miraculous Apparitions.
    7. Accounts of Marvelous and Remarkable Events.
    8. Portrait Broadsheets.
    9. Accounts of Comets.
    10. Anti-Semitic Broadsheets.
    11. Local Events in Strasbourg, Festivals, and Celebrations.
    12. Accounts of Floods.
    13. Broadsheets Illustrating Coinage.
    14. Anti-Catholic Polemical Broadsheets.
    15. Historical Broadsheets.

V11. Accounts of Recent Events.
    1. Imperial Politics and Neighboring Events, Knights and Historical Wars.
    2. The War against the Turks.
    3. The Revolt of the Netherlands.
    4. The Wars of Religion in France.
    5. The Bishops' War.

S. Science.
  S1. Medicine.
    1. Memory Books.
    2. Gynecology.
    3. Health Rules and Regimens.

    4. Plague.

    5. Surgery.

    6. Syphilis.

    7. General Medical Treatises.

    8. Baths.

    9. Pharmaceutical Books.

    10. Anatomies.

    11. Medical Treatises Based on Greek Sources.

    12. Specific Medical Treatises.

    13. Medical Treatises Based on Arabic Sources.

    14. Works by Theophrastus Bombastus Paracelsus.

    15. Medical Theses.

S2. Books on Distilling.

S3. Botany and Herbals.

S4. Astronomy.

    1. Traditional Astronomical Texts.

    2. Planetary Theory.

    3. Eclipses.

    4. Meteors, Comets, and Bright Stars.

    5. Astronomical Techniques.

    6. Meteorology.

    7. Treatises on the Strasbourg Clock.

    8. Debate over the Gregorian Calendar.

S5. Mathematics and Physics.

    1. Traditional Encyclopedias.

    2. Books on Scientific Measurement.

    3. Physics.

    4. Applied Mathematics.

    5. Geometry.

    6. Orations on Studying Mathematics.

    7. Arithmetic.

    8. Mathematical Texts.

    9. Scientific Theses.

S6. Geography, Travel and Exploration.

    1. Traditional Voyages and Descriptions.

    2. Descriptions of Voyages to the New World and East Indies.

    3. General Geographies and Cosmographies.

    4. Maps, Itineraries, and How to Use Them.

    5. Descriptions of Particular Regions.

S7. Natural History.

S8. Agronomy.

S9. Veterinary Texts.

S10. Hunting Manuals.

S11. Technical Manuals.

    1. Cookbooks.

    3. Gunpowder.
    4. Mining and Metal Working.
    5. Textile Dyes.
    6. Models for Design.
    7. Making and Preservation of Wine.
    8. Sundials.
    9. Architecture.
    10. Surveying.
    11. Embroidery.
S12. Calendars and Prognostications for Popular Use.
S13. Astronomical Calendars.
S14. Ecclesiastical Calendars.
S15. Astrology and Chiromancy.
    1. Astrology.
    2. Chiromancy and Physiognomy.
    3. Dream Books.
S16. Alchemy.
S17. Witchcraft.

P. Protestant Publication.
   P1. Protestant Doctrine and Theology.
    1. Luther's Statements of Doctrine.
    2. The Eucharist.
    3. Melanchthon's Statements of Doctrine.
    4. Other Protestant Theology.
    5. Religious Councils and Attempts at Religious Settlement.
    6. Catechisms and Other Books of Instruction.
    7. Marriage.
    8. Strasbourg Theologians.
    9. Confessions of Faith.
   P2. Protestant Sermons.
    1. Sermons by Luther.
    2. Local Reformers.
    3. Other Sermons.
    4. Funeral Sermons.
   P3. Anti-Catholic Polemic.
    1. Luther.
    2. Ulrich von Hutten.
    3. Laymen.
    4. English Polemic and Statements of Faith.
    5. General Polemic by Other German and Swiss Reformers.
    6. Anti-Papal Polemic.
    7. Marriage of the Clergy.
    8. Appeals to the German Nation for Ecclesiastical Reform.
    9. Defenses of Luther.
    10. Melanchthon and Other Wittenberg Theologians.

11. Strasbourg Reformers.
12. Polemic by Otto Brunfels.
13. Polemic against Episcopal Authority.
14. French Tracts and Treatises.
15. Polemic against the Council of Trent.
16. Polemic by Johannes Fischart.
17. The Bishops' War.

P4. Intra-Protestant Controversy and Anabaptism.
1. Anabaptist, Spiritualist, and Sectarian Tracts.
2. Polemic against Anabaptists and Sectarians.
3. Reports on the Anabaptists.
4. Sturm-Pappus Controversy and Others.

P5. Protestant Devotionals, Prayerbooks and Service Books for Lay Use.

P6. Protestant Hymnals and Devotional Songs.
1. Collections of Hymns for Congregational Singing.
2. Liturgies.
3. Popular Religious Songs.

P7. Protestant Manuals for the Clergy.
1. Protestant Postils.
2. Liturgies.
3. Sermon Manuals.

P8. Protestant Martyrologies.

APPENDIX B · GYMNASIUM AND ACADEMY FACULTIES

FACULTY OF THE GYMNASIUM AND
UPPER CLASSES, 1538–1548

Faculty members whose works were published are indicated by a star.

Latin Classes
Class I   ★Peter Dasypodius (1538–45) Gerhard Sevenus (1545–59)
Class II   ★Simon Lithonius (1538–45) Christopher Kerlin (ca. 1540)
Class III ★Johann Sapidus (1538–41) Michael Toxites (1541–45) Theobald Dietrich
          (ca. 1545)
Class IV   Jacob Villicus (1538–41) Valentin Erythraeus (ca. 1550–75)
Class V   Peter Schriessheimer (1538–45) Lorenz Engler (ca. 1545)
Class VI   Johann Schwebel (1538–45) Georg Hitzler (ca. 1545)
   ★Theophilus Gol joined the faculty of the Latin Classes in 1548. He would move
    up through the ranks, serving eventually as Professor of Ethics in the Academy
    until his death in 1600.
   Peter Dasypodius appointed vice-rector in 1545.

Upper Classes and Lectures
Theology   ★Wolfgang Capito (1538–41)
             ★Caspar Hedio (1538–52)
             ★Martin Bucer (1538–49)
             ★Fontanus (ca. 1538)
             ★Jean Calvin (1538–41)
             ★Peter Vermigli (Peter Martyr) (1542–47)
             ★Paul Fagius (1544–49)
             ★Johann Marbach (1546–81)
Greek   ★Jacob Bedrotus (1538–41)
             Christopher Kerlin (1541–48/49)
             ★Peter Dasypodius (1548/49–59)
             Gerhard Sevenus (1559–61)
             Paola Lacisio
             Claudius Féraeus   lectured intermittently 1538–1545
             ★Johann Guinther von Andernach
Hebrew   Michael Délius (1535–54)
             ★Immanuel Trémellio (1541–49)
Mathematics ★Christian Herlin (1538–62)
Law   ★Wendelin Bittelbron (1538–41)
             ★Ludwig Bebio (1541–45)
             Kilian Vogler (1545–52)
Philosophy   ★Justus Velsius (1545–50)

Rhetoric   *Johann Sturm (1537–81)
                *Valentin Erythraeus (ca. 1550–75)
Medicine   *Sebald Hawenreuter (1545–53)
SOURCE: Charles Engel, *L'école latine,* pp. 24–55; Johann Sturm, *Classicae Epistolae,* trans. and
ed. Jean Rott; and Anton Schindling, *Humanistische Hochschule.*

FACULTY OF THE ACADEMY, 1566–1599

Faculty members whose works were published are indicated by a star.

Rhetoric   *Melchior Junius (1575–1604)

Philosophy: Dialectics, Ethics, and Physics
  Dialectics   Johann Reinhard (1568–70)
                *Andreas Planer (1570–72)
                *Johann Ludwig Hawenreuter (1572–73)
  Organon   *Johann Bentz (1597–99)
  Ethics   *Ernst Regius (1565–70)
                *Hubert Giphanius (1570–72)
                *Theophilus Gol (1572–1601)
                *Marcus Florus
  Physics   Johannes Bruno (1567–71)
                Andreas Planer (1571–78)
                *Johann Ludwig Hawenreuter (1572–88)
                Henning Oldendorp (1588–89)
                *Johann Ludwig Hawenreuter (1595–1618)
  Mathematics   *Conrad Dasypodius (1562–1600)
                Johann Bruno, assistant (1567–71)
                *David Wolckenstein (1574–92)

Philology: Hebrew, Greek, and Poetry
  Hebrew   Elias Kyber (1565–69)
                *Johann Pappus (1569–75)
                Henning Oldendorp (1575–89)
                *Elias Schad (1589–93)
                Tobias Speccer (1594–1615)
  Greek   Johann Wilvesheim (1564?–89)
                Laurentius Siphanus (1568)
                Ernst Regius (1565–67)
                Philipp Glaser (1587–89)
                *Michael Bosch (1591–1608)
  Poetry   *Michael Beuther (1565)
                Ernst Regius (1565–67)
                Laurentius Siphanus (ca. 1568)
                Nikolaus Reusner (1585–88)
                Joseph Lang (1588–89)
                Philipp Glaser (1589–91)

History	*Michael Beuther (1565–87)
	*Johann Pappus (1587–91)
	Philipp Glaser (1591–1601)

Law	Philipp Custosius (1570–74)
	Hubert Giphanius (?)
	*Georg Obrecht (1575–1612)
	Laurentius Tuppius (1572–1600)
	*Nikolaus Reusner (1583–88)
	Paul Graseck (1588–1600)
	Denys Godefroy (1591–1600)

Medicine	*Andreas Planer (1572–78)
	Open 1578–1585
	*Johann Ludwig Hawenreuter (1586)
	*Melchior Sebiz (1586–1612)
	*Israel Spach (1589–1600)

Theology	*Johann Marbach (1546–81)
	Elias Kyber (1566–69)
	*Melchior Speccer (1566–69)
	*Johann Pappus (1576–1610)
	Johann Piscator (1571)
	*Erasmus Marbach (1574–93)
	*Philipp Marbach (1593–1611)
	*Nikolaus Florus (1569?–87)
	Elias Schad (1586–93)
	Johann Faber (1593–96)
	Bartholomaeus Nasse (1596–1614)

SOURCE: Anton Schindling, *Humanistische Hochschule,* passim.

APPENDIX C · CATEGORIES OF BOOKS FOR SPECIAL MARKETS

CATEGORIES OF BOOKS FOR THE CLERICAL MARKET

Old Testament
New Testament
Bibles
Gospels and epistles
Psalters
Biblical commentary
Lives of the saints
Church fathers and philosophy
Catholic doctrine and theology
Catholic sermons
Catholic curates' manuals

Catholic missals for the orders
Catholic religious verse
Intra-Catholic controversy
Protestant doctrine and theology
Protestant sermons
Protestant catechisms
Protestant postills for clerical use
Intra-Protestant controversy
Canon law and ecclesiastical politics
Ecclesiastical calendars

CATEGORIES OF BOOKS FOR THE SCHOLARLY MARKET

Old Testament
New Testament
Entire Bibles
Psalms
Biblical commentary
Humanist works in Latin
Pedagological treatises
Dictionaries
Latin classics in Latin
Greek classics in Latin
Greek classics in Greek

Classical historians in Latin or Greek
Contemporary or medieval historians
   in Latin
Moral treatises
Math and physics
Natural history
Catholic doctrine and theology
Protestant doctrine and theology
Church fathers and philosophy
Geography and exploration

CATEGORIES OF BOOKS FOR THE PROFESSIONAL MARKET (DOCTORS, LAWYERS, NOTARIES, CIVIL SERVANTS)

Gospels and epistles
Latin classics in Latin
Greek classics in Latin
Classical historians in Latin
Contemporary and medieval
   historians in Latin
Moral treatises
Medicine
Distilling
Botany and herbals

Math and physics
Geography and exploration
Natural history
Veterinary texts
Technical manuals
Alchemy
Catholic doctrine and theology
Protestant doctrine and theology
Law and Politics

CATEGORIES OF BOOKS FOR THE POPULAR MARKET

Bible stories
Humanist works in German
Latin classics in German
Greek classics in German
Textbooks for adults
Lives of the saints
Contemporary and medieval
    historians in German
Accounts of recent events
Medieval romances and knightly tales

Popular literature
Popular journalism (Wunderzeichen)
Music including popular songs
Calendars and prognostications
Catholic liturgies for laymen
Protestant liturgies for laymen
Protestant hymnals and devotional songs
Biblical plays
Psalms set to music

NOTES

INTRODUCTION

1. Henri-Jean Martin was the first to recognize that the whole mass of books published in a given time would provide new insights into the cultural and social forces operating in that period. Martin's work was one point of departure for this study. Henri-Jean Martin, *Livres, pouvoirs et société à Paris au XVIIᵉ siècle (1598–1701)*, vol. 1, p. 3.

Elizabeth L. Eisenstein's recent book *The Printing Press as an Agent of Change* is an important contribution to a new attitude toward book culture. She recognizes printing as a major transformation in communications and examines this change in many of its ramifications.

2. The assumption that published books mirror intellectual tastes and interests is already well established and accepted. Ernest Goldschmidt, in his study of incunabula, stated that from the very beginning books were made to sell and that the publisher had to be able to judge the market: "There has never been a book that went to press unless the printer, rightly or wrongly, believed he would make a profit." E. P. Goldschmidt, *Medieval Texts and Their First Appearance in Print*, p. 13. See also Margaret Bingham Stillwell, *The Awakening Interest in Science during the First Century of Printing, 1450–1550*, p. xii, and George Sarton, "The Scientific Literature Transmitted through the Incunabula," p. 55, on scientific publication.

3. In his classic definition of cultural anthropology, Bronislaw Malinowski states that the discipline involves the study of man's social heritage, his language, habits, ideas, and beliefs, as they are incorporated into a particular organizational and cultural setting. Language is a distinct element of any culture, not a mere tool but a body of vocal customs vital to a person's understanding of his social environment. *Encyclopedia of the Social Sciences*, ed. Edwin R. A. Seligman, 15 vols. (New York: Macmillan, 1930–35), vol. 4, pp. 621–23. Contemporary anthropologists are less willing to accept any one definition of what culture means. "Culture," writes one, "is the patterned behavior learned by each individual from the day of his birth as he or she is educated . . . by parents or peers to become and remain a member of the particular group into which he or she was born or joined." *Encyclopedia of Anthropology*, ed. David E. Hunter and Phillip Whittler (New York: Harper & Row, 1976), p. 103. Language is still considered a vital part of this acculturation.

4. Most scholars agree that books belonging to the libraries of such institutions as Catholic convents or Protestant schools, where they were in the care of librarians, had a greater chance of being preserved.

Martin pointed out that a large proportion of the seventeenth-century books now in the collection of the Bibliothèque nationale in Paris, which was the basis of his study, came from monastic houses secularized during the French Revolution. These ecclesiastical libraries had, however, received donations from private secular libraries. Martin, *Livres, pouvoirs et société*, vol. 1, p. 68.

Rudolf Hirsch also believed that conditions for preservation were more favorable for religious books and scholarly works. His list of books more likely to have disappeared were almost all vernacular works: small or cheap editions, household books, almanacs, prognostications, dream books, technical and medical books, school books, vernacular popular literature or popular legends, books for private devotions, books judged heretical, and news tracts. Rudolf Hirsch, *Printing, Selling and Reading, 1450–1550,* p. 11.

In the light of these assumptions the strong showing of vernacular literature in Strasbourg appears even more compelling. The popular books that survived may be a smaller proportion of the total number printed than is the case for scholarly and religious books.

5. Josef Benzing, in *Die Buchdrucker des 16. und 17. Jahrhunderts im Deutschen Sprachgebiet,* lists the ten major centers in German-speaking areas in the sixteenth century as follows:

City	Number of Printers
Cologne	93
Nuremberg	62
Strasbourg	57
Basel	54
Wittenberg	38
Frankfurt am Main	37
Augsburg	32
Leipzig	29
Erfurt	28
Vienna	22

A list of French printing centers assigns to Paris, Lyons, and Rouen many more printers than are found in the German cities. Note the different French and German estimates for the total number of printers in Strasbourg. My own figure, a count of printers who each published at least one book under his own name, is 77. The French figure, which is somewhat higher than the German figure, may include journeymen printers who did not print under their own names.

City	Number of Printers
Paris	903
Lyons	466
Rouen	145
Strasbourg	64
Poitiers	36
Troyes	33

SOURCE: Jean Muller, *Dictionnaire abrégé des imprimeurs/éditeurs français du seizième siècle,* p. 4.

6. Jean-Pierre Kintz, "Notes sur quelques aspects démographiques de la ville de Strasbourg," in *Strasbourg au coeur religieux du XVIe siècle,* p. 13.

7. Philippe Dollinger, "L'apogée médiéval," in *Histoire de l'Alsace,* p. 116.

8. Ibid., p. 91.

9. Miriam Usher Chrisman, *Strasbourg and the Reform,* p. 16.

10. Ibid., p. 32.

11. François-Joseph Fuchs, "L'immigration artisanale à Strasbourg de 1544 à 1565," in *Artisans et ouvriers d'Alsace*, pp. 185–97.

12. ADB 13, p. 456.

13. Chrisman, *Strasbourg and the Reform*, pp. 14–26.

14. Thomas A. Brady, Jr., *Ruling Class, Regime and Reformation in Strasbourg, 1520–1555*, pp. 96–97.

15. François-Joseph Fuchs, "Le droit de bourgeoisie à Strasbourg," *Revue d'Alsace* 101 (1962): 19–50.

16. Ibid., p. 20.

17. Brady, *Ruling Class, Regime and Reformation*. This study provides a comprehensive description of the upper class social groups in the city and a compelling analysis of the political power of the patriciate. My account in this introduction is based on Brady's work.

18. *Der Statt Strassburg: Policey-Ordnung* (Strasbourg: Johann Carolus, 1628).

19. See the city ordinances on marriage (L2.1.26a–h), which were meant to protect the handworkers from imprudent expenditures, the market ordinances (L2.1.22) which were meant to protect them from speculators, and the Anabaptist ordinances (L2.1.19a–b). See also L2.1.45.

20. Brady, *Ruling Class, Regime and Reformation*, p. 72.

21. Ibid., p. 56.

22. Ibid., pp. 51, 59–61.

23. Ibid., pp. 72–76.

24. Ibid., pp. 61–62.

25. Ibid., pp. 33–35. Percy Stafford Allen, ed., *Opus Epistolarum Des. Erasmi Roterodami*, 10:223, epist. 2808.

26. Brady, *Ruling Class, Regime and Reformation*, pp. 110–12.

27. Ibid., p. 111. See also ibid., appendix, pp. 329, 340, 349.

28. Ibid., pp. 209–210, 239.

29. Ibid., p. 112.

30. Ibid., p. 120.

31. Luther's father was a miner. Of the Strasbourg reformers, Martin Bucer's father was a shoemaker; Wolfgang Capito's father was a smith who served on the city council of Hagenau; and Matthias Zell and Caspar Hedio both came from middle-level burgher families. See Chrisman, *Strasbourg and the Reform*, p. 83, or the more recent study by Bernard Vogler, "Recrutement et carrière des pasteurs strasbourgeois au XVIᵉ siècle," pp. 150–60.

32. Johann Sturm, who established the Strasbourg Gymnasium, was the son of a civil servant in the court of the Count of Manderscheid. Christian Herlin, who taught mathematics in the school, came from a Strasbourg merchant family; his uncle was ammeister. Michael Beuther was the son of a civil servant in Würzburg. Paul Olinger, Jonas Bitner, and Theophilus Goll all came from Strasbourg burgher families of the middle rank. At the end of the century J. L. Hawenreuter, Melchior Junius, Isaac Malleolus, and Tobias Speccer were the second generation of teachers in their families, their fathers having served on the faculty before them. For bio-

graphical details see François Edouard Sitzmann, *Dictionnaire de biographie des hommes célèbres de l'Alsace; Allgemeine Deutsche Biographie;* or Marie-Joseph Bopp, *Die Evangelischen Geistlichen und Theologen in Elsass und Lothringen.*

33. *Der Statt Strassburg Policey-Ordnung,* 1628.

34. Chrisman, *Strasbourg and the Reform,* p. 9.

35. The changing demands and the concerted group action of some journeyman printers in Lyons from 1550 to 1572 are well described in the essay "Strikes and Salvation in Lyons," by Natalie Zemon Davis, *Society and Culture in Early Modern France,* pp. 1–16.

36. Brady, *Ruling Class, Regime and Reformation,* pp. 303, 308, 315, 317, 319, 326, 327, 334, 334–35, 336, 347, 351, 352–53.

37. Ibid., pp. 300, 316, 323, 332, 350.

38. AMS, VI, 695, 21. Mémoire sur les écoles élémentaires.

CHAPTER ONE

1. The problem of establishing markets faced the printers from the very earliest period. See Florence Edler de Roover, "New Facets on the Financing and Marketing of Early Printed Books," pp. 222–30.

2. The list of printers who are not known to have printed any books under their own names appears in the notes to François Ritter, *L'imprimerie alsacienne,* pp. 355–57.

3. In the sixteenth century most books were paginated by leaves and the terms recto and verso were used to differentiate the sides of the leaf. In modern pagination, there are two pages for every leaf. In this study all references to length are made in leaves, since this is the way most sixteenth-century books were numbered.

4. Leon Voet, *The Golden Compasses,* vol. 2, app. 8, pp. 540–47, provides a clear set of diagrams showing basic folding patterns and then more complex systems.

5. Length of materials like song sheets, municipal ordinances, or broadsheets is rarely given in the bibliographies. These, however, would not add significantly to the oeuvre of any printer. Three major catalogues provide no information about the length of the books: François Ritter, *Catalogue des livres du XVIe siècle ne figurant pas à la Bibliothèque nationale et universitaire de Strasbourg;* the British Museum, *Short-title Catalogue;* and the Pegg catalogue. Nevertheless, of a total of 5,684 books foliosheet data is available for 3,911 editions, or 68 percent. Of the 1,773 books about which data are missing, 505 are one-page sheets, broadsheets, or polemic tracts that rarely went over four foliosheets. Thus the actual missing data may affect only 1,268 editions, or 22 percent.

6. A large volume of sermons came to about 125 foliosheets; a lawbook to 160–300; a volume of Cicero to 36–40; a volume of Erasmus to 18–24; a Lutheran tract to 10–30.

7. The number of copies printed of any one book could vary from 800 to 2,000. An edition of 1,250 copies was the most efficient use of the press, because a printing team could pull 1,250 sheets off the press in a day. If only 800 copies of a book were printed, the formes had to be changed in the middle of the day to permit a run of 450 copies (or fewer) of the next page or of some other work. Records from the Plantin

press in Antwerp show that for the period 1563–67, 40 percent of their production was in press runs of 1,250 copies. From 1590 to 1600, 31 percent was at 1,250 and another 31 percent at 1,500. Voet, *Golden Compasses,* vol. 2, pp. 169, 172.

8. Adolphe Rusch (1466–1489), an important printer of the early period, falls into the study only in the very last years of his life, when his production was greatly diminished. There is no information on his foliosheet production. There is a similar lack of information for Johann Eber (ca. 1481). Heirs who merely closed out a printing shop have not been included.

9. They are also comparable to the description of Paris printing shops described by Lucien Febvre and Henri-Jean Martin in *The Coming of the Book,* p. 110.

10. Voet, *Golden Compasses,* vol. 2, pp. 313, 318. Voet notes that until 1563 two compositors worked on each forme at the Plantin press. It was normal in small and medium shops for two compositors to work on a continuous text in this way. After 1565 in the Plantin shop, which was larger than average, the system was made more efficient and one compositor worked on both sides of a forme.

11. Ibid., p. 315.

12. Herman van der Wee, *The Growth of the Antwerp Market,* vol. 1, p. 50. Antwerp was a Catholic city and would have continued to observe the Catholic saints' days. There is little indication, however, that the abolition of these feast days did much to change the work year. In Strasbourg work would still have been suspended for the two great fairs in June and December. The 260-day figure probably remains a viable estimate.

13. Voet, *Golden Compasses,* vol. 1, pp. 69, 88, 200.

14. Arius Montanus supervised Plantin's proofreaders for the great polyglot Bible. Frans Raphelengius, a scholar in oriental languages, was principal proofreader. Voet, *Golden Compasses,* vol. 1, pp. 63, 115. In Strasbourg Nicolaus Gerbel, a member of the *sodalitas literaria,* served as proofreader for Matthias Schürer. Johannes Ficker and Otto Winckelmann, *Handschriftenproben des sechzehnten Jahrhunderts nach Strassburger Originalen,* vol. 2, p. 77. Later, from 1573 to 1578, Johann Fischart served as proofreader for his brother-in-law, Bernard Jobin. Adolf Hauffen, *Johann Fischart, Ein Literaturbild aus der Zeit der Gegenreformation,* vol. 1, p. 50. Johannes Nubling, the former chaplain at St. Erhart, is listed in the *Bürgerbuch* as a printer's corrector. Charles Wittmer and J. Charles Meyer, *Livre de bourgeoisie,* vol. 2, p. 684, no. 7261; p. 739, no. 8022.

15. Voet, *Golden Compasses,* vol. 2, pp. 329–30.

16. Benzing, *Buchdrucker 16 und 17 Jahrhunderts,* pp. 410, 411, 412.

17. F. Ritter, *L'imprimerie alsacienne,* pp. 352–53.

18. Knoblochtzer was active from 1474 to 1484 in Strasbourg. Thus he appears in this study only at the end of his career. Between 1480 and 1484 he published nine books under his own signature. Ritter attributes thirty-one other works to him. Thus, he may have operated at the level of a minor printer. F. Ritter, *L'imprimerie alsacienne,* p. 55.

19. Charles G. A. Schmidt, *Répertoire bibliographique strasbourgeois jusqu'a vers 1530,* vol. 4, p. 1. See L1.2.3; V5.2.2a.

20. Ibid. C4.1.9a. For Anshelm's career in Tübingen, see Heiko Augustinus Oberman, *Werden und Wertung der Reformation,* pp. 19–24.

21. Ibid., p. 15. V1.1.5.
22. Ibid., p. vi. C3.1.50c; T1.1.5c; C5.1.9d.
23. F. Ritter, *L'imprimerie alsacienne*, pp. 323; 466, n. 462.
24. C6.2.5; C4.1.15.
25. F. Ritter, *L'imprimerie alsacienne*, p. 312. H1.2.23.
26. Ibid., pp. 320–21.
27. Rodolphe Peter, "Les premiers ouvrages français imprimés à Strasbourg," vol. 1, p. 90, n. 77. B4.1.9; S1.4.12; S1.4.13.
28. Eugénie Droz, ed., *Chemins de l'hérésie*, vol. 3, p. 105.
29. Rodolphe Peter, "Les premiers ouvrages français imprimés à Strasbourg (suite)," pp. 22–23.
30. V9.1.19; P2.3.14; V9.3.7b; V9.3.8.
31. Peter, "Premiers ouvrages français (suite)," p. 23. Peter's search has uncovered yet four more French works by Strasbourg printers. A translation of Luther, *Livre tresutile de la vraye et parfaite subjection des chrestiens,* Johann Schott for Wolfgang Köpfel, 1525; (Valérand Poullain), *Oraison chrestienne au Seigneur Dieu faicte par maniere de complaincte sur le temps present,* Jacob Fröhlich, 1544–45; *L'instruction et creance des chrestiens: contenant l'oraison de Iesus-Christ, les articles de la foy, les dix commandemens . . . ,* Rémy Guédon, 1546; Philipp Melanchthon, *Confession de la foi presentée à l'empereur Charles V,* Christian Mylius(?), 1555(?). Rodolphe Peter, "Les premiers ouvrages francais, (2e suite)," 35–46.
32. L1.7.4.
33. V11.5.2; V11.5.3.
34. The ten native born printers were:

> Martin Schott, son of the Strasbourg sculptor, Friedrich Schott.
> Matthias Brant, assumed to be the brother of Sebastian Brant.
> Martin Flach II, son of Martin Flach.
> Johann Knobloch II, son of Johann Knobloch.
> Johann Schott, son of Martin Schott.
> Johann Prüss II, son of Johann Prüss.
> Beatus and Sixtus Murner, thought to be the brothers of Thomas·Murner.
> Josias Rihel, son of Wendelin Rihel.
> Theodosius Rihel, son of Wendelin Rihel.

In addition to these men who printed in their own names, Bartholomäus Grüninger and Paul and Philip Köpfel carried on their fathers' businesses for several years, but used the names and imprints of their fathers.

35. Eight immigrant printers whose place of birth appears in, or is known from, other records, with dates of activity in Strasbourg:

> Heinrich Knoblochtzer (1476–84), b. Ettenheim (F. Ritter, *L'imprimerie alsacienne*, p. 55).
> Matthias Hupfuff (1492–1520), b. Württemberg (F. Ritter, *L'imprimerie alsacienne*, p. 145).
> Wilhelm Schaffner (1498–1515), b. Roperswiler (Schmidt, *Alte Bibliotheken*, p. 119).

Wolfgang Köpfel (1522–54), b. Haguenau (Benzing, *Buchdrucker 16/17 Jh.*, p. 414).

Christian Egenolff (1528–30), b. Hademar, Nassau (Benzing, *Buchdrucker 16/17 Jh.*, p. 415).

Matthias Biener (1533–37), b. Berchinger, Franconia (Benzing, *Buchdrucker 16/17 Jh.*, p. 417).

Crato Mylius (1536–47), b. Sélestat (F. Ritter, *L'imprimerie alsacienne*, p. 251).

Augustin Fries (1550–56), b. Francken, Ostfriesland (Benzing, *Buchdrucker 16/17 Jh.*, p. 419).

The scarcity of information after 1530 is due in part to a lacuna in the Strasbourg *Bürgerbuch* for the years 1530–43.

36. Sixteen printers active in the period 1480–1599 who acquired bürgherrecht through purchase, chronologically by date of purchase (from Wittmer and Meyer, *Livre de bourgeoisie* and AMS, *Bürgerbuch, 1559–1730*):

Heinrich Eggestein, 9 August 1459 (*Livre de bourgeoisie,* vol. 1, p. 156, no. 1475).

Adolphe Rusch, 8 January 1460? (*Livre de bourgeoisie,* vol. 1, p. 363, no. 3216).

Peter Attendorn, 12 March 1476 (*Livre de bourgeoisie,* vol. 1, p. 327, no. 2932).

Johann Grüninger, 2 October 1482 (*Livre de bourgeoisie,* vol. 1, p. 390, no. 3439).

37. Printers who acquired citizenship by marriage (The last two men married burgher wives during the period of the *Bürgerbuch* lacuna, but would have acquired citizenship automatically.) (From AMS, *Bürgerbuch,* vol. 3, *1559–1730*; AMS, *Kontracktstube*; AMS, *Registres de St. Nicolas*; F. Ritter, *L'imprimerie alsacienne*; and Wittmer and Meyer, *Livre de bourgeoisie*):

Georg Husner m. Agnes, d. of Claus Honowe, goldsmith, 13 September 1470 (*Livre de bourgeoisie,* vol. 1, p. 267, no. 2439).

Martin Flach m. Catherine, d. of Johann Dammerer, shoemaker, 3 November 1472 (*Livre de bourgeoisie,* vol. 1, p. 289, no. 2616).

Johann Eber m. Adelheit, d. of Erhart Kannels, cartwright, 9 November 1473 (*Livre de bourgeoisie,* vol. 2, p. 303, no. 2740).

Johann Knobloch m. Catherine Dammerer, w. of Martin Flach, printer, 29 May 1501 (*Livre de bourgeoisie,* vol. 2, p. 520, no. 5103).

Konrad Kerner m. Noppurg, d. of Matthias Brant, printer, 14 January 1511 (*Livre de bourgeoisie,* vol. 2, p. 591, no. 6042).

Ulrich Morhard m. Barbara, d. of Michael Burger, paymaster, 26 June 1518 (*Livre de bourgeoisie,* vol. 2, p. 645, no. 6750).

Johann Schwann m. Margarethe Prüss, w. of Reinhardt Beck, printer, 2 June 1524 (*Livre de bourgeoisie,* vol. 2, p. 696, no. 7416).

Johann Schwintzer m. Apolonia, w. of Hans Niblung, corrector, 3 January 1525 (*Livre de bourgeoisie,* vol. 2, p. 739, no. 8002) (See chap. 1, n. 14.).

Balthasar Beck m. Margarethe Prüss, w. of Johann Schwann, printer, 1527 (*Livre de bourgeoisie,* vol. 2, p. 764, no. 8380).

Peter Schöffer m. Anna Pfintzer, w. of Blase Wechter, furrier, 14 December 1529 (*Livre de bourgeoisie,* vol. 2, p. 805, no. 8908).

Johann Albrecht m. widow of Johann Knobloch, printer, 1532 (*L'imprimerie alsacienne,* p. 210).

Jacob Frölich m. Magdalene, d. of Hans Schnyder von Haslach, no profession given, November 1546 (*Kontracktstube,* K.S. 56, fol. 304).

Nikolaus Wyriot m. Rachel Scheuflin, d. of Conrad von Weil, no profession given, 21 October 1555 (*Registres de St. Nicolas,* M50/41b).

Samuel Emmel m. Sarah Rihel, w. of Johann Esslinger and d. of Wendelin Rihel, printer, 11 October 1558 (*Registres de St. Nicolas,* M50/55a).

Nikolaus Faber m. Aurelia, w. of Peter Hugg, printer, 17 November 1573 (*Bürgerbuch, 1543–1618,* vol. 2, p. 388).

Anton Bertram m. Johanna, d. of Nikolaus Wyriot, printer, 10 June 1583 (*Bürgerbuch, 1543–1618,* vol. 2, p. 533).

Jost Martin m. Barbara, d. of Wilhelm Reinbolt, fisherman, 4 September 1585 (*Bürgerbuch, 1543–1618,* vol. 2, p. 551).

Jacob Cammerlander m. Catherine, d. of Catherine von Offenburg and Wolff Bissenger, ca. 1531.

Blase Fabricius m. Ottilia Crafft, w. of Crato Mylius, printer, ca. 1549.

38. Jean-Pierre Kintz, *La société strasbourgeoise 1560–1650,* pp. 154–155.

39. Fuchs, "L'immigration artisanale," pp. 191–93.

40. Places of origin are given by Josef Benzing in *Buchdrucker des 16 und 17 Jahrhunderts,* pp. 409–23. The following examples show the geographic spread: Johann Prüss, Württemberg; Grüninger, Württemberg; Kistler, Speyer; Hupfuff, Württemberg; Knobloch, Zofingen, Switzerland; Köpfel, Haguenau; B. Beck, Kircheim an der Eck; Egenolff, Hadamar, Nassau; Cammerlander, Mainz; Frölich, Baden; Biener, Franconia; Rihel, Haguenau; Guidon, Lorraine; Fabricius, Chemnitz; Wyriot, Lorraine; Jobin, Porrentray, Switzerland; Bertram, Linz (Rhineland).

41. F. Ritter, *L'imprimerie alsacienne,* pp. 51, 137, 281, 288, 304.

42. Ibid., pp. 81, 261, 317, 330.

43. Ibid., pp. 75, 160, 220.

44. R. Hirsch, *Printing, Selling and Reading,* p. 27.

45. This conclusion is further confirmed by the wording of the censorship edicts during the century. The Magistrat never directed their ordinances to the Steltz. The edict is directed to "our painters, printers, booksellers." See AMS, R3, 124, 1524. Thomas A. Brady, Jr., concurs with my conclusion.

46. Adolph Seyboth, *Das Alte Strasbourg,* pp. 44, 149, 151. Seyboth describes buildings and shops street by street in the city.

47. Karl Schottenloher found that few printing families carried on for three generations in this early period. Surveying the family relationships for presses in all European countries he found only six three-generation presses in the sixteenth century: four in Cologne, one in Frankfurt am Main, and one in Venice. He then lists four "small publishing houses" that continued for three generations in Augsburg, Münster, Erfurt, and Wittenberg. He does not define "small." See Karl Schottenloher, "Die Druckersippen der Frühdruckzeit," p. 236.

48. F. Ritter, *L'imprimerie alsacienne,* pp. 46, 70.

49. C6.2.1; C6.2.3–4; C6.2.6a–b; C6.2.8–12.

50. F. Ritter, *L'imprimerie alsacienne,* pp. 218, 220.

51. Wittmer and Meyer, *Livre de bourgeoisie,* vol. 2, p. 696, no. 7416. Benzing, *Buckdrucker des 16 und 17 Jahrhunderts,* p. 415.

52. Wittmer and Meyer, *Livre de bourgeoisie,* vol. 2, p. 764, no. 8380.

53. F. Ritter, *L'imprimerie alsacienne,* p. 76.

54. Ibid., p. 187.

55. Ibid.

56. Benzing, *Buckdrucker des 16 und 17 Jahrhunderts,* p. 412.

57. C4.2.14a.

58. See, for example, P3.1.2a; P3.5.2a; P4.1.1–2; P3.2.3; P2.1.2–8; P3.1.3a–b.

59. F. Ritter, *L'imprimerie alsacienne,* p. 192.

60. Schmidt, *Répertoire bibliographique,* vol. 6, p. viii.

61. Benzing, *Buckdrucker des 16 und 17 Jahrhunderts,* p. 417.

62. L1.3.4i–j; S8.1.3c; B8.5.6; P4.1.35.

63. Benzing states in *Buchdrucker des 16 und 17 Jahrhunderts,* p. 416, that Johann Knobloch II continued to publish until 1557. Calvin's and Marot's *Aulcuns pseaulmes et cantiques mys en chant* of 1539 bears the tag "en l'imprimerie de Jean Knobloch jun." Rodolphe Peter notes that Knobloch II continued to direct the press but from a distance, the actual work being done by Johann Albrecht and Georg Messerschmidt (Peter, *Premiers ouvrages français,* p. 81). I am hesitant to assume that Knobloch II played an active role in the Messerschmidt shop on the basis of one book.

64. L1.3.5d–e; L1.3.4k–l; S15.2.4c–e; A4.1.8; A1.5.9; H1.4.22; H1.3.58; H3.1.18.

65. Benzing, *Buchdrucker des 16 und 17 Jahrhunderts,* p. 418.

66. The tentative agreement with regard to the division of the inheritance is printed in F. Ritter, *L'imprimerie alsacienne,* appendix, pp. 541–42, n. 284.

67. See, for example, his publications of Ernst Regius, A5.1.17; of Conrad Dasypodius, S5.8.1, S5.8.3, S5.8.5; of J. L. Hawenreuter, S5.9.3–4; of Theophilus Goll, T1.1.40, T2.1.5d–i, T1.4.12a–c; and of Melchior Junius, T1.3.34. These were in addition to his publication of editions and texts by Johann Sturm.

68. H5.3.10d–k.

69. L1.2.23a–j.

70. A5.2.15a–h; A5.2.14a–g.

71. I am indebted to Professor Thomas A. Brady, Jr. of the University of Oregon for the information with regard to the paper mill.

72. AMS, *Registres du Temple Neuf,* N 213, 53a.

73. François-Joseph Fuchs, "Une association d'imprimeurs-libraires à Strasbourg au XVIᵉ siècle," p. 2.

74. Ibid.

75. Ibid., p. 7.

76. B8.6.1–8.

77. Fuchs, "Association d'imprimeurs-libraires," p. 5.

78. F. Ritter, *L'imprimerie alsacienne,* p. 338.

79. Fuchs, "Association d'imprimeurs-libraires," pp. 6–7.

80. Benzing, *Buckdrucker des 16 und 17 Jahrhunderts,* p. 418.
81. H1.1.39a–d; H1.1.44a–b; H1.1.48; T1.6.6c–e; S5.7.2; S5.6.1c; T1.3.9a–d; T1.2.6b–d; S1.12.11; B7.6.18; B7.6.20; B7.6.22a; B7.3.4a–b; S1.10.10.
82. Ficker and Winckelmann, *Handschriftenproben,* vol. 2, p. 101.
83. AMS, *Registres de St. Guillaume,* N25/II, 5a.
84. AMS, *Bürgerbuch, 1543–1618,* vol. 2, p. 46, 12 May 1549.
85. Benzing, *Buckdrucker des 16 und 17 Jahrhunderts,* p. 420.
86. Ficker and Winckelmann, *Handschriftenproben,* vol. 2, p. 101. F. Ritter, *L'imprimerie alsacienne,* p. 254. Benzing, *Buchdrucker des 16 und 17 Jahrhunderts,* p. 420. The important document, indeed the only one that throws any light on the matter, is the baptismal record of Crato Mylius's son.

> 6 Aprilis 1546
> Baptizar: Phillipum Joachimum
> Filium Cratonis et Otiliae Uxoris
> Compatres H. Johann Meyer, Stattschreiber
> H. Christianus, H. Jacob Fröwlichs, doctermann
> Commater Jola von Nidenburg
> Uxor H. Johans Schleidant.

SOURCE: AMS, *Registres de St. Guillaume,* N25/II, 5a.

The H. Christians (Herr Christianus) listed as here the son-in-law of Jacob Frölich, is the Christian Mylius who began to print in 1555, when he took over Frölich's shop. But his relation to Crato remains undetermined.
87. S5.5.10a–b; S5.5.11.
88. Christian's children by his second wife, Margaret Stür, are listed in a contract drawn up at the time of her remarriage after his death. The contract lists seven children, the second a boy named Christman (AMS, *Kontraktstube,* KS 169, fol. 596, 1573). The baptismal record of the same child at the Neue Kirche, December 4, 1558, gives the name as Christopher (AMS, *Registres du Temple Neuf,* 1558, p. 93). It is difficult to believe that Christman-Christopher took over his father's shop in 1570 at the age of twelve. If Christian II is the son of Christian, he must have been the child of the first marriage, and the child of the second marriage must have been given an identical or similar name.
89. F. Ritter, *L'imprimerie alsacienne,* p. 416.
90. Ibid., p. 250.
91. Widows through whom property was transferred:

> Margarethe Prüss (w. of Reinhardt Beck) m. Johann Schwann (Wittmer and Meyer, *Livre de bourgeoisie,* vol. 2, p. 696, no. 7416).
> Margarethe Prüss (w. of Johann Schwann) m. Balthasar Beck (Wittmer and Meyer, *Livre de bourgeoisie,* vol. 2, p. 764, no. 8380).
> Catherine Dammerer (w. of Martin Flach) m. Johann Knobloch (Wittmer and Meyer, *Livre de bourgeoisie,* vol. 2, p. 520, no. 5103).
> Magdalene Vogler (w. of Johann Knobloch) m. Johann Albrecht (F. Ritter, *L'imprimerie alsacienne,* p. 209).
> Ottilia Crafft (w. of Crato Mylius) m. Blaise Fabricius (AMS, *Bürgerbuch, 1543–1618,* vol. 2, p. 46).

Aurelia (w. of Peter Hugg) m. Nicholas Faber (AMS, *Bürgerbuch, 1543–1618,* vol. 2, p. 388).

Rachel Schäufelin (w. of Nikolaus Wyriot) m. Anton Bertram (AMS, *Bürgerbuch, 1543–1618,* vol. 2, p. 533).

92. F. Ritter, *L'imprimerie alsacienne,* p. 311.

93. Printers' daughters through whom property was transferred:

Salome Mentelin (d. of Johann Mentelin) m. Adolphe Rusch (F. Ritter, *L'imprimerie alsacienne,* p. 46).

Younger Mentelin daughter (d. of Johann Mentelin) m. Martin Schott (F. Ritter, *L'imprimerie alsacienne,* p. 69).

Margarethe Prüss (d. of Johann Prüss) m. Reinhardt Beck (Wittmer and Meyer, *Livre de bourgeoisie,* vol. 2, p. 593, no. 6070).

Daughter of Jacob Frölich m. Christian Mylius (See baptismal record, chap. 1, n. 92).

Printers' daughters whose marriages did not result in transfers of property:

Sarah Rihel (d. of Wendelin Rihel) m. Samuel Emmel (AMS, *Registres de St. Nicolas,* H 50/55a).

Suzanne Berger (d. of Theobald Berger?) m. Nicholaus Waldt (F. Ritter, *L'imprimerie alsacienne,* p. 347).

Marguerite Wähinger (d. of Johann Wähinger?) m. Martin Flach II (F. Ritter, *L'imprimerie alsacienne,* p. 187).

Ursula Beck (d. of Reinhardt Beck) m. Wolfgang Fortier, who helped to run the Prüss-Beck press (Wittmer and Meyer, *Livre de bourgeoisie,* vol. 2).

Noppurg Brandt m. Conrad Kerner (Wittmer and Meyer, *Livre de bourgeoisie,* vol. 2, p. 591).

Catherine Bissinger Cammerlander (d. of Wolff Bissinger) m. Josias Rihel (F. Ritter, *L'imprimerie alsacienne,* p. 272).

94. Jean-Pierre Kintz, "La Ville."

95. Voet, *Golden Compasses,* vol. 1, pp. 142–44. The role of women in the printing industry is discussed in general terms by Annemarie Meiner, "Die Frau im Druckgewerbe," pp. 333–43; Otto Bettman, "Frauen in Buchgewerbe," passim; more specifically by Natalie Zemon Davis, "Women in the *Arts Mécaniques;*" and by Beatrice Beech, "Charlotte Guillard, a XVIth century business woman," a paper delivered at the Fourteenth International Congress on Medieval Studies, Kalamazoo, Mich., 1979.

96. Manfred Krebs and Hans Georg Rott, *Quellen zur Geschichte der Täufer, Elsass,* vol. 1, p. 588.

97. AMS, *Kontraktstube,* 46A, fol. 69, 23 May 1542.

98. Wittmer and Meyer, *Livre de bourgeoisie,* vol. 2, p. 729, no. 7883.

99. Charles Schmidt, *Histoire littéraire de l'Alsace,* vol. 1, p. 211. There is nothing in the sources to confirm this relationship, which has, nevertheless, been accepted traditionally.

100. Ibid., vol. 2, p. 227.

101. Ibid., vol. 1, p. 21.
102. F. Ritter, *L'imprimerie alsacienne,* p. 317.
103. Ibid., p. 320.
104. Ibid., p. 324.
105. Ficker and Winckelmann, *Handschriftenproben,* vol. 2, p. 65.
106. F. Ritter, *L'imprimerie alsacienne,* p. 354; p. 577, n. 416.
107. Sitzmann, *Dictionnaire de biographie* vol. 2, p. 580; F. Ritter, *L'imprimerie alsacienne,* p. 167.
108. Hauffen, *Johann Fischart,* p. 50.
109. S1.10.1; S6.3.4; A4.2.1.
110. Sitzmann, *Dictionnaire de biographie,* vol. 2, p. 580.
111. Schmidt, *Histoire littéraire de l'Alsace,* vol. 2, p. 407. H1.3.32c; A4.1.3; S6.3.7.
112. Ibid., p. 183. A1.5.6c.
113. Ficker and Winckelmann, *Handschriftenproben,* vol. 2, p. 84. The Livy was printed by Augustin Fries for the Spanish publisher Pedro de Porres. F. Ritter, *L'imprimerie alsacienne,* p. 335.
114. Hauffen, *Johann Fischart,* p. 50.
115. Kenneth Thibodeau, "Science in an Urban Perspective," pp. 168–69.
116. S3.1.10E, title page. S3.1.10j, fol. BV[v].
117. S1.14.1; S1.14.4; S1.14.9; S1.14.19; S1.14.24–25.
118. F. Ritter, *L'imprimerie alsacienne,* p. 268.
119. H4.1.14; H4.1.15; H4.1.16a–e; H4.1.12; H4.1.13; H4.1.14a–e.
120. AMS, *Registres de St. Thomas, 1551–1670,* N245/49a, 1553. AMS, *Registres du Temple Neuf, 1551–72,* N213–50a, 1557.
121. S5.8.1a–b; S5.8.3; S5.8.5.
122. F. Ritter, *L'imprimerie alsacienne,* p. 277.
123. A1.6.12d–h; A1.6.13d–h; A1.6.15d–g; A1.6.17d–j; A1.6.20d–i; A1.6.25a–c; T1.3.21a–e; T1.3.24; T1.5.5a–n.
124. H5.3.10a–n.
125. AMS, *Registres de St. Guillaume,* N25/II 5a, 1546.
126. Chrisman, *Strasbourg and the Reform,* p. 83.
127. I am indebted for information on the clergy and the Magistrat to Jean-Pierre Kintz and Jane Abray.
Godparental relations within the printing trade:

Date	Father (Position)	Baby's Name	Sponsor (Position)
1551	Leonard Beck (worker-printer)	(son)	Josias Rihel[a] (large-scale printer)
1553	Christophel Rüdlinger (book-binder and book seller)	Emanuel	Frau Rihel[b] (wife of Wendelin Rihel, large-scale printer)
1555	Johann Messerschmidt[c] (son of printer)	Georg	Jung Frau Margreth Knobloch[d] (daughter of former owner of Messerschmidt's press)

1555	Peter Hugg (typographer in Emmel or Frölich shop, later had one-man shop)	Peter	Magdalene Frölich[c] (wife of Jacob, medium-scale printer)
1559	Nicholas Wyriot (medium-scale printer)	Nicholas	Hieronymus Rihel[f] (brother of large-scale printer)

[a]AMS, *Registre de St. Guillaume*, 1545–1551, N25/III, 98a, 16 August.

[b]AMS, *Registres de St. Thomas*, 1551–1570, N245/49b, Domin. 14 Post Trinit., 1553 (3 sects.).

[c]The relationship between Johann and Georg is indicated by another baptismal record in which "Hans Messerschmidt, son of Georg, the buchdrucker" stands as a godfather. AMS, *Registres de St. Thomas*, 1551–1570 N245/25a, 7 August 1552.

[d]AMS, *Registres de St. Nicolas*, 1550–1569, N104/105b, 21 July.

[e]AMS, *Registres de St. Thomas*, 1551–1570, N245/68b, 13 October.

[f]AMS, *Registres du Temple Neuf*, N213/103a, 15 March.

128. Schmidt, *Répertoire bibliographique*, vol. 2, pp. v–vi. See also Brady, *Ruling Class, Regime and Reformation*, pp. 80–82, 365, 396.

129. Jacques Hatt, *Liste des membres du Grand Sénat de Strasbourg* (Strasbourg, 1963), p. 521.

130. Schmidt, *Répertoire bibliographique*, vol. 2, p. vi.

131. L2.1.15.

132. Jane Abray, "The Long Reformation," p. 43.

133. Schmidt, *Répertoire bibliographique*, vol. 1, p. XI.

134. F. Ritter, *L'imprimerie alsacienne*, p. 231.

135. AMS, RP, folio 73v, 12 Feb. 1550.

136. Abray, "The Long Reformation," p. 67.

137. P1.1.1–15; P3.2.1–16.

138. P4.1.20–39; P4.1.33–37.

139. P3.6.9–12; P3.15.1–9.

140. P3.14.12–14; V11.4.1–24.

141. V11.3.1–10; P3.16.1; P3.16.3–4; P3.16.7–8.

142. P3.1.1a.

143. P3.1.3a–b; P3.1.8.

144. P3.1.6a–b; P3.1.7a.

145. Josef Benzing, *Ulrich von Hutten und seine Drucker*, p. xiii.

146. Schmidt, *Répertoire bibliographique*, vol. 3, p. 38.

147. Peter, "Premiers ouvrages français," pp. 75–80.

148. B7.3.1–3; B7.4.3–5; B7.5.1–7; B7.6.1.

149. P3.1.23.

150. P3.7.9; P3.7.10.

151. This statement is based on a hand count of Lutheran publication by city and by printer from Josef Benzing's *Lutherbibliographie*.

152. P4.1.1–3; P4.1.5–6; P4.1.10; P4.1.12–13; P4.1.16.

153. P4.1.22; P4.1.24a–26; P4.1.33–34; V9.1.7.

154. P4.1.27; P4.1.38a; P4.1.32. For Schwintzer's participation in the Schwenck-feld circle see Daniel Hüsser, "Caspar Schwenckfeld et des adeptes entres l'église et le sectes à Strasbourg," p. 522.

155. P3.16.1–12; V11.4.8a–e; V11.4.9; V11.4.11–14.

156. Droz, *Chemins de l'hérésie*, vol. 1, p. 174.

157. F. Ritter, *L'imprimerie alsacienne*, pp. 276–77.

158. Rudolf Hirsch provides further evidence of specialization by printers even in the incunabula period. Regiomontanus (Johann Müller von Königsberg) printed mathematical and astronomical works in Nuremberg from 1473 to 1475. Rykert Paffraet of Deventer published classical and humanist works and textbooks for the British market after 1488. Günther Zainer of Augsburg specialized in books in the vernacular after 1470. See Hirsch, *Printing, Selling and Reading*, p. 50.

CHAPTER TWO

1. The concept of intellectual generations has been a theoretical tool for sociolo-gists of knowledge and literary scholars since Karl Mannheim identified the genera-tional phenomenon as one of the dynamic elements in the historic process. Defining who is included in a given generation, however, has been difficult. Mannheim assumed that all men of the same generations would share the same class status and the same cultural experience (e.g., European culture or Chinese culture). Given these similarities, a generation would be composed of a group of contemporaries who participated in a common destiny, sharing the ideas and concepts bound up in that destiny. Mannheim concluded, however, that establishing the actual member-ship of a particular generation would be problematical.

Ortega y Gasset and Julián Marías believed that a particular group would share similar customs, traditions, and beliefs because they faced the same life experience. For them close contiguity of age was an essential element in the creation of a generation. Henri Peyre agreed and defined a literary generation as a group of men, born within two or three years of each other, who shared the same aspirations, ideas, and beliefs. These definitions based on age have recently been criticized by the historian Alan Spitzer as vague, ambiguous, and inexact, particularly when used to explain political behavior.

See Karl Mannheim, *Essays on the Sociology of Knowledge*, pp. 309–20; Julián Marías, *Generations, A Historical Method*, trans. H. C. Raley, p. 81; Henri Peyre, *Les générations littéraires*, p. 48; Alan B. Spitzer, "The Historical Problem of Genera-tions," pp. 1353–85.

2. See C3.2.1–31; C5.1.11–12.

3. Schmidt, *Histoire littéraire*, vol. 2, pp. 2–35, 51–54, 58–60.

4. Ibid., vol. 1, p. 376; vol. 2, pp. 133–49.

5. The best sources on Geiler are the biography by Leon Dacheux, *Un réformateur catholique à la fin du XVᵉ siècle, Jean Geiler;* Rapp, *Réformes et réformation*, pp. 150–60, 347–71; and E. Jane Dempsey Douglass, *Justification in Late Medieval Preaching. A Study of John Geiler of Keisersberg.*

6. Chrisman, *Strasbourg and the Reform*, pp. 81–93.

7. James M. Kittelson, *Wolfgang Capito from Humanist to Reformer*, pp. 23–83.

8. Ficker and Winckelmann, *Handschriftenproben,* vol. 2, pp. 62, 63.

9. Ibid., vol. 1, p. 38.

10. George H. Williams, *The Radical Reformation,* pp. 241–78, 328–41.

11. See sections P3.1–P3.12.

12. See P1.8.1; P1.8.6; P1.2.12; P7.2.10–16; P1.6.6.

13. See P1.5.7–10; P1.5.12–13b; P1.6.12; P1.8.13–14; P3.11.29–34.

14. For the failure of the attempt to introduce the Interim religion in Strasbourg, see Erdmann Weyrauch, *Konfessionelle Krise und soziale Stabilität. Das Interim in Strassburg (1548–1562).*

15. Bernard Vogler, "Recrutement et carrière," pp. 151–55.

16. See P1.8.21; P1.8.23; P1.8.25–26; P1.2.23; P1.2.24; P1.6.13; P7.2.25.

17. See P1.6.15a–e; P1.9.4; P1.9.6; P1.9.7.

18. Anthony F. C. Wallace, "Revitalization Movements," pp. 273–75.

19. The major biographical and critical source for this group remains Charles Schmidt's *Histoire littéraire.*

20. See H5.2.3; H5.3.4; V9.3.2; V9.3.3; A4.1.3; A4.2.1; H3.1.3–4a–g; T1.1.24a–d; T1.3.1a–e.

21. See H1.2.1–31.

22. See C7.1.8; C7.1.16; C7.1.19.

23. H1.2.11, passim.

24. G. Livet, L. Greiner, and A. Van Seggelen, "Sélestat, l'école humaniste et Beatus Rhenanus," p. 41.

25. See B7.2.5–10; B7.3.1–3; B7.4.1–12; B7.5.1–7; B7.6.1–9; B7.7.1–6.

26. The exceptions were Luther's commentaries on Deuteronomy, Jonah, and Habbakkuk, in German. All the rest of Luther's vernacular commentaries were on short sections of the Bible. See B8.1.1–18.

27. See B8.3.1; B8.4.2–3.

28. See B8.5.1–8.

29. Kittelson, *Wolfgang Capito,* pp. 227–29. For the development of Capito's method of biblical commentary see also Beate Stierle, *Capito als Humanist.*

30. See appendix C.

31. The best description of the school and the faculty was in Charles Engel, *L'école latine et l'ancienne Académie de Strasbourg, 1538–1621.* This has now been replaced by Anton Schindling's *Humanistische Hochschule und Freie Reichstadt, Gymnasium und Akademie in Strassburg 1538–1621,* which gives a particularly detailed account of the Academy.

32. See T1.3.8; T1.3.10–18; T1.6.8–10; A1.6.12–24; A2.2.22–26; A2.3.8; A2.4.2–4; A2.5.1–2.

33. Engel, *L'ecole latine,* p. 66, fn. 1.

34. Schindling, *Humanistische Hochschule,* p. 56.

35. Ibid., p. 9.

36. See appendix C.

37. Schindling, *Humanistische Hochschule,* p. 321.

38. See T1.1.37–38; T1.2.16–17; T1.3.27–31; A2.4.6.

39. See section T4.1.

40. Schindling, *Humanistische Hochschule,* pp. 247–48, 251–53.

41. Ibid., p. 391.
42. Schmidt, *Histoire littéraire,* vol. 2, pp. 87–133; 133–48; 159–74.
43. S6.2.2–3; S6.3.3; S6.3.5. See Georges Livet, "Geographes et cartographes en Alsace à l'epoque de la Renaissance," pp. 183–201.
44. S6.3.4; S1.7.4; S1.10.1.
45. S5.3.1.
46. S6.3.5–7.
47. Sitzmann, *Dictionnaire de biographie,* vol. 1, pp. 249, 598.
48. S2.1.3a–d; S2.1.4a–k.
49. S1.5.2a–h.
50. Sitzmann, *Dictionnaire de biographie,* vol. 1, 533–34.
51. F. Ritter, *Histoire de l'imprimerie alsacienne,* pp. 315–16.
52. P. Antonin Passman, "Die Kartause zu Strassburg," pp. 143–50.
53. Ernest Wickersheimer, "Paracelse à Strasbourg," pp. 356, 363.
54. Ficker and Winckelmann, *Handschriftenproben,* vol. 2, p. 82; Sitzmann, *Dictionnaire de biographie,* vol. 1, p. 718.
55. Ernest Wickersheimer, "Laurent Fries et la querelle de l'arabisme en médicine," pp. 97–100.
56. S1.7.14, fol. 33r.
57. S3.1.8a, introduction.
58. S7.1.11.
59. S1.7.1–2; S1.12.1–4.
60. S1.2.3–4.
61. S1.10.3.
62. Sitzmann, *Dictionnaire de biographie,* vol. 2, p. 470.
63. F. Ritter, *Histoire de l'imprimerie alsacienne,* pp. 280–83.
64. Sitzmann, *Dictionnaire de biographie,* vol. 2, p. 629.
65. S1.7.18a; S1.7.19a–d.
66. S8.1.4; S8.1.5a–e.
67. See S9.1.3; S10.1.3–4.
68. See S11.6.1a–c; S11.6.2; S11.6.3; S11.9.1.
69. See S5.4.3–4; S5.4.7; S11.4.1–3.
70. Cyril Stanley Smith, "Metallurgy and Assaying," p. 68.
71. The lectures given by these men are summarized in detail by Schindling in *Humanistische Hochschule,* pp. 255–57, 330–31, 332–34.
72. Ficker and Winckelmann, *Handschriftenproben,* vol. 2, p. 93.
73. Sitzmann, *Dictionnaire de biographie,* vol. 2, p. 548.
74. S5.3.5a–b.
75. S5.5.5–12; S5.8.1; S5.8.3–5; S5.8.2.
76. S5.9.1–13.
77. Charles G. A. Schmidt, *Michael Schütz genannt Toxites,* pp. 55–56, 81.
78. See section S1.14.
79. I am indebted to Steven Nelson for this information.
80. S12.1.63a–h.
81. S6.5.10; S15.1.10; S15.1.15.
82. S11.9.3.

83. S11.9.4.
84. S8.1.7a–d; S10.1.5; S10.1.6.
85. Schmidt, *Histoire littéraire,* pp. 209–59.
86. V9.1.3a–b; V9.3.2.
87. V6.2.1a–d; V6.2.4a–d; V6.2.8.
88. Jörg Wickram, *Das Rollwagenbüchlein,* trans. Franz Hirtler, pp. 10–14.
89. Sitzmann, *Dictionnaire de biographie,* vol. 1, p. 526.
90. Ibid., p. 802.
91. Ibid., p. 565.
92. Ibid., vol. 2, pp. 1062–63.
93. Ibid., p. 945.
94. Ibid., p. 493.
95. See V6.3.4–5; V6.3.7; V6.3.8–12; V6.3.16.
96. See V6.3.17–20.
97. See section V8.
98. See sections V7.1 and V7.3.
99. Hauffen, *Johann Fischart,* vol. 1, pp. 5–44.
100. V6.2.12a–d.
101. V10.14.1–4; V11.4.4–14; V11.4.16–21; V11.3.4–V11.3.6; V11.3.9–11.
102. Eisenstein, *The Printing Press,* vol. 2, pp. 523 ff.
103. See chapter 3.
104. V6.1.1d. *Kurzweiliges Loos,* title page.
105. V6.3.7a. *Der Jungen Knaben Spiegel,* fol. a^i.

CHAPTER THREE

1. In a recent study Rolf Engelsing attempted to estimate the number of readers in Germany in the incunabula period. He has established a rough figure of 1 percent of the total population of the Holy Roman Empire, or about 5 percent of the urban population. See Rolf Engelsing, *Analphabetentum und Lektüre,* p. 19.

2. Rott, "L'ancienne bibliothèque de Strasbourg, détruite en 1870: Les catalogues qui en subsistent," p. 426.

3. Bucer, *Martin Bucers Deutsche Schriften,* ed. Robert Stupperich, vol. 1, pp. 281–84. See also *Correspondence de Martin Bucer,* ed. Jean Rott, vol. 1, pp. 42–58.

4. At the time of Bucer's death in Cambridge, the books were divided into three lots. Presumably, two lots were sold, but one was probably given to the Duchess of Suffolk, who had served as Bucer's patron in England. M. Jean Rott, with his indefatigable energy, has tracked down this third lot after four centuries. The books probably went from the Suffolk family to Westminster College and may form part of a collection recently turned over by Westminster to the Bodleian Library in Oxford. The story is a good illustration of the difficulties involved in studying sixteenth-century libraries. I am indebted for this information to M. Rott.

5. KS 98/II, fols. 78^v–86^v. Katherine Zell's testament.

6. For several books owned by Conrad Dasypodius see Rott, *L'ancienne bibliothèque,* p. 437, n. 34. Kenneth Thibodeau has informed me that Conrad Dasypodius

left numerous manuscripts and a library, which was purchased by the Duke of Braunschweig-Wolfenbüttel.

7. Adolf Hauffen, "Uber die Bibliothek Johann Fischarts," pp. 21–32. Unfortunately this article, which sounds so promising, is based on the discovery at the Darmstadt Library of seven books with Fischart's name in them and marginal notes in his hand. While two of them, Joannes Gropius's *Becanus* and a *Sprichworter* of 1565, reflect Fischart's etymological and linguistic interests, the sample of seven books is too small to be useful. Hauffen believes that by 1580 Fischart had established an important library. He bases this conclusion on Fischart's description of the library of the Abbey of Thélème, which was added to the 1582 edition of the *Geschichtklitterung*.

8. Rott, *L'ancienne bibliothèque*, p. 426.

9. Schmidt, *Altesten Bibliotheken*, pp. 67–70.

10. Ibid., pp. 70–74.

11. I am indebted to M. Jean Rott, who discovered the inventory of the estate of Thomas Wolf Senior in the Archives Saint Thomas. The manuscript is now in AST, supp. 1.

12. AST, supps. 1, 138, 172.

13. See note 83, below.

14. Sitzmann, *Dictionnaire de biographie*, vol. 1, pp. 646–47.

15. F. Ritter, *L'imprimerie alsacienne*, p. 335.

16. AMS, V 132, 123. Liste des livres reliés par Louis Gremp.

17. Ibid.

18. Joseph Walter, *Catalogue général de la Bibliothèque municipale de la ville de Sélestat*, vol. 3. Beatus Rhenanus's collection is included in the general listing of sixteenth-century books. Books from his library are indicated by the notation "B.Rh."

19. Gustav Knod, "Aus der Bibliothek des Beatus Rhenanus, 1500–1507," pp. 57, 70. See also Walter, *Bibliothèque municipale de Sélestat*.

20. Knod, "Bibliothek des Beatus Rhenanus," pp. 76–77. See also Walter, *Bibliothèque municipale de Sélestat*.

21. Walter's catalogue includes the following works on Ethiopia:

> Varthema, *Novum itinararium Aethiopiae Aegiptae, utriusque Arabia Persidis*, Mediolani, n.d.
>
> Ludovicis, *Novum itinerarium Aethiopiae*, n.d.
>
> Goes, *Damianus, Fides, Religio, Moresque Aethiopam sub imperi preciosi Joannis* (. . . Presbyterum Joannem), 1540.
>
> Heliodorus, *Historia Aethiopicae*, Basel, 1534.

22. Walter, *Bibliothèque municipale de Sélestat*.

23. Ibid.

24. John Patrick Donnelly, *Calvinism and Scholasticism in Vermigli's Doctrine of Man and Grace*, pp. 208–09. Donnelly compiled his list from Gardy and Ganoczy.

25. Donnelly, *Calvinism and Scholasticism*, p. 212, n. 9.

26. Ibid., p. 213.

27. Ibid., p. 214.

28. Ibid., p. 212.

29. Lina Baillet, "Recherches sur la bibliothèque des Seigneurs de Ribeaupierre: La Bibliothèque du premier pasteur Protestant de Ribeauvillé," pp. 51–63.

30. Ibid., pp. 54–55.

31. Ibid.

32. Ibid., p. 52.

33. Ibid., pp. 56, 57, 54, 55, 59.

34. His grandfather had served as ammeister in 1500, 1506, 1512, and 1518. See Brady, *Ruling Class, Regime and Reformation,* p. 306.

35. Sitzmann, *Dictionnaire de biographie,* vol. 2, pp. 672–73. A full biography of Schenckbecher is in Gustav Knod, *Johann Schenckbecher: Ein Strassburger Ratsherr der Reformationzeit.*

36. See Edmund Ungerer, *Elsässische Altertümer in Burg und Haus, in Kloster und Kirche,* vol. 2, pp. 140–46, for the complete inventory of the library.

37. These portraits are in the collection of the Muśee de l'oeuvre de Notre Dame in Strasbourg. The first portrait is attributed to Mathis Nithart [Mathis Grunewald]. I am grateful to Monique Fuchs for identifying the donor in this portrait as a canon.

38. Natalie Z. Davis in her chapter "Printing and the People," in *Society and Culture,* p. 209, states that there were thirty-eight male teachers of reading, writing, and arithmetic in Lyons between 1550 and 1560. We know of at least five *Rechenmeister,* teachers of arithmetic and accounting, in Strasbourg. Teachers of reading were more common. See chapter 8.

39. Hans Holbein the Younger (1497/98–1543), *Aushängeschild eines Schulmeisters,* 1516 (Kunstmuseum, Basel).

40. Ungerer, *Elsässische Altertümer,* vol. 2, pp. 78–161.

41. I am indebted to Steven Nelson, Thomas A. Brady, Jr., and Edmond Ponsing for help in working on the Kontraktstube inventories. The liasses of the Kontraktstube have not yet been inventoried, and they contain a wide variety of materials, including exchanges of property, marriage contracts, wills and testaments, and purchases of land. The following liasses were consulted:

> AMS, V, 5, 8, 9, 132, 138–41.
> AMS, IV, 132.
> AMS, II, 22b, 123.
> AMS, VI, 145.
> AMS, KS, 9, 12, 43/I, 44, 63/I, 127, 223, 229.
> AMS, Not. 775. Daniel Strinz registers.

42. Roger Doucet, *Les bibliothèques parisiennes au XVIe siècle,* pp. 171–75.

43. Davis, *Society and Culture,* p. 327, n. 11.

44. AMS, Not. 775 (1598, part 2), Inventory of Georges Flügel, furrier, 19 July 1598.

45. AMS, Not. 775 (1598, part 2), Inventory and papers of Ludwig Bozen, February 1598.

46. Ungerer, *Elsässische Altertümer,* vol. 2, p. 78.

47. Ibid., p. 106.

48. AMS, H 10, 433. Inventory of Hannsen Hecklin, 1556.

49. AMS, Not. 775 (1598, part 1); 22 February 1598.

50. AMS, Not. 775 (1600); 28 May 1600.

51. AMS, KS 44, 1541, fol. 103.

52. Ungerer, *Elsässische Altertümer,* vol. 2, p. 151.

53. AMS, Not. 775 (1600); 14 May 1600.

54. Cf. Kalendar der Strassburger Domherren, Gestelt durch D. Lucam Bathodium Medicum und Astronomiae studiosum zu Pfalzburg. Strassburg, Nicolaus Waldt, 1584. AMS, VI 464/3a.

55. AMS, Not. 775 (1598, part 1); 4 April 1598.

56. AMS, Not. 775 (1598, part 2); 18 October 1598.

57. Ungerer, *Elsässische Altertümer,* vol. 2, p. 83.

58. Ibid., pp. 92–93.

59. See Brady, *Ruling Class, Regime, and Reformation,* pp. 159, 376.

60. Ungerer, *Elsässische Altertümer,* vol. 2, pp. 93–96.

61. Ibid., p. 124.

62. Ibid., p. 157.

63. AMS, Not. 775 (1598, part 2); 19 July 1598.

64. AMS, Not. 775 (1598, part 2); 22 February 1598.

65. AMS, Not. 775 (1600); 27 May 1600. For Hans Schott, who had served on the XV, see Brady, *Ruling Class, Regime, and Reformation,* p. 391.

66. AMS, H 4745; 1545.

67. AMS, Not. 775 (1600); 23 May 1600.

68. AMS, Not. 775 (1598, part 2); 26 January 1598.

69. AMS, Not. 775 (1600); 14 April 1600.

70. AMS, Not. 775 (1598, part 2); 19 September 1598.

71. AMS, Not. 775 (1601); January 1601.

72. AMS, Not. 775 (1601); 8 November 1601.

73. AMS, Not. 775 (1598, part 2); June 1598.

74. AMS, Not. 775 (1601); 24 July 1601.

75. AMS, II 22b/7; 5 March 1541.

76. H. Neu, "Freiherrlich von Türckheimisches Archiv auf Schoss Marberg, Bezirkamts Ettenheim," p. 55, n. 1. I am grateful to Thomas Brady for passing information about the Hebrew Bible on to me. For biographical data see Brady, *Ruling Class, Regime and Reformation,* p. 125.

77. AMS, II, 22b/8; 10 February 1546.

78. AMS, VI, 145, 8; 1563.

79. AMS, VI, 145, 2; n.d.

80. Ungerer, *Elsässische Altertümer,* vol. 2, pp. 85–90.

81. Wittmer and Meyer, *Livre de bourgeoisie,* vol. 2, p. 615, no. 6366.

82. AMS, H 1218; 29 March 1543.

83. AMS, H 4701; 11 February 1600.

84. AMS, Not. 775 (1601); 10 December 1601.

85. AMS, Ratsprotokolle, 12 June 1570, 5ᵛ–6ʳ. I am indebted for this reference and the next to Jane Abray. For Adolf Braun see Brady, *Ruling Class, Regime and Reformation.*

86. AMS, Ratsprotokolle, 8 April 1566, 139ʳ.

87. Private libraries are recorded in the following studies:

Baillet, "Bibliothèque de Ribeaupierre," pp. 9–15.
Baillet, "Bibliothèque du premier pasteur," pp. 51–63.
Bartholdi, "Bibliothèque des Seigneurs de Ribeaupierre," pp. 36–51.
Burmeister, *Achilles Pirmin Gasser,* vol. 1, p. 122.
Doucet, *Bibliothèques parisiennes.*
Engelsing, *Burger als Leser.*
Knod, "Bibliothek des Beatus Rhenanus," pp. 47–85.
Kolb, "Caspar Peucer's Library."
Schmidt, *Altesten Bibliotheken.*
Ungerer, *Elsässische Altertümer,* vol. 20.
Walter, *Bibliothèque municipale de Sélestat,* part 3.
Ernst Wickersheimer, *Livres léguées par Jean Protzer.*

88. Catholic Parish or Preaching Clergy
Matthias Brunck, churchman of Blienswiler (d. ca. 1520).
36 books:

Catholic theology	11
Sermon collections	7
Biblical commentaries	4
Breviaries	3
History of Lombardy	1

SOURCE: Ungerer, *Elsässische Altertümer,* vol. 2, p. 90.

Canons
Paul Munthart, Canon of Saint Thomas (d. 1480)
43 manuscript books and 20 printed books:

legal treatises	80%

SOURCE: Schmidt, *Ältesten Bibliotheken,* pp. 67–70.

Ludwig von Odratzheim, Dean of Old St. Peter (d. 1499)
127 books:

legal treatises	49%
Greek and Latin classics and humanism	10%
religious and philosophical works	10%
medical and scientific treatises	11%

SOURCE: Schmidt, *Ältesten Bibliotheken,* pp. 70–74.

Thomas Wolf, senior, Canon of St. Thomas (d. 1511)
274 books:

legal treatises	46%
humanist works and Greek and Latin classics	25%
Catholic works (philosophy, sermons)	14%
biblical texts and commentaries	4%
history	4%
science and medicine	4%

SOURCE: AST supp. 1.

Protestant Clergy
Peter Vermigli (Peter Martyr), resident of Strasbourg, 1542–48, 1553–56
135 books:

Protestant theology and sermons	25%
Catholic theology	20%
Bibles and biblical commentary	12%
humanism and Greek and Latin classics	28%

SOURCE: Donnelly, *Calvin and Scholasticism*, pp. 211–17.

Georg Federer (Georgius Pennarius), first Protestant pastor of Ribeauvillé (d. after 1560)
134 books:

Bibles and biblical commentary	26%
Protestant doctrine	12%
Catholic church fathers	8%
rhetoric and grammar	11%
Greek and Latin classics and humanism	23%
science	6%

SOURCE: Baillet, "Bibliothèque du premier pasteur," pp. 51–60.

Professional Men (Lawyers and Civil Servants)
Nicole Gilles, notary and secretary to the king, Comptroller of the Treasury, in Paris (d. 1499)
72 books:

law books	(1 book?)
religious books (devotionals, prayerbooks, lives of the saints, psalters)	37%
humanism, Greek and Latin classics	15%
history and biography	12%
popular literature and moral treatises	15%

SOURCE: Doucet, *Bibliothèques parisiennes*, pp. 83–89.

Jean Janot, bookseller to the University of Paris (d. 1522)
140 books:

law and politics	7%
religious books	27%
humanism and Greek and Latin classics	4%
popular literature and moral treatises	34%
scientific works	7%
music	3%

SOURCE: Doucet, *Bibliothèques parisiennes*, pp. 91–104.

Johann Protzer, lawyer of Nördlingen (d. 1528)
290 books:

canon and civil law	33%
theological works	18%
humanism and Greek and Latin classics	27%
science and medicine	3%

SOURCE: Wickersheimer, "Livres léguées par Jean Protzer," pp. 1–9.

Jean de Feron, lawyer of the Parliament of Paris (d. 1547–48)
670 books:

law	20%
humanism and Greek and Latin classics	20%
history and biography	7%
popular literature and moral treatises	7%
scientific works	10%

SOURCE: Doucet, *Bibliothèques parisiennes*, pp. 105–164.

Lay People
Les Seigneurs de Ribeaupierre (Herren von Rappoltstein)
225 books:

Protestant theology	29%
science	16%
history	14%
law and politics	12%
popular literature, including plays and moral treatises	12%
Greek and Latin classics and humanism	8%

SOURCE: List made by Bartholdi, corrected by Baillet. Though Bartholdi gives 227 titles, an unpublished manuscript catalogue shows 265 titles. Bartholdi's list is probably based on a part of the library that was sent by Egenolph von Rappoltstein to be bound between 1560 and 1580.

Klaus Stallburger, Frankfurt merchant (d. 1524)
30+ books:

Bible and religious books	43%
science	16%
Greek and Latin classics	16%
history	13%
vernacular literature	10%

SOURCE: R. Engelsing, *Burger als Leser*, pp. 13–14. For biographical information on Stallburger see Alexander Dietz, *Frankfurter Handelsgeschichte*, 4 vols. (Frankfurt/ M, 1910–25), vol. 1.

Scholar-Humanists
Beatus Rhenanus (d. 1547)
1,020 books:

humanism and the Greek and Latin classics		40%
Greek and Latin classics	10%	
contemporary Italian humanists	12%	
contemporary German humanists	9%	
Erasmus	9%	
Catholic theology		11%
other Catholic works		5%
science		10%
history		9%
Protestant works		5%
school texts		4%

SOURCE: Walter, *Bibliothèque municipale de Sélestat,* part 3. Walter states in the index to the catalogue that there are 1,165 books which belonged to Rhenanus. Since he counted each two-volume work as two books, and I counted it as one, I have based the percentages on my total of 1,020 books.

Men of Science

Caspar Peucer, professor of mathematics and medicine at the University of Wittenberg (d. 1602)

1,455 books:

medicine	29%
other science	7%
history	25%
humanism, Greek and Latin classics	21%
Protestant theology	15%
law	2%

SOURCE: Kolb, "Caspar Peucer's Library."

Achilles Pirmin Gasser, doctor, scientist, and humanist (d. 1577)

2,844 books:

medicine	31%
other science	13%
history and geography	20%
humanism, Greek and Latin classics	11%
Latin theology	11%
German theology	10%

SOURCE: Burmeister, *Achilles Pirmin Gasser,* vol. I, p. 122. The actual catalogue of the library has not been printed; therefore, I have had to use Burmeister's categories.

Tycho Brahe, astronomer (d. 1601)

59 books:

science	75%
Greek and Latin classics	10%

SOURCE: Engelsing, *Burger als Leser,* p. 32. This sample does not represent Brahe's entire library.

PART II

1. For the political and diplomatic history of the city in this period see Willy Andreas, *Strassburg an der Wende vom Mittelalter zur Neuzeit,* pp. 10–30; Rodolphe Reuss, *Histoire de l'Alsace,* pp. 55–65; Rodolphe Reuss, *Histoire de Strasbourg depuis ses origine jusqu'à nos jours,* pp. 100–15; François Rapp, "Humanisme, Renaissance et Réforme," in *Histoire de l'Alsace,* ed. Phillipe Dollinger, pp. 171–75.

2. For the ecclesiastical history of the period see Rapp, *Réformes et réformation,* pp. 347–93. For the failure of the bishops to respond to the need for reform, see ibid., p. 159.

CHAPTER FOUR

1. For Peter Schott, Jacob Han, Johann Hug, Jacob Otther, and Thomas Wolf, Jr., see Schmidt, *Histoire littéraire,* vol. 1, pp. 131, 376; vol. 2, pp. 36–86.

2. Douglass, *Justification,* p. 208.

3. A5.1.1; A2.2.2; B7.1.8; C1.2.19; C7.2.2.

4. Schmidt, *Histoire littéraire,* vol. 2, p. 18.

5. C9.1.18b.

6. François J. Himly, *Atlas des villes médiévales d'Alsace,* p. 42.

7. C6.1.2; C6.2.1; C6.1.3; C6.2.9; C6.1.10; C6.2.4; C6.1.11; C6.2.12; C6.1.18; C6.2.7.

8. C6.1.5; C6.1.12; C6.1.16.

9. C6.2.5; C6.2.13; C6.2.15; C6.2.8.

10. C6.2.2; C6.2.14; C6.2.11; C6.1.4; C6.1.9.

11. F. Ritter, *L'imprimerie alsacienne,* p. 41.

12. Ibid., p. 173.

13. C3.1.37a, Bitonto, *Sermones dominicales,* last page (unpaginated).

14. C1.3.6b, Antonius Florentinus, *Confessionale,* fol. a².

15. C3.1.21, Vincentius Ferrerius, *Sermones de tempore, pars hyemalis,* fol. b.

16. C5.1.7a, Salectitus, *Antidotarius anime,* title page.

17. Schmidt, *Répertoire bibliographique,* vol. 1, p. 4.

18. British Museum, *General Catalogue of Printed Books,* vol. 249, cols. 191–92; vol. 33, cols. 763–67; vol. 219, cols. 357–58.

19. *Lexicon für Theologie und Kirche,* vol. 2, col. 750.

20. C3.1.23. Caracciolo, *Sermones per adventum,* cap. xxx, cap. xxxi, cap. xxxiiii.

21. C. Piana, "Antonius di Bitonto," *Franciscan Studies* (1953): 176.

22. C3.1.37c.

23. Piana, "Antonius di Bitonto," p. 179.

24. C3.1.5f.

25. *Lexicon für Theologie und Kirche,* vol. 10, cols. 630–31.

26. Paludanus, general of the Dominican order in 1317, was actively involved in French and papal politics, serving for a time as patriarch of Jerusalem. In the last decades of the fifteenth century, twenty-eight editions of various collections of his sermons were published in Strasbourg. Close examination, however, reveals they could not have been his work, since they contain references to Pope Martin V, Wycliff, and Hus, who were active after his death. Furthermore, the sermons supported the Immaculate Conception and the doctrine that Christ would have been incarnate even if man had not sinned, both of which were inimical to orthodox Thomism and the Dominican school. Since Strasbourg was a center of the Marian controversy, the sermons may have been published under the name of the long-dead Dominican to give added force to the protagonists of Mary and the Immaculate Conception. See "Petrus de Paludanas," *Histoire littéraire de la France* 37 (1938): 83.

27. C3.1.10c. Paludanus, *Sermones . . . novi de tempore,* 1486, weeks 1, 2, 4, and 12.

28. C3.1.18f.

29. *Lexicon für Theologie und Kirche,* vol. 5, col. 1036.

30. Editions were printed in Venice in 1486, 1495, and 1500; in Rome in 1486 and 1496; in Cologne in 1492 and 1498; and in London in 1498 and 1500.

31. C4.1.1.

32. C4.1.8.

33. C4.1.6c. Guido de Monte Rocheri, *Manipulus curatorum*, part 1, sections 1–4; part 3, sections 1–2.

34. See C3.1.3; C3.1.4; C3.1.6a–i; C3.1.11; C3.1.30; C3.1.31; C3.1.39; C3.2.22a–c; C3.2.31; C4.1.2; C4.1.3; C4.1.9a–h; C4.1.29a–b.

35. C4.2.1j, Varagine, *Legenda Aurea*, fols. a^v–a6; h3–h6.

36. B1.1.1a–g; B1.1.2.

37. B7.1.3; B7.1.2b.

38. Schmidt, *Altesten Bibliotheken*, pp. 67–70.

39. Ibid., pp. 70–71.

40. Ungerer, *Elsässische Altertümer*, vol. 2, p. 90.

41. Schmidt, *Altesten Bibliotheken*, pp. 51–67.

42. Ibid., pp. 58–59, 62, 63.

43. Ibid., p. 62.

44. C5.1.9b. *Hortulus animae*, 1500.

45. C5.1.9a–l.

46. C5.1.9m–u.

47. C5.1.3a–b; C5.1.12a–e; C5.1.14a–c; C5.1.24; C5.1.25; C5.1.15a–b; C5.1.18; C5.1.22.

48. C5.1.2e. *Trostspiegel*, 1510, fol. aaiii.

49. Ibid., fols. aaiii, aaiii^v, BB, BBiii^v–BBiiii.

50. Douglass, *Justification*, pp. 21, 24, 25.

51. C3.2.10. *Das Buch Granatapfel*, 1510 (Augsburg edition), fol. aii^v.

52. C3.2.8a. *Das Irrig Schaf*, fol. xxix^v.

53. C3.2.22a. *Das Evangelibuch*, fol. xxiii^v.

54. Ibid., fol. xxix^v.

55. Douglass, *Justification*, p. 144.

56. Ibid., p. 206.

57. Ibid., p. 176.

58. Rapp, *Réformes et réformation*, p. 169.

59. C5.2.1–8.

60. C4.1.20a. *Manuale curatorum*, fol. 7. See also: Bornert, *La Réforme protestante du culte*, p. 29.

61. Ibid., folio 56^v.

62. C6.3.7a. *Hymni de tempore et de sanctis*.

63. C1.3.25. *Concordia curatorum*, fols. iv–vii.

64. Schmidt, *Histoire littéraire*, vol. 2, pp. 340–72. Of 171 editions of Brant's work listed by Schmidt, only 22 were published after 1501.

65. Ibid., vol. 1, pp. 27, 88–89.

66. Chrisman, *Strasbourg and the Reform*, p. 51.

67. Schmidt, *Histoire littéraire*, vol. 2, pp. 174, 177.

68. Desiderius Erasmus, *Opus epistolarum*, ed. P. S. Allen, vol. 2, pp. 7–9. For full biographical material on these men see the forthcoming biographical volume of the *Collected Works of Erasmus*, University of Toronto Press.

69. Ibid., vol. 3, Ep. 606, Ep. 633, Ep. 731, Ep. 797, Ep. 858, Ep. 867, Ep. 883; vol. 7, Ep. 2166.

70. Francis Rapp, "L'humanisme et le problème de l'église," p. 48.

71. Ibid., p. 49.

72. Ciriaco Morón-Arroyo, "The Reformation and Its Impact on Spanish Thought," in *Social Groups and Religious Ideas in the Sixteenth Century*, p. 126.

73. Figure XX combines three classes of books—humanist works, Greek and Latin classics, and school texts—to show the aggregate of the humanist oeuvre.

74. T1.1.4a–r; T1.1.2a–e.

75. Lina Baillet, "Aspects et richesses de l'humanisme à Colmar et en Haute-Alsace," p. 73.

76. T1.1.20a–c; T1.1.22a–g; T1.1.23a–c; T1.1.28a–k.

77. T1.1.24b.

78. T1.1.28a.

79. Matthias Ringmann, *Die grammatica figurata,* ed. R. V. Wieser, pp. 14, 30, 37, 45, 48, 53, 57, 60.

80. Schmidt, *Histoire littéraire,* vol. 2, p. 183.

81. A2.2.8–10; A2.2.18–19.

82. T2.1.4a.

83. H1.3.54, Valla, *Elegantiae,* fols. XIII^v–XVI^v.

84. H1.3.24a–e.

85. H1.3.3a–i; H1.3.19a–h.

86. There were thirteen editions of his *Bucolica* (H1.3.9a–m), three editions of his poem *Calamitates* (H1.3.7a–c), and two editions of a collection of his poetry, *Fastorum libri XII* (H1.3.53a–b). There was one single edition of H1.3.8.

87. H1.3.9a. Mantuanus, *Bucolica,* fols. lxviii^v, lxxii, lxxiiii–lxxiiii^v.

88. Schmidt, *Histoire littéraire,* vol. 1, p. 27.

89. H1.3.10; H1.3.13; H1.3.15a–b; H1.3.21; H1.3.43.

90. Baillet, "Aspects et richesses," p. 64.

91. Lewis Spitz, "The Third Generation of German Renaissance Humanism," p. 105.

92. H1.4.2a–l; H1.4.5a–b; H1.4.7; H1.4.8a–e; H1.4.10a–c; H1.4.11; H1.4.12.

93. A1.3.2a–e; A1.3.3a–e; A1.3.4a–b, d–e; A1.3.6a–b.

94. A1.6.1a–c; A1.6.2a–b; A1.6.3a–c; A1.6.4a–b; A1.6.5a–c, e; A1.6.6a–b.

95. A1.1.1a–b; A1.1.3a–g; A1.2.1–5; A1.4.1–6; A1.5.1; A1.5.2; A1.5.3a; A1.5.4; A1.5.5; A1.5.6.

96. A1.7.1–6.

97. Livet, "Vers une nouvelle définition," p. 317.

98. H3.1.4a. Wimpheling, *Adolescentia,* fol. viii.

99. Wackernagel points out that Alsatian humanism was a movement within the Roman church. See Baillet, "Aspects et richesses," p. 64.

100. Jacob Wimpheling, *Jakob Wimpfeling's Adolescentia,* ed. Otto Herding, p. 200.

101. Ibid., pp. 208–09.

102. H1.2.11.

103. Schmidt, *Histoire littéraire,* vol. 1, pp. 144–50.

104. Wimpheling, *Jakob Wimpfeling's Adolescentia,* ed. Otto Herding, pp. 241–380.

105. S5.3.1.

106. H3.1.6a–h.

107. Johan Huizinga, *Erasmus and the Age of Reformation*, p. 27.

108. H3.1.16.

109. H3.1.16. Also see Madeleine Lang, "Erasme et la pédagogie strasbourgeoise," pp. 57–60.

110. H3.1.9. Brunfels, *De corrigendis studiis*, caps. VII–IX, unpaginated. For Brunfels's pedagogical writing in this period, see Jean-Claude Margolin, "Otto Brunfels dans le milieu évangélique Rhénan," pp. 129–31.

111. Philippe Ariés, *Centuries of Childhood*, p. 177.

112. Schmidt, *Histoire littéraire*, vol. 1, pp. 31–46, 57–67, 68–74.

113. This phenomenon is very clear in the correspondence of Erasmus. For specific examples see the accounts of Erasmus's relations with Ottmar Nachtigall, Martin Bucer, and Otto Brunfels in the forthcoming biographical volume of the *Collected Works of Erasmus*, and the accounts of Jacob Wimpheling and Thomas Murner in Schmidt's *Histoire littéraire*, vol. 1, pp. 31–75; vol. 2, pp. 226–38.

114. H1.2.4; H1.2.9; H1.2.22; H1.2.27; H1.2.30; H1.2.31; H1.1.12; H1.1.26.

115. H1.1.22; H1.2.11.

116. *Epithoma Rerum Germanicarum*, A5.1.1, caps. I, VI, VIII, IX, LXV, LXVII, LXVIII, LXIX, LXX, LXVI.

117. Hajo Holborn, *History of Modern Germany*, vol. 1, pp. 107–08.

118. H1.1.10a–e; H1.1.17a–c.

119. V9.3.2a–c; H5.3.4.

120. Miriam U. Chrisman, "La pensée et la main: Mathias Schürer humaniste-imprimeur," pp. 161–62, 164.

121. Lorie Leininger, "The Jacobean Bind," Ph.D. dissertation, University of Massachusetts, 1974, p. 295. Leininger develops the point that rhetoric became a means of establishing and maintaining order.

CHAPTER FIVE

1. F. Ritter, *L'Imprimerie alsacienne*, pp. 54–62, 69–72.

2. V6.2.1a. Brant, *Narrenschiff*, stanzas 3, 12, 14.

3. Ibid., stanzas 11, 8, 22, 36, 42, 54. Five different stanzas, scattered throughout the poem, deal with the theme of the lack of wisdom.

4. Ibid., stanzas 43, 58, 56, 66.

5. V6.2.3a–c; V6.2.4a–c; V6.2.5a–b; V6.2.7a–b; V6.2.8. Modern editions of Murner's works can be found in Thomas Murner's *Deutsche Schriften mit den Holzschnitten der Erstdrucke*, vols. 1–9. References below are to these editions.

6. Thomas Murner, *Narrenbeschwörung*, vol. 2, ed. M. Spanier, pp. 120–21.

7. Ibid., pp. 124–25, 127, 216–17, 149.

8. V6.2.8.

9. Thomas Murner, *Die Mühle von Schwindelsheim*, vol. 4, ed. Gustav Bebermeyer, pp. 58–61.

10. V6.2.3a–c.

11. Thomas Murner, *Badenfahrt*, Vol. I/II, ed. Ernst Martin, pp. 2, 7, 9, 22, 23.

12. Engelsing, *Analphabetentum*, p. 22. See also David Kunzle, *The Early Comic Strip*, p. 18.

13. Ibid., p. 23.

14. Ibid.

15. F. Ritter, *L'imprimerie alsacienne*, pp. 56–57.

16. See sections V1, V2.1, and V2.3.

17. F. Ritter, *L'imprimerie alsacienne*, p. 69.

18. Ibid., p. 70.

19. Ibid., p. 85.

20. Ibid., p. 86.

21. Ibid., p. 141.

22. V2.1.1. *Melusine*, title page.

23. V2.1.2. *Peter Diemringer*, title page.

24. V2.1.13. *Hug Schapler*, title page.

25. V2.1.25a. *Ritter vom Turn*, title page.

26. V2.3.1–V2.3.7.

27. V2.3.1a–f.

28. *Gesta Romanorum*, trans. Charles Swan, pp. 239–41.

29. V2.3.3a–c.

30. Schmidt, *Répertoire bibliographique*, vol. 2, p. 5.

31. V2.3.3d–j.

32. V2.3.1e; V2.3.1f; V2.3.3b.

33. V2.3.3f. *Historia Alexandri Magni*, fols. fiv, fviᵛ; gᵛ; h.

34. Ibid., fols. hviᵛ; qiiiᵛ.

35. V2.1.19a–e.

36. Paul Heitz, ed., *Strassburger Holzschnitte zu Dietrich von Bern, Herzog Ernst, Der Hürnen Seyfrid, Marcolphus*, pp. 3–8.

37. V2.1.10. *Salman and Morolf*, fol. a3ᵛ.

38. Ibid., fols. 6ᵛ, Biᵛ.

39. Ibid., fols. 23–66.

40. V2.1.1a; *Melusine*, fols. b4, b4ᵛ, f4, f2ᵛ.

41. V2.1.12a. *Küniges tochter von Frankreich*, fols. xiiiᵛ, xiv, xxvᵛ, xxiᵛ, xlii, xlivᵛ.

42. Ibid., fols. lxiii, xxxii, lxvii.

43. V2.1.13c.

44. Theodor Hampe, ed., *Gedichte vom Hausrat aus dem XV und XVI Jahrhundert*, p. 10.

45. Ibid., pp. 6–7.

46. Ibid., p. 13.

47. Ibid., opposite p. 16.

48. V6.3.1. *Nüwen Jar einen Hausrat*, fol. iiᵛ. (In facsimile edition in *Hausrat*, ed. Theodor Hampe.)

49. Ibid., folios iiiᵛ, iiiiᵛ, B, Bᵛ.

50. Ibid., folios Bii, Bvᵛ, Cii.

51. Ibid., Cvᵛ.

52. See *Ein schönes büchlin darinnen allerley haussrat zu haushalten notig kurtzlich begriffen wurt*, 1531 (Hagenau edition), and V6.3.6.

53. Arthur M. Hind, *An Introduction to a History of the Woodcut,* vol. I, pp. 207–09.
54. *Biblia pauperum,* ed. Elisabeth Soltés, p. 2. The themes of each picture are outlined on pp. xxix–xxxi.
55. V1.1.1–V1.1.5; V1.1.9.
56. V1.1.4. *Somnia Daniel,* title page.
57. Ibid., title page^v.
58. Ibid., passim (unpaginated).
59. V3.1.2a–e.
60. V3.1.7a–e; V3.1.8; V3.1.10a–b; V3.1.11a–b.
61. V3.1.14a–d.
62. See chapter 3.
63. V1.1.6a; B3.1.4a.
64. Schmidt, *Répertoire bibliographique,* vol. 7, 6.
65. V1.1.6b–c; B3.1.4b–c.
66. V1.1.6d–e; B3.1.4d. See Schmidt, *Répertoire bibliographique,* vol. 1, pp. 47, 48.
67. V1.1.6a. *Der Text des Passions,* end page.
68. Ibid., fols. aii–aiii.
69. Ibid., fol. aiii^v.
70. Ibid., fols. aiiii^v, bv^v.
71. Ibid., fols. ci^v, fi^v.
72. Ibid., aii. See Kunzle, *The Early Comic Strip,* p. 21, on the anti-Semitism in sequences on the Passion.
73. Ibid., b^v.
74. Ibid., dii^v, div^v.
75. Ibid., fvi^v.
76. Lucien Febvre, *A New Kind of History,* pp. 61–65. Leon Dacheux, *Un réformateur catholique,* p. 561.
77. It is extremely difficult to sort out the publication history of the different editions of the Passion that appeared between 1506 and 1514; the same is true of the provenance of the biblical texts. According to Leon Dacheux, Johann Wechtelin drew illustrations for a life of Jesus, which were used by Johann Knobloch in a 1506 Latin edition that included poems by Chelidonius (B3.1.4a). In the same year that he published the Latin edition, Knobloch printed another version, illustrated by Urs Graf. He asked Geiler to furnish a Latin text. Geiler provided a text drawn from Gerson's *Montesseron* and from the Gospels. Knobloch then had Matthias Ringmann translate the Latin into German. This text became Strasbourg's most popular version of the Passion. Knobloch printed it in 1506, 1507, and 1508. Grüninger copied it in 1509; Hupfuff in 1513 (V1.1.6a–e). Dacheux, *Un réformateur catholique, Jean Geiler,* p. 561. See also Schmidt, *Répertoire bibliographique,* vol. 7, pp. 6–8, 11, 18; vol. 1, pp. 47–48; vol. 5, p. 32.
   In addition to the harmonic version, Geiler preached a lenten sermon on the Passion in the form of a trial. This was translated into German by Johann Adelphus Müling and published without indication of a place of publication in 1509. It was reprinted by Grüninger in 1514 (V1.1.7). There was also a volume based on Geiler's sermons, entitled *Doctor Keiserpergs Passion des Herrn Jesu Furgeben und gepredigt*

. . . *und geteilt in stückes weisz eins süssen lebkuchen,* published by Grüninger in 1514 (C3.2.16a–b). The text had a good deal more of Geiler than of the Bible. For example, in describing the descent from the cross, Geiler pointed out that just as Joseph of Arimathea took Christ from the cross into his arms, so does the individual Christian take Christ into his mouth during communion (C3.2.16a, folio cvii^v).

The evidence indicates that the initiative for these editions came from the printers. Geiler did not approach Knobloch with a manuscript. Instead, Knobloch asked Geiler to provide the text. Ringmann was working for Knobloch as a translator at the time, and he rendered the Latin into German. Knobloch (or Schott) commissioned the artists. Grüninger and Hupfuff took the step of pirating Knobloch's text. The use of Geiler's name for the harmonic editions is interesting; obviously, his name sold books and was used whenever possible, even if he had had very little to do with the book.

78. Erasmus, *Opus epistolarum,* ed. Allen, vol. 6, p. 85.
79. Febvre and Martin, *The Coming of the Book,* p. 285.
80. C3.2.22a. *Das Evangelibuch,* folio clix^v.
81. Ibid., fol. xxviii^v.
82. Ibid., fol. lv.
83. Ibid., fol. cxxiii.
84. C3.2.23. *Die Emeis,* fol. viii.
85. Ibid., fol. xxv.
86. Oberman, *Werden und Wertung,* pp. 145–49, 171–75, 202–08.
87. Rapp, *Réformes et réformation,* pp. 440–44.
88. Febvre, *A New Kind of History,* p. 68.
89. Rapp, *Réformes et réformation,* p. 446.
90. Eisenstein, *The Printing Press,* vol. 1, p. 88. Eisenstein emphasizes the role the printers played in the development of these how-to books.
91. V4.1.1a–f.
92. V4.1.1. *Formulare und tütsch Rhetorica,* passim.
93. V4.1.4; V4.1.7; V4.1.12.
94. V4.1.2.
95. V4.1.8. *Vocabularius . . . in lingua vernacula,* title page.

CHAPTER SIX

1. A problem arises concerning definitions and terminology. To call books of this period "scientific" and the men who wrote them "scientists" is misleading, given the modern meanings of these words. "Science," meaning a connected body of demonstrated truths or observed facts systematically classified and considered together under general laws, according to the *Oxford English Dictionary,* does not appear in English until 1725. In the sixteenth century the more accurate term is natural philosophy, because mathematics, physics, and astronomy had traditionally been regarded as part of philosophy. Thus, this category of books might have been called "medicine, botany, and natural philosophy"; because of awkwardness in phrasing, however, I will refer to "scientific books." Since it is cumbersome to refer to the writers as "natural philosophers," I will use the term "scientists." While the

term "science" is an anachronism, it is so completely accepted that to discard it altogether would result in *preciosité*.

2. Marie Boas, *The Scientific Renaissance, 1450–1630*, p. 25.
3. F. Ritter, *L'imprimerie alsacienne*, pp. 104, 159, 192, 130.
4. S6.3.5.
5. M. Boas, *Scientific Renaissance*, p. 25.
6. Arturo Castiglioni, *A History of Medicine*, p. 501.
7. Thibodeau, *Science in an Urban Perspective*, pp. 45–46.
8. Castiglioni, *History of Medicine*, p. 470.
9. Thibodeau, *Science in an Urban Perspective*, p. 44.
10. S15.1.2.
11. S1.5.1; S1.5.2.
12. M. Boas, *Scientific Renaissance*, p. 29.
13. S5.1.3b. Reisch, *Margarita philosophica*, 1504, unpaginated.
14. Ibid., fols. miiii, lvi.
15. Ibid., fol. q.
16. Ibid., fol. u viii. See M. Boas, *Scientific Renaissance*, p. 31.
17. Reisch, *Margarita philosophica*, fol. y iii^v.
18. Ibid., S5.1.3b, ff–ffv^v.
19. Ibid., aai–aav.
20. George Boas, "Philosophies of Science in Florentine Platonism," pp. 242–43.
21. Castiglioni, *History of Medicine*, p. 366.
22. S3.1.1a–d; S3.1.4a–c; S3.1.5a–c.
23. S3.1.1a, *Ortus sanitatis*, n.d., fol. xiv.
24. Ibid., fol. xvii.
25. Ibid., fol. xv^v.
26. Ibid., fol. di^v.
27. Ibid., fol. n^v.
28. S1.3.2; S1.3.3; S1.3.4a–c; S1.3.5; S1.3.7; S1.7.4.
29. S1.7.3. Tollat, *Margarita medicinae*, 1512, fol. v.
30. Ibid., fols. vi, vii, xxiiii.
31. S1.11.1a–b.
32. S1.7.3d. Tollat, *Margarita medicinae*, 1512, preface (unpaginated).
33. Castiglioni, *History of Medicine*, p. 501.
34. Friedrich Wieger, *Geschichte der Medecin und ihrer Lehranstalten in Strassburg vom 1497–1872*, p. 3.
35. Sitzmann, *Dictionnaire de biographie*, vol. 1, p. 249.
36. S1.5.1a–b; S1.4.2.
37. R. J. Forbes, *Short History of the Art of Distillation*, pp. 56–69, 95.
38. S2.1.3a–d; S2.1.4a–k.
39. Forbes, *Short History of Distillation*, pp. 101–05.
40. S2.1.4a. Brunschwig, *Liber de arte distillandi*, 1512, book IV.
41. Ibid., fols. xl, xli^v.
42. M. Boas, *Scientific Renaissance*, p. 160.
43. S1.5.2a–h. Two Strasbourg editions by unknown printers, one in 1524, the

other in 1542, are listed by Heinrich Haeser, in *Grundriss der Geschichte der Medicin*, vol. 2, p. 162, and Ernst Julius Gurlt, in *Geschichte der Chirurgie und ihrer Ausübung*, vol. 2, pp. 222–23. A modern facsimile of the 1517 edition was printed by Editions Medicine Rara, Ltd (*Feldtbuch des Wunderartzney* [Weiler im Allgäu: Druckerei Holzer, n.d.]). Pagination below is based on the facsimile edition.

44. Hans Gersdorff, *Feldtbuch*, facsimile edition, verso of title page.

45. Ibid., fols. xix^v, xviii^v.

46. René Burgun, "La syphilis à Strasbourg au XVme et XVIme siècles," part 1, p. 86.

47. Gersdorff, *Feldtbuch*, unpaginated.

48. Ibid., folio xviii^v. I am grateful to Dr. George Snook for helping me to interpret this figure.

49. Wieger, in *Geschichte der Medicin*, p. 9, describes the instrument as a trephine rather than the ordinary trepan. The illustration in the Gersdorff/Schott edition is on fols. xxii–xxii^v.

50. Gersdorff, *Feldtbuch*, fol. xxx.

51. Ibid., fols. xxxiii^v, xxxv, following xxxiiii.

52. Ibid., fol. xiii.

53. Wieger, *Geschichte der Medicin*, p. 5.

54. See Guido Majno, *The Healing Hand*, p. 403.

55. Castiglioni, *History of Medicine*, p. 476.

56. Wieger, *Geschichte der Medicin*, p. 23.

57. S1.10.1. Mondino dei Luzzi, *Anathomia*, title page.

58. Appointed physician to the Duke of Württemberg, Hock spent most of his professional life in Rome. He gave his treatise on gout to Schott to publish, and this may have been the cause of his visit to Strasbourg.

59. Gersdorff, *Feldtbuch*, folio xiii^v. Wieger, *Geschichte der Medicin*, p. 24.

60. Wieger, *Geschichte der Medicin*, p. 24

61. Castiglioni, *History of Medicine*, p. 409.

62. S1.7.6c. Fries, *Spiegel der Artzney*, 1526, fol. xiiii.

63. Ibid., fols. cxxvii–cxxxvii^v.

64. Castiglioni, *History of Medicine*, p. 465.

65. S1.4.2–S1.4.8.

66. S1.4.5. Beroaldus, *Opusculum de . . . Pestilentia*, fols. di–dii.

67. Wittmer and Meyer, *Livre de bourgeoisie*, vol. 2, p. 400, no. 3534.

68. S1.4.6c. Wydman, *Wie man sich in pestil luft . . .* , 1519, fol. aii.

69. Ibid.

70. Ibid., fol. aiv.

71. Ibid., fols. biii–c.

72. Burgun, "Le syphilis," part 1, p. 67.

73. Whether the Spanish troops were infected by Columbus's returning sailors is still a matter of scholarly debate. Alfred Crosby, Jr., reviews the Columbian and the Unitarian theories that syphilis was the same disease as yaws, or treponematosis, which had long been globally distributed. Crosby concludes that neither thesis can be finally proved with the present biological evidence. There are, however, contem-

porary documents which consistently state that this was a new disease. Also, the only pre-Columbian bones with clear lesions of treponematosis are found in America. See Alfred W. Crosby, Jr., *The Columbian Exchange,* pp. 124, 127–39, 141–43.

74. For a full description of the city's reaction to the new menace, see René Burgun, "Strasbourg, sa contribution à l'histoire de la médecine," parts 2, 3, 4, *Journal Médicale de Strasbourg,* 1973, 4:237–51; 5:53–64, 717–27.

75. Castiglioni, *History of Medicine,* p. 456.

76. S1.6.1. Widmann, *Tractatus de pustulis,* unpaginated.

77. S1.4.2.

78. S1.6.2. Hock, *De causis . . . et cura morbi Gallica.*

79. S1.6.3. Hutten, *Von . . . des Holtz Guaiacan,* passim. See also S1.6.4a–b.

80. Burgun, "Strasbourg, sa contribution," part 2, 4:249–50.

81. Castiglioni, *History of Medicine,* p. 465.

82. S1.2.2b. Roesslin, *Der Schwangeren Frauen Rosengarten,* fols. div, div^v, e, eii^v–eiii.

83. Castiglioni, *History of Medicine,* p. 482.

84. August Hirsch, ed., *Biographisches Lexikon der hervorragenden Ärtzte aller Zeiter und Volker,* vol. 4, p. 850.

85. See S4.1.1a–h; S4.1.2; S5.1.1a–c; S5.1.2; S5.2.1; S5.4.1; S5.5.1.

86. Febvre and Martin, by contrast, found there was little interest in geographic discoveries until 1550. The French printers continued to publish John de Mandeville. See Febvre and Martin, *The Coming of the Book,* p. 279.

87. S6.2.2–3; S6.2.4; S6.2.5–6.

88. M. Boas, *Scientific Renaissance,* pp. 32–33.

89. S6.3.1. See Hugh Honour, "America as Seen in the Fanciful Vision of Europe," p. 55. See also Georges Livet, "Géographes et cartographes," pp. 193–97.

90. S6.3.5.

91. E. G. R. Taylor, "Cartography, Survey and Navigation, 1400–1750," pp. 537–38.

92. Ibid.

93. S6.3.6.

94. S6.3.7.

95. A. E. Nordenskiöld, *Facsimile Atlas with Reproductions of the Most Important Maps Printed in the XV and XVI Centuries,* p. 24.

96. S6.4.1. Treatise published to accompany the map.

97. Taylor, "Cartography," pp. 537–38.

98. S6.4.4.

99. Schmidt, *Répertoire bibliographique,* vol. 1, p. 95.

100. S6.4.3.

101. Steven Ozment, *The Reformation in the Cities,* p. 9.

102. Rapp, *Réformes et réformation,* p. 442.

103. V1.1.6a–e.

104. V5.2.2–V5.2.7.

105. L2.1.1; L2.1.2. These edicts were somewhat compromised by the fact that, at the same time, the Magistrat rented municipal property for a house of prostitution. I am indebted to Thomas A. Brady, Jr., for this information.

106. L2.1.5a.
107. L2.1.10.
108. S6.4.1.
109. S6.2.1; S6.2.3–6.

PART III

1. Marc Leinhard and Jean Rott, "Die Anfänge der evangelischen Predigt in Strassburg und ihr erstes Mainfest: der Aufruf des Karmeliterlesemeisters Tilman von Lyn (anfang 1522)," *Bucer und seine Zeit*, ed. Marijn de Kroon and Friedhelm Krüger (Weisbaden: Steiner Verlag, 1976), pp. 54–73. For a description of the beginnings of the Reform see Chrisman, *Strasbourg and the Reform*, chap. 6.

2. Heinrich Bornkamm, *Martin Bucers Bedeutung für die europäische Reformationsgeschichte*, p. 12.

3. Kittelson, *Wolfgang Capito*, pp. 146–47.

4. Ibid., pp. 154–55.

5. François Wendel, *L'eglise de Strasbourg, sa constitution et son organization*, pp. 246–47.

6. The following account is based on chapters 9 and 10 of my earlier study, *Strasbourg and the Reform*.

7. Quoted in James M. Kittelson, "Wolfgang Capito, the Council and Reform Strasbourg," p. 133.

8. Wendel, *L'église de Strasbourg*, p. 67.

9. Brady, *Ruling Class, Regime and Reformation*, p. 237.

10. Ibid., pp. 239–41.

11. François Wendel, *Le mariage à Strasbourg à l'époque de la réforme, 1520–1692*, p. 76.

12. Brady, *Ruling Class, Regime and Reformation*, p. 270.

13. Ibid., p. 241.

14. Ibid., chap. 8.

CHAPTER SEVEN

1. Albert Rabil, Jr., *Erasmus and the New Testament*, p. 91.

2. Ibid., pp. 115–16.

3. B5.1.1–3; B7.2.2–10.

4. Erasmian New Testament in Latin: B5.1.3a–f. Other Erasmus editions, 1522–23: H1.4.5f–g; H1.4.8d–e; H1.4.9b; H1.4.10c; H1.4.13c–f; H1.4.14c; H1.4.16; H1.4.17; H1.4.18a–c; B5.1.2b; B5.1.3b–e; B7.2.3–7. Of these last 25 editions, 15 (60%) were Christian humanist texts or treatises.

5. C10.1.43.

6. Kittelson, *Wolfgang Capito*, p. 110.

7. C10.1.49.

8. Jean Rott points out that in 1530, Bucer, replying to the attack leveled in the *Epistola contra quodam*, tried to be as open as possible, and the Strasbourg reformers let the debate drop rather than prolong a public difference of opinion with a man

whom they deeply respected. Rott also notes that Erasmus continued to correspond with Jacob Sturm and Caspar Hedio until his own death, and that Capito translated Erasmus's *Treatise on Ecclesiastical Unity* into German in 1533. Jean Rott, "Erasme et les réformateurs de Strasbourg," p. 50.

9. B7.2.9–10; B7.3.2f; B7.4.6–9; B7.5.2b; B7.5.4–5; B7.6.4–7; B8.1.9–10; B8.2.8–10; B8.3.2b; B8.3.3; B5.1.5c; B6.1.3.

10. B1.1.3; B5.1.5a–e; B2.1.7a–c; B6.1.1.

11. B5.1.6; B6.1.5; B6.1.4; B2.1.10.

12. B7.4.1–5b; B7.3.1–3b; B7.6.1–5.

13. F. W. Hassencamp, *Franciscus Lambert von Avignon,* pp. 16, 19.

14. Section B7.5.

15. Bopp, *Evangelischen Theologen,* vol. 2, p. 322.

16. B7.7.2–3.

17. B7.7.5–6.

18. B7.7.1; B7.7.4.

19. Kittelson, *Wolfgang Capito,* pp. 179–81.

20. B8.1.1–8; B8.1.10; B8.1.13–18.

21. B7.8.2; B7.8.5; B7.4.2.

22. B7.8.2. Brunfels, *Pandectarum,* fols. 2, 4, 8–9.

23. Ibid., fols. 39–42^v.

24. Latin version, B7.8.6. German version, B8.4.3. Brunfels, *Helden Büchlin,* fols. ii–xiv, xiv^v–xviii^v, xviii^v–xxv.

25. B7.8.1a–b; B7.8.2; B7.8.5a–b; B7.8.6; B8.4.2; B8.4.3.

26. Section B8.6.

27. Klaus Deppermann, "Melchior Hoffman à Strasbourg," p. 502.

28. B8.3.1a–b; B8.5.1–8.

29. B1.1.3–6.

30. British Museum, *Short-title Catalogue,* pp. 89–91.

31. Herbert Moller, "Population and Society during the Old Regime, c. 1640–1770," p. 5. Moller gives an estimate of 18 million in 1600 for the area occupied by Germany in 1871. I have reduced this to produce a very conservative figure.

32. See chapter 3.

33. See section B4.1. Thirteen editions of Luther's psalms alone were set to music, but after 1569 (B4.1.11a–m). See also B2.1.7a–c for the German psalter without music.

34. B5.1.5a–i; B5.1.7; B5.1.8a–c; B5.1.9.

35. D. Martin Luthers *Deutsche Bibel,* II, vol. 2. *Bibliographie der Drucke der Lutherbibel, 1522–1546,* Paul Pietsch, ed., in the Weimar edition of Luther's works. These figures do call into question Lucien Febvre's estimate that one million copies of the entire Bible may have been printed between 1500 and 1550, and furthermore, Febvre does not make it completely clear how he arrived at this estimate. Febvre and Martin, *The Coming of the Book,* pp. 294–95.

36. The criterion for polemic in this study was that the given treatise presented an argument or defense or was controversial in nature. This included books specifically critical of the Roman Catholic church, of the pope, bishops, or other ecclesiastical

officers, or of established doctrines or customs of the church. Tracts that defended Luther's leadership and Luther's actions, particularly those that extolled his position, and treatises that set forth the Protestant program while attacking traditional doctrines were also included. Although some Protestant sermons or statements of doctrine were argumentative in nature, they were not included under the heading of polemic.

37. P3.1.1; P3.1.6–7; P3.1.30; P3.11.13.
38. P3.1.4.
39. P3.2.1a–d; P3.2.5a; P3.2.6a–b.
40. Benzing, *Ulrich von Hutten,* p. 123.
41. P3.4.1.
42. P3.6.2.
43. P3.6.5.
44. P3.6.4; P3.9.11.
45. William Stafford, *Domesticating the Clergy: the Inception of the Reformation in Strasbourg* (Missoula, Mont.: Scholars Press, 1976), pp. 20–26.
46. P3.2.1; P3.2.7; P3.8.1; P3.8.3; P3.11.2; P3.11.4.
47. P3.7.5.
48. P3.7.9; P3.7.10.
49. P2.2.2. Zell, *Collation . . . M. Anthonii,* fols. III–VII.
50. P3.3.20. Zell, K., *Entschuldigung . . . für Mathias Zell,* folios XVIII, XXIV.
51. P3.1.17.
52. P3.11.10–11; P3.11.14.
53. P2.2.1. Bucer, *Das ym selbs niemant,* fol. c.
54. P3.3.13. Wurm von Geudertheim, *Christlich schreiben,* fols. i^v–ii.
55. Ibid., fols. xiii–xxv.
56. Ibid., fol. lxii.
57. P3.3.22. Schenck, *Sendtbrieff an seyne Geschwyen,* passim.
58. P3.1.28.
59. Martin Luther, *Works,* trans. Eric Gritsch and Ruth Gritsch, vol. 39, p. 305.
60. P3.3.9. Excerpts from the treatise are translated in Roland Bainton, *Women of the Reformation in Germany and Italy,* p. 97.
61. P3.3.4a–c; P3.3.19; P5.1.14.
62. P3.3.19. Treubel, *Christelich lob und vermanung,* fols. aii–iv, biv.
63. *Niklaus Manuel,* Jakob Baechthold (Fravenfeld: J. Huber, 1878), pp. 33–34.
64. Ozment, *Reformation in the Cities,* pp. 118–20.
65. See Bucer's statement of this ideal in P2.2.1.
66. P3.1.2a.
67. P3.2.4.
68. P3.3.1b. Gemigger, *Zu lob dem Luther,* title page.
69. Ibid., p. aiiii^v.
70. P3.1.11; P3.1.12; P3.1.16.
71. P3.9.6–8; see also P3.9.3–4.
72. P3.12.2a–b.
73. P3.3.15. Buellheim, *Brüderliche warnung,* fol. Bii. This pamphlet has been edited with scholarly notes by Marc Lienhard in an article entitled "Mentalité popu-

laire, gens d'église et mouvements évangelique à Strasbourg en 1523," in *Horizons européens de la Réforme en Alsace, Mélanges Jean Rott,* (Leiden: E. J. Brill, 1980), pp. 42–62.

74. P1.1.2–4; P1.2.1–3.

75. P1.1.6; P1.2.4.

76. P1.1.7; P1.1.12.

77. P1.1.5.

78. P1.1.16; P1.4.2; P2.1.2.

79. P1.7.1; P2.1.1; P2.1.17; P2.1.49.

80. For the significance of Bucer's treatise see Stafford, *Domestication of the Clergy,* pp. 48ff.

81. This attitude can be seen in the municipal ordinances, particularly those concerning marriage, the controls on marketing practices, and edicts calling for days of prayer. See L2.1.5; L2.1.17; L2.1.20; L2.1.22; L2.1.26; L2.1.28; L2.1.30, etc. The petitions presented by laymen asking for abolition of the Mass point to the fact that men's sinfulness prevents them from seeing the public good. Chrisman, *Strasbourg and the Reform,* pp. 167, 173.

82. P5.1.14. Treubel, *Ein vetterliche gedruge lere,* folio a iv^v.

83. *Niklaus Manuel,* Jakob Baechthold, p. 101.

84. P1.2.5–28; P1.8.6; P1.8.7; P1.8.14.

85. P1.3.6; P1.4.18; P1.4.19; P1.4.23; P1.8.27.

86. P1.2.1–4.

87. P4.2.3–4.

88. Kittelson, *Wolfgang Capito,* p. 145.

89. P1.2.6.

90. P1.2.5a–b.

91. Hastings Eells, *Martin Bucer* (New Haven: Yale University Press, 1931), p. 71. See pp. 73–78 for the early development of the controversy.

92. *Martin Luthers Werke,* Weimar edition, 19, p. 466.

93. Ibid., pp. 471–72.

94. P1.8.7.

95. Ernest G. Schwiebert, *Luther and His Times,* p. 699.

96. Kittelson, *Wolfgang Capito,* p. 152; see P1.2.12.

97. Schwiebert, *Luther and His Times,* p. 713.

98. P1.9.2; P1.5.3.

99. See P1.7.2 and P1.7.3.

100. P5.1.1–4.

101. P7.2.6–7. For a full discussion of the development of the new liturgy, see René Bornert, *La réforme protestante du culte à Strasbourg au XVIe siècle.*

102. P7.2.8–15; P7.2.17.

103. Charles Garside, *Calvin's Theology of Music,* p. 11.

104. Ibid., p. 12. The singing in the Strasbourg churches made a deep impression on John Calvin who, while serving as pastor to the French congregation in Strasbourg, began work on a French psalter that incorporated Marot's psalms. On his return to Geneva, congregational singing was made part of the new liturgy there. See Garside, pp. 14–16.

105. See section B4, which lists more than 40 editions of psalms for congregational singing. See also P6.1.1–13, which lists 23 editions of hymns for congregational singing.

106. P5.1.32; P6.1.1.

107. P5.1.5; P5.1.7; P5.1.9; P5.1.13–15; P5.1.17.

108. P1.6.5.

109. P5.1.13.

110. P5.1.26.

111. P1.6.13b. *Vermanung an die jungen Knaben.*

112. Ibid., Aiiii–Aiiii^v.

113. Garside, *Calvin's Theology of Music,* p. 18.

114. Wallace, "Revitalization Movements," p. 265.

115. Ibid.

116. Ibid., pp. 268–69.

117. Ibid., p. 266.

118. Ibid., pp. 270–73.

119. Ibid., pp. 273–75.

CHAPTER EIGHT

1. Kenneth Thibodeau, "Science and the Reformation," p. 40. For further development of his theme see his doctoral dissertation, "Science in an Urban Perspective."

2. Having contributed a major share of Lutheran polemic and the majority of the Strasbourg editions of Hutten, Schott published only seven works by a Strasbourg reformer, namely Martin Bucer. See P1.8.1, P2.2.1, P3.11.5–6, P3.11.13–14. All these were published before 1524, before the controversy over the Eucharist had become bitter.

3. The combination of Anabaptist and Spiritualist publications with scientific and technological treatises can be found in the work of P. Schöffer, B. Beck, J. Schwann, M. Apiarius.

4. Peter, "Les premiers ouvrages française," p. 90, n. 77.

5. Thibodeau, "Science and the Reformation," p. 43. For Paracelsus, see Wittmer and Meyer, *Livre de bourgeoisie,* vol. 2, p. 754, no. 8326, and Karl Bittel, "Die elsässer Zeit des Paracelsus."

6. Wittmer and Meyer, *Livre de bourgeoisie,* vol. 2, p. 770, no. 8456.

7. F. Ritter, *L'imprimerie alsacienne,* p. 316.

8. Ficker and Winckelmann, *Handschriftenproben,* vol. 2, p. 82.

9. Schindling, *Humanistische Hochschule,* p. 323; Ficker and Winckelmann, *Handschriftenproben,* vol. 2, p. 82.

10. Schindling, *Humanistische Hochschule,* p. 180.

11. Sitzmann, *Dictionnaire de biographie,* vol. 1, p. 755.

12. Wickersheimer, "Laurent Fries," p. 97.

13. S1.13.1.

14. Wickersheimer, "Laurent Fries," pp. 99–100.

15. See S1.11.2–6; S1.9.9; S1.9.11; section S1.13.

16. S1.13.6, a translation of S1.13.2. Schmidt notes that Gerald of Cremona disfigured the Arab names. The Arab doctors referred to in S1.13.2 were, respectively, Abul Hafsan al Mukhtar of Bagdad, Ibn Wafid al Lakhmi, and Kindi al Abu Jusus Jaqub.

17. S1.7.14. On the reverse of the title page there is an elegaic poem addressed to Fuchs by Nicolaus Gerbel, the Strasbourg lawyer. This, as well as the fact that other of his books were printed in Strasbourg, indicates Fuchs's close ties with the city. For biographical data on Fuchs, see *ADB,* vol. 8, p. 169.

18. S1.7.14. Fuchs, *Compendiaria,* fol. 3.

19. J. F. Michael, *Biographie universelle,* vol. 24 (1968), p. 377.

20. S1.9.11; S1.11.3; S1.11.4.

21. J. L. Heiberg, *Beiträge zur Geschichte Georg Vallas,* p. 381.

22. S1.7.1. Valla, *De inventa Medicina,* fols. A2–A4ᵛ, B5–B6.

23. S1.9.6; S1.9.10.

24. *Nouvelle biographie générale,* (reprint 1968), vol. 39–40, cols. 388–89.

25. S1.9.9. See *Nouvelle biographie générale,* vol. 41–42, col. 865.

26. Gregorius Reisch, author of the *Margarita philosophica,* discussed in chapter 5, was prior of the Carthusian house in Freiburg. Brunfels obviously knew him and respected him, since he dedicated his second book, a pedagogical treatise, to Reisch in 1519. See Passman, "Die Kartause," vol. 14, p. 146.

27. Ibid., pp. 146–47.

28. I am grateful to Kenneth Thibodeau for this information.

29. P. W. E. Roth, "Otto Brunfels, nach seinem Leben und literarischen Werken," p. 289.

30. Wittmer and Meyer, *Livre de bourgeoisie,* vol. 2, p. 694, no. 7388.

31. F. Ritter, *L'imprimerie alsacienne,* pp. 182–83.

32. Ibid., p. 182.

33. S3.1.9a. Brunfels, *Contrafayt kreuterbuch,* 1532, fols. biiᵛ, ciᵛ, cvi.

34. Wittmer and Meyer, *Livre de bourgeoisie,* vol. 2, p. 787, no. 8676.

35. Thibodeau, "Science and the Reformation," p. 42.

36. Thibodeau, "Science in an Urban Perspective," pp. 159–60.

37. S3.1.8. Brunfels, *Herbarium vivae Icones,* vol. 3, 1536, verso of frontispiece.

38. Vesalius, *De humani corporis fabrica,* published by J. Oporinus in Basel in 1543, provides an even greater effect on the modern viewer, in part because Vesalius recognized the need to break down each organ or each part of the skeleton to its very smallest component part; thus there are illustrations of separate arteries and each bone of the hand. This move from the view of the whole to that of its finite parts was an essential step toward modern scientific analysis.

39. S3.1.8a. Brunfels, *Herbarum vivae Icones,* 1530, vol. 1, fols. 23–25.

40. An early sixth-century manuscript of Dioscorides, *De Materia medica* (Vienna: National Bibliothek, Cod. Med. g.r.l) depicted the plant with the root as well as the bud and the flower. By the tenth century the plant had become generalized. Although the root and the bud were still shown, they were not clearly identifiable. Dioscorides, *De Materia medica,* Pierpont Morgan Library, M562.

41. Brunfels, *Herbarum vivae Icones,* vol. 1, fol. 28.

42. S3.1.8d; S3.1.9c.

43. S3.1.9b. Brunfels, *Contrafayt Kreuterbuch,* 1537, vol. 2, fol. xvi.

44. S6.2.7; S8.1.5a.

45. S7.1.11. Herr, *Aller vierfüssigen thier,* fols. aiii, bii–biiᵛ.

46. Sitzmann, *Dictionnaire de biographie,* vol. 2, p. 629.

47. Josef Benzing, *Walther H. Ryff und sein literarisches Werk, Eine Bibliographie,* pp. 5–6. See also Wieger, *Geschichte der Medicin,* p. 31.

48. S1.9.7. Brunschwig and Schrick, *Apotek für den gemeinen man,* introduction. S1.12.13. Bock, *Kurtz Regiment für Hauptweh,* introduction.

49. S1.5.7a–b; S1.7.16; S1.7.17a–b; S1.7.18a–b; S1.7.19a–d; S1.7.20a–b; S1.7.22; S1.7.26a–i; S1.9.16a–d; S1.9.17a–b; S1.10.7; S1.10.8; S1.10.19; S1.12.12.

50. S1.9.16a. Ryff, *Kleynen Teütschen Apoteck.*

51. S1.10.4. Castiglioni, *History of Medicine,* p. 418. M. Boas, *Scientific Renaissance,* p. 142.

52. I am indebted to Kenneth Thibodeau for the information regarding this plagiarism.

53. S1.10.6b. Vogtherr, *Anathomia,* 1539, unpaginated.

54. S1.10.5b. Vogtherr, *Krankheyten der Augen,* title page.

55. S1.10.8. Benzing states that this edition had nineteen woodcuts and was twenty pages in length, and that Beck printed two editions in one year (Benzing, *Luther Bibl.,* # 90, p. 24). François Ritter says that this and S1.10.9 were the work of Hans Baldung Grien (*Livres ne figurant pas,* no. 3134). I have used this later edition, which was a folio in size and seventy-seven pages in length, and which contained twenty-five full-page illustrations. The vascular system is shown on pp. Diiᵛ–Diii. The organ *situs* is on folio lii. Friedrich Wieger, in *Geschichte der Medicin,* discusses the Ryff anatomy on pp. 30–31. Ryff's work antedated Vesalius's *Tabulae sex,* published in 1538, which included six plates (three skeletal views and three views of the vascular system). Vesalius's main work, *De humani corporis fabrica,* was not published until 1543. See John Bertrand de C. M. Saunders and Charles D. O'Malley, *The Illustrations from the Works of Andreas Vesalius of Brussels,* pp. 17 and 19. Vesalius felt that the reduction in size of his plates in the Ryff work was abominable (the latter from Kenneth Thibodeau).

56. For instance, S1.5.7.

57. Josef Benzing, "Christian Egenolff zu Strassburg und seine Drucke (1528 bis 1530)," pp. 88–92.

58. *Das Feuerwerkbuch von 1420,* ed. and trans. Wilhelm Hassenstein, p. 89. *Bergwerk-und Probierbüchlein,* ed. and trans. Anneliese Grünhaldt Sisco and Cyril Stanley Smith, pp. 8–9.

59. Abbott Payson Usher, *A History of Mechanical Inventions,* p. 108.

60. S10.1.1–4.

61. S11.2.1; S11.2.2.

62. S11.11.1a–b. The fact that the women of the household were constantly using their skills in embroidery is borne out in the inventories discussed in chapter 3, in which embroidered cushions were a major item. The scene depicted on the cushion was often described in the inventory.

63. S5.4.1–13.

64. S11.3.1; S11.4.1–3; S11.5.1–2.

65. S11.10.1.

66. S11.7.1–3; see also S2.1.2a–f.

67. S11.8.1a–c; S11.8.2a–c.

68. François J. Fuchs, "Quelques aspects de la vie économique à Strasbourg" (Paper presented at the Colloque Internationale, Strasbourg, May 1975).

69. I am indebted to M. Fuchs for directing me to this material. The Seydenschuher petition can be found in AMS, V 32; 1559.

70. V7.3.3. Heckel, *Lauten-buch*, title page.

71. Fuchs, "Quelques aspects de la vie économique."

72. S5.4.13. Höflin, *Rechenbüchlin*, title page.

73. For a discussion of the work of French reckonmasters in the period see Natalie Zemon Davis, "Sixteenth-Century French Arithmetics on the Business Life," pp. 18–48. Davis indicates that it was not until after 1550 that French reckonmasters wrote texts that met the specific requirements of businessmen by providing practical examples of buying and selling, profit and loss. Even at that date the French commercial mathematicians, unlike their German counterparts, had not adopted algebra.

74. The name "cossists" was derived from the Arab term for an equation containing an unknown. These men spoke of themselves as cossists and of algebra as "the rules of coss."

75. S5.4.2. Rudolph von Jauer, *Rechnung . . . durch die Cosz.*

76. Rudolph's work, in turn, drew on the unpublished work of Adam Riese and the published treatises of Johann Widmann. See Moritz Cantor, *Vorlesungen über Geschichte der Mathematik*, vol. 2, p. 387.

77. Alexandre Koyré, "The Beginnings of Modern Science from 1450 to 1800," in Taton, *History of Science*, vol. 2, p. 32.

78. Louis Charles Karpinski, *The History of Arithmetic*, p. 130.

79. Salomon Bochner, *The Role of Mathematics in the Rise of Science*, p. 185.

80. S5.4.6. Waelckl, *Die Wälsch Practica.*

81. Ibid., fol. aii^v.

82. Ibid., fol. aiii^v.

83. Ibid., fol. aiiii^v.

84. Ibid., fol. bvi.

85. Ibid., fols. ciii, diiii^v.

86. S5.4.5. Kern, *Visierbuch.*

87. Ibid., fol. ai^v.

88. Ibid., last section (unpaginated).

89. V4.1.10a–d. *Vocabularius latinis, gallicis et theutonicis.*

90. Peter, "Les premiers ouvrages francais (suite)," II, pp. 13–14.

91. S11.9.1; S11.9.2a–b.

92. Françoise Lévy-Coblentz, *L'art du meuble en Alsace*, vol. 1, p. 62.

93. Ibid., p. 52.

94. Lévy-Coblentz includes the full texts of the ordinances for the cabinetmakers' guild from 1519, 1544, and 1571 (pp. 465–68), as well as a German/French version of the 1571 ordinance (pp. 92–93). The importance of these guild regulations, which

show significant changes in the attitudes of the cabinetmakers and an increasing professional and artistic sophistication, can hardly be overstressed.

95. Ibid., pp. 95–96.

96. S11.6.1a–f; S11.6.2. Vogtherr, *Kunstbüchlein.*

97. Lévy-Coblentz, *L'art du meuble,* vol. 1, p. 40.

98. S11.3.1.

99. *Das Feuerwerkbuch,* ed. Wilhelm Hassenstein, p. 89.

100. Ibid., p. 91.

101. S11.4.1.

102. *Bergwerk und Probierbüchlien,* ed. A. Sisco and C. S. Smith, pp. 8–9.

103. Ibid., p. 6.

104. Egenolff, *Probierbüchlein,* fols. 3–7^v.

105. Ibid., fols. 11^v–12.

106. Ibid., fols. 14–14^v.

107. Ibid., fols. 12^v–18^v.

108. Ibid., fols. 33–37.

109. Ibid., fols. 44–46.

110. S11.4.2a–b.

111. S11.4.2a. *Von stahel und eisën,* 1539, fol. Aii.

112. Ibid., fol. Aiii^v. Ox-tongue is the popular name of several plants, chiefly bugloss, borage, and ackanet (O.E.D.).

113. Ibid., fols. Aiiii^v–B^v.

114. S11.5.1–2.

115. S5.4.1; V10.13.1.

116. S11.10.1.

117. S8.1.1a; S8.1.1c; S8.1.2; S8.1.3a, b, d.

118. S8.1.5a–e.

119. S8.1.5a. Cassianus Bassus, *Der Veldbaw,* fols. 2–6.

120. Ibid., passim.

121. S11.1.1a–c.

122. I am indebted for the information about the Rhine river crabs to Edmond Ponsing of the Archives municipales de Strasbourg.

123. S11.1.1b. *Kuchenmeistery,* 1516, fols. cii–cix.

124. S11.8.1a–c; S11.8.2a–c.

125. S11.11.1a–b.

126. See chapter 12.

127. M. Boas, *Scientific Renaissance,* pp. 53–54.

128. Quoted in Elisabeth Feist Hirsch, "The Discoveries and the Humanists," p. 42.

CHAPTER NINE

1. William J. Bouwsma, "The Two Faces of Humanism," p. 4.

2. Ibid., p. 10.

3. Ibid., pp. 10–11.

4. Ibid., p. 28.

5. Ibid., pp. 42, 44.

6. Ernst-Wilhelm Kohls, *Die Schule bei Martin Bucer in ihrem Verhältnis zu Kirche und Obrigkeit*, p. 50.

7. Charles Engel, *L'école latine*, p. 9.

8. Vorentwurf des Ratschlags in *Martin Bucers Deutsche Schriften*, ed. Robert Stupperich, vol. 7, pp. 558–59.

9. In this discussion the secondary classes in the period before 1563 will be called the Latin Classes, the advanced classes will be called the Upper Classes, and the school as a whole will be called the Gymnasium. Following local custom, I will refer to the Latin Classes after 1563 as the Gymnasium and the degree-granting institution as the Academy.

10. Engel, *L'école latine*, p. 24.

11. Ficker and Winckelmann, *Handschriftenproben*, vol. 2, p. 78.

12. Ibid., p. 79.

13. Jean Sturm, *Classicae epistolae*, p. 70, n. 1. Engel, *L'école latine*, p. 55.

14. See appendix B for lists of school faculty.

15. Charles G. A. Schmidt, *La vie et les travaux de Jean Sturm*, p. 307; and Schindling, *Humanistische Hochschule*, p. 386.

16. Quoted in Bouwsma, "Two Faces of Humanism," p. 32.

17. Sturm, *Classicae epistolae*, p. 31.

18. Ibid.

19. Cicero, *De Inventione*, pp. 5–7.

20. Bouwsma, "Two Faces of Humanism," p. 17.

21. Sturm, *Classicae epistolae*, pp. 63, 71, 73.

22. Cicero, *De Inventione*, p. 13.

23. Cicero, *Philippics*, pp. 107–15, 123, 127–29. See Sturm, *Classicae epistolae*, pp. 68–69, for Sturm's assignment of the *Philippics* to the second class.

24. A2.2.24; A2.2.25; A2.4.2. See table 16.

25. Sturm, *Classicae epistolae*, p. 73.

26. Johannes Crüger, "Zur Strassburger Schulkomödie," vol. 1, pp. 314, 315.

27. Ibid., p. 315.

28. Ibid.

29. A1.6.16a–c; A1.6.17a–c; A1.6.24a; T1.3.8a–c; T1.6.8a–d; A2.5.1a–b; A1.6.13a–c; A1.6.14a–b; A1.6.15a–c; A1.6.12a–b.

30. A2.4.2–4; A1.6.18a–b; A1.6.19a–b; A1.6.20a–b; A2.2.24–25.

31. See A1.6.12–A1.6.25.

32. Jean Rott, *Bibliographie des oeuvres imprimés du recteur Strasbourgeois Jean Sturm, 1507–1589*, vol. 1, pp. 319–404.

33. T1.6.8a–m.

34. T1.6.9a–e. See Schindling, *Humanistische Hochschule*, p. 206.

35. Schindling, *Humanistische Hochschule*, p. 166.

36. T1.5.5a–n.

37. A2.3.8; A2.5.2a–b.

38. T2.1.5a–i.

39. T1.3.10a–b.

40. T1.3.13–18.
41. S5.5.5. This was not printed until 1557 when Herlin's student, Conrad Dasypodius, aided his former teacher by publishing his work.
42. S5.6.2.
43. H4.1.12.
44. H4.1.13.
45. H4.1.14a–d.
46. P1.6.8a–b.
47. B7.6.16.
48. B7.6.21.
49. A1.2.1–5; A1.3.1–6; A1.4.1–7; A1.7.1–7; A1.3.2f; A1.2.6; A1.4.7.
50. A2.2.22a–d; A2.2.23–25.
51. Schindling, *Humanistische Hochschule*, p. 220.
52. Ibid., pp. 176–77.
53. Ibid., p. 392.
54. Ibid.

PART IV

1. Chrisman, *Strasbourg and the Reform,* chapter 9.
2. Werner Bellardi, *Die Geschichte der "Christlichen Gemeinschaft" in Strassburg (1546–1550),* chapters 1 and 2.
3. Johann Adam, *Evangelische Kirchengeschichte der Stadt Strassburg bis zur Französischen Revolution,* pp. 285–90. For a detailed account of the crisis over the Interim see Weyrauch, *Konfessionelle Krise.*
4. Abray, "Long Reformation," p. 161.

CHAPTER TEN

1. Abray, "Long Reformation," p. 161.
2. A1.6.24–32; A2.2.25–34; A2.4.5; A4.3.4–7.
3. T1.2.8–13; T1.3.24–26.
4. T1.1.37–38.
5. Franz Hirtler, "Lebensbild des Dichters," in Wickram, *Das Rollwagenbüchlein,* p. 11.
6. Ibid., p. 13.
7. Ibid., p. 14.
8. V2.3.1q–r; V2.3.106; V2.1.6f.
9. Gertrude Fauth, *Jörg Wickram's Romane,* pp. 4–6.
10. V6.3.4a.
11. V6.3.7a–b. Wickram, *Der Jungen Knaben Spiegel.* The modern facsimile edition, volume 3 of Georg Wickram, *Sämtliche Werke,* is edited by Hans Gert Roloff. See p. 13. All page numbers below refer to the modern edition.
12. Ibid., p. 15.
13. Ibid., p. 9.
14. Ibid., p. 13.
15. Ibid., p. 119.

16. Leon Battista Alberti, *The Family in Renaissance Florence,* trans. Renée New Watkins, pp. 4–5.

17. Wickram, *Der Jungen Knaben Spiegel,* p. 104.

18. Ibid., p. 119.

19. V6.3.11. Georg Wickram, *Von Güten und Bösen Nachbaurn.* The modern facsimile edition is volume 4 of *Sämtliche Werke,* ed. Hans Gert Roloff. See pp. 16–20. All page numbers refer to this edition.

20. Ibid., p. 24.

21. Ibid., pp. 30, 40–41.

22. Ibid., pp. 46–68.

23. V6.3.9–10; V6.3.14.

24. Georg Wickram, *Der Irr Reitende–Pilger,* in *Sämtliche Werke,* ed. Hans Gert Roloff, vol. 6, p. 136.

25. V6.1.1a–g; V6.1.9a–c.

26. Franz Podleiszek, *Anfänge der bürgerliche Prosaromans in Deutschland,* ed. Walter Brecht and Dietrich Kralik, pp. 23–25.

27. Cf. Franz Joseph Mone, ed., *Schauspiele des Mittelalters aus Handschriften herausgegeben und erklärt,* and Adelbert von Keller, ed., *Fastnachspiele aus dem fünfzehnten Jahrhundert,* with the plays discussed below.

28. V8.1.8a.

29. Hirtler, "Lebensbild des Dichters," p. 11.

30. Martin Vogeleis, *Quellen und Baustein zu einer Geschichte der Musik, und des Theaters im Elsass, 1500–1800,* p. 243.

31. Sitzmann, *Dictionnaire de biographie,* vol. 1, p. 802.

32. Ibid., p. 526.

33. Ibid., p. 565.

34. See the sparse publication of Protestant sermons from 1530–70 (sections P2.2 and P2.3). Polemic writing was substantially reduced after 1530. The major religious publications for the laity were prayer books and devotionals, of which fourteen were published in German between 1530 and 1570 (P5.1.16–29). Two treatises on marriage were published in German (P3.7.16; P1.7.4a–b).

35. August Jundt, *Die dramatischen Aufführungen im Gymnasium zu Strassburg ein Beitrag zur Geschichte des Schuldramas in XVI. und XVII. Jahrhundert.*

36. Edith Weber, *Le théatre humaniste et scolaire dans les pays Rhénans,* in *Musique et théatre dans les pays Rhénans,* vol. 2, pp. 90ff.

37. Ibid., p. 45; Crüger, "Zur Strassburger Schulkomödie," p. 314.

38. Weber, *Le théatre humaniste et scolaire,* vol. 2, p. 45.

39. Crüger, "Zur Strassburger Schulkomödie," p. 315.

40. V8.1.3. Georg Wickram, *Die Zehen Alter . . . ausz der Bibel gezogen, von newem gespilt, gemert und gebessert worden,* title page.

41. The following plays contain notes that they were performed by townspeople:

> 1538 Wickram's *Das Narrengiessen,* presented by the burghers of Colmar.
>
> 1541 Birck's *Susanna,* presented by the apprentices of the furrier's guild. (Crüger, "Zur Strassburger Schulkomödie," p. 308).
>
> 1546 Gart's *Joseph,* presented at Sélestat in 1540.

1554   Wickram's *Tobias*, presented at Colmar.
1556   Frey's *Fastnachtspil*, presented at Marmoutier.
1558   Rouf's *Job*, presented by the burghers of Strasbourg.
1562   Wickram's *Tobias*, presented by the burghers of Strasbourg.
1564   *Judith*, presented by "young burghers of Strasbourg."
1568   Walliser's *Esther*, presented in Strasbourg.
1572   Zyrl's *Rebecca*, presented at Weissenburg.
1573   Rasser's *Johannis . . . des Täuffers*, presented by the burghers of Colmar.
1575   Meyenbrunn's *Johannis des Heiligen Täuffers*, presented by the burghers of Colmar.

42. V8.1.4. See *ADB*, 33, pp. 487–88.

43. V8.1.7. See *ADB*, 33, p. 653. See also Alexander Seitz, *Sämtliche Schriften*, ed. Peter Ukena, vol. 1.

44. V8.1.15. See *ADB*, 37, p. 158.

45. *ADB*, 29, pp. 591–93.

46. *ADB*, 23, pp. 245–50; Jöcher, AGL, 2, 1702; *ADB*, 2, p. 656; Sitzmann, *Dictionnaire de biographie*, vol. 2, p. 945.

47. V8.1.26–27. See *ADB*, 45, p. 579.

48. V8.1.30. See Karl Goedeke, *Grundrisz zur Geschichte der Deutschen Dichtung*, vol. 2, p. 391.

49. V8.1.31. See *ADB*, 47, pp. 562–63.

50. V8.1.29. See *ADB*, 32, p. 126.

51. See V8.1.24.

52. V8.1.3–25. Cf. B4.1.4–11b.

53. V8.1.8a–c; V8.1.27a–b; V8.1.31. The Joseph plays are the subject of an important thesis by Jean Lebeau, presented and accepted in 1976 at the Sorbonne. Copies of the thesis are available at the Bibliothèque Universitaire at Strasbourg and at the Archives Municipale.

54. V8.1.1; V8.1.4; V8.1.30. Georg Wickram, *Sämtliche Werke*, ed. Hans Gert Roloff, vol. 11, p. 120.

55. Jean Lebeau, "Thiébolt Gart de Sélestat," p. 223.

56. Theobald Gart, *Joseph*, in *Elsässische Litteraturdenkmäler aus dem XVI–XVII Jahrhundert*, ed. Ernst Martin and Erich Schmidt, 5 vols. (Strassburg: K. J. Trübner, 1878–88), vol. 2, pp. 44, 47, 60–61.

57. *ADB*, 47, p. 563.

58. Theobald Gart, *Joseph*, ed. Martin and Schmidt, *Elsässische Litteraturdenkmäler*, vol. 2, pp. 87–89, 96.

59. Ibid., p. 105.

60. Ibid., p. 120.

61. Luther, *Works*, trans. Eric Gritsch and Ruth Gritsch, vol. 6, pp. 359–60; vol. 8, p. 74. In a few instances Luther makes a comparison between Joseph and Christ. Joseph's brothers acted like the Jews who persecuted Christ (vol. 6, p. 326; the price for which Joseph was sold was less than the price given for Christ (vol. 6, p. 391). There is no comparison between Joseph in the pit and Christ in the tomb, nor is there any development of the comparison with the Eucharist.

62. B8.2.13; B8.2.14.
63. Goedeke, *Grundrisz*, vol. 2, p. 347.
64. V8.1.4. Gnapheus, *Acolastus*, act 3, sc. 5.
65. Ibid., act 4, sc. 2.
66. Ibid., act 5, sc. 5.
67. *Der Verlorener Sohn*, in Georg Wickram, *Sämtliche Werke*, ed. Hans Gert Roloff, vol. 11. Edith Weber mistakenly includes the *Verlorener Sohn* in her list of plays published in Strasbourg.
68. Ibid., p. 73.
69. Ibid., pp. 56–86.
70. Ibid., pp. 118–20.
71. *Tobias*, in Georg Wickram, *Sämtliche Werke*, ed. Hans Gert Roloff, vol. 11, p. 238.
72. Ibid., pp. 290, 291, 309.
73. Ibid., pp. 217–18.
74. Ibid., p. 220.
75. Ibid., p. 251.
76. Ibid., p. 247.
77. Ibid., p. 272.
78. Ibid., p. 227.
79. Ibid., pp. 243–44.
80. Ibid., p. 304.
81. T3.2.5. Walter, *Nabal*.
82. V8.1.23.
83. V8.1.26. Zyrl, *Rebecca*.
84. V8.1.19; V8.1.21; V8.1.24; T3.2.11; T3.2.14.
85. V8.1.15; T3.2.1. Frey, *Von dem armen Lazaro*.
86. V8.1.26. Zyrl, *Rebecca*, title page.
87. Ibid., fol. aii^v.
88. Ibid., fol. Eii^v.
89. Implicit in these marriage plays was the idea that the young couple must have the consent of their parents, as Luther had taught. Thomas Robisheaux, in his recent work, has discovered the importance of this doctrine among the peasants of Hohenlohe. While the peasants were unwilling to adopt Protestant doctrine as a whole, they quickly accepted those elements that supported the patriarchal family. Their response to the Reform was, then, highly selective. See Thomas Robisheaux, "Peasants and Pastors: Rural Youth Control and the Reformation in Hohenlohe, 1540–1560," *Social History* 6 (1981):281–300.
90. V8.2.11. Montanus, *Von zweien Römern*, fol. a.
91. Ibid., act 3.
92. This theme was developed by Montanus in another play, *Ein Untrew Knecht* (V8.2.10), in which the hero seduces the wife of a friend. She eventually returns to her husband, avowing her loyalty and obedience to him. In the epilogue Montanus uses this as an example of the weakness of women.
93. A5.2.4a–h; A5.2.5a–b.
94. A5.2.14a–g; A5.2.15a–h.

95. V9.4.2a–b; V9.4.3.

96. Modern writers tend to develop the drama of the scene at Worms and the confrontation between Luther and Cajetan. Sleidan provided an unadorned narrative. His version of Luther's final words at Worms was conciliatory in tone: "I will never seem to refuse the judgment of Caesar and the States of the Empire if it may be done by Scripture and according to God's word." Jean Sleidan, *Commentaries concerning the State of Religion . . . during the Reign of Emperor Charles V*, fol. xxxi^v.

97. Ibid., fols. iiii ff.

98. Ibid., fols. Biiii–iv.

99. V9.1.18a–b; V9.1.10; V9.1.13–15.

100. V11.1.15; V11.1.16; V11.1.19; V11.2.5–11.

101. V11.3.1–2; V11.4.1–4.

102. S5.5.5–10; S4.2.6–7.

103. S4.6.1; S5.3.2; S7.1.14–15.

104. S16.1.5–10.

105. Lucien Braun, "Paracelse (1493–1541), un antihumaniste parmi les humanistes," p. 228.

106. S16.1.9a. Paracelsus, *Archidoxa*, fols. iiii–iiii^v.

107. Georges Cattaui, "Paracelse et sa posterité," in *Paracelse, l'homme—le médecin—l'alchimiste* (Paris: La Table Ronde, 1966), p. 9.

108. John Mason Stillman, *The Story of Early Chemistry*, pp. 308–09.

109. Otto Zekert, *Paracelsus*, pp. 19–21.

110. Bittel, "Die elsässer Zeit des Paracelsus," p. 158.

111. Wittmer and Meyer, *Livre de bourgeoisie*, vol. 2, p. 754, no. 8326.

112. Wickersheimer, "Paracelse," p. 363.

113. Zekert, *Paracelsus*, pp. 53–61.

114. Schmidt, *Michael Schütz genannt Toxites*, pp. 33–36.

115. Ibid., pp. 52–55.

116. Ibid., pp. 81–84.

117. Stillman, *Early Chemistry*, p. 310.

118. KS, 100, fol. 231; 1558. Margaret Stör was Christian Mylius's second wife. Michael Toxites was the second husband of Veronica, the mother of Margaret Stör.

119. Theophratus von Hohenheim genannt Paracelsus, *Sämtliche Werke*, ed. Karl Sudhoff, vol. 3, p. xxxviii.

120. Manfred Fleischer, "The Institutionalization of Humanism in Protestant Silesia," p. 258.

121. S16.1.9a. Paracelsus, *Archidoxa*, fols. Bii^v–Biiii.

122. Ibid., p. Bv.

123. Charles Singer, *A Short History of Scientific Ideas*, p. 200.

124. Stillman, *Early Chemistry*, p. 320.

125. S16.1.9a. Paracelsus, *Archidoxa*, fols. Eiv–Ev.

126. Schmidt, *Michael Schütz genannt Toxites*, p. 85.

127. S16.1.9a. Paracelsus, *Archidoxa*, fols. Di^v ff.

128. Stillman, *Early Chemistry*, pp. 316–17.

129. Allen G. Debus, *The Chemical Philosophy, Paracelsian Science and Medicine in the Sixteenth and Seventeenth Centuries*, vol. 1, pp. 52, 61.

130. Ibid., p. 52.
131. Ibid., p. 53.
132. S3.1.10a–l.
133. S3.1.10k. Bock, *Kreütterbuch*, 1587, fol. bvi.
134. Ibid.
135. Ibid.
136. S3.1.12a. Bock, *Teütsche Speiszkammer*, introduction. (unpaginated).
137. S3.1.10b. Bock, *Kreütterbuch*, 1546, fol. b.
138. S3.1.10j. Bock, *Kreütterbuch*, 1587, fol. bv^v.
139. S3.1.10b, fol. b^v.
140. Ibid.
141. S3.1.10c. Bock, *Kreütterbuch*, 1550.
142. Ibid.
143. For Paracelsus, see Debus, *The Chemical Philosophy*, I, p. 126.

PART V

1. These issues are fully explored by Jane Abray in "The Long Reformation," chaps. 5–7. The materials from the Ratsprotokolle which appear in this chapter were given to me by Jane Abray. I am more than grateful for her willingness to share her work with me.
2. This account is summarized from Marcel Fournier and Charles Engel, *Gymnase, Académie et Université de Strasbourg*, part 1, pp. 203–04.
3. Jane Abray, "The Long Reformation," pp. 209–10.
4. Jean Rott, "L'eglise des réfugiés de langue française à Strasbourg," pp. 533–39.
5. Abray, "The Long Reformation," p. 236.
6. Ibid., p. 238.
7. Ibid., pp. 240–42.
8. Ibid., pp. 246–48.
9. Ibid., pp. 255–58.

CHAPTER ELEVEN

1. V7.1.56–57; V7.1.73. See also V10.1.8.
2. V7.1.63; V7.1.77.
3. P6.3.8. See also P6.3.14; P6.3.21; P6.3.26.
4. J. Adam, *Evangelische Kirchengeschichte*, pp. 227–35.
5. Ibid., p. 236. See Roger Mehl, "Strasbourg et Luther: la Tétrapolitane," pp. 147–51, for the attitude of the Strassburgers toward the Tetrapolitana.
6. J. Adam, *Evangelische Kirchengeschichte*, pp. 237–38.
7. Ficker and Winckelmann, *Handschriftenproben*, vol. 2, p. 67.
8. Bopp, *Evangelischen Theologen*, vol. 1, pp. 31, 75.
9. The major posts were:

Cathedral	Johann Flinner, 1559–78
	Johann Pappus, 1578–93
New Saint Peter	Lorenz Offner, 1549–72
	Johann Liptiz, 1577–98

Saint Thomas	Melchior Specker, 1557–69
	Bartholomäus Nasser, 1569–93
Old Saint Peter	Isaak Kessler, 1560–77
	Elias Schad, 1577–86
	Pankratius Keffel, 1586–1609
Saint Aurelien	Nikolaus Florus, 1558–87
	Johann Rottman, 1587–1604
Saint Nicolaus	Jacob Glocker, 1557–66
	Johann Thomas, 1566–93
	Tobias Specker, 1593–1622

See Bopp, *Evangelischen Theologen,* vol. 1, pp. 31, 34, 71. The continuity was further strengthened by the emergence of pastoral families. Marbach, Schad, Florus, Specker, and Thomas all had sons who eventually received appointments to the Strasbourg churches. This is well developed in Vogler, "Recrutement et carrière," pp. 151–65.

10. P1.9.5; P3.15.7.

11. James M. Kittelson, "Marbach vs. Zanchi," pp. 40–43.

12. P4.4.1; P4.4.2.

13. Kittelson, "Marbach vs. Zanchi," pp. 32ff.

14. P1.1.26; P1.2.15b; P1.6.15b–f; P1.6.16a–b; P1.6.21.

15. See P1.8.23–26.

16. P1.9.6.

17. P1.9.6. Erythraeus, *Augustanae Confessionis,* pp. 2–3.

18. P1.2.24. Johann Marbach, *Underricht . . . Das Jhesus Christus . . . warhafftig und mit der That, erhaben und gesetzt seye,* unpaginated.

19. Ibid., fol. b2.

20. Ibid., fol. c2^v.

21. Ibid., fol. c3.

22. Rott, "L'église des réfugiés," p. 544.

23. P7.2.25. *Kirchenordnung . . . in der Kirchen zu Straszburg,* 1598, p. 23.

24. Ibid., p. 24.

25. Ibid., p. 26.

26. Ibid., p. 27.

27. Ibid., p. 28.

28. Ibid., p. 44.

29. Ibid., p. 48.

30. P1.9.7. Pappus, *Articuli . . . doctrinae christianae.*

31. Ibid., pp. 10–11. See Bouwsma, "Two Faces of Humanism," pp. 56–57.

32. B5.1.8b–c; B1.1.6.

33. F. Ritter, *L'imprimerie alsacienne,* p. 276.

34. B5.1.12; B6.1.8.

35. B7.6.22–28; B7.7.11.

36. B8.4.5–6; B8.4.8.

37. B8.6.1–8.

38. P6.1.6b. *Newer . . . Gesangbüchlein,* 1560, fol. aiiii.

39. P5.1.26. *Tischgebete für die Kinder,* fol. aiii.

40. See B4.1.11e; P5.1.23.
41. P5.1.27; P5.1.30a–d.
42. P5.1.25d. Luther, *Betbüchlein*, 1580.
43. P1.6.3a. See Gerald Strauss, *Luther's House of Learning*, p. 157.
44. P1.6.6; P1.6.8a–b.
45. P1.6.15a–e; P1.6.19; P1.6.16a–b; P1.6.21.
46. P1.6.18.
47. P1.6.13b. *Vermanung an die Jungen Knaben* . . . , fols. aiiii–aviv, avv–avii.
48. Strauss, *Luther's House of Learning*, pp. 166–71.
49. Abray, "The Long Reformation," pp. 275, 280.
50. Ibid., pp. 201, 207. See also municipal ordinances L2.1.45 and L2.1.61. The latter ordinance states that, even if people did not like the foreigners who had come to the city, everyone was required to be polite to them.
51. AMS, RP, 21 Sept. 1579, 439v–440r.
52. Alcuin Hollaender, "Der Theologe Matthias Flacius Illyricus in Strassburg 1567–1573," pp. 203–18.
53. Hauffen, *Johann Fischart*, vol. 1, p. 49.
54. AMS, Rat und XXI, 27 Sept. 1570, fol. 736v.
55. Ficker and Winckelmann, *Handschriftenproben*, vol. 2, p. 91.
56. Ibid.
57. P3.6.16.
58. Sitzmann, *Dictionnaire de biographie*, vol. 2, p. 799.
59. B8.6.1–8.
60. B8.6.2a. *Epistel . . . an Titum*, fol. aiiiv.
61. Ibid., fol. xiiiv.
62. Ibid., fol. avv.
63. B8.6.7. *Epistel . . . an die Corinthier*, preface (unpaginated), fols. i, iii.
64. Ibid., fol. cxvir.
65. Sitzmann, *Dictionnaire de biographie*, vol. 2, p. 799.
66. Hauffen, *Johann Fischart*, vol. 1, pp. 10–40.
67. AMS, Rat und XXI, 26 May 1527, fol. 385r.
68. *ADB*, 8, p. 96.
69. T3.1.12b. Frischlin, *Phasma*, fol. a4.
70. Ibid., fol. G5v.

CHAPTER TWELVE

1. Schindling, *Humanistische Hochschule*, p. 14.
2. Ibid., p. 90.
3. Chrisman, *Strasbourg and the Reform*, p. 265.
4. Engel, *L'école latine*, p. 8.
5. Schindling, *Humanistische Hochschule*, pp. 35–37.
6. Ibid., p. 39.
7. Kittelson, "Marbach vs. Zanchi," pp. 36–37.
8. Schindling, *Humanistische Hochschule*, pp. 46–47.
9. Ibid., pp. 51–55.

10. Ibid., pp. 63 ff.

11. Ibid., p. 87.

12. For biographical information on Jonas Bitner, see Ficker and Winckelmann, *Handschriftenproben,* vol. 2, p. 89; for Theophilus Gol, see ibid., p. 61; for Johann Ludwig Hawenreuter, see ibid., p. 95; for Melchior Junius, see ibid., p. 94; for Johann Pappus, see ibid., p. 90; for Melchior Sebiz, see Sitzmann, *Dictionnaire de biographie,* vol. 2, p. 766; for Conrad Dasypodius, see ibid., vol. 1, p. 350, and Ernst Zinner, *Geschichte und Bibliographie der Astronomischen Literatur,* pp. 35–36.

13. For biographical information on Andreas Planer, see Melchior Adam, *Vitae Germanorum Juriconsultorum . . . Medicorum . . . etc.,* vol. 2, p. 404; for Nikolaus Reusner, see Sitzmann, *Dictionnaire de biographie,* vol. 2, p. 548; for Ernst Regius, see Engel, *L'école latine,* p. 186; for Hubert Giphanius, see ibid., pp. 187, 227.

14. Engel, *L'école latine,* pp. 189–90.

15. Schindling, *Humanistische Hochschule,* p. 60 ff.

16. Ibid., pp. 106–09.

17. Fournier and Engel, *Gymnase, Académie et Université,* p. 252.

18. Schindling, *Humanistische Hochschule,* p. 101.

19. "Statutes de l'Académie de Strasbourg, 1568," in Fournier and Engel, *Gymnase, Académie et Université,* p. 145.

20. Ibid.

21. "Propositions de la Commission de Convents Academique . . . à la discipline et à l'enseignement," in ibid., p. 258. See also Schindling, *Humanistische Hochschule,* pp. 158–61, for a discussion of the magistrate's authority over the schools. A school *konvent* brought together the rectors, the deacons, and the visitors to discuss disciplinary matters affecting both faculty and students. See Schindling, *Humanistische Hochschule,* p. 155.

22. Schindling, *Humanistische Hochschule,* pp. 210–11.

23. The curriculum of the Academy included lectures on rhetoric; Aristotelian philosophy (dialectics, ethics, and physics); mathematics; philology (Hebrew, Greek, and Poetics); and history; as well as the specialized work in law, medicine, and theology. Anton Schindling's book includes a meticulous description of the content of these lectures, as well as the textbooks which were used. There is a separate chapter for each field.

24. Walter J. Ong, *Ramus, Method and the Decay of Dialogue,* p. 27.

25. Schindling, *Humanistische Hochschule,* p. 204, n. 43.

26. Jean Rott notes that in the year 1565/66 Sturm's production of texts and theoretical manuals was as important as that of the years 1538–41. Jean Rott, "Jean Sturm, le premier recteur du Gymnase et de l'Academie," p. 187.

27. T1.3.12c–g; T1.6.8e–j, l–m.

28. Ong, *Ramus,* p. 234.

29. Schindling, *Humanistische Hochschule,* p. 205.

30. Ong, *Ramus,* pp. 230–39.

31. T1.6.9a–e; T1.3.10a; P1.9.6.

32. Schindling, *Humanistische Hochschule,* p. 206.

33. Ficker and Winckelmann, *Handschriftenproben,* vol. 2, p. 91.

34. See section T4.1.

35. A2.1.6; A6.1.17; A2.2.33.

36. A2.4.6–7.

37. A2.5.1d–f.

38. Ficker and Winckelmann, *Handschriftenproben*, vol. 2, p. 91.

39. T1.3.28; T1.3.27; T1.3.30–31; T1.3.25.

40. Schindling, *Humanistische Hochschule*, p. 240. T1.3.29; T1.3.34; T1.4.13.

41. S3.1.10e; S3.1.13.

42. Ficker and Winckelmann, *Handschriftenproben*, vol. 2, p. 90. Pappus also served as professor of Hebrew after the death of Kyber. He was pushed into the post at that time (he was only twenty-one) by his mentor, Johann Marbach. François Ritter, *L'imprimerie alsacienne*, p. 548, n. 306. H5.2.6.

43. Ficker and Winckelmann, *Handschriftenproben*, vol. 2, p. 95. Schindling, *Humanistische Hochschule*, pp. 248–49.

44. Ficker and Winckelmann, *Handschriftenproben*, vol. 2, p. 93. S4.5.2; S4.8.2.

45. S8.1.7a–d. Planer also published *Analysis libri primum physicorum Aristotelis*, 1571, and *Questionarum dialectarum;* see M. Adam, *Vitae Germanorum*, vol. 2, p. 404.

46. Sitzmann, *Dictionnaire de biographie*, vol. 1, p. 590.

47. *ADB*, 2, p. 590.

48. H5.4.18.

49. Schindling, *Humanistische Hochschule*, pp. 275–76.

50. H5.2.6a–b.

51. H5.3.19a–c.

52. H5.3.19c. Reusner, *Icones*. . . .

53. Crüger, "Zur Strassburger Schulkomödie," p. 315. Crüger cites all the instances in the Ratsprotokolle in which the students appear before the Rat to ask for permission to put on a play publicly. The first request was made by the students of the Gymnasium in February 1557. Crüger notes that after 1574 Greek tragedies, presented in Greek, were more frequent than performances in the vernacular, p. 319. T3.1.8–16.

54. V8.1.24; V8.1.30.

55. A4.3.13. There is a discussion of this production in Eugen Wagner, *Zur Geschichte des Strassburger Schultheater von 1598 bis 1620*, mss. copy (1935) in the possession of the Strasbourg Archives Municipale, IX.

56. A4.3.13. Euripides, *Medea*, fol. Biiii ff.

57. Ibid., blank page preceding act 4.

58. Sitzmann, *Dictionnaire de biographie*, vol. 2, p. 945. These were not published in Strasbourg.

59. Ibid., p. 1011. B4.1.17; B4.1.19.

60. Edith Weber, *La musique mesurée à l'antique en Allemagne*, part 1, pp. 531, 781.

61. Schindling, *Humanistische Hochschule*, p. 247.

62. "Avis de Michel Beuther," in Fournier and Engel, *Gymnase, Académie et Université*, p. 123.

63. S5.3.2a–b; S4.6.1; S7.1.14.

64. Fournier and Engel, *Gymnase, Académie et Université*, p. 123.

65. Schindling, *Humanistische Hochschule*, p. 248.

66. Ibid.

67. S5.3.5a–b.
68. Schindling, *Humanistische Hochschule*, p. 249.
69. S5.5.6–9; S5.5.11–12.
70. AMS, V, 14, 188; 1570. Proclamation Maximilian II.
71. S5.8.1a–b; S5.8.3.
72. S5.8.3. Dasypodius, *Institutionum mathematicarum*.
73. S5.8.2.
74. Schindling, *Humanistische Hochschule*, p. 258.
75. S5.8.3. Dasypodius, *Institutionum mathematicarum*, pp. 222–23.
76. Ibid., p. 124.
77. Ibid., pp. 144–46.
78. S4.2.7; see Schindling, *Humanistische Hochschule*, p. 259.
79. S4.4.8. Dasypodius, *De Cometis*, fols. ci ff, Div ff.
80. M. Adam, *Vitae Germanorum*, vol. 2, p. 404.
81. Ficker and Winckelmann, *Handschriftenproben*, vol. 2, p. 95.
82. Sitzmann, *Dictionnaire de biographie*, vol. 2, p. 766.
83. Schindling, *Humanistische Hochschule*, pp. 328–30.
84. S1.15.1–24.
85. S1.2.8. Spach, *Gynaeciorum*.
86. Kohls, *Die Schule bei Martin Bucer*, p. 59.
87. Schindling, *Humanistische Hochschule*, pp. 297–311.
88. L1.2.22–30; L1.8.1–24.
89. Schindling, *Humanistische Hochschule*, p. 386.
90. Ibid., pp. 394–97.

CHAPTER THIRTEEN

1. Jane Abray, in chapter 8 of her thesis, "The Long Reformation," indicates that very few laymen put their religious beliefs in writing, and when they did they were vague. Thus, Daniel Sudermann, who was attached to the cathedral canons, wrote, "First I was a Catholic, . . . but soon I went to the Calvinist school. I attended Lutheran services as well. Heard the Anabaptists. In 1594 I came to understand the truth." The truth for him was the teachings of Caspar Schwenckfeld (pp. 271–272). The Catholic magistrate Adolf Braun wrote in the official record that he "subscribed to the Old and New Testaments, and to the Apostles', Nicean, and Athanasian creeds. He believed he was saved by the unique sacrifice of Jesus Christ, the son of God and man. And of the sacraments he believed what scripture tells us" (p. 286). The Protestant Wolfgang Schütterlin, in a speech, stated that "he learned his catechism in the Saint Lawrence chapel [from Matthias Zell]. He was neither Zwinglian, Calvinist, nor Lutheran, for he followed Christ who saved him. He believed in the teachings of the Christian faith, simple and unbeclouded. He believed that God created him, Christ saved him, and that the Holy Ghost leads us to the truth. As for the sacraments, he believed what every Christian can and should believe from God's word" (p. 286). It is important to note that these men, as members of the Magistrat, were among the wealthiest, best educated, and most articulate citizens.
2. Gerald Strauss, "Success and Failure in the Lutheran Reformation," p. 56.

3. P6.3.6; P6.3.22; P6.3.29; P6.3.33.

4. Two different kinds of journalistic accounts were present in the Strasbourg repertoire. Note that the term newspaper or *Zeitung* cannot be used because in modern scholarly usage it means a paper published regularly and sequentially. *Zeitung* of this sort did not appear in Germany until after 1606. The newssheets of the sixteenth century covered a single event and were rarely sequential, although we do have one set of five accounts, published over several weeks, describing the siege of Vienna. One set of newssheets were called, in the language of the time, *Wunderzeichen,* literally miraculous signs. These covered accounts of natural disasters, such as storms, comets, amazing appearances in the heavens, floods, earthquakes, and terrible human events such as murders, suicides, and robberies. The other type of newssheet provided factual accounts of recent political or religious events. One can think of one group as the *National Enquirer,* the other as the *New York Times.* Even the make-up of the sheets reflects these differences.

The *Wunderzeichen* were usually printed on one folio sheet with an illustration that took up about half the page. The picture was in color and the woodcut or copper engraving was often done by a major artist. The accounts of recent events or *Zeitung* were usually octavo in size, although the number of sheets used depended on the length of the account. These were rarely illustrated and, if they were, the woodcut never occupied a whole page.

The greatest number of newssheets appear in the decades from 1560 to 1580. This is, in part, due to the efforts of Johann Jacob Wick, a Protestant preacher and canon of Zürich, who preserved a collection of newssheets from these years. Wick, deeply moved by the religious and political divisions of his time, began in about 1560 to collect materials supporting his belief that the end of the world was at hand. What he gathered, with the help of his friends and correspondents, was a compendium of catastrophe—war, murders, heavenly signs, earthquakes, floods, human violence. Since the entire collection of newssheets runs to over five hundred items, they provide a valid sample, and the modern reader can balance the catastrophic events with the sober news accounts which are also included in the collection. While a few newssheets from the Strasbourg presses are in the Strasbourg libraries, the largest number extant are in the Wick collection.

The Wick collection is housed in the Zentralbibliothek, Zürich. The folders containing Wick's own notes and the octavo-size newssheets which he included with them are available in the Manuscript Room. The illustrated newssheets are in the Graphics Collection. The first modern study of the illustrated broadsheets was done by Marlies Stäheli, who divided the accounts into eighteen different subject matter groups and catalogued them using the code PAS II followed by the number of the file and the number of the broadsheet in that file: for example, 12/3. Insofar as possible I have given these numbers in my own citations since the Ritter numbers do not apply to the Zürich collection. Essentially the collection is a mine of information on everyday, sixteenth-century life, and is especially useful to anyone studying popular printing in Nuremberg, Augsburg, or other cities. For further information about Wick and a sample of some of the materials, see Bruno Weber, *Wunderzeichen und Winkeldrucker, 1543–1586,* and Matthias Senn, *Johann Jakob Wick (1522–1588) und seine Sammlung von Nachrichten zur Zeitgeschichte.*

5. V10.6.11. *Wundergesicht am Himmel . . . auf den Schwartzwald* (PAS II 12/73).

6. *Ein erschrockliches Wunderzeichen zu Dinckelspühel geschehen,* 1554; this was probably printed in Strasbourg. No printer is listed.

7. V10.9.2. *Warhafftige beschriebung was auff einen Cometen. . .* (PAS II 2/15).

8. V10.9.1. *Verzeichnuss des Cometen . . . 1556* (PAS II 12/52).

9. V10.5.3. *Abbildung des wunderbaren . . . Weitzenstocks* (PAS II 12/69).

10. V10.5.5. *Zwey seltzam Wundergewechs* (PAS II 4/10).

11. V10.3.4. *Beschreibung einer Wundergeburt* (PAS II 617; 616). In another account of the same event, the mother is portrayed as quite cheerful and happy.

12. P6.3.28; P6.3.36; P6.3.10; P6.3.24; P6.3.45; P6.3.49.

13. P6.3.14; P6.3.32; P6.3.54.

14. P6.3.33.

15. Martin Luther, *Betbüchlein,* in *Luther's Works,* vol. 43, ed. J. Pelikan and H. Lehman, p. 12.

16. Ibid., pp. 13–23.

17. Ibid., pp. 24–29.

18. Ibid., pp. 29–38.

19. *Johannes Hus,* no printer, n.d. (PAS II 13/20).

20. V10.8.7. Fischart, *Eigentliche Conterfahtung . . . Bullingers* (PAS II 12/11).

21. V10.1.3. *Ein schöner spruch von zweyen Junckfrawen . . . in Delden* (PAS II 1/2).

22. AMS, *Bürgerbuch,* III, 1559–1730, 19; 27 April 1560.

23. Pierre Besson, *Etude sur Jean Fischart,* p. 290.

24. V10.14.3. *Malchopapo.* Pierre Besson attributed this and the following broadsheet to Fischart, an attribution which has been accepted. See Besson, *Etude sur Jean Fischart,* p. 208.

25. V10.14.1. *Gorgonkopf* (PAS II 13/8).

26. V10.14.4. *Von Römischen Abgotsdienst* (PAS II 14/10).

27. Besson, *Etude sur Jean Fischart,* p. 191.

28. P3.16.7. *Beschriebung . . . des abgeführten, quartirten . . . Viereckechten Hütleins.*

29. V11.3.1a. *Newe, unchristliche Spannisch Zeitung,* 1568, fol. aii^v.

30. Ibid., fol. aiii.

31. V11.3.2. *Zeitung aus den Niederlanden,* fols. aii–aiii.

32. Ibid., fol. aiii.

33. Ibid., fol. aiii^v.

34. V11.4.6. *Bericht von der unerhörten . . . Mordery zu Paris.*

35. One of the first attempts at censorship was initiated against Martin Flach in 1515/16 for publishing obscene songs (*Annales Sebastian Brant*). The Ratsprotokolle of 7 Sept. 1545 and 14 Sept. 1545 are concerned by the appearance of a new song, AMS, Ratsprotokolle, 1545, 358^v, 371^v.

36. V7.1.19–28.

37. V7.1.31; V7.1.34; V7.1.39; V7.1.59; V7.1.62; V7.1.72–77.

38. V7.1.73; V7.1.77.

39. V7.1.73. *Lied von der Lothringischen Bezalung,* fols. ai^v–aii^v.

40. V7.1.77. *Lied von dem Elsazsischen Krieg,* fol. aii.

41. A5.2.13a–g.

42. A5.2.14a–g; A5.2.15a–h.

43. See section V9.2.
44. V9.3.7g–m.
45. V9.3.10; V9.3.12; V9.3.15; V9.3.11; V9.3.13.
46. *NDB*, 8, p. 719.
47. V9.3.14. Hertzog, *Chronicon alsatiae*, passim.
48. S6.5.10. Rösslin, *Der Elsasz . . .* , title page.
49. Ibid., a–bvi^v.
50. Ibid., pp. 69–100.
51. Ibid., pp. 111–60.
52. V9.1.25.
53. V9.1.22; V9.1.26 (see translation V9.3.13).
54. V11.2.8–11.
55. V11.2.7. Guevara, *Neuwe Zeitung . . . von Malta*, fols. aii^v–aiii.
56. V11.2.13. *Zeytung ausz Constantinopel*, fols. aii^v–aiii.
57. V10.7.2. *Abzaichnus der fremden Ehrenbegrabnus des . . . Kaisers Selyni.*
58. V10.2.6. *Erschrocklichen Brandt auff der Insel Pyru.*
59. *Warhafftige Beschreibung aines graussamen . . . Wurms*, ca. 1558 (PAS II, 6/3).
60. V10.7.3.
61. *Moscowitterische Bottschafft oder Legation an die Rom: Kays: Mayestat*, M. Petterle, Prague, n.d. (PAS 13/10–13).
62. *Contrafactur: Der Kirchen Ceremonien, so die Moscoviter bey irem Gottesdienst gebrauchen*, M. Petterle, Prague, n.d. (PAS 13/14).
63. Ficker and Winckelmann, *Handschriftenproben*, vol. 2, p. 81.
64. AMS, *Bürgerbuch*, 1563–1614, II, 231. Sitzmann, *Dictionnaire de biographie*, vol. 1, p. 462.
65. AMS, *Bürgerbuch*, 1563–1614, III, 465. Sitzmann, *Dictionnaire de biographie*, vol. 2, p. 597.
66. I am indebted to Steven Nelson for this information.
67. Castiglioni, *History of Medicine*, p. 450.
68. S1.14.8–26.
69. S1.8.9a–c.
70. S16.1.6–13.
71. S12.1.63.
72. S1.7.26b–i.
73. S1.12.15–17.
74. S1.10.10–11.
75. S5.4.13.
76. S8.1.7a–d.
77. S8.1.7. I used the English translation, John Libault and Charles Stevens [sic], *Maison Rustique or the Country Farm*, Adam Islip for John Bull, London, 1616; see book 5, especially pp. 528–29.
78. S11.10.1.
79. S9.1.4–6. Reuschel, *Hippopronia*. See especially S9.1.5a.
80. S10.1.5; S10.1.6.
81. S4.7.3. Dasypodius, *Beschreybung des Astronomischen Urwercks*, fol. aii.
82. Ibid., fol. aii^v.

83. Ibid., fol. b^v.

84. Ibid., fol. biv.

85. Ibid., fol. c.

86. See V8.1.25–36; V8.2.15–20.

87. Vogeleis, *Quellen und Bausteine*, pp. 305–07.

88. Ibid., pp. 308, 323.

89. V7.3.4–13; V7.2.4–7.

90. Vogeleis, *Quellen und Bausteine*, pp. 375, 381–82.

91. Hugo Sommerhalder, "Nachwort," in *Johann Fischart's Geschichtklitterung*, ed. Hugo Sommerhalder, p. 433. See also François Joseph Fuchs, "Jean Fischart," in *Grandes figures de l'humanisme alsacien courants milieux destins*, pp. 109–14.

92. V10.11.4. Fischart, *Das Glückhafft Schiff von Zürich*.

93. Ibid., unpaginated.

94. V6.2.11c. Fischart, *Der Flüh Hatz, Weiber Tratz*.

95. Fischart, *Geschichtklitterung*, title page.

96. Sommerhalder, "Nachwort," in *Geschichtklitterung*, p. 435.

97. François Rabelais, *Les oevvres . . . contenant cinq livres de la vie, faicts et dicts heroiques de Gargantua, et de son Fils Pantagruel*. Lyon: Jean Martin, 1558, p. 71.

98. Fischart, *Geschichtklitterung*, pp. 256–57.

99. Rabelais, *Oevvres*, p. 76; Fischart, *Geschichtklitterung*, p. 269.

100. Fischart, *Geschichtklitterung*, p. 255.

101. Ibid., pp. 417, 421.

CHAPTER FOURTEEN

1. Abray, "The Long Reformation," p. 271.

APPENDIX A

1. Full bibliographical references appear at the beginning of the companion volume, *Bibliography of Strasbourg Imprints, 1480–1599* (New Haven: Yale University Press, 1982).

2. Norman H. Nie, Dale H. Bent, and C. Hadlai Hull, *Statistical Package for the Social Sciences*, 2nd ed. (New York: McGraw-Hill, 1975).

3. Ibid., p. 199.

4. The program for these calculations was developed by Wayne Johnson of the University of Massachusetts Computer Center, using Fortran.

5. SPSS, pp. 219–22.

BIBLIOGRAPHY

PRIMARY SOURCES

The primary sources for the study were the books published in Strasbourg from 1480 to 1599. These are arranged in a separate bibliography which appears as a companion volume to this study, entitled *Bibliography of Strasbourg Imprints, 1480–1599*.

The archival sources of the Archives Municipales de la Ville de Strasbourg were used for biographical data, inventories, and wills.

SECONDARY SOURCES

Abray, Jane. "The Long Reformation: Magistrates, Clergy and People in Strasbourg 1520–1598." Dissertation, Yale University, 1978.

Adam, Johann. *Evangelische Kirchengeschichte der Stadt Strassburg bis zur Französischen Revolution*. Strasbourg: J. H. Ed. Heitz, 1922.

Adam, Melchior. *Vitae Germanorum Jureconsultorum et Politicorum; Vitae Germanorum Medicorum; Vitae Germanorum Superiori et quod excurrit seculo philosophicis et humanioribus literis clarorum*. 3 vols. Frankfurt: N. Hoffman, 1602–15.

Alberti, Leon Battista. *The Family in Renaissance Florence*. Translated by Renée New Watkins with an introduction by the translator. Columbia, S.C.: University of South Carolina Press, 1969.

Allen, Percy Stafford, ed. *Opus epistolarum Des. Erasmi Roterdami*. 12 vols. Oxford: Clarendon Press, 1905–06.

Allgemeine Deutsche Biographie. 56 vols. Berlin: Duncker und Humbolt, 1967–71.

Allgemeines Gelehrten Lexicon. 4 vols. Edited by Christian Gottlieb Jöcher. Leipzig: J. F. Gleditschen, 1750. New edition edited by Johann Christoph Adelung. A–R. Hildesheim: Georg Olm, 1960–61.

Andreas, Willy. *Strassburg an der Wende vom Mittelalter zur Neuzeit*. Leipzig: Köhler und Amelang, 1940.

Apel, Karl Otto. "Die Idee der Sprache in der Tradition des Humanismus von Dante bis Vico." *Archiv für Begriffsgeschichte* 8 (1963): 1–397.

Ariès, Philippe. *Centuries of Childhood: A Social History of Family Life*. Translated by Robert Baldick. New York: Alfred A. Knopf, 1962.

Aristotle. *De generatione animalum*. Translated and edited by T. A. Smith and W. D. Ross. Works, vol. 5. Oxford: Clarendon Press, 1949.

Artisans et ouvriers d'Alsace. Publications de la Société savante d'Alsace et des Régions de l'Est, vol. 9. Strasbourg: Librairie Istra, 1965.

Association Guillaume Budé, ed., *L'humanisme en Alsace*. Congrès de Strasbourg, 20–22 avril, 1937. Paris: Société d'édition "Les Belles-Lettres," 1939.

Baillet, Lina. "Aspects et richesses de l'humanisme à Colmar et en Haute-Alsace." In *Grandes figures de l'humanisme alsacien courants milieux destins*. Société savante d'Alsace et des Régions de l'Est, 14 (1978): 63–108.

_____. "Recherches sur la bibliothèque des Seigneurs de Ribeaupierre: La bibliothèque du premier pasteur protestant de Ribeauvillé." *Bulletin de la société d'histoire et d'archéologie de Ribeauvillé* 23 (1961): 51–63.

_____. "Recherches sur la bibliothèque des Seigneurs de Ribeaupierre: La catalogue de la bibliothèque de Ribeaupierre selon Charles Bartholdi." *Bulletin de la société d'histoire et d'archéologie de Ribeauvillé* 22 (1959–60): 9–15.

Bainton, Roland. *Women of the Reformation in Germany and Italy.* Minneapolis: Augsburg Publishing House, 1971.

Bartholdi, Charles. "Catalogue de la bibliothèque des Seigneurs de Ribeaupierre au seizième siècle." *Curiosités d'Alsace* (1861–62): 36–51.

Baudrier, Henri. *Bibliographie lyonnaise, recherches sur les imprimeurs, libraires, relieurs, et fondeurs de lettres de Lyon au XVIᵐᵉ siècle.* 12 vols. Published and continued by J. Baudrier. Lyons: Brun, 1895–1921. Tables by George Tricou. Genève: Droz, 1950.

Baum, Adolf. *Magistrat und Reformation in Strassburg bis 1529.* Strasbourg: J. H. Ed. Heitz, 1887.

Becker, Oskar. *Grundlagen der Mathematik in geschichtlicher Entwicklung.* Freiburg: K. Alber, 1954.

Bellardi, Werner. *Die Geschichte der "Christlichen Gemeinschaft" in Strassburg (1546–1550).* Quellen und Forschungen zur Reformationsgeschichte 18. Leipzig: M. Heinsius Nachfolger, 1934.

Benzing, Josef. *Die Buchdrucker des 16. und 17. Jahrhunderts im Deutschen Sprachgebiet.* Beiträge zum Buch- und Bibliothekswesen, vol. 12. Edited by Walter Bauhuis. Wiesbaden: Otto Harrassowitz, 1963.

_____. "Christian Egenolff zu Strassburg und seine Drucke (1528 bis 1530)." *Das Antiquariat* 9 Jahrgang 8 (April 1954): 88–92.

_____. *Die Drucke Jacob Cammerlanders zu Strassburg 1531–1548.* Vienna: Walter Krieg Verlag, 1963.

_____. "Die Druckerei der Matthias Schürer Erben zu Strassburg (1520–1525)." *Archiv für Geschichte des Buchwesens* 2 (1960): 170–74.

_____. *Jörg Wickram, Die Zehn Alter der Welt.* Facsimile of the original edition of Jakob Frölich with a postscript by Josef Benzing. Wiesbaden: Guido Pressler, 1961.

_____. *Lutherbibliographie; Verzeichnis der gedruckten Schriften Martin Luthers bis zu dessen Tod.* Baden-Baden: Heitz, 1965–66.

_____. "Zum Leben und Werk des Strassburger Druckers Jakob Cammerlander." In *Festschrift für Claus Nissen.* Wiesbaden: Guido Pressler, 1963.

_____. "Die Presse der Kartäuser zu Strassburg (1518–1533)." *Stultifera Navis* 14 (1957): 112–16.

_____. "Die Reformationspresse der Mathius Schürer Erben in Strassburg (1520–1525)." In *Refugium animae bibliotheca, Festschrift für Albert Kolb.* Wiesbaden: Guido Pressler, 1969.

_____. *Ulrich von Hutten und seine Drucker; eine Bibliographie der Schriften Huttens im 16. Jahrhundert.* Wiesbaden: O. Harrassowitz, 1956.

_____. *Walther H. Ryff und sein literarisches Werk, Eine Bibliographie.* Hamburg: Dr. Ernst Hauswedell, 1959.

Bergwerk und Probierbüchlein. Translated and edited by Anneliese Grünhaldt Sisco and Cyril Stanley Smith. The Seeley W. Mudd Series. New York: American Institute of Mining and Metallurgical Engineers, 1949.

Bernays, J. "Zur Biographie Johann Winthers von Andernach." *Zeitschrift für die Geschichte des Oberrheins.* N. F., 16 (1901): 28–59.

Besson, Pierre. *Etude sur Jean Fischart.* Paris: Librairie Hachette, 1889.

Bettman, Otto. "Frauen im Buchgewerbe." *Archiv für Buchgewerbe und Gebrauchsgraphik* 68 (1931): 65–71.

Besterman, Theodore. *Early Printed Books to the end of the Sixteenth Century.* 2nd ed. Genève: Librairie Droz, 1961.

Biblia Pauperum. Facsimile edition of the forty-page block-printed Bible for the poor. Hanau, Main: Werner Dausein, 1967.

Bietenholz, Peter G. *Basle and France in the Sixteenth Century: The Basle Humanists and Printers in their Contacts with Francophone Culture.* Toronto: Univ. of Toronto Press, 1971. Genève: Librairie Droz, 1971.

Biographie Universelle. Edited by J. F. Michaud. Paris, 1968 edition.

Biographisches Lexikon der hervorragenden Ärtze aller Zeiten und Völker. 6 vols. Edited by E. Gurlt, A. Wernich and A. Hirsch. Berlin: Urban und Schwarzenberg, 1929–34.

Bittel, Karl. "Die elsässer Zeit des Paracelsus, Hohenheims Wirken in Strassburg und Kolmar, sowie sein Beziehungen zu Lorenz Fries." *Elsass-Lothringisches Jahrbuch* 21 (1943): 157–86.

Blench, J. W. *Preaching in England in the late Fifteenth and Sixteenth Centuries.* New York: Barnes and Noble, Inc., 1964.

Blumhof, J. G. L. *Vom alten Mathematiker Conrad Dasypodius.* Göttingen, J. C. D. Schneider, 1796.

Boas, George. "Philosophies of Science in Florentine Platonism." In *Art, Science and History in the Renaissance.* Edited by Charles S. Singleton. Baltimore: The Johns Hopkins Press, 1967.

Boas, Marie. *The Scientific Renaissance, 1450–1630.* New York: Harper and Row, 1962.

Bochner, Salomon. *The Role of Mathematics in the Rise of Science.* Princeton: Princeton University Press, 1966.

Bogeng, Gustav A. E., et al. *Geschichte der Buchdruckerkunst.* 2 vols. Dresden, 1930–41.

Bopp, Marie-Joseph. *Die Evangelischen, Geistlichen, und Theologen in Elsass und Lothringen.* 3 vols. Neustadt a. d. Aisch: Degener und Co., 1959.

Bornert, René. *La réforme protestante du culte à Strasbourg au XVIᵉ siècle (1523–1598).* Leiden: E. J. Brill, 1981.

Bosse, Friedrich. *Illustriertes Wörterbuch der Gebräuchlichsten Kunst. Ausdrücke aus dem Gebiete der Architektur, Chromatik, Malerei . . . für den Buchdruck und verwandte Zwiege.* Leipzig: A. Waldow, 1884.

La bourgeoisie alsacienne, études d'histoire sociale. Publications de la Société savante d'Alsace et des Régions de l'Est, 5. Strasbourg: Librairie Istra, 1967.

Bouwsma, William J. "The Two Faces of Humanism." In *Itinerarium Italicum,* pp.

1–60. Festschrift for P. O. Kristeller. Edited by Heiko Obermann and Thomas A. Brady, Jr. Leiden: E. J. Brill, 1975.

Boyer, Carl. *A History of Mathematics.* New York: Wiley and Co., 1968.

Brady, Thomas A., Jr. *Ruling Class, Regime and Reformation in Strasbourg, 1520–1555.* Leiden: E. J. Brill, 1978.

Brant, Sebastian. *The Ship of Fools.* English translation by Edwin Zeydel. New York: Columbia University Press, 1944.

Braudel, Fernand. *Capitalism and Material Life, 1400–1800.* Translated by Miriam Kochan. New York: Harper and Row, 1973.

Braun, Lucien. "Paracelse (1493–1541), un anti-humaniste parmi les humanistes." *Grandes figures de l'humanisme alsacien courants milieux destins,* pp. 227–36. Strasbourg: Librairie Istra, 1978.

Brinkmann, Hennig. *Anfänge des modernen dramas in Deutschland: Versuch über die beziehungen zwischen Drama und Bürgertum im 16. Jahrhundert.* Jena: Verlag der Frommannschen Buchhandlung (Walter Biedermann), 1933.

British Museum. *Short-title Catalogue of Books Printed in the German-speaking Countries and German Books Printed in other Countries from 1455–1600 now in the British Museum.* London: Trustees of the British Museum, 1962.

Bucer, Martin. *Correspondance.* Tome I (jusqu'en 1524). Edited by Jean Rott. Leiden: E. J. Brill, 1979.

_____ *Martin Bucers Deutsche Schriften.* 7 vols. Edited by Robert Stupperich. Gütersloh: Gerd Mohn, 1960–78.

Burgun, René. "La syphilis à Strasbourg au XVme et XVIme siècles." Part 1. *Etudes Alsaciennes,* pp. 63–97. Publications de la Société savante d'Alsace et des Régions de l'Est. Strasbourg-Paris: F-X le Roux, 1947.

_____. "La syphilis à Strasbourg au XVme et XVIme siècles." In "Strasbourg, sa contribution à l'histoire de la médecine," parts 2, 3, 4. *Journal Médicale de Strasbourg* 4 (1973): 237–51; 5 (1973): 53–64; 5 (1973): 717–27.

Burmeister, K. H. *Achilles Pirmin Gasser.* 2 vols. Wiesbaden: Guido Pressler Verlag, 1970.

Cantor, Moritz. *Vorlesungen über die Geschichte der Mathematik.* 3 vols. Leipzig: B. G. Teubner, 1892.

Castiglioni, Arturo. *A History of Medicine.* Translated by E. B. Krumbhaar. New York: Alfred A. Knopf, 1941.

Chrisman, Miriam Usher. "La pensée et la main: Mathias Schürer humaniste-imprimeur." *Grandes figures de l'humanisme alsacien courants milieux destins,* pp. 59–72. Publications de la Société savante d'Alsace et des Régions de l'Est, 14. 1978.

_____. *Strasbourg and the Reform.* New Haven: Yale University Press, 1967.

Cicero. *De Inventione.* English translation by H. M. Hubbell. Loeb Classical Library. Cambridge: Harvard University Press, 1968.

_____. *Philippics.* English translation by Walter C. A. Kee. Loeb Classical Library. Cambridge: Harvard University Press, 1926.

Claudin, Anatole. *Histoire de l'imprimerie en France au XVme et XVIme siècle.* 5 vols. Paris: Imprimerie Nationale, 1900–15.

Crämer, Ulrich. *Die Verfassung und Verwaltung Strassburgs von der Reformationszeit bis zum Fall der Reichsstadt, 1521–1681.* Schriften des Wissenschaftlichen Instituts der Elsass-Lothringer im Reich an der Universität Frankfurt, neue Folge, 3. Frankfurt a. M.: Selbstverlag des Elsass-Lothringen-Instituts, 1931.

Crosby, Alfred W., Jr. *The Columbian Exchange: Biological and Cultural Consequences of 1492.* Contributions in American Studies, 2. Westport, Conn.: Greenwood Publishing Co., 1972.

Cruel, Rudolf. *Geschichte der Deutschen Predigt im Mittelalter.* Hildesheim: Georg Olms, 1966 [Nachdruck der Ausgabe Detmold, 1879].

Crüger, Johannes. "Zur Strassburger Schulkomödie." In *Festschrift zur Feier des 350 Jahrigen Bestehens des Protestantinischen Gymnasiums zu Strassburg.* 2 vols. Strasbourg: J. H. Ed. Heitz, 1888.

Dacheux, Léon. *Un réformateur catholique à la fin du XVᵉ siècle, Jean Geiler.* Paris: C. Delagrave, 1876.

Dargan, Edwin Charles. *A History of Preaching.* 2 vols. London: Hodder and Stoughton; New York: G. H. Doran, 1905–12.

Davis, Natalie Zemon. "Sixteenth-Century French Arithmetics on the Business Life." *Journal of the History of Ideas* 21 (1961): 18–48.

_____. "Women in the *Arts Mécaniques,*" in *Lyon et l'Europe: hommes et sociétés.* Mélanges d'histoire offerts à Richart Gascon. Lyon: Presses Universitaires de Lyon, 1980.

_____. *Society and Culture in Early Modern France.* Stanford: Stanford University Press, 1975.

Debus, Allen G. *The Chemical Philosophy, Paracelsian Science and Medicine in the Sixteenth and Seventeenth Centuries.* 2 vols. New York: Science History Publications, 1977.

Deppermann, Klaus. *Melchior Hoffman. Soziale Unruhen und apokalyptische Visionen im Zeitalter der Reformation.* Göttingen: Vandenhoeck und Ruprecht, 1979.

_____. "Melchior Hoffman à Strasbourg." *Strasbourg au coeur religieux du XVIᵉ siècle,* pp. 501–10. Strasbourg: Librairie Istra, 1977.

Desgraves, Louis. *Les livres imprimés à Bordeaux au XVIIᵐᵉ siècle.* Genève: Droz, 1971.

Dibdin, Thomas Frognall. *An Introduction to the Knowledge of Rare and Valuable Editions of the Greek and Latin Classics, including the Scriptores de Re Rustica, Greek Romances and Lexicons and Grammars.* 2nd ed. London: W. Dwyer, 1804.

Die Deutschen Dichtungen von Salomon und Markolff. Edited by Friedrich Vogt. Halle: Max Niemeyer, 1880.

Dollinger, Philippe, ed. *Histoire de l'Alsace.* Univers de la France, Collections d'histoire régionale. Toulouse: Edouard Privat, 1970.

_____. "L'apogée médiéval," in *Histoire de l'Alsace.* Toulouse: Edouard Privat, 1970.

_____. "Le sens social dans *La Nef des Fous* de Sebastian Brant." *Grandes figures de l'humanisme alsacien courants milieux destins,* pp. 13–22. Strasbourg: Librairie Istra, 1978.

Donnelly, John Patrick. *Calvinism and Scholasticism in Vermigli's Doctrine of Man and Grace.* Leiden: E. J. Brill, 1976.

Doucet, Roger. *Les bibliothèques parisiennes au XVIᵉ siècle.* Paris: A. et J. Picard, 1956.

Douglass, E. Jane Dempsey. *Justification in Late Medieval Preaching: A Study of John Geiler of Keisersberg.* Studies in Medieval and Reformation Thought 1. Leiden: E. J. Brill, 1966.

Drake, Stillman and Drabkin, I. E., trans. and ed. *Mechanics in Sixteenth-Century Italy.* Selections from Tartuglia, Benedetti, Guido Ubaldo and Galileo. Madison: University of Wisconsin Press, 1969.

Droz, Elizabeth and Desgraves, Louis. *L'imprimerie à La Rochelle.* 3 vols. Geneva: Droz, 1960.

Droz, Eugénie, ed. *Chemins de l'hérésie, textes et documents.* Geneva: Slatkine Reprints, 1970–76.

Eis, Gerhard. *Forschungen zur Fachprosa: ausgewählte Beiträge.* Bern/Munich: Francke, 1971.

Eisenstein, Elizabeth L. "The Advent of Printing and the Problem of the Renaissance." *Past and Present* 45 (November 1969): 19–89.

———. "L'avenement de l'imprimerie et la Réforme." *Annales* 26 (1971): 1355–82.

———. *The Printing Press as an Agent of Change: Communications and Cultural Transformations in Early-modern Europe.* 2 vols. Cambridge: Cambridge University Press, 1979.

———. "Some Conjectures about the Impact of Printing on Western Society and Thought: A Preliminary Report." *Journal of Modern History* 40 (1968): 1–56.

Ellinger, G. *Geschichte der neulateinischen Literatur Deutschlands im 16ten Jahrhundert.* 3 vols. Berlin u. Leipzig: W. de Gruyter, Co., 1929–33.

Engel, Charles. *L'école latine et l'ancienne Académie de Strasbourg, 1538–1621.* Paris: Librairie Fischbacher, 1900.

Engelsing, Rolf. *Analphabetentum und Lektüre.* Stuttgart: J. B. Metzlersche Verhandlung, 1973.

———. *Der Bürger als Leser.* Stuttgart: J. B. Metzlersche Verlagsbuchhandlung, 1974.

Erasme, L'Alsace et son temps. Catalogue of the exposition at the Bibliothèque nationale et universitaire de Strasbourg, November 1970. Publications de la Société savante d'Alsace et des Régions de l'Est, Strasbourg. Collections "Recherches et Documents" 8 (1970).

Erasmus, Desiderius. *The Correspondence of Erasmus,* vols. 1–4. Collected Works of Erasmus. Translated by R. A. B. Mynois and D. F. S. Thomson. Toronto: University of Toronto Press, 1974.

Ercker, Lazarus. *Treatise on Ores and Assaying.* Translated and annotated by Annaliese G. Sisco and Cyril Stanley Smith. Chicago: University of Chicago Press, 1951.

Etudes alsaciennes. Publications de la Société savante d'Alsace et des Régions de l'Est, 1. Strasbourg-Paris: F. X. le Roux, 1947.

Fauth, Gertrud. *Jörg Wickrams Romane.* Einzelschrifte zur Elsässischen Geistesund Kulturgeschichte, 2. Strasbourg: Karl J. Trübner, 1916.

Febvre, Lucien. *A New Kind of History.* Edited by Peter Burke, translated by K. Folca. New York: Harper and Row, 1973.

Febvre, Lucien, and Martin, Henri-Jean. *The Coming of the Book: The Impact of Printing, 1450–1800.* Translated by David Gerard. London: NLB, 1976.

_____ *L'apparition du Livre*. Paris: A. Michel, 1958.

Fehr, Hans. *Massenkunst im 16. Jahrhundert*. Flugblätter aus der Sammlung Wickiana. Berlin: Herbert Stubenrauch, 1924.

Das Feuerwerkbuch von 1420. Ed. and trans. by Wilhelm Hassenstein. New edition from first edition of 1529. Munich: Verlag der Deutschen Technik GMBH, 1941.

Ficker, Johannes, and Winckelmann, Otto. *Handschriftenproben des sechzehnten Jahrhunderts nach Strassburger Originalen*. 2 vols. Strasbourg: Karl J. Trübner, 1905.

Fischart, Johann. *Geschichtklitterung*. With a postscript by Hugo Sommerhalder. Düsseldorf: Karl Rauch Verlag, 1963.

Fischer, Charles. *Ein beitrag zur Geschichte der Astronomie im Elsass*. Strasbourg: Dactylographié, 1975. Copy of Dr. Jean Rott.

Fleisher, Manfred. "The Institutionalization of Humanism in Protestant Silesia." *Archive for Reformation History* 66 (1975): 256–74.

Forbes, R. J. *Short History of the Art of Distillation*. Leiden: E. J. Brill, 1948.

Fournier, Marcel, and Engel, Charles. *Gymnase, Académie et Université de Strasbourg, première partie: 1525–1621*. Paris: L. Larose; Strasbourg: E. d'Oleire, 1894.

The Frankfort Book Fair, the Francofordiense Emporium of Henri Estienne. Edited with historical introduction by James Westfall Thompson. Chicago, 1911.

Fuchs, François-Joseph. "Une association d'imprimeurs-libraires à Strasbourg au XVIᵐᵉ siècle: Samuel Emmel, Christophe Riedlinger, Jacques Froschesser." In *Festschrift für Kurt Köster*. Frankfurt-am-Main: Klostermann, 1977.

_____. "Le droit de bourgeoisie à Strasbourg." *Revue d'Alsace* 101 (1962): 19–50.

_____. "L'immigration artisanale à Strasbourg de 1544 à 1565." In *Artisans et ouvriers d'Alsace*, pp. 185–97. Strasbourg: Librairie Istra, 1965.

_____. "Jean Fischart (1546/47–1590/91), auteur du Gargantua, chantre du peuple et de la cité." *Grandes figures de l'humanisme alsacien courants milieux destins*, pp. 109–14. Strasbourg: Librairie Istra, 1978.

Fuchs, François-Joseph, and Rott, Jean. *Humanisme et réforme à Strasbourg*. Exposition organized by the Archives, the Library and the Museums of the city of Strasbourg, 5 May–10 June, 1973.

Ganoczy, Alexandre. *La bibliothéque de l'Académie de Calvin*. Geneva: Droz, 1969.

Garrett, Christina. "The Resurrection of the Masse by Hugh Hilarie or John Bale." *The Library* (London), 4th series, 21 (1941): 143–59.

Garside, Charles, Jr. "The Origins of Calvin's Theology of Music: 1536–1543." *Transactions of the American Philosophical Society* 69 (1979): 5–35.

Genschmer, Fred. *The Treatment of the Social Classes in the Satires of Brant, Murner and Fischart*. An abstract of a thesis in the Graduate School of the University of Illinois. Urbana: University of Illinois Press, 1934.

Gesta Romanorum. Translated by Charles Swan, edited by Wynnard Hooper. London: George Bell and Sons, 1906.

Gilbert, William. "Sebastian Brant: Conservative Humanist." *Archiv für Reformationsgeschichte* 46 (1955): 145–67.

Goedeke, Karl. *Deutsche Dichter des XVI jahrhundert*. Leipzig: F. A. Brockhaus, 1865–68.

_____. *Grundrisz zur Geschichte der Deutschen Dichtung.* 3 vols. Dresden: L. S. Ehlermann, 1884–86.

Goldschmidt, Ernest P. *The Printed Book of the Renaissance.* Cambridge: Cambridge University Press, 1950.

_____. *Medieval Texts and Their First Appearance in Print.* Bibliographical Society, London, Supplement to the Transactions 16 (1943).

Grandes figures de l'humanisme alsacien courants milieux destins. Publications de la Société savante d'Alsace et des Régions de l'Est, 14. Strasbourg: Librairie Istra, 1978.

Gurlt, Ernst Julius. *Geschichte der Chirurgie und ihrer Ausübung; Volkschirurgie; Altherthum; Mittelalter; Renaissance.* 3 vols. Berlin: A. Hirschwald, 1898.

Haffen, Louis. "Johann Fischart, humanist alsacien, Rabelais de l'Allemagne." *Europe,* 2nd series, 31² (December, 1953): 159–66.

Hampe, Theodor, ed. *Gedichte vom Hausrat aus dem XV und XVI Jahrhundert.* Printed work and woodcuts of the fifteenth and sixteenth centuries after the originals. Strasbourg: J. H. Ed. Heitz, 1899.

Haeser, Heinrich. *Grundriss der Geschichte der Medicin.* Jena: G. Fischer, 1887.

Hassencamp, F. W. *Franciscus Lambert von Avignon.* Leben und ausgewählte Schriften der Väter und Begründer der Reformierten Kirche. Elberfeld: R. L. Friderichs, 1860.

Hatt, Jacques. *Liste des membres du Grand Sénat de Strasbourg.* Strasbourg: no printer, 1963.

Hauffen, Adolf. *Johann Fischart, ein Literaturbild aus der Zeit der Gegenreformation.* 2 vols. Berlin and Leipzig: Walter de Gruyter & Co., 1921.

_____. "Über die Bibliothek Johann Fischarts." *Zeitschrift für Bücherfreunde* 2 (1899), Band 1:21–32.

Heiberg, J. L. *Beiträge zur Geschichte Georg Vallas und seiner Bibliothek.* Leipzig: Otto Harrassowitz, 1896.

Heitz, Paul. *Basler Büchermarken bis zum Anfang des 17. Jahrhunderts.* Strasbourg: J. H. Ed. Heitz, 1895.

_____. *Frankfurter und Mainzer Drucker und Verlegerzeichen bis in das 17. Jahrhundert.* Strasbourg: J. H. Ed. Heitz, 1896.

_____. *Die Kölner Büchermarken bis Anfang des XVII Jahrhunderts.* Strasbourg: J. H. Ed. Heitz, 1898.

_____, ed. *Strassburger Holzschnitte zu Dietrich von Bern, Herzog Ernst, Der Hürnen Seyfrid, Marcolphus.* Strasbourg: J. H. Ed. Heitz, 1922.

Heitz, Paul, and Ritter, François. *Versuch einer Zusammenstellung der deutschen Volksbücher der XV und XVI Jahrhunderts.* Strasbourg: J. H. Ed. Heitz, 1924.

Herding, Otto. "Der elsässische Humanist Jacob Wimpheling und seine Erziehungsschrift Adolescentia." *Zeitschrift für Württemburgische Landesgeschichte* (1963): 1–18.

Hermelink, Heinrich. *Die religiösen Reformbestrebungen des deutschen Humanismus.* Tübingen: J. C. B. Mohr (P. Siebeck), 1907.

Himly, François J. "L'activité intellectuelle en Alsace au moyen age, répertoire des auteurs." *Revue d'Alsace* 96 (1957): 46–52.

_____. *Atlas des villes médiévales d'Alsace.* Publications de la Fédération des societés d'histoire et d'archéologie d'Alsace, 6. Strasbourg: Fédération des societés d'histoire et d'archéologie d'Alsace, 1970.

Hind, Arthur M. *An Introduction to a History of the Woodcut.* 2 vols. New York: Dover Publications, 1963.

Hirsch, August, ed. *Biographisches Lexikon der hervorragenden Ärtzte aller Zeiter und Völker.* 2nd ed., 5 vols. Berlin/Vienna: Urban und Schwarzenberg, 1929–34.

Hirsch, Elisabeth Feist. "The Discoveries and the Humanists." In *Merchants and Scholars,* pp. 35–46. Essays in the History of Exploration and Trade, collected in memory of James Ford Bell. Edited by John Parker. Minneapolis: University of Minnesota Press, 1965.

Hirsch, Rudolf. *Preliminary Check-list of Chemical and Alchemical Books Printed 1470–1536.* Philadelphia, 1949.

———. *Printing, Selling and Reading, 1450–1550.* Wiesbaden: Otto Harrassowitz, 1967.

Histoire littéraire de la France. A study begun by the Religious Benedictines of the Congregation of Saint-Maur and continued by members of the Institute. Académie des Inscriptions et Belles-Lettres 37 (1938).

Holborn, Hajo. *History of Modern Germany.* 3 vols. New York: Alfred A. Knopf, 1964.

Hollaender, Alcuin. "Der Theologe Mathias Flacius Illyricus." *Deutsche Zeitschrift für Geschichtswissenschaft* n.f. 2 (1897–98): 203–24.

———. *Strassburg im Schmalkaldischen Kriege.* Strasbourg: K. H. Trübner, 1881.

Honour, Hugh. "America as Seen in the Fanciful Vision of Europe." *Smithsonian* (February 1976): 51–56.

Horizons européens de la réforme en Alsace, edited by Marijn de Kroon and Marc Lienhard. Mélanges offerts à Jean Rott. Strasbourg: Librairie Istra, 1980.

Horning, Wilhelm, ed. *Briefe von Strassburger Reformatoren, ihren Mitarbeitern und Freunden über die Einführung des "Interims" in Strassburg (1548–1554).* Strasbourg: R. Schultz und Co., 1887.

Hüsser, Daniel. "Caspar Schwenckfeld et ses adeptes entre l'église et les sectes à Strasbourg." *Strasbourg au coeur religieux du XVIe siècle,* pp. 511–38. Strasbourg: Librairie Istra, 1977.

Huizinga, Johan. *Erasmus and the Age of Reformation.* Translated by F. Hopman. New York: Harper and Row, 1957.

Jahrbuch für Geschichte, Sprache und Literatur Elsass-Lothringens. Historisch-Litterarischen Zweigverein des Vogesen-Clubs. Strasbourg: J. H. Ed. Heitz, Jahrgang 5, 15, 16, 22, 25 (1885).

Jundt, August. *Die dramatischen Aufführungen im Gymnasium zu Strassburg ein Beitrag zur Geschichte des Schuldramas in XVI. und XVII. Jahrhundert.* In Programm auf das Schuljahr 1881–82. Protestant Gymnasium zu Strassburg. Strasbourg: C. F. Schmidt, 1881. Programme no. 441.

Karpinski, Louis Charles. *The History of Arithmetic.* New York: Rand McNally, 1925.

Keller, Adelbert von, ed. *Fastnachtspiele aus dem fünfzehnten Jahrhundert.* Bibliothek des Literarischen Vereins in Stuttgart, vols. 28–30. Stuttgart: Literarischer Verein, 1853.

Kiessling, Elmer Carl. *The Early Sermons of Luther and their Relation to the Pre-Reformation Sermon*. Grand Rapids, Mich.: Zondervan Publ. House, 1935.

Kintz, Jean-Pierre. "Notes zur quelques aspects démographiques de la ville de Strasbourg," in *Strasbourg au coeur religieux du XVI⁵ siècle*. Strasbourg: Librairie Istra, 1977.

———. "La société strasbourgeoise 1560–1650: Essai d'histoire démographique et sociale." Thèse presentée pour le doctorat ès lettres, l'Université des Sciences Humaines de Strasbourg, 1980.

Kittelson, James M. "Marbach vs. Zanchi, The Resolution of Controversy in Late Reformation Strasbourg." *The Sixteenth Century Journal* vol. 8, no. 3 (1977): 31–47.

———. *Wolfgang Capito, from Humanist to Reformer*. Leiden: E. J. Brill, 1975.

———. "Wolfgang Capito, the Council and Reform Strasbourg." *Archiv für Reformationsgeschichte* 63 (1972): 126–40.

Knepper, Joseph. *Jakob Wimpheling, sein Leben und seine Werke nach den Quellen dargestellt*. Nieuwkoop: De Graaf, 1965.

Knod, Gustav. *Johann Schwenckbecker: Ein Strassburger Ratsherr der Reformationszeit*. Strasbourg: Dumont Schauberg, 1906.

Köhler, Hans-Joachim. "Fragstellen und Methoden zur Interpretation frühneuzeitlicher Flugschriften," in *Flugschriften als Massenmedium der Reformationszeit*, edited by Hans-Joachim Köhler, pp. 1–27. Beiträge zum Tübinger Symposion 1980. Stuttgart: Klett-Cotta, 1981.

Kohls, Ernst-Wilhelm. *Die Schule bei Martin Bucer in ihrem Verhältnis zu Kirche und Obrigkeit*. Pädagogische Forschungen, 22. Heidelberg, 1963.

Kolb, Robert. "Caspar Peucer's Library: Portrait of a Wittemberg Professor of the Sixteenth Century." *Sixteenth Century Bibliography*, 5. St. Louis: Center for Reformation Research, 1976.

Koyré, Alexandre. *Mystiques, spirituels, alchimistes du XVI siécle allemand*. Paris: Gallimard, 1971.

Krebs, Manfred, and Rott, Hans Georg, eds., *Quellen zur Geschichte der Täufer, Elsass*. 2 vols. Gütersloh: Gerd Mohn, 1959.

Kroon, Marijn de, and Krüger, Friedhelm, eds. *Bucer und seine Zeit*. Veröffentlichungen des Instituts für Europäische Geschichte Mainz, 80. Wiesbaden: Franz Steiner Verlag, 1976.

Krüger, Friedhelm. *Bucer und Erasmus*. Wiesbaden: F. Steiner, 1970.

Kunzle, David. *The Early Comic Strip: Narrative Strips and Picture Stories in the European Broadsheet from c. 1450 to 1825*. Berkeley: University of California Press, 1973.

Lang, Madeleine. "Erasme et la pédagogie strasbourgeoise." In *Erasme, l'Alsace et son temps*. Publications de la Société savante d'Alsace et des Régions de l'Est. Collections "Recherches et Documents," 8. Strasbourg: Librairie Istra, 1970.

Lebeau, Jean. "Thiébolt Gart de Sélestat, et l'essor de la comédie biblique au XVI⁵ siècle." *Grandes figures de l'humanisme alsacien courants milieux destins*, pp. 221–26. Strasbourg: Librairie Istra, 1978.

Lenhart, John M. "Pre-Reformation Printed Books: A Study in Statistical and Applied Bibliography." *Franciscan Studies* 14 (1935).

Lévy-Coblentz, Françoise. *L'art du meuble en Alsace*. Vol. 1, *Du Gothique au Baroque, 1480–1698*. Strasbourg: Librairie Istra et Editions des Dernières Nouvelles l'Alsace, 1976.

Lienhard, Marc. "Mentalité populaire, gens d'Eglise et mouvement évangélique à Strasbourg en 1522–1523: Le pamphlet 'Ein brüderlich warnung an Meister Mathis' de Steffan von Büllheym." In *Horizons européens de la réforme en Alsace*. Strasbourg: Librairie Istra, 1980, pp. 37–68.

Livet, Georges. "Geographes et cartographs en Alsace à l'époche de la Renaissance." *Grandes figures de l'humanisme alsacien courants milieux destins*, pp. 183–201. Strasbourg: Librairie Istra, 1978.

———. "Vers une nouvelle définition de l'humanisme alsacien." In *Grandes figures de l'humanisme alsacien courants milieux destins*, pp. 315–26. Strasbourg: Librairie Istra, 1978.

Livet, Georges, Greiner, L., and Van Seggelen, A. "Sélestat, l'école humaniste et Beatus Rhenanus." In *Erasme, l'Alsace et son temps*. Collections "Recherches et documents," 8. Strasbourg, Librairie Istra, 1970.

Lobstein, J. F. *Beiträge zur Geschichte der Musik im Elsass und besonders in Strassburg, von der ältesten bis auf die neueste Zeit*. Strasbourg: P. H. Dannbach, 1840.

Luther, Martin. *Die Deutsche Bibel*. Kritische gesammtausgabe, II, vol. 2. *Bibliographie der Drucke der Lutherbibel, 1522–1546*. Edited by Paul Pietsch. Weimar: H. Böhlau, 1909.

———. *D. Martin Luther's Werke*. Kritische gesammtausgabe. 94 vols. in 109. Weimar: H. Böhlau, 1883–1980.

———. *Works*. Edited by Jaroslav Pelikan and H. T. Lehmann. 55 vols. Saint Louis: Concordia Publishing House, 1955–1976.

Majno, Guido. *The Healing Hand: Man and Wound in the Ancient World*. Cambridge: Harvard University Press, 1975.

Mannheim, Karl. *Essays on the Sociology of Knowledge*. Edited by Paul Kecskemeti. New York: Oxford University Press, 1952.

Margolin, Jean-Claude. "Otto Brunfels dans le milieu évangélique rhénan." In *Strasbourg au coeur religieux du XVIᵉ siècle*, pp. 111–44. Strasbourg: Librairie Istra, 1977.

Mariás, Julián. *Generations, A Historical Method*. Translated by Harold C. Raley. University, Alabama: University of Alabama Press, 1970.

Martin, E. "Landsknechte und Hofleute im elsässichen Dramen des 16. Jahr." *Jahrbuch für Geschichte, Sprache und Literatur Elsass-Lothringens* 5 (1885): 90–106.

Martin, Henri-Jean. *Livres, pouvoirs et société à Paris au XVIIᵉ siècle (1598–1701)*. 2 vols. Geneva: Droz, 1969.

"Mass Culture and Mass Media." *Daedalus* (Spring 1960).

Meiner, Annemarie. "Die Frau im Drückgewerbe." *Gutenberg Jahrbuch* (1933): 333–43.

Mehl, Roger. "Strasbourg et Luther: la Tétrapolitane." *Strasbourg au coeur religieux du XVIᵉ siècle*, pp. 145–52. Strasbourg: Librairie Istra, 1977.

Meister, Aloys. *Der Strassburger Kapitelstreit 1583–92*. Strasbourg: J. H. Ed. Heitz, 1899.

Moller, Herbert. "Population and Society During the Old Regime, c. 1640–1770."

Population Movements in History. Edited by Herbert Moller. New York: Macmillan, 1964.

Mone, Franz Joseph, ed. *Schauspiele des Mittelalters aus Handschriften herausgegeben und erklärt*. 2 vols. Mannheim: J. Bensheimer, 1852.

Morón-Arroyo, Ciriaco. "The Reformation and Its Impact on Spanish Thought." In *Social Groups and Religious Ideas in the Sixteenth Century*. Studies in Medieval Culture, 13. The Medieval Institute, Western Michigan University, 1978.

Muller, Jean. *Dictionnaire abrégé des imprimeurs/éditeurs français du seizième siècle*. Bibliotheca Bibliographica Aureliane, 30. Baden-Baden: Valentin Koerner, 1970.

Murner, Thomas. *Badenfahrt*. New edition from the Strasbourg edition of 1514. Edited by Ernst Martin. Strasbourg: J. H. Ed. Heitz, 1887.

———. *Deutsche Schriften mit den Holzschnitten der Erstdrucke*. 9 vols. Berlin: Walter de Gruyter, 1918–31.

Nauert, Charles G., Jr. "Humanists, Scientists and Pliny: Changing Approaches to a Classical Author." *American Historical Review* 84 (1979): 72–86.

Neu, Heinrich, ed. "Freiherrlich von Türckheimisches Archiv in Altdorf, Bezirksamt Ettenheim." *Mitteilungen der Badischen Historischen Kommission*, 29 (1907): m49–m82.

Neue Deutsche Biographie. 10 vols. Berlin: Duncker und Humblot, 1953–74.

Nie, Norman H., Bent, Dale H., and Hull, C. Hadlai. *Statistical Package for the Social Sciences*. New York: McGraw-Hill, 1970.

Nordenskiöld, A. E. *Facsimile Atlas with Reproductions of the Most Important Maps Printed in the XV and XVI Centuries*. New York: Dover Press, 1973.

Nouvelle Biographie Générale. Edited by Hoeffer. Paris: Firmin Didot, 1968, reprint.

Oberman, Heiko Augustinus. Werden und Wertung der Reformation. Tübingen: J. C. B. Mohr, 1977.

Ong, Walter S. *Ramus, Method and the Decay of Dialogue*. Cambridge, Mass.: Harvard University Press, 1958.

Ozment, Steven. *The Reformation in the Cities: The Appeal of Protestantism to Sixteenth-Century Germany and Switzerland*. New Haven: Yale University Press, 1975.

———. "The Social History of the Reformation: What Can We Learn from Pamphlets?" *Flugschriften als Massenmedium der Reformationszeit*, edited by Hans-Joachim Köhler, pp. 171–240. Beiträge zum Tübinger Symposion. Stuttgart: Klett-Cotta, 1981.

Pagel, Walter. *Paracelsus*. Basel and New York: S. Karger, 1958.

Paracelsus (Theophrast von Hohenheim, gen. Paracelsus). *Sämtliche Werke*. ed. Karl Sudhoff, 3 vols. München and Berlin, 1929–30.

Passman, P. Antonin. "Die Kartause zu Strassburg V, Kunst und Wissenschaft," *Archives de l'église d'Alsace* 10 (1959): 141–51; 14 (1964): 143–66.

Peter, Rodolphe. "Le jardinier Clement Ziegler, l'homme et son oeuvre." Unpublished thèse de baccalaureate en theologie, l'Université de Strasbourg, 1954.

———. "Les premiers ouvrages français imprimés à Strasbourg," *L'Annuaire des Amis du Vieux-Strasbourg*, 4 (1974): 73–108.

———. "Les premiers ouvrages français imprimés à Strasbourg (suite)." *L'Annuaire des Amis du Vieux-Strasbourg*, 8 (1978): 11–75.

_____. "Les premiers ouvrages français imprimés à Strasbourg" (suite). *L'Annuaire des Amis du Vieux-Strasbourg,* 9 (1979): 11–108.

_____. "Les premiers ouvrages français imprimés à Strasbourg" (2ᵉ suite). *Annuaire des Amis de Vieux-Strasbourg,* 10 (1980): 35–46.

Peyre, Henri. *Les générations littéraires.* Paris: Boivin et Cie, 1948.

Podleiszek, Franz. *Anfänge der bürgerlichen Prosaromans in Deutschland.* Deutsche Literatur; Sammlung literarischer Kunst- und Kulturdenkmäler in Entwicklungsreihe. Edited by Walter Brecht and Dietrich Kralik. Reihe Volks- und Schwankbücher, 7. Leipzig: Philipp Reclam, 1933.

Pottinger, David T. *The French Book Trade in the Ancien Régime, 1500–1891.* Cambridge: Harvard University Press, 1958.

Rabelais, François. *Les Oevvres . . . contenant cinq livres, de la vie, faicts et dicts heroiques de Gargantua, et de son Fils Pantagruel.* Lyon: Jean Marin, 1558.

Rabil, Albert, Jr. *Erasmus and the New Testament, the Mind of a Christian Humanist.* San Antonio: Trinity University Press, 1973.

Rapp, Francis. "Discipline et prospérité (1530–1618)." In *Histoire de l'Alsace.* Edited by Philippe Dollinger. Toulouse: Edouard Privat, 1970.

_____. "Humanisme, Renaissance et Réforme." In *Histoire de l'Alsace.* Edited by Philippe Dollinger. Toulouse: Edouard Privat, 1970.

_____. "L'humanisme et le problème de l'église." *Strasbourg au coeur religieux du XVIᵉ siècle,* pp. 45–50. Strasbourg: Librairie Istra, 1977.

_____. *Réformes et réformation à Strasbourg: Eglise et société dans le diocèse de Strasbourg (1450–1525).* Paris: Edit. Ophrys, 1974.

Rehermann, Ernest Heinrich. *Das Predigtexempel bei protestantische Theologen des 16. und 17. Jahrhundert.* Schr. zur Niedert. Volkskunde, 8. Göttingen: O. Schwartz, 1977.

Reusch, Franz Heinrich. *Der Index der verbotenen Bücher.* 2 vols. Bonn: Cohen, 1883.

Reuss, Rodolphe. *Histoire de Strasbourg depuis ses origine jusqu'à nos jours.* Paris: Librairie Fischbacher, 1922.

_____. *Strassburg im sechzehnten jahrhundert (1500–1594). Auszug aus der Imlinschen Familienchronik.* Colmar: E. Barth, 1875.

Rhenanus, Beatus. *Briefwechsel des Beatus Rhenanus.* Collected and edited by Adalbert Horawitz and Karl Hartfelder. Leipzig: B. G. Teubner, 1886.

Ringmann, Mathias. *Die grammatica figurata.* Edited by Fr. R. v. Wieser. Printed works and woodcuts of the fifteenth and sixteenth centuries after the originals. Facsimile edition. Strasbourg: J. H. Ed. Heitz, 1905.

Ritter, François. *Catalogue des incunables et livres du XVIᵉ siècle de la Bibliothèque municipale de Strasbourg.* Strasbourg: P. H. Heitz, 1948.

_____. "Catalogue des incunables et livres du XVIᵉ siècle (jusqu'en 1530) de la bibliothèque du Grand Séminaire de Strasbourg." *Archives de l'église d'Alsace* 5 (1953–54): 69–133.

_____. *Catalogue des livres du XVIᵉ siècle ne figurant pas à la Bibliothèque nationale et universitaire de Strasbourg.* Strasbourg: P. H. Heitz, 1960.

_____. *Histoire de l'imprimerie alsacienne, au XVᵉ et XVIᵉ siècles.* Strasbourg-Paris: Editions F-X. Le Roux, 1955.

_____. *Répertoire bibliographique des livres imprimés en Alsace au XVIᵉ siècle de la*

Bibliothèque nationale et universitaire de Strasbourg. 4 vols. Strasbourg: Heitz et Cie., 1932–45.

———. "Elsässische Buchdrucker im Dienste der Strassburger Sektenbewegungen zur Zeit der Reformation." *Gutenberg Jahrbuch* (1963): 97–108.

Ritter, Gerhard. "Die geschichtliche Bedeutung des deutschen Humanismus." *Historische Zeitschrift* 127 (1932).

Röhrich, Timotheus Wilhelm. *Mittheilungen aus der Geschichte der Evangelischen Kirche des Elsasses.* 3 vols. Strasbourg: Treuttel und Würtz, 1855.

de Roover, Florence Edler. "New Facets on the Financing and Marketing of Early Printed Books." *Bulletin of the Business Historical Society* 28 (1953): 222–30.

Rostenberg, Leona. "The printers of Strasbourg and humanism from 1401 until the advent of the Reformation." *Papers of the Bibliographical Society of America* 34 (1940): 68–77.

Roth, P. W. E. "Otto Brunfels, nach seinem Leben und literarischen Werken." *Zeitschrift für die Geschichte des Oberrheins.* n.f. 9 (1894): 284–321.

Rott, Jean. "L'ancienne bibliothèque de Strasbourg, détruite en 1870: Les catalogues qui en subsistent." In *Refugium animae bibliotheca,* pp. 426–37. Mélanges Albert Kolb Festschrift. Wiesbaden: G. Pressler, 1969.

———. *Bibliographie des oeuvres imprimées du recteur Strasbourgeois Jean Sturm, 1507–1589.* Actes du 95ᵉ Congrés National des Sociétés Savantes (Reims, 1970), pp. 319–404. Paris: Bibliothèque nationale, 1975, I.

———. "Erasme et les reformateurs de Strasbourg." In *Erasme, l'Alsace et son temps.* Publications de la Société savante d'Alsace et des Régions de l'Est. "Collections Recherches et Documents," 8 (1970): 49–56.

———. "Jean Sturm, premier recteur du Gymnase et de l'Académie de Strasbourg (1507–1589)." *Strasbourg au coeur religieux du XVIᵉ siècle,* pp. 185–89. Strasbourg: Librairie Istra, 1977.

———. "L'église de réfugiés de langue française à Strasbourg au XVIᵉ siècle." *Bulletin historique et littéraire de la Société de l'histoire du Protestantisme français* 122 (1976): 525–50.

———. "L'humanisme et la réforme pédagogique en Alsace." In *L'humanisme en Alsace.* Etudes de l'Association Guillaume Budé. Paris: Société d'édition "Les Belles Lettres," 1939.

———. "Nouveaux documents sur Jean Sleidan, historien de la Réforme (1506–1556)." *Bulletin Philologique et Historique* 2 (1967): 551–648.

———. "Radikale und gemässigte Evangelische im Kampf um Strassburg: das 'Judicium' des Pacatius von 1523." *Flugschriften als Massenmedium der Reformationszeit,* edited by Hans-Joachim Köhler, pp. 373–96. Beiträge zum Tübinger Symposion 1980. Stuttgart: Klett-Cotta, 1981.

———. "Ulrich de Hutten et les débuts de la Réforme à Strasbourg." *L'Annuaire des Amis du Vieux-Strasbourg,* 4 (1974): 40–72.

Roudié, P. "Inventaire de la bibliothèque du Lancelot Dufau." *Bulletin et Mémorial Societé Archéologique de Bordeaux* 61, Groupe Jules Delpit, 1 (1957–59): 41–45.

Sarton, George. "The Scientific Literature Transmitted through the Incunabula." *Osiris* 5 (1938): 41–245.

Saunders, John Bertrand de C. M., and O'Malley, Charles D. *The Illustrations from the Works of Andreas Vesalius of Brussels.* Cleveland: World Publ. Co., 1950.

Schaff, Georges. "Jean Gonthier d'Andernach (1497–1574) et la médicine de son temps," in *Médecine et assistance en Alsace, XVIᵉ–XXᵉ siècle,* pp. 21–40. Recherches sur l'histoire de la santé. Strasbourg: Librairie Istra, 1976.

Schindling, Anton. *Humanistische Hochschule und Freie Reichstadt, Gymnasium und Akademie in Strassburg 1538–1621.* Veröffentlichungen des Instituts für Europäische Geschichte in Mainz, 77. Wiesbaden: Franz Steiner, 1977.

Schmidt, Charles G. A. *Histoire littéraire de l'Alsace à la fin du XVᵉ et au commencement du XVIᵉ siècle.* 2 vols. Nachdruck der Ausgabe Paris: Sandox et Fischbacher, 1879. Nieuwkoop: B. De Graaf, 1966.

———. *Michael Schütz gennant Toxites.* Strasbourg: C. F. Schmidt's Universitäts-Buchhandlung, 1888.

———. *Répertoire bibliographique strasbourgeois jusqu'à vers 1530.* 9 vols. Strasbourg: J. H. Ed. Heitz (Heitz & Mändel), 1894.

———. *La vie et les travaux de Jean Sturm.* 2nd ed. Nieuwkoop: B. De Graaf, 1970.

———. *Zur Geschichte der Ältesten Bibliotheken und der Ersten Buchdrucker zu Strassburg.* Strasbourg: C. F. Schmidt's Universität-Buchhandlung, 1882.

Schönbach, Anton Emanuel. *Studien zur Geschichte der Altdeutschen Predigt.* 8 vols. Wien: G. Gerold's Sohn, 1896–1907.

Schottenloher, Karl. "Die Druckersippen der Frühdruckzeit." *Zentralblatt für Bibliothekswesen* 57 (1940): 232–40.

Schultz, Franz. *Thomas Murners Deutsche Schriften mit den Holzschnitten der Erstdrucke.* Vol. 1¹, *Von den fier Ketzeren.* Edited by E. Fuchs, 1929. Vol. 1², *Badenfart.* Edited by Victor Michels, 1927. Vol. 2, *Narrenbeschwörung.* Edited by M. Spanier, 1926. Vol. 3, *Die Schelmenzunft.* Edited by M. Spanier, 1925. Vol. 4, *Die Mühle von Schwindelsheim.* Edited by Gustav Bebermeyer. Vol. 5, *Die Geuchmat.* Edited by Eduard Fuchs, 1931. Vols. 6–8, *Kleine Schriften.* 1927–28. Vol. 9, *Von dem grossen Lutherischen Narren.* Edited by Paul Merker, 1918. Berlin: Walter de Gruyter, 1918–31.

Schutz, A. H. *Vernacular Books in Parisian Libraries of the Sixteenth Century.* Chapel Hill: University of North Carolina Press, 1955.

Schwiebert, Ernest G. *Luther and His Times.* St. Louis: Corcordia Publishing House, 1950.

Sélestat, Ville de. *Catalogue général de la Bibliothéque Municipale.* Premiére Série, "Les livres imprimés." Troisième Partie: "Incunables et XVIᵐᵉ Siècle." Edited by Joseph Walter, Librarian. Colmar: Imprimerie Alsatia, 1929.

Senn, Matthias. *Johann Jakob Wick (1522–1588) und seine Sammlung von Nachrichten zur Zeitgeschichte.* Mitteilungen der Antiquarischen Gesellschaft in Zürich, vol. 46, section 138. Neujahrsblatt. Zurich: Druck Leeman AG, 1974.

Seyboth, Adolph. *Das Alte Strassburg vom 13 Jahrhundert bis zum jahre 1870.* Strasbourg: J. H. Ed. Heitz und Mündel, 1890.

Singleton, Charles S., ed. *Art, Science and History in the Renaissance.* Baltimore: The Johns Hopkins Press, 1967.

Sitzmann, François Edouard. *Dictionnaire de biographie des hommes célèbres de l'Alsace.* 2 vols. Rixheim: F. Sutter et Cie., 1910.

Smith, Cyril Stanley. "Metallurgy and Assaying." *A History of Technology*. 3 vols. Vol. 3, pp. 27–71. Edited by Charles Singer. Oxford: Oxford University Press, 1956–57.

Sohn, Walter. *Die Schule Johann Sturms und die Kirche Strassburgs in ihrem gegenseitigen Verhältnis, 1530–1581.* München: R. Oldenbourg, 1912.

Sommerhalder, Hugo. *Johann Fischarts Werk.* Quellen und Forschungen zur Sprach- und Kulturgeschichte der Germanischen Völker, Neue Folge. Edited by Hermann Kunisch, 4 (128). Berlin: Walter de Gruyter & Co., 1960.

Spitz, Lewis. "The Third Generation of German Renaissance Humanism." In *Aspects of the Renaissance.* Edited by Archibald R. Lewis. Austin: University of Texas Press, 1967.

Spitzer, Alan B. "The Historical Problem of Generations." *American Historical Review* 78 (1973): 1353–85.

Stäheli, Marlies. "Beschreibender Katalog der Einblattdrucke aus der Sammlung Wickiana in der Zentralbibliothek Zuerich." Dissertation, Universität Zeurich, 1950.

Steele, Robert. "What Fifteenth Century Books are About." *The Library,* ser. 2 (1903–07), 4: 337–54; 5: 337–58; 6: 137–55; 8: 225–38.

Stierle, Beate. *Capito als Humanist.* Quellen für Reformationsgeschichte. Gütersloh: Gerd Mohn, 1974.

Stillman, John Mason. *The Story of Early Chemistry.* New York: D. Appleton & Co., 1924.

Stillwell, Margaret Bingham. *The Awakening Interest in Science during the First Century of Printing, 1450–1550.* New York: The Bibliographical Society of America, 1970.

Stolberg, August. *Tobias Stimmers Malereien an der astronomischen Münsteruhr zu Strassburg.* Strasbourg: J. H. Ed. Heitz, 1898.

Strauss, Gerald. *Luther's House of Learning: Indoctrination of the Young in the German Reformation.* Baltimore: Johns Hopkins University Press, 1978.

––––––. "Success and Failure in the Lutheran Reformation." *Past and Present* 67 (1975): 30–63.

Sturm, Johann. *Classicae epistolae: sive, Scholae argentinenses restitutae.* Translated and edited by Jean Rott. Paris: Librairie E. Droz, 1938.

Taton, René. *History of Science.* Translated by A. J. Pomerans. Vol. 1, *The Beginnings of Modern Science.* New York: Basic Books, Inc., 1964.

Taylor, E. G. R. "Cartography, Survey and Navigation, 1400–1750." In *A History of Technology,* vol. 3, pp. 530–57. Edited by Charles Singer, E. J. Holmyard, A. R. Hall, and Trevor Williams. Oxford: Clarendon Press, 1957.

Thibodeau, Kenneth. "Science and the Reformation: The Case of Strasbourg." *Sixteenth Century Journal* 7 (1976): 35–80.

––––––. "Science in an Urban Perspective: Social and Cultural Parameters of the Sciences in Sixteenth Century Strasbourg." Dissertation, University of Pennsylvania, 1974.

Tiedge, Hermann. *Jörg Wickram und die Volksbücher.* Hannover: Emil Homann, 1904.

Ungerer, Alfred. *L'horloge astronomique de la cathédrale de Strasbourg.* Paris: Societé astronomique de France, 1922.

Ungerer, Edmund. *Elsässische Altertümer in Burg und Haus, in Kloster und Kirche.* Inventare vom Ausgang des Mittelalters bis zum dreissig-jährigen Kriege aus Stadt und Bistum Strassburg. 3 vols. Strasbourg: Karl J. Trübner, 1911–17.

Usher, Abbott Payson. *A History of Mechanical Inventions.* 2nd ed. Cambridge: Harvard University Press, 1954.

van der Wee, Herman. *The Growth of the Antwerp Market and the European Economy (Fourteenth–Sixteenth Centuries).* 3 vols. The Hague: Martinus Nijhoff, 1963.

Voet, Leon. *The Golden Compasses.* 2 vols. Amsterdam: Vangendt and Co., 1972.

Vogeleis, Martin. *Quellen und Bausteine zu einer Geschichte der Musik und des Theaters im Elsass 1500–1800.* Strasbourg: F. X. Le Roux, 1911.

Vogler, Bernard. *Le clergé protestant Rhénan au siècle de la réforme (1555–1619).* Paris: Editions Ophrys, 1976.

_____. *Vie religieuse en pays Rhénan dans la seconde moitié du XVIᵉ siècle (1556–1619).* 3 vols. Lille: Service de Reproduction des Theses, Université de Lille, 1974.

_____. "Recrutement et carrière des pasteurs strasbourgeois au XVIᵉ siècle." *Revue d'histoire et de philosophie religieuses* 48 (1968): 151–74.

Voullième, Ernst. *Die Deutschen Drucker des fünfzehnten Jahrhunderts.* 2nd ed. Berlin, 1922.

Wallace, Anthony F. C. "Revitalization Movements." *American Anthropologist* 57 (1956): 264–81.

Walter, Joseph. *Catalogue général de la Bibliothèque municipale de la ville de Sélestat.* Trois parties. Colmar: Imprimerie Alsatia, 1929.

Weber, Bruno. *Erschröckliche und warhafftige Wunderzeichen, 1543–1586.* 2 vols. Zürich: Graf, 1971–72.

_____. "'Die Welt Begeret allezeit Wunder' Versuch einer Bibliographie der Einblattdrucke von Bernhard Jobin in Strassburg." *Gutenberg-Jahrbuch* (1976), pp. 270–90.

Weber, Edith. *Musique et théatre dans les pays Rhénans.* Vol. 1, *La musique mesurée à l'antique en Allemagne,* in two parts. Vol. 2, *Le théatre humaniste et scolaire dans les pays Rhénans.* Paris: Klincksieck, 1974.

Wendel, François. *L'église de Strasbourg, sa constitution et son organization.* Paris: Etudes d'histoire publiés par la Faculté Protestante de l'Université de Strasbourg, 1942.

_____. *Le mariage à Strasbourg à l'époche de la réforme, 1520–1692.* Collection d'études sur l'histoire du droit et des institutions de l'Alsace, 4. Strasbourg: Imprimerie alsacienne, 1928.

Westman, Robert S. *Magical Reform and Astronomical Reform: The Yates Thesis Reconsidered.* W. A. Clark Memorial Library, 1976.

_____. "The Melanchthon Circle, Rheticus and the Wittenberg Interpretation of the Copernican Theory." *Isis* 66 (1975): 165–93.

Weyrauch, Erdmann. *Konfessionelle Krise und soziale Stabilität: Das Interim in Strassburg (1548–1562).* Spätmittellalter und Frühe Neuzeit. Tübinger Beiträge zur Geschichtsforschung, 7. Stuttgart: Klett-Cotta, 1978.

Wickersheimer, Ernest. "Catalogue des livres légués par Jean Protzer a l'hôpital du St. Esprit de Noerdlingen," *Revue des Bibliothèques* (7–12), 1921, pp. 1–9.

———. "Laurent Fries et la querelle de l'arabisme en médicine (1530)." *Les Cahiers de Tunisie, Revue de Sciences humaines* (1955): 96–103.

———. "Paracelse à Strasbourg." *Centaurus* 1 (1951): 356–65.

Wickram, Georg. *Sämtliche Werke.* Edited by Hans Gert Roloff. Vol. 1, *Ritter Galmy.* Vol. 2, *Gabriotto und Reinhart.* Vol. 3, *Knaben Spiegel. Dialog vom ungeratnen Sohn.* Vol. 4, *Von Güten und Bösen Nachbaurn.* Vol. 5, *Der Goldtfaden.* Vol. 6, *Der Irr Reitende Pilger.* Vol. 8, *Der Siben Hauptlaster.* Vol. 12, *Apostelspiel. Knaben Spiegel.* Berlin: W. de Gruyter, 1967–72.

———. *Das Rollwagenbüchlein.* A new translation with a biography of the poet by Franz Hirtler. München: Zinnen-Verlag, 1943.

Wieger, Friederich. *Geschichte der Medicin und ihrer Lehranstalten in Strassburg vom 1497–1872.* Strasbourg: Karl J. Trübner, 1885.

Wilder, Raymond L. *Evolution of Mathematical Concepts.* New York: Wiley, 1968.

Wildhaber, Robert. *Jakob Ruf. Ein Zürcher Dramatiker des 16. Jahrhunderts.* St. Gallen: Gebr. Wildhaber, 1929.

Williams, George H. *The Radical Reformation.* London: Weidenfeld and Nicholson, 1962.

Wimpheling, Jacob. *Jakob Wimpfeling's Adolescentia.* Edited by Otto Herding. Munich: Wilhelm Fink, 1965.

Winkler, Eberhard. *Die Leichenpredigt im deutschen Luthertum bis Spener.* Forschungen zur Geschichte und Lehre des Protestantismus, series 10, vol. 34. Munich: Chr. Kaiser Verlag, 1967.

Wittmer, Charles and Meyer, J. Charles, eds. *Le livre de bourgeoisie de la ville de Strasbourg, 1440–1530.* 3 vols. Strasbourg: P. H. Heitz, 1948–61.

Yates, Frances A. "The Hermetic Tradition in Renaissance Science." In *Art, Science and History in the Renaissance*, pp. 255–75. Edited by Charles S. Singleton. The Johns Hopkins Humanities Seminars. Baltimore: The Johns Hopkins University Press, 1967.

———. *The Art of Memory.* London: Routledge & Kegan Paul Ltd., 1966.

———. *The Rosicrucian Enlightenment.* London: Routledge & Kegan Paul, 1972.

Zinner, Ernst. *Geschichte und Bibliographie der Astronomischen Literatur in Deutschland zur Zeit der Renaissance.* Stuttgart: Anton Hiersemann, 1964.

INDEX